Reference use only
not for loan

THE GLOBAL BUSINESS HANDBOOK

The Global Business Handbook
The Eight Dimensions of International Management

Edited by

DAVID J. NEWLANDS

and

MARK J. HOOPER

GOWER

Published by
Gower Publishing Limited
Wey Court East
Union Road
Farnham
Surrey GU9 7PT
England

Gower Publishing Company
Suite 420
101 Cherry Street
Burlington, VT 05401-4405
USA

www.gowerpublishing.com

British Library Cataloguing in Publication Data

The global business handbook : the eight dimensions of
  international management
  1. International business enterprises - Management
  I. Newlands, David J. II. Hooper, Mark J.
  658'.049

ISBN-13: 9780566087479

Library of Congress Cataloging-in-Publication Data

The global business handbook : the eight dimensions of international management /
[edited] by David Newlands and Mark J. Hooper.
  p. cm.
  ISBN 978-0-566-08747-9
  1. International business enterprises--Management. 2. International trade. I. Newlands,
David J. II. Hooper, Mark J.

  HD62.4.G536 2008
  658'.049--dc22

2008031193

Mixed Sources
Product group from well-managed
forests and other controlled sources
www.fsc.org Cert no. SA-COC-1565
© 1996 Forest Stewardship Council

Printed and bound in Great Britain by
MPG Books Ltd, Bodmin, Cornwall.

Contents

List of Figures

List of Tables

Contributors

The Editors

Dr. David J. Newlands has worked in various industrial positions, from his apprenticeship through sales, system calibration, test engineering, to lecturing and research into supply chain issues. He gained a BTEC and HNC in engineering while an apprentice, B.Eng. (Hons) in Manufacturing Systems Engineering and his PhD in developing supply chain methodologies that focused on supplier development.

Dr Newlands is Senior Assistant Professor of Opérations and Industrial Management at the Institute d'Économie Scientifique et Gestion. IÉSEG School of Management is part of the Catholic University of Lille, North France.

Contact: d.newlands@ieseg.fr; d.newlands@hotmail.fr
Telephone +33 320 54 58 92

Dr Mark J. Hooper is a Senior Lecturer in the Faculty of Engineering and Computing at Coventry University. In addition to his teaching in the UK, he has lectured in America, Hong Kong, China and India. He is an active researcher in a diverse range of organizational subjects which currently include innovation cluster dynamics, privatization in the UAE and human-centred change paradigms. He is a visiting professor of Operations Management at IÉSEG where he teaches the core subjects of Change and Environmental Management. Prior to entering academia he worked in a number of organizations centred in the defence and aerospace industries.

Contact: cex212@coventry.ac.uk
Telephone +44 24 7688 7688

The Contributors

Dr Zoltán Antal-Mokos is Associate Professor of Strategy and Executive MBA programme director at the European School of Management and Technology, Berlin, Germany (www.esmt. org). Prior to joining ESMT, he held the McKinsey & Co. Chair in Strategy at the Budapest University of Economic Sciences. He completed his PhD at London Business School. The results of his PhD research were published by Cambridge University Press. Professor Antal-Mokos has published extensively and run successful courses on corporate strategy, privatization, mergers and acquisitions, and strategic alliances, and consulted international corporations in various business sectors across Europe.

Contact: antal-mokos@esmt.org

Dr Erkan Bayraktar earned his PhD in Industrial Engineering from the University of Iowa. After working several years in industry as a consultant, he has been lecturing in a number of business and engineering schools in the area of operations management, supply chain management, quantitative methods and re-engineering. Dr Bayraktar currently serves as an associate professor of Operations Management at Bahcesehir University, Istanbul, Turkey.

His principal research areas include supply chain management, lean production, layout studies and re-engineering. He has published in several academic journals including the *International Journal of Production Economics* and *Industrial Management and Data Systems*, among others. He is a member of INFORMS, AOM and AIB.
Contact: erkanb@bahcesehir.edu.tr

Dr Chumpitaz is Full Professor and Head of the Department of Marketing at the IÉSEG School of Management at the Catholic University of Lille. He earned his MBA in 1995 and his PhD in 1998, both from the Louvain School of Management at the Catholic University of Louvain in Belgium.

Dr Chumpitaz is currently a professor of Marketing and has taught such courses as Strategic Marketing and Company Observation, Marketing Research Seminar, Multivariate Data Analysis and Forecasting Methods for Marketing. His teaching experience includes executive and MBA programmes in Argentina, Belgium, France, Paraguay, Peru, Spain and Uruguay.

Prior to entering academia, Dr Chumpitaz worked for several years in management in the telecommunication industrial sector and for almost fifteen years he has served as an analytical consultant for marketing research projects and agencies. Dr Chumpitaz's research focuses on customer satisfaction, brand loyalty market orientation and service recovery. His research has been published in academic and professional journals such as the *Managing Service Quality*, *International Review of Retail, Distribution and Consumer Research*, *European Business Forum*, *European Journal of Marketing* and *Recherche et Application en Marketing*.
Contact: r.chumpitaz@ieseg.fr

Dr Keith Dawes is a psychologist and management educator in NSW Australia. He works closely with senior management in several prominent Australian organizations on strategic planning and organizational development. He currently teaches university courses in the Management of Innovation and Technical Change, Managing People and Organizations, Introduction to Contemporary Business Practice and Strategic Planning for Business Coaches. His research interest is in Tacit Knowledge. He teaches the course Tacit Knowledge and Implicit Learning for IÉSEG in Lille and conducts research on Tacit Knowledge and Innovation in Australian organizations.
Contact: dawescon1@bigpond.com

Dr Isabel Fernández has been professor of Logistics and Production Organization at the Engineering University in Oviedo (Spain) since 1997. Professor Fernández earned her PhD in Reverse Logistics at both the University of Vaasa (Finland) and the University of Oviedo. She also earned the title of European Doctor. Prof. Fernández obtained an MSc from the University of Vasque Country and MBA from University of Oviedo. Her major research interests are logistics management, reverse logistics, cost analysis, inventory control and time series analysis. She has published over fifty articles in academic journals and conference proceedings and has participated in several research projects and books. She acts as external referee for several scientific journals and is a member of FAL (Asturian Logistics Foundation), ADINGOR (Association of Production Organization Engineers) and board member of the International Society for Productivity and Quality Research. She has consulting experience in private companies.
Contact: ifq@uniovi.es

Dr Peter Firkola is an Associate Professor of International Management and Director of the Hokkaido University Short-Term Exchange Program at the International Student Center, Hokkaido University in Sapporo, Japan. He received his PhD from the Graduate School of Economics and Business Administration at Hokkaido University. In addition, he received his MBA specializing in International Business at McMaster University in Canada. His research focuses on human resource management practices in Japanese organizations, career development practices and cross-cultural management, and he has published several articles in these areas.
Contact: firkola@gmail.com

Dr Sandra Jones is the Professor of Employment Relations at RMIT. Professor Jones earned a PhD and is a renowned international researcher in the fields of employment relations and knowledge strategy. Professor Jones is the recipient of an Australian National Award Citation for Outstanding Contribution to Student Learning for her design and development of innovative Virtual Situated Learning Environments. Professor Jones has been invited as an international expert to teach and research in many countries including France, Canada and the UK, as well as Hong Kong, Malaysia and Singapore.
Contact: Sandra.jones@rmit.edu.au

Dr María D. De Juan has a PhD in Marketing. She is an assistant professor in Marketing at the University of Alicante (Spain) and a visiting assistant professor at IÉSEG School of Management (Institute d'Économie Scientifique et Gestion, France), one of the top ranking French Grande École (French Elitist University). Dr De Juan has been a lecturer at the University of Florida (USA), Southampton Business School SSU (Southampton Solent University, UK) and Spanish Business Schools including ESIC (Madrid) and ESADE (Barcelona). She is the author of three books in Spanish: *Shopping Centre Attraction toward Consumers*, *Sales Promotions* and *Channels and Retailing: Commercial Distribution in Practice*. She has published articles about retailing and consumer behaviour in several journals and edited books including the *Journal of the Academy of Marketing Science* and the *Journal of Consumer Psychology*. Her research focuses on consumer behaviour, retailing, merchandising and store patronage.
Contact: Mayo@ua.es

Dr Brooks C. Holtom is an Associate Professor of Management at McDonough School of Business, Georgetown University, USA. Dr Holtom's recent publications on negotiation have appeared in Harvard University's *Negotiation Journal* as well as the *International Journal of Conflict Management*, the *Journal of Management Education* and *Decision Sciences Journal of Innovative Education*. He was named the 2005 Ascendant Scholar of the Year for the Western Academy of Management and is a multiple-time recipient of the Professor of the Year award for the Georgetown University Executive Masters of Leadership Program, where he teaches International Negotiation. He has also served as a consultant to many organizations including Capital One, Citibank, Nordstrom, NorthWestern Mutual, POSCO, Rolls Royce, Sprint/Nextel, US Chamber of Commerce and the World Bank.
Contact: BCH6@msb.edu

Dr David Kimber is visiting Professor at IÉSEG School of Management, France and at the Indian Institute of Management – Bangalore in India. He teaches courses in International Business Ethics, International Corporate Governance, Ethics and Governance. He was the former associate dean and director of postgraduate studies and joint programme coordinator

for the Doctor of Business Administration at RMIT's Business Faculty. With Fran Siemensma, his teaching and research interests are in the areas of business ethics, corporate governance and citizenship, international alliances, cross-cultural studies, business/society relationships and values in management and leadership. He has taught at universities and colleges in China, Malaysia, Singapore, France, India, Bangladesh and Australia. He has undertaken research and published papers with Fran Siemensma on corporate governance and social responsibility, values in management and leadership, ethics and integrity systems.
Contact: dkimber@bigpond.net.au; fransiemensma@yahoo.com.au

Dr Kevin Laframboise has been a recognized and successful educator for several decades. A long-standing member of the American Society for Quality, he was awarded an MSc and a PhD in Quality Management from Concordia University in Montreal, Canada. He has presented at many highly rated international business conferences. He has also authored or co-authored articles in several business publications including the *European Journal of Operational Research*, *International Journal of Intelligent Information Technologies*, *International Journal of Enterprise Information Systems*, *International Journal of Knowledge Management*, *International Journal of Information and Operations Management Education*, *Journal of Supply Chain Management* and *Leadership Quarterly*.
Contact: la.fr.ak@hotmail.com

Tim Lyons is an experienced senior manager who has worked extensively in the Asia Pacific region. His primary background is in sales and marketing in the consumer industries, with additional expertise in finance and banking and TV media. Since the early 1990s he has gained additional experience in higher education at undergraduate and postgraduate levels, both in Australia and internationally. His academic work has taken him to Singapore, Hong Kong, Vietnam, China, Australia and France. He is currently an Assistant Professor of Marketing at the International School of Management (ISM) in Paris (www.ism.edu) and Executive Director of Chinese-based consultancy firm, Manage China (www.managechina.com). His research interests are in SMEs and online marketing.
Contact: tim@managechina.com

Douglas K. Macbeth is full Professor of Purchasing and Supply Management in the School of Management. University of Southampton, UK. From 1994, Professor MacBeth was CIPS/SCMG Ltd Professor of Supply Chain Management at the University of Glasgow and he is the founding Director of SCMG Ltd, a consulting company specializing in Supply Chain Management, Procurement and Logistics. This business was spun out of the University of Glasgow in 1990.

His research interests include supply chain management and strategy, applications of change management and chaos theory to supply chains and logistics and the globalization of supply chains. He is Associate Editor of the *European Management Journal*.
Contact: D.K.Macbeth@soton.ac.uk

Dr Hedley Malloch, PhD, MSc (Administrative Sciences), BSc (Econs) is Professor of Management at IÉSEG School of Management, the Catholic University of Lille, France, where he teaches international HRM and strategy. Previously he taught in business schools in the UK, Turkey and Cyprus. He has worked professionally in many other countries including Poland and The Netherlands. His research interests include international vocational education and training, cross-cultural leadership styles and HRM in firms operated by monastic

orders. He has published widely in many journals including *International Journal of Human Resource Management*, *Personnel Review* and the *Journal of Management Inquiry*. He serves on the Management and Editorial Boards of *Personnel Review*, *Human Resource Development International* and the *Journal of Vocational Education and Training*.
Contact: h.malloch@ieseg.fr

Dr Simon A. Mercado is Head of Strategy and International Business at Nottingham Business School (NBS), Nottingham Trent University (NTU). He holds a PhD in International Political Economics and is author of various papers and principal author (with R. Welford and K. Prescott) of *European Business*, 5th edition (Harlow: Pearson Education Ltd, 2007). Dr Mercado has professional and industrial experience in the fields of journalism and food marketing. He is an active consultant on HE internationalization.
Contact: simon.mercado@ntu.ac.uk

Dr Steve Molloy is an Associate Professor of Management at the Wehle School of Business, Canisius College in Buffalo, New York. Dr Molloy earned his PhD in Business Strategy and MIS from Indiana University. His research interests focus on entrepreneurship, not for profit organizations and the strategic impacts of information technology. Dr Molloy currently teaches Strategic Management of Not-for-Profit Organizations as a visiting Professor at IÉSEG School of Management.
Contact: molloy@canisius.edu

Olga Muzychenko is a lecturer at the University of Adelaide Business School. Her areas of expertise and research interests span across Cross-cultural Management, Entrepreneurship and International Business. Her past research looked at various aspects of internationalization of small and medium-sized enterprises, entrepreneurship education and training and cross-cultural dimensions of organizational behaviour. After commencing her academic career she has retained a link with the business community, acting as a consultant to small and medium-sized enterprises in Europe and Australia as well as the Enterprise Development Section of the International Labor Organization (ILO).
Contact: olga.muzychenko@adelaide.edu.au

Dr Nicholas G. Paparoidamis earned his PhD in 2001 from Cardiff Business School, Wales. He is an Associate Professor of Marketing at the IÉSEG School of Management, Catholic University of Lille. Dr Paparoidamis' research curriculum includes a number of publications in top American and European marketing journals such as the *International Business Review*, *Industrial Marketing Management*, *European Journal of Marketing*, *Managing Service Quality* and *Management Decision*. He has participated in many major marketing conferences worldwide and he is a member of a number of distinguished marketing organizations including the Academy of Marketing Science, the European Marketing Academy, the American Marketing Association and the French Marketing Association. He also worked for a number of years as a marketing consultant and research and development expert at EFG Eurobank S.and European Dynamics SA in Greece.
Contact: n.paparoidamis@ieseg.fr

Dr J. Phillip Scott is currently Deputy Dean of the Graduate School of Business and Co-Director of the Centre for Supply Chain Research at the University of Wollongong, Australia. Prior to accepting this position, Dr Scott was the Head of the School of Management and Marketing and Deputy Director of the Graduate School of Business and Professional Development at the University of Wollongong. He has been teaching in Australia since the early 1990s. Contact: pscott@uow.edu.au

Dr Fran Siemensma is visiting Professor at IÉSEG School of Management, France and at the Indian Institute of Management – Bangalore in India. She teaches courses in International Business Ethics, International Corporate Governance, Ethics and Governance and was a faculty member at the School of Management at Victoria University. With David Kimber, her teaching and research interests are in the areas of business ethics, corporate governance and citizenship, international alliances, cross-cultural studies, business/society relationships and values in management and leadership. She has taught at universities and colleges in China, Malaysia, Singapore, France, India, Bangladesh and Australia. She has undertaken research and published papers with David Kimber on corporate governance and social responsibility, values in management and leadership, ethics and integrity systems.

Dr Coral R. Snodgrass is a visiting professor at IÉSEG School of Management, Catholic University of Lille, France. She earned her PhD from the University of Pittsburgh in 1984. She is a professor of International Business at Canisius College in Buffalo, NY where she is also the Director of the International Business Program. She specializes in the teaching of International Strategy with an emphasis on business in North America. Most recently she has been studying the impact of increased security measures at the Canada–US border on cross-border trade. This project, funded by the Canadian government, has concentrated on the functioning of cross-border supply chains that support the most vibrant bilateral trade relationship in the world.

Professor Snodgrass is the faculty director for student exchanges and study abroad projects. She is presently the Project Director of an Atlantis Grant from the US Department of Education and the European Union which supports EU and US students to complete dual degrees in International Business at Canisius College, the University of Strasbourg and the University of Antwerp. she leads groups of students on study tours of Mexico and the European Union. Contact: snodgras@canisius.edu

David Trigg has been an academic for a number of years, working in the fields of international business and strategy. He has taught at graduate and undergraduate levels in Australia – his home country – as well as in Hong Kong, China, Thailand, USA and France. He currently has an adjunct position with the University of Ballarat. He also conducts a management consultancy practice in the area of management training to international business. His research interests lie in governance issues of multinational companies and published widely. He is a board member of a number of commercial organizations. He has held the position of Board President. His most recent appointment is to the education board of a national agribusiness company. Contact: dtrigg@netspace.net.au

Marie C. Trigg is a member of the postgraduate Deakin Business School in Australia and the Faculty Chair of International Business Management and Program Director of the China International Study Program. She has taught in both graduate and undergraduate programmes in many parts of the world including the USA, Thailand, Hong Kong, China, The Netherlands and France. While she has published in the areas of corporate and national culture and experiential learning, she is best known for the two editions *International Business: A*

Managerial Perspective, which she co-authored with a colleague. The second edition was awarded the prestigious Australian tertiary textbook of the year 2002. Her theoretical background is balanced by her practical involvement the breeding of stud cattle and her importing and exporting of genetic material.
Contact: marie.trigg@deakin.edu.au

Dr Alkiviadis Tromaras originates from Thessaloniki, Greece. He studied Aerospace Manufacturing Engineering at the University of the West of England and obtained a Masters degree in Competitive Manufacturing at Coventry University. He was awarded a PhD from Coventry University for studying the application of Stakeholder Theory in Environmental Management related to the Aerospace Industry. He currently works on environmental matters at Cummins UK.

Dr Maria de Lurdes Martinez Veludo holds a PhD in Management from the University of Glasgow with a specialization in Partnering Relationships within a Multinational and Subsidiary Context. Dr Veludo's academic experience as a lecturer, programme designer and researcher is extensive. She teaches supply chain management courses in postgraduate and executive programs at Groupe ESC Rouen, where she is also responsible for the design and implementation of Masters programmes on supply chain management. Additionally, she has taught purchasing, supplier development and business relationship management in various countries as a visiting professor. Dr Veludo has led research on the automotive and health industries and services logistics. Her international research projects cover areas such as sustainable purchasing, reverse logistics, traceability, waste management, fair trade and intermodal transportation.
Contact: mlv29@orange.fr

Dr Nada Zupan is an associate professor at the Faculty of Economics, University of Ljubljana, department of Management and Organization. She completed her Master's studies in 1990 at Cornell University in the field of Organizational Behaviour and her doctoral studies in 1999 at the Faculty of Economics in Ljubljana in the field of Human Resource Management. Her main research interests include strategic HRM, performance management and compensation. Besides teaching and research, she is also involved in management training programmes and consulting projects. She has published over forty articles and monographs and she regularly attends international conferences. She is also the vice-president of Slovenian Human Resource Association.
Contact: nada.zupan@ef.uni-lj.si

Acknowledgements

This volume would not have been realized without the understanding, foresight and patience of Mr Jonathan Norman, Publisher and Commissioning Editor at Gower Publishing. He brought significant subtlety, many suggestions and a keen eye for detail to this project that was a diamond in the rough.

We would like to thank Professor John Saee for helping to assure Mr Norman of the merit of the project and his insistence on quality contributions.

We owe a debt of thanks to each of the contributors, both in this volume and those that we had to turn down. In alphabetical order of lead contributors: Zoltan Antol-Mokos, Erkan Bayraktar, Ruben Chumpitaz and Nicolas Paproidamis, Isabel Fenandez, Peter Firkola, Brooks C. Holtom, Sandra Jones, David Kimber and Fran Siemensma, Kevin Laframboise, Tim Lyons, Douglas K. MacBeth, Hedley Malloch, Simon A. Mercado, Steve Molloy, Olga Musychenko, Roby B. Sawyers, Phil Scott, Coral R. Snodgrass, David Trigg and Marie C. Trigg, Maria Lourdes de Veludo, Mayo de Juan Vigaray and Beyza Gültekin and Nada Zupan.

The Eight Dimensions of International Business

David J. Newlands and Mark J. Hooper

There are so many things going on in international business at a global level that it would be impossible to list and describe them all in a single volume. Rather than do so many things an injustice, we will concentrate on the big developments that currently are happening and consider how managers operating in the global business landscape must change what they do to create advantages and remain competitive.

Most business schools have functional specialisms known as majors or concentrations. The most usual of these are marketing, finance, operations management and research, information systems, human resource management and audit and managerial control. Students and practitioners tend to specialize in their chosen fields. Some commit to a field prior to higher education study. As a result of taking obligatory courses in each concentration, in Europe it is possible to be a generalist up until the final stages of a Bachelors degree.

We as editors have 'cherry picked' and invited contributions from academics that have been invited to develop and deliver elective courses at IÉSEG School of Management in Lille, France. The number of electives on offer has developed rapidly since 2005 when 35 courses were run. For academic year 2008–2009 we plan in excess of 200 subjects that deal with specific issues and managerial decision making. Specialist subject titles offered vary greatly with time given to specific issues. In assessing the larger picture, eight dimensions or clusters were identified. These dimensions further enabled other potential electives to be identified, developed and tested by delivering courses.

A volume of this size can not possibly cover all aspects of a single subject area or business major. Such an endeavour would require a series of volumes dedicated to each. This bound volume aims to combine the essential knowledge and value add discussions of the contributors into a structured sequence of chapters. We have brought together the 'need to know' elements that will support specialists when dealing with issues outside their functional or departmental 'comfort zone'. We aim to further enhance this selection with online contributions.

Introduction

This handbook comprises of a collection grouped and sequenced chapters. This volume of contributed chapters directly stems from a set of intensive electives delivered at IÉSEG[1] School of Management, Lille and Paris, France. The number of electives has grown organically in recent years as a result of the strategy to identify specific course titles, provide choices to

---

1   IÉSEG – Institut d'Économie Scientifique et de Gestion. This school is a member of the Grande Ecole system of elitist business schools in France. The course electives are offered as part of the Masters Degrees in Business.

participants and to fulfil the learning needs of both an international audience and businesses that operate in a global context.

Eight dimensions were identified during a strategic skills and needs analysis. A visiting professor programme academic committee then started to set the framework for identifying and commissioning new courses. The framework has been used to identify the mix and subject portfolio appropriate to the industries and sectors of business activity that postgraduate students tend to go into.

The team identified that it is important to be aware of the international community. Awareness provides a guide and sense of the difficulties that lie ahead. Knowing and understanding these limitations, business leaders may then create limits and rules of thumb that can help control over enthusiastic, or perhaps rather uncontrolled, endeavours. The chapters in this volume help identify some of the most important 'show stoppers' to implementing globalization strategies. Hence, this first edition of the *Global Business Handbook* has focused on international business and supply chain management.

Volumes of this sort can identify the key issues and start to colour-in important details. Reviews that have a wide scope may suffer in depth. Within the boundaries of the chapter working titles, each contributor has selected the most pressing issues that currently affect business managers in today's global trading environment.

The Eight Dimensions Model

We have depicted the eight dimensions identified thus:

8 *Business transformation*	
6 *Cost management*	7 *Innovation and quality*
4 *Regional and country specific differences*	5 *Marketing and sales*
2 *Relationship management*	3 *Supply chain management*
1 *International perspectives*	

Figure 0.1   The eight dimensions of international management

Each of these subject areas represent a significant phase of managerial attention when management is building multinational, international and global enterprises. The design is symbolic of the tradition to build firm foundations and have a strong roof. International perspectives are firstly identified. This asks: Who could we work with? and how do they differ from us? Relationship management is important in order to foster understanding, set expectations, generate trust and negotiate initial agreements. Once the initial introductions and contracts are signed, work needs to be done to set up and design the chains supply of businesses involved. This may start internally and then spread to suppliers; equally, different teams may be charged with improving a specific section and they must trust other teams to do their allotted work too. Managing supply chains starts to forge long-term relationships by coordinating value-added activities for mutual benefit. Supply chains are required to produce goods for market. Supply chain management tends to take the stream toward suppliers.

Dimension 4 sets out issues of employing staff at home and abroad. Probably the biggest sources of show stoppers or enablers of superior performance are a company's employees. Growing and establishing both internationally and globally requires companies to understand the relationship between employees and performance, the issues of international human resourcing, the context and processes of different human relations models in use. Japan is perceived by many as a foreign country, with specific cultural and work placed traditions, expectations, customs and norms. Specific differences are identified and contrasts are made with more familiar Western situations.

Dimension 5 looks down toward the point of sale; to trade customers or dealers and consumers. Issues relating to doing business within the EU and NAFTA economic regions are discussed. Businesses may target their marketing directly at individuals in order to set up dialogues to identify needs, present solutions and then proceed to negotiations. Equally, businesses may set up front end retailing environments to take advantage of passing trade such as airport terminals and the high street, as well as individuals that make planned purchasing trips. Many of these trips are to buy physical goods, including gift tokens. Services marketing issues round off this dimension. This chapter builds theory around the direct marketing approach and focuses on attitudes and perspectives to intangible services.

Dimension 6 sets out issues related to cost management and economic viability of an activity. Many organizations exist that do not have profit as an objective. Hence, their specific issues are treated.

Dimension 7 fundamentally is about learning and improving. Emphasis is placed on doing jobs effectively and efficiently, making better products and providing superior services. The final two chapters focus on managing what is known – explicit knowledge, and identifying and recording ideas, perceptions and other cogitations that have yet to be written down and analysed.

The first seven dimensions aid in providing a company with its context, contacts, cost structure, chains of linked together companies and processes, and corporate structures. Dimension 8 is operational in nature. These issues focus less on what is and more on what could be. Industries such as retail, banking and financial, transportation, medical and hospitality are examples of service oriented business activity. A large proportion of so-called modern society is based on the provision of services. Emphasis initially is placed on managing services. We need to understand issues of bringing goods made in low cost countries to markets around the world requires international transportation. These activities rely on accurate data to coordinate production and distribution. Where ever companies buy from, they rely on suppliers efforts to improve quality, cost and delivery reliability in order to remain competitive. A review of supplier development is made because few benchmarking, re-engineering and supplier development schemes seem to achieve their expected results. Most of these efforts to improve supply chain performance focus on existing companies that have already been selected by purchasing and categorized as capable, even if they could reduce cost, improve quality and other performance metrics. Building on the explicit and tacit knowledge issues and attempts to help others, some individuals may feel they have the ideas and competitive advantage 'to go it alone' and set up their own company to supply goods and services. There are cultural issues that affect intrapreneurs and entrepreneurialism. For example, in China people understand there is little profit in working for someone else. Hence many Chinese create new supplier companies that are micro, small and medium sized enterprises.

Supplier development tends to focus on improving against specific key performance indicators. This assumes the environment and competitive forces will remain constant. Taking a step back, we examine questions that define the purpose, identify the risks, thus challenging the justification for making what is produced, providing existing and the way work is done. Change management may be the result of autocratic and democratic processes. Specific individuals may be heralded as company saviours, such as Carlos Ghosn at Nissan. Equally, collective behaviour may generate impetus to set new agendas, behavioural norms and expectations.

Supply chain games can be used to facilitate learning, aid communication, identify potential strategies and understand effects of potential solutions. A chapter discusses benefits of using live supply chain games versus financial and decision analysis based computer simulations. This enables versions to be intuitively understood that represent mass production, lean manufacturing and agile customization.

Products can subtly differ between these modes because supply chains design for manufacture and assembly in their existing supply chains. Changing mode from mass, to lean to agile can require producers to modify designs in order obtain expected benefits.

The Eight Dimensions

Dimension 1 – International Perspectives

Dimension 1 focuses on the macro level multicultural business environment and the philosophical underpinnings required to sustain ethical business. The aim of the section is to review in what context and why the business exists, how organizations plan their long-term programmes. International Business Ethics reviews what the company will and will not do. Managing the ethical company puts these Dos and Don'ts into context based on many case examples. Organizations in many countries are now legally required to consider environmental management.

Chapters 1–3 relate to the context of international business – the external realities and influences that provoke responses by senior management within an organization. Chapters 1 and 2 focus on the reactions and values of management. Particular focus is placed on the validity of decisions, taking responsibility for what is done now, and what will need to be done in the future to rectify or reduce the consequences of what has been done or made.

Chapter 1: Visiting Professors David Trigg and Marie C. Trigg introduce international business environmental factors to develop strategies to internationalize a corporation's activities.

Chapter 2: Dr Mark J. Hooper reviews international strategic management that should be considered when working up a plan to operate globally.

In Chapter 3: International Business Ethics, Dr David Kimber and Dr Fran Siemensma review a current framework of business ethics. They reflect on philosophical, social, political, and organizational theories and consider their practical application in an international context. As a subject which directly relates to all forms of personal and organizational decision-making, it is a practical and extremely relevant area for current or potential managers who are or wish to work with a multinational corporation or in an international business environment. It is an essential element of business knowledge, one which may help avoid future turmoil as evidenced by recent major corporation collapses in the US and elsewhere.

Dimension 2 – Relationship Management

Dimension 2 is concerned with conflict management. The chapters introduce best practice negotiations, making contacts, hiring people, motivation, different countries employee's expectations, supplier's human resources, etc.

Chapter 4: Dr Maria Veludo reviews contributions and describes a case study concerning business to business relationship management. Companies may have relationships ranging from traditional adversarial aggressive negotiations through to collaboration on projects and genuine partnering that is considered a basis of world class business. This chapter reviews literature from several fields of research and models a wide range factors relating to inter-firm collaboration and partnering. Clarifications are provided to order the development process of inter-firm collaboration and partnering.

This chapter reviews a variety of definitions of inter-firm collaboration and partnering. This provides the reader an idea of the complexity of these concepts.

Then it will review main contributions of some theoretical perspectives to the understanding of these topics. These are: the resource based view theory, transaction cost analysis and network theory. The chapter will go on providing a short overview of partnering related issues, including disciplinary perspectives, characteristics and influencing factors.

In Chapter 5: International Negotiation, Dr Brooks C. Holtom examines the art and science of international negotiations with the aim of developing negotiation abilities. Three key assumptions are reviewed: first, international negotiation is a comprehensible social process. It is not a mystical process in a black box; it can be analysed, understood and modelled. Second, negotiation is a learnable and teachable skill. Negotiators are made, not born, and skills can be improved and relearned throughout life. Third, change and improvement in negotiating behaviour require a combination of intellectual training and behavioural skill development. The purpose of this chapter is to review the practices and strategies of negotiation skills used in both personal and professional settings. The chapter is designed to provide:

1. an understanding of the decision-making processes that influence negotiation outcomes;
2. applied theoretical frameworks for principled negotiation in the international context;
3. opportunities to develop effective negotiation skills.

Dimension 3 – Business-to-Business Coordination

Dimension 3 looks at the physical assets involved in delivering products to the major markets of the world. SCM and purchasing are mutually exclusive yet mutually supporting.

Chapter 6: Dr Mark J. Hooper and Alkiviadis Tromaras delve into social and environmental responsibilities. Given the legal and environmental pressure, companies must ensure they and their business partners go green. This chapter analyses the relationship between business strategy and the ecological environment. Legal requirements are noted including ISO 14000.

Chapter 7: Dr Zoltán Antal-Mokos identifies managerial issues that impact on successful mergers and acquisition projects. Pre-, during and post-phase difficulties and challenges are considered.

Chapter 8: Prof Douglas Macbeth introduces the concepts and benefits of organizing businesses into efficient supply chains. The chapter explores issues posed by organizations that operate in supply chains around the globe. The intention is to understand the strategic and operational aspects of such organizations and therefore to recognize the interdependence of any solutions.

The chapter:

- addresses critical areas of knowledge about the organizational context in which international business takes place;

- describes and compare examples of current good practice in managing extended supply chains;
- reviews the use such knowledge to understand situations in organizations;
- critically evaluates current practice to draw useful lessons.

Chapter 9: Dr David J. Newlands examines purchasing activities from a perspective of fast moving consumer goods producers, where new products are developed and introduced with increasing regularity. This differs from conventional purchasing that also focuses on order placement and materials control. This chapter focuses on preparing to purchase for a given product, where the product attributes and process characteristics are yet to be defined.

Chapter 10: Dr Isabel Fernández builds on the preceding chapters and discusses the technical practicalities of reverse logistics in order to ensure goods at the end of there service contracts and service lives are managed in environmentally responsible ways. This chapter introduces key aspects related to reverse logistics (RL). This field has been coined as 'the last frontier for companies to cut down costs'. The discipline is extremely necessary to create sustainable development. It is estimated there is sufficient steel already in a refined state to eliminate all iron ore extraction activities for the next 400 years. This chapter provides strategies to reduce, reuse and recycle materials.

Dimension 4 – Regional and Country Specific Differences

Dimension 4 reviews specific regions and countries requirements, expectations and core differences. They show how international companies truly need to manage their staff in an international context, rather than simply operating the same way in multiple countries.

Chapter 11: Dr Nada Zupan explores the correlation between human resource management practices and company's abilities to achieve and sustain peak performance. This chapter is based on the premise, that decisions about managing people make a difference: The decisions you make as a manager affect not only your own success but also employee behaviours, their performance and well being, their focus on satisfying customers, their sense of fair treatment, and ultimately, the efficiency and effectiveness of entire organization. The link between human resource management (HRM) and company performance is thus intensively studied and models of strategic HRM are developed. Of course, performance starts with every individual and thus employment relationships and psychological contracts become important. The main objective is to present theoretical background for critical analysis of various concepts and models, thus providing a framework for making good decisions.

Chapter 12: Prof Hedley Malloch reviews issues of recruiting and retaining managerial talent within an international context. The primary question is 'Should the company recruit locally or second staff from their home country to take control?' The chapter examines corporate ways of motivating employees to take ex-patriot assignments and compares this type of strategy to recruiting locally.

Chapter 13: Dr Sandra Jones examines employee relations management within an international context. Rather than taking control, the primary question here is 'How can management become more inclusive, reduce conflict and increase the employee number of ideas and learning in order to contribute to the firm's success?'

Chapter 14: Dr Peter Firkola emphasizes the key differences between Western and the Japanese' approaches to management. This chapter introduces Japanese human resource management systems from a variety of perspectives. Japanese management are examined from a historical and cultural perspective. The characteristics of traditional and modern management practices in Japan will then be discussed. An examination of the current situation and emerging management trends in Japan is included. This chapter discusses how to do business with the Japanese as well as the transferability of these management practices. This chapter offers practical and relevant knowledge for students planning to work in an international business environment.

Dimension 5 – Markets, Marketing Modes and Sales

Dimension 5 builds on the knowledge of the macro level market, in Dimension 3, by analysing individuals, groups and cliques. Once these are understood, the philosophies and processes of getting the message across, and then how these can be managed. Marketing creates many forms of data. They include 'voice of the customer', actual orders, requests for special products? These chapters focus on learning, recording information, observations and data mining. The data then can support focused creativity to identify new niche market segments and produce new product specifications that later become fully developed commercialized products of appropriate quality. In this context, quality is not only the eradication of process variances, but more importantly conformance to customers' expectations and requirements.

Chapter 15: Dr Simon A. Mercado examines the issues and complications of doing business in the pre-enlarged fifteen countries of the European Union. Further difficulties and differences clearly are evident with the accession of the twelve new countries. It is too early to evaluate the long term consequences of these changes. For example, the number of 'new countries' such as Kosovo on Sunday 17 February 2008 are changing the political and business map. Hence the chapter focuses on the pre-enlarged group of relatively wealthy nations.

Chapter 16: Prof Coral R. Snodgrass examines issues to doing business and when considering marketing goods and services in NAFTA. A key recent issue that touched many businesses is the subject of border crossing delays experienced since the 9/11 attacks on the United States.

Chapter 17: Visiting Professor Tim Lyons looks at developments in direct and e-marketing. As a founder of a consultancy that facilitates international business expansion in China, his team make use of these techniques to leverage there position and maximize returns on marketing Dollar investments. The point of sale in effect can be over the internet, or the result of being hosted when international business management visits the country. The chapter aims are:

- to identify the difference between direct marketing and more traditional marketing methods, and the potential role for direct marketing within organization's overall marketing strategy;
- to use a conceptual framework for the planning, integrating and control of the direct marketing process;
- to construct realistic objectives for different types of direct marketing;
- to provide relevant input towards creative strategy;
- to set a direct marketing budget and allocate resources to the direct communication elements within this budget;
- to demonstrate the strategic use of each of the direct marketing elements and critically analyse and evaluate the elements of a direct marketing campaign;
- identify the need for evaluating the effectiveness of the direct marketing communication plan;
- to determine the role of direct marketing in branding;
- to understand the role of technology in the ongoing development of direct marketing.

Chapter 18: Dr Mayo de Juan Vigaray and Beyza Gültekin describe retail industry strategies and effects of well designed points of sale venues. These may be high street stores, stalls in exhibition halls and other locations. Individuals may feel compelled to buy because dates such as Valentines Day create expectations that people anticipate receiving a good. To clinch the deal, each of the five senses may be stimulated in store, as well as maintaining displays of goods in flattering arrangements.

Chapter 19: Prof Ruben Chumpitaz and Dr Nicholas G. Paparoidamis examine service marketing issues. The key question asked is 'Will customers be dissuaded from continuing to buy from a given supplier even if they recently have had a bad experience purchasing?' The objectives of this chapter are twofold: First, to shed light in the theory underlying the concepts of service quality, customer satisfaction, service recovery and loyalty, and second to bring into focus the business-to-business field, presenting the theoretical grounds upon which the relationship marketing concepts of relationship quality, relationship satisfaction, trust and commitment are developed.

Dimension 6 – Money Matters

Dimension 6 examines raising capital, financial appraisal, policies and risks. These verify the sensitivity and profitability of doing business internationally.

Chapter 20: Prof Roby B. Sawyers identifies strategic cost management issues common to most companies and supply chains. Costs may be direct and immediate, or the result of total cost of ownership or life cycle costs included in servicing and disposal of goods. These latter issues relate to reverse logistics and environmental responsibility of producers. This chapter on cost management considers the long-term competitive success of the firm. Each successful firm maintains a competitive advantage based on a unique strategy. The strategy identifies the critical success factors that the firm must achieve. Cost management provides the information managers need to develop and implement successful strategies.

Chapter 21: Prof Steve Molloy examines cost management from a not-for-profit (NFP) perspective. By reducing costs, NFPs can offer more services and buy and distribute more aid with the same revenue. The objectives of the chapter are to:

- understand the nature of non-for-profits – why they not only survive, but dominate certain industries such as health, education, social services and the arts;
- craft strategies for improving the effectiveness and efficiency of the nonprofit organization; and
- develop control mechanisms for an organization for which there is often no 'bottom line'.

Dimension 7 – Perfection and Performance

Dimension 7 is of key importance in existing businesses. It is insufficient to simply analyse without plans or action. Action without analysis and a plan leads to unexpected consequences. Businesses must start to improve. Once started, they must accelerate the rate of learning, creativity and strive toward excellence, providing error-free products and services to gratify and delight customers.

Chapter 22: Dr Kevin Laframboise examines total quality management (TQM) philosophies. These set the scene for effective management by defining problem solving methodologies and vocabulary that is common to all international satellite operations. In so doing, managers will be able to communicate to their workforces, despite location or national and international cultural differences. This chapter examined total quality management, its principles and applications, strengths and drawbacks, and with a focus on the effects for the broad enterprise.

A complementary chapter available online from Gower Publishing's website reviews quantitative techniques used to optimize and monitor process quality.

Chapter 23: Dr David J. Newlands introduces key technology and innovation management issues for companies that have to push the boundaries of what seems possible – so-called 'technology challengers', while ensuring that they convert inventions and process capabilities into viable commercial products.

Chapter 24: Dr Sandra Jones examines organization's ability to harvest, collate, store and use data for commercial gains. The core principles of this chapter are that all employees are involved and that discussions are based on negotiation rather than autocratic senior management decrees.

Chapter 25: Dr Keith Dawes reviews the field of tacit knowledge and converting this unspoken information into communicated and recorded data. This is the basis of explicit knowledge management practices.

Dimension 8 – Making it Happen

All the chapters up to now have focused on locations, people, philosophies, relationships, infrastructure and tools. These are 'what could be' and 'what is'.

The chapters in Dimension 8 focus on getting started, growing the business from concept through to sustainability, creating further change, managing transitions to move away from 'me too' to sustainable competitive advantage, segment leadership and profitability.

These chapters focus on operationalizing international business. The scope includes identifying the initial need, developing plans, getting started, testing initial assumptions, planning next stages, making it happen.

Chapter 26: Dr Erkan Bayraktar explores service provision management within an international context. These types of activities make up the majority of commercial job positions in mature economies. This chapter also examines how services and manufacturing complement each other. Service facilities locations, quality, experience and other criteria are examined.

Chapter 27: Dr Phil Scott introduces all of the significant components of an integrated international logistics system and how to manage each activity and combine them in a strategic manner. This chapter addresses the logistical channel, which handles the physical flow of products and service.

Chapter 28: Dr David J. Newlands examines supplier development specific literature models and inhibitors to implementation are identified. Recruitment of suppliers to supplier development programmes is a significant challenge. Supplier development models have focused on the activities undertaken by purchasing staff. As with other intra- and inter-company improvement initiatives, the number of supplier development initiatives undertaken and the success rate are comparatively low. Tacit and explicit knowledge, training, development and facilitating are identified as core concepts typically omitted from conventional supplier development literature.

Chapter 29: Visiting Professor Olga Muzychenko explores the influence of the cross-cultural environment on the behaviour of international entrepreneurs and their effectiveness. The chapter reviews effects of growing cross-cultural and cross-border interaction on the content of entrepreneurial tasks and competencies.

Chapter 30: Dr David J. Newlands introduces the key issues associated with planning, forming a task force, implementing, monitoring and sustaining change. The aim is to identify key questions that must be answered in order to justify the present position or to identify questions that must be answered, and then analyse proposed solutions.

Chapter 31: Dr David J. Newlands discusses a realistic supply chain game. The game structure is based on the mobile phone market and was originally conceived to teach managers and logistics planners the benefits of selecting various operating strategies. This constituted design *of* logistics. The author then took this basic game and developed various options that represented more accurately the reality of the industry. These versions can be used to explain design *for* logistics, cost control, site location decisions, just-in-time, total quality management, supply chain and purchasing, change management and support other improvement initiatives.

We hope you enjoy and benefit from this combined effort. Good luck!

David Newlands and Mark Hooper
Lille, February, 2008

DIMENSION 1

International Perspectives

Chapter 1

International Business – Operating Abroad

David Trigg and Marie C. Trigg

A nation's economic success depends on the capacity for its companies and trading organizations to develop business relationships, trade and do business in the international arena. We introduce conceptual and practical material necessary to consider the issues and techniques associated with doing business internationally. Components of the topic embrace:

- why countries and companies need to trade internationally;
- comparative frameworks for international environmental assessment, especially country risk assessment; and
- international operations, including market entry strategies for multinational corporations (MNCs).

In an era of growing globalization, understanding contemporary international trade theory and how it applies to the development of MNCs are essential tools.

Application of business analysis to foreign market entry, the potential international mix of company operations and longer-term investment decisions by companies in a global context are also fundamental, as is an understanding of the volatility of exchange rate risk.

Managers and specialists increasingly require a need to:

- formulate scenarios to analyse risky situations in times of rapid, often discontinuous technological, political and social change in both the domestic and international environments;
- plan for the future in a systematic way; and
- retain flexibility and responsiveness where risks and change are unprecedented and unexpected.

These represent major challenges for managers and specialists at all levels of an organization. Their main focus in such a context should be on the development of international business and the successful conduct of that business.

The aim of this chapter is twofold: to develop an understanding of the international business environment and to develop and refine knowledge of business in an international setting. This chapter builds basic knowledge with a particular emphasis on the skills or competencies needed to ensure the successful development and implementation of operational processes applicable to the international environment.

Introduction

International business is commerce or trade that is carried on by a company beyond its domestic borders (Mahoney et al. 2001). It is often called cross-border trade. In most cases it is business conducted between different companies in different countries. However, as will be seen later, it may involve business conducted between different elements of the same company in different countries.

When people contemplate international business it is most common to think in terms of bulk carriers with oil or minerals or manufactured goods in a container on a cargo ship. However, items traded in routine and spot purchase international transactions are many and varied.

Perhaps the most common internationally traded item is information. Information ranges from everyday events in the nightly TV news service to confidential trading reports on market conditions in foreign countries. Other objects of international business include services such as consulting on foreign aid projects and capital for foreign investment projects. The employment of personnel from foreign sources is an increasingly important object of international business as companies seek skilled and professional managers and specialists to perform in the international arena. The ownership rights to goods, land, resources, information and businesses may be traded without transporting goods on container ships or trains, etc. For instance, Sony bought a movie studio in California; banks sell insurance policies on guarantees they made that underwrite loans they made to clients. Technology also is a much traded object of international business as companies all over the world strive to compete with each other on the basis of quality or low cost. Finally, we must not forget manufactured goods, because although their relative importance as a percentage of international business may be decreasing, they still are a vital element of business and will continue to be so into the future.

Companies involved in international business range from small enterprises making goods for export through to very large MNCs that are household names. To put the scale of international business into context, the combined revenues of the top 200 corporations constitute one quarter of the world's GDP. Their total revenues approach US$ 10 trillion.[1] This can be compared to the combined revenues of the poorest 80 per cent of countries, which are around US$ 4 trillion. Whilst the total global workforce is over two and a half billion people, the combined employment of the top 200 corporations is fewer than 20 million employees.[2] These figures have to be seen in the light of the fact that one of the largest employers in any country which has high social security contributions is the nation's health service provider. This sector alone accounts for around 17 per cent of the economy and increasingly, international 'health tourism', where individuals travel to other countries to undergo operations more quickly than they can be undertaken, or where they are unavailable, in their home country, have dental treatment and buy prescription glasses at much lower prices than are available at home.

One of the least visible international trades is known as the 'brain drain'. Qualified individuals who have the competence to move internationally can obtain jobs in other countries. They may have studied in one or more countries and now provide value-added services to their clients in other countries. These flows of employees are examined by Prof. Malloch in 'International Human Resource Management', Chapter 12 in this volume.

Terminology

There are many terms used in international business. The most common term is 'globalization'. There are many definitions of globalization and these are covered in a subsequent section. In its broadest sense, globalization is the worldwide trend of economies of the world becoming borderless and interlinked (Hill 2005). The extensions to the European Union typify this trend.

---

1   http://money.cnn.com/magazines/fortune/global500/2006/.
2   http://www.ilo.org/public/english/bureau/stat/portal/topics.htm#paidemp.

The globalization process allows businesses to expand beyond their domestic (national) borders. At a different level, globalization is the creation of standardized management practices and products that companies apply on a worldwide basis.

The important process covered in this chapter is that of internationalization (Welch and Luostarinin 1988). Such progressions occur when a company extends its operations beyond its domestic borders. In effect it is developing into an MNC. An MNC is a company that engages in foreign direct investment (FDI). In essence, it owns and controls value-adding processes in more than one country.

Another term that may be used to describe MNCs is a global corporation Mahoney et al. 2001, p. 869). These are companies that view the world as a single marketplace and strive to create standardized goods and services to meet customers' needs worldwide. A transnational corporation (TNC) is a company that seeks to combine global scale efficiencies with local responsiveness. One last expression to note at this stage is a wholly owned foreign subsidiary. This is an enterprise that is subordinate to a parent company in another country. Assembly and manufacturing facilities owned by the parent corporation that build identical or similar products closer to the market are known as transplants.

When referring to different countries, there are specific terms to denote what we are talking about. The country in which an MNC is based and has its head office is referred to as the parent or home country (ibid., p. 878). The country in which subsidiary operations are conducted is referred to as the host country.

In this chapter, we limit our argument to the nature of international business under four different headings (Hill 2005):

1. cultural differences;
2. politico-legal environment;
3. commercial environments;
4. financial issues.

Each of these areas of business is significant and raises issues that international managers must get right in order for their businesses to be successful.

The first of these is that when dealing between different countries there are cultural differences to be considered (Shenkar and Luo 2004, p. 149). The most obvious cultural difference is that of language. Management must consider things like people's social customs. For example, the way people greet each other, their concepts of hierarchy, personal space, work ethic, customer service, face, being an insider, cooperation and individual versus collectivism. Some social cultural aspects would never be accepted in private, yet are the accepted way for business and management practices.

The second aspect of international business that must be covered is the politico-legal environment in which business must be conducted. Each country has its own political system and its own legal system (ibid., p. 175). Whilst these may be classified under major categories, they are nevertheless quite different. Other aspects that need to be considered are issues such as employment regulations, contracts and dispute resolution.

The commercial environments of each country are also different from each other. Firstly, there are different levels of development, ranging from highly industrialized countries through to emerging economies (ibid., p. 119). Economies may be at different levels in cycles. Some countries are growing rapidly whilst others are in decline. Resource availability differs from country to country, as does the infrastructure and support necessary for the conduct of business. Emerging economies may be able to jump ahead because they adopt modern solutions without scrolling through obsolete phases. They can do this at lower cost because they have not invested in, and do not need to get rid of, historic legacy infrastructure, conditions and inefficient practices.

The last aspect that must be considered is that of financial issues (ibid., p. 226). Countries have to trade with each other and most countries have unique currencies at variable exchange rates that need to be taken into account. In essence, parties to transactions must use different currencies. Many currencies are quite volatile and as they fluctuate, business decisions to invest in a specific location can be the difference between success and failure. Ford Motor Company's sales of Aston Martin, Volvo and Land Rover are the result of the devaluation of the US dollar and tye comparative strength of sterling. Emerging economies, by contrast, may not have access to tradable currencies.

Classic Concepts

There are many differences between domestic and international business. It may seem trite to say that the major difference is clearly the range of activities that need to be performed. However, this is indeed true. A domestic business need concern itself with operating only in its home market where the managers are very conversant with local business practices. Management must try to ward off the inbound competition from transplants and cheap imports of substitute brands that may or may not be inferior. International business, on the other hand, involves operating in host countries where conditions, laws and business practices may be significantly different. Some of the major differences are now outlined.

Cultural Factors

One of the very first differences to note when conducting business internationally is whether to just export or operate a wholly owned foreign subsidiary, is that employees will be dealing with people who have different attitudes and perceptions about doing business (Mahoney et al. 2001). From the very outset people talk different languages. Whilst English may be the *lingua franca* of international business, there are many thousands of different languages around the world. Because people need to communicate, this means that one of the two parties involved in business is going to have to use a different language or else both parties will need to find a common language, such as English. The common axiom is that 'the British and the United States are two countries separated by the same language!' The rate of change in both spoken and written forms of language has significantly increased since the widespread take-up of the internet. Text message codes are the most significant example of this phenomenon.

We need to be very careful when it comes to speaking different languages. Just because another person speaks English as a native tongue is not a reason to think there will be no confusion. English is spoken very differently in different parts of the world and not all English words are in universal usage. Take for example the word 'fortnight'. In the United Kingdom and other countries of the British Commonwealth the word 'fortnight' is used to denote a period of two weeks. However, in the United States the word 'fortnight' is virtually unknown. So if an English person is dealing with the American and says that the details of a project will be available in a fortnight's time, the American may not understand and the result will lead to uncertainty. A black coffee in the UK means coffee without milk. In Israel, it means filter coffee put in a cup, to which hot water is added to make a mixture that settles at the bottom of the cup as a sludge. Israelis use the term 'Nes'' to indicate a coffee drink made with instant powder. 'Arctic' to the British means the North Pole region and implies polar bears. Israelis use it to mean an ice cream. The word 'lolly' to British means money or frozen juice on a stick. To Australians, it means confectionary.

Each country will have its own customs and the way people interact with each other varies enormously. Take, for example, a simple greeting.[3] In France, when entering a room, even if someone is late and the meeting is in full flow, they will greet everyone in turn. The British are more likely to 'just slip in' and try to not interrupt the flow. They may then apologize at a convenient moment, typically a pause or the first time they would like to contribute to the discussion. Many countries use the basic handshake where people will clasp each other's right hand. However, there are very many variations on even this simple gesture. It is customary for Muslim men to shake hands and then touch their chest in front of their heart. People in some countries bow to each other; in others they embrace. Other nationalities not only embrace, but kiss each other on the cheek (in Britain once, France twice, Spain three kisses, Russia six!) although regional differences also apply in the same country. Convention dictates which cheek to start the sequence with. In some cultures males embrace each other when greeting. If a businessman comes from a culture where embracing another male in public is unacceptable, that person may have difficulties in undertaking a simple greeting in a foreign country. Impressions of each other on first meeting are very important and if a person perceives rudeness in the form of greeting then it may be difficult to proceed to a business relationship. Giving business cards in two hands and receiving them reverently, placing them on the desk and making frequent glances to them is the norm in Japan. Other cultures flick them across the desk at each other. They may then put the cards in a trouser pocket – a big 'no, no' in certain Far Eastern cultures.

Perceptions and attitudes vary between different national groups (Catalyst 2006). In some Western cultures there is a perception that when business people meet they are there to do business. Other aspects of relationships are of a secondary nature. However, in other cultures, such as Asian, Middle Eastern or Latin American, people spend much time in creating a relationship in which they feel comfortable to do business. In France, the relationship is the aspect that must be maintained as a priority, even if there are frustrating issues that seem urgent and important that it would be efficient to sort out immediately. In most Western cultures, it is easy for a business person to cold call and thus make contact with a potential client previously unknown to them. In other cultures people will most likely only do business after they are formerly introduced by mutual acquaintances or agencies.

Commercial Environments

Each country has a different commercial environment in which business operates. First of all, each country is at a different level of development.[4] The level will vary from the highly industrialized, such as Western Europe, through to emerging economies, such as those in Africa. One of the important ways in which the level of development will affect the way business operates is the infrastructure support that is vital to business. Highly industrialized countries have well-developed transport and communication systems. They have strong legal and financial systems and the capacity to enforce these systems where necessary. Emerging economies, on the other hand, typically do not enjoy systems that are as well developed. Therefore, business people will have to take into account that some countries do not have these systems to facilitate the conduct of business at the same level they are used to in their own countries.

---

3 http://www.executiveplanet.com/index.php?title=Main_Page.
4 http://www.worldwatch.org/node/3893.

Each country will have different resource availability.[5] Some countries have a large skilled workforce, particularly where the education system is well-developed. Other countries have a large but poorly educated workforce. Labour in such countries will typically be quite cheap relative to that in other countries[6] and may be used in simple, repetitive manual activities. In wealthy countries, private loan capital will be more readily available than in poor countries. As a result, capital can be more readily raised to undertake new ventures. The credit crisis of 2007 stemmed from NINJA (no income, no job or assets) mortgages given to people who couldn't afford to repay the loan or even service the interest.

Economic and business conditions vary between countries.[7] Just as countries are at different levels of development so they will be at different stages in their business cycles. Growth in some countries is at double digit levels whilst at the same time other countries may be in recession. Inflation, for example, may be very low in some countries (Japan especially), yet quite rampant in others (Zimbabwe, at the time of writing. Previously Poland, Russia and Israel have suffered crippling inflation).

Politico-Legal

There are many forms of political and legal systems throughout the world.[8] There are over 270 countries in the world today and each has a different political and legal system. Whilst all these different systems may be classified under common headings, there are still differences between countries. Spain's accounting system is copied from the French, which itself is borrowed from Germany. There are countries, for example, whose legal system is based on the British system of law. However, every country that adopts a system will have variations. So the law as it is applied in the United Kingdom or in Australia is different and this must be taken into account when doing business in other countries, even though they may be common law countries. Other forms of legal systems include code law and theocracy.

Because business has to operate within the political and legal systems of each country there is necessarily political risk.[9] Political risk is the effect on a firm's ability to conduct value-adding operations to production due to the nature of a country's political and legal environment. Political risk can extend from a change in government policy towards business through to civil unrest and also include civil war and foreign wars.

There are many other aspects of operating within the legal environment, including simple things like employment law. For example, the duration of the working week varies around the world. In France the working week is 35 hours,[10] although President Sarkozi has indicated that more flexibility will be introduced in order to reward hardworking people and enable the economy to compete. In Australia it is 38 hours. UK workers are limited to 48 hours, except for certain types of employment such as truck drivers and airline pilots, where specific legislation is in operation. Other countries can have as many as 60 hours in the working week. The benefits and conditions available to workers, including such things as meal and rest breaks, vary from country to country.

The formulation of contracts for business also varies according to legal systems. The enforcement of those contracts varies around the world. The adherence to international treaty

---

5   http://www.iiasa.ac.at/Research/ECS/docs/book_st/node7.html.
6   http://yaleglobal.yale.edu/display.articlechapter?id=3231.
7   http://www.nber.org/papers/W9859.
8   http://garnet.acns.fsu.edu/~phensel/intlpoli.html.
9   http://www.political-risk.net/framesBase.htm.
10   http://www.triplet.com/50-10_employment/50-20_workingtime.asp.

obligations also varies.[11] A country's membership of various treaty organizations, such as the World Trade Organization (WTO), will result in the need for different business practices.

Financial

Most countries in the world have their own unique currency, although more and more member countries of the European Union are adopting a common currency, the Euro (€). This means that when companies wish to trade with each other around the world, they have to exchange their currency for that of the other country. An alternative is to use a common currency, such as the US dollar. Oil and aircraft are sold in US dollars. The US dollar depreciation – from about $0.80/€ in 2002 to $1.30/€ by 2007 – hampered Airbus in marketing, designing and producing their A380, sustained Boeing sales and made exports from European producers difficult. When the exchange rate stood at about $1.5/£, business was great. At the time of writing it is around $2/£. Consequently, Ford's profitability as a result of producing Jaguar and Land Rover vehicles in the UK has dropped drastically.[12]

Some currencies, such as the US$ and the Hong Kong dollar, are tied to each other in their exchange rate.[13] Most currencies, however, have a floating value. That is, their value against other currencies will fluctuate periodically. Some currencies are quite volatile, particularly measured over time. Because normal international business is not carried out instantaneously, it is necessary to agree on prices for the delivery of goods and services that will occur at some time in the future. Payment for goods is most often made upon delivery. This means that payment of goods to be made in the future has to be worked out in the present.[14]

To facilitate the negotiation of contracts it is necessary to use forward prices of currencies. These forward prices are the predictions of bankers and foreign exchange (Forex) traders of what they think the price will be at a future date.[15] Business people have to agree on the value of currency at a future delivery date. If a price is struck and the currency moves in an adverse direction, this can result in failure to make a profit. Companies can insure and hedge against such currency movements, although this can incur extra expense.

The nature of currencies varies around the world. Many countries have what is called hard currency that is readily tradable currency.[16] The currencies of countries such as the United States and the countries of Western Europe are readily tradable on a worldwide basis. On the other hand, emerging economies may have currencies that are not always readily tradable. These are called soft currencies. Indeed, some countries do not have cash available to trade and therefore must adopt other methods. Counter-trade, that is the exchange of one lot of goods for another, is still widely used in international business. This is an international form of the barter system. While they were trading, Massey Ferguson exchanged tractors for sesame seeds. These were then sold to fast food restaurant chains in exchange for cash. This approach avoids currency exchange risks and can include an element of fair trade and sustainable development.

---

11 http://www.cailaw.org/ita/publications.html.

12 http://www.oanda.com.

13 http://www.expatfacts.com/topics/Foreign-Currency-Exchange.html.

14 Companies are now finding they must compete on time. The faster they can fulfil an order, the less risk there is that dramatic changes will occur. Suppliers can stipulate they wish to be paid in their own currency. Another strategy is to demand payment in a currency that is relatively more stable. This is not only limited to selling goods. ABBA, the Swedish pop group from the 1970s dictated the currency and the exchange rate they required.

15 http://www.dailyreckoning.com/rpt/SpotCurrencyMarket.html.

16 http://www.oanda.com/channels/business/business.shtml#data.

Technological

Highly industrialized countries have access to advanced technology and generally have a skilled workforce that can readily use state-of-the-art technology. Other countries may not have ready access to advanced technology and nor do they have skilled workforce able to use advanced technology. When companies set up business in foreign countries, managers need to take into account whether technology available in the home country is also available in the host country. Indeed, one of the functions of multinational corporations is to export technology from their home country to the host countries where it conducts business (Hill 2005, p. 245).

Some countries are blacklisted. Trading is prohibited between US organizations and Cuba. The US also prohibits its companies and governmental agencies from trading with companies that trade with Cuba.

Internationalization Process

Almost every company begins life as a domestic operation. If that company enjoys success in its home market it will seek to expand that market locally. Soon, the managers will perceive the home market as being insufficient to sustain growth and will need to expand their horizons (ibid., p. 536). Home markets may become saturated or new opportunities appear that offer promise of growth and higher returns. This is the impetus for internationalization.

A simple definition of internationalization is the development of an international profile (Shenkar and Luo 2004, p. 133). A more complete definition is the increasing structural complexity of the organization as more resources are needed for cross-border operations (ibid., p. 67). It is a move outwards from the home base which may proceed at any pace and, in fact, may be reversed depending on management commitment. The success of the satellite business may depend on the comparative strengths of the organizations in the target economy. Foreign supermarket chains find it very difficult to operate in Germany and the US, for example, because of the strength of the indigenous brands.

There are a number of models that examine the process. A company may stop its internationalization process at any stage of development. It may even skip stages, depending on the nature of the market. Just because a firm commences the internationalization process does not mean that it will proceed to the ultimate stage of a wholly owned foreign subsidiary involved in the full manufacturing process.

The level of internationalization will depend on the commitment of managers (Hill 2005, p. 246). Resources available to a company are scarce. Access to resource availability changes over time. As a result, firms do not always proceed with their internationalization plans at a constant pace. Not all firms are equally resource endowed. It is rare to see firms in the same industry advance their international plans at the same rate.

Internationalization can occur at two levels (ibid., 212–37). The first, and easiest, of the internationalization processes is through non-equity methods. Non-equity methods of market entry do not involve the investment of the firm's capital. Nevertheless, it can still be an expensive exercise as expenditure of resources is made into foreign markets. The other method of internationalization is through equity methods. As the name equity implies, there is the investment of capital in international operations. Firms take control and ownership of resources used to add value to their operations (Mahoney et al. 2001, p. 485).

Stages Model

The first of these models is the 'stages model' (Shenkar and Luo 2004, p. 67). This model states that firms engage in a distinct pattern of movement outwards from their home base. The parameters that affect this movement rate of involvement are ownership and the risk of investment, along with the complexity of the investment.

The stages model has been developed from examination of the growth of manufacturing firms. The model seeks to explain increasing long-term revenue – that is, growth – and at the same time keeping risk-taking costs low. It is problematic whether this model can be used for service industries such as hospitality.

Figure 1.1 shows a typical evolution of a multinational corporation from its embryonic beginning. On the horizontal axis is a time scale, although no absolute measures are used. There is no set pattern of time during which a multinational may evolve. Some firms may evolve into multinationals over several decades, whilst others evolve very quickly. For example, there are many firms in high technology, communications and pharmaceuticals that have developed into large MNCs in a very short space of time.

On the vertical axis is the factor of complexity. Each successive stage in the evolution of a multinational involves operations of a more complex nature. According to our definition, internationalization is the increasing complexity of international operations. The options to deal with this issue are to 'keep it simple' by retaining all decision-making and control functions at the parent site, or to develop strong leadership locally.

The most typical initial foray into international activity is by means of exporting or importing (Hill 2005, pp. 534–53). This may be by means of deliberate strategy or by pursuing a casual foreign enquiry. The local activities focus on buying or selling products and components. If this initial foray into international activity is successful, managers will continue the practice.

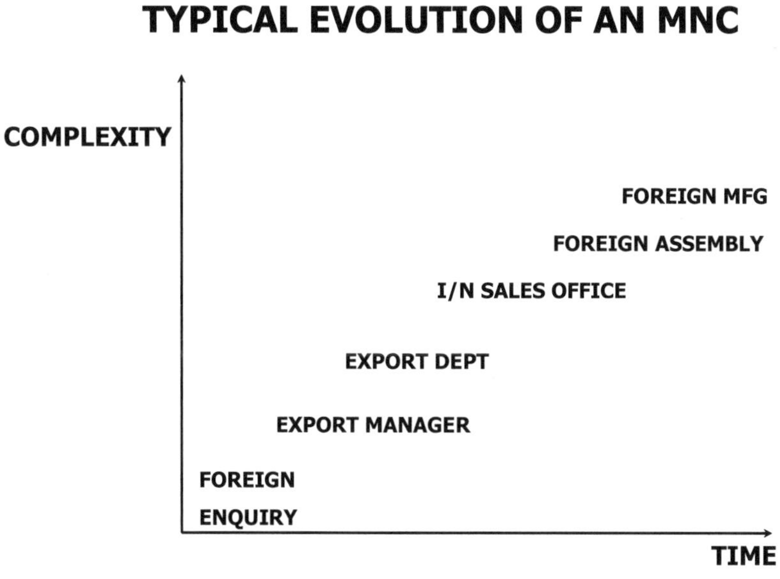

TYPICAL EVOLUTION OF AN MNC

Figure 1.1   Typical evolution of multinational corporation

As more resources are needed to sustain this export activity, managers will need to establish a structural response and create an export-oriented work unit.

It may become necessary for the firm to create international sales offices in host countries where the firm operates. This will lead to the first level of investment (ibid., pp. 468–9). International business develops the managers it needs to explore further options for conducting activities in foreign countries. As the business grows, operations become more complex as the firm moves into assembly, perhaps from knock-down kits, through to campus-based parts production for full manufacture.

These operations can be divided into the two categories of equity and non-equity operations. It will be remembered that the distinction between these two methods is the pattern of capital for investment or merely an expense of doing business.

Taking the equity option first, the two axes will refer to ownership and control on the horizontal axis and complexity and risk of operations on the vertical axis. Although it will be reported as a non-equity method of entry, most firms start with exporting or importing as their first venture into international operations. If the export-import activity is successful, a firm will open a foreign sales office, which is a wholly-owned foreign subsidiary. The purpose of these sales offices is to facilitate sales in host countries and to have representatives on the ground. As further sales are made, managers may deem it more efficient for products to be sent to the host country in a 'knocked down' state and assembled for sale in the host country. This is most often a precursor to full manufacture. Such a strategy can significantly reduce the pipeline liability costs and cost of finished goods that are in the distribution channels. This consequently increases speed to market, introduces variants only to replenish sales of stored goods, or assembles goods to exact customer specifications and thus avoids the cost of full value inventory. The strategy, however, seems to be ignored by companies that mass produce in low-cost countries because they primarily focus on unit price rather than supply chain total cost, product flexibility and obsolescence risk.

For reasons that will be discussed in the international strategy section, firms may not wish to create a wholly-owned foreign subsidiary to manufacture their products. For political or legal reasons it may be more advantageous to seek a local partner. Creating a joint venture with a local company is a way of sharing risk, depending on the stability of the operating environment in the host country (Shenkar Luo 2004, p. 130). Managers may consider that sharing resources with a host country firm is a better way to operate. This gives rise to a joint-venture operation that is a way of sharing resources, which is generally done on a 50/50 basis.

In the non-equity model, the graph represents the involvement and a risk involved in equity methods of the internationalization process. The horizontal axis is an indication of the degree of involvement and control of the operation. The vertical axis is an indication of the risk and complexity of the particular types of operation. The various methods of non-equity entry are given as a progression. However, it is not necessary for a multinational to progress from one method of operation to a higher level unless there are strategic imperatives and corporate commitment to do so.

It has been stated previously that exporting and importing is the least risky of all forms of international activity. It does, however, have associated risk. There are issues of non-payment, delivery time and actual delivery.

Licensing is the legal use of intellectual property and brand identity by another firm (Mahoney et al. 2001, pp. 643–6). One firm, the licensor, creates intellectual property such as a formula, a recipe or other patent. The Body Shop grew as a result of this strategy into a multinational with significant brand presence. While production was centralized, goods sales were expanded across a wider geographic area and revenue was generated from franchise agreements. Perhaps the most common forms of intellectual property are software, recorded music or film. Another firm – the licensee – purchases the legal right to use this intellectual property to create product(s) that they then sell into the marketplace. A useful example of this process is the manufacture of yoghurt. The original recipe was created by a French firm that then sold the right to use this recipe to companies in many other countries for production and sale.

Franchising is essentially an advanced form of licensing where one company – the franchisor – owns intellectual property and allows other companies – franchisees – to use that property (ibid., pp. 480–81). The biggest difference between franchising and licensing is that the franchisee uses the name of the franchisor. The most prominent examples of franchising are perhaps found in the fast food restaurant industry, such as McDonald's Corporation. Individual restaurants are owned by private companies and enter into royalty agreements with McDonald's Corporation for the use of their intellectual property and their trading name. As can be seen, the degree of risk and complexity in operating a franchise is much greater than that of operating a licence. Therefore the degree of involvement and control by the franchisor needs to be much greater as they are protecting their intellectual property and their name and reputation.

Higher-level entry strategies such as subcontracting and turnkey operations are far more complex because of specifications written into contracts. For example, if a company is building a utility complex, such as a power generating plant, for a client company – which is a turnkey operation – the risk is very high and the degree of control by the contracting company needs to be much greater.

Whilst this model is useful as showing the development of international firms, there are some difficulties with it. Even casual observation of the development of multinational corporations indicates that there is some leapfrogging. That is, firms may not go through every stage as set out in the model. As a firm gains experience in foreign markets it is possible that in subsequent markets a firm will move to an advanced stage of the model without going through the early stages.

Some companies increase their global presence by taking over ailing businesses. These may be competitors or in other sectors that would widen their business portfolio or bolster strategic weaknesses with their strengths. An issue noted by Lamming (1993) is that vertically integrated firms that buy and sell within the group perceive less commercial pressure and hence may provide worse service and lower quality than that available from external competitors.

Another variable that impacts on the rate internationalization is 'psychic distance'. Psychic distance is defined as the perceived remoteness and cultural differences of the host country. With the advent of increased and improved transport and communications the phenomenon of psychic distance is becoming less of an issue.

Transaction Cost Analysis (TCA) Model

The objective for all firms is to provide revenue growth and/or reduce costs. This objective is the basis of explanation for structural decisions.

Transaction costs consist of *ex-ante* costs plus *ex-post* costs. The former comprise search and contracting costs. The search costs consist of gathering information to identify and evaluate potential international opportunities. Contracting costs are associated with negotiating and writing agreements between sellers and buyers.

Ex-post costs comprise monitoring costs and enforcement costs. Monitoring costs are associated with fulfilling predetermined sets of obligations. Enforcement costs are associated with sanctioning a trading partner for not performing in accordance with the agreement. The obvious goal is to minimize the combination of these costs. Therefore, a firm will internalize these costs where it can see a benefit to itself. It will undertake the value-adding operations under its own auspices if it believes the operation will be cheaper than contracting it out to another firm. Intellectual property is a key consideration. All vehicle manufacturers produce the pressings and assemble the vehicle. The shape of the car is their trademark design feature and early adoption of innovative methods to increase quality, strength, rigidity and production efficiencies reduce labour requirements.

Some of the parameters that guide the TCA (Hill 2005, p. 683) model include bounded rationality, which refers to be framework in which managers think. Because of their experience in business operations, managers tend to contemplate ways that have provided effective, efficient or elegant solutions to them in the past. Although managers are expected to think 'outside the box', only a few ever really do this. If managers are expected to take last year's model and modify it 2 or 3 per cent, they will essentially only tweak what they did and not really think differently. If managers are challenged to create radically different or superior results, hundreds or thousands of percentage point differences for example, they will think differently because the 'glass ceiling' has been removed. It is not enough simply to have the ideas. Managers must be able to sell their solutions or convince others that the change needs to be undertaken and soon. The fear of what will be done should be less than the fear of failure and business collapse if nothing is done or if they continue on as if nothing was untoward.

Business decisions are beset with uncertainty because risks are only just being identified. They also are ambiguous because there are more questions than solutions. There is internal uncertainty within the company that is controllable by managers, such as the availability of resources and the framing of budgets. There is also external uncertainty such as demand for product. Whilst uncontrollable by managers, it is certainly still manageable. Information may be asymmetrical with information coming from different sources. Because sources may differ both in their collection of data and its interpretation, there will always be a need to reconcile these differences to make useful and meaningful decisions. Despite the best market research and planning there is no guarantee that all information is accurate. There are also underlying factors such as management commitment to a certain plan of action as we saw in the stages model. Business decisions affect the future. They are made in the present based on historic data and predictions or forecasts. Clearly, as time goes by, more will be learned and insights will be clarified. As a result, the strategic commitment to a decision will need to be revised and new strategies and decisions made to fit with the scenarios and contexts businesses have to operate in.

International Strategy

An expression often used in the international context is 'going global' (Shenkar and Luo 2004, p. 88). This refers to the potential scope for all of the organization's operations to be uniform around the world and its ability to compete on a worldwide basis.

There are two ways that a multinational corporation can direct its offering of products and services. The first of these is by standardization, where a company sees its market as a homogenized, uniform place for trade (Mahoney et al. 2001, pp. 643–6). It assumes that customer preferences are universal. On the other hand, companies may see a need for customization of goods and services and the adaptation of these according to national or regional preferences. The differences between the two are that the latter is customer driven rather than being product and production efficiency driven.

Companies will expand according to their resource availability and their core competencies. Management commitment and decision-making companies can position themselves as they wish along the value-adding chain. Hence, companies are also capable of organizational learning. That is, as managers gain experience in different types of international operations they can expand their activities according to the extent of that knowledge and experience. Managers don't have a script. Some may rely on facts and evidence. Others rely on intuition and 'gut feeling'. All managers must make the effort to convert tacit knowledge that is in the heads and experience of their supply-chain participants into explicit recorded data that then can be analysed, debated and then plans decided upon. Chapters by Jones and also by Dawes in this volume debate tacit and explicit knowledge management issues and processes.

One useful device is known as a life cycle (Shenkar and Luo 2004, p. 61). We are familiar with this process from study of such things as marketing. Products are all fully developed in the domestic market and available for sale in that market. As a firm seeks expansion it will exploit that product to enter likely foreign markets. As the product succeeds in the host country markets, competitors will also start production of similar products. As the product matures in global markets, companies tend to seek to reduce costs and start a search procedure to reduce production costs. For example, if labour is a major cost of production a company may seek out lower labour wage countries and transfer production. They also benefit from tax holidays and other incentives when doing so. The key potential drawback is the increased downstream distribution time and the consequent increase in pipeline stock value, which is a risk to profit.

As mentioned above, the choices available for a company to expand its operations internationally will depend on the resources available to it and also its current operating position. These aspects are internal to the company and therefore controllable by the managers. Management should consider the resources and assets that managers currently have available and their effectiveness in acquiring extra resources and assets. These may be generated internally by sales revenue or else be acquired from shareholders and/or lenders, such as banks. Experience in international operations is also a variable asset. Managers acquire experience by actually doing business in foreign markets. However, companies can acquire experience by recruiting appropriately skilled personnel. The former method takes time, while the latter can provide a much quicker access to growth.

External to the company but still manageable are various industry drivers. These industry drivers include issues such as the nature of the market, government regulation, the nature of competition and industry cost structures.

The nature of the market will depend on the host country's level of industrialization. Companies from developed countries are more likely to trade with companies from other industrialized countries. As a result we see the highest levels of international business being conducted between Western Europe, Eastern Asia and North America. These are trading groups of countries that have high per capita income and large levels of disposable income. These markets also are highly sophisticated with very cosmopolitan tastes.

Governments in all countries are the major players in international business, whether they are taking part in business themselves or merely acting as regulators. There is international cooperation between countries under the auspices of organizations such as the WTO (Hill 2005, p. 180). Countries may go into partnership with others such as the European Union (EU) or the North America Free Trade Association (NAFTA). Markets that were once closed or centrally planned are opening up to be more market driven and provide many opportunities for foreign companies.

Putting these two issues together, managers have available to them a number of strategy levers. These include the nature of the product/service offerings. There are many ways in which managers can participate in the market. Managers can also make choices about the location of activities, whether it is production or sales. They also can make a choice about which competitors they choose to compete with and the nature of that competition. For example, there are companies that choose to compete on a head-to-head basis, such as Coca-Cola and Pepsi in the soft drink industry or Hertz and Avis in the rental car industry.

Conclusions

This chapter has introduced various themes that are examined in detail within subsequent contributions of this volume. To become a successful manager in the international context requires a wide range of knowledge and understanding. These fields include cultural differences, the politico-legal environment, commercial environments and financial issues.

There is no unique solution – a 'one size fits all' strategy. Corporations are staying small, evolving, growing or collapsing, adapting or remaining as stalwarts, competing or making their own unique market where they dominate a new niche. Large monolithic corporations such as IBM have broken up. Their single company solution is now a myriad of niche players that each provide the best on offer and enable clients to choose an individual custom-made solution.

A business cannot exist on its forecasts. It must have orders. A company's business is the orders it receives. Key to success is how the company organizes internal and external resources to satisfy those orders while ensuring that the many key performance indicators show they are doing this competitively. To acquire orders with a minimum of capital investment, franchising and licensing may be a viable option. McDonald's and The Body Shop are key examples of this strategy successfully applied.

References

Catalyst (2006), 'Different Cultures, Similar Perceptions: Stereotyping of Western European Business Leaders', http://www.docuticker.com/?p=5589.

Hill, C.W.L. (2005), *International Business: Competing in the Global Marketplace* (New York: McGraw Hill).

Lamming, R. (1993), *Beyond Partnership – Strategies for Innovation and Lean Supply* (London: Prentice Hall International).

Mahoney, D., Trigg, M.C., Griffin, R. and Pustay, M. (2001), *International Business: A Managerial Perspective*, 2nd edn (Frenchs Forest: Prentice Hall).

Shenkar, O. and Luo, Y. (2004), *International Business* (Danvers: Wiley).

Welch, L.S. and Luostarinen, R. (1988), 'Internationalization: The Evolution of a Concept', *Journal of General Management* 14(2) (Winter), pp. 36–64.

Chapter 2
International Strategy Management

Mark J. Hooper

Strategic Management in the International Arena

As firms position themselves to compete on a worldwide basis, they will continue to seek external reinforcement of their efforts, such as international trade agreements and favourable national industrial policies. Going global raises several internal issues that need to be successfully managed. This chapter discusses multinational corporations and explores international operations from the strategic management perspective: analysing the environment, establishing organizational direction, formulating strategy, implementing strategy, and exerting strategic control.

Multinational Corporations

Asserted by contributors to Wikipedia,[1] a *multinational corporation* (MNC) is an 'enterprise that manages production establishments or delivers services in at least two countries'. MNCs are also known as *multinational enterprise* (MNE), *transnational corporation* (TNC) and *multinational organization* (MNO).

MNCs can be divided into three distinct subgroups:

1. *Horizontally integrated multinational corporations* manage production establishments located in different countries to produce the same or similar products.
2. *Vertically integrated multinational corporations* manage production establishments in certain countries to produce products that serve as inputs to production establishments in other countries.
3. *Diversified multinational corporations* manage production establishments located in different countries that are neither horizontally nor vertically integrated.

Given their large economic influence as well as their extensive financial resources available for public relations and political lobbying, MNCs can exert a powerful influence over international relations. Analysis of the 100 largest economic entities reveals the economic power of MNCs (Anderson and Cavanagh 2000).[2] Table 2.1 shows key findings.

The Economic Power of MNCs

Multinationals have played an important role in globalization. Given their international reach and mobility, prospective countries, and sometimes regions within countries, must compete

---

1 http://en.wikipedia.org/wiki/Multinational_corporation.
2 http://www.webeurope.co.uk/corporate-power-the-facts.htm.

Table 2.1   The economic power of MNCs

- 51 are now corporations and 49 are countries.

- The world's top 200 corporations account for over a quarter of economic activity on the globe while employing less than one per cent of its workforce.

- The Top 200 corporations' combined sales are bigger than the combined economies of all countries minus the biggest 10.

- The Top 200s' combined sales are 18 times the size of the combined annual income of the 1.2 billion people (24 per cent of the total world population) living in 'severe' poverty.

- Between 1983 and 1999, the profits of the Top 200 firms grew 362.4 per cent, while the number of people they employ grew by only 14.4 per cent.

- A full 5 per cent of the Top 200s' combined workforce is employed by Wal-Mart.

- United States (U.S.) corporations dominate the Top 200, with 82 slots (41 per cent of the total). Japanese firms are second, with only 41 slots.

- Between 1983 and 1999, the share of total sales of the Top 200 made up by service sector corporations increased from 33.8 per cent to 46.7 per cent.

with each other to have MNCs locate their facilities within their region. Once installed, spin-off benefits for regions when MNCs set up include future tax revenues, employment and stimulated economic activity. 'To compete, countries and regional political districts offer incentives to MNCs such as tax breaks or holidays, pledges of governmental assistance and improved infrastructure. They may relax environmental and labour standards. This process of becoming more attractive to foreign investment can be characterized as "a race to the bottom".'[3]

There is no clear consensus on the origin of the first MNC. Some have argued that the Knights Templar, founded in 1118, became a multinational when the order started providing banking services in 1135. However, others claim that the honour goes to the Dutch East India Company (Vereenigde Oostindische Compagnie) when it first appeared in 1602.

Since the expression MNC first appeared in 1974, the term has been used to describe organizations that have significant operations in more than one country. The organization that invests in international operations is called the parent company; the country in which the parent company makes the investment is called the host company. If the facility is a production unit that replicates existing infrastructure, this is called a transplant. The multinational corporation views its diverse activities as a whole and develops and implements a unified strategy to encompass all of them.

At the end of World War II, the US was the most powerful industrial nation and for the next 35 years US enterprises ranked among the largest in the world. In 1975, 126 of the world's 260 multinational organizations were based in the US, including 15 of the largest 25 multinationals. In the 1980s and 1990s, things began to change rapidly. Japanese, British, German, French,

---

3   http://www.answers.com/topic/multinational-corporation.

Dutch, Italian and South Korean multinational organizations grew in strength and size and began challenging US companies, even in the North American market.

Transforming into Multinational Corporations

Some organizations accomplish the transformation into multinational corporations in stages: their early foreign operations rely on exporting and they progress gradually through licensing to direct investment. Today, however, progress in technology and global interdependence has freed organizations that do not rank with MNCs to exploit the potential of international markets. For example, Alpha Electronics is a small- to medium-sized enterprise employing 38 people with an annual turnover of £1.8 million. Based in the industrial centre of Coventry, United Kingdom (UK), they manufacture printed circuit boards for a broad base of end customers in the aerospace, automotive, telecommunication and research industries in the UK. In an increasingly competitive global environment the UK has seen a significant reduction in its PCB industry resulting from low-cost/high-volume manufacturers in the Far East importing direct to the UK marketplace.

By virtue of its size and most importantly its focus on delivering total solution products to customers, Alpha Electronics has established itself as a leading provider of prototype and low volume circuits with a reputation for delivering reliability, responsiveness and expertise. This focus is the key to its future survival and competitiveness (Hooper et al. 2001). Irrespective of size, all companies competing on a global basis must perform the main steps of the strategic management process.

International Environmental Analysis

Environmental analysis is the process of monitoring the conditions in which an organization operates. The framework typically used to aid this systematic discussion is 'SWOT analysis' that allows the present and future Strengths, Weaknesses, Opportunities and Threats that affect the progress of an organization toward its goals (Ansoff 1965; Andrews 1987). This complicated process involves analysing:

1. the general environment – social, economic, technological, ethical and political/legal conditions;
2. the operating environment – suppliers, competitors, customers and labour conditions;
3. the internal environment – conditions within the organization;

Table 2.2 shows a possible SWOT analysis for two MNCs, Apple Computers Inc. and Canon Inc.

SWOT analysis has been criticized for its apparent simplicity which has lead to a check list mentality to be applied to strategic analysis. Hill and Westbrook (1997) and later McDonald (1999) contend that SWOT analyses often yield only 'shallow extemporaneous inventories' that are as likely to detract from critical issues, themes, and forces that enable them to be identified. Alternative models to identify and analyse strategic issues have been proposed including resource-based SWOT analysis that draws on Porter's work (1979, 1980, 1991a) and Brandenburger and Nalebuff's value net (1995). From a resource-based perspective, strategic implications determine strategic significance. Therefore, identifying significant SWOT attributes and deriving their strategic implications are interactive rather than sequential tasks. Further,

Table 2.2   Example SWOT analysis for Apple Computers and Canon

Strengths	Weaknesses
Global presence	Low returns
Brand image	Dependency for key components
Synergistic portfolio	
Strong media content	

Opportunities	Threats
Wireless products	Strong competition
New digital platform	Slow Eurozone economy
MP3 player market	Lawsuits

Apple Computers Inc.

Strengths	Weaknesses
Strong brand image	High dependence on Hewlett-Packard
Wide range of products	Low growth in Japan
R&D capability	
Strong financial performance	

Opportunities	Threats
Growing digital SLR camera market	Embedded cameras in mobile phones
Expanding Asia Pacific market	Counterfeit Canon products
	Intense competition
	Emergence of new recording formats

Canon Inc.

strengths and weaknesses commonly define and are defined by opportunities and threats. Hence, the importance and status (favourable or unfavourable) of many factors that comprise a business' internal and external domains are contextually determined and far from apparent at first glance.

Analysis of MNCs strategic environmental context needs to be more complex than that of a purely domestic firm. Fombrun and Wally (1993) suggest that this complexity can be expressed as a function of three forces:

1. worldwide infrastructure;
2. worldwide socio-structure;
3. worldwide superstructure.

Figure 2.1 illustrates some of the relationships between the forces of change, emerging trends and the issues that affect environmental analysis of international operations. For example changes in socio-structure may lead to the emergence of regional trading blocs. In turn, each bloc implies a unique set of market changes, competitive changes, and regulatory changes that guide the organization's environmental analysis. This demands that the multinational organization acquires additional skills, flexibility and expertise that the purely domestic organization does not require because it does not encounter these environmental complexities.

Within the general model for the links between the forces of change and emerging trends in Figure 2.1, several specific trends affect all multinational organizations' environmental analysis efforts. Porter's analysis (1991b) identifies several of these trends:

- *Fewer differences among countries.* Differences in such areas as income, energy costs, marketing practices, and channels of distribution seem to be narrowing. In many industries, it is no longer meaningful to separate the European market from the American market or the Asian market. Consumers are becoming increasingly alike (Ohmae 1991).

Figure 2.1   The relationship of change forces to organizational actions

- *More aggressive industrial policies.* The governments of such countries as Japan, Germany and Taiwan have developed fiercely competitive attitudes toward international business. The future policies of these governments will probably make the international environment more and more competitive. For example, aggressive planning has moved Taiwan from an agricultural economy in the 1960s to being a worldwide economic power in the 1990s. This performance has brought so much success that in 1992, Taiwan had tangible assets worth $3.5 billion on the Chinese mainland; $5 billion in Malaysia, $3.4 billion in Thailand, $2.8 billion in Indonesia. Probably the next country to be a star performer in the region will be Vietnam. In general terms, pick any Asian country with cheap land and labour from the Philippines to Sri Lanka, and a Taiwanese business is probably putting up a factory there to make umbrellas, toys, wigs, textiles or goods for sale in markets across the globe.
- *More vigorous protection for distinctive assets.* More and more countries, and some individual business leaders, seem to be focusing on determining their own unique assets and exploiting this uniqueness to best advantage. An example of this trend was the formation of the oil cartel, the Organization of Oil Exporting Countries (OPEC). Although the effectiveness of this cartel has varied over time, its primary purpose is

still clear: to protect the return its members can generate on a scarce natural resource – oil. Despite the fact that less than 50 per cent of the world's oil comes from OPEC nations, this cartel is blamed for price rises that stem from traders' concerns relating to global capacity. Richard Branson, founder of the Virgin Group, is now entering the oil exploration and refining sector with the establishment of Virgin Fuels, in collaboration with other partner businesses. His goal is to reduce the price of fuel globally through such ventures (*Business Week* 2005).

*   *Emerging, large-scale markets.* In volume terms, world trade expanded at an average annual rate of 5.6 per cent between 1953–1963 and 8.5 per cent between 1963–1973. This is much higher than the average rate of 3.5 per cent between 1873–1913 and the 0.9 per cent in the inter-war period of 1919–1939. This unprecedented expansion in world output and trade in the post-war era provided the Asia Pacific economies like Japan and the four newly industrializing economies (NIEs) South Korea, Taiwan, Hong Kong and Singapore, with a conducive and stable environment for export-led growth. Consequently, during the past three decades, the four East Asian NIEs have become the most dynamic middle-income economies in the world. Their annual growth rates in terms of GNP per capita between 1965–1995 averaged 6 to 8 per cent, triple the average rate of 2.3 per cent for middle-income economies of the world and almost double the 4 per cent average for countries in the Association of South East Asian Nations (ASEAN), excluding Singapore.

*   *Competition from developing countries.* Now, more than ever before, smaller developing countries are becoming competitors in international markets. Malaysia, for example, is the largest exporter of semiconductor chips in the world. Environmental analysts for multinational corporations cannot stop after evaluating the larger, more established competitors; they must consider threats from developing countries, as well.

International Organizational Direction

The complexity of the international environment, magnified by several significant trends, affects the multinational firm's analysis of its environment. Based on this environmental analysis, managers must establish a direction for organizations that operate internationally. Figure 2.2 illustrates the most significant environmental factors together with the possible strategic reactions.

As with the wholly domestic enterprise, the multinational organization must carefully evaluate the results of environmental analyses and then develop an organizational vision and mission. Managers must decide on the type and extent of international involvement they want to pursue, because this decision guides the establishment of appropriate organizational goals.

After clarifying a vision and defining a mission, managers provide further direction for a multinational organization by developing long-term goals and short-term tactics. Naturally, these reflect the type and extent of international involvement outlined in the company mission statement. However, host countries often impose constraints that affect the goals of multinational organizations. Such constraints can take many forms:

*   a host country may require that a local person or firm maintain a major or controlling interest;
*   host countries commonly demand that their own citizens hold certain management and technology positions;

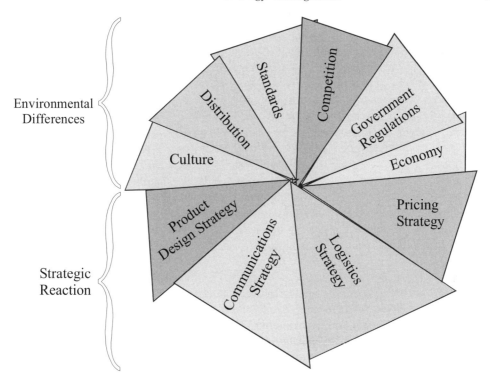

Figure 2.2   Environmental forces and strategic reaction

- host countries normally require some level of training for all their citizens employed by a foreign multinational;
- host countries seek technology-based businesses and strive to raise the technology levels of multinational organizations within their borders.

International Strategy Formulation

Following the general model of the strategic management process, managers formulate a strategy that reflects organizational goals, that in turn reflects the organization's mission. Whether the organization limits itself to domestic operations or enters into international operations, the purpose of strategy is the same. Over the years many different companies have formulated and successfully implemented numerous international strategies. All of these specific strategies fall into three broad categories:

1. trade-related;
2. transfer-related;
3. direct investment.

These strategies require different commitments from parent companies to foreign markets and offer parent companies varying levels of control over foreign operations (see Figure 2.3).

Inflexible multinational organizations' initial foreign operations involve trade-related activities such as exporting and, as the organization grows, progression is made though transfer

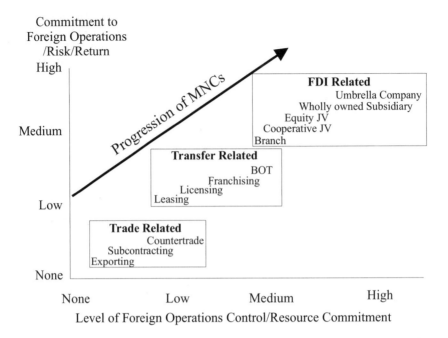

Figure 2.3　Strategic commitment options available to companies

activities leading ultimately to direct investment. Regardless of the stage and the direction of a MNC's progress, strategy formulation needs to involve an assessment of the level of commitment to, and control of, foreign operations that the organization's mission demands.

Trade-related business can be defined as selling goods or services to customers in a foreign country. This strategy leaves an organization's production facilities at home, from where it transfers products abroad. This strategy minimizes foreign investment, since the firm usually hires a foreign agent to act on its behalf and products are often shipped directly to customers' warehouses. This strategy exposes the exporter to high transportation costs, however, and it must deal with government regulations and other operational and strategic issues from a distance.

Transfer-related business grants one company's right to its brand name, product specifications and the like, to another company. The recipient then sells the goods or services. The purchaser of the licence hopes to profit from selling the products, whereas the seller of the licence profits from the fees charged for the it. At the international level, the purchaser and the seller of a licence are from different countries, or the purchaser will sell the products in a country other than the one in which it bought the item. For example, today all of the South Korean automobile manufacturers licence technology from Japanese companies such as Nissan, Toyota and Honda. This is in direct contrast to the 1950s and 1960s, when almost all Japanese auto makers set up technology and product transfer agreements with American and European producers. The notable exception to this trend was Toyota. They developed by reverse engineering products and benchmarking, then developing their own component and product variants. This kept Toyota's technology acquisition costs low. In fact, many of the Japanese auto makers did not fully reimburse their Western technology suppliers.

Franchising is a form of licensing that usually covers access to a wider range of rights and resources, perhaps including production equipment, managerial system, operating procedures, advertising and trademarks. McDonald's and Kentucky Fried Chicken (KFC) branded outlets are good examples of MNCs that sell franchises around the world.

An extension of this approach is Build-Operate-Transfer (BOT). Sometimes this is referred to as turnkey, where a business undertakes and supervises the construction of a manufacturing or business system and then delivers this to the desired geographical location.

Foreign direct investment (FDI) is the term used to describe organizations' acquisition and operation of assets in a foreign country. This may involve purchasing existing factories and equipment or constructing new plants and purchasing new equipment. MNCs often implement direct investment strategies by entering into cooperative or joint equity ventures, in which two companies contribute to the costs of creating a third business entity. Both firms usually share in the ownership of the joint venture and in its returns (Contractor and Lorange 1988; Gulati 1988). New United Motor Manufacturing Inc. (NUMMI), a joint venture formed by Toyota Motor Corporation and General Motors in Fremont, California, is an example.

MNCs often form joint ventures to create synergy between the different skills sets of the two parent companies. In the NUMMI example, General Motors (GM) tried to access Toyota's expertise in the manufacture of small cars, whilst Toyota tried to gain GM's knowledge of manufacturing and selling cars in the US market. When joint ventures are driven by this logic, the strategy formulation is guided by each parent company's desire to learn and internalize the skills of the other (Hamel 1991). This desire can also transcend business sectors, as is shown in the case of the joint venture between Nestle and Coca-Cola. Here, both companies exploited their respective skills and knowledge in marketing canned goods and coffee production in order to manufacture and distribute canned coffee in Hong Kong and Korea (Barney 1997).

Direct investment can also create a wholly owned subsidiary. An example of this direct investment strategy led various companies to start manufacturing and selling their products in Japan. Kodak, IBM, Procter & Gamble, and Motorola are examples of American companies that have successfully launched wholly owned subsidiaries in Japan.

International Strategy Implementation

After conducting an environmental analysis, establishing an appropriate organizational direction, and carefully formulating a strategy to take the firm in that direction, managers of international operations must implement the strategy they devise. Implementing an international strategy is generally considered a much greater challenge than implementing a purely domestic strategy. Managers in multinational organizations have to design administrative systems for their employees across the globe, and then provide the management leadership in those locations to ensure results are achieved.[4]

The design of an administrative system is driven by two imperatives: the need to align the systems with the overall strategy of the organization, and the need to accommodate the cultural characteristics of each host country. Table 2.3 illustrates some inherent difficulties in trying to satisfy these imperatives. Although the table describes the cultural characteristics of only Japanese, North American and Latin American managers, it demonstrates the complexities of designing systems to suit multiple host countries.

---

4   See Chapter 11 by Nada Zupan, in this volume.

Table 2.3   A comparison of cultural values

Japanese values	North American values	Latin American values
Emotional sensitivity highly valued	Emotional sensitivity not highly valued	Emotional sensitivity valued
Restrained emotions	Straightforward or impersonal relationships	Emotional passion
Subtle power plays; conciliation	Litigation; little emphasis on conciliation	Overt power plays; exploitation of weakness
Loyalty to employers; employers carrying for employees	Lack of commitment from employees and employers	Loyalty to employer
Group or team decision-making; co-conscious	Team or group work provides input to single decision maker	Decisions handed down from one individual
Face Saving is critical	Decisions based on cost-benefit	Face saving critical
Open special interest influence	Influence of special interests, but often not considered ethical	Satisfying special interests expected and condoned
Non-confrontational	Confrontational; impersonal	Confrontational; passionate
Accurate written statements; must be valid	Documentation seen as evidential proof	Documentation seen as obstructive to understanding and enacting general principles
Incremental approach to decision-making	System based decision-making	Impulsive, spontaneous decision-making
Team or group seen as paramount concern	Individual	

International Strategic Control

Controlling an international strategy must follow its implementation. Control ensures that the strategy is effective, given organizational conditions. Comparing this effectiveness to some predetermined standard and making any necessary changes are both part of strategic control.

Managers refer to the same financial standards at the international level to establish the appropriateness of performance as at the domestic level. Business people often mention return on investment as the most important financial measurement by which to evaluate the performance of foreign operations.

Applying such financial measurement is complicated, however, for operations in different countries. The comparison must take into account different currencies, different rates of inflation, and different tax laws, all of which contribute to this complexity. In the final analysis, comparing the financial performance of operations in different countries is very difficult and commonly somewhat subjective.

Conclusions

Any organization that operates internationally must adjust its strategic management process to account for the complexities of cross-border transactions. International business has grown in importance in recent years and this trend will only accelerate as national markets become more integrated and trade between them increases.

International trade agreements define much of the structural background for this trade. The World Trade Organization (WTO) is a broad, multilateral organization that establishes rules for international trade through consensus among its member states. It aims to manage international trade, negotiate market regulation and resolve disputes between its members. Regional trade agreements (RTAs) function within guidelines defined by the WTO to promote trade between neighbouring countries without excluding products from outside the region. The North American Free Trade Agreement (NAFTA),[5] the European Union (EU), and the Asia-Pacific Economic Cooperation forum are three prominent RTAs amongst the 211 that currently exist as of September 2006 (Figure 2.4).

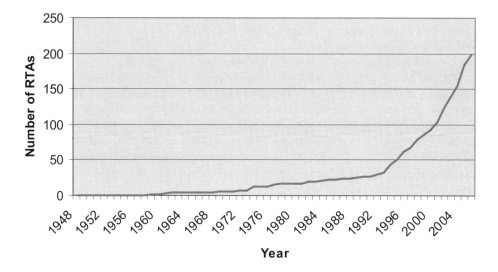

Figure 2.4   The evolution of RTAs 1948–2006 (WTO Secretariat)

Within the provisions of these agreements, national governments develop and implement industrial policies to promote the competitive success of native organizations. These policies can seek to achieve broad, nationwide objectives or target specific industries for special attention.

Multinational corporations react to the pressures of international operations by adjusting their procedures to complete the strategic management process. Environmental analysis for such an organization must expand its scope to evaluate conditions and trends in distant, often idiosyncratic markets. Its vision and mission statements must guide decisions about the appropriate type and extent of international involvement, given the results of the environmental analysis.

Managers then formulate strategies designed to move the firm in this chosen organizational direction, often following the traditional progression from exporting through licensing to direct investment in foreign operations. Implementing a previously formulated strategy becomes vastly more complex when it leads the firm across international borders; cultural differences can demand changes to the most successful strategy. Finally, strategic control of international

---

5   See Chapter 16 by Coral Snodgrass, in this volume.

operations faces problems to adjust familiar financial standards, especially return on investment, for differences in currencies, inflation levels, and tax laws, among other factors.

References

Anderson, S. and Cavanagh, J. (2000), *The Rise of Corporate Global Power* (Washington, DC: Institute for Policy Studies).

Andrews, K.R. (1987), *The Concept of Corporate Strategy* (Homewood, IL: Irwin).

Ansoff, H.I. (1965), *Corporate Strategy* (New York: McGraw-Hill).

Barney, J.B. (1997), *Gaining and Sustaining Competitive Advantage* (Reading, MA: Addison-Wesley).

Brandenburger, A.M. and Nalebuff, B.J. (1995), 'The Right Game: Use Game Theory to Shape Strategy', *Harvard Business Review* 73 (July–August), pp. 57–71.

Business Week (2005), 20 September.

Contractor, F.J. and Lorange, P. (1988), *Competitive Strategies in International Business* (Lexington, MA: Lexington Books).

Fombru, C.J. and Wally, S. (1993), 'Global Entanglements: The Structure of Corporate Transnationalism', in Pucik, V., Tichy, N.M. and Barnett, C.K. (eds), *Globalizing Management: Creating and Leading the Competitive Organization* (New York: John Wiley & Sons).

Gulati, R. (1998), 'Networks and Alliances', *Strategic Management Journal* 19, pp. 293–318.

Hamel, G. (1991), 'Competition for Competence and Interpartner Learning within International Strategic Alliances', *Strategic Management Journal* 12, pp. 83–103.

Hill, T. and Westbrook, R. (1997), 'SWOT Analysis: It's Time for a Product Recall', *Long Range Planning* 30 (February), pp. 46–52.

Hooper, M.J., Steeple, D. and Winters, C.N. (2001), 'Costing Customer Value: An Approach for the Agile Enterprise', *International Journal of Operations and Production Management* 21(5/6), pp. 630–44.

McDonald, M. (1999), *Marketing Plans* (Oxford: Butterworth-Heinemann).

Ohmae, K. (1991), 'Becoming a Triad Power: The New Global Corporation', in Vernon-Wortzel, H. and Wortzel, L.H. (eds) *Global Strategic Management: The Essentials* (New York: John Wiley & Sons).

Porter, M.E. (1979), 'How Competitive Forces Shape Strategy', *Harvard Business Review* 57 (March–April), pp. 137–45.

Porter, M.E. (1980), *Competitive Strategy* (New York: Free Press).

Porter, M.E. (1991a), 'Toward a Dynamic Theory of Strategy', *Strategic Management Journal* 12, pp. 95–117.

Porter, M.E. (1991b), 'Changing Patterns of International Competition', in Vernon-Wortzel, H. and Wortzel, L.H. (eds) *Global Strategic Management: The Essentials* (New York: John Wiley & Sons).

Chapter 3
International Business Ethics

David Kimber and Fran Siemensma

Introduction

This chapter reviews frameworks of international business ethics and demonstrates the philosophical, social, political and organizational theories adopted in this programme and how they apply to business. The approach emphasizes self-awareness, using case study analysis, experiential exercises, reflective questioning and discussion. As ethics relates to all forms of personal and organizational decision-making, it is an essential element of business knowledge, one that may assist future managers to avoid the personal and organizational turmoil associated with the corporate collapses recently seen in Europe and the USA. The international applications of business ethics concern those who wish to work with multinational corporations or in any form of international business.

Values and Ethics

Values and ethics are often claimed to be the fundamental basis of good business behaviour, both in boardrooms as well as operational areas of organizations only after fraud or financial disaster has shaken business practice and confidence. Ethical frameworks aim to demonstrate that business practitioners can be more successful over the longer term by taking a proactive rather than a reactive attitude to ethics. A definition of business ethics helps to position this discussion.

Ethics can be defined as reflecting on the question 'What ought I (we) do?' In business, as in any context, this question is about making a decision and commitment to a course of action based on principles and beliefs. The concept of 'ought' is normative. It is not descriptive. It rather seeks to determine what 'ought' or 'should' mean in a specific situation. The notions of should and ought represent personal responsibility that is associated with the responsibility an individual fills as a result of their role in an organizational a certain time and place.

For example, the issue could be:

- the closure of a manufacturing plant in one country in order to relocate to a region with lower labour costs;
- the development of an organizational culture dedicated to promoting and maintaining integrity. The aim being to ensure decisions are reached only after all ethical considerations have been addressed.

In both cases, those responsible for making such decisions have to consider what the 'right' course of action is. This is a judgement that involves understanding all those who are affected directly or indirectly by the implications of that choice.

Much discussion in business ethics centres round the resolution of ethical dilemmas. These involve the prospect of 'bad consequences' when, no matter which choice is selected, some ethical principles are likely to be violated. For example, the reduction of an organization's workforce in order to avoid collapse has to be balanced against the hardships imposed on redundant employees. Corporations in a globalized world increasingly confront such dilemmas. Some cognitive dissonance may be reached to rationalize their decision and ease malcontents in the management tea. The management may justify their actions because they base their judgement and place trust in economists' arguments that freed labour will transfer to other jobs and continue to add value to society.

Values can be identified as one of the bases for determining 'right action'. The values defined and described by a society, an organization, or held by an individual are likely to be reviewed to determine an appropriate policy or action. They will emerge from a number of viewpoints – moral philosophy (e.g., distributive justice), a political or social framework (beliefs underpinning democracy), or cultural heritage (values emerging from a Christian or Confucian understanding).

Petrick and Quinn (1997, pp. 46, 48) identified different orientations to business ethics. They have developed a model which creates a typology of organizations, using two variables – flexible/control oriented and internal/externally focused. This enabled them to define four types of businesses which coincide with four orientations to business ethics. Table 3.1 summarizes their model.

Table 3.1   Petrick and Quinn's business ethics orientation model

Organization type	Business ethics orientation
Flexible and internally focussed	Virtue ethics
Control oriented and internally focused	Deontology
Control oriented and externally focused	Teleology
Flexible and externally focused	Systems ethics

This model summarizes the different orientations to business ethics which are discussed in this chapter.

Virtue Ethics

Virtue ethics is often associated with personal ethics. This approach, drawn from Aristotles notions relating to a 'good life'[1] is commonly identified with individual decision-making and behaviour. It involves questions such as 'How should I act to become the person I want to be?' or 'How should I behave to lead *a good life?*' These questions are commonly framed in terms of personal values and morality – the aspects of personality or character that drive one to behave in a 'virtuous' way. They were defined by Aristotle as 'habits' to be cultivated in order to be worthy of the status of 'citizen'. The refined practice of such habits would lead to *eudemonia*, the happiness of a 'good life' pursued by all.

---

1   Aristotle, a Greek Philospher of the third century BC outlined, his understanding of what makes a 'good life' or 'eudemonia' in his writings, published under the title *Nicomachean Ethics* (2000, pp. 577–86).

This orientation to ethics has an individualistic focus. Robert Solomon has reinterpreted virtue ethics for contemporary secular societies where many choose to pursue a professional career in business.[2] In this context, ethical considerations, including the pursuit of personal identity and satisfaction, involve responsibilities associated with being an employee. Solomon, an American business ethicist, reworked Aristotle's original virtue ethics to be applicable in an organizational setting, adapting the six dimensions to the moulding of the 'character' of an employee, manager or executive, rather than the citizen role to which Athenians aspired. The new virtue ethics are community, holism, role identity, excellence, judgement and integrity.

Community   Working individuals join organizations. These in turn provide income, status and a sense of identity. Organizations are 'communities' or 'sites of mutual interdependency' that fit within society. By agreeing to 'belong' to them, and signing on as an employee, individuals become responsible for preserving that community. Allegiance to one's community is an element of personal identity and pride. Some individuals move from country to country, community to community and business to business. They may derive identity and pride by maintaining their network of contacts and learning. Career progression may require individuals to pursue job titles as a form of personal identity.

Role identity   This dimension of virtue ethics encourages each individual to consider organizational role identity, and its associated duties, before choosing to act. Individuals are paid to fulfil specific duties and their associated responsibilities. Consider the different roles played by accounting, information technology, human resource management and marketing within a company. To be effective, each employee must behave as required to fulfil specific role requirements. There may be role conflicts either between role fulfilment within an organization or between one's role as an employee and for example that of a parent, sibling or citizen.

Excellence   To act 'virtuously' in an organization, individuals must do their best and seek to excel, not merely comply at the lowest level. Peters and Waterman emphasized the importance of this theme in business in their book *In Search of Excellence* (2004). This approach shows how organizations are able to survive, and even thrive, in a competitive environment. As a personal philosophy, it encourages individuals to be fully and creatively engaged in their work.

Holism   This dimension requires each individual to recognize and apply core human values. These include respect for life and the rights of strangers to the decisions they make in their working lives. Holism encourages managers and decision makers to treat the rights and needs of their employees, suppliers and customers as respectfully as they would those of their family and friends.

Judgement   The ability to judge effectively is an essential business 'virtue'. It is a product of upbringing, education and professional development. Managers and decision makers are continually required to master facts and approaches so that they may make sound judgements. Solomon sees this as the 'linchpin of all the virtues' because it seeks to balance and mediate conflicts.

Integrity   Solomon regards integrity as the ability to demonstrate 'courage under fire', where people display the ability to act properly when core principles are threatened. In the context of

---

2   For further details of Solomon's writing on virtue ethics see Solomon (1993).

the individual's corporate duties and responsibilities, integrity is demonstrated when someone knows whether to 'conform' to organizational demands or to 'rebel' against them. Managers possessing integrity in this sense will make the hard decisions, will be prepared to face up to difficult situations and will acknowledge ethical dilemmas.

Virtue ethics, as identified above, reflects an approach that is most appropriate in organizations where flexibility is required and personal autonomy is high. The types of organizations that strongly emphasize virtue ethics are likely to be consulting firms and accounting and law practices. Virtue is a powerful and pertinent area of ethical analysis for senior executives – CEOs and board members. Corporate scandals and collapses often are associated with organizations whose senior managers seemed to disregard the concerns outlined above in virtue ethics.

Deontology

Deontology is the arena of ethics associated with seeking to answer the question 'Is it right?' and searches for 'rightness'. Traditionally, deontology has involved reference to a set of principles, defined 'rights', duties, or obligations. In a business sense, it has become associated with adherence to appropriate rules and regulations and their associated processes. Hence, an organization that emphasizes a deontological approach to 'right' behaviour is likely to be, in Petrick and Quinn's terms, control oriented and internally focused – such as a hospital, a prison, or a bank. Such organizations have a clear and well defined understanding of their principles and are able to manage and create 'ethical' behaviour because they create guidelines on how the principles should be upheld and implemented. Examples include:

- hospitals making people well;
- governments agencies that protect society;
- financial institutions that manage depositors' funds prudentially.

Kant's 'categorical imperative'[3] is another example of deontology. According to this perspective, one can determine 'right action' by reflecting on whether or not that behaviour should be universally applied. This could be determined by referring to three 'laws':

1. 'act as if the maxim of thy action were to become by thy will a universal law of nature';
2. 'act that you use humanity, whether in your own person or in the person of any other, always at the same time as an end, never merely as a means';
3. 'act that we may think of ourselves as legislating universal laws through our maxims'.[4]

Thus, the determination to act in a certain way is based on the judgement that the decision taken would become a moral obligation for every person facing the same circumstances, based on the respect due to every human being.

In the business context, Kant's categorical imperative can help resolve questions about whether to purchase goods made by indentured labour or that cause environmental damage.

---

3   Emmanuel Kant was an eighteenth century German philosopher who established a framework for deontology, breaking away from doctrinal thinking which emanated from religion and suggesting that logic and reasoning could clarify guiding principles.

4   See the Wikpedia website on Kant http://en.wikipedia.org/wiki/Immanuel_Kant, accessed 24 February 2006.

'Kantian' corporate directors recognize that the implications of decisions reached should be morally and universally compelling.

Roles and responsibility – principles and process   The increased reliance on regulation as a means of improving corporate governance recently has given deontological approaches greater and wider prominence. There are two significant reasons for this increased recognition. Firstly, with globalization and the growth of multinational corporations, initiatives have emerged to regulate and control business behaviour. Responses range from aspiration based principles being expressed by groups such as the UN,[5] and The Caux Round Table[6] attempts to regulate MNC activities through home country legislation such as anti-corruption legislation or the US laws prohibiting American corporations from engaging in corruption in foreign countries.[7] The aim is to raise awareness and thus discourage business managers from undertaking activities incompatible with good business and social justice around the world.

Secondly, since the corporate collapses in 2000–2001 (Enron, WorldCom, Parmalat and Arthur Andersen) several different countries have passed legislation to encourage directors and executives to act more 'ethically'. The Sarbanes Oxley Act[8] in the USA places particular emphasis on compliance practices in corporations. Such processes are being developed and instituted to increase the confidence of shareholders and other stakeholders in corporations. One example is the legal requirement that senior executives now personally endorse accurate annual statements relating to solvency, transparency and accountability.

Both approaches noted above aimed at promoting good business behaviour can be seen as grounded in deontological theory.

Teleology

Teleology is the study of the end or purpose of things.[9] In the ethical context, it involves the pursuit of the best outcome. The question involves the notion of 'good' understood as the best possible result of an action or decision. It is a term derived from the two Greek words, *telos*, meaning 'purpose or end' and *logos*, meaning 'word'. It is often seen in terms of individualism from two perspectives – first, the 'self', often known as ethical egoism – 'what is best for me' and second, the 'other' – altruism, 'what is best for the other(s)'. John Stuart Mill[10] suggested that teleology can also relate to 'the group' – utilitarianism, 'what is best for all of us'. He described an ethical action as that which produces 'the greatest good for the greatest number'.

---

5   See *The Global Compact* website for details of 10 business principles which the UN is encouraging multinational corporations to follow: http://www.unglobalcompact.org/, accessed 20 February 2006.

6   See *The Caux Round Table* website for details of business principles promulgated by the Caux Round Table Council: http://www.cauxroundtable.org/, accessed 20 February 2006.

7   See International Anti-Bribery and Fair Competition Act of 1998, http://usinfo.state.gov/usa/ infousa/laws/majorlaw/antibrib.htm, accessed 20 February 2006.

8   The Sarbanes Oxley Act or SOX was legislated in the USA in 2002. It was a response to major corporate failures which took place in 2000–2001. It has had considerable influence on emphasizing the role of corporate governance in the management of corporations. For further details and discussion see http://www.sarbanes-oxley.com/, accessed 20 February 2006.

9   See website dictionary definition www.theapologiaproject.org/glossary.htm, accessed 20 February 2006.

10   John Stuart Mill was a nineteenth century English philosopher who was the prime proponent of and writer on the concept of utilitarianism. For further details see http://www.utilitarianism.com/jsmill. htm, accessed 24 April 2006.

This way of conceptualizing ethics is also known as consequentialism. Emphasis is on 'What are the consequences of my/our actions?'

In business, much decision-making is concerned with outcomes such as how to improve profitability, how to increase sales, how to make products that consumers want or need. The goal-oriented focus of many business decisions corresponds with teleology. Business managers tend to be comfortable with this approach

Tensions emerge when business decisions have different impacts on stakeholders, especially when they create winners and losers. Executives continually have to make decisions that must be balanced in terms of their outcomes. Those who understand teleological analysis and practice it, consciously taking account of the impact on all stakeholders, are likely to be seen as ethical decision makers. Those who are unable to foresee the inevitable 'unintended consequences' of decisions are more likely to be tripped up by unwanted and unexpected ethical dilemmas.

Conversely, considerable tension in organizations can emerge because managers are conscious of outcomes. Decisions, that seen 'too hard' may be shelved. The drive for self-preservation may mean that people seek to avoid responsibility because of their awareness of inevitable 'bad' outcomes. Often 'good' managers, those who can 'just do it', are those prepared to make 'the tough choices'. Equally, the situation in which they find themselves may permit them to direct actions of others that they themselves wouldn't undertake. The question of who has responsibility for the strategy and who is responsible for 'getting the job done' may be divorced. This can permit a level of cognitive dissonance to creep into the decision-making process and commitment to tasks. Given that business demands that decisions must be made, when they are made 'consciously' and recognize all consequences, the chance of balanced outcomes is increased. Anticipated tangible results of actions may be assessed using decision-making tools such as cost/benefit analysis or SWOT[11] analysis. Hence, this approach to ethics is appropriate when organizations undertake strategic planning, risk assessment and performance monitoring and evaluation. It is also directly connected to stakeholder theory, a theme discussed below.

Systems Ethics

As business systems and processes become more complex and supply chain networks enable improved organizational performance, a systemic approach to ethics has also become more necessary. This area involves ways that an organization develops and maintains its ethical culture. The approaches covered by virtue ethics, deontology and teleology together combine to develop an appropriate and effective ethical culture. This approach is described as the formulation of an integrity system for an organization. It is a relatively new field of organizational development that is increasing in importance as establishments either works jointly in different countries and regions.

Systems ethics can be seen from both an internal and external perspective. Internal systems relate to the development, within organizations, of:

- codes of conduct;
- clear structures and systems which encourage ethical behaviours;
- ethics training and development for both managers and executives;
- ethics monitoring and reporting; and
- 'whistleblower' protection.

---

11 Undertaking a scenario planning which identifies the Strengths, Weaknesses, Opportunities, Threats which emerge from each set of decisions.

External systems within countries relate to:

- effective legal systems;
- appropriate public service agencies which encourage integrity in public policy;
- well developed oversight agencies, that protect the rights of the public in both the public and private sectors.

Following the corporate collapses noted above, corporate law enforcement in many countries have been strengthened. Research in this field suggests it is approached with different levels of intensity and interest in different countries and in different industries.[12]

Another theme of systems ethics relates to the increased economic and social significance of multinational corporations. A more holistic notion of systems theory considers the interaction between economic, socio-cultural and environmental systems both locally and globally. This ethical approach to organizations involves themes such as corporate social responsibility, sustainability and 'triple bottom line' analysis.

Ethical Decision-making in Business – An Integrated Approach

Drawing on the above analysis, an appropriate approach to making ethical decisions takes all perspectives into account. All ethical theories are interrelated. If applied in isolation they cease to be effective. Personal values and behaviour, principles and processes, impacts and outcomes and overall systems must all be considered before making business decisions. In response to the basic initial question 'What ought to be done?', the subsidiary questions, could be considered in sequence, starting from those related to virtue ethics. This highlights the need to recognize the micro, personal ethical position, through the organizational impact, to systemic considerations and social/environmental implications. Depending on the situation, the sequence could start at either the individual end (virtue ethics) or from the worldview perspective. If managers followed this process of analysis, they are likely to diminish the risk of making short term decisions which threaten sustainability.

Personal values and behaviour, principles and processes, impacts and outcomes and overall systems must all be considered before making business decisions. In response to the basic initial question 'What ought to be done?', the subsidiary questions, noted in Figure 3.1, could be considered in sequence, starting from those related to virtue ethics. This highlights the need to recognize the micro, personal ethical position, through the organizational impact, to systemic considerations and social/environmental implications. Depending on the situation, the sequence could also start at either the individual end (virtue ethics) or from the world view perspective. If managers followed this process of analysis, it would likely decrease the risk that stems from short-term decisions that are not sustainable social or when economical consequences are not foreseen.

---

12 See Transparency International, http://www.transparency.org/, which considers the role of corruption in public and private sectors and the impact on social systems. TI is a non-government agency set up to help counteract corruption in the world.

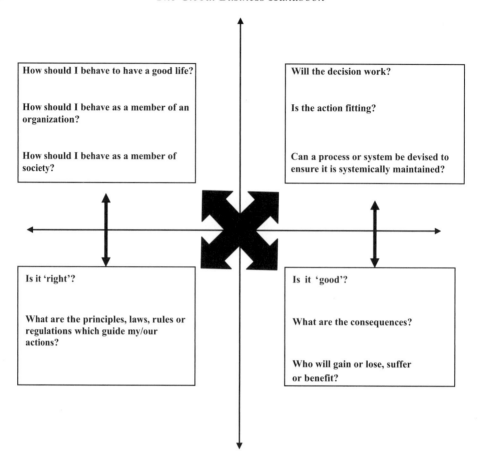

How should I behave to have a good life?

How should I behave as a member of an organization?

How should I behave as a member of society?

Will the decision work?

Is the action fitting?

Can a process or system be devised to ensure it is systemically maintained?

Is it 'right'?

What are the principles, laws, rules or regulations which guide my/our actions?

Is it 'good'?

What are the consequences?

Who will gain or lose, suffer or benefit?

Figure 3.1   A decision-making diagram

Stakeholder Theory

Stakeholders are increasingly recognized by corporations as influencing relates to good business ethics.

The concept of 'stakeholder engagement'[13] describes the interaction of an organization with members of a number of groupings. These include those who have a direct economic relationship as well as those who have an indirect involvement and interest in the entity's activities. Stakeholders are characterized in two groups, namely, primary (direct) and indirect (secondary):

Primary–Direct:
- financial investors;
- shareholder/security holders;
- banks and other finance providers;

---

13 For more detailed discussion regarding the stakeholder concept, see http://en.wikipedia.org/wiki/Stakeholder_concept, accessed 24 April 2006.

- employees – management/non-management;
- customers and suppliers;
- government bodies such as the taxation department and business or corporate regulation agencies.

Indirect–Social:
- local communities, represented by local and state government agencies and lobby groups;
- regional, national and global communities, represented by non-government organizations (NGOs), churches, lobby groups etc.

Indirect–Environmental:
- government agencies such as environmental protection and planning authorities;
- non-government bodies representing environmental interests – NGOs, research institutes, etc.

Business most commonly considers direct stakeholders. Such interests may be represented by others, for example, directors acting on behalf of shareholders. The interests of direct stakeholders can be positively influenced by an organization's actions. Consequently, while seeking to ensure protection, they are keen to see business in a positive way. However, the environment and the community are more likely to limit or control the impact of business growth.

In the past these interests often have been ignored or negatively affected by business decisions. For this reason the environment is often referred to as the 'silent stakeholder'.[14] Advocates often act on behalf of social or environmental threats, especially those posed to future generations. The growing power and concern of such people or groups has forced business managers to become increasingly sensitive to critics portrayed as primarily 'negative' influences, who oppose their decisions. Decision makers who apply stakeholder theory may come to realize that negotiating with those stakeholders who could frustrate their business purpose is as important as gaining support from, say, financial backers.

The Figure 3.2 identifies the relationships between a business and its stakeholders. Whilst the stakeholders in the outer circle both can be direct and indirect, those relating to the social and environmental considerations tend to be represented by advocates.

Sustainability, Corporate Social Responsibility (CSR) and the 'Triple Bottom Line'.

Traditionally businesses 'accounted for their actions' by producing annual financial reports. Such documents show the economic impact – companies' profits or losses and their status in terms of assets and liabilities at a given point in time. Growing concerns about the social and environmental impact of business and the sustainability of current patterns of production and consumption have increased the demands that business must take a broader view of its impact. As such there have been growing calls for corporations, especially those operating globally, to incorporate social and environmental, as well as economic, responsibility as part of their mission.

---

14 See also discussions relating to sustainability at http://en.wikipedia.org/wiki/Sustainability, accessed 24 April 2006.

Triple Bottom Line View of Stakeholders

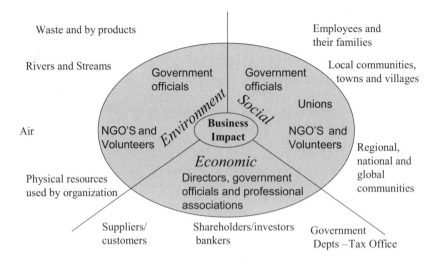

Figure 3.2   A stakeholder map

Such concerns led to the concept of the 'triple bottom line', namely that businesses should report on their social and environmental activities and the financial 'bottom line'.[15] Such disclosure has proved difficult and little headway has been made to introduce standards for reporting such broad scale data. However, there is a growing recognition of the need, and the feasibility, for CSR[16] as a basis of ensuring sustainability.

Figure 3.3 identifies the relationship between the concepts of the triple bottom line, corporate social responsibility and sustainability.

Conclusions

In the final analysis, ethics is essential for individuals, business corporations and well functioning societies. People who maintain high standards of personal ethics are often noted as those who are able to 'sleep well' – they are confident and happy that their behaviour is well founded and will not lead to future dilemmas. This notion is often related to the 'sunshine test' which suggests that an action or decision should be avoided if its disclosure would lead to embarrassment or shame.

Organizations known for their high standards of ethics often are identified as those people are proud to work for. In that sense they become 'employers of choice'. Most employees prefer to work for ethical organizations and are attracted to them. They are likely to be easier and

---

15 The term 'triple bottom line' was coined by John Elkington in his book *Cannibals with Forks: The Triple Bottom Line of 21st Century Business* (1998).

16 CSR (corporate social responsibility) is the term used by a growing community of academics and social commentators who are critical of the focus on business on serving its primary stakeholder, in particular the shareholders. For further details relating to this debate see http://en.wikipedia.org/wiki/Corporate_Social_Responsibility, accessed 25 April 2006.

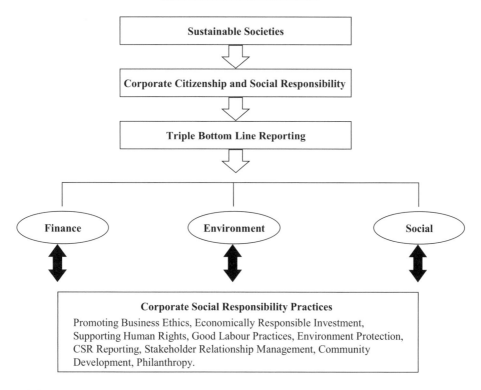

Figure 3.3   A sustainability diagram

more pleasant places to work in as the behaviour of others usually is predictable and based on socially accepted norms.

When ethical behaviour becomes the norm in societies are inevitably more harmonious, predictable and enjoyable environments to live in. Each citizen leads a 'good life'. Social capital is high and people enjoy high levels of social trust.[17] Businesses function effectively and people are able to develop positively and to their best ability in such environments.

As far as business is concerned, product and service reputation, customer and vendor preferences, employee recruitment and retention, financial market recognition, international partnering and so on, all testify to the need for good social standing. The creation of corporate wealth, important as it is, is admired only when it is achieved in ways judged to be ethical, fair and legitimate. The oft-cited maxim that the ends do not justify the means is never more amply demonstrated than in the market assessment of a corporation's business behaviour. Usually, scandals and financial crisis are found in corporations which have lost touch with business ethics. As evidenced in the last decade, they often decline significantly or collapse. Alternatively, many well-regarded corporations that suffered business downturns or have even blundered strategically are more likely to be supported by the markets and their shareholders. In the final judgement, it can be seen that many were given the time or the money to recover because they were admired and respected for doing the right thing.

---

17 Social capital and trust are terms which have been identified with good ethics in society. For further details see http://en.wikipedia.org/wiki/Social_capital, accessed 24 April 2006.

References

Aristotle (2000), *Nihomachean Ethics*, in ed. Cohen, S.M., Curd, P. and Reeve, C.D.C. *Readings in Ancient Greek Philosophy* (Cambridge, MA: Hackett), pp. 577–86.

Elkington, J. (1998), *Cannibals with Forks: The Triple Bottom Line of 21st Century Business* (Gabriola, BC: New Society Publishers).

Peters, T. and Waterman, R. (1982), *In Search of Excellence: Lessons from America's Best-Run Companies* (New York: HarperCollins).

Petrick, J.A. and Quinn, J.F. (1997), *Management Ethics: Integrity at Work* (Thousand Oaks, CA: Sage Publications).

Solomon, R.C. (1993), 'Corporate Roles, Personal Virtues, Moral Mazes: An Aristotelian Approach to Virtue Ethics', in Coady, A. and Sampford, C. (eds) *Business, Ethics and the Law* (St Leonards, NSW: Federation Press), pp. 24 –51.

DIMENSION 2

Relationship Management

Chapter 4

Inter-Firm Collaboration and Partnering: A Key Competence to Satisfy Demand

Maria Veludo

This chapter examines literature from several fields of research and models a wide range factors relating to inter-firm collaboration and partnering. Clarifications are provided to order the development process of inter-firm collaboration and partnering.

Definitions of inter-firm collaboration and partnering are considered. This provides the reader an idea of the complexity of these concepts.

Then it will review main contributions of some theoretical perspectives to the understanding of these topics. These are the resource-based view theory, transaction cost analysis and network theory. This chapter then provides a brief overview of partnering related issues, including disciplinary perspectives, characteristics and influencing factors.

> The understanding of the partnering concept is important for the manager's decision-making process.
>
> Rui Pinho (Managing Director of Group Ficosa)

Introduction

Anderson, Håkansson and Johanson (1994) relate the primary functions of the relationships between buying and supplying companies to actors, resources and activities on the basis of: (a) efficiency through interlinking of activities; (b) creative enhancement of resource heterogeneity; and (c) mutuality based on self-interest of actors. These functions appear to have common features with those associated to the partnering concept.

Lambert, Cooper and Pagh (1998) asserted that the inter-related nature of supply chain management includes three inter-related elements: (a) the structure of the supply chain; (b) the supply chain business processes; and (c) the supply chain management components. The supply chain structure consists of the network of members and links between the firms. Business processes are the activities that produce a specific output of value to the customer. The management components are the managerial variables by which the business processes are integrated and managed across the supply chain.

Partnering is a central construct in supply chain management (SCM) and has been used as the basis of the dyadic relationship perspective. It is not, however, used in the network perspective. In the framework that this researcher proposes, partnering provides a bridge between the dyadic and the network perspectives. This is done by structuring the defining characteristics of partnering in such a way that they are translated into actor bonds, resource ties and activity links, which are concepts associated with the network approach.

Buyer–Supplier Relationships

A great amount of research on buyer–supplier relationships (BSR) has focused on the need for closer relationships between buyers and suppliers (Lamming 1996). Most arguments start with Coase's (1937) theory of the firm and Williamson's (1975) transactional economics. The concepts of inter-organizational relationships (Van de Ven et al. 1975) are at the basis of the development of a 'network concept' that has been designed to surpass supply chains (Lamming 1996).

Research interest relating to inter-firm collaboration and partnering has accompanied the many changes and competitive trends in recent years, particularly championed by the world's automotive assembly giants. They have created competitive forces that oblige many firms now to continually review how they add value and reduce costs. These changes and trends include increased globalization of both sources of supply and markets and higher levels of quality consciousness (Hendrick and Ellram 1993). The companies must act as a cohesive entity, learning from each other, transferring staff and equipment between them, reducing costs, improving coordination and process efficiency, designing products to suit their production processes and ensuring adequate supply to the assembly plant and after-market spares and repair workshops. Above all, management of each firm must accept that they do not operate in isolation: no single company can develop, produce and deliver all parts and own the processes to produce the goods and services their clients require. Networks of companies now compete against other networks in the marketplace. The businesses that make up these networks may supply more than one trade customer or assembler. They have to improve performance against a myriad of key indicators, or they face losing market share to competitors as a result of dual or like-for-like purchase policy decisions to switch supply to more competitive suppliers, or entirely lose the contract for the next product variant.

Womack, Jones and Roos (1990) asserted these changes have created conditions for sustainable cost reduction programmes, quality improvement initiatives, inventory reduction programs, early supplier involvement in product design and an increased emphasis on cycle-time reduction. Japanese firms, followed by Western companies, found that a way to reduce costs was to work more closely with their suppliers.

The philosophical underpinnings of this approach can be designated by:

- collaboration and cooperation (Young and Wilkinson 1997);
- closeness (Ford 1998);
- partnership, partnering, strategic alliance (Spekman 1988) or co-makership (Bevan 1987); and
- Deming's (1986) 14 points on quality. These were developed in the late 1940s. Deming argued that firms should work more closely with fewer suppliers to facilitate communication flows and to achieve the maximum of synergy from their relationship.

Partnering

Literature does not seem to provide a coherent picture of partnering. The study of partnering resulted in a degree of frustration for this researcher, as definitions and characteristics are broad and idiosyncratically selected by researchers dependent on their particular background or area of research. Moreover, much of the literature uses terms like 'partnering', 'partnership' and 'collaboration' interchangeably, adding to the broadness and confusion surrounding the term itself. This reveals a patchy understanding of the nature of the concept and of how it operates. Hill (1996) summarizes the topic by stating that partnering is the relationship between two organizations in order for them to survive within the marketplace.

For the purposes of this review the researcher will explore the broadness of the concept that guide the remainder of the chapter. This section will provide a short overview of: (a) partnering related literature; (b) disciplinary perspectives on partnering; (c) partnering characteristics; and (d) influencing factors on partnering.

Disciplinary Perspectives on Partnering

This section will discuss the way in which partnering has been viewed within a variety of disciplines with an interest on the topic. In this way, the researcher expects to (a) give to the reader the disciplinary contexts in which inter-firm collaboration and partnering have been studied and (b) identify where further research is required and the broad principles of how it should be conducted. Much of the literature written on inter firm collaboration and partnering can be traced to three disciplines: supply chain management, purchasing and industrial marketing.

Supply Chain Management

The concept of supply chain management (SCM) has its roots in the 1960s concept of logistics management (Lazzarini et al. 2001) and has evolved since then. The concept of SCM has been used to represent a variety of different meanings, some related to management processes, others to the structural organization of businesses (Harland 1996).

Lazzarini, Chaddad and Cook (2001) found that, despite divergences that may exist on its conceptualization, the literature on SCM has generally emphasized the role of management to coordinate the flow of products, information and decisions in supply chains in order to minimize costs, optimize production flows, or capture value along the chain. Despite this view on SCM, it seems that the term 'supply chain' is increasingly giving place to 'supply network', which takes into account the complex non-linear network of relationships that exists for any product or service that is provided for an end customer (Cox et al. 2001).

According to Harland, Lamming, Zheng and Johnsen (2001), the supply network concept appears to be more complex than the traditional supply chain concept. They argued that, whilst SCM tends to concentrate on more simplistic, linear, and unidirectional flows of materials and associated information, supply networks encompass the complexity of networks involving lateral links and two-way exchanges. Christopher (1998) recognized a lack of precision in the term 'chain', suggesting that the term 'network' is more realistic and that ideally it should be 'demand' and not 'supply'. However, for Christopher, more important than the words is the way firms manage upstream and downstream relationships with suppliers and customers on an integrated basis. The distinction between supply chain and supply network seems to become clearer when taking into account the different levels of analysis within supply chain management, as considered by Harland (1996). These are:

- the internal supply chain, which integrates business functions involved in the flow of materials and information within the firm;
- the dyadic relationship level, which involves the management of dyadic or two-party relationships with immediate suppliers;

- the external chain level, with the management of a chain of businesses also being described as a pipeline;[1] and
- the inter-business network level, which relates to the management of a network of inter-connected businesses in the supply of products and services.

For Christopher (1998), one of the most significant breakthroughs in SCM thinking has been the realization that individual firms no longer compete as stand-alone entities, but rather as supply chains (as formed by suppliers and alliance partners). Christopher views the opportunities for achieving sustainable competitive advantage through the supply chain, which he believes are considerable, as the basis for competition switches from the individual firm to the network. He further suggests that in today's increasingly global markets, the way to reach sustainable competitive advantage lies in managing the complex web of relationships that link highly focused providers of specific elements in a cost-effective value-added chain. In the view of Stock and Lambert (1992), this can be achieved only if traditional adversarial relationships between channel members are abandoned and replaced by a partnership based on mutual trust and the desire to increase performance within the entire pipeline. Chopra and Meindl (2001) reinforce this idea, arguing that effectively managed supply chain relationships foster cooperation and thus support increasing supply chain coordination.

This importance given to relationships is demonstrated by the increasing emphasis on the establishment and management of supply chain partnerships (Wyatt 2001). Partnerships are increasingly viewed in terms of the dyadic relationships between two organizations, and also as core elements of competitive advantage in supply networks (ibid.).

Ellram (1991) recognized that the relative 'newness' of supply chain management and its multidisciplinary nature had resulted in difficulties for researchers in the area. This view is shared by Monczka and Morgan (1997), who emphasize the fragmentation that exists within the discipline and assert that, after almost a decade of existence, supply chain management continues to be a poorly understood, badly explained and wretchedly implemented concept. In relation to partnering research, Stannack (1997) states there is, as yet, no comprehensive model that can be used to explain inter-firm relationships. For Stannack, as a result, partnership strategies may well be self-defeating.

Purchasing

Today, moves towards collaboration have expanded the approach taken by purchasing to supplier management and supplier development activities (Wyatt 2001). However, much of the literature on partnering within the purchasing domain reflects the enduring belief in the dominant role of the buyer in buyer–supplier relationships (ibid.). For instance, supplier development practice, which is associated to a collaborative approach (Krause and Ellram 1997), has its essence in an active partner (the buyer) who puts resources into improving its suppliers (New and Burnes 1998). As a consequence of this buyer-centric perspective, much of research on partnering has tended to focus on the role of the customer in establishing and managing partnering relationships (ibid.). The purchasing discipline is itself dominant in the research of buyer–supplier relationships and partnering in particular, producing the most papers and owning highly respected journals (Wyatt 2001).

---

1   The term was introduced by Farmer and van Amstel (1991).

Industrial Marketing

Over the last two decades research in industrial marketing has moved steadily away from an emphasis on analysing organizational purchasing decisions in discrete transactions to the study of how organizations interact in industrial markets. In a brief literature review, Ford (1980) considered that the majority of the research in industrial marketing, particularly in the US, had fallen into a general research tradition, which he labelled the 'industrial buying'. This approach focused on two main areas: (a) the understanding of the industrial purchasing decision and the supplier choice process; and (b) the understanding of the impact of different elements of the marketing mix on industrial markets. He also mentioned a tendency to isolate the study of the industrial buying process and industrial marketing activities, rather than look at the interplay between the two. Dissatisfaction with this state of affairs, and the recognition of the importance of interdependence of buyers and suppliers in industrial markets, led to a new approach to the study of industrial marketing and purchasing that attempted to redress some of the imbalances pointed out by Ford. One of the starting points of the new approach, labelled the 'interaction approach', was to view the process of industrial marketing as 'the mirror image of the industrial purchasing process and to look at the interaction between two active partners in a buying/selling episode' (Araujo 1990, p. 29). A significant legacy of this approach is Håkansson's (1982) interaction model.

According to the interaction approach, each interaction between companies, whether for product, service, financial, social, or information exchange, is an episode within the relationship between the companies. Each episode within the relationship (which may be close or distant, complex or simple) is affected by the relationship and in turn may affect the relationship itself. The relationship between the companies consists of learned rules and behaviours that provide the atmosphere within which interaction takes place. Individuals will approach each episode on the basis of their experience within the relationship and elsewhere and on the basis of the values that they hold, both in general and in regard to the particular relationship. The interaction approach has introduced the concept of atmosphere to capture the subtle co-existence of conflict and cooperation within a business relationship (Håkansson 1982; Turnbell and Valla 1985).

There have, of course, been criticisms of the interaction approach, among which are that it demonstrates 'the tendency to over emphasize harmony in buyer–seller relationships and neglect, to some extent, the disruptive impact of competitive forces on a relationship' (Ford 1980, p. 236) and that it offers very little guidance on adaptation decisions (Brennan and Turnbull 1998). Wyatt (2001) noticed that its application to the study of the European automotive industry has been limited. According to Wyatt, that the model also has a theoretical basis as it was developed from concepts and assumptions taken from inter-organizational theory and new institutional economics as well as trends in marketing and purchasing literature.

Based on the knowledge accumulated in the study of exchange relationships in industrial markets, and recognizing the limitations of a dyadic level of analysis, a number of Swedish researchers proposed a 'network approach' to the study of industrial systems (Johanson and Mattsson 1987). The network approach has become a major research direction in industrial marketing (Cheung and Turnbull 1998). This is due to the fact that more and more researchers in industrial marketing are aware that dyads are only part of an overall picture and that with a dyadic approach the network view is lost, since connectedness is assumed away (Backhaus and Buschken 1997. According to Purchase (2000), researchers (Axelson and Easton 1992; Araujo and Easton 1996) within the network approach have begun to consolidate their research around the actors-resources-activities (ARA) model originally developed by Håkansson and Johanson (1992) and further extended by Håkansson and Snehota (1995). The ARA model was developed to describe industrial networks and to integrate network stability and development into a single model.

The network approach adds to the interaction approach the awareness that the focal relationships cannot be managed in isolation from a firm's other relationships (Moller and Halinen 1999) and that these focal relationships represent a conduit to other relationships through which resources may be accessed (Easton 1992). The network approach emphasizes cooperation, complementarity in relationships and coordination. Within this approach, cooperation depends on the relationships between the firms' objectives. For Easton, competition and cooperation are two 'dialectical processes in networks'. He considered two types of cooperation: (a) instrumental, in that each firm seeks to gain different ends from the same means; and (b) complementary in the objectives both parties held. The author assumed that firms buying and selling from one another have to have a minimum level of cooperation.

According to Low (1997), the network structure and the positions occupied by the actors in the network are a result of mutual cooperation and adaptation. Easton (1992) and Easton and Araujo (1992) have included both vertical and horizontal relationships in network analysis. Horizontal, competitive interactions are mediated by vertical, cooperative relationships between buyers and suppliers. The recognition of the interdependence between horizontal, competitive relationships and vertical buyer–supplier relationships reinforces the argument for moving beyond a dyadic to a network level of analysis.

According to Johnston, Lewin and Spekman (1999), the complexity of relationships increases when business relationships occur at an international level. From an industrial network perspective, internationalization of the firm means that the firm establishes and develops network positions in foreign markets (Johanson and Mattsson 1987). For Fletcher and Barrett (2001), in the international business context, business transactions are embedded in networks of relationships that cut across cultural boundaries. In addition, they observed that these relationships, in turn, are embedded in different national as well as global business environments. Furthermore, these environments include social networks, institutional networks and market networks. This means that: (a) there are likely to be differences in the political environment; (b) there will be different institutions and organizations to deal with; and (c) the nature of the market is likely to be different. Johnston, Lewin and Spekman (1999) believe that a changing global environment is forcing firms to move closer to their exchange partners, form international alliances and participate in complex multinational networks.

Partnering Characteristics

Studies have been conducted that look at the nature of partnering in terms of its main characteristics. Academics have been describing the boundaries of partnering by defining the concept through the consideration of the so-called dimensions, attributes, features, critical success factors or indicators of partnering success. The identification in the literature of the defining characteristics of partnering is not an easy task, because different authors use different constructs to express similar ideas, which creates methodological problems in establishing comparisons and in looking for similarities. Perhaps this happens because the literature on partnering characteristics does not appear to represent a common stream of research. In spite of the divergences concerning the key characteristics of partnering, some commonalities emerge. Authors appear to converge to consider joint work, sharing of resources and mutual benefits as key defining characteristics of partnering. Key partnering characteristics extracted from literature and respective authors include:

Table 4.1 A framework for understanding partnering

Dimension(s)	Characteristic(s)	Indicator(s)
Commitment	Formal commitment	Type of contracts
Trust	An inherent trust	Type of contracts Negotiation Ordering procedure Technology transfer Quality inspection Information disclosure
Win-Win	Sharing of risks Sharing of benefits Increase in joint competitiveness	
Long-term orientation	Expectation of continuity	Type of contracts Substitutability of suppliers Length of contracts Information disclosure on long-term forecasting Assessment schemes
	A continuous improvement focus	Multi-functional teams Assessment schemes Payment performance Cost reduction projects
	Supplier development	Supplier development programme
	Joint strategy setting	
	Joint planning	Planning product mix Management of capacity Joint cost planning
Coordination	Joint R&D	Joint design Prototyping Joint product development Joint process definition
	Two-way communication	Channels of communication Frequency of interaction
Joint problem-solving	Willingness to help one another	
	Personnel allocation	
	Conflict resolution	
Flexibility	Two-way flexibility	Flexibility in agreements Flexibility in delivery
	A reduced supply base	Proportion of buyer total demand provided by the supplier Importance of this item/product class to buyer Number of suppliers for this item/product class bought Number of alternative sources
Mutual dependence		
	A reduced customer base	Supplying on an exclusivity basis Proportion of buyer's purchases

- commitment
- communication: two-way communication
- conflict resolution
- continuous improvement focus
- flexibility
- information disclosure and sharing
- joint planning
- joint problem solving
- joint R&D

- long-term orientation
- mutual dependence
- sharing benefits
- sharing risks
- sharing goals
- supplier development
- trust
- willingness to help one another
- win-win

Based on these characteristics, this researcher developed a framework for partnering that is illustrated in Table 4.1. This framework was developed by the researcher to provide guidance in exploring and analysing partnering relationships and thus aid further discussion. In this framework the dimensions correspond to the defining features of partnering, that in turn can be defined though a number of characteristics. It is not the objective of the researcher to explore in detail what has been written on each construct that would extend this thesis beyond what the researcher believes to be necessary to the understanding of the concept of partnering following a constructivist and grounded approach, and as a basis for the fieldwork.

Factors Influencing Partnering

In the literature there is a lack of emphasis and of a clear distinction between the factors that motivate the choice of a partnering relationship-type (i.e., the motivational aspects of partnering or partnering drivers), the factors that influence partnering as a dynamic process and the success factors of partnering implementation. The researcher proposes in this section to bring some insights into these factors and briefly discuss the work that has been developed.

Partnering Drivers

Empirical studies have indicated a wide variety of driving forces behind the development of partnering relationships (Hendrick and Ellman 1993). These drivers are not mutually exclusive and a participant can manifest more than one at different times or in different circumstances (Ford et al. 1998). According to some authors, partnerships are motivated primarily to gain competitive advantage (Mudambi and Helper 1998; Vlosky et al. 1998) through the development of potentially important synergies between firms with different capabilities (Dodgson 1992). According to other authors, although partnering relationships can be implemented for a variety of strategic and operational goals (Ellram 1991; Monczka and Trent 1991), it is agreed that the improvement of the product development process and access to innovative technologies are of paramount importance (Håkansson and Eriksson 1993). Firms may choose to collaborate with respect to some goals and not with respect to others (Young and Wilkinson 1997). This may explain the myriad ways in which buyer–supplier partnerships begin and are developed (Hendrick and Ellram 1993). For example, a partnership focused on the trading partners with a long-term horizon differs from a project-based partnership; in this case two firms may jointly work towards a common goal and dissolve their agreement after achieving the goal. The main drivers or motivations for partnering (i.e., partnering drivers) emphasized in the literature include:

- linking of the complementary contributions of the partners in the value chain (e.g., access to technology, materials, labour and capital) (Contractor and Lorange 1988);
- the promotion of synergies between firms with different capabilities (Dodgson 1992);
- the development of partnership philosophy appears as a result of firms' need to reduce costs (Cousins 1994);
- better integration of design efforts, improvement of specific areas, increased stability of supply (Mudambi and Schrunder 1996);
- technology is increasingly the focus of collaboration. However, there are broad differences in the actual focus of collaboration between industries. In some industries the focus can be in product development and in others it can be in process development. Moreover, the focus of collaboration changes over time, sometimes with product life cycles (Beecham and Cordey-Hayes 1998);
- cost reductions, improves product quality, productivity and lead-time (Langfield-Smith and Greenwood 1998);
- ultimately firms are driven by the desire of greater competitive advantage (Mudambi and Helper 1998);
- the ultimate goal of collaborative relationships is to develop strategic advantage by pooling resources, gaining access to market and/or technical information, leveraging of complementary strengths and achieving of economies of scale (Vlosky and Wilson 1997);
- firms collaborate not only to safeguard assets and enhance adaptation, but also to lower the costs of conducting development tasks by joining together to exploit scale economies better (Bello et al. 1999);
- collaborative relationships with suppliers can be a means for buyers to scan the technological knowledge base of related industries and to keep its progress under control (Calabrese 2000);
- increased market share; inventory reductions; improved delivery service; improved quality; shorter product development cycles (Corbett et al. 2001).

According to Biong, Wathne and Parvatiyar (1997), resistance of firms to engage in partnering relationships is driven by:

- fear of dependency – firms will be reluctant to engage in partnering relationships when they fear unilateral dependency on the other party due to: (a) loss of flexibility in strategic choices (e.g., in choice of suppliers); (b) fear of opportunistic behaviour of the partner, and (c) loss of personal or organizational control;
- lack of perceived value in the relationship – firms will be reluctant to engage in partnering relationships unless significant value added is proposed in terms of: (a) cost reductions; (b) new sources of revenue such as development of new products and access to new markets; (c) superior market position; (d) development of new competencies (i.e., new technological solutions can provide advantages for both the customer and the supplier); and (e) social rewards (e.g., the effect on company's reputation);
- lack of credibility of partners – firms will be reluctant to partner with other firms that: (a) are small relative to the firm's total demand in terms of size and capacity; (b) are unreliable in fulfilling agreements (e.g., related to delivery, quality); (c) lack an innovative outlook; and (d) have a generally low reputation;
- rapid technological changes – in industries with rapid technological changes, large growth and many actors, firms will resist engaging in partnering relationships;

- lack of relational orientation in the buying company – firms with low relational orientation will be less inclined to engage in partnering relationships. This low relational orientation could be due to: (a) inhibitive firm policies; (b) transactional-based reward systems; (c) corporate belief systems; (d) rigid organization structure; and (e) restricted flows of communication.

Factors Influencing Partnering Process Implementations

Literature has identified a large number of factors that shape inter-organizational relationships and has offered numerous categorizations for investigating each set of factors. For example, the literature suggests that to fully understand buyer–supplier relationships one must consider the characteristics and behaviour of the supplier, the characteristics and behaviour of the buying organization, the interaction process between buyer and supplier (Wren and Simpson 1996), the network where the dyad is embedded (Håkansson and Johanson 1992), the political and socio-economic environment under which both parties are operating (Håkansson 1982) and the characteristics of the industry both buyer and supplier are associated with (Campbell 1985). Such categorizations are apparent in models of buyer–supplier relationships and in many studies, either conceptual and/or empirical. Some of these models have brought together many significant influencing factors related to inter-firm collaboration and partnering. Such models follow Fynes's (1998) classification in order to facilitate their identification. They have appeared in several disciplines such as channel management, operations management, supply chain management, relationship marketing, and industrial marketing and purchasing. It happens that not all focus on the same aspects of relationship management and when addressing the same issues, they examine them from a different perspective and even use a different terminology. Classifying models into discrete streams is an inexact task due to the level of duplication across literature.

A review of the literature revealed four groups of models exploring the influencing factors of buyer–supplier relationships: one exploring the behaviour of only one party (Sheth 1973), another exploring the buyer–supplier dyad (e.g., the IMP interaction model), a third group emphasizing the network in which the firm is embedded (Håkansson and Johanson 1992) and a fourth group attempting to bring together the dyadic and the network elements (Håkansson and Snehota 1995). Unfortunately this research has not been evolutionary, which means that the resulting models of buyer–supplier relationships have not built on previous models (Wren and Simpson 1996). This has led to a body of research which is rather disjointed, as well as confused and confusing (Cheung and Turnbull 1998). The use of different terms to express the same category of factor is illustrative of this. In some cases, the categorizations and labels given to constructs not only confuse meaning, but also make it difficult to compare and summarize. Another example is found on the lack of clarity of the type of influence a factor may exert on buyer–supplier relationships. It often remains to be explained if a factor is influencing the overall buyer–supplier relationship or a particular feature of a relationship. At other times, impacts on collaborative or partnering relationships are mentioned without specification of the feature in question.

Models and studies refer to factors influencing buyer–supplier relationships, yet often ignore factors that will affect each relationship uniquely and to a varying extent (Veludo et al. 2001). It seems that in these cases the complexity of relationships is not fully taken into account.

Success Factors of Partnering Implementation

For Sako, Lamming and Helper (1994) it takes time to develop partnerships. There are authors, such as Leverick and Cooper (1998), who suggest that building partnerships should be a step-by-step approach or, in other words, should be built gradually, as familiarity and trust between companies increase. Cousins (1994) shares a similar opinion, but justifies his view by arguing that organizations will find the change easier to implement if they go about it one step at a time. For Cousins important changes need to occur (e.g., an organizational cultural change) in both parties because if changes are not properly prepared, the move towards the adoption of partnering relationships can be compromised. New and Burnes (1998) have referred to the need for considerable changes in the behaviour of both buyer and supplier to develop a viable long-term and close business relationship.

The notion of change is at the centre of the change model developed by Macbeth, Boddy, Wagner and Charles (1998), which recognizes the need to allow for the dynamics of change and consider the combination of people and institutional mechanisms as part of an implementation route for change. This model takes into account the dynamic and developmental process aspects of partnering, that do not often appear to be emphasized in the literature.

Bensaou (1999) suggested that a partnering relationship should be carefully planned and chosen as a type of relationship which is costly to develop and maintain, as well as risky, given the specialized investments it requires. This aside, the choice affects how a firm defines its boundaries and core activities. Leverick and Cooper (1998) pointed out that partnering has risks that can be lessened by good partnership management, that takes into account the factors that influence the process of collaboration.

A Case Study of Partnering in the Automotive Sector

A detailed investigation was undertaken to investigate business to business partnering activities between Opel and its European suppliers. The research was based on surveys and in-depth interviews.

The complexity and variety of relationships between an assembler and its first tier supplier are typically characterized by the existence of collaborative and non-collaborative elements. The predominant collaboration form usually is formal and enforceable through contracts. Such relationships are not necessarily the full responsibility of the parent assembler's subsidiary (transplant or more recently set up capacity expansion facility).

Defining constructs were useful in determining the extent to which, if at all, the parties were moving in the direction of a more integrated and mutually considerate process. The research project undertaken with Opel in Portugal singularly failed to observe partnering concerning the items supplied to OP (Opel Portugal). Partnering agreements instead were established between Opel Germany, where a centralized purchasing department and R&D facilities are located, and the suppliers' division or specific people charged with the negotiation of these types of contracts.

This research revealed that, for the buyer, drivers for partnering agreements were the access to innovative technologies and capital, while for the suppliers were the increasing stability in supply and the gaining of access to the market. This study showed that project-based partnering relationships are much more common than partnering relationships with a long-term horizon.

When considering the complexity demonstrated in OP's focal network and its links back to the US, it is clear that the network effects are significant. Of importance is that the nature of the MNC decision processes and structures have enabling (or in this case more often constricting) influences on the freedom of action of their Portugal-based branch. Thus it comes as little surprise that the journey along the path to a more explicitly partnering relationship has a limited and insignificant status. The local management, even if they wished to get closer and become more integrated with local suppliers were not empowered through their parent company network to commit to such processes. The role of OP was also constrained through the level and location of decision-making authority across the European network. These are structural and procedural issues within the customer organization about which local suppliers (i.e., Portuguese-based direct suppliers – PBDS) can do little at their level. One however has to recognize that some of the PBDSs are of themselves part of more extended networks including MNCs. As such they have alternative influencing routes. Local suppliers, without the backing of their own MNCs, in order to influence decisions at a distance have opted for strategic alliances and/or agents close the customer's purchasing decision centre (in this case Germany).

Opel, by following in GM's footsteps, was taking an arm's length approach to its relationship strategy. Evidence has shown that Opel has been a company trying to find ingenious ways of exploiting upstream companies (i.e., first tier, second tier suppliers) and, furthermore, not looking at the opportunities offered by collaborative practices and behaviour. The logic of inter-firm collaboration is value enhancement and through collaboration there are opportunities to reduce operational costs. The researcher suggests that the leadership of Opel should be attuned to develop an overall strategic view of where the industry is going and to consider the benefits of a truly collaborative approach to business relationships.

Implications for Practice and Policy

The findings have shown some critical areas, which deserve some attention from OP and Opel (in particular, at head office and where maximum authority in the decision-making process lies), from its PBDS (some of which are Portuguese-owned companies while others are subsidiaries of MNCs) and from governmental institutions.

The fast-changing competitive environment, with its shortened product life cycles and fast technological innovation, faced by automotive companies has created a demand for high levels of flexibility and the ability to cope with greater environmental change and uncertainty. A current issue for management is how to develop a more flexible company. Similarly to Hyun (1994), this researcher asserts that one way for final assemblers to achieve this would be through the synchronization of their activities with their suppliers' activities.

Delivery and the subsequent need for flexibility are critical issues in the relationships between OP and its PBDS. The practices required by OP were likely to demand substantial efforts on behalf of the supplier to achieve just-in-time (JIT) delivery but were being performed without significant support and commitment from the buyer. Delivery was practised in a context where OP, and ultimately Opel, were seeking some advantages (e.g., cost reduction) and influence over suppliers. In addition, it seems that the buyer was attempting to optimize its performance at the expense of its suppliers, who were trying to accommodate the need to be flexible. Although OP's level of satisfaction with suppliers' delivery was high, it was based on a low level of synchronization as demonstrated by the low level of coordination between parties and, in particular, by the absence of joint planning (in terms of production planning and management of capacity).

OP's inefficient disclosure of information related to production volumes, production schedules and volume of stocks required, did not allow the supplier to plan far enough in advance (e.g., production), which created difficulties for the suppliers and affected the climate of the relationship. The researcher, based on the evidence, infers that the managerial practices that Opel established for OP had effects in terms of performance, costs and ultimately competitiveness, with negative impacts for all parties involved. The researcher sees the alignment of processes and information flows, for which joint planning, increased information sharing and improved communication channels would be fundamental prerequisites, as beneficial for the buyers and suppliers. The potential sensitivity of sharing information between the buyer and its suppliers was known: however, it is prudent that there should be a balance between limiting the extent of commercially or competitively sensitive information exchange to that which is absolutely necessary while still achieving an open relationship. A successful synchronization of OP's activities with its PBDS's activities also depends on the synchronization between firms within the business network of OP. This notion seems to be compatible with the view held by Lagendijk (1997). who claimed that an automotive subsidiary should be based on the positive-sum type of partnership and be attuned to a full exploitation of economies of specialization and integration throughout the production chain. It also appears that the PBDSs are constrained in what they can do to synchronize their supply chains given the limited amount of information coming from OP.

Evidence has shown that the internal relationships within Opel affected the performance of both the MNC and buyer–supplier relationships. The main problems of intra-organizational relationships within Opel, felt by both OP and its PBDS, were communication, power relationships and the cultural differences between individuals. Opel should perhaps investigate its intra-organizational relationships, whose problems may be a result of the implementation of policies (e.g., human resources management) and of the perceived, unclear definition of its subsidiaries' roles (e.g., responsibilities between Opel in Spain and Opel in Germany).

PBDS had a significant understanding of Opel's requirements and systems. This could help Opel in many of its improvements. Opel could benefit from being much closer to its suppliers and by establishing a more collaborative approach to them (e.g., cost reductions, knowledge transfer).

Historically, GM has taken an arm's length approach towards supplier relations (Kim and Mitchell 1999). Opel, by following in GM's footsteps, was also taking an arm's length approach to its relationship strategy. Evidence has shown that Opel has been a company trying to find ingenious ways of exploiting upstream companies (i.e., first tier, second tier suppliers) and, furthermore, not looking at the opportunities offered by collaborative practices and behaviour. The logic of inter-firm collaboration is value enhancement and through collaboration there are opportunities to reduce operational costs. Perhaps the leadership of Opel should be motivated to develop an overall strategic view of where the industry is going and to consider the benefits of a truly collaborative approach to business relationships. There have been strong recommendations for the final assembler to collaborate with suppliers (Testore 1998). This need for inter-firm collaboration is driven by the challenges and numerous pressures faced by the industry, including pressure to reduce cost and increase responsiveness (this requires suppliers to achieve challenging targets for which they need help from their customer). GM and Opel have been operating under the shadow of their collective history. Such a historical legacy must be overcome if this vehicle manufacturer is to succeed in developing more inter-firm collaborative relationships and genuine partnerships with its key suppliers. The researcher suggests that profound change within this MNC requires changes in the underlying culture. A renewed collaborative culture needs to be created. The cultural gulf which needs to be bridged is vast, because other multinational networks need to be involved.

The process of creating a cooperative inter-organizational culture between two companies that interact at multiple levels (i.e., local, regional, head office) in different functional areas, and with individuals from different cultural backgrounds should not be underestimated. The researcher believes that in such a process of change the suppliers may be of great help to Opel; through the understanding they have about Opel and through their self-interest in remaining, or becoming, the Opel's preferred supplier. Opel must also consider whether their current behaviour supports their being a supplier's preferred customer. From findings in this study that is, at the time of writing, unlikely, and whilst suppliers may not choose to refuse business from Opel, their truly innovative efforts may be directed towards other customers. This was not tested in the study but is a possibility referred to in other situations (Macbeth 1998).

The evidence implies that Opel is not getting the best effort from suppliers. Opel has been a difficult customer for many suppliers. Based on other survey findings in this study, Opel is perceived as forming relationships with their suppliers that are not based on trust and commitment, trust and satisfaction nor on continuity. Furthermore, Opel has been relying on procedures and policies for relationship building rather than on the development of close personal relationships. Blois (1997) argued that certain relationships, such as those established by Opel, have been shown to have certain advantages such as control over whom the company deals with, (ultimately) profit gains and the ability to use opportunism to obtain advantage over suppliers. The researcher believes that Opel's behaviour can lead to unsustainable situations for suppliers and to suppliers' opportunistic behaviour. Perhaps if suppliers had a better alternative they would not choose Opel as a key customer.

For some PBDS the efforts the suppliers make to please OP are notable given the low volume of demand and turnover they get from OP in comparison to other final assemblers. In the view of the researcher the attractiveness of OP as a key customer is relative. On the one hand PBDS, through OP, can get access to other subsidiaries of Opel such as OS and Opel Germany (OG), but on the other hand the business relationships they can build and the activities they can implement with OP are limited due to the subsidiary's boundaries. In other words, the multinational network of OP offers to PBDS opportunities and constraints.

An awareness of both opportunities and constraints has strategic implications for suppliers and impact on the development of their expectations. Evidence indicates that the strategy-structure strategies, defined at the coordination centre of OP and applied in cascade through OG and OS, have influenced and affected the choices of inter-firm collaborative activities and relationship interactions at the dyadic level in Portugal. Hence, the entrepreneurial initiatives of OP have been limited. This should not be surprising, having taken Birkinshaw's (2000) view into account, which was that 'despite the compelling logic for tapping into local markets through the subsidiary network many corporations appear to neglect the creative potential of their subsidiaries'.

Potential entrepreneurial initiatives undertaken by OP have been underestimated. This belief is based on findings, which have shown, for example, that OP's initiatives for quality improvements, which were instigated by levels high in the Opel organizational hierarchy, brought positive results in the performance of both OP and PBDS. The measures that Opel applied elsewhere did not have such positive impacts on quality management. This is a sign that at the dyadic level in Portugal, performance improvement may be more dependent on Opel's internal interactions than on the locally permitted activity. When looking closely at the organizational design of the internal network of OP and specifically the linkages between OP, Opel Spain (OS) and OG (Opel Germany), the researcher has found that Opel's practices when in managing subsidiaries in a supply chain have been wasteful of resources and have been holding performance back. It remains a question as to what extent Opel has been aware of the impact that its strategic and dynamic allocation of resources to different units has been having and to what extent performance has been properly evaluated. This researcher argues that if the collaboration effort has not been well targeted then performance levels will be impacted, at all levels of Opel's multinational network.

A Model of the Supply Chain Relationship

Findings and conclusions from research with OP lead to the development of the framework shown in Figure 4.1. This includes a number of factors that can be used to analyse varying relationship types when the actors involved are subsidiaries of a MNC and/or actors in a network. Although these factors are context specific (the reason why the framework has been conceived as a contextual factors framework), the researcher claims that these factors can be used as explainers of the dynamics and processes associated with buyer–supplier interaction. Many of the factors that emerged from the case study are mentioned in the literature, albeit in a scattered and fragmented form.

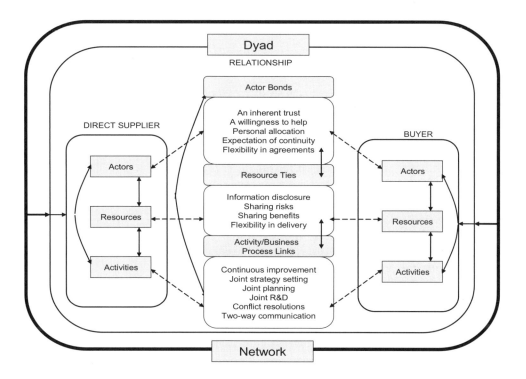

Figure 4.1   A conceptual framework to analyse inter-firm collaboration in industrial markets

The main components of this conceptual framework are: (a) the focal company; (b) the relationship; (c) actor bonds; (d) resource ties; and (e) activity links. These components will now be defined and discussed, taking into account existing literature so that uniformity in terms and notions can be maintained.

The Focal Company

The focal company is an organization that performs activities and employs resources. It is formed by actors, resources and activities which are inter-related. This interdependence is indicated through the vertical arrows in Figure 4.1.

Actors are defined as entities involved in activities to convert resources to finished goods and services for consumption by end users. In other words, actors are defined by the activities they perform and the resources they control. Therefore, actors are both resource holders and resource users. Actors possess different resources, depending upon the nature of the global environment they are working in and the position they hold in the network (Harland 1996). There are many different types of resources. They can be tangible or intangible (O'Donnell 1999). Actors carry out activities in the pursuit of their own goals. Actors possess their own perceptions of the interacting party (Håkansson and Snehota 1989). The two main types of activities are transformation activities and transfer activities (Johnston et al. 1999). Through transformation activities resources are changed in some way. Transfer activities link the transformation activities of different actors to each other.

The Relationship

Similarly to the AAR model, in this framework three interdependent substance layers identify a relationship. These result from the interaction process between two dyadic actors: actor bonds, resource ties and activity links. Actor bonds describe the connections between the actors, either individual or organizational, through their perceptions of each other. Resource ties describe the organizational connections that are developed through resource inputs and outputs. Activity links describe the connections formed by activities and business processes, which the actors develop with each other. There is a large variety in the substance, which depends on the existence, type and strength of actor bonds, resource ties and activity links. The differences may reflect the type of industrial activity or company specific circumstances. The functions of a relationship can be formulated in terms of the effects produced by the relationship on the dyad, on each of the involved parties and on third parties. Relationships make it possible for an organization to access, and exploit, the resources of other parties, and to connect the parties' activities together.

The substance layers are inter-related with each other, implying that an occurrence in one substance layer will affect other substance layers, as indicated by the vertical arrows in Figure 4.1. The connectedness of the focal relationship with other actors is indicated by outward facing horizontal arrows from each substance layer.

Actor Bonds

Actor bonds occur when two actors interact with each other through an exchange process (Håkansson and Snehota 1995). The following partnering characteristics are used as a measure of actor bonds: an inherent trust, willingness to help one another, personnel allocation, expectation of continuity and flexibility in agreements.

Resource Ties

The researcher considers resources as including all assets, capabilities, organizational processes, and information knowledge controlled by the firm and which enable it to conceive and implement strategies that improve its efficiency and effectiveness. Resources are also seen as commodities that actors use during activity links to produce their goods and/or services. Ties are created through the production process as resource inputs and resource outputs go from one company to another. Through inter-firm linkages, firms can obtain access to assets that create value, that are not available for purchase in the market, and that require time to build up. Thus, a firm can use inter-firm linkages to access assets stocked by other firms, and share its assets.

The following partnering characteristics are used as a measure of resource ties: information disclosure, the sharing of risks and benefits, and flexibility in delivery.

Activity Links

Activity is assumed to be a sequence of acts directed towards a purpose (Håkansson and Snehota 1995). Activity becomes the generator of a continuously emerging context. The activity link construct includes the actions done together by the actors, through the exchange process (Håkansson and Johanson 1992). According to Håkansson and Snehota (1995), activity links in a dyadic relationship are affected by adjustments in the activity structures of the companies involved. In addition, activity links affect the activity structures of the buyer and the supplier, as well as the activity pattern in the business network. The following partnering characteristics are used as a measure of activity links: continuous improvement, joint strategy setting, joint planning, joint R&D, conflict resolution and two-way communication.

Contextual Factors Framework

As findings have shown, relationships can vary. The researcher has found that various factors influence inter-firm collaborative relationships between OP and its PBDS and that these factors did not have the same importance for all companies. Based on this, the researcher infers that various combinations of factors can explain the variety of inter-firm collaborative relationships, which companies may implement. Findings and conclusions led the researcher to develop a framework, which includes a number of factors that can be used to analyse varying relationship types when the actors involved are subsidiaries of a MNC and/or actors in a network. Although these factors are context specific (the reason why the framework has been conceived as a contextual factors framework), this researcher claims that these factors can be used as explainers of the dynamics and processes associated with buyer–supplier interaction. This claim is based on the fact that most of the factors that came out from the case study are mentioned in the literature, albeit in a scattered and fragmented view.

One implication from the framework is that it combines both inter- and intra-organizational relationships. The researcher claims that both perspectives are needed to develop a thorough understanding of relationship strategies undertaken by actors. The IMP researchers have concentrated on the inter-organizational aspects and MNC researchers have looked mainly at the intra-organizational aspects. This framework combines the two streams of research to develop a holistic picture of relationship development by MNC subsidiaries. The literature relating to contextuality (Mittila 2000) was of great influence in the development of the framework.

This researcher does not suggest that this framework has the power to explain all buyer–supplier relationships within a multinational network context. However, the merit of this framework should be seen in the light of its ability to speak specifically for the population from which it was derived and in the light of the understanding one can get from it.

Bringing together both inter- and intra-organizational relationships, the framework develops a wider network perspective than considered at the start of the research project. The wider network perspective is particularly applicable to the automotive industry, where MNCs dominate the assembly processes through multiple plants and utilizing large numbers of suppliers through a number of different tiers. As in the case illustrated in this study, the parent headquarters may be some distance (geographically and structurally) from the subsidiary and therefore an intra-organizational approach is necessary.

By bringing the inter- and intra-organizational aspects of relationships, it can be seen that actors operate within four contexts: (a) organizational; (b) relational; (c) spatial; and (d) network. These groups and their linkages are illustrated in Figure 4.2.

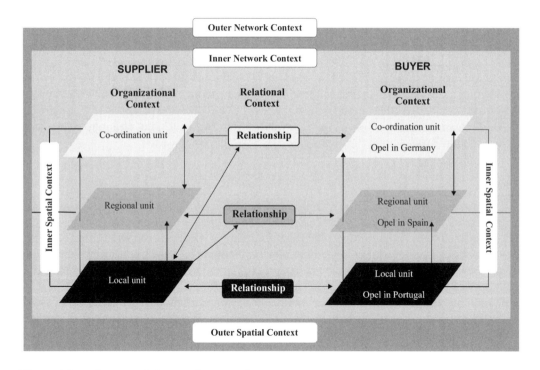

Figure 4.2   Contextual factors framework

The key modules are comprised of the following:

Organizational context:
– Corporate Culture
– Employment System Links
– Strategy
– Policies
– Organizational Structure

- Actors
- Resources
- Activities.

Relational context:
- product
- service
- information
- finance
- communication
- personal relations
- atmosphere (trust, climate of pressure, buyer's conflict behaviour)
- relationship specific investments.

Inner spatial context:
- position in the network
- geographical location (e.g., local, regional, head office).

Inner network context:
- network of actors
- network of resources
- network of activities.

Forces that bind the network:
- embeddedness
- connectedness
- interdependence.

The organizational context refers to the specific features of a company that affect the focal relationship. Therefore, this context is limited by the activities and resources internal to the organization. Håkansson and Ford (2002) indicate that the internal processes of the actor are influenced by the relationships it has and it also influences its relationships. Factors that operate within this context include: corporate culture, employment system links, strategy, subsidiary policies and strategy, actors, resources and activities.

The relational context is the frame in which inter-organizational relationships develop. These relationships operate between a subsidiary and external dyad partners such as customers and suppliers. These relationships types are characterized by collaborative and non-collaborative elements. The factors that operate within this context include: components which effect the dyadic interaction process (product, service, information, finance), communication related issues, the personal relations established between buyer and suppliers, the atmosphere affecting and being affected by buyer–supplier interaction, and the relationship specific investments made by both parties. Atmosphere is considered to be an intervening group of variables, which reflect the behaviour of the parties involved and the mutual expectation each of the parties holds, in relation to the other. Relationship specific investments include, the activities performed within the relationship (e.g., adjustments in transportation and payment routines), the activities performed by the respective companies (e.g., reallocation in the production processes and product customization), and those tangible (e.g., building and tools), and intangible (e.g., time allocated to the buyer) specific investments, either strategically planned and implemented, or occurring in an unconscious manner. The factors also include those depicted in Figure 4.1 as the actor bonds, activity links and resource ties. All interaction occurs externally at the dyadic level with the subsidiary having the ability to influence the relationship, but perhaps limited in its ability to control the relationship to its liking.

The inner spatial context is the space, both in terms of geographical location and network position, in which a firm resides. For instance, in the case study investigated in this research, the inner spatial context consists of three layers (Portugal, Spain and Germany) where the buyer and its PBDS (through direct or indirect subsidiaries of their own MNC networks) undertake business relationships.

The inner network context includes the network of actors, resources and activities of a subsidiary's (i.e., focal) business network and the intra-organizational relationships of the companies involved. The network, as configurations of actors carrying out activities, forms the contextual domain in which all the companies (i.e., buyer and suppliers) operate. Embeddedness, connectedness and interdependence, are the forces that bind the network components. Network's influence embraces the factors, which reflect the actors' inducements, constraints, and availability of opportunities to form relationships and alliances, either vertical or horizontal.

The inner spatial context and the inner network context correspond to the internal parts of a subsidiary's (i.e., focal) business network, rather than the MNC (e.g., GM's multinational network) in general. The external context would be formed by all organization sets of the different units of the MNC. However, the focal subsidiary's capabilities, and therefore its position within the MNC, are primarily shaped by its role in the whole network (Andersson and Forsgren 2000). The outer spatial and outer networks contexts include all the remaining factors that may influence the subsidiary's (i.e., focal) business network.

The external network context is the context that develops externally to the subsidiary with all external organizations, that is, its external business network. This context includes suppliers (all tiers), government departments, union organizations and customers that form part of the wider business network.

The links in the network context (i.e., internal and external) are of a relational nature with the subsidiary influencing and being influenced by the network effects that flow through the network. The factors that operate within the network context are activity patterns, web of actors and resource constellations (Håkansson and Snehota 1995).

Each context will require a different approach to strategy development due to the differing relationships developed in each situation. For example, the hierarchical relationships developed within the spatial context may require strategies aimed at changing policy development and influencing resource allocation. Measures used to achieve these aims could be through developing closer ties with regional units, indicating the subsidiaries' ability to undertake higher level tasks and developing personal relations with employees within the closely linked units. The four contexts are not independent and consideration needs to be given to how changing aspects of one context will affect the other three contexts.

Managers may find they can identify factors vary in relation to the others in differing contexts. By analysing those factors affecting each context, actors will be able to develop a greater understanding of how they can influence relationships within each context. Moreover, the ability to influence the relationships will vary between contexts. For example, the ability for an actor to exert some influence at the network level will be much less then its ability to influence the organizational context.

Conclusions

Despite the extensive work on inter-firm collaboration (IFC) and partnering, a review of literature revealed that most studies have focused on IFC and partnering without taking into account the ownership ties of firms, which is the case of the MNC and respective subsidiaries. Largely missing from the literature is a clear understanding of how IFC and partnering are implemented at different points within a MNC network. This research, by exploring these subjects within the context of a an automotive subsidiary in Portugal of which no study has been developed yet, has brought some context specific insights which allow a better understanding of real-life practices on the referred subjects.

Literature review revealed that partnering has been, for years, a competitive strategy pursued by the vehicle manufacturers (VMs) and their motor vehicle parts and components suppliers. Long practiced in Japan, VM–supplier partnering relationships have increased in the US and Europe. In a market characterized by changing regulations, intense cost pressures, and discriminating consumer preferences, VMs have developed partnering relationships with their supply base as a means to attain resources and achieve goals that elude these companies when operating alone. The increasing importance given to partnering within the automotive industry has been accompanied by a great number of studies on this topic, as this chapter tried to illustrate. However, lack of clarity, misunderstanding, controversy, partial views of phenomena, lack of an integrated and multidisciplinary approach to research are evident. Overall, the picture painted is one of a sense of confusion with the concept and a lack of empirical studies taking into account both perspectives of VMs and respective suppliers as well as the organizational structure of the parties involved in the business relationships they establish. Thus, only partially reliable insights can be drawn from the existing literature. This may be explained by: (a) the assumptions researchers based their research on and the different objectives that they were set to achieve; (b) the limitations on the research design; (c) a static perspective, which took 'snapshots' of the organization at particular points in time and described the organization at that point in time only; and (d) a focus on dyadic relationships without taking into account the network context and the ownership ties of the companies involved.

The purpose of the literature review was to develop an understanding of the relevant work on inter-firm collaboration and partnering and to identify areas where further research is required. Literature review was explored to unearth the research objectives. These 'grew out' of the discussion as gaps in the body of knowledge were discovered. In so doing, the aim is to help the reader to grasp the novelty of the work conducted by the researcher. It is therefore important to select particular areas on which to focus the research. An area not yet explored and discussed is the one that refers to inter-firm vertical collaboration and partnering, taking into account the ownership ties of firms, such as those of MNCs. It is based on this gap that the researcher has defined the following objectives previously referred to: (a) to explore how inter-firm and partnering operates between a subsidiary of a motor vehicle manufacturer and its direct suppliers in Portugal and (b) to explore the influencing factors on inter-firm collaboration and partnering between a subsidiary of a motor vehicle manufacturer and its direct suppliers in Portugal.

Core Findings

Four major findings from this research are:

1. relationships can be characterized by several dimensions, each of which is a mix of collaborative and non-collaborative elements;
2. a diversified scenario of relationships can be explained by the different combinations of several factors; the importance of each needs to be weighted and hierarchicalized;
3. the wider network affects both to enable and constrain the freedom of action at the level of the customer–supplier dyad:
4. partnering is contingent on the position, role and influence at different points in the network.

References

Andersson, U. and Forsgren, M. (2000), 'In Search of Centre of Excellence: Network Embeddedness and Subsidiary Roles in Multinational Corporations', *Management International Review* 20(4), pp. 329–350.

Anderson, J., Håkansson, H. and Johanson, J. (1994), 'Dyadic Business Relationships within a Business Network Context', *Journal of Marketing* 58, pp. 1–15.

Araujo, L. (1990), 'Interorganisational Relationships in Industrial Markets', PhD Thesis, University of Lancaster.

Araujo, L. and Easton, G. (1996), 'Networks in Socio-economic Systems', in Iacobucci, D. (ed.) *Networks in Marketing* (London: Sage), pp. 63–107.

Axelsson, B. and Easton, G. (1992), *Industrial Networks: A New View of Reality* (London: Routledge).

Backhaus, K. and Buschken, J. (1997), 'What Do We Know about Business-to-Business Interactions', in Gemünden, H., Ritter, T. and Walter, A. (eds) *Relationships and Networks in International Markets* (Oxford: Pergamon), pp. 13–36.

Beecham, M. and Cordey-Hayes, M. (1998), 'Partnering and Knowledge Transfer in the UK Motor Industry', *Technovation* 18(3), pp. 191–205.

Bello, D., Lohtia, R. and Dant, S. (1999), 'Collaborative Relationships for Component Development: The Role of Strategic Issues, Production Costs, and Transaction Costs', *Journal of Business Research*, 45, pp. 15–31.

Bensaou, M. (1999), 'Portfolios of Buyer-Supplier Relationships', *Sloan Management Review* 8(2), pp. 35–44.

Bevan J. (1987), 'What is Co-makership?', *International Journal of Quality and Reliability Management* 4(3), pp. 47–56.

Biong, H., Wathne, K. and Parvatiyar, A. (1997), 'Why Do Some Companies Not Want to Engage in Partnering Relationships?', in Gemünden, H., Ritter, T. and Walter, A. (eds) *Relationships and Networks in International Markets* (Oxford: Pergamon), pp. 91–107.

Birkinshaw, J. (2000), 'Network Relationships Inside and Outside: The Form, and the Development of Capabilities', in Birkinshaw, J. and Hagstrom, P. (eds) *Capability Management in Network Organizations* (New York: Oxford University Press), pp. 4–18.

Blois, K. (1997), 'Don't All Firms Have Relationships?', *Journal of Business and Industrial Marketing* 13(3), pp. 256–70.

Brennan, R. and Turnbull, P. (1998), 'Adaptations in Buyer-Seller Relationships', in Naudé, P. and Turnbull, P. (eds) *Network Dynamics in International Marketing* (Oxford: Elsevier Science Ltd), pp. 26–41.

Burnes, B. and New, S. (1998), 'Developing the Partnership Concept for the Future', in Burnes, B. and Dale, B. (eds) *Working in Partnership: Best Practice in Customer-Supplier Relations* (Aldershot: Gower), pp. 101–9.

Calabrese, G. (2000), 'Small-Medium Supplier-Buyer Relationships in the Car Industry: Evidence from Italy', *European Journal of Purchasing and Supply Management* 6, pp. 59–65.

Campbell, N. (1985), 'An Interaction Approach to Organizational Buying Behaviour', *Journal of Business Research* 13, pp. 35–49.

Cheung, M. and Turnbull, P. (1998), 'A Review of the Nature and Development of Inter-organisational Relationships: A Network Perspective', in Naudé, P. and Turnbull, P. (eds) *Network Dynamics in International Marketing* (Oxford: Elsevier Science Ltd), pp. 42–69.

Chopra, S. and Meindle, P. (2001), *Supply Chain Management: Strategy, Planning and Operation* (Upper Saddle River, NJ: Prentice Hall).

Christopher, M. (1998), *Logistics and Supply Chain Management* (London: Financial Times Management).

Coase, R. (1937), 'The Nature of the Firm', *Economica* 4 (November), pp. 386–405.

Contractor, F. and Lorange, P. (eds) (1988), *Cooperative Strategies in International Business*, (Lexington, MA: Lexington Books).

Corbett, C., Blackburn, J. and van Wassenhove, L. (2001), 'Pellton International: Developing a Supply-Chain Partnership', *Supply Chain Forum* 2(1), pp. 60–65.

Cousins, P. (1994), 'A Conceptual Model for Managing Long-term Inter-organisational Relationships', *European Journal of Purchasing and Supply Management* 8, pp. 71–82.

Cox, A., Sanderson, J. and Watson, G. (2001), 'Supply Chains and Power Regimes: Toward and Analytic Framework for Managing Extended Networks of Buyer and Supplier Relationships', *Journal of Supply Chain Management* 37(2), pp. 28–35.

Deming, W. (1986), *Out of the Crisis: Quality, Productivity and Competitive Position* (Cambridge: Cambridge University Press).

Dodgson, M. (1992), 'Technological Collaboration: Problems and Pitfalls', *Technology Analysis and Strategic Management* 4(1), pp. 83–8.

Easton, G. (1992), 'A Model of Industrial Networks', in Axelsson, B. and Easton, G. (eds) *Industrial Networks: A New View of Reality* (London: Routledge), pp. 1–27.

Easton, G. and Araujo, L. (1992), 'Non-economic Exchange in Industrial Networks', in Industrial Networks: A New View of Reality', in Axelsson, B. and Easton, G. (eds) *Industrial Networks. A New View of Reality* (London: Routledge), pp. 62–84.

Ellram, L. (1991), 'Supply Chain Management: The Industrial Organization Perspective', *International Journal of Physical Distribution and Logistics Management* 21(1), pp. 13–22.

Farmer, D. and van Amstel, P. (1991), *Effective Pipeline Management* (Aldershot: Gower).

Fletcher, R. and Barrett, N. (2001), 'Embeddedness and the Evolution of Global Networks: An Australian Case Study', *Industrial Marketing Management* 30, pp. 561–73.

Ford, D. (1998), 'Two Decades of Interaction, Relationships and Networks', in Naudé, P. and Turnbull, P. (eds) *Network Dynamics in International Marketing* (Oxford: Elsevier Science Ltd), pp. 3–15.

Ford, D. (1980), 'The Development of Buyer-Seller Relationships in Industrial Markets', *European Journal of Marketing* 14(5/6), pp. 339–53.

Ford, D., Mcdowell, R. and Tomkins, C. (1998), 'Exploring Relationship Strategy', in Naudé, P. and Turnbull, P. (eds) *Network Dynamics in International Marketing* (Oxford: Elsevier Science Ltd), pp. 251–71.

Fynes, B. (1998), 'Quality Management Practices: A Review of the Literature', *Irish Business and Administration Research* 19/20(2), pp. 113–38.

Håkansson, H. (ed.) (1982), *International Marketing and Purchasing of Industrial Goods: An Interaction Approach* (Chichester: John Wiley).

Håkansson, H. and Eriksson, A. (1993), 'Getting Innovations out of Supplier Networks', *Journal of Business-to-Business Marketing* 1(3), pp. 30–37.

Håkansson, H. and Ford, D. (2002), 'How Should Companies Interact in Business Networks', *Journal of Business Research* 55(2), pp. 133–9.

Håkansson, H. and Johanson, J. (1992), 'A Model of Industrial Networks', in Axelsson, B. and Easton, G. (eds) *Industrial Networks. A New View of Reality* (London: Routledge), pp. 28–36.

Håkansson H. and Snehota, I. (1989), 'No Business is an Island: The Network Concept of Business Strategy', *Scandinavian Journal of Management* 5(3), p. 18.

Håkansson, H. and Snehota, I. (1995), *Developing Relationships in Business Networks* (London: Routledge).

Harland, C. (1996), 'Supply Chain Management: Relationships, Chains and Networks', *Journal of Management*, March (Special Issue) 7, SS63–S80.

Harland, C., Lamming, R., Zheng, J. and Johnsen, T. (2001), 'A Taxonomy of Supply Networks', *Journal of Supply Chain Management* (Fall), pp. 21–7.

Hendrick, T. and Ellram, L. (1993), *Strategic Supplier Partnerships: An International Study* (Tempe, AZ: Center for Advance Purchasing Studies).

Hill, S. (1996), 'Success through Partnership', *Logistics Focus* (April), pp. 18–20.

Hyun, J. (1994), 'Buyer-Supplier Relations in the European Automobile Component Industry', *Long Range Planning* 27(2), pp. 66–75.

Johanson, J. and Mattsson, L. (1987), 'Interorganizational Relations in Industrial Systems: A Network Approach Compared with the Transaction-Cost Approach', *International Studies of Management and Organization* 17(1), pp. 34–48.

Johnston, W., Lewin, J. and Spekman, R. (1999), 'International Industrial Marketing Interactions', *Journal of Business Research* 46, pp. 259–71.

Kim, J. and Michell, P. (1999), 'Relationship Marketing in Japan: The Buyer-Supplier Relationships of Four Automakers', *Journal of Business and Industrial Marketing* 14(2), pp. 118–29.

Krause, D. and Ellram, L. (1997), 'Success Factors in Supplier Development', *International Journal of Physical Distribution and Logistics Management* 27(1), pp. 39–52.

Lagendijk, A. (1997), 'Towards an Integrated Automotive Industry in Europe: A Merging Filiere Perspective', *European Urban and Regional Studies* 4(1), pp. 5–18.

Lambert, D., Cooper, M. and Pagh, J. (1998), 'Supply Chain Management: Implementation Issues and Research Opportunities', *International Journal of Logistics Management* 9(2), pp. 1–19.

Lamming, R. (1996), 'Squaring Lean Supply with Supply Chain Management', *International Journal of Operations and Production Management* 16(2), pp. 183–96.

Langfield-Smith, K. and Greenwood, M. (1998), 'Developing Co-operative Buyer-Supplier Relationships: A Case Study of Toyota', *Journal of Management Studies* 35(3), pp. 331–52.

Lazzarini, S. Chaddad, F. and Cook, M. (2001), 'Integrating Supply Chain and Network Analysis: The Study of Netchains', *Journal on Netchain and Network Science* 1(1), pp. 7–22.

Leverick, F. and Cooper, R. (1998), 'Partnerships in the Motor Industry: Opportunities and Risks for Suppliers', *Long Range Planning* 31(1), pp. 72–81.

Low, B. (1997), 'Managing Business Relationships and Positions in Industrial Networks', *Industrial Marketing Management* 26(2), pp. 189–202.

Macbeth, D. (1998), 'Partnering – Why Not?', in *Proceedings* of the 2nd Worldwide Research Symposium on Purchasing and Supply Chain Management, London

Macbeth, D., Boddy, D., Wagner, B. and Charles, M. (1998), 'Implementing Partnering Relationships: A Change Process Model', report, University of Glasgow.

Mittila, T. (2000), *Relation Trine* (Tampere, Finland: University of Tampere).

Moller, K. and Halinen, A. (1999), 'Business Relationships and Networks: Managerial Challenge of Network Era', *Industrial Marketing Management* 28, pp. 413–27.

Monczka, R. and Morgan, J. (1997), 'What's Wrong with Supply Chain Management?', *Purchasing* 16 (January), pp. 69–72.

Monczka, R. and Trent, R. (1991), 'Evolving Sourcing Strategies for the 1990s', *International Journal of Physical Distribution and Logistics Management* 21(5), pp. 4–12.

Mudambi, R. and Helper, S. (1998), 'The "Close but Adversarial" Model of Supplier Relations in the US Auto Industry', *Strategic Management Journal* 19, pp. 775–92.

Mudambi, R. and Schrunder, C. (1996), 'Progress towards Buyer-Supplier Partnerships: Evidence from Small and Medium-sized Manufacturing Firms', *European Journal of Purchasing and Supply Management* 2(3),pp. 119–127.

New, S. and Burnes, B. (1998), 'Developing Effective Customer-Supplier Relationships: More than One Way to Skin a Cat', *International Journal of Quality and Reliability Management* 15(4), pp. 377–88.

O'Donnell, S. (1999), 'Managing Foreign Subsidiaries: Agents of Headquarters, or an Interdependent Network?', *Strategic Management Journal* 21, pp. 525–48.

Purchase, S. (2000), 'Developing Networks through the Use of Network Catalysts', in *Proceedings* of ANZMAC Conference, Gold Coast, Australia, pp. 1014–18.

Sako, M., Lamming, R. and Helper, S. (1994), 'Supplier Relations in the UK Car Industry: Good News – Bad News', *European Journal of Purchasing and Supply Management* 1, pp. 237–48.

Sheth, J. (1973), 'A Model of Industrial Buyer Behaviour', Journal of Marketing 37, pp. 50–56.

Spekman, R. (1988), 'Strategic Supplier Selection: Understanding Long-term Buyer Relationships', *Business Horizon* (July/August), pp. 75–81.

Stannack, P. (1997), 'The Dimensions of Value – A Ghost in the Machine of Supply Management?', in *Proceedings* of the International Annual Conference of the IPSERA, Italy.

Stock, J. and Lambert, D. (1992), 'Becoming a World Class Company with Logistics Service Quality', *International Journal of Logistics Management* 3(1), pp. 73–81.

Testore, R. (1998), 'World Class Manufacturing Demands World Class Suppliers', European *Journal of Purchasing and Supply Management* 4, pp. 3–5.

Turnbull, P. and Valla, J. (eds) (1985), *Strategies for International Industrial Marketing* (London: Croom Helm).

Van de Ven, A., Emmit, D. and Koenig, R. (1975), 'Frameworks for Interorganizational Analysis', in Negandni, A. (ed.), *Interorganizational Theory* (Kent, OH: Kent State University Press).

Veludo, M., Purchase, S. and Macbeth, D. (2001), 'Relationship Drivers Influencing the Nature and Development of Dyadic Relationships in Industrial Markets: Empirical Evidence from Portugal', in *Proceedings* of the International Annual IMP Conference, Oslo, Norway.

Vlosky, R. and Wilson, E. (1997), 'Partnering and Traditional Relationships in Business Marketing: An Introduction to the Special Issue', *Journal of Business Research* 39, pp. 1–4.

Vlosky, R.P., Wilson, E.J., Cohen, D.H., Fontenot, R., Johnston, W.J., Kozak, R.A., Lawson, D., Lewin, J.E., Paun, D.A., Ross, E.S., Simpson, J.T., Smith, P.M., Smith T. and Wren, B.M. (1998), 'Partnerships versus Typical Relationships between Wood Products Distributors and their Manufacturer Suppliers', *Forest Products Journal* 48(3), pp. 27–35.

Williamson, O. (1975), *Markets and Hierarchies: Analysis and Antitrust Implications* (New York: The Free Press).

Womack, J., Jones, D. and Roos, D. (1990), *The Machine that Changed the World* (New York: Macmillan).

Wren, B. and Simpson, J. (1996), 'A Dyadic Model of Relationships in Organizational Buying: A Synthesis of Research Results', *Journal of Business and Industrial Marketing* 11(3/4), pp. 63–79.

Wyatt, C. (2001), 'An Exploration of Partnerships in the European Automotive Industry', PhD Thesis, Cranfield University.

Young, L. and Wilkinson, I. (1997), 'The Space Between: Towards a Typology of Interfirm Relations', *Journal of Business-to-Business Marketing* 4(2), pp. 53–97.

Chapter 5
International Negotiation

Brooks C. Holtom

Mixed Signals?

Perry worked for a large multinational company that was divesting a portion of its portfolio. As part of its restructuring, the company offered Perry and many of his fellow employees in the same division a generous severance package including outplacement assistance. Perry was making €50,000 per year at the time. After finding a new job that fit his talents well, Perry asked his executive coach at the outplacement firm for negotiation advice regarding the job offer. The executive coach counselled him to be quiet at the bargaining table. Perry remained silent when the new firm offered him €53,000 per year. The recruiter interpreted the silence as disappointment and immediately increased the offer to €55,000.

How many ways could Perry's silence be interpreted by the new firm? Delight? Dissatisfaction? Disbelief? In a short moment, the recruiter making the offer had to analyse her options (e.g., Do we have other acceptable candidates who might work for €53,000 or less?), consult her salary range for this position (evidently it goes up to at least €55,000) and interpret Perry's nonverbal communication. While we don't know exactly what she was thinking, what we do know is that in this case Perry's reward for his silence was €2,000 – per year – as long as he is with the firm. Because future raises will build on this base, the value of this concession is more than €132,000 (based on an assumption of 5 per cent annual pay increases and a 30-year career).

Introduction

People are negotiating all the time. In many circumstances they are unaware of their active or passive role in a negotiation process. Companies negotiate contracts to buy and sell products. Governments negotiate agreements on free trade, environmental performance, technology transfer and entice organizations to set up facilities within their borders. Spouses negotiate over household chores and where to go on vacation. Parents negotiate bed times or allowances with children. Friends negotiate to determine where to go out in the evening. They do it over email, instant messaging, text messaging or even occasionally through letters. Other times they have phone conversations, speak face to face or simply gesture.

Because people are constantly negotiating, it is important for business and personal success to understand the fundamental processes of negotiation, particularly within an international context. That is the purpose of this chapter. After examining the core principles involved in preparing to negotiate almost anything (ranging from deciding who will clean the apartment to delicate diplomatic relations), the focus will then shift to how the principles are adapted to fit different national or cultural contexts.

Prepare, Prepare, Prepare

> Failing to prepare is preparing to fail.
>
> John Wooden (USA Basketball Hall of Fame Coach)

Recognize Negotiation Opportunities

The first step in preparing is to recognize negotiation situations. Many people fail to negotiate effectively because they have not foreseen the scenario where discussion is required to resolve differences. As a result, they haven't spent time to identify opportunities and go into the bargaining session less prepared than their 'opposite number'. Some proactive people see negotiation as an expedient way of resolving conflict when there are two or more parties that perceive and react in a conflictual manner because their interests are negatively affects. Others, in contrast, propose negotiated terms that could benefit both sides if they work together. They assume that they can persuade the other side to offer a better deal than they would have without such persuasion. They also assume that there will be some give and take – both sides will modify their demands or give in on some of their opening requests.

By definition, negotiating parties need each other. That is to say, they are interdependent. For example, a buyer cannot obtain a good unless someone is willing to sell it. An employee cannot negotiate over a position unless an employer needs the work done in-house. The level of mutual dependency may vary. In other words, one party may have more power than the other in any given interaction. This is a topic that will be further addressed in detail. In short, the two parties have interlocking goals and they depend symbiotically on the other to fulfil these goals.

Assess Interests of Both Parties

The second step in effective negotiation preparation is to carefully assess one's own interests and priorities as well as those of the other party. Fisher, Ury and Patton (1991), in their famous book *Getting to Yes*, take great care to differentiate interests from positions. The interests are the needs, desires and fears that drive negotiations. Positions, by comparison, are the assertions, demands or offers that parties make during a negotiation. To be successful in a negotiation, it is not enough to argue for a position. A negotiated outcome should satisfy the *interests* of both parties.

Some people mistakenly believe that preparation involves thinking only about what they want. Not so. A possible agreement that would meet only their needs will not be sustainable and will likely result in further and more bitter conflicts if it doesn't also meet the needs of the other side well enough so that they are willing to accept it. Further, interests include substantive issues (e.g., price or delivery terms), relationship issues (e.g., trust) and principles (e.g., honesty or fairness).

For each negotiation proposal – either demand or offer, that a person makes, he or she should ask 'why?' or 'for what purpose?' Why do I want payment by the end of the month? What is the purpose behind asking for payment in cash? These questions reveal the interests, needs and drivers that underlie these demands. If there is doubt or uncertainty relating to whether something is a position or interest, individuals should determine whether there are alternative ways to satisfy the proposal or demand. If not, it is a position (for example 'I demand a private office'). If there are several ways to satisfy a demand (e.g., 'I need a quiet place to do my work' or 'I would like more status in the organization'), it is probably an interest.

Once interests are identified, they should be prioritized. This will aid the process of comparing proposed options more efficiently and also may help achieve an optimal result. If a deadline is looming, prioritizing interests will highlight the issues on which one should spend the remaining time. Finally, prioritizing helps in making concessions. Ideally individuals will identify high priority interests for the other side that can be met with little difficulty on their own side. When this occurs on both sides of the equation, the resulting exchange creates value – the key to most successful negotiations.

Determine Your Best Alternative to a Negotiated Agreement (BATNA)

Not every negotiation concludes with an agreement. Not every negation should. Occasionally, a party can do no better than by abandoning the process when the costs of the proposed agreement exceed its benefits or because someone else is in a position to offer a better deal.

In most negotiation situations, there may be multiple alternatives for satisfying your interests. For example, when someone is interested in buying an automobile shortly after graduation from the university and they approach Dealer A (the Audi dealer in your hometown) to discuss Car 1 (a new four-door sedan), there are many alternatives to making this purchase. One alternative is to buy the same model from Dealer B (the Audi dealer in a neighbouring town). Another alternative is to consider buying Car 2 (a slightly used four-door sedan) from Dealer A *or* from Dealer B. In short, in this example there are many possible alternatives. To increase the number of available options in any given negotiation interaction, it is critical to understand *better alternatives to a negotiated agreement* (BATNA) with the other party before. If one believes that Dealer B will sell Car 1 to you for €21,000, then one should not pay any more than that amount to Dealer A for the car. In other words, if Dealer A will not come down below €21,000 for the car, the BATNA (Car 1 from Dealer B) will give the individual the power to walk away from the proposed deal.

Alternatives are one of the greatest sources of power or leverage that a negotiator can develop. Of course, it takes time to study the market, to talk to various dealers, and to compare all of the alternatives. However, this is time well spent if the negotiation is important. Think for a moment about how it would feel to walking into a job interview with no other job offers. Think about how the salary discussion would go. Now contrast that with how it would feel walking into the discussion with two other job offers. How would the salary discussion go? The difference is power.

The well-prepared negotiator seeks to understand and strengthen their own BATNA, and analyses the BATNA for the other party at the negotiating table. While it may not be possible to know their BATNA with perfect confidence, through research and reasonable forecasts it may be possible to estimate their BATNA or at very least make an educated guess at what it might be.

Explicit and Tacit Negotiation Assumptions

A contemporary expression follows that:

When you *assume* something, you make an 'ass' out of 'u' and 'me'.

When it is necessary to make a number of assumptions in the course of preparing to negotiate, individuals may find themselves somewhat outside their comfort zone once they commence negotiations. Thus, it is important to keep track of assumptions and periodically test them in the course of the negotiation. By sharing information with the other party, it is possible to create an environment where it's possible to request information to test the assumptions. As these assumptions are affirmed or refuted, estimates can be updated or refined.

The opponent's BATNA may be better for them than any fair solution one can offer. Further, if both sides have attractive BATNAs, the best outcome of the negotiation for both parties may well be not to reach agreement. If the parting is amicable, both groups will likely preserve the possibility of negotiating again in the future. In summary, understanding the BATNAs on both sides is critical to successful negotiation preparation.

Choose an Appropriate Negotiation Strategy

The fourth step in effective negotiating is to strategically assess the best approach to resolve the issues. One of the most popular approaches for determining negotiation strategy is known as the dual concerns model (Pruitt and Rubin 1986). The model asserts that parties in conflict have two types of independent concerns: a level of concern for their own outcomes and a level of concern for the other party's outcomes.

Figure 5.1 shows the level of concern can vary from low to high on either dimension. In effect, the stronger a person's concern for his or her own outcome, the more likely the person will be to pursue strategies located on the right side of the diagram. The stronger a person's concern for the other party, the more likely he or she will pursue strategies located at the top of the chart. While there are many potential points of intersection between the assertiveness dimension (the horizontal dimension) and the cooperativeness dimension (the vertical dimension), scholars have identified five major strategies for conflict management.

Integrating (also called *collaborating* or *problem solving*) is the strategy in the upper right corner. Pursuing an integrative strategy means that the negotiator is both assertive and cooperative. When collaborating, an individual attempts to work with the other person to find a solution that fully satisfies the concerns of both. It involves investigating an issue comprehensively to clearly understand the underlying concerns of both parties and then searching for alternatives that meet both sets of concerns. In enacting an integrative strategy, the parties will often explore a disagreement to learn from each other's insights, resolving some condition that would otherwise have them competing for resources, or confronting and trying to find a creative solution to an interpersonal problem. This approach frequently is referred to as a 'win-win' approach because of its focus on maximizing the joint outcomes for the parties.

Accommodating (also called *yielding* or *obliging*) is the strategy in the upper left corner. When accommodating, an individual neglects his or her own concerns to satisfy the concerns of the other person. This mode relies on a profound level of self-sacrifice. Accommodating involves lowering one's own aspirations to let the other win. Though many people might think it a strange strategy, it has definite advantages in conflict scenarios. For example, when an issue is relatively unimportant to one party and very important to the other party, the first may increase trust or goodwill with the second by accommodating the latter's request. Alternatively, after accommodating another's request, the first may claim value in a subsequent interaction because of a sense of obligation on the part of the second to reciprocate the favour.

Avoidance (also called *yielding* or *inaction*) is the strategy in the lower left corner. It is unassertive and uncooperative. When avoiding, a person does not immediately pursue his or her own concerns or those of the other person. He or she does not address the conflict. Avoiding might take the form of diplomatically side-stepping an issue, postponing an issue until an appropriate time, or simply withdrawing from a threatening situation. In Japan, he or she may state 'this is very difficult'. Translated into assertive language, this expression means 'there is no point continuing. We have made up our minds and there is no chance you will get what you want. We are done talking except for the niceties demanded by protocol.'

Distributive (also called *competing* or *contending*) is the strategy in the lower right corner. It is assertive and uncooperative. It is a power-oriented mode. When competing, an individual pursues his or her own concerns at the other person's expense using whatever power seems appropriate to win his or her position – the ability to argue, rank, economic sanctions, and so on. Competing might mean standing up for your rights, defending a position one believes is correct, or simply trying to win. This approach is sometimes called the 'win-lose' approach

Compromise is the strategy in the middle of the dual concerns model. It is intermediate in both assertiveness and cooperativeness. When compromising, the objective is to find an expedient, mutually acceptable solution that partially satisfies both parties. Compromising falls on a middle ground between competing and accommodating. Likewise, it addresses an issue more directly than avoiding though doesn't explore it is as much depth as collaborating. Compromising might mean splitting the difference, exchanging concessions, or seeking a quick middle-ground position.

These negotiation strategies should not be confused with personal negotiation styles. As can be observed in the box below, there are a wide variety of ways of describing a person's style of negotiation. As a thought exercise, take a few minutes to consider how the various styles might be useful in implementing one of the negotiation strategies outlined by the dual concerns model. For example, an aggressive style might suit a distributive strategy well and

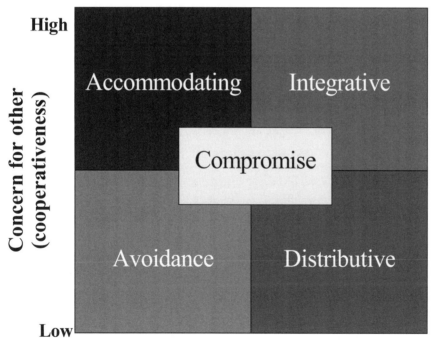

Figure 5.1   Dual concerns model

also seriously hinder an integrative strategy. As a second example, a vague communication style on the part of one negotiator would reduce the probability that two parties could clearly understand the underlying needs involved in the negotiation and thereby preclude win-win outcomes that come most frequently from an integrative strategy.

Negotiation Styles

1. Behaviours vary between aggressive versus assertive versus submissive versus unconditionally constructive.
2. Precise versus vague → specified solutions versus 'We now know what the questions are that need answers, and potential solutions will be identified and evaluated. What we know evolve and what we decide will need reconsideration in the light of new knowledge over time'.
3. Legalistic versus casual, ad hoc and exploring opportunities based on trust that the other will do the right thing and principled behaviour.
4. Tolerance of ambiguity versus need for precision, specifications and clarity.
5. Open and honest about what is relevant versus conniving, contriving, cunning or playing games – one against another.
6. Taking responsibility versus placing blame → 'I'm sorry, I made a mistake' versus 'It's your fault!'
7. Demonstrating respect versus superficial expressions of cordial politeness.
8. Terms based (e.g., price, delivery) versus principles based (e.g., honesty, openness).
9. Long-term versus short-term focus → 'We are building something together' versus 'I want it now!'
10. Telling rather versus selling ideas → Tayloristic instructions 'I think, you do!' versus 'What do you think? How would you do it. Do have a go and let me know what happened'.
11. Intellectual versus emotional arguments → logic versus sensitivity.

Each conflict management strategy has its advantages and disadvantages. Each is more or less appropriate given the type of conflict and situation in which the dispute occurs. For example, if a fast decision is needed, a distributive approach is likely to be superior to a collaborative approach. In contrast, if the issues are complex and one party alone cannot solve the problem, then a collaborative approach is preferred. In summary, careful and systematic consideration of the level of concern for the outcomes for oneself and for the other party should point to the most appropriate strategy for negotiation.

Situation Assessment

One of the key considerations in determining one's level of concern for the other party's outcomes is the expected length of the relationship. In the case where they anticipate interacting for many years into the future on many different issues, then the parties are well advised to have a high level of concern for the other party's outcomes. The full range of the parties' respective interests need careful assessment. Key attributes of this scenario include:

1. Is the negotiation one-shot, long-term, or repetitive?
2. Do the negotiations involve scarce resources, *ideologies*, *dogma* or *objectives*?
3. Is the negotiation one of necessity or opportunity?

4. Is the negotiation an exchange of dialogue or a dispute situation?
5. Is this negotiation linked to other negotiations?
6. Is agreement required?
7. Are there time constraints or time-related costs?
8. Where do the negotiations take place?
9. Is third-party intervention (e.g., mediators, arbitrators, courts) possible?
10. Are there norms or conventions that apply to this negotiation?
11. Do negotiations involve more than one offer? Who should make the first offer?
12. Do negotiators communicate explicitly or tacitly?
13. Are precedents relevant and important?
14. Do we know everything to make a confident proposal?
15. What unanticipated consequences could occur from the agreement?
16. Is what we are going to propose provocative, a surprise, difficult to accept, urgent, in direct conflict with the principals, beliefs and concerns of the other party?

While providing detailed discussion about each of these points is beyond the scope of this chapter, skilled negotiators will consider the ramifications of each as they prepare to negotiate. There are a number of excellent negotiation texts that will analyse these issues in depth and great clarity (Thompson 2004; Lewicki et al. 2005).

Accreditation of Proposal

Two important parts of actual negotiations are 1) the ability to present a case clearly that is supported by facts and solid arguments, and 2) the ability to refute the other party's arguments with persuasive counter-arguments. While the wide breadth of issues that can be included in negotiations makes it almost impossible to delineate all of the procedures that can be used to assemble the necessary information, there are some helpful general questions to guide a negotiator's preparation (Lewicki et al. 2004).

1. What facts support my point of view? What substantiates or validates this information as factual?
2. With whom may I clarify the facts? What records, files or data may exist to support these arguments?
3. Have these issues been negotiated before by others? Can I speak with them? What records exist of these interactions?
4. What are the other party's views likely to be? How can I respond to them as well as develop creative positions that might bridge our collective interests?
5. How can I best present the facts in my case? Are there charts, graphs, pictures or expert testimony that will be helpful to me in making the case?

Opening Offer

Preparing a compelling case for your opening offer is vital to success because opening offers have been demonstrated to have such a strong impact on the final outcomes in negotiation, it is critical that negotiators carefully consider their opening offers. In contrast to the widely accepted model of reality, research evidence overwhelmingly asserts that negotiators that make an opening offer have the upper hand. The metaphor to describe this is that he or she 'sets the anchor' from which all other offers are considered an adjustment.

Consider the following example. Deepa is in her second year of university studies. She would like to purchase a used textbook from a third year student, Daniela. Like most students, Deepa would like to buy the book for as little as possible. She sets her goal at €6. She is not sure she will be able to get it for that little, though she definitely will try. This goal is also known as a target. Deepa knows of a number of students who are selling this textbook for €15. That is the lowest a price of which she is aware. Because this is her best known alternative (BATNA), she sets €15 as her resistance point or walk-away point in the upcoming negotiation with Daniela. Independently, Daniela has also been gathering information from friends and the web to get a sense of the market for this book. Daniela has an offer for the book from another student for €11. However, she has heard of at least one sale that took place for €20. She sets €20 as her target and €11 as her resistance point. Figure 5.2 shows that the buyer's bargaining range is €6 to €15 whereas the sellers bargaining range is from €11 to €20. The area of overlap (€11 to €15) is known as a positive bargaining zone or zone of potential agreement. Identifying this overlap is essential for negotiators. Typically, negotiators' target points do not overlap. However, it is often the case that their reservation points do. The challenge of negotiation is to reach a settlement that is most favourable to oneself and does not give up too much of the bargaining zone. If the parties fail to reach agreement in this situation, the outcome is an impasse and is suboptimal because they leave money on the table and are worse off not reaching an agreement than reaching agreement.

In the event the bargaining ranges do not overlap (Figure 5.3), there is a negative bargaining zone. Put differently, the negotiators never will be able to reach an agreement. The sooner they realize this, the sooner they should exercise their BATNA. Because negotiations are costly to prolong, it is in both parties interests to determine whether there is a positive bargaining zone. If not, they should stop negotiating and pursue other opportunities.

The positive bargaining zone is the amount of overlap in the parties' reservation points. It is a measure of the 'pie' (at least in a single-issue negotiation) as well as the value created by entering into the agreement. The fact that negotiated settlements fall somewhere in the bargaining zone and that each negotiator tries to maximize his share of the bargaining surplus illustrates the mixed motive nature of negotiation. Put differently:

1. negotiators are motivated to cooperate with the other party to get a settlement;
2. but they are also motivated to claim as much of the bargaining surplus as possible.

One of the most frequently asked questions about negotiation is: How can I get most of the bargaining surplus for myself? The simple answer is to determine the other party's resistance point and offer him the option that represents this reservation point. However, this is easier said than done. Most negotiators never reveal their reservation point, but it may emerge unintentionally. Examples of a direct request for information about the other party's reservation point are: 'Tell me the bare minimum you would accept from me, and I'll see if I can throw in something extra' and 'Why don't you tell me the very maximum you would be willing to pay and I'll see if I can shave off a bit?' Even when someone reveals his reservation point, there is no way to verify he is telling the truth. Thus, trust is important. However, when someone tells you something that is not in their interest, you may have more reason to believe it.

Returning to our example, if in initiating the discussion Deepa offers to pay €6 (her target), we would expect Daniela to return a counter-offer of €20 (her target). After going back and forth, if Deepa makes a final offer to Daniela of €13 for the text, it is likely that Daniela will accept it because it is better than her best alternative (€11). This price is also likely to satisfy Deepa as it is €2 less than her best alternative. In sum, in this example, the buyer's surplus is

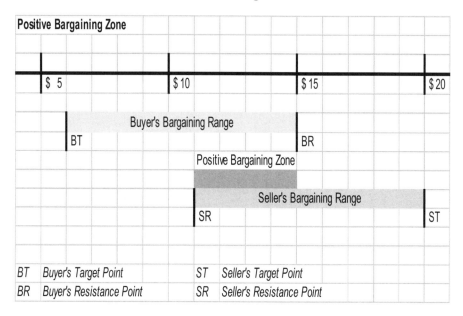

Figure 5.2   Used textbook negotiation (a)

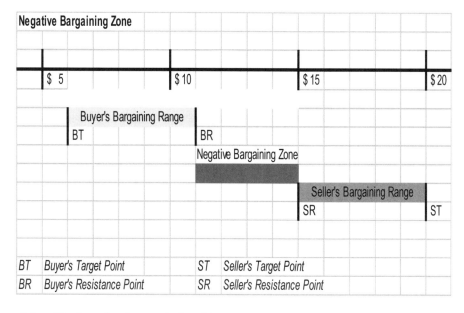

Figure 5.3   Used textbook negotiation (b)

€2 and seller's surplus is €2. While life is rarely this fair, in this example the two parties are better-off trading with each other than any of their alternatives and the benefits are shared equally as can be seen in Figure 5.4.

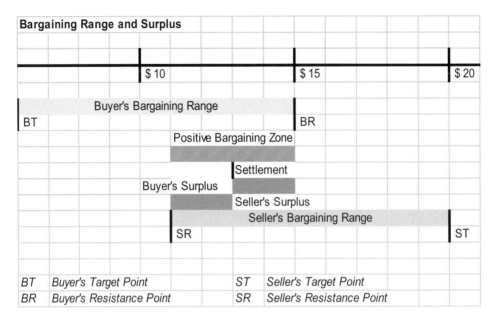

Figure 5.4   Used textbook negotiation (c)

Concessions

What was not discussed explicitly in the example above was the pattern of concessions that Deepa and Daniela made in the course of their conversation. Most scholars believe that the timing and amount of concessions constitute an important part of the 'negotiation dance' (Raiffa 2000). However, there are significant differences across cultures regarding the interpretation of the messages conveyed by the concessions. For example, in some contexts, it is believed to be more effective to make progressively smaller concessions to signal that you are getting close to the walk-away or resistance point. In the case of Deepa, this might have been represented by the following pattern of offers: €6, €9, €11, €11.75, €12.40, €12.80 and €13. Other cultures, by contrast, often start with extreme opening offers to provide ample room for many large concessions as a signal of willingness to sacrifice for the other. The same pattern may apply even if the size of the concessions would generally be larger.

An alternative concession pattern that has received some empirical support is the Black Hat, White Hat (BH, WH) strategy. The essence of this strategy is to make a number of small, but equal concessions and then make one final large concession in an attempt to signal, 'Hey, let's get to the bottom of this process, I am going to my 'bottom line' and I hope you'll agree.' If Daniela followed such a pattern in the example above, it might look something like this: €20, €19, €18, €17, €16, and €13. The key point to take away from this example is the need to identify the cultural norms that govern where you will negotiate as will be discussed in greater detail later in this chapter.

A third strategy is straight away to express the lowest acceptable and sustainable bottom line and maintain a take it or leave it aptitude.

Western manufacturing organizations typically bought based on lowest purchase price paid. Suppliers had then to justify price increases as a result of the customer's modified specifications and expectations. By contrast, Japanese companies recognize supplier's rights to make a reasonable profit provided the customer's expectations are satisfied. The Japanese focus on costs rather than profit. They will accept a higher initial price provided both agree that they will examine non-value-added waste that is part of the cost structure. They agree to work together to identify and do something about these wastes. Both agree at the beginning of the process what they are prepared to contribute to the improvement process and what they expect to achieve. Both agree also how the benefits of reduced cost will be shared. Customers reduce their purchasing budgets and suppliers increase their profits for a given turnover. The supplier knows also that they can transfer the techniques, tools and philosophies to other lines that satisfy their other customers. This reduces the overheads absorbed by the company and increases their competitive advantage. Newlands discusses the process of supplier development in Chapter 28 in this volume.

Closing the Deal

Before sitting down at the negotiation table, the parties should determine what is needed to tie down the deal. In many western societies (e.g., USA, Western Europe, Australia), the end result of negotiation will be a binding contract. While *contracts* may be obtained in other parts of the world, negotiators will also want to take special care to develop meaningful *contacts*. Put differently, when doing business internationally, negotiators are best served by seeking to develop relationships – not simply 'doing a deal' (Griffin and Daggatt 1990).

In addition to this helpful general advice, there are a number of key questions that should be answered before negotiators conclude discussions. Among these questions are the following:

1. What are the final terms agreed upon:
    a) price and cost structure;
    b) goods or services to be provided;
    c) timing of delivery or service;
    d) payment terms (e.g., date due, interest charges);
    e) other material components of the transaction (e.g., service to provided with equipment purchased, options for future purchases);
    f) ownership of any copyrights, patents or other limitations on usage?
2. If there is a dispute, how will it be resolved (e.g., further discussion, courts, mediation, arbitration)?
3. Can the outcome of the negotiation be discussed publicly (e.g., press release announcing new joint venture)?

Measuring the Utility

The final aspect of negotiation preparation is to determine how you will measure the value of the deal. Untrained negotiators tend to focus on one simple factor that is used to define success or failure: price. However, as you have learned in this chapter, there is much more to negotiation than price. The skilled negotiator will review the various interests in the case and place a value on each. Especially when negotiating deals across cultural boundaries, he must find a way to measure the quality of the terms of the deal as well as the foundation of trust or relationship that is developed. Future deals will depend as much or more on the latter as they do the former. Another reason to prepare to quantify the quality of the deal is so that it can be explained to other parties with a stake in the outcome but who were not part of the process (e.g., one's boss or peer). Finally, knowing clearly what you want and how success will be measured and obtained will help a negotiator resist the other party's attempts to assign the value in any given proposal.

Enacting an Integrative Negotiation Strategy

> Let us not be blind to our differences – but let us also direct attention to our common interests and the means by which those differences can be resolved.
>
> John F. Kennedy

The quote by US President John F. Kennedy revolves around differences of preference and opinion that exist between two parties. He insightfully directs attention to the importance of understanding our common interests and commitment to a process that leads to beneficial outcomes for each side. The fundamental structure of an integrative negotiation situation is such that it allows both sides to reach its objectives. Following is a discussion of the key processes involved in crafting integrative agreements.

Create a Free Flow of Information

Effective information exchange promotes the development of good integrative solutions. For the exchange to occur, the negotiators must be willing to reveal their true objectives and to listen to each other carefully. Willingness to share information is not a characteristic of distributive bargaining situations, in which the parties distrust one another, conceal and manipulate information, and attempt to learn about the other for their own competitive advantage.

Attempt to Understand the Other Negotiator's Real Needs and Objectives

To help satisfy another's needs, first one must understand them. Integrative agreements are most likely when the parties exchange information about their priorities for certain issues.

Emphasize Commonalities between the Parties and Minimize the Differences

Many times a new frame of reference is needed for the parties to share information and understand others' needs. Individual goals may need to be redefined as best achievable through collaborative efforts directed toward a collective goal.

Search for Solutions that meet the Goals and Objectives of Both Sides

In the process of developing solutions that meet the objectives and needs of all parties, negotiators need to be both firm (around their primary interests) and flexible (around the manner in which these interests are met). Successful integrative negotiation requires each negotiator to define and pursue his own goals and be mindful of the other's goals and search for solutions that meet the needs of both sides. Outcomes are measured by the degree to which they meet both negotiators' goals – not by determining whether one party is doing better than the other.

Introduce Other Issues and Explore Differences in Preferences across the Issues

Most negotiation situations present themselves as single-issue negotiations. By definition, single-issue negotiations are not win-win because whatever one party gains, the other loses. In even the simplest negotiations it is possible to identify more than one issue. Similarly, it can be valuable to bring other issues into the negotiation or make side deals. While many people feel threatened by differences, diversity can be valuable in crafting integrative deals – especially when the negotiators are able to determine the other party's preferences and devise a means of satisfying each party's most important interests while inducing them to make concessions on lower-priority issues. Asking diagnostic questions, providing information, making package deals rather than single-issue offers and using contingent contracts (based on differences in valuation, expectations, risk attitudes or time preferences) are additional tactics that facilitate integrative settlements.

Enacting a Distributive Negotiation Strategy

> Effectiveness at the conference table depends upon overstating one's demands.
> Henry Kissinger (US Secretary of State, 1973 Noble Prize Winner)

The prime objective in distributive bargaining is to maximize the value of this single deal (Thompson 2004). The following are tactics designed to increase the probability that a negotiator will 'win' the negotiation or obtain the most favourable possible slice of the pie.

Know your BATNA

Before entering the negotiation, be clear about your alternatives. Then seek to improve those alternatives. Also, exercise caution not to disclose those alternatives – unless one is willing to accept terms identical to the best alternative. Further, do not lie about your BATNA. Not only does it raise ethical concerns but lying also reduces the size of the bargaining zone – which cause the negotiation to end in impasse when it otherwise would have been beneficial to both sides.

Research the Other Party's BATNA

Whilst this may prove difficult, clearly it will define the bargaining zone as well as provide insight into the lowest possible offer they should be willing to accept. There are a variety of ways of anticipating or learning about an opponent's alternatives including public information sources (e.g., newspapers, trade journals), the internet, competitors, suppliers, and customers.

Set High Aspirations

Aspirations or targets have been demonstrated to influence final demands more than BATNAs. Negotiators who set higher targets tend to get more of the opportunities than those who set low targets. High goals also help negotiators to avoid the 'winner's curse' that occurs when your first offer is immediately accepted by the other side because it is too generous.

Make the First Offer

As discussed previously, making the first offer confers an advantage by setting the anchor. Research shows that first offers correlate with final outcomes at least .85 – suggesting they are very important. Also, it is important to wait for a counter-offer before reducing stated expectations. In certain situations patience and silence can be important negotiation tools (as they were in our opening example).

Counter-offer Immediately

Making a counter-offer immediately has the effect of diminishing the prominence of the opponent's offer.

Avoid Stating Ranges

Stating a range gives up valuable bargaining ground. Opponents will consider the lower end of the range as your target and negotiate down from there. A better response if asked to provide a range is to give a number of offers that would be equally satisfying to you.

Make Bilateral Concessions

It is an almost universal norm that concessions take place in a back-and-forth exchange. Do not offer more than one at a time. Wait for the other party to concede before going further.

Appeal to Norms of Fairness

Fairness is a key issue in negotiation as most negotiators view themselves as fair. It is critical, however, to determine which norms of fairness would be appropriate to the situations (e.g., equality, equity, needs based). The following example of the needs-based standard for fairness that exists in Vietnam has important implications for business.

Needs Based Fairness Rules

An Executive MBA group was assigned to study the viability of 'self-drive car rental' in Vietnam. Currently nearly all rentals in Vietnam employ the 'car and driver' model. In the course of the study, the students learned that in Vietnam, when two parties are involved in an accident, it is the party that is perceived to be the most affluent who must take financial responsibility for damages. In the case of a foreigner being involved in an accident with a local resident, it is always the foreigner who is perceived to be the wealthier party, and thus the foreigner is always responsible financially.

While there were other factors considered before recommending against the self-drive car rental model, this issue was the largest obstacle. The concern was validated when the students visited Vietnam and met with expatriate American business managers. They indicated that they would never drive a car there under any circumstances and this was one of the main reasons.

Critical Considerations When Negotiating Internationally

When negotiators work across borders, they are likely to also confront differences in culture. As discussed in earlier chapters, culture is the unique character of a social group. Cultures consist of psychological elements, the values and norms shared by members of a group as well as social structural elements like the economic, social, political, and religious institutions that are the context for social interaction. Cultural values point to what issues are more or less important (as can be seen in the story below about the Mexican fisherman) and influence a negotiator's interests and priorities. Cultural norms define what behaviours are appropriate and inappropriate in negotiation and influence negotiators' strategies.

Mexican Fisherman

An American investment banker was at the pier of a small coastal Mexican village when a small boat with just one fisherman docked. Inside the small boat were several large yellow fin tuna.

The American complimented the Mexican on the quality of his fish and asked how long it took to catch them.

The Mexican replied, 'Only a little while.'

The American then asked, 'Why didn't you stay out longer and catch more fish?'

The Mexican said, 'With this I have more than enough to support my family's needs.'

The American then asked, 'But what do you do with the rest of your time?'

The Mexican fisherman said, 'I sleep late, fish a little, play with my children, take siesta with my wife, Maria, stroll into the village each evening where I sip wine and play guitar with my amigos, I have a full and busy life.'

The American responded, 'I am a Georgetown MBA and could help you. You should spend more time fishing; and with the proceeds, buy a bigger boat. With the proceeds from the bigger boat you could buy several boats. Eventually you would have a fleet of fishing boats. Instead of selling your catch to a middleman you would sell directly to the processor; eventually you will open your own cannery. You would control the product, processing and distribution. You would need to leave this small coastal fishing village and move to Mexico City, then Los Angeles and eventually New York where you will run your ever-expanding enterprise.'

The Mexican fisherman asked, 'But, how long will this all take?'

To which the American replied, '15 to 20 years.'

'But what then?' asked the Mexican.

The American laughed and said 'That's the best part. When the time is right you would announce an IPO and sell your company stock to the public and become very rich, you would make millions.'

'Millions? Then what?'

The American said, 'Then you would retire. Move to a small coastal fishing village where you would sleep late, fish a little, play with your kids, take siesta with your wife, stroll to the village in the evenings where you could sip wine and play your guitar with your amigos.'

Author unknown

Cultural values may reveal the interests underlying negotiators' requests. Negotiators who value tradition over change may be less enthusiastic about economic development that threatens valued ways of life than negotiators from cultures that value change and development. This was the case with Disney when it tried to buy a large tract of land south of Paris to construct EuroDisney.

When people negotiate, their behaviours are strategic and their strategies may be culturally based. This is the case because cultures develop norms to facilitate social interaction. Norms function because they reduce the number of choices a person has to make about how to behave and because they provide expectations about how others in the culture will behave. For example, in some cultures negotiations are not direct verbal interactions. Sometimes the verbal message is indirect because disagreement or confrontation would be rude and result in loss of face (e.g., in China) (Wilhelm 1994). Other alternatives include communicating through nonverbal behaviour or a third party. Other norms have evolved over what constitutes a 'reasonable' opening offer. In some cultures, negotiators make 'extreme' opening offers with the expectation that they will later make large concessions to signal their good faith in bargaining. However, other cultures encourage opening offers that are very near expected settlement points in a sign of their interest in saving time and energy. Sometimes this is called 'getting straight to the point'. In either case, it is important to anticipate the ranges created by opening offers by studying the prevailing cultural norms across countries.

Another instance where culture influences negotiators is motivation. Negotiators from countries characterized as *individualistic* may be most concerned about their own interests or those of their immediate group. In contrast, negotiators from countries characterized as *collectivistic* may be more concerned about collective interests that extend beyond the parties at the negotiation table. Negotiators who work across national and cultural boundaries will need to be sensitive to these differences in motivations among potential partners so as to be able to clearly identify and prioritize all of the potential interests to be addressed in the negotiation.

Cultures are distinguished by the difference observed between their *hierarchical* or *egalitarian* tendencies. In hierarchical cultures, social status implies social power. Social inferiors are expected to defer to social superiors. Thus, in hierarchical cultures, people may be reluctant to confront another directly because it implies a lack of respect. In contrast, in more egalitarian cultures, BATNA may very well be the key source of power. Because neither party is assumed to be superior, the quality of a person's alternatives will dictate how dependent or beholden he is to the other party. In short, the flexible nature of BATNAs fits well with egalitarian cultures whereas status-based power tends to dominate in hierarchical cultures.

People in *low-context* cultures (e.g., Germany, Scandinavian countries, United States) tend to communicate directly. Information is explicit, without nuance, and relatively context free. Put differently, the meaning is on the surface of the message. In contrast, people in *high-context* cultures (Arab cultures, France, Japan, and Russia) tend to communicate indirectly. Meaning is rooted in the context of the message and must be inferred to be understood. Many times, high-context cultures are characterized by extensive information networks among friends, family, colleagues, and clients. Important information oftentimes comes through an informal channel to complement information that comes through more formal channels. Thus, when people outside the network enter into negotiations in high-context cultures, time spend building a relationship is especially valuable. A recent conversation with a wise Brazilian businessman sheds light in the importance of making personal connections. When asked why negotiations move so slowly in the early stages in South America, he answered, 'We don't negotiate with strangers. Until we know the person, it is pointless to discuss matters of substance'. This is because the population understand that three types of agreements are required. Recognition agreements are concerned with who can participate. Does each party recognize the right and authority of the other to participate in the negotiation. A second level relates to agreements on the process – arbitration for example. The third level of agreement relates to the substantive negotiation concerning what they want out of the deal – lower price, more profit, faster, higher quality etc.

Language barriers also can complicate negotiations. Sometimes it is the inability of a negotiator to clearly express him or herself that causes problems. Other times overconfidence that the message truly has been understood and agreed upon that undermines the negotiation (as can be seen in the example below about Nissan). One way negotiators seek to overcome language issues is to involve professional translators. However, introducing translators to the equation adds complexity and some potentially unintended consequences. One risk when using a translator is that he or she may be more loyal to their countrymen than to the foreigner they are to serve. This points to the critical role of trust in negotiation. As another example, though many Asians will understand English very well, to avoid losing face by making a mistake they will employ a translator. Because they understand the English when first spoken by their counterparts, these negotiators will have a time-based advantage because they can think about the implications of the communication while the translator is taking time to translate. In the 'negotiation dance' this may be very helpful in buying time to formulate superior responses or counter-offers.

Nissan

When a person learns Japanese, she will come across some basic Japanese vocabulary words that sound like words in English. *Hai* is one example. It does not mean 'hi!' In fact, it means 'yes', and it is equivalent to an American saying 'hmm' or 'I see' in a conversational setting – a verbal cue to let the speaker know that the listener is following what is being said. (It is important to understand that *hai* does not necessarily mean that the listener agrees with the speaker!) Consider the exchange below that might have taken place when Carlos Ghosn was leading a major turnaround effort at Nissan in Japan (Magee 2003). Imagine the outcome might have been different if he believed that his Japanese partner was saying 'Yes, I agree' versus 'Yes, I see.'

Ghosn:	We need to radically change.
Partner:	Yes.
Ghosn:	We need to cut jobs.
Partner:	Yes.
Ghosn:	We need to do it quickly.
Partner:	Yes.

Perspectives on time also influence the behaviours of negotiators from different cultures. In some cultures, time is seen as being a limited resource which is constantly being used up. It is like having a sink full of water which can never be replaced, and which is running down the drain. You have to use it as it runs down the drain or it is wasted. In other cultures, time is perceived to be more plentiful. In societies where time is limited, punctuality becomes a virtue. It is insulting to waste someone's time. In the United States you frequently hear people say, 'Time is money.' In cultures where time is plentiful, like India or Latin American, there is no problem with making people wait all day and then telling them to come back the next day.

Time-plentiful cultures tend to rely on trust to do business. Time-limited cultures often do not have time to develop trust and so create other mechanisms to replace trust (such as strong legal protections).

The particularly American desire for expeditious entry into the heart of the matter was exhibited by Franklin Roosevelt at the end of World War II at the famous Yalta conference. Before the meeting, Roosevelt and Churchill met to discuss strategy. Roosevelt expressed his hope that the meetings with Stalin would not last more than five or six days. Churchill replied: 'I do not see any way of realizing our hopes about world organization in five or six days. Even the Almighty took seven.' The extent to which American expectations of the duration of a negotiation can differ from those of a foreign foe was demonstrated yet again when peace talks to end the Vietnam War began in Paris. The American negotiators, led by Averell Harriman, checked into the Ritz Hotel, while the North Vietnamese leased a villa for two years.

Conclusions

In this chapter, we have explored the key points for successfully preparing to negotiate across cultures. As should be evident by now, the most successful negotiators internationally are not those schooled in the art of advanced table pounding or making loud threats. Instead those who are willing to invest time and energy to prepare thoroughly are more likely to succeed. Excellent cross-cultural negotiators will proceed slowly in negotiations, testing their assumptions about what strategy and tactics will be effective with the other party (Brett 2001). They are willing to adjust their use of negotiation strategy to achieve their goals but do not compromise on their goals.

References

Brett, J.M. (2001), *Negotiating Globally* (San Francisco, CA: Jossey-Bass).

Fisher, R., Ury, W. and Patton, B. (1991), *Getting to Yes: Negotiating Agreement without Giving In* (New York: Penguin Books).

Griffin, T.J. and Daggatt, W.R. (1990), *The Global Negotiator* (New York: Harper Business).

Lewicki, R.J., Saunders, D.M. and Barry, B. (2005), *Negotiation* (New York: McGraw-Hill Irwin).

Lewicki, R.J., Barry, B., Saunders, D.M. and Minton, J.W. (2004), *Essentials of Negotiation* (New York: McGraw-Hill Irwin).

Magee, D. (2003), *Turnaround: How Carlos Ghosn Rescued Nissan* (New York: HarperCollins).

Pruitt, D.G. and Rubin, J.Z. (1986), *Social Conflict: Escalation, Stalemate and Settlement* (New York: Random House).

Raiffa, H. (2000), *The Art and Science of Negotiation* (Cambridge, MA: Harvard University Press).

Thompson, L.L. (2004), *The Mind and Heart of the Negotiator* (Upper Saddle River, NJ: Prentice Hall).

Wilhelm, A.D. (1994), *The Chinese at the Negotiating Table* (Washington, DC: National Defense University Press).

DIMENSION 3
Supply Chain Management

Chapter 6
Social and Environmental Management

Mark J. Hooper with Alkiviadis Tromaras

The world we have made, as a result of the level of thinking we have done thus far, creates problems we cannot solve at the same level of thinking at which we created them.

Albert Einstein

Humanity, as a species, has developed a unique ability to shape whole environments for its benefit. Simultaneously, humanity is has endangered its current success as a result of activities to dispose of its waste by dumping materials. This chapter brings together arguments and evidence of the negative environmental impact. The aim of this chapter is to give a brief overview of the range of issues that challenge companies and organizations in the field of environmental management.

Introduction

Four distinct phases of environmental development can be seen. The first encompasses the pre-industrial era. This period had the following characteristics:

* artisanship-based production systems production;
* agrarian-based economies;
* limited division of labour – in pre-industrial societies, production was relatively simple and thus the number of specialized crafts was limited;
* limited variation of social classes;
* parochialism – communications were limited between communities. Few had a chance to see or hear beyond their own village.

During this phase limited local, national and international development occurred. Humanity lived within the natural limits of the environment.

The transition to the second phase resulted from the developments instigated by the Industrial Revolution. The catalyst for this change was the availability of information and knowledge. Once the domain of the skilled worker, this knowledge could now be transferred from the individual to the mechanism of machines. Skilled craftsmen were usurped by unskilled labour, allowing a wider pattern of economic participation. Towns and cities developed to provide this labour, changing the nature of cultures and societies. The new cities not only provided the source for goods but created markets for the new mass produced products. The cycle of consumerism was now in operation. The advent of the Second Industrial Revolution (1871–1914) further developed humanity's ability to produce. Technological and economic progress gained momentum with the development of steam-powered ships, railways, and later in the nineteenth century the internal combustion engine and electrical power generation. This increasing production, however, produced conditions that precipitated the Long Depression and international turmoil that encompassed the two World Wars. The environment played only a small part in these industrial developments. Diseases were conquered and nature suppressed. The environment was seen as a source of wealth that was available for exploitation and control. Its conservation was of secondary importance to the economic benefits that could be gained.

The advent of the third phase is associated with the international focus on stability and an end to economic nationalism following World War II. To meet these demands, international mechanism were created to aid communication and trade. The United Nations developed a world form for debate between nation, and mechanisms for conflict resolution. The need for post-war Western economic order was resolved with the agreements made on monetary order and an open trade at the 1944 United Nations Monetary and Financial Conference (Bretton Woods Conference). The agreement allowed for the synthesis of a British desire for full employment and economic stability and the United States' desire for free trade. In order to achieve these aims, two fundamental approaches where adopted; the notion of open markets and the joint management of the Western political-economic order. Countries would maintain their national interest, but trade blocks and economic spheres of influence would no longer be legitimate means of control. These two principles informed the design and operation of three international bodies, the International Monetary Fund (IMF), the World Bank and the General Agreement on Trades and Tariffs (GATT, later transformed into the World Trade Organization (WTO)). Through the action of these bodies economies prospered and entered a period described as the post-war economic boom. Production exploded in a wave of consumerism, with little regard for the environmental consequences. However, as scientific methods became more sophisticated a clearer picture of the harm that was resulting from meeting these demands became evident. The social changes that had started in the Industrial Revolution had produced ever more sophisticated populations with increased levels of education who had a wide engagement with the democratic and political process. These two factors started to create increasing pressure for action at a governmental and inter-governmental level. The age of environmental activism was born.

In the late twentieth and early twenty-first centuries, progression towards a fourth phase is underway. As in phases 2 and 3, the focus is on economic growth as the paramount driver for organizations and economies. Consumerism is accelerating on a global scale with the advent of increasingly sophisticated products and services utilizing more and more intense methods of production. However, the environmental and social costs of this progress are being questioned and challenged. The central dichotomy that is facing societies today is how to maintain economic growth and progress whilst protecting and enhancing the environment. This contradiction goes to the very heart of modernity and questions the fundamental tenets of large-scale integration:

- increased movement of goods, capital, people and information among formerly separate areas;
- increased influence that reaches beyond local to global.
- increased formalization of mobile elements, development of 'channels' on which those elements and influences travel and standardization of many aspects of the society in general that is conducive to the mobility.
- increased specialization of different segments of society.

These growing demands for conservation and sustainability have driven nations to deliver solutions using regulation and legislation. Companies have responded, evidenced by the substantial rise in corporate awareness of environmental and social issues (Morhardt et al.

2002). Companies seek to adopt environmental management in order to show that their activities are legitimate and that they comply with all the environmental conventions (Bansal and Roth 2000; Sharma 2000) and also to show that they are aware of the societal norms that currently lean towards environmentalism (IPCC 1999, p. 343; Bansal and Roth 2000). Compliance to regulations, especially in cases where sanctions of non-compliance are invoked (King and Lenox 2000; Stafford 1996; Berman et al. 1999; Cormier and Magnan 1999; Henriques and Sadorsky 1999; Reinhart 1999; Reivera-Camino 2001; Waddock and Graves 2000) and cost reduction at the operational, tactical and strategic level have been the most significant drivers the companies (Decahnt et al. 1994; Ghobadian et al. 1995; Prinn et al. 1990; Shrivastana 1995; Hart 1995; Ghobanian et al. 1998); Dias-Sardhina and Reijinders 2001; Reivera-Camino 2001). Additional benefits can be found by a proactive approach to industry codes allowing flexibility to be designed into operations. Many companies have found that an advanced relationship with stakeholders can enhance a company's image, gain new markets creating a significant comparative competitive advantage (Bansal and Roth 2000; Hart 1995; Reinhart 1999; Shrivastana 1995). The power of the environmental movement on businesses is illustrated by the case of TXU.

TXU, which has its headquarters in Dallas, Texas, provides electricity and related services to more than 2.2 million electricity customers in the state. TXU Power has over 18,300 MW of generation in Texas, including 2,300 MW of nuclear and 5,800 MW of coal-fired generation capacity. In April TXU announced plans to build 11 coal-fired power plants in Texas. The group Environmental Defense, led by Fred Krupp, mobilized an intense grassroots campaign targeting TXU and the Governor of Texas, Rick Perry. Nearly 50,000 Environmental Defense members and activists took action, sending emails, attending public hearings across Texas and submitting public comments against the plants. More than 50 community and environmental groups signed letters urging TXU to change its course.

They took out television, billboard and online advertisements. These efforts were designed to achieve three goals:

1. stop as many of the plants as possible;
2. prevent TXU from exporting its coal plant build-out to other states; and
3. send a national message to other utility companies that the TXU plan is one they should reject.

In February 2007, private equity firms Kohlberg Kravis Roberts & Co (KKR), Texas Pacific Group and Goldman Sachs announced their intention to purchase TXU by way of leveraged buyout for $45 billion. A precondition of the sale was a requirement to negotiate and reach an agreement regarding the issues raised by Environmental Defense. As a result a new environmental strategy for TXU was agreed:

- terminate plans for the construction of eight of 11 coal-fired power plants TXU had hoped to build;
- abandon TXU's plans to expand coal operations in other states;
- TXU to endorse the US Climate Action Partnership (USCAP) platform, including the call for a mandatory federal cap on carbon emissions; and
- reduce the TXU's carbon dioxide emissions to 1990 levels by 2020.

The case of TXU clearly indicates the future pressures that organizations will experience and the strategic barriers that will have to be overcome.

Global Warming

The main concern of climate change centres on the global warming effect. The predicted warming is called green house effect which can be directly associated with human industrial activities, particularly the burning of fossil fuels such as oil, coal and natural gas. The earth's global average temperature during the last two centuries has risen by between 0.4–0.8°C (Lomborg 2001). The primary cause is the release of large quantities of greenhouse gases in the atmosphere.

The main gas of concern is carbon dioxide (CO_2), a product of the burning of fossil fuels and non-renewable biomass. Carbon dioxide plays an important role within the atmosphere providing a means of transferring carbon within ecosystems, allowing photosynthesis to take place and even allowing humans to breathe. Concentrations of this gas have varied during the evolution of the earth. High concentrations were present during the Cretaceous Period, approximately 136 million years ago. Coral, sponges and other small sea creatures used the gas to build and reinforce their bodies or shells. When they died, they sank to the bottom of the sea, eventually being transformed into sedimentary rock. The micro shells of these ancient creatures can be found today in chalk cliffs that greet visitors to British shores in Dover, Cap Gris-Nez in northern France or the French champagne that is consumed around the world which relies on the soil conditions provided by this chalk.

CO_2 is not alone in creating a warming effect; methane (CH_4), Nitrous Oxide (N_2O), ozone and CFC gases all create, to a larger or smaller extent, the same result. Most of these gases exist naturally in the atmosphere and are responsible for making the planet habitable. Without greenhouse gases, the Earth would be approximately 33°C colder (ibid.) and the diversity of life that exists today would not have developed. At the other extreme, large amounts of these gases tend to trap heat and increase the Earth's temperature.

The Greenhouse Effect

The greenhouse effect is a relatively simple and well understood natural phenomenon. It was originally described in 1827 by the physicist-mathematician Jean-Baptiste Fourier. The effect takes its name from the its resemblance to a garden greenhouse, where glass panels let in visible (short wave) radiation and impede the exit of long wave thermal radiation. This increases the indoor temperature. The Earth receives a relatively constant amount of energy in the form of 'incoming' radiation. Light consists of visible spectrum, ultra violet and infrared. Some of this energy is reflected directly back out to space by the atmosphere and the surface, but approximately 70 per cent is absorbed. This absorption raises the temperature of the Earth's surface and consequently that of the atmosphere. The same amount of energy is emitted back into space as thermal or 'outgoing' radiation. This balance between incoming and outgoing energy is necessary to maintain average temperature levels of approximately 15°C (Makhijani and Gurney 1995).

Concern about the greenhouse effect generally focuses on the increase in the concentration of greenhouse gases from anthropogenic processes. An increase in Earth's average temperature will raise sea levels through melting of the polar ice and thermal expansion of the oceans thus having disastrous consequences for people living in low-lying countries or coastal regions.

Were the rate of temperature increase to be rapid, organisms would not be able to adapt quickly enough, jeopardizing the survival of numerous species.

Approximately 80 per cent of the extra CO_2 originates from fuel combustion such as oil, coal and gas. The remaining 20 per cent is emitted from 'slash and burn' deforestation methods, natural forest fires, volcanic activity and other changes in the tropics. About 55 per cent of the CO_2 is absorbed by the oceans, by northern hemisphere forest and more generally by plant growth. Overall, the concentration of CO_2 has increased since pre-industrial revolution times by 33 per cent (Lomborg 2001). Figure 6.1 shows the increase in CO_2 emissions from 1751 to 2003.

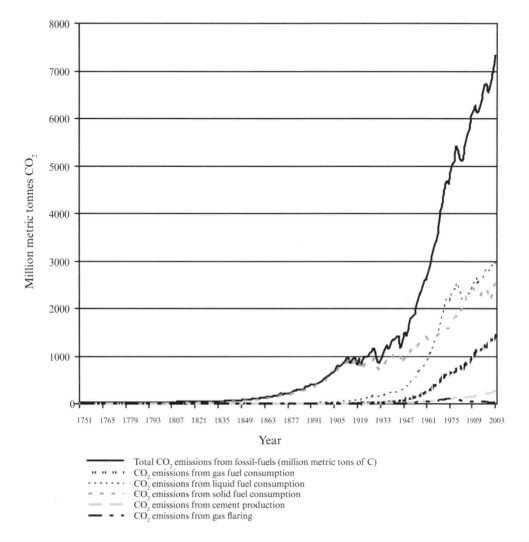

Figure 6.1   The increase in CO_2 emissions from 1751 to 2003

Source: Marland et al. 2006.

Since 1751 approximately 305 billion tons of carbon have been released into the atmosphere from the consumption of fossil fuels and cement production. Half of these emissions have occurred since the mid 1970s. The 2003 global fossil-fuel CO_2 emission estimate, 7303 million metric tons of carbon, represents an all-time high and a 4.5 per cent increase from 2002.

Greenhouse gases affect global temperatures both directly and indirectly. Direct effects happen because the gas itself is a greenhouse gas and indirectly because the climate acts as a natural chemistry set. The atmospheric transformation processes that break the gases into less harmful compounds can produce other greenhouse gases.

Although different scenarios have been published regarding global warming and temperature rises, it is difficult to make accurate predictions. Some scenarios are more dramatic; others are more optimistic. These perspectives stem from differences with respect to predicted CO_2 levels, the level of sophistication of climate model being used together with variations in initial model variables. The Inter-governmental Panel on Climate Change (IPCC) prediction an increase of 1.5–4.5°C in global temperature has remained constant since 1970 (IPCC 1990, p. 135; 2002, 2006, p. 43). No predictions over the last 25 years have suggested conditions will improve, rather they confirm an evermore pessimistic view of future temperature change.

The Ozone Hole

The catalytic destruction of ozone from ozone depleting compounds (ODCs) in the stratosphere originally was theorized and proposed in 1974 by Mario Molina and Sherwood Rowland. The ozone hole above Antarctica was first confirmed in 1982 by the British Antarctic Survey Team and was brought to light in the British Science journal *Nature* in 1985. Since then, research on the principles of ozone depletion have made significant advances and helped to create a global environmental awareness and consensus for action. Within two years of its publication in *Nature*, the Montreal protocol in 1987 took steps to ban ODCs such as CFCs.

Significance of Ozone

Ozone, derived from the Greek '*ozein*' ('to smell'), is a natural gas in the earth's atmosphere. It is considered to be a trace gas, naturally existing in extremely small amounts (approximately 0.000008 per cent). Ozone is a 'Janus faced' molecule. In the lower atmosphere it is a toxic oxidizing agent that causes lung irritation. In the upper atmosphere it is transformed into a guardian of life on the earth.

Approximately 90 per cent of ozone lies within the stratosphere. Maximum ozone concentration occurs in the middle of the stratosphere in the so-called ozone layer.

Sunlight consists of radiation of various wavelengths that can be harmful to humans, such as ultraviolet. As altitude increases so radiation levels rise. Oxygen and ozone help to absorb this ultraviolet radiation from passing through the atmosphere and preventing it from reaching the surface and causing damage.

Homogeneous Ozone Depletion

Human activities are causing an imbalance between natural production and destruction of stratospheric ozone. Nitrous oxide from increased fertilizer usage results in an estimated 0.28 percent increase in NO_2 concentrations every year (Prinn et al. 1990). The production of foam and refrigerant coolant relied heavily on compounds that containing the ozone depleting chemicals chlorine (Cl_2) and bromine (Br_2). When emitted into the atmosphere, these compounds migrate from the troposphere through the tropopause and accumulate in the stratosphere. Here they are broken down by ultraviolet radiation.

The reaction between chlorine and ozone is:

$$Cl + O_3 \rightarrow ClO + O_2$$
$$Cl\,O + O \rightarrow Cl + O_2$$

$$O_3 + O + Cl \rightarrow O_2 + O_2 + Cl$$

(Warneck 1988, pp. 125–30).

Bromine is emitted in smaller quantities since it is present in smaller concentrations in ODCs, however, it is more effective in depleting the ozone layer. The reaction between bromine and ozone is:

$$Br + O_3 \rightarrow BrO + O_2$$
$$BrO + O \rightarrow Br + O_2$$

$$O_3 + O + Br \rightarrow O_2 + O_2 + Cl$$

(ibid.).

It takes many years for the ODCs to reach the stratosphere and undergo destruction. Despite the abandonment of these materials by the older industrialized nations, this long life cycle allows the release of chlorine to continue for many decades.

Another mechanism for ozone depletion involves hydrogen chloride (HCl). HCl is formed by reactions with methane, a gas created from sources varied sources such as decompositions of organic materials, natural gas emissions, cattle, coal mining and oil extraction and refining. The reaction between chlorine and methane is:

$$CH_4 + Cl \rightarrow CH_3 + HCl$$

Stratospheric chlorine can be incorporated into other inactive forms in addition to HCl. The most important of these is chlorine nitrate ($ClONO_2$) that can be formed by the reaction:

$$ClO + NO_2 + M \rightarrow ClONO_2 + M$$

(Makhijiani and Gurney 1995, p. 15).

Over half of the stratospheric chlorine is stored in these two forms – HCl and $ClONO_2$. Unfortunately, stratospheric chlorine diffuses when it passes through the tropopause back to the troposphere, a process that takes about two to five years (WMO 1991, p. 8.41). Before removal, HCl and $ClONO_2$ act as a catalyst that facilitates the release of reactive chlorine approximately 20–200 times through photo-dissociation or reaction with OH that further destroys ozone (Rowland 1990, p. 284).

Heterogeneous Ozone Depletion

Homogeneous infers all depleting compounds are gases. Heterogeneous depletion covers ODCs in dual or triple phases, that is, gas + ice, gas and liquid, liquid and ice, and gas, liquid and ice. These phenomena are more likely to occur in the polar regions and over middle latitudes.

The seasonal thinning of ozone in the Antarctic polar stratosphere involves a more intensive process than homogeneous depletion. The theories suggest that the same total concentration of all chlorine containing compounds can deplete ozone considerably more under certain conditions like those that prevail in the Arctic during winter and summer. These conditions can make HCl and ClONO$_2$ become very active Cl and ClO as they react to aerosol surfaces and therefore increase ozone depletion. Figure 6.2 shows the 2005 seasonal depletion and recovery cycle of the ozone layer over Antarctica. Readers should note the scale of the ozone hole and its proximity to Australia, South Africa, Chile and Argentina. Weather systems drive the boundary gaseous areas out and mix low ozone and high ozone concentrations. This makes it very important for humans to protect against high ultraviolet (UV) radiation. Australians are advised to 'slip, slap, slop'. They should slip on a shirt, slap on a hat and slop on high UV factor sun cream.

Effect of Ozone Depletion

Depletion of the ozone layer, discussed in the previous sections, allows greater amounts of radiation to reach the Earth's surface. But not all radiation has the same effect on living organisms. Partial exposure to UV radiation is necessary for the formation of Vitamin D in humans. There are three classes of UV radiation: UV-A (wavelength above 320 nanometres), UV-B (290–320nm) and UV-C (40–290nm). The latter two can be extremely harmful and cause severe biological injury. UV-B will be discussed further because, even if small amounts reach the surface, it causes skin aging, skin cancer and other illnesses (Makhijiani and Gurney 1995, p. 50).

UV-B radiation   UV-B radiation is responsible for DNA damage. The extent to which this occurs depends on the duration of the exposure, tolerance of the exposed organism and the biological coping reactions that take place. The main effects on human are skin cancer, cataracts and immuno-suppresion. Cataracts and cataract-related blindness is related to long-term and cumulative exposure to UV-B. Acute exposure can cause photokeratitis or 'snow-blindness' (Sliney 2001; Roberts 2001; Johnson 2004). Damaged skin becomes more susceptible to skin tumours as a result of widespread immunological defence reductions (Young 2006). In 1993, Bentham (1993) concurred that there is sufficient evidence that links UV-B to cutaneous malignant melanoma and non-melonoma skin cancers. The immuno-suppression from UV-B radiation may exacerbate infectious diseases. The magnitude of these effects depends on the ethnic racial skin colour and age.

Air Pollution

Of all the different types of pollution, air contaminants are the most significant. In a consolidation of 39 regional, state and local comparative risk analysis studies, air pollution invariably came out as the most important environmental concern for human health (Konisky 1999). One might assume this phenomenon is a comparatively recent and the result of Western countries use of fossil fuels. A background level of air contaminants has existed throughout traceable human history. However, since the Industrial Revolution, air pollution has increased dramatically.

Air pollution from lead can be traced back 6,000 years to its peak during the Greek and Roman eras. Seneca in ancient Rome complained of 'the stink, soot and heavy air' in the city (Miller and Tyler 1998, p. 466). In 1285 King Edward I established the world's first air pollution commission and 25 years later banned coal burning. However, this law was not enforced and subsequently was eliminated from the statutes (Brimblecombe 1987, p. 9). Throughout the eighteenth century the city of London had 40 per cent less sunshine than surrounding towns due to the pollution-laden 'smelly fog', a contraction of which gives us the term we use today, smog. A fog-bound London has become an iconic image for the city, frequently depicted in the novels of Conan Doyle, films and famously inspiring Monet's 1903 composition, '*Le Parlement Londres*'. Even today, foreign visitors to London can be heard to comment on the lack of fog in the city. Despite these romantic images the reality of air pollution in London was grim. The Great Smog (Big Smoke) that befell London in December 1952 illustrates this reality.

Early in December 1952, a cold fog descended upon London. Because of the cold, Londoners began to burn more coal than usual to heat their homes. At the time the UK economy was under great strain and required high value exports to provide valuable foreign currency to ease these pressures. High quality coal was diverted from domestic consumption to export markets, leaving only poorer low-quality high-sulphur coal available to heat homes. The resulting air pollution was trapped by the inversion layer formed by the dense mass of cold air. Concentrations of pollutants, coal smoke in particular, built up dramatically creating a thick chemical laden 'fog,' or smog, so thick that driving became difficult or impossible (Figure 6.2). Its density and opacity was such that it easily entered buildings, obscuring theatre and cinema performances to such an extent that they were disrupted or cancellation.

In the weeks that followed, the statistics showed that the smog had killed 4,000 people; predominantly the very young or elderly, or those with pre-existing respiratory conditions. Deaths in the majority of cases were due to hypoxia (low blood oxygen levels) caused by respiratory tract infections that obstructed breathing. The lung infections were predominantly bronchopneumonia or acute purulent bronchitis superimposed upon chronic bronchitis. These shocking statistics led to a re-evaluation of air pollution and generated a political will within the UK to instigate new regulations restricting the use of dirty fuels in industry and banning black smoke.

The principal air pollutants are (Lomborg 2001, p. 165):

- particles (smoke and soot from industrial plants, diesel engines and volcanic ash);
- sulphur dioxide (SO_2) that creates acid rain;
- ozone (O_3);
- lead;
- nitrogen oxides (NO and NO_2, NO_x);
- carbon monoxide (CO).

The main sources of these pollutants are transportation (cars, trucks, and motorcycles), aviation and industry. Overall there are efforts to reduce emissions into the atmosphere through different regulations described in the later legal issues section of this chapter. Although there has been some progress in obtaining reductions, air pollutions and emissions remain a problem that has not been fully addressed. This lack of progress is illustrated by the work of Benjamin Chauveau. Chauveau carried out a series air pollution recordings on the top level of the Eiffel Tower in the 1890s. The findings published in his book, *L'Electricité atmosphérique* (1925), showed that in the period 1896 to 1898 the Parisian atmosphere contained on average between 30 and 90 micrograms of particulate (smoke, soot and ashes) per cubic metre of air, a figure that is roughly equivalent to that generated in Paris today (Harrison and Aplin 2003; Miserey 2003).

This type of pollution can be seen in all major modern cities and has been cited as a key factor in the growing incidence of pulmonary disorders, particularly amongst children. If we consider

The Global Business Handbook

the UK, 5.2m people are currently receiving treatment for asthma of which 1.1m are children. This translates into one person in every five UK households being affected by asthma.

Figure 6.2 shows a picture taken from the Kowloon peninsula of Victoria harbor in Hong Kong. The contrast between the clear foreground and hazy background clearly illustrates the pollution present in the modern urban setting.

The incomplete combustion of fossil fuels (such as diesel) and wood releases black carbon into the air. Though black carbon, most of which is soot, is an extremely small component of air pollution at land surface levels, the phenomenon has a significant heating effect on the atmosphere at altitudes above 2 km (6,562 feet). Also, it dims the surface of the ocean by absorbing solar radiation.

Experiments in the Maldives (comparing the atmosphere over the northern and southern islands) in the 1990s showed that the effect of macroscopic pollutants in the atmosphere at that time (blown south from India) caused about a 10 per cent reduction in sunlight reaching the surface in the area under the pollution cloud – a much greater reduction than expected from the presence of the particles themselves (Srinivasan and Gadgil 2002). Prior to the research being undertaken, predictions were of a 0.5–1 per cent effect from particulate matter; the variation from prediction may be explained by cloud formation with the particles acting as the focus for droplet creation. Clouds are very effective at reflecting light back out into space.

The rate of dimming varies around the world but is on average estimated at around 2–3 per cent per decade, with the possibility that the trend reversed in the early 1990s. It is

Figure 6.2   Air pollution in Hong Kong observed in February 2008

Source: Photograph by kind permission of Dr Mark Hooper.

difficult to make a precise measurement, due to the difficulty in accurately calibrating the instruments used, and the problem of spatial coverage. Nonetheless, the effect is almost certainly present.

The effect (2–3 per cent, as above) is due to changes within the Earth's atmosphere; the value of the solar radiation at the top of the atmosphere has not changed by more than a fraction of this amount.

The effect varies greatly over the planet, but estimates of the terrestrial surface average value are:

- 5.3 per cent (9 W/m²); over 1958–1985 (Stanhill and Moreshet 2004);
- 2 per cent/decade over 1964–1993 (Hilgen et al. 1998);
- 2.7 per cent/decade (total 20 W/m²); up to 2000 (Stanhill and Cohen 2001);
- 4 per cent over 1961–1990 (Liepert 2002).

The phenomenon underlying global dimming may also have regional effects. While most of the earth has warmed, the regions that are downwind from major sources of air pollution (specifically SO_2 emissions) have generally cooled. This may explain the cooling of the eastern United States relative to the warming western part.

Some climate scientists have theorized that aircraft contrails (vapour trails) are implicated in global dimming, but the constant flow of air traffic previously meant that this could not be tested. Figure 6.3 shows an image pair, acquired on 9 December 2003, by the Aqua and the Terra satellites, visualizing numerous aeroplane contrails crisscrossing the English Channel.

Figure 6.3   Aeroplane condensation trails across the English Channel

Source: Jacques Descloitres, MODIS Rapid Response Team, NASA/GSFC.

The shutdown of civil air traffic during the three days following the 11 September 2001 attacks provided an opportunity to observe the climate of the United States in the absence of the effect of contrails. During this period, an increase in diurnal temperature variation of over 1°C was observed in some parts of the US, that is, aircraft contrails may have been raising nighttime temperatures and/or lowering daytime temperatures by much more than previously thought (Travis 2002).

Airborne volcanic ash can reflect the sun's rays back out into space and cool the planet. Dips in earth temperatures have been observed from large volcano eruptions such as Mount Agung in Bali that erupted in 1963, El Chichon (Mexico) 1983, Ruiz (Colombia) 1985 and Pinatubo (Philippines) 1991. But even for major eruptions, the ash clouds remain only for relatively short periods.

Some scientists now consider that the effects of global dimming have masked the effect of global warming to some extent and that resolving global dimming may therefore lead to increases in predictions of future temperature rise.

Global warming and global dimming are not mutually exclusive or contradictory. This point is supported by the work of Romanou et al. (2007) in showing that the apparently opposing forces of global warming and global dimming can occur at the same time. Global dimming interacts with global warming by blocking sunlight that would otherwise cause evaporation and the particulates bind to water droplets. This reduces the amount of water vapor in the atmosphere. Water vapour, being a greenhouse gas, is reduced decreasing the heating effect. In an opposite parallel process, global dimming is affected by evaporation and rain. Rain has the effect of clearing particulate pollution.

Climatologists are stressing that the roots of both global dimming causing pollutants and global warming causing greenhouse gases have to be dealt with together and soon.

Acid Rain

The term *pluie acide* was first used by the French chemist Ducros in 1845 (Wellburn 1994, p. 97). It was only later, in 1872, that Robert Angus Smith, the Chief Alkali Inspector of the UK, introduced the phrase 'acid rain' to described the acidic nature of rain falling around Manchester (Smith 1872). The term acid rain describes acid depositions in the atmosphere, which can occur in two ways: wet and dry (Figure 6.4).

Wet deposition refers to acidic rain, fog and snow (Wellburn 1994). In fact all rain has been acidic so the term acid rain has been related to acid that is produced when NO_x or SO_2 produced by pollution, reacts with water creating sulphuric or nitric acid.

Dry deposition refers to acidic gases and particles (ibid.). Acid in the atmosphere returns to soil through acid deposition. This process describes the acid gases and particles that return to earth with the aid of wind. Acid deposition can also occur through the washed out particles and gases on different surfaces. These acids would be added to the water from acid rain, making the impact more severe.

Acid rain occurs when sulphur dioxide (SO_2) and nitrogen oxides (NO_x) react with water, oxygen and other chemicals in the atmosphere to form acidic compounds such as sulphuric or nitric acid. Sunlight can enhance the rate of reaction between these compounds. The main source of SO_2 and NO_x is fossil fuel combustion.

The phenomenon of acid rain became noticeable in the 1960s when air pollution from British coal combustion brought acid rain to Sweden and Norway that affected their rivers and lakes. The main pollutant was identified as sulphur dioxide. A belt from Birmingham to

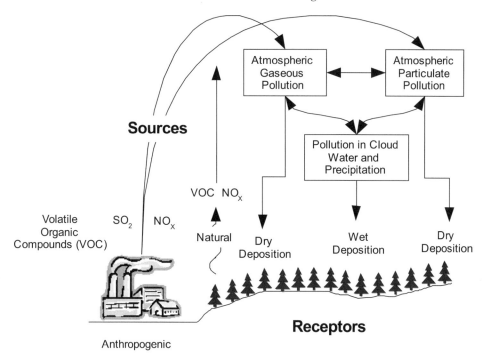

Figure 6.4   The cycle of acidic compounds and acid rain types

Source: US Environmental Protection Agency.

Bratislava was affected by acidification of soils and waters. Two factors drove this pollution: the concentration of heavy industry and vehicles in this region and the tall smokestacks constructed by industry in order to reduce local air pollution. Releasing gases further up into the atmosphere allowed them to migrate into other countries. This acidification of water affected Nordic forests, killing tree leaves and needles and leaving plants weak and vulnerable to disease. Native fish stocks in Finland's many lakes died out because of the change in acidity. The power of this acidic pollution can be clearly seen in the damage it causes to buildings, dissolving limestone, sandstone, marble and granite to form gypsum, which then flakes off.

The phenomenon of transboundary pollution occurs in any area where acidic emissions occur. It is particularly problematical in East Asia, where Japan and Taiwan are showered by acid rain from Korea, China, Philippines and Taiwan. In 1980, half of Canada's SO_2 came from US. Given the damaging nature of this pollution, considerable work has been done to reduce such pollution, focusing on flue gas desulphurization and low sulphur based fuels. Notable successes in reducing sulphur oxide emissions have taken place in Europe, with a decrease of 15 per cent taking place between 1980 and 1995 (Murley 1995, p. 387). Reductions have occurred in US Great Lakes and Ohio River regions emissions are down by one-third from those of the 1980s.

Soil Pollution

In the twentieth century, significant soil pollution has been created by the metallurgical industries that grew rapidly in Europe, Eastern North America, the ex-Soviet Union states and Japan. Major sources include the refining, smelting and mining of metals such as lead, cadmium, mercury and zinc. Although these metals are important for industry, they have proved to be dangerous toxins for humans. Some of these substances enter soil first as air pollutants or directly enter the top soil. After entry into the soil strata, contaminants either migrate into the water bed, entering the food chain, or enter directly into the food chain as a result of herbivorous animals' consumption of arable products such as grass, hay and silage.

Japan provides numerous examples of this type of pollution in particular copper contamination from smelting and mining operations occurring in several Japanese river basins during the early twentieth century. In the Jinzu river valley, clusters of bone disease cases occurred, later being diagnosed as cadmium poisoning.

Aside from metals, other chemical pollutants can challenge the environment. It is estimated that 10 million chemical compounds have been produced since 1900. Between 1940 and 1982, synthetic chemical production volumes expanded more than 350 times (Makhijiani and Gurney 1995, p. 50). A large proportion of those, perhaps 50–70 per cent, ended up in landfills. Metallurgical, petroleum and pharmaceutical companies dumped wastes directly and untreated into pits that were not lined to prevent migration into the strata.

Probably the most widely reported case of the chemical pollution took place in the Love Canal area located in Niagara Falls region of New York State. Starting in the early 1920s, Hooker Chemical, along with fellow chemical companies located along the Niagara River, used Love Canal to dispose of 21,800 tons of hazardous chemicals, including 130 tons of dioxins (Charlier 2000). In 1953 the waste was capped with soil and by the late 1950s around 100 homes and an elementary school had been built on the site.

In the years that followed, residents of the Love Canal housing estate complained about strange odours coming from their basements, gardens and sometimes their sewers. In other cases liquids came out from the ground. Residents started to complain of respiratory conditions, skin irritation, miscarriages and birth defects. In 1978, 800 chemical compounds buried at the site were identified. Medical tests were performed on residents, most of which remain confidential. Birth rates declined and some children were malformed. In May 1981 President Carter declared Love Canal a national emergency and residents were relocated (*Niagara Gazette*, 23 May 1980).

In other cases, the US and some European countries have exported hazardous waste. During the 1970s this exchange of hazardous waste became an international business. For example, Mexico and some West African countries accepted waste for US. In the same manner Morocco and West African countries took waste from Europe and Southeast Asian countries received materials from Japan (McNeil 2001, p. 29).

Water Pollution

Approximately 71 per cent of the Earth's surface is covered by sea water, while a further 0.5 per cent is covered by lakes. Half of these lakes are freshwater, while rivers constitute 0.26 per cent of the area (Shiklomanov 2000). This section focuses on the impact human activities have on ocean habitats, rivers and lakes and the environmental signs of human activities.

Oil Pollution in the Seas and Oceans

Oil slicks and dumping waste are an all too common phenomena along sea lanes. It was estimated that in 1985 approximately 60 per cent of the marine sources of oil pollution came from routine oil tanker transport operation, while 20 per cent came from oil spills from tankers or other ships. Only 15 per cent could be accounted for by seepage from natural oil deposits (NRC 1975, p. 82).

Oil pollution from routine tanker transportation is due to the fact that ships use sea water as ballast to stabilize the vessel while they sail unloaded. When the tanker arrives at its destination it flushes away the water into the harbour. This discharge contains oil and potentially other trace elements from previous cargos. This has been a serious problem. International agreements have been signed to regulate discharges. New technologies were developed to treat pollutant residues differently and waste treatment facilities in ports have improved (International Maritime Organization, http://www.imo.org/). Since oil spills can occur from cracks in the bottom of the sea from natural oil reserves, it is presumed that oil exploration and extraction has reduced the magnitude of the phenomenon because it has relieved the pressure from these reservoirs (Goudie 1993). Today, major oil spills are exclusively the result of accidents (ITOPF 2000).

The impact from oil spills directly effect animals that populate the polluted area. The human food chain is indirectly affected as a result of reduced fish stocks in the area. Birds and other sea-going mammals are affected and overall coastal life diminishes. One of the main catastrophes in recent history was the Gulf War in 1991. Some 6 to 8 million tons of oil were spilled into the Gulf (Dodson et al. 1994). These shallow waters made the impact more devastating because most of the fauna and flora in the sea were destroyed, leaving little food for creatures in the marine biosystem.

Numerous incidents have occurred that underline these points, but the accident that befell the Exxon Valdez on 24 March 1989 exemplifies best the hazards that oil pollution can carry. Following its collision in Prince William Sound in Alaska, 266,000 barrels of oil were released (Lomborg 2001, p. 192). The cost in animal life was 2,800 sea otters, 250,000 sea birds, 250 bald eagles, 300 harbour seals and probably 22 killer whales (ibid.). The oil spill ruined 300 kilometres of coastline and light oil was found along 1,700 kilometres of coast line (ibid.). Studies in the area later showed that most species recovered to some extent and the ecosystem is well on its recovery. The long-term impacts on species may take decades to be fully mitigated (Knickerbocker 1991). A significant financial package was put together to support the restoration and clean up of the oil from the area. Exxon paid $3.5 billion in total as a result of the accident, of which $2.1 billion were spent on the clean up operation (Exxon Valdez Oil Spill Trustee Committee, http://www.evostc.state.ak.us/). Oil is one of the pollutants that tend to be found in seas and oceans. Chemicals from factories and municipal waste, however, are dumped close to shore, typically in bays and estuaries. These will be reviewed in the next section.

Pollution in Seas and Oceans

Seas have been used as convenient locations for the disposal of municipal and industrial waste. Two significant drivers for this behaviour have been the low cost relative to other disposal paths and the absence of technology to treat waste biologically. This is especially true of cities that were situated near the sea. New York is a notable example, sending immense barges out to sea where they dumped untreated waste. Despite the convenience of this mode of disposal some of this waste washes back to shore or enters into food chains. These actions can have considerable effects on ecosystems and those who interact with them. This interaction is illustrated by the events that occurred in Minamata Bay in Japan. From 1932 Nippon Chisso produced acetaldehyde using mercury as a catalyst. Waste Mercury was dumped into the bay through the factory's waste where bacteria converted it to the organic compound methyl mercury that is an organic compound, which eventually found its way up to the food chain. Fish started to die unexpectedly in the late 1940s. Domestic and wild cats of the area started to act strangely, as if drunk, started to vomit and eventually died. In 1956 children of the area began developing brain diseases and numerous cases of deformed babies. It was finally confirmed that the cause of the effects was mercury poisoning. After eliminating the source of pollution and many years of monitoring, the bay was declared mercury free in 1997 (McNeil 2001, pp. 138–9).

Larger-scale effects can also be seen. In the last few centuries, humanity has done much to alter the Mediterranean. It was a superhighway of transport in ancient times, allowing for trade and cultural exchange between emergent peoples. Structures have been built all along the coastlines, exacerbating and rerouting natural erosion patterns. Many pollution-producing boats travel the sea that unbalances the natural chemical balance of the region. Beaches have been mismanaged, and the overuse of the sea's natural and marine resources continues to be a problem. Fresh water inflows from rivers are insufficient to counteract the high evaporation rate. In the twentieth century the sea has become highly polluted to the point where serious health issues have been created. These changes are most clearly illustrated by the fate of the old harbours of Piraeus, Alexandria and Ostia. Once thriving hubs of commerce, they are now empty and abandoned, silted up with waste and garbage.

The main pollutants included microbes, synthetic organic compounds such as DDT or PCBs, oil, litter, heavy metals and radionuclides. Cities such as Athens and Thessaloniki in Greece as late as 1990 did not have sewage treatment and waste was dumped untreated into the sea as biological effluent. The main problem area was concentrated in industrial basins such as Ebro, Rhone, Genoa and the northern Adriatic coast from the Po delta to Trieste. These were cities with heavy industry that released heavy metals such as mercury, arsenic and lead along with PCBs into the sea (ibid.).

River Pollution

Pollution in rivers is of major concern because they form the major source of water for drinking, agricultural irrigation, and everyday use for human activities. In order for water to be suitable for use there are some certain criteria. Water must not contain E-coli bacteria or any other water-borne enzymes and viruses. There is some correlation between the wealth of a country and how polluted its rivers are. This is due to the fact that poorer countries have not invested in the technologies required to treat waste and hence dump them untreated directly into rivers. This correlation is not always valid because wealthy countries still have some polluted rivers. El Griffo in Bilbao, the industrial city in the Basque region of Northern Iberia is a case in point. After a century of intense industrial activity the river, especially the final 25km, was ecologically dead with oxygen levels 20 per cent below the norm, being one of the most polluted rivers in the world. The Thames, which flows through London, used to be a toxic soup described as a dark, turgid slurry of industrial toxins and coal power station discharges that was 'too thick to swim in and to thin to plough'. Today both rivers have undergone extensive cleanups resulting in each having extensive marine ecosystems, including species such as salmon, which have an ultra low tolerance to toxins.

Another criterion for judging the quality of water is its oxygen content. In a dissolved form oxygen is vital for organisms living in rivers, including fish, crabs and zoo-plankton. Oxygen also affects water in terms of odour, clarity and taste. Again there is a correlation between the wealth of a country and oxygen levels present in rivers.

Chemicals are another issue concerning river pollution. Fertilizers used in agriculture illustrate these concerns. A principle constituent of these products is Nitrogen which if allowed to accumulate in drinking water leads to health problems such as stomach cancer. Oxygen asphyxiation also can occur as a result of a high concentration of nitrates in the blood, which inhibits the absorption of oxygen. Nitrate can be dangerous, because bacteria can convert it into nitrite which oxidizes the blood's haemoglobin, impeding the transport of oxygen (methemoglobinemia) (IRIS 1991). Due to these risks in 1980 the EU and the US set standards for levels of nitrates in water (EU 1980; IRIS 1991). These standards have been mainly set for more vulnerable members of society such as babies. This was due to cases of 'blue baby' syndrome which describes the reduction of oxygen in blood causing cyanosis (Lack 1999).

Conclusion

In this section of chapter, the impacts of anthropogenic actions on the environment have been discussed. The aim was to introduce the different types of pollution and these effect the environment and living organisms. Issues such as global warming, ozone depletion, acid rain and air, water and soil pollution were reviewed to present the effect of human actions on the environment. Due to this impact it was demonstrated that there is a growing concern and scepticism for the state of the environment. Despite our sophistication, human beings are still a single species living within a series of ecosystems linked at a global scale. If these systems are damaged or polluted we ourselves are affected. This section of the chapter has focused on the mechanism of pollution and key issues related to them.

The remainder of this chapter will review the actions of regulatory bodies and governments and will consider what efforts have been made to reduce the impact on the environment discussed above.

Global Environmental Initiatives

The last two decades have been marked by the efforts of the United Nations and European Union to produce legislation that would help the conservation of the environment at a global rather than local scale. Although the first steps towards a sustainable environment and future were done back in the 1970s, the efforts were only isolated in countries holding International meetings and mainly discussing environmental issues. The decade of 1980s marked a more serious and concerted approach to environmental stewardship. Events such as the discovery of the ozone zone hole over Antarctica, made people realize that if certain measures were not introduced, the Earth could become a much more hostile home. The United Nations Environment Programme (UNEP) and the United Nations Framework Convention on Climate Change (UNFCC) produced a series of protocols, which will be discussed later, such as the Montreal and Kyoto Protocols, which are considered to be the most significant. These can be seen as the most systematic efforts of world governments to create a sustainable future. Parallel to this endeavour the EU has created its own set of directives which attempt to minimize the anthropogenic impact on the environment and promote sustainability. This section of the chapter is dedicated to the most significant environmental Protocols and Directives.

Vienna Convention

In 1985 the United Nations Environmental Programme (UNEP) Governing Council set up a working group that would prepare the framework for a convention for the protection of the ozone layer. The main objective was to create a protocol that would give the basis for preventing ozone depletion.

The negotiations of creating a treaty that would help to tackle the problem of ozone depletion proved to be a difficult task. Finally, 1985, the Protocol was signed in Vienna, by 20 nations but not many ratified it immediately. The protocol did not specify any ways of achieving any target, but mentioned ways of monitoring and doing scientific research on ozone depletion. This was the main target – to boost and promote research and cooperation between countries.

Specifically, all the parties are asked to undertake, as appropriate, to initiate and cooperate in conducting research and scientific assessment on:

- physical and chemical processes that may affect the ozone as a whole;
- the human health and other biological effects that might derive from modification of ozone depletion and specifically from UV-B radiation;
- climate changes due to ozone layer modification;
- effects that derive from ozone depletion and UV-B radiation and have effect on natural and synthetic materials useful to humans;
- substances, practices, processes and activities that can affect the ozone layer and their cumulative effects;
- alternative substances and technologies;
- related socio-economic matters.

For the first time ozone depletion substances and their possible effects were discussed in the proceedings. These were substances such as carbon substances, CO_2, CO, CH_4, non-methane hydrocarbon species, Nitrogen substances, N_2O, NO_x, chlorine substances, fully halogenated alkanes, partially halogenated alkanes, bromine substances, hydrogen substances and H_2O.

Despite the endless disputes, the Vienna Convention provided the foundations for the Montreal Protocol in 1987. 'For the first time nations agreed in principle to tackle a global environmental problem before its effects were felt or even scientifically proven' (UNFCC 2002). Later on, in the journal *Nature* (Farman et al. 1985), Dr Joe Farman, a British scientist, would write about severe ozone depletion in the Antarctic and his findings would be confirmed by American satellite observations. This resulted in governments taking dramatic, transnational, measures in the form of the Montreal Protocol.

For further details of the Vienna Protocol for the Protection of the Ozone Layer see UNEP 2001.

Montreal Protocol

The discovery of the 'ozone hole' and the first publication regarding its evidence in 1985 (Farman et al. 1985) triggered the current wave of environmental awareness. Ozone depletion was no longer a theory but a real phenomenon that could not be dismissed and which posed a significant threat to the environment. Within a year of the ozone hole's discovery, the Vienna Convention for the Protection of the Ozone Layer took place, taking the first steps towards relating ozone depletion to human health. Stratospheric ozone depletion was recognized as a legitimate international environmental issue for further negotiation. Unfortunately, no protocol on controlling CFCs was established due to a dispute between USA, Canada, Sweden, Norway and Finland.

Within the next two years, governments from all over the world were called to take drastic measures to control and minimize the effect of ozone depletion resulting from human activities. This showed a move against the toleration of the environmental pollution that had become suddenly so obvious. On 16 September 1987 the Montreal Protocol on Substance that Deplete the Ozone Layer was signed by 24 countries (United Nations Environment Programme (UNEP, http://www.unep.org/). The Protocol focused on compounds such as CFCs, halons, carbon tetrachloride, 1,1,1-trichlorofluorocarbons (methyl chloroform), hydrochlorofluorocarbons, hydrobromofluorocarbons, methyl bromide and bromochloromethane. These compounds would all have to be phased out by the 24 countries that had signed the treaty.

On 1 January 1989 the protocol came into force (ibid.). All the parties agreed to freeze production and consumption of CFCs and halons along with the other compounds mentioned before, within seven months from the protocol's entry into force. Different amendments were made during subsequent years in order to accelerate the phase out, namely in London 1990, Copenhagen 1992, Vienna 1995, Montreal 1997 and Beijing 1999 (UNEP 2000).

Under the Copenhagen amendment, developed countries agreed to phase out CFCs by 1 January 1996, halons were to be totally phased out by 1 January 1994 and carbon tetrachloride and methyl chloroform by 1 January 1996. In consideration of the fact that application of these agreements might be constrained by factors such as social conditions and the level of infrastructure, developing countries were given dispensation to produce and purchase CFCS and carbon tetrachloride for use until 2010 and methyl chloroform until 2015–2016. Developing countries would also be allowed to produce up to 10 per cent of their calculated level of emissions in 1986 for domestic and essential use. Later amendments followed and focused on refining initially agreed values for the percentage reduction of substances towards their complete proscription (for further information on the Montreal Protocol, see UNEP 2000).

Rio Declaration on Environment and Development

The United Nations Conference on Environment and Development also known as the 'Earth Summit' took place in Rio de Janeiro between 3 and 14 June 1992. This was the largest-ever meeting of world's leaders who came from 179 countries to discuss and take action on the environment. The Summit essentially reaffirmed the UNCED Declaration adopted at Stockholm on 16 June 1972 and sought to build on it (UNEP, http://www.unep.org/). Concern had been growing over the previous two decades about the huge discrepancy between developed and Third World nations. This inequality was seen as symptomatic of a degrading global relationship between environmental stakeholders which could not be sustained for the long term without radical realignment. This would influence the 1990s culture which made societies start to consider that, while societies must continued to develop and grow, the environment must be sustained. The challenge in this concept is how to make more people more aware of environmental issues and at the same time move towards sustainable forms of development and lifestyles.

The goal of the Rio Declaration was to 'establish a new equitable global partnership through the creation of new levels of cooperation among States, key sectors of societies and people', in order to 'work towards international agreements which respect the interests of all and protect the integrity of the global environmental and developmental system, recognizing the integral and interdependent nature of the Earth our home' (UNEP 1992).

The Declaration consisted of 27 anthropocentric principles. Specifically, it stipulated that people were entitled to health and productive life in harmony with nature (IISD, http://www.iisd.org/) and any further developments should not undermine the environment of future generations. All countries would have the right to exploit their resources without causing damage to the environment outside their borders and they should create international laws that should compensate those countries whose environment had been damaged because of their negligence.

Moreover, in order to achieve sustainable development, environmental protection should be an integral part of the development process. This development process should be aiming for the eradication of poverty, since there can be no sustainable development while the rest of the world is living under the average standard of living. Therefore, public awareness of the environment was to be encouraged by government and people should put pressure on societies to pursue sustainable development.

Hence, nations should create national laws that would protect the environment from pollution and the polluter should bear the cost of pollution. There should be cooperation between nations to create an open international economic system to support economic growth and sustainable development in all countries. These environmental policies should not create barriers to international trade and countries should exchange technological knowledge to achieve sustainability.

Finally, war is destructive of sustainable development and all nations should respect international environmental laws. On the other hand peace, development and environmental protection are independent and indivisible (further information on the Earth Summit can be obtained from UNEP 1992).

Kyoto Protocol

Five years after the Rio de Janeiro Summit, the first legally binding treaty aimed at cutting emissions of the main greenhouse gas was signed in Kyoto, Japan on 11 December 1997. Building on the UN Framework of the Convention Climate Change, the Kyoto Protocol 'broke new ground with its legally-binding constraints on greenhouse gas emissions and its innovative "mechanisms" aimed at cutting the cost of curbing emissions' (UNFCC 2002). At the time of writing, 164 countries have ratified the protocol (UNFCC, http://www.unfcc.int/), more than any other environmental treaty, and it entered into force on 16 February 2005. The USA is not a signatory: although they signed the treaty on 12 November 1998 under the Clinton administration (Fletcher 2000), in 2001 the current Bush administration decided against ratification.

The Kyoto Protocol commits all parties to individual, legal binding targets to limit or reduce their greenhouse gas emissions up to a total cut of at least 5 per cent from the 1990 baseline to 2008–2012. Each country has agreed a different target, while some of them have shown more initiative by agreeing a higher reduction of emissions.

The greenhouse gases that the parties would have to reduce were carbon dioxide (CO_2), methane (CH_4), nitrous oxide (N_2O), hydrofluorocarbons (HFCs), perfluorocarbons (PFCs) and sulphur heaxafluoride (SF_6). Emission targets must be met by the so-called commitment period of 2008–2012. However, progress must be made by 2005 and all countries must submit a progress report by the beginning of 2006.

The Protocol does not oblige parties to follow specific strategies in achieving their emission targets but has set out a list of policies and measures that can help to mitigate climate change and promote sustainable development. These polices are:

- enhancing energy efficiency;
- protecting and enhancing greenhouse gas sinks;
- promote sustainable agriculture;
- promoting renewable energy, carbon sequestration and other environmentally-friendly technologies;
- removing subsidies and other market imperfections for environmentally-damaging activities;
- encouraging reforms in relevant sectors to promote emission reductions;
- tackling transport sector emissions;
- controlling methane emissions through recovery and use in waste management (UNFCC 2002).

Countries can reduce their emissions by increasing the removal of greenhouse gases by carbon sinks in the land use, land-use change and forestry (LULUCF) sector. The Protocol proposed the removal of emission through afforestation, reforestation and deforestation.

In addition, three 'innovative mechanisms' were introduced: joint implementation, the clean development mechanism and emissions trading. All these methods can be used by member parties to reduce the cost of meeting their targets, in order to ease the economic cost of emissions' removal by finding different means that would cost less but would have the same effect on the atmosphere.

The mechanism of joint implementation allows member parties to implement projects that reduce emissions or increase removals by sinks, in the territories of other member parties, for example, by replacing a coal-fired power plant with a more efficient combined heat and power plant or reforesting land. These joint implementation plans are more likely to occur in economies in transition (EITs) such as the ex-Soviet Union countries.

Emissions' trading is a programme that allows member parties to buy emissions from another member, in order for the first to meet their targets. Emissions can be bought from countries that have less emissions and no heavy industries. By doing so, the party that buys the emissions are not reducing pollution but simply paying for the privilege to emit more.

Clean development mechanism allows member countries to implement projects that can help reduce emissions in other countries. The reduction achieved by the project can contribute towards the member party meeting its target emissions.

The Treaty was widely hailed as a major international success. It certainly can be described in such terms if one considers the difficult nature of gaining so many countries' consent. However, the Treaty is limited in both its effect on global warming and the coverage it gives to carbon emission. Growing transportation sectors such as international aviation and marine bunker fuels used for international transport are not included in the Treaty and are reported separately from the overall emission total of the parties under the Convention (ibid.). The Protocol requires these countries to deal with International Civil Aviation Organization (ICAO) to control their emissions.

Despite its ambition, the Treaty can only be seen as a first step in the confrontation of global warming. The Protocol does not consider emissions of oxides of nitrogen and water vapour which, at high altitude, can cause more damage to the atmosphere than carbon dioxide (Royal Commission on Environmental Pollution 2002). Despite these limitations the Kyoto protocol finally came into operation in 16 February 2005 (see UNFCC website, http://unfccc.int/ for further information on the Kyoto Protocol).

The challenge for nations is to develop beyond the current protocol and take further steps towards the reduction of global warming gasses. The future direction of policy is illustrated by the non-binding G8+5 Climate Change Dialogue 'Washington Declaration' agreed on 16 February 2007. Presidents or Prime Ministers from Canada, France, Germany, Italy, Japan, Russia, United Kingdom, the United States, Brazil, China, India, Mexico and South Africa agreed in principle on the outline of a successor to the Kyoto Protocol. They envisage a global cap-and-trade system that would apply to both industrialized nations and developing countries and hope that this would be in place by 2009.

WEEE and ROHS Directives

The European Commission has prepared legislation to oblige manufacturers to pay for the treatment and recovery of white and brown waste from electrical and electronic equipment. The proposals are divided in two separate directives, one focussing on waste recovery and the other on hazardous substance restriction. Waste Electrical and Electronic Equipment (WEEE) (2002/96/EC) (EP/CEU 2003a) and Restriction of Hazardous Substances in Electrical and Electronic Equipment (ROHS) (2002/95/EC) (EP/CEU 2003b) are the EU directives that aim to minimize the impact of electrical and electronic goods on the environment, by increasing re-use and recycling, reducing the amount of WEEE going to landfill and reducing the quantities of four heavy metals and two brominated flame retardants which electronic equipment may contain. WEEE seeks to achieve this by making producers responsible for financing the collection, treatment and recovery of waste electrical equipment, and by obliging distributors to allow consumers to return their waste equipment free of charge. Some of the major issues in negotiation are when the Directive will come into action, the recovery process and financing. Under the ROHS directive all member states of the EU must have substituted the use of lead, mercury, hexavalent chromium, polybrominated bihenyls (PBB) and polybrominated diphenylethers (PBDEs) in electrical and electronic equipment that enters the market from 1 July 2006. Exemptions will be made if any of those are not scientifically or technically replaceable.

The main aims of the directives are:

- minimize waste from the end of electrical and electronic equipment's life cycle in order to reduce land fill and the impact on the environment;
- engage re-use, recycling and other forms of recovery of brown and white goods from electronic and electrical equipment that have come to the end of their life cycle;
- minimize the risk and impact to the environment and human health of using hazardous substances in the production-manufacture, treatment and disposal.

The Directives hold the manufacturers responsible for taking back and recovering electrical and electronic goods. This changes the relationship between customers and business from one based on a one-way transfer of goods to one where manufacturers take the responsibility for treating, recovering and disposing of the goods, which has to be free of charge for the customer and with the is possibility of collection from their household as well. Both directives became European Law on 13 August 2004.

In order for the products to be suitable for collection and disposal in this way, they must be designed to be more environmentally friendly. The products would have to be recyclable, more durable and be able to be upgraded. Therefore they must have a longer life cycle. Currently the European Parliament is proposing a 60 to 80 per cent recycle ability depending on the product.

The data shown in Table 6.1 are derived by the Industry Council for Electronic Equipment Recycling (ICEER) on the volumes on domestic WEEE in the UK. This table illustrates the significance of the directive when it comes into action for all the members of the EU. If all this volume of products could be recycled or re-used in different ways the impact on the environment could significantly be reduced (for further information on the directives see EP/CEU 2003a).

EU Landfill Directive

The EU Landfill Directive (1999/31/EC) (CEU 1999a) was adopted on 16 July 1999. The objective of the directive is to prevent or reduce the impact to the environment from waste of all type that come from anthropogenic activities. This would be achieved by strict regulations on materials that can be dumped and better and strict control of landfills, by setting standards in their design, operation and aftercare.

The aim of the directive is to control the impact on the environment from landfill waste by preventing pollution that could affect the surface groundwater, soil, air and human health.

All waste would have to be defined according to its type such as municipal, hazardous, non-hazardous and inert. This would apply to the landfills as well, which would be labelled depending on what type of waste they could accept. This means that no co-disposal of waste is allowed. The landfills can be characterized as:

- landfills for hazardous waste;
- landfills for non-hazardous waste;
- landfills for inert waste.

Table 6.1   Data from ICEER from 2005 in UK

Equipment	Tonnage discarded ('000tones)		Units discarded (millions)	
Large household appliances	644	69%	14	16%
Small household appliances	80	8%	30	31%
IT/telecoms equipment	68	7%	21	23%
Consumer equipment	120	13%	12	13%
Tools	23	2%	5	5%
Toys, leisure and sports equipment	2	<1%	2	2%
Lighting*	2	<1%	9	10%
Monitoring and control equipment	<1	<1%	<1	1%
Total domestic WEEE	939	100%	93	100%

*   Lighting arisings relate only to discarded domestic lamps, which make up only 10% of total lamps discarded.

Source: ICEER 2005.

In contrast, the Directive does not apply to some types of waste such as:

•   disposal on the soil of sludges including sewage sludges and sludges resulting from dredging operations;
•   the use of inert waste which is suitable in development/restoration and filling-in work, or for construction purposes, in landfills;
•   the deposit of non-hazardous dredging sludges alongside small waterways from where they have been dredged out and non hazardous sludges in surface water including the bed and its subsoil;
•   the deposit of unpolluted soil or non-hazardous inert waste resulting from prospecting and extraction, treatment and storage of mineral resources as well as from the operation of quarries.

Hence, the waste that the landfills will accept have to comply to certain specifications:

•   all waste must be treated, with the exception of inert waste, which it is not feasible to treat;
•   hazardous waste as defined by the Directive must be disposed only in landfills designed for this type of waste;
•   landfills for non-hazardous waste must be used for municipal waste, non-hazardous waste as defined by the Directive and stable non-reactive hazardous waste that meet the criteria of the Directive.

The types of waste that are not allowed to be disposed of in landfills are:

•   liquid waste;
•   flammable waste, explosive or oxidizing waste;
•   hospital and other clinical waste which is infectious;
•   whole used tyres manufactured two years from the date that the Directive came into force, excluding tyres that have been used as engineering material and shredded tyres manufactured five years from the date that the Directive came into force.

Also, in order to continue their operation all the existing landfills need to comply with the new regulations and after their closure they have to be treated properly to reduce the impact on the environment.

Finally the Directive sets out targets for reducing biodegradable municipal waste (BMW). This has to be reduced to 75 per cent of the 1995 baseline by 2010, 50 per cent by 2013 and 35 per cent by 2020. The directive also requires that member states must set up national strategies for implementing these targets (for further information regarding the directive see CEU 1999a).

EU Hazardous Waste Directive

The EU Hazardous Waste Directive (HWD) (1991/689/EEC) was signed on 12 December 1991 and came in to force on 20 January 1992. The aim of the Directive is the management, recovery and proper disposal of hazardous waste. This is achieved by ensuring that all European member states comprehend the definition of hazardous waste and to comply with the regulation on how they manage hazardous waste.

The contents of the Directive define a list of hazardous waste (also called Hazardous Waste List or HWL) depending on category, constituents and properties. Domestic waste is not covered by the Directive, although it was covered in Directive 75/442/EEC, released in 1975 which dealt with all types waste (CEC 1975).

All member states have to record and identify their hazardous waste to ensure that it is not mixed with non-hazardous and does not cause any problems to human health. All member states must ensure that they treat hazardous waste differently to non-hazardous ones.

Any establishment or undertaking that disposes of hazardous waste has to be authorized by permit from the Commission. The same applies to recovery operations which must be undertaken according to regulations and through communication with the Commission. All of these operations need to be recorded properly by the transporters, producers, establishments and undertakings. Hence, all the organizations involved with hazardous waste have to be inspected and must be able to certify the origin and destination of the waste. Finally, any breach of the Directive by any member state should be stated to the Commission and the violation of the Directive should not create any threat to human health (for further information regarding the directive see CEC, p. 20).

EU Solvents Emissions Directive

The European Union has agreed Council Directive 1999/13/EC on 'the limitation of emissions of volatile organic compounds due to the use of organic solvents in certain activities and installationsor' or also called the Solvent Emissions Directive (SED). The directive was proposed on the 11 March 1999 (CEU 1999b, pp. 0001–22).

> The aim of the SED is to prevent or reduce the indirect effects of emissions of volatile organic compounds (VOCs) into the environment, mainly into air and the potential risks to human health, by providing measures and procedures to be implemented. (DEFRA 2002)

The Directive aims at the reduction of VOCs, which can contribute to ozone depletion by supporting the convention of nitrogen to nitrogen oxide. VOCs are chemical compounds produced by road traffic, production processes, storage and distribution of mineral oil products, solvents and other natural sources such as vegetation. Therefore, in order to tackle ozone depletion the EU has targeted the reduction of nitrogen oxides and VOCs in the atmosphere. Hence, the Directive targets emissions from solvents produced from industrial processes. Despite this fact, emissions for domestic use are not covered by the Directive.

The sectors covered by the directive are the following (ibid.; CEU 1999b, pp. 0001–22):

- adhesive coating, metal and plastic coating, coil coating, paper coating, vehicle coating, vehicle refinishing, wood coating, leather coating, textile coating;
- winding wire coating;
- dry cleaning;
- footwear manufacture;
- vegetable oil and animal fat extraction and vegetable oil refining;
- manufacturing of pharmaceutical products;
- rubber convention;
- surface cleaning;
- wood impregnation;
- manufacturing of coating preparations, varnishes, inks and adhesives;
- heatset web offset printing;
- publication rotogravure.

The aim of SED is to reduce the above emissions from EC members by 57 per cent by 2007, based on their 1990 levels. Individual emission levels apply for all those categories mentioned above.

The methods that are stated by the SED for reducing emissions are:

- meet emission levels stated in Annex IIA of the Directive;
- introduce a solvent directive scheme;
- create a National Plan Approach (excluding dry cleaning and surface cleaning);
- all installations have to be authorized or require being subject to an authorization or general binding rules (unless the previous option is implemented).

Strict regulation will apply for halogenated VOCs or VOCs that are classified as carcinogenic, mutagenic or toxic to reproduction. Some of the definitions that have been given to these substances are:

- R40 = possible risk of irreversible effects;
- R45 = carcinogenic;
- R46 = may cause heritable genetic damage or mutagenic;
- R49 = may cause cancer by inhalation;
- R60 = may impair fertility;
- R61 = may cause harm to the unborn child (DEFRA 2002).

The Directive also states that EU member states should cooperate and exchange information about the use of organic substances and their potential substitutes. This information should be tested for fitness for use, potential effect on human health, environmental and economic consequences of the substitutes and whether their potential impact on the environment, ecosystem and human health is less. All this information must also be published and a solvent management scheme has to be created within the member states according to available knowledge (for further information regarding the directive check (CEU 1999b, pp. 0001–22).

ISO14000

In this era of growing environmental concerns there are two types of environmental regulations: mandatory requirements and voluntary initiatives. Mandatory requirements refer to obligations of companies to comply with the law, while voluntary initiatives 'are an integral part of corporate social responsibilities which demonstrate corporations' commitment to environmental consciousness and obligations' (Rezaee and Elam 2000, p. 60). ISO 14000 comprises a series of standards that model an environmental management system (EMS). It is built around 21 standards intended to assist organizations manage their environmental issues and to ensure that their environmental policies align with their missions and goals. The environmental standards are divided into six categories:

1. environmental management system;
2. environmental auditing;
3. environmental performance evaluation;
4. environmental labelling;
5. life cycle assessment;
6. environmental aspects in product standards.

Despite that, ISO 14000 is not about 'environmentalism' or being 'green'. An effective EMS (ISO14001) is simply a systemic way of controlling procedures and operations related to environmental issues, based on an outline devised by the ISO 14000 standard. It is concerned with environmental performance but it is about effective corporate management. Therefore, the EMS should encourage organizations to consider implementation of the best available techniques, in order to achieve environmental objectives. Hence ISO 14000 cannot substitute any environmental regulations or laws created by any country. Virtually every company from small to large is suitable for certification by the standard, but usually it is medium and large companies that are registered, due to the expense of certification.

In order for a company to be ISO 14000 certified there is a series of steps that must comply with the following standards.

Initially a company should have an environmental policy which is defined by senior management and is appropriate to the nature, scale and environmental impacts of the activities, products and services that are to be defined within the scope of the EMS. The policy should be committed to continual improvement and prevention of pollution and comply with applicable environmental legal requirements and other similar requirements to which the organization subscribes. Also, all the environmental objectives and targets of the organization should be related to the environmental policy. Hence, all employees of the organization should be aware of the policy, which must also be available to the public.

In order for organizations to formulate an environmental policy they first have to review their current one. This includes reviewing all the current regulations and international policies and the organization's extant work practices, processes and operations. Afterwards the company has to create a strategic plan for implementing the EMS. In the same way environmental aspects have to be identified.

Organizations need to identify their environmental aspects and determine the most significant ones. Environmental aspects are defined as the elements of an organization's activities, products or services that can interact with the environment. In order to identify the environmental aspects the organization has to consider the following:

- emissions to air;
- releases to water;
- aspects related to waste management;
- releases to land;
- aspects related to extraction and distribution of raw materials and natural resources;
- use of raw materials and natural resources;
- other local/community environmental issues.
- use of energy;
- aspects related to distribution, use and end life of products.

But, after qualifying and being registered with ISO 14000, companies must also maintain their conformance to this standard and work on continuous improvement. This is why EMS must be integrated into all the organization's activities. The environmental objectives and targets must be part of the routine operations and activities of the company.

Among the main criticisms levelled at the ISO standard are that it has been developed with very little consultation and participation of public interest groups, non-governmental organizations, workers or governments and that it does not require the public disclosure of environmental information. The resulting democratic deficit has important implications for the stakeholder credibility of the standard. ISO 14001 is further criticized for the considerable degree of flexibility it allows, which make it a weaker, less stringent EMS standard than its peers, EMAS and BS 7750.

Irrespective of the arguments for or against environmental standards, they can only be judged by their effectiveness in delivering enhanced environmental performance and by the extent to which they succeed in meeting stakeholders' expectations.

Conclusion

This section of the chapter was a review of different protocols and directives that have been proposed by national regulators and other private regulatory bodies in a worldwide effort to preserve and protect the planet for current and future generations. Among the Protocols that have been reviewed are the Montreal Protocol in 1987 and the Kyoto Protocol 1997. The Vienna Convention set the foundations for Montreal Protocol, while the Rio Declaration on Environment and Development created the momentum for the Kyoto Protocol. These specific protocols show that governments have become more environmentally aware and have decided that environmental improvements must be made. The focuses for these two protocols are ozone depletion and global warming and the reductions of specific pollutants and ODCs in the environment. The fact that these protocols are set at a global scale makes them more significant. In a parallel set of initiatives, the European Union has instigated its own legislation which suggests a framework for future manufacturing activities and how organizational strategies need to change in response to the new environmental business dynamic. ISO 14000 has been discussed in this section to suggest that companies can demonstrate that they can have their own initiatives in managing environmental issues apart from simple compliance with legislation. Governments are increasingly using the latter to control markets adding to competitive and productivity pressure; however regulations set the minimum case for sustaining the environment since they are intrinsically designed not to overburden industries with heavy costs of change and compliance.

The Way Forward

The progress we have witnessed in the modern world has resulted from the synergistic interaction of events and innovations. As we have moved through history, the number of these events and innovations has increased. This has created a complex network of interconnections that not only create innovation but accelerate its pace. We have become ever more dependent on these innovation cycles to create competitive advantage in organizations. Each invention demands its own follow-up: technological change is driven by the momentum created by the previous change; once started, it is hard to stop. The example of Kuwait, where society has leapt from a level reminiscent of ancient Egypt to the technology of today in 30 years, illustrates this increased change cycle.

However, the pace of change has allowed competitive advantage to be more rapidly eroded, requiring more innovation to replace it and an increasing reliance on it. Twenty-first century organizations and the lifestyle they create could not exist without these systems and the underlying technology and advancement processes. The nature of this dependence is illustrated by the failure of the Niagara generating station Sir Adam Beck Station No. 2 in Queenston, Ontario and Southern Ontario which precipitated the New York City power blackouts of 1965. The support systems that were taken for granted failed and for many people life almost came to a standstill.

Environmental degradation by businesses and societies is an outcome of this relentless change. The scientific evidence is compelling beyond reasonable doubt that unless we radically transform our businesses and economies, then future generations will pay a heavy price. This chapter has outlined the signs and signals that are already present and has discussed the changes that have been made to mitigate these impacts. Despite these efforts, every sign suggests that we must be prepared for wholesale change. Our environmental future will at the outset be mixed, with regions seeing both positive and negative outcomes. However, as time progresses the negative impacts will come to dominate all regions. An example of this future is demonstrated by the heat wave that hit northern and central France in the first two weeks of August 2003. During this period 8,000 deaths over and above the average for the period were recorded in France, and a total of 35,000 additional deaths were recorded in Switzerland, northern Italy and southern Germany. Many of the dead were elderly with breathing difficulties who collapsed when night-time temperatures stayed above 80°F. The irony is that the earliest and heaviest burdens will fall on the poorest countries, who are least able to adapt and who have contributed least to the problems.

The view taken by many is that we should look for technological solutions, alternative energy sources, new materials and cleaner processes. However, this misses the point. By simply focusing on the outcomes – the pollution, the harm and the inequality we generate – we can never achieve any form of solution. All that can be done is to create another set of outcomes that present further problems that feed into a new set of challenges for the future.

We must look beyond outcomes to their underlying causes. The cycle of progress and the network of technological acts insulates our day-to-day lives to the extent that individuals can believe they are detached from the wider environment, but that is an illusion. This decoupling is clearly present when we consider the challenge of climate change which, unmitigated, will magnify many of the existing scourges of humanity: deprivation, drought, flood, sickness and conflict.

Internationalization, structural changes and increasingly active customers and consumers have changed the nature of business in recent years. Demands for faster, more reliable and cheaper products are forcing companies to improve the efficiency of the flow of goods, services and information. These changes reflect the structural changes in modern societies based on the development of highly specialized, self-sustaining and prescriptive systems which serve identifiable social functions (Luhman 1987). Society is nothing but reflexive, self-recursive communication. The social still constitutes a whole, but one without centre or unity, where systems sit side-by-side, differentiated by function and stabilized by communication. Thus society is split into fields of practice where differentiation occurs between the powerful and powerless, with individuals estranged from both their traditional communities and other people in general. This atomization leads to shallower relations between individuals and creates barriers to understanding and adapting to each others' uniqueness. Demand is created without reference to a greater good: whereas a majority may support activities which would help to stem our headlong plunge toward extermination as a species, the majority engages in activities which have the opposite effect. The market is everything, a self-directing automatic system where everyone pursues their own gain and there is no room for altruism.

This market-led approach has been adopted by governments in taking a supply-side economics approach to improving companies' environmental performance, based on the structural elements of competition, innovation, enterprise, investment, skills and legislation. However, environmental productivity is not primarily a function of inputs but the complex, human social processes of transforming them into usable outputs. These supply elements are further diminished by their disconnection from the value chain within firms: the supply of skills may increase, but employers' ability to use them has not; supply-side push has little effect. At a corporate level the concept of best or world-class practices has been pursued. The notion is based on the ability to transfer one set of practices from one business context to another. This is simplistic at best and the weakness of the argument is demonstrated by the domination of Toyota and its lean manufacturing system, despite all attempts at imitation. Instead, companies need to look within themselves as much as outside to develop their own unique processes that can define unique environmental competitive advantages.

The root causes of environmental damage are the hidden social forces which form a network of mutually supportive feedback loops that drive markets, formulate competitive advantages and direct consumers. We find ourselves in the world similar to that in which people found themselves before Newton. At that time, it was believed that if things moved or changed direction it was due to an object's internal animation. Newton showed that it was because they were acted upon by a network of invisible forces which could nevertheless be qualified, quantified, and harnessed. Only by understanding these forces and directing them can we move forward towards true environmental stewardship, where markets and society can be balanced.

References

Bansal, P. and Roth, K. (2000), 'Why Companies Go Green: A Model of Ecological Responsiveness', *Academy of Management Journal* 43(4), pp. 717–36.

Bentham, G. (1993), 'Depletion of the Ozone Layer: Consequences for Non-infectious Human Diseases', *Parasitology* 106, S39–S44.

Berman, S.L., Wicks, A.C., Kotha, S. and Jones, T.M. (1999), 'Does Stakeholder Orientation Matter? The Relationship between Stakeholder Management Models and Firm Financial Performance', *Academy of Management Journal* 42(5), pp. 488–506.

Brimblecombe, P. (1987), *The Big Smoke: A History of Air Pollution in London since Medieval Times* (London: Methuen).

Charlier H.R. (2000), 'From Green to Brown: Is Brownfields Use Risk Taking?', *Environmental Management and Health* 11(1), pp. 20–26.

Cormier, D. and Magnan, M. (1999), 'Corporate Environmental Disclosure Strategies: Determinants, Costs, Benefits', *Journal of Accounting Auditing and Finance* 14(4), pp. 429–51.

Council of European Communities (CEC) (1975), Council Directive of 15 July 1975 on Waste (75/442/EEC), Official Journal, L194, 25/07/1975.

Council of the European Communities (CEC) (1991), Council Directive of 12 December 1991 on Hazardous Waste (91/689/EEC), *Official Journal of the European Communities* L377, 31/12/1991.

Council of the European Union (CEU) (1999a), Council Directive 1999/31/EC of 26 April 1999 on the Landfill of Waste, *Official Journal of the European Communities* I182/1, 16/7/1999.

Council of the European Communities (CEU) (1999b), Council Directive 1999/13/EC of 11 March 1999 on the Limitation of Emissions of Volatile Organic Compounds due to the use of Organic Solvents in Certain Activities and Installations, *Official Journal of the European Communities*, L085, 29/03/1999.

Decahnt, K., Altman, B., Downing, R.M. and Keeney, T. (1994), 'Environmental Leadership: From Compliance to Competitive Advantage', *Academy of Management Executive* 8(3), pp. 7–28.

Department for Environment Food and Rural Affairs (DEFRA) (2002), Guidance Note from the Department of Environment Food and Rural Affairs and the National Assembly for Wales on the Implementation of Solvent Emissions Directive, Department for Environment Food and Rural Affairs, London.

Dias-Sardinha, I. and Reijinders, L. (2001), 'Environmental Performance Evaluation and Sustainability Performance Evaluation of Organizations: An Evolutionary Framework', *Eco-Management and Auditing* 8, pp. 71–9.

Dodson, M.C., Kwarteng, A.Y and Ulaby, F.T. (1997), 'Use of SIR-C/X-SAR to Monitor Environmental Damages of the 1991 Gulf War in Kuwait', IGARSS'97, 1997 International Geoscience and Remote Sensing Symposium. Remote Sensing – A scientific vision for sustainable Development (Cat. No. 97CH6042) Vol. 1, pp. 119–21.

European Parliament and the Council of the European Union (EU/CEU) (2003a), Directive 2002/96/EC of the European Parliament and of Council of 27 January 2003 on Waste Electrical and Electronic Equipment (WEEE), *Official Journal of European Union*, 13/2/2003.

European Parliament and the Council of the European Union (EU/CEU) (2003b), Directive 2002/95/EC of the European Parliament and of the Council of 27 January 2003 on the Restriction of the Use of Certain Hazardous Substances in Electrical and Electronic Equipment, *Official Journal of European Union* L37, 13/02/2003.

European Union (EU) (1980), Council Directive 80/77/EEC of 15 July 1980 relating to the Quality of Water Intended for Human Consumption.

Farman J.C., Gardiner, B.G. and Shanklin, J.D. (1985), 'Large Losses of the Total Ozone in Antarctica Reveal Seasonal ClOx/NOx Interaction', *Nature* 315, pp. 207–10.

Fletcher, R.S. (2000), *CRS Report for Congress: 98–2: Global Climate Change Treaty: The Kyoto Protocol* (Washington, DC: National Council for Science and the Environment).

Ghobadian, A., Viney, H., James, P. and Liu, J. (1995), 'The Influence of Environmental Issues in Strategic Analysis and Choice', *Management Decision* 333(10), pp. 46–58.

Ghobadian, A., Viney, H., Liu, J. and James, P. (1998), 'Extended Linear Approaches to Mapping Corporate Environmental Behavior', *Business Strategy and the Environment* 7, pp. 13–23.

Gilgen, H., Wild, M. and Ohmura, A. (1998), 'Means and Trends of Shortwave Irradiance at the Surface Estimated from Global Energy Balance Archive Data', *Journal of Climate* 11(8), pp. 2042–61.

Goudie, A. (1993), *The Human Impact on the Natural Environment* (Oxford: Blackwell).

Harrison, R.G. and Aplin, K.L. (2003), 'Nineteenth-century Parisian Smoke Variations Inferred from Eiffel Tower Atmospheric Electrical Observations', *Atmospheric Environment* 37, 5319–24.

Hart, S.L. (1995), 'A Natural-resource-based View of the Firm', *Academy of Management Review* 20(4), pp. 986–1014.

Henriques, I. and Sadorsky, P. (1999), 'The Relationship between Environmental Commitment and Managerial Perceptions of Stakeholder Importance', *Academy of Management Journal* 42(1), pp. 87–99.

Industry Council for Electronic Equipment Recycling (ICEER)(2005), 'Status Report on Waste Electrical and Electronic Equipment in the UK 2005', Interim Report.

Integrated Risk Information System (IRIS) (1991), *Nitrate*, Integrated Risk Information System, US Environmental Protection Agency, CASRN 14797-55-8.

Intergovernmental Panel on Climate Change (IPCC) (1990), *Climate Change – The IPCC Scientific Assessment. Report of IPCC Working Group 1* (Cambridge: Cambridge University Press).

Intergovernmental Panel on Climate Change (IPCC) (1999), *Aviation and the Global Atmosphere* (Cambridge: Cambridge University Press).

Intergovernmental Panel on Climate Change (IPCC) (2002), *Climate Change 2001: The Scientific Basis. Contribution of Working Group 1 to the Third Assessment Report of the Intergovernmental Panel on Climate Change*, Houghton, J.T. (ed.), Ding, Y., Griggs, D.J., Noguer, M., Linden, P.J. van der and Xiaosu, D. (Cambridge: Cambridge University Press).

Intergovernmental Panel on Climate Change (IPCC) (2006), *Climate Change 1995 – The Science of Climate Change. Report of IPCC Working Group 1* (Cambridge: Cambridge University Press).

International Tanker Owners Pollution Federation (ITOPF) (2000), *Tanker Oil Spill Statistics* (London: International Tanker Owners Pollution Federation Ltd).

Johnson, G.J. (2004), 'The Environment and the Eye', *Eye* 18, pp. 1235–50.

King, A.A. and Lenox, M.J. (2000), 'Industry Self-regulation without Sanctions: The Chemical Industry's Responsible Care Program', *Academy of Management Journal* 43(4), pp. 698–716.

Knickerbocker, B. (1999), 'The Big Spill', *Christian Science Monitor* 91(79).

Konisky, D.M. (1999), 'Comparative Risk Projects: A Methodology for Cross-Project Analysis of Human Health Risk Rankings', Discussion Paper 99–46, Resources for the Future, Washington DC.

Lack, T. (1999), 'Water and Health in Europe: An Overview', *British Medical Journal* 318(1), pp. 678–82.

Liepert, B.G. (2002), 'Observed Reductions in Surface Solar Radiation in the United States and Worldwide from 1961 to 1990', *Geophysical Research Letters* 29(12), pp. 1421.

Lomborg, B. (2001), *The Sceptical Environmentalist* (Cambridge: Cambridge University Press).

Luhmann, N. (1987), 'The Evolutionary Differentiation between Society and Interaction', in Alexander, J.C., Giesen, B., Münch, R. and Smelser, N.J. (eds) *The Micro-Macro Link* (Berkeley and Los Angeles: University of California Press), pp. 112–31.

Makhijiani, A. and Gurney, R.K. (1995), *Mending the Ozone Hole: Science, Technology and Policy* (Cambridge, MA: MIT Press).

Marland, G., Boden, T.A. and Andres, R.J. (2006), *Global, Regional, and National CO_2 Emissions. In Trends: A Compendium of Data on Global Change* (Oak Ridge, TN: Carbon Dioxide Information Analysis Center, Oak Ridge National Laboratory, US Department of Energy).

McNeil J. (2001), *Something New Under the Sun: An Environmental History of the Twentieth Century* (London: Penguin Books).

Miller, G.T. Jr (1998), *Living in the Environment: Principles, Connections and Solutions* (Belmont CA: Wadsworth).

Miserey, Y. (2003), 'Paris was as Polluted at the End of the 19th Century as it is Today', *Le Figaro*, 21 November.

Molina, M.J and Rowland, F.S. (1974), 'The Stratospheric Sink for Chlorofuoromethanes: Chlorine Atom-Catalysed Destruction of Ozone', *Nature* 239, pp. 810–12.

Morhardt, J.E, Baird, S. and Freeman, K. (2002), 'Scoring Corporate Environmental and Sustainability Reports Using GRI2000, ISO 14031 and Other Criteria', *Corporate Social Responsibility and Environmental Management* 9, pp. 215–33.

Murley, L. (ed.) (1995), *Clean Air Around The World* (Brighton: International Union of Air Pollution Prevention and Environmental Protection Associations).

National Research Council (NRC) (1985), *Oil in the Sea: Inputs, Fates and Effects* (Washington, DC: National Academy Press).

Niagara Gazette (1980), 23 May.

Prinn, R.G., Cunnold, D., Rasmussen, R., Simmonds, P., Alyea, F., Crawford, A., Fraser, P. and Rosen, R. (1990), 'Atmospheric Emissions and Trends of Nitrous Oxide Deduced from 10 Years of ALE-GAGE Data', *Journal of Geophysical Research* 95(D11), pp. 18,369–85.

Reinhart, F. (1999), 'Market Failure and the Environmental Policies of Firms: Economic Rationales for "Beyond Compliance" Behavior', *Journal of Industrial Ecology* 3(1), pp. 9–21.

Reivera-Camino, J. (2001), 'What Motivates European Firms to Adopt Environmental Management Systems?', *Eco-Management and Auditing* 8, pp. 134–43.

Rezaee, Z. and Elam, R. (2000), 'Emerging ISO 14000 Environmental Standards: A Step by Step Implementation Guide', *Managerial Auditing Journal* 15(1/2), pp. 60–67.

Roberts, J.E. (2001), 'Ocular Phototoxicity', *Journal of Photochemistry and Photobiology* B64, pp. 136–43.

Romanou, A., Liepert, B., Schmidt, G.A., Rossow, W.B., Ruedy, R.A. and Zhang, Y. (2007), '20th-century Changes in Surface Solar Irradiance in Simulations and Observations', *Geophysical Research Letters*, 34.

Rowland, F.S. (1990), 'Stratospheric Ozone Depletion by Chlorofluorocarbons', *Ambio* 19(6–7), pp. 281–92.

Royal Commission on Environmental Pollution (2002), *The Environmental Effects of Civil Aircraft in Flight* (London: Royal Commission on Environmental Pollution).

Sharma, S. (2000), 'Managerial Interpretations and Organizational Context as Predictors of Corporate Choice of Environmental Strategy', *Academy of Management Journal* 43(4), pp. 681–97.

Shiklomanov, I.A. (2000), 'Appraisal and Assessment of World Water Resources', *Water International* 25(1), pp. 11–32.

Shrivastana, P. (1995), 'The Role of Corporations in Achieving Ecological Sustainability', *Academy of Management Review* 20(4), pp. 936–60.

Sliney, D.H. (2001), 'Photoprotection of Eye-UV Radiation and Sunglasses', *Journal of Photochemistry and Photobiology* B64, pp. 166–75.

Smith, A.R. (1872), *Air and Rain – The Beginning of a Chemical Climatology* (London: Longmans, Green).

Srinivasan, J. and Gadgil, S. (2002), 'On the Asian Brown Cloud Controversy', *Current Science* 83, pp. 586–92.

Stafford, E.R. (1996), 'Green Alliances: Strategic Relations between Business and Environmental Groups', *Business Horizons* 39(2), pp. 50–59.

Stanhill, G. and Cohen, S. (2001), 'Global Dimming: A Review of the Evidence for a Widespread and Significant Reduction in Global Radiation with Discussion of its Probable Causes and Possible Agricultural Consequences', *Agricultural and Forest Meteorology* 107: pp. 255–78.

Stanhill, G. and Moreshet, S. (2004), 'Global Radiation Climate Changes in Israel', *Climatic Change* 22, pp. 121–38.

Travis, D.J. (2002), 'Contrails Reduce Daily Temperature Range', *Nature* 418, p. 601.

United Nations Environmental Programme (UNEP) (1992), Rio Declaration on Environment and Development (Stockholm: UNEP).

United Nations Environmental Programme (UNEP) (2000), *The Montreal Protocol on Substances that Deplete the Ozone Layer as either Adjusted and/or Amended in London 1990, Copenhagen 1992, Vienna 1995, Montreal 1997, Beijing 1999* (Nairobi: UNEP).

United Nations Environmental Programme (UNEP) (2001), *Vienna Protocol for the Protection of the Ozone Layer* (Nairobi: UNEP).

United Nations Framework on Climate Change (UNFCC) (2002), *A Guide to the Climate Change Convention and its Kyoto Protocol* (Bonn: UNFCC).

Waddock, S.A. and Graves, S.B. (2000), 'Performance Characteristics of Social and Traditional Investments', *Journal of Investing* 9(2), pp. 27–41.

Warneck, P. (1988), *Chemistry of the Natural Atmosphere: An Introductory Survey* (London: Academic Press).

Wellburn, A. (1994), *Air Pollution and Climate: The Biological Impact* (London: Longman).

World Meteorological Organisation (WMO) (1985), Atmospheric Ozone1985: Assessment of our Understanding of the Process Controlling its Present Distribution and Change (Geneva: WMO).

World Meteorological Organisation (WMO) (1991), *Scientific Assessment of Ozone Depletion: 1991* (Geneva: WMO).

Young, A.R (2006), 'Acute Effects of UVR on Eyes and Skin', *Progress in Biophysics and Molecular Biology* 92, pp. 80 85.

Chapter 7
Managing Mergers and Acquisitions

Zoltán Antal-Mokos[1]

Introduction

Mergers and acquisitions continue to be a key option for corporate strategy. Many countries' official statistics suggest that they fail more often than they create wealth. It is also apparent that doing the right deal in the right way can override other potential strategic pathways to growth. Mergers and acquisitions (M&A) have captured the interest of executives, policy-makers, regulators, and scholars and are prime candidates to make headlines because:

- staggering amounts are often involved;
- these deals have a significant impact on people and their organizations;
- executives the glamour may enjoy at signing ceremonies;
- high stakes and thrills often surround the deal-making processes.

Given the variety of issues related to M&A, this chapter can only provide a brief overview of some of the most important themes and attributes. A general management perspective of strategic M&A is taken, focusing on two at least analytically distinct phases of acquisition processes: developing a strategic rationale and striking the deal, and managing the integration. From a meta-analysis of research evidence and numerous published cases, several general rules of thumb and premises emerge to which proficient business acquirers seem to adhere in developing the rationale and managing the process after the deal closes, thus achieving consistently superior results through M&A. The first two sections of this chapter will highlight the key issues and potential pitfalls. Key overarching principles are formulated in the concluding section.

Why Embark on the Journey?

As there are typically various ways to achieve similar objectives, the rationale for any strategic decision must include a consideration of different options. Cultivating alternatives can only improve the quality of decision-making. For M&A, alliances represent the most expedient alternative. The choice between the two requires an analysis of the resources and the type of potential synergies, the competitive environment, and the collaborative competences of the involved firms (Dyer et al. 2004). Alliances can often result in sharing and combining resources and thus creating new value without the risks of a takeover being involved. A systematic comparison between the options of pursuing an acquisition or entering into an alliance is likely to lead to more prudent decisions and a better chance of successful acquisitions.

1   The author wishes to thank the Peter Curtius Foundation for their generous support.

Successful deals are typically made by what Sirower (2003/4) calls 'prepared' acquirers, that are 'always on'. These companies are not grabbed by opportunities presented to them in an obsessive search for top-line growth. Instead they develop and consistently utilize a road map to strategically create and plan for opportunities. M&A planning must be rooted in the overall strategy process of the company, rather than triggered in a cursory fashion by a prospect that looks 'interesting'. Being constantly alert is also a safeguard against being driven into making deals unprepared by a perceived pressure to keep up with competitors.

Even with the best preparation, mergers and acquisitions are risky. There may be strong motives, however, for the management of a firm to take the risk and embark on the rough journey of making an acquisition. Perhaps the most strongly felt, in the era of globalization and consolidation in many industries, is the urge to merge for the sake of getting bigger. Take the example of Chrysler which, at the time of merging with Daimler-Benz, was the third largest automotive company in the world's largest market, yet not large enough to effectively compete globally. Their relatively low competitiveness lead the merger to break down and Chrysler were sold off in 2007. General Motors acquired Lotus Engineering in 1986. Once they had transferred lessons to learn, the group sold Lotus to ACBN Holdings SA in 1993. Proton subsequently bought the majority shareholding in 1996.[2] Then BMW bought Rover not so much to buy production capacity in the UK or the brands such as Land Rover and Mini, but to get access to Honda. Honda had exchanged equity with Rover. Once BMW had Rover, Honda let go its shares in Rover. Rover bosses at the time were claiming it was a reverse takeover. Rover now had its hands on a benevolent owner that would guide and take care of them.

Recent mergers in banking, IT, telecoms, pharmaceuticals, energy and other sectors provide numerous further examples. There is a compelling logic behind mergers that are envisaged to catapult the firm to the top of the industry. Size may increase market power and it can yield opportunities for significant cost savings owing to scale economies. In an otherwise slowly growing industry, doing the deal seems to offer a fast way to gain advantage over the competition and please the investors. All too often, however, demonstrating fast growth through M&A is mistakenly believed to be easier than organic growth: size is mistaken for competitive leadership, and mergers are mistaken for a sound strategy for achieving that position. M&A is not a strategy on its own.

> You can relatively quickly merge yourself into being big, but you cannot merge yourself into being great.

Merger Mania

A range of motives to actively engage in M&A revolves around diversification, relatedness, complementarity, and synergies – in all forms and shades. A number of different types of synergy, from operating performance through to managerial to financial viability, have been analytically distinguished and used in practice to build a convincing argument for making deals. Recent studies suggest that synergies most often remain potential benefits that are often used to justify deals. Christofferson et al. (2004) noted that they have seldom delivered up to the expected, or promised, levels.

---

2   http://en.wikipedia.org/wiki/Lotus_Cars, accessed 1 February 2008.

'Relatedness', when viewed from a simple product or market perspective, may mislead decision-makers. The concept of reinforcing sources of competitive advantage may better serve executives who contemplate whether to go ahead with an acquisition. Deals often are ill-fated when they contradict the fundamental way the acquirer achieves competitive advantage.

Acquisitions frequently are justified with the need to gain access to new technologies, or other skills of another firm (Gammelgaard 2004). This approach has worked for Cisco, Microsoft, Intel, Siemens and many others (Mitchell and Capron 2002). Through organizational learning, acquisitions can even spark new sources of advantage for an acquirer with relatively strong foundations and a balancing dose of organic growth. However, excessive reliance on M&A for skills can become a dangerous illusion inasmuch as it may also appear to give an otherwise ailing firm the chance to reinvigorate itself by infusing new skills, great people, and new perspectives of the acquired firm. M&A then can change the whole foundation of the acquiring company (Harding and Rovit 2004). Skills might evaporate as people abandon ship, while acquired organizational capabilities may get entrapped in the web of the budgets and policies of the acquirer, suggesting that the problem in effect lies in the integration phase. Employees in the newly acquired business typically want to have the same benefits and pay scales as employees of the parent. Consequently, recommendations focus on organizational safeguarding *ex-ante* status quo to preserve capabilities and enticing key people to stay. No matter how carefully the integration is planned, these deals are most likely to fail because of the weak rationale in the first place. Rarely can an ailing core business be completely transformed by simply acquiring a team of movers and shakers, or by buying into a promising technology. An acquisition best serves the interest of the stakeholders not by increasing the size of the company. Its contribution to the competitive advantage of the business principally should be the result of achieving superior a cost position, fortifying brand power or customer loyalty.

Differences between Deals

Overcoming these difficulties requires managers to understand differences between successful and underperforming deals. Consider, for example, and compare acquisitive growth strategies of Vodafone (Anderson and Antal-Mokos 2007; Antal-Mokos and Bauer 2007) and Deutsche Telekom (Antal-Mokos and Bauer 2007), and the strategies that E.ON and the Hungarian MOL Group are pursuing in the consolidation of various segments of the formerly fragmented Central-East European energy markets (Antal-Mokos and Tóth 2006). These environments require markedly different competitive strategies and consequently different M&A approaches. Bower (2001), for example, distinguishes between five major reasons that motivate and justify takeover deals:

1. the 'overcapacity M&A' copes with industry consolidation;
2. the 'geographic roll-up M&A' eliminates competitors in geographically fragmented industries;
3. the 'product and market extension M&A' augments the business portfolio;
4. the 'M&A as R&D' is a substitute for growth through in-house research and development; and
5. the 'industry convergence' R&D exploits value chain reconfigurations by inventing a new industry.

No matter how M&A varieties are delineated, different strategic rationales will drive many aspects of what follows in an acquisition process, and management are well advised to develop a consistent approach to making a deal and achieving expected results by maintaining a strong fit between motives, due diligence questions, negotiation style and integration mode.

Due diligence and negotiation often are viewed as activities in the acquisition process that pave the way toward (and are, to some extent, the last hurdle one has to overcome before) striking the deal and, eventually, changing who is in control. If that is the case, due diligence can easily become a routine exercise that has to be done to check accuracy of financial statements and hidden liabilities. At the same time, negotiations may be dominated by establishing a final, often increased, price and hammering out legal clauses. In European cross-border deals where regulators, unions and other stakeholders also play a crucial role in negotiations, potential acquirers may be forced to enter into lengthy discussions and to assume restrictions on any future restructuring efforts. Such was the case in recent deals in the European banking sector (Härlc 2005). Eventually clinching the deal, then, may not be the reason for declaring immediate success, but the point of no return away from the path to probable failure.

Experience of successful frequent acquirers invariably suggests that due diligence and negotiations can and should serve purposes well beyond the legal and financial aspects. Due diligence may discover any potential deal-breakers or issues that eliminate the initial acquisition rationale altogether (Rovit and Lemire 2003). This requires the establishment of the walk-away price, a constant and dispassionate checking of the strategic rationale in the light of new information and, most importantly, the willingness to kill a deal if its terms no longer fit a set of pre-established criteria. While negotiators can orchestrate an agreement for the parties to sign, a social contract based on the 'spirit' of the deal is also formed, that should be managed to reinforce the economic contract (Fortgang et al. 2003).

Post-Merger Acquisition: How to Move Forward?

Post-merger acquisition can be a daunting task, as many examples suggest. As an introduction to the issues, we take three illustrative examples below.

As early as when there were only rumours that PepsiCo might bid for French Group Danone, analysts speculated about the difficulties of integration, should the acquisition proceed (Matlack 2005). Among the potential hurdles were negative reactions from French customers and cultural barriers to a smooth organizational integration. It was also assumed that Danone managers would depart *en masse* in the case of a hostile takeover as Danone, with its small-firm culture and substantial managerial ownership, was felt by many to be a company run by and for employees.

Similarly, when Oracle concluded its 18-month fight for PeopleSoft, the challenge to make the deal really work included a need to prevent a mass departure of talent of those whom Oracle wanted to keep, while also winning over the customers of PeopleSoft who had been known for their loyalty (Kerstetter 2004). More than a year after the PeopleSoft deal, and after spending about $19 billion on taking over 14 rivals in two years, melding the acquired companies was reportedly one of the toughest jobs in the software industry (Lacy 2006). Analysts appeared sceptical as to how Oracle could implement 'Project Fusion' and create a package of corporate applications that would eventually overtake SAP of Germany. The task is far beyond the integration of software codes; it involves drawing on the best technologies and best talent of the acquired companies and making them work together, as well as convincing customers to wait until the product is ready and not to desert to SAP. Given the importance of retaining talent and customers, it is a critical task of post-merger management to clearly and frequently communicate with employees who wonder how, if at all, they can fit into the new reality, and with customers, who may wonder how, if at all, the company will continue to be able to provide them with enough attention and seamless service.

Finally, as corporate social responsibility advances, it also appears as an issue of the integration agenda. Telefónica of Spain, is a former monopoly that had been fined for abusing its market dominance. It was believed to have a risk based approach to social responsibility, whereas the British company O2 was viewed by many as an industry leader in corporate responsibility in the UK. When Telefónica announced its intention to bid for O2, the potential acquisition was considered as an example in which the experience of the acquired company could provide an opportunity for the acquirer to learn and improve corporate social responsibility (CSR) practices. Indeed, it was reported that the two firms had already been communicating on ethical issues before the closure of the deal (Russel 2005).

As these examples indicate, managerial challenges in the post-deal period are sizeable and diverse. According to Heinrich von Pierer, then CEO of Siemens, 'the real work' begins with integration in the post-merger period (Javidan 2002). The importance of post-merger integration has often been repeated as possibly the most crucial learning from all the failures the corporate M&A world has ever witnessed. It remains to be seen whether integration of itself is responsible for all the disappointment that it has been attributed to, or a brief know-it-all reference to 'soft' issues and 'unforeseen cultural challenges' is offered only to hide lack of robust justification in the first place. Either way, experienced M&A leaders and scholars unanimously assert that creation of much of the new value can only take place in the integration phase. This is precisely where some of the expected synergies fail to materialize; competitive positions of the core business deteriorate, and disgruntled customers and even key employees divert to rivals. Surely, good integration management cannot save a bad deal. Even a good deal can be derailed if integration is managed badly.

It appears to be the dominant view that human integration poses a greater challenge in the course of the post-merger phase than task integration. Yet it is task integration that often receives the most attention in practice, so as to achieve the expected benefits of value creation quickly (Birkinshaw et al. 2000). Relegating the 'people side' of the deal to a position of secondary importance inevitably leads to uncertainty, 'us' and 'them' conflicts and employee resistance. This in turn is likely to limit their ability to realize synergy (Larsson and Finkelstein 1999).

What is referred to as clash of cultures may involve a broad range of differences in the way things get done in merging organizations. Consider the reported difficulties San Francisco-based Del Monte Food was faced with when merging with units of Pittsburgh-based H.J. Heinz. As Harding, Rovit and Corbett (2004) illustrate, the differences between the ways things get done in the two firms (between 'tomato' and 'tomahto' as one executive referred to it) were articulated and strongly felt across the board from organizational philosophies through sales strategies to operating practices.

Wal-Mart's adventure in Germany in the late 1990s, when it acquired many Wertkauf and Interspar stores, also illustrates the importance of cultural issues. While the culture of the acquirer strongly relied on cost controls, the local management teams of these stores found it unacceptable to share hotel rooms, not to mention what they thought of the motivation exercises every morning. Many left their jobs soon after the acquisition (Bert et al. 2003).

Observers of the planned Reebok–Adidas merger also highlighted the different cultures of the two firms, which could make it difficult for a combined firm to achieve the strategic rationale for the deal, namely to increase their chances to compete with Nike by combining forces. The difference between Adidas's focus on sport and its German culture that emphasized control, engineering and production on the one hand, and Reebok's lifestyle-based approach and its US market-driven culture suggested that business integration would not be a simple task (Kiley 2005).

Beyond anecdotal evidence, one of the key persistent questions of integration clearly is that of merging cultures (Cartwright and Cooper 1993). How management deal with this issue depends largely on why the deal has been made in the first place (Kaplan 2001). The best way to approach integration in a merger driven by scale economies significantly differs from that of a scope deal (Vestring et al. 2003). In the former, total integration is needed to achieve expected cost savings that justify the premium the acquirer pays. This involves imposing the culture of the acquirer onto the target organization to expedite absorption. In the latter, quasi-separation or the creation of a completely new culture would result in greater benefit, depending on the overlap between the businesses of the merged companies. A hands-off approach works best only if there is minimal overlap. When there is significant overlap, building a winning culture calls for a blending approach, carefully guarding those values and unique organizational characteristics of the acquired firm that made the deal appear rational at the beginning.

Beyond different approaches to cultural integration lies another important consideration concerning the capabilities of the merging firms. Viewing culture as the container of some of the capabilities whose combination provides the rationale for the transaction, the approach to cultural integration has a direct impact on its economic success or failure. The strategic rationale may be based on a combination of capabilities, whereas in other cases it is the preservation of capabilities, and thus some autonomy of the acquired organization, that is required for the acquisition to create value. The necessary degree of strategic interdependence between the acquirer and the acquired business, and the need for the acquired firm's continuing organizational autonomy together create different integration modes of absorption, preservation, and symbiotic acquisitions (Haspeslagh and Jemison 1991). This also indicates that the merits of different approaches to cultural integration cannot be discussed and explained without bearing in mind the strategic objectives of the transaction.

Considerations outlined above surely are pertinent to a recent acquisition, in which Paris-based L'Oréal, the global leader in cosmetics, took over British-based retailer The Body Shop. This move gave the acquirer, a primarily manufacturing company, access to a retail chain of about 2,000 stores worldwide, which seemed to call for some degree of integration. However, L'Oréal have promised to keep both the brand and the distinct values of The Body Shop intact (*Business Week Online*).

If we consider differences between national cultures and we accept the suggestion that the administrative heritage of organizations is culturally bound (Lubatkin et al. 1998), then the challenge of cultural integration is clearly exacerbated in cross-border deals. If they are done well, however, greater national cultural distance may then enhance cross-border acquisition performance by providing the two merged companies with access to diverse organizational routines and repertoires (Morosini et al. 1998).

As GE Capital learnt by repeated experience, there are a number of issues an acquirer can prepare for before the deal closes. Integration, or at least integration planning, starts well before the ink dries on the paper (Ashkenas et al. 1998). GE Capital was probably also one of the first companies that made serious efforts to institutionalize what it could learn from each and every acquisition it made. Post-acquisition integration management thus became an organizational capability, continuously improved as the company intentionally capitalized on the experience it accumulated and strengthened by dedicated integration managers (Ashkenas and Francis 2000).

In many cases, particularly in scale-driven deals, speed is of the essence, if for no other reason than the detrimental effects of prolonged uncertainty. Management structure, positions and reporting relationships and expected lay-offs can easily preoccupy the mind, diverting efforts from customer relationships towards managing relationships internally. Delaying tough decisions and waiting for the right time to communicate them often result in exactly what the acquirer may want to avoid: declining morale, losing unknown talents, or lack of buy-in into a common vision. Even more deceptive is to believe that a merger can be a neat and clean routine process. Anyone who thinks they have seen a merger without pain has probably not looked around hard enough. The sooner the 'organizational fog' clears, the sooner the firms can set out to focus on true integration by mutual learning, improving processes and creating new business opportunities. On the other hand, acquisitions for unique capabilities, values and processes and will probably benefit from a more gradual and measured approach.

Even moving fast should not mean lack of respect and unwillingness to listen and learn. Yet acquirers often follow an exclusively 'telling' approach to post-merger communication. Particularly in scale acquisitions of familiar businesses and in cross-border investments in emerging economies, it is tempting to believe that the acquirer possesses the key to business wisdom and the acquired company is there to learn and accept the way it is, which may explain why the immediate post-acquisition period is often characterized by imposed one-way knowledge transfer from the acquirer to the acquired and why high-quality reciprocal knowledge transfer occurs only in the long run (Bresman et al. 1999).

Conclusions

In this concluding section we attempt to formulate three overarching principles that are applicable throughout the various phases and activities of the acquisition process to ensure doing the right deal in the right way. In particular, we emphasize the importance of process discipline, prudent decision-making and integrative leadership.

Mergers and acquisitions require a great deal of *discipline* throughout the process. Serial acquirers build safeguards in the process to ensure that the deal in the making indeed contributes to building a great company, and develop organizational routines to avoid costly mistakes. These include:

- having each potential deal scrutinized by executives without direct interest in either making or breaking the deal;
- requiring board-level approval for deals of certain size and type;
- insisting on careful comparisons with alternative forms such as alliances and entrepreneurship;
- sticking to the walk-away price instead of 'fitting' the investment thesis to the requirements of the sellers or negotiating away expected synergies in return of gaining approval from host country governments or unions;
- establishing incentives for long-term success of acquisitions rather than for closing the deal itself

These safeguards are all traits of disciplined acquirers.

Management must understand that, in an era of industry-wide merger mania, finding good deals comes second to avoiding bad ones.

Prudence in M&A decision-making calls for having options and paying attention to detail. Avoiding bad deals is certainly more likely when there are other options to walk away to. Continuously considering and evaluating a number of options is a trait not only of private equity firms but also of many successful acquirers. Having options on the table for the management to consider can also reduce efforts and costs spent on the detailed evaluation of, and planning for, a series of single options that may prove to be wrong and are rejected. Experience suggests that meticulous attention to detail can improve the odds better than focusing on a few masterstrokes. This goes way beyond doing a detailed legal and financial due diligence and should involve building a robust business case for the deal to happen, understanding the drivers and dynamics of competition and how the merger will change that, developing a solid model to check increased earnings potential and substantiating all the key assumptions on which the deal rationale rests. A similarly thorough approach in the negotiations will help avoid too many skeletons in the cupboard, while an exhaustive planning for post-merger integration should start well before the deal is closed.

Finally, *integrative leadership* is perhaps the one single most important prerequisite to a successful deal. M&A processes present numerous conflicts and trade-offs that need to be carefully managed and balanced. Emotions can rise, hype may escalate, pressure can heighten, idea champions argue and interests clash, employees of the acquired company look for security, managers may be in need of a compelling vision, key customers may require top level assurance. A wide range of ethical issues – as manifested through accounting practices, negotiation and communication tactics and managerial behaviour – may arise from conflicts of interests between managers and owners and from conflicts between members of the broader stakeholder community. Honesty in communication with external as well as internal stakeholders, the ability to provide vision and achieve alignment and the personal power to take charge and supreme integrity are key characteristics of M&A process leaders. They understand that their task and responsibility are much broader than conjuring up a master plan and engineering an agreement.

References

Anderson, J. and Antal-Mokos, Z. (2007), 'M&A in Mobile Telephony: Industry Dynamics', in Meyer, K.E. and Estrin, S. (eds) *Acquisition Strategies in European Emerging Economies* (Basingstoke: Palgrave Macmillan).

Antal-Mokos, Z. and Bauer, A. (2007), 'T-Mobile Hungary and the Hungarian Mobile Telecommunications Market', in Meyer, K.E. and Estrin, S. (eds) *Acquisition Strategies in European Emerging Economies* (Basingstoke: Palgrave Macmillan).

Antal-Mokos, Z., and Tóth, K. (2007), 'MOL: The Emergence of the Central European MNE', in Meyer, K.E. and Estrin, S. (eds) *Acquisition Strategies in European Emerging Economies* (Basingstoke: Palgrave Macmillan).

Ashkenas, R.N. and Francis, S.C. (2000), 'Integration Managers: Special Leaders for Special Times', *Harvard Business Review* November–December, pp. 108–16.

Ashkenas, R.N., DeMonaco, L.J. and Francis, S.C. (1998), 'Making the Deal Real: How GE Capital Integrates Acquisitions', *Harvard Business Review* January–February, pp. 5–15.

Bert, A., MacDonald, T. and Herd, T. (2003), 'Two Merger Integration Imperatives: Urgency and Execution', *Strategy and Leadership* 31(3), pp. 42–9.

Birkinshaw, J., Bresman, H. and Hakanson, L. (2000), 'Managing the Post-acquisition Integration Process: How the Human Integration and Task Integration Processes Interact to Foster Value Creation', *Journal of Management Studies* 37, pp. 395–425.

Bower, J.L. (2001), 'Not all M&As are Alike – and that Matters', *Harvard Business Review* March, pp. 93–101.

Bresman, H., Birkinshaw, J. and Nobel, R. (1999), 'Knowledge Transfer in International Acquisitions', *Journal of International Business Studies* 30(3) (Fall), pp. 439–52.

Business Week Online (2006), 'L'Oréal's Latest Leap', 17 March, http://www.businessweek. com.

Cartwright, S. and Cooper, C.L. (1993), 'The Role of Culture Compatibility in Successful Organizational Marriage', *Academy of Management Executive* 7(2), pp. 57–70.

Christofferson, S.A., McNish, R.S. and Sias, D.L. (2004), 'Where Mergers Go Wrong', *McKinsey on Finance* Winter, pp. 1–6.

Dyer, J.H., Kale, P. and Singh, H. (2004), 'When to Ally and When to Acquire', *Harvard Business Review* July–August, pp. 109–15.

Fortgang, R.S., Lax, D.A. and Sebenius, J.K. (2003), 'Negotiating the Spirit of the Deal', *Harvard Business Review OnPoint*, February.

Gammelgaard, J. (2004), 'Access to Competence: An Emerging Acquisition Motive', *European Business Forum* Spring, pp. 44–7.

Harding, D. and Rovit, S. (2004), 'Building Deals on Bedrock', *Harvard Business Review* September, pp. 124–8.

Harding, D., Rovit, S. and Corbett, A. (2004), 'Avoid Merger Meltdown: Lessons from Mergers and Acquisitions Leaders', *Strategy and Innovation Newsletter* September–October, pp. 3–5.

Härle, P. (2005), 'Negotiating Better Cross-border Banking Mergers in Europe', *McKinsey Quarterly*, web exclusive, November, http://www.mckinseyquarterly.com.

Haspeslagh, P. and Jemison, D.B. (1991), *Creating Value through Corporate Renewal* (New York: The Free Press).

Javidan, M. (2002), 'Siemens CEO Heinrich von Pierer on Cross-border Acquisitions', interview, *Academy of Management Executive* 16(1), pp. 13–15.

Kaplan, N. (2001), 'Assimilate, Integrate, or Leave Alone', *Journal of Business Strategy* January–February, pp. 23–5.

Kerstetter, J. (2004), 'Finally, Oracle Nails PeopleSoft', *Business Week Online* 13 December, http://www.businessweek.com.

Kiley, D. (2005), 'Reebok and Adidas: A Good Fit', *Business Week Online* 4 August, http://www.businessweek.com.

Lacy, S. (2006), 'The Hardest Job in Silicon Valley', *Business Week Online* 23 January, http://www.businessweek.com.

Larsson, R. and Finkelstein. S. (1999), 'Integrating Strategic, Organizational, and Human Resource Perspectives on Mergers and Acquisitions: A Case Survey of Synergy Realization', *Organization Science* 10(1) (January–February), pp. 1–26.

Lubatkin, M., Calori, R., Very, P. and Veiga, J.F. (1998), 'Managing Mergers across Borders: A Two-nation Exploration of Nationally Bound Administrative Heritage', *Organization Science* 9(6), pp. 670–84.

Matlack, C. (2005), 'Could PepsiCo Digest Danone?', *Business Week Online* 21 July, http://www.businessweek.com.

Mitchell, W. and Capron. L. (2002), 'Managing Acquisitions to Change and Survive', *European Business Forum* Spring, pp. 51–5.

Morosini, P., Shane, S. and Singh, H. (1998), 'National Cultural Distance and Cross-border Acquisition Performance', *Journal of International Business Studies* 29(1) (Spring), pp. 137–49.

Rovit, S. and Lemire, C. (2003), 'Your Best M&A Strategy', *Harvard Business Review* March, pp. 16–17.

Russel, J. (2005), 'Mergers and Acquisitions – Madrid Calling for O2', *Ethical Corporation Online* 17 November, http://www.ethicalcorp.com

Sirower, M. (2003/4), 'Becoming a Prepared Acquirer', *European Business Forum* Winter, pp. 55–9.

Vestring, T., King, B. and Rouse, T. (2003), 'Should You Always Merge Cultures?', *Harvard Management Update* May, pp. 3–4.

Chapter 8
Supply Chain Management

Douglas MacBeth

Introduction: The Supply Chain Concept

A supply chain 'consists of all parties involved, directly or indirectly, in fulfilling a customer request. The supply chain includes not only the manufacturers and suppliers, but also transporters, warehouses, retailers and even customers themselves. Within each organization, such as a manufacturer, the supply chain includes all functions involved in receiving and fulfilling a customer request. These functions include, but are not limited to, new product development, marketing, operations, distribution, finance and customer service' (Chopra and Meindl 2007, p. 3). It has also been described as a 'network of materials, information and services processing links' (Chen and Paulraj 2004), 'an integrative approach to manage the total flow of the distribution channel from supplier to ultimate user (Cooper and Ellram 1993), or as 'a logistics network consisting of suppliers, manufacturing centres, warehouses, distribution centres and retail outlets as well as the raw material, work in process and finished goods that flow between the facilities' (Simchi-Levi et al. 2000). Therefore, supply chains are more like units of analysis rather than a single entity. Even the term *chain* limits the scope since a particular organization is likely to have multiple customers and many suppliers. It also may be active to differing degrees in multiple chains. In this sense the chain is really one of many routes through the organization and the other firms involved that contribute to satisfying many final customers. Technically we should talk of networks but so far we do not know how to manage such complexity and so we can try to improve single chains and hope that the interactions between chains at the level of the single organization is manageable.

What has brought this into focus is the realization, in Thomas Freidman's (2005) terms, that 'the world is flat'. What he means is that the competitive playing field has been levelled such that countries that once had competitive advantages are now being challenged by newly emerging countries who are able to create advantages from the forces that reduce the comparable advantage of competitors in global markets. The essence of the argument is that global communications networks (interlinked software that allows parallel and efficient joint working across time zones) have permitted low labour cost countries to become significant players. Added to this is the opening of these countries' markets as they join the World Trade Organization. This permits, facilitates and demands the freer flow of internationally mobile investments as multinational companies look to these countries as places to utilize low cost labour. As local populations gain more disposable income, supportive government policies must be in place to enable companies to produce their products and services and potentially provide new buyers. China and India are of major interest in the early years of the twenty-first century for these reasons. Of course, many countries have the potential to become significant global players and a number of them are featured in this international business handbook.

In the case of India and China we might talk of newly developing countries. Viewed over the longer term, we have to realize that both these countries have traded globally for centuries. These countries are experiencing more of a re-emergence into world trade after long being constrained by political regimes from interacting in this way (see Deloitte Research 2006). The trends are impressive. Goldman Sachs (2003) predicted that China will overtake the gross domestic product (GDP) of Japan by 2006 and Germany in 2009. India lags China in this respect by about 15 years. China is forecast to overtake the USA in 2041.

China has taken a large share of recent foreign direct investments (FDIs). Western companies have rushed to become part of the bandwagon of its expansion and growth. China developed into manufactured goods while India developed more along the IT service and call centre directions. Increasingly, both compete against each other in all areas. Thus the global supply chains are proving to be somewhat mobile as newly emerging and cheaper countries gain some short-term advantage. Other aspects of the supply chain begin to have greater impact as rapid salary inflation erodes the labour cost benefits. The cost and time of transporting goods that have relatively short sales windows (time sensitive and fashion goods such as high technology goods where goods are superseded frequently) across oceans limits responsiveness. Proximity, in geographical and culture terms, becomes more important than simply low labour cost production. For these reasons, most automobile and computer producers in Europe are Japanese or American.

Supply Chain Concepts and Architecture

Market behaviour that results from capitalism has a long history. The nature of economic thought largely is built on the belief that competition for resources is both necessary and efficient in propelling progress and benefits society generally as well as entrepreneurs. Adam Smith (1776) is much quoted as one of the main proponents of Free Market principles, recognizes that greed on its own is a powerful motivator:

> It is not from the benevolence of the butcher, the brewer or the baker that we expect our dinner, but from their regard to their own interest. We address ourselves, not to their humanity, but to their self-love, and never talk to them of our own necessities, but of their advantages. (Smith 1776, i.ii.2)

Greed, however, is not the only factor, as Smith also observes:

> How selfish ... man may be supposed, there are evidently some principles in his nature, which interest him in the fortune of others, and render their happiness necessary to him, though he derives nothing from it except the pleasure of seeing it. (Smith 1759)

Thus we can recognize that in the final market place, where a consumer makes a choice to buy from only one supplier, by definition, that supplier wins the business and all others must lose that opportunity. It is a win-lose, or zero sum, game. That is to say, if player A wins ten units, player B must lose ten units, +10 and –10 = zero. This logic is clear and unchallenged. What has changed is that this is not the only logic possible when repeated games take place between players who are in the business of working together as supplier and customer over a more extended period of time. Cooperation provides the possibility that both players may get some benefit from their business transactions such that we can describe a win-win game or non-zero sum game. We will return to these points later when we consider the managerial choices open to companies as they decide how they want to play the supply chain game.

When Henry Ford first developed his mass production car company (c. 1910), he would not have talked about supply chains. To his credit, he did understand the need to coordinate all of the factors of production from raw materials taken from the ground to finished product in the ownership of the customer. In technical terms his industrial structure or architecture can be described as complete vertical integration. Ford owned all of the facilities required to produce vehicles all the way along the inbound supply chain and out to distributors. With ownership came control. An unfortunate side effect was corporate and manufacturing system rigidity – an inflexibility to respond to external forces. The Model T was hugely significant in creating both a new and powerful industry and the means for working people to buy the product since its price reduced from around $850 to $220 over its manufacturing lifetime. Ford adapted the meat disassembly activities at abattoirs to create a moving assembly chain. In this way, the car came past workers at a fixed rate. The 'any colour as long as it is black' mentality and dedicated production equipment meant, however, that Ford was not able to introduce significant product variety. When consumers demanded more choice and variety, the monopoly Ford had created in low-cost cars was challenged by a new industrial model operated by General Motors.

In the meantime Toyota was beginning to build cars but, following a trip to learn how Ford did it, they went home more impressed with the American supermarkets where a simple shelf stock replenishment method was developed into the Toyota production system (Monden 1983). Today this is called Kanban and is integral to the Just-in-Time approach to synchronize assembly operations. Toyota developed a different architecture that focuses on what the product brand owning/assembly company does well and allows others in their chain to concentrate on what they do well. This division of labour is reminiscent of work by Adam Smith described in his *Wealth of Nations* (1776). Toyota's architecture is built on a series of tiers, like a multi-level wedding cake, with Toyota only interacting with first-tier suppliers while they become responsible for all of the supply chain leading into them. Toyota still buys the same number of parts. They buy them from 200 to 300 first tier suppliers or system integrators who in turn deal with the many thousands of lower tier suppliers. Being on the first tier means continuous and meaningful access to the customer (Toyota) and maintaining a co-destiny relationship with them. If the Toyota chain succeeds, so too do all the participating companies in that chain. However, in Japan it is very unlikely that a first-tier supplier will be allowed to supply one of Toyota's competitors. In a sense this is a form of outsourcing – often buying from organizations within the equity share 'family' group known as a *keiretsu*. There is a high level of control and it also can often involve exchanges of shareholdings and staff. It is close in concept to vertical integration but the ownership boundaries are more blurred.

A variation on this model has become popular in electronics production where major brand companies progressively have decided that manufacturing is not core to their competitive advantage. They have outsourced very many of the features associated with design, production, distribution and service to systems integrators. System integrators are tend to be massive companies that deal with many customers across the globe. The brand companies do not have the same 'control' as in the Toyota case and so have to influence and manage their suppliers in more considered ways.

The final architecture is best shown by the Smart car (now part of Daimler–Chrysler) which has taken the equivalent first-tier suppliers and made them even more important so that they can be described as 0.5 tiers (Siekman 2002). In this model, eight integrators are co-located on the Smart production line and are jointly responsible for output and quality such that none is paid if there is a quality problem in a car. They were also responsible for design and manufacturing of their module, investing much of their own money in solving the initial problems so that each module joins together into the finished car. They have to be responsible for all inbound materials and the management of the upstream supply chain. With two other companies involved in support services the whole vehicle is built by only ten supply chains.

Each of these configurations of manufacturing operations demonstrate the need for close coordination and integration of information flows and joint decision-making in order to avoid wastes of over or underproduction and delays, while quality must be high and continually improving to reduce waste and add value wherever possible.

Figure 8.1 indicates the nature of all of these changes. In Ford's system (especially at the River Rouge Plant) all of the stages (except the recycling one perhaps) were owned by Ford.

Subsequent models of manufacturing implemented variations on the boundaries of the firm so that by the time we get to the Smart example or perhaps even more by the story of the launch of the Microsoft Xbox (O'Brien 2001) it is possible to think of a production system where the nominal owner of the brand does no manufacturing at all and does not in any way own the other parties on whom it is completely dependent. Nike is perhaps the most famous organization of this type.

In such circumstance a number of issues become paramount, as below.

- How to choose partner organizations.
- How to ensure that they wish to cooperate with you.
- How to create a structure that is effective and provides a fair economic return for efforts.
- How to manage for efficiency and effectiveness in satisfying the chosen customers.

We will return to some of these issues in the final section of this chapter.

Physical Logistics

The movement of materials and information in these situations is the glue that joins disparate groups together and at the same time is the oil that keeps the whole system moving and minimizing friction, both in the physical and the managerial sense.

In all logistics operations there are common considerations.

- There often is a direct relationship between costs and volume/weight as well as speed.
- Efficiency in the movement of goods means building bigger loads to use space better, otherwise we are paying to move air.

You do not need to own all of the factors of production
You need to be sure that they are activated when you need them

Figure 8.1   Organizational tasks

- A transport vehicle's journey is more economic if it is loaded in both directions.
- The quality of a finished good for dispatch to customers must be protected from damage in transit. Theft of anything of value must be protected against.

Logistics systems are built around inventory storage and goods movement and, as Figure 8.2 shows, the concept of hub and spoke, which is one of the key principles.

Small amounts of supplies are collected at a hub where they are aggregated into bigger loads (building bulk). These loads then are transported along relatively fixed routes and efficient transport modes (water, rail, road and air) until they reach the destination hub where they are disaggregated (break bulk) back into their individual sizes and delivered by very flexible means (delivery vans) to their ultimate destinations. Of course the logistics companies are trying at the same time to find loads that can be sent in the opposite direction and help pay for the transport infrastructure (marginal revenue).

The need for the hub also highlights the need for warehousing since this is where the conversion of bulk and packaging often take place. However, while some elements of the logistic processes add place value for a customer the number of times a package is lifted and laid, counted, put away, retrieved, repacked and reloaded to a vehicle can be very wasteful of resources and a potential source of handling damage. Given the effort to produce high quality material in the factory, the worst thing to do would be to damage them en route to the customers. This is a major focus of the logistics effort. The cost in the design, recycling and re-use of appropriate packaging may quickly be amortized as they will lower returns and increase available stock for sale at the full ticket value. Packaging has to protect goods from transport and handling damage and degradation through contact with other substances such as salty sea air, and often there is the need to ensure that theft of the item is made more difficult. Labelling parts can be an element of a joint marketing and operations strategy. Labelling using RFID tags can facilitate rapid storing and picking, life cycle tracking and delivery process assurance for customers who want to check on the status of their goods. RFID are radio frequency identifiers

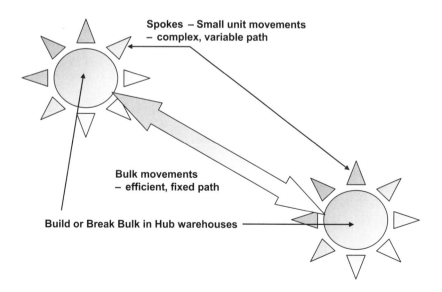

Figure 8.2   Logistics hub and spoke

that can provide identity and other information, often in adverse conditions, without human intervention or even close proximity between tag and reader.

One significant development from Wal-Mart was in the way they built their store expansion process was based on the hub and spoke logic. Their hub is a Wal-Mart distribution centre and the spokes are the routes to the stores. In order to keep stores replenished and without large on-site inventories, they introduced the concept of cross-docking in the distribution centres (DCs). This works by bringing bulk goods into one side of the DC. Rather than putting them onto shelves in the warehouse, the goods go straight across from the inbound dock to be loaded into vehicles at the outbound dock. These consignments are sent with other required goods to replenish goods sold at retail outlets. In this way time and cost is saved in the warehouse. This reduces the handling costs. However, vehicles on the inbound side can be made to wait longer to be unloaded and to some extent the inventory has been moved from warehouse to vehicle. The trade-off of having extra vehicles is more than offset by reductions in inventory holding costs and improved response rates to actual demand in the stores, on an overnight replenishment cycle.

Away from the retail sector, the logistics impact of different physical assembly or production processes is also worth considering. If demand has to be forecast and the uniqueness of a product is determined close to its point of origin, there is a great danger of having too much inventory of goods for which there is no real demand. Conversely, too much demand cannot be satisfied because it takes too long to go through all of the serial processes to produce the product. Thus in some fashion sectors' plans have to be made for many months ahead and are difficult to change without changes in technology. For example, Benetton found an acceptable way to colour woollen garments rather than have to depend on orders placed on the wool yarn producers many months earlier. In this way they could react to actual customer requests and fill them by dying garments to order. In other products this idea is called postponement, where the final configuration (based on real customer demand) is done as late in the overall cycle as possible so that a relatively standardized product is converted into one that is more unique to the individual customers.

Whenever suppliers and customers are in different countries, another key factor comes into play. It is important to recognize that in any business exchange, companies must know when the exchange actually takes place, that is to say, when a supplier passes ownership of their goods to the customer. Of course, the supplier also has to feel confident that the agreed terms of trade are adhered to and that payment promises will be honoured. Transfer of ownership is important as each party needs to know if they are responsible for paying freight charges to a carrier or insurance cover to an insurance company. Figure 8.3 lists some of these key terms (see http://www.sitpro.org.uk/trade/incoterms.html).

It is also important to understand these terms of trade when costs of supply are being evaluated for different suppliers in different geographical regions. In the UK, some of the supermarkets are now asking to be quoted ex works or, as they describe it, factory gate prices. In this way they can begin to evaluate whether they, as buyers, might be able to get better 'deals' from logistics providers rather than have their suppliers organize the physical distribution for them.

Another level of bureaucracy involves customs regulations and approvals for exporting and importing. Some of the INCO terms include these costs. More important are the time delays that can occur as trade tries to cross national borders. For this reason many of the system integrators working for global customers have local customs clearance facilities either close by their plants or in many cases on the same production campus location (e.g., Flextronics who were launch suppliers for the Microsoft Xbox).

Group E - Departure	Group F – Main Carriage Unpaid
Available at Sellers premises	Seller delivers to Carrier
	–FCA Free Carrier
	–FAS Free Alongside Ship
ExW Ex Works (No export duty paid)	–FOB Free on Board
Group C – Main Carriage Paid	Group D – Arrival
Seller contracts carriage but not risk after delivery to shipper	Seller assumes all costs and risks until destination
–CFR Cost and Freight	–DAF Delivered at Frontier
–CIF Cost Insurance and Freight	–DES Delivered Ex Ship
–CPT Carriage Paid To	–DEQ Delivered Ex Quay
–CIP Carriage and Insurance Paid	–DDU Delivered Duty Unpaid
	–DDP Delivered (Import) Duty Paid

Figure 8.3   International Trade INCO terms

Logistics brings into sharp focus the trade-off between inventory and information. Inventory is needed for a variety of reasons. Stores are a repository of resources that companies anticipate will be needed, for which there are no immediate orders. Of itself, therefore, inventory is wasteful since it consumes resources and requires more resources to look after and hold securely. The essence of the Toyota method is to reduce the need for inventory by reacting to actual customer demand and only producing when there is a direct need. Physical movement of goods is not instantaneous and there are many potential delays that may vary in duration in the overall process. In order to ensure some defined level of customer service it is necessary to decouple demand from supply by having stores of inventory in different forms and at different points in the chain. Good information, particularly about real demand and the time to move materials, reduces the need to have excessive inventory and so reduces the cost of operating the logistics system. The point at which actual customer orders become clear in the system is described as the order entry point. Measuring order fulfilment performance enables organizations to establish benchmarks for efficiency and responsiveness in the overall chain. Before the order entry point, it makes sense to be efficient and perhaps source from low cost sources around the world. Once firm customer orders are received, perhaps a more locally based and responsive system is required. Often inventory will also be needed here. At its most responsive, the time limit for a supply system to react may be zero. That is, if your product is not on the shelf for the customer to choose then the sale can be lost to a competitor. If however you had some visibility of the customer needing that product in a certain future time period, it may have been possible to initiate production, just in time to meet that demand. The just in time system is one of the key messages out of the Toyota experience and it is to that we now turn.

Understanding the Messages of Lean Thinking

For a number of decades while Toyota was developing its Toyota Production System, its competitors in the West were looking at Japan and did not understand what they observed. They saw individual activities make extensive use of, for example, robotics, quality circles, just-in-time and Kanban activations but they did not perceive the big picture. When they raised their eyes they saw a production sector that was closely aligned with and by a governmental process (MITI) that supported production and exports but limited the opportunity for outside companies to compete in the Japanese home market. The justification made was that when an example of good performance by a Japanese company was reported, the typical reaction was that this was a uniquely Japanese result. It was *JAPAN Inc.* and was not a serious threat to international business because it was so geographically and culturally proscribed.

However, a research team coordinated by MIT in the USA had seen methods and tools in Japanese automobile assembly plants that they recognized as being so different from current practice that they felt the need to research and understand what was going on. Thus grew a research project that resulted in the publication of a book that was to change the world though perhaps not in the ways the authors envisaged. That book was *The Machine that Changed the World* (Womack et al. 1990), soon to be followed by another, *Lean Thinking* (Womack and Jones 2003). These volumes expanded the areas of application outside the automotive industry and into many other sectors.

One of the most important effects of the first of these books was that, in the global benchmarking exercise on which it reported, the best of the companies was Toyota in Japan. The second best plant was a Ford facility in Mexico (albeit one they operated with Mazda of Japan). At a stroke this blew all the Western excuses away. Here was a plant, at that time, in a developing country that was operated by an arch advocate of the old ways of thinking – mass production that was developed by Ford for the River Rouge plant. The Toyota system was found not to be uniquely Japanese, it was a system that was transferable and effective in other areas of the world without the need for local government support of the type previously suggested. Womack et al. (1990) called it *lean production*, because it used many fewer resources to produce more variety, more quickly and effectively than any other. More recently Liker (2005, pp. 37–41) tried to capture the essence of 'the Toyota Way' in 14 management principles, as follows:

1. Base management decisions on a long-term philosophy, even at the expense of short-term financial goals.
2. Create continuous process flows to bring problems to the surface.
3. Use 'pull' systems to avoid over production.
4. Level out the work load (*heijunka*).
5. Build a culture of stopping to fix problems, to get quality right the first time.
6. Standardized tasks are the foundation for continuous improvement and employee empowerment.
7. Use visual control so no problems are hidden.
8. Use only reliable, thoroughly tested technology that serves your people and processes
9. Grow leaders who thoroughly understand the work, live the philosophy and teach it to others.
10. Develop exceptional people and teams who follow your company's philosophy.
11. Respect your extended network of partners and suppliers by challenging them and helping them improve.
12. Go and see for yourself to understand the situation thoroughly (*genchi genbutsu*).
13. Make decisions slowly by consensus, thoroughly considering all options; implement decisions rapidly (*hoshin kanri*).
14. Become a learning organization through relentless reflection (*hansei*) and continuous improvement (*kaizen*).

Liker (2005) emphasizes the cultural aspects of the system for good reason. It is the facilitating aspect of interpersonal and inter-organizational negotiation and collaboration. There are other aspects of equal importance that come more from the earlier study and represent a coherent approach to thinking in chain terms and make it attractive to be a supplier member of such a chain. We can divide these into three areas. Firstly, there is the treatment of suppliers on the inbound side. Secondly, there is all the internal best practice about how to make factories, (and indirect activities as well) flow and continually improve. What is important in this is the means of promoting and developing the design concepts and putting them into practice in terms of product and processes. Thirdly, the way in which the distribution process and the customer orientation is translated to make real the belief in a 'customer for life'.

Our earlier discussion of supply chain architectures indicated the major contribution of tiering and use of the first-tier suppliers as system integrators. In this way Toyota retain control while allowing the supplier to excel at what they are good at. This requires a long-term perspective that recognizes suppliers must make a margin on their business to stay economically viable, to be able to grow and develop and become preferred providers. Making a profit provides confidence in the future relationship and enables them to invest in the continuous improvements that are so necessary for Toyota to outperform competitors' chains. Toyota only want to pay suppliers for work done by the supplier for Toyota; they thus examine the supplier's cost structure to determine that they are not cross-subsidizing competitors' production lines which require more indirect costs such as obsolescence, supervision, poor quality and rework. Building on suppliers' expertise means that they provide much of the technological insight into their part of new product designs and, as a result, design trade-offs and compromises are made in the light of considered opinion and implementation is rapid in line with Liker's Principle 13. Suppliers are set target cost standards for supplied parts. To achieve these goals, they are expected to innovate to reduce the costs of production continuously. Toyota supports them by ensuring an agreed profit margin so that they can plan sensibly for their own future investments and development. By approving the profit margins between Toyota and the suppliers, concentration moves onto the real and total cost of doing the business. Both sides then collaboratively explore ways to reduce these costs and share in the benefits of doing so. Suppliers may transfer their knowledge internally to product lines making competitors goods. Simultaneously, this allows suppliers to make larger profits from goods sold to competitors and reduces their overheads.

Design is one area that spans inbound supply, material processing and assembly, and through sales to after-sales involvement. In this process the chief engineer, Shusa or respected leader takes full responsibility for the team for a particular product and stays with that product through each of its redesigns and re-aunches as the product evolves over time. The Shusa selects the team. Individuals' career advancement is dependent on performance in the team rather than the core discipline from which the individual is drawn. It is the responsibility of the individual to ensure that they network with others. They gauge their efforts by trying to answer two questions: 'who will vouch that I worked today?' and 'who else knows what I did today?' Of course supplier and customer representatives will be on the team as will be representatives from all production stages so that all the inter-dependencies in the design decisions are fully investigated and agreed. Once the product is launched the Shusa's core team will follow the product into the market place to see if the promise to the customer was met and identify what lessons can be learnt that lead to changing the way things are done for the next incarnation. In traditional Western business practice, customer contact would be restricted to sales or marketing and would exclude technical engineering experts. Toyota by contrast place great importance of customer satisfaction and the direct learning opportunity of talking with real customers. This opportunity is one that should not be delegated or allocated to those who do not understand the technological implications of the information gathered.

In terms of the level of specification given to suppliers this is more likely to be at the level of functional specifications, that is what the part of the system is required to do rather than how it is to be done. The supplier is regarded as the expert in translating the functional specification into the detailed specifications of what and how things are to be made to deliver the required performance. Also important is an understanding of where individual contributions come into contact with other systems so that when these disparate systems are brought together at assembly they can join together seamlessly and quickly without delays or malfunctions.

Another aspect of the importance of design is the realization that if organizations believe cost of retaining a customer is cheaper than the costs of finding new ones, suppliers should never give the end user cause to defect to another brand. This means that even if the new car warranty period has expired it still makes sense to fix the problem. If this is the practice then repairs costs are more the supplier's responsibility than the customer's or Toyota. The effect is that the design mindset shifts from designing for a limited warranty period in a planned obsolescence way and more to designing so that the likelihood of any failure is very small indeed hence the costs of any repairs are not borne by Toyota. Consequently, the reliability of their products is both a marketing edge and production costs are reduced.

The final link in this chain is out to distributors and customers. Here again Toyota works with reduced numbers of distributors to reach as many loyal customers as they can. For many years they have sold the integrated package of product and services (in terms of financial support to facilitate the purchasing process, insurance, etc.) as well as tracking the needs of their product users so that as the customers' situations develop, Toyota's sales people are able to suggest different versions of the product that best suit their new needs. This tracking of *customer requirement evolution* is only now being used extensively in the West through customer loyalty programmes that allow for the same tracking of spending patterns and the associated targeted marketing of a unique selling proposition.

In some senses, the challenges of operating in this way are relatively easier for the automobile industry. It is. after all. a relatively mature product line with a life cycle measured in years rather than months and with an efficient mix of volume production of standardized parts assembled to order and 'pulled' out of the system by actual customer demand. Toyota still represents one of the best examples of a supply chain in action with links through from supplier's supplier through to distribution's customer and as such it demonstrates much of the joined-up thinking that supply chains are all about. However, the spread of the lean production approach has not been as extensive as Womack et al. (1990) predicted. In many cases products need to be more customized from less standardized parts. It can also be argued that more service-oriented businesses need even more flexibility in satisfying customers than is implied in an overly lean approach. These arguments still rage. There remain many advocates who say that thinking in process and continuous improvement terms and using all of the skills of the people in the extended team are principles that are completely transferable to other geographies and to other business activities.

Toyota demonstrated the benefits of cooperation with their first-tier suppliers. Organizations have to choose those with whom they want to collaborate over a significant time period and those where competition is still the most sensible option because goods are spot purchased.

Managing Cooperation and Competition

Pareto described the property of the distribution of value or wealth in a population according to his 80:20 rule. This asserts that 80 per cent of the total value is contributed by only 20 per cent of the participants. This principle allows the division of the population of suppliers (and customers) on the basis of their relative attractiveness and contribution to the economic wellbeing of the analysing party.

For suppliers we can use a portfolio approach modelled on the original work by Kraljic (1983). For many companies, once their purchasing spend is analysed, it is possible to recognize the relative importance of some suppliers compared to others. Strategic contractors are those on whom the customer is highly dependent. Typically they have *turnkey contracts* to provide integrated systems. If they did not support the customer then the customer's business would be at serious risk of failure. Such suppliers need to be managed very carefully and if possible a partnering, cooperative approach is implemented. All of the Toyota first-tier suppliers are in this quadrant. At the other extreme are generic activities where many suppliers sell standardized products and commodities. They only differentiate themselves by the unit price. Here the appropriate tactic is to make the market as efficient as possible and to compete aggressively to reduce prices since, if one supplier fails there are lots more to take their place.

Bottleneck items are those that are unique to the customer and are not of great interest to the supplier as their value or volume is too low to validate decisions to build a dedicated business stream. In such circumstances, it is better, where possible, for the customer to replace the unique requirement with a generic specification or alternatively ask a commodity supplier also to manage bottleneck items as part of a wider group of items they supply. This approach enables customers to get better service and suppliers adds more value and may become strategically important to the customer.

Leverage is where value and or volume are such that winning the customer's business is attractive for a number of suppliers. The spot market is likely to be the source for the best price. In commodity and leverage sourcing, the use of e-auctions or reverse auctions (where the price is bid down until the auction is ended) has proved a useful technique to establish low market prices on single transactions. What also seems to be a reality is that the next attempt to reduce prices this way is less likely to show the same benefits, because this is a win-lose game. Suppliers do not want to be under pressure on prices all the time so auctions and commodity markets are less attractive than being a preferred supplier. Thus suppliers have similar versions of the matrix to establish which customers are most attractive and with whom they wish to align themselves. In an ideal situation a customer would choose their preferred supplier who would in turn consider the customer as their preferred customer. In such circumstances cooperative behaviour can flourish.

Cooperative behaviour largely mirrors that indicated in the Toyota case except that the single customer linkage in the Toyota case is replaced by multiple customers and multiple suppliers. Here again, the need is to influence good suppliers by being a good customer so that the innovative ideas from the supplier expert are offered to the good or preferred customer before their other customers. Capturing the most innovative and productive suppliers is a good way to build competitive supply chains.

At this point we realize the limitations of the chain analogy for many organizations. Both customer and supplier are active in a number of chains, even in different industry sectors at the same time.

The network view (Gadde et al. 2003) argues that individual firms should not be the focus of attention since they are embedded in extended networks from where opportunities and threats

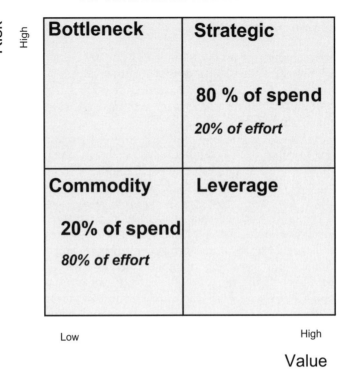

Figure 8.4   Modified Kraljic portfolio

emanate and that these have both an economic and a social dimension. It is the relationships and interactions focal firms have with their extended network that defines the business opportunity. The portfolio argument suggests that some of these relationships should be operating according to the original rules of transaction cost economics (Coase 1937; Williamson 1985) that is in the area of commodities and leverage. For the strategic quadrant, organizations need to operate more collaboratively and use the network logic to position their business where they can best influence the future. This will require access to complementary resources from customers and suppliers to build a robust and dynamically adaptive chain.

A useful framework to consider is that proposed by Håkansson and Snehota (1995) which uses three main concepts to describe a network process:

Resource ties:
* relationships use but also develop resources;
* relationships require investment;
* interdependence creates 'lock-in';
* relationships enable learning.

Activity links:
* activities join actors together interdependently;
* recognize mutuality in plans and actions;
* firms are not free to act alone.

Actor bonds:

- network position affects ability to influence and depends on perceptions being input by other actors;
- mutual trust and commitment are enabled by interaction and social exchange;
- all participants benefit.

This provides a useful summary of the principal features needed to manage in a more holistic way. These elements recognize that individual companies cannot normally compete on their own. They need to build alliances – relationships and network connections with others that offer products, services and capabilities that they have chosen not to have inside their own organization but which are still required by customers as a package. Given that all of this is subject to competitive pressures and actions by competitors and the onward rush of new technological possibilities, it is clear that these decisions have to be fluid and reactive to change. This in itself is an argument not to build rigid fixed structures that are difficult to change when needed. Rather, it is better to see the extended network as continuously forming and dissolving sets of relationships as the need arises. Some of the links will endure through many changes while others will be more transient as each party finds a better fit with their needs. Respect and intellectual property rights therefore are considerations that must be included in the analysis and interactions between the supply chain participants.

Conclusions

This chapter has described an evolving field of study as the chain or the network becomes the focus rather that the individual firm or organization. These changes are driven by new opportunities in global markets, advanced communications and computer technology as well as the opening of world trade arrangements and the financial support made possible by governments and institutions.

Organizations try to structure their immediate environments to keep a measure of control and influence over their key business activities and how the nature of both physical and information flows can permit logistics to link potentially disparate groups together into a coherent chain. Toyota stands out as an example of a company that understands and has demonstrated this process to be effective. The challenges are real and substantial, especially if the change agent organization that drives these initiatives is not of the scale and influence of Toyota. Once the size is more equal and the relative power more evenly distributed, companies are faced with a shifting ground of relationship links that form and change as the business requirements change.

The management challenges of organizing and being effective in such situations are severe indeed. The opportunities are there for those who move more cohesively and quickly than their competitors. After all, it was only in 1935 that the first Toyota car was produced and in 2006 it is regarded as fast overtaking General Motors to be the biggest car producer by volume in the world.

References

Chen, I.J. and Paulraj, A. (2004), 'Understanding Supply Chain Management: Critical Research and Theoretical Framework', *International Journal of Production Research* 42(1), pp. 131–61.

Chopra, S. and Meindl, P. (2007), *Supply Chain Management, Strategy, Planning and Operation*, 3rd edn (New York: Pearson).

Coase, R.H. (1937), 'The Nature of the Firm', *Economica N.S.* 4, pp. 386–405.

Cooper, M. and Ellram, L. (1993), 'Characteristics of Supply Chain Management and Implications for Purchasing and Logistics Strategy', *International Journal of Logistics Management* 4(2), pp. 13–24.

Deloitte Research (2006), *China and India: The Reality Beyond the Hype*, http://www.deloitte. com/dtt/research, accessed 22 May 2006.

Freidman T.L. (2005), *The World is Flat: A Brief History of the Twenty-first Century* (New York: Farrar, Straus and Giroux).

Gadde, L-E., Heumer, L. and Håkansson, H. (2003), 'Strategising in Industrial Networks' *Industrial Marketing Management* 32, pp. 357–64.

Goldman Sachs (2003), *Global Economics Paper 99* (New York: Goldman Sachs).

Håkansson, H. and Snehota, I. (1995), *Developing Relationships in Business Networks* (London: International Thompson Business Press).

Kraljic, P. (1983), 'Purchasing Must Become Supply Management', *Harvard Business Review* 61(5) September–October, pp. 109–17.

Liker, J.K. (2004), *The Toyota Way: 14 Management Principles from the World's Greatest Manufacturer* (New York: McGraw-Hill).

Monden, Y. (1983), *The Toyota Production System* (Portland, OR: Productivity Press).

O'Brien, J.M. (2001), 'The Making of the Xbox', *Wired* 9 November.

Siekman, P. (2002), 'The Smart Car is Looking More So', *Fortune* 4 April.

Simchi-Levi, D., Kaminsky, P. and Simchi-Levi, E. (2000), *Designing and Managing the Supply Chain* (New York: McGraw-Hill).

Smith, A. (1776), *An Inquiry into the Nature and Causes of the Wealth of Nations* (Edinburgh).

Smith, A. (1759), *The Theory of the Moral Sentiments* (Edinburgh).

Womack, J.P. and Jones, D.T. (2003), *Lean Thinking*, 2nd edn (New York: Simon and Schuster).

Williamson, O.E. (1985), *The Economic Institutions of Capitalism* (New York: Free Press).

Womack, J.P., Jones, D.T. and Roos, D. (1990), *The Machine that Changed the World* (London: Macmillan).

Chapter 9

International Purchasing Management

David J. Newlands

Introduction

Purchasing provides an acquisition service for the company while not requiring the goods itself. The role has changed from the 1980s administrative oriented activity management to today, with its emphasis on strategic supply chain facilitating and provides value adding activities such as quality improvement and cost reduction. Purchasing no longer needs to focus on order placement and economic ordering. Materials management specialists typically now take control of these issues, using advanced planning and control software such as SAP or BAAN. With reduced product life cycles, an ever increasing rate of new design releases and the constant search both internally and within the existing and potential supply base, purchasing must focus on preparing for the next product and improving performance while producing the existing good. Purchasing agents must work with process engineering to implement best practices, quality engineers that focus on process verification and stability, cost engineering that focus on efficient operations, transportation and other third party value-adding service providers.

Marketing and design have always been managed as projects. Purchasing is migrating from repetitive procedures to project-based value-adding services. Purchasing must contribute at strategic and tactical levels. Purchasing today is required not to be a cost centre. Most agents' performance is measured against the aim to reduce costs rather than the function costs. Some companies require up to 15 times the agent's salary in proposed cost reductions, in order to create the budget for their salary for the following year. The aim of this chapter is not to review conventional purchasing. Instead, the emerging challenges and roles purchasing agents face are discussed.

Purchasing Perspective Shifts

Purchasing, like sales and marketing, operates at two levels:[1]

1. Knowing the name of the Target (person or company) in advance that will be involved in the transaction; the goods in question will be created and delivered to fulfil unique order requirements. The lead-time between order and delivery, or the frequency of orders placed, allow for the provision of significant variety and variability (Slack et al. 1998, p. 29). Typically, a make-to-order or assemble-to-order contract is established.
2. Not knowing the name of the person or company in advance. As a consequence lower variety or a limited range of goods are provided usually on a make-to-stock basis. Making

---

1   This insight was provided by Kenneth Gervase Williams, Founder of Gervase Instruments Ltd, now part of Spirax Sarco.

to stock is typically in response to forecasting, which in itself is inherently inaccurate and subject to variables.

Purchasers must select and use appropriate strategies that fit with the organization's needs, current order profiles, development projects and the requirement to be actively involved or operate at arm's length:

- High-value fixed asset investments and tooling management activities include contractor selection, process analysis, benchmarking activities and business process re-engineering, detail design, construction approval, commissioning, process verification, operator training and formal process hand-over, laying roads, pipelines, high voltage electricity lines, constructing purpose-built manufacturing or distribution centres, assembly of customized point-of-sale building (e.g., McDonald's and other restaurant's 'drive thrus'). High performance dedicated tooling may be only sourced from specialized engineering firms. An automotive example is to put a car tyre on a wheel, fit the valve, inflate and balance the assembly in seven seconds. The equivalent operation for tractor tires can take as little as 23 seconds!
- Project-based purchasing for branded fast-moving consumer goods. Different applications or market segment definitions frequently use the same core technology. The result is a series of differentiated products that use the same components, or variants that have been modified as a result of a number of engineering requests.
- Purchasing of non-core activities and services. Makers make. Stores store. They focus on their core activities to turn the every day into something special. Everything that they are weak at, and some other company can do better, faster, cheaper, greener and more often, is outsourced. Examples of outsourced activities for manufacturing companies include cleaning, management and booking of business travel arrangements, catering, buildings and gardens, data archiving, information system development, headhunting and personnel management activities such as pay roll, process development and change management projects undertaken by consultants.
- Consultancy and marketing services contract management. IBM had over 70 advertising agencies under contract worldwide. When Louis V. Gerstner Jr (2002) took over as CEO, he discovered this and determined to contract with only one agency for advertising to create and manage a single global message.
- Low-volume commodities can be purchased at a spot price. Standard parts and equipment may be standardized worldwide. Single company agreements may be made. Negotiations are handled by a single purchasing agent for the total worldwide demand in the corporation for particular types of equipment. A global demand forecast or commitment is made. This encourages the supplier to stock the same equipment at various sites and rapidly deliver upon request. The price is standardized, regardless of annual volume per site. The purchasing agent with the highest demand is responsible for the contract and relations with the supplier(s).
- Spares and repair requirements may include service provision as well as traceability. Pattern or genuine parts may be selected. The aim being to ensure operations run with the minimum disruption possible.
- High technology parts may be sourced. These can be mock-ups, prototypes, made during pre-production run process verifications, production versions. Cost and consequently price reduction profiles should be defined in order to provide a guideline and objectives for process improvement, quality enhancement and non-value-adding cost elimination.

Purchasing emphasis at its most tangible level is product-centred purchasing which has the objectives: to obtain goods at:

1. the right quality;
2. arriving consistently on time;
3. delivered to the right location;
4. in the right quantities; and
5. at the right cost (Baily and Farmer 1982).

Stannack and Scheuing (1996) identify three further levels that define purchasing activities. At a second level, buyers focus on process-centred purchasing which emphasizes the nature of the processes that provide goods and services to the customer company. The third level is 'relational purchasing'. This involves activities focusing on the exchange of a variety of 'items' (including money, relationships, longer contracts, supplier development programmes and so forth) for changes in behaviour and improvements in quality, reliability, consistency and cost. The fourth level is performance-centred purchasing, based on the exchange of items for performance – undertaking activities outside the remit of the customer's core activities. This fourth level corresponds to full outsourcing. These levels highlight purchasers' perspective shifts from tangible goods and services acquired to the supplier's organization and subsequently to the more intangible performance advantages suppliers can create.

Adversarial Contracting

Customers engaged in adversarial contracting encourage their suppliers to oppose their competitors' acquisition of contracts by cutting piece prices. Competition in effect becomes 'cut-throat' at a micro-economic level. In these scenarios, suppliers may not make a profit on the initial quotation though they will chase every opportunity to increase the piece price based on complications due to customers' engineering change requests (ECRs). Simultaneously, any development work undertaken by the supplier will likely be financed as a non-recurring expenditure (NRE), funded by the customer on a contract basis agreed in advance. Focus on low price and short-term contracts are perceived either to reduce supplier's motivation, or as a hygiene factor, thus reducing the probability that the supplier will invest in capital equipment that reduces the unit cost of production.

Contracting During Product Development

Secondly, product development is perceived as a strategic core competence (Susman 1992; Medhat and Bell 1996; Cusumano and Nobeoka 1993). Product development has evolved with the adoption of concurrent engineering, composed of five key elements in an industrial system: process, people, tools, structure and control (Brookes and Backhouse 1997). Brookes and Backhouse (ibid.) suggest that efficiency, proficiency, radical innovation, incremental change and focus are key external driving forces acting to stimulate concurrent engineering.

Purchasing representatives working for product development programmes during concurrent engineering projects aim to provide a set of solutions for operations' purchasing. It is during this preparatory phase that purchasing negotiations typically take place for bespoke components and modules. As company-specific items, the customer company has the strategic opportunity to single, sole, dual or multi-source the goods required. This decision affects whether the supplier receives an order for all or a portion of the goods for either a limited period or for the production lifetime of the product in operation.

Updated traditional purchasing literature (Baily and Farmer 1982; Dobler and Burt 1996) augmented the consideration of adversarial trading and negotiation with scenarios between active buyers who gain control and passive sales representatives regarding relationships.

Partnership Sourcing

Partnership sourcing (Partnership Sourcing Ltd 1992; MacBeth and Ferguson 1994) or co-makership (Bevan 1998; Deans and Rajagopal 1991; Merli 1991) became the alternative to adversarial trading, and is considered a more powerful paradigm (Reck and Long 1988). The approach uses outsourcing for long-term service provision rather than merely a one-time acquisition of goods or services against a specification (Nutt 1991). An updated traditional purchasing text (Baily et al. 1994) provides clarity on purchasing objectives:

- to supply the organization with a steady flow of materials and services to meet its needs;
- to ensure continuity of supply by maintaining effective relationships with existing sources of supply and by developing other sources either as alternatives or to meet emerging or planned needs;
- to buy efficiently and wisely, obtaining by ethical means the best value for every unit of currency spent;
- to maintain sound cooperative relationships with other departments (internal customers), providing information and advice as necessary to ensure the effective operation of the organization as a whole;
- to develop staff, policies, procedures and organization to ensure the achievement of these objectives;
- to select the best suppliers in the market;
- to help the effective development of new products;
- to protect the organization's cost structure;
- to monitor supply market trends;
- to negotiate effectively in order to work with suppliers who will seek mutual benefit through superior performance.

Webster and Wind (1972a) developed a model of organizational buyer behaviour. They define four classes of variables that determine corporate buying behaviour as *individual*, *social*, *organizational* and *environmental*; these are divided into task and non-task related dimensions, of which one is likely to dominate (Webster and Wind 1972b). Argyris (1993) noted similar effects when examining tacit defensive routines. Webster and Winds' hierarchy is defined from macro to micro levels:

- starting with environmental impact and external sources;
- determining the organizational boundary defined by its technological, structural, and directional attributes that are formed by the principal participants;
- focusing on functional activities and interpersonal determinants of behaviour;
- task and non-task (value-adding and non-value-adding) activities;

- psycho-sociological determinants of individual behaviour that underpin the preferred styles of knowledge workers; and
- individual or group (Janis 1972, 1983) decision-making processes.

Webster and Wind's model creates a hierarchy of dependencies from various domains and impacts on the company through controlling processes, the individual and the results of the decision. They note that 'the buyer (or purchase agent) is in most cases the final decision maker and the target of influence attempts' and expand further by stating that 'It is the specific individual who is the target for marketing effort, not the abstract organization'.

Sheth (1973) also developed a model of organizational buying behaviour. Sheth identified information sources, experience, purchasing process, product development issues, conflict resolution processes and situational factors, and links them in a closed loop cycle that has functional similarity to the learning cycle by Kolb, Rubin and MacIntyre (1979).

By convention, the initial part of analysis using Sheth's model focuses on perception and expectations of participants that form the inter- and intra-organizational business scenario. Functional roles augment the framework supporting a decision-making process. The model is based on adversarial negotiation practices and does not attempt to transfer knowledge, techniques or technology to suppliers. In its place, a comparison is made between expectations and actual performance assessed in terms of 'satisfaction' with the purchase. In scenarios where expectations are unchanging, the variable is supplier performance against set criteria. The model omits production process factors. Given the introduction of continuous improvement stemming from the total quality paradigm, from a supplier development perspective this simple model requires either an additional element that allows the customer to improve the supplier, or a mechanism by which the supplier can gauge customer's requirements and autonomously respond.

Håkansson's (1982) interaction model contextualized approaches taken by customer and supplier organizations and individuals representing them. Håkansson's model is used to form a bridge between a purchasing relationship and functional process gestalt to an interactive, development and improvement based relationship with network partners. To achieve the key performance indicators that define world-class manufacturers requires a significantly greater level of sustained collaborative effort both internally within each company and department, and throughout the supply chain between trading partners. The common objective is to have a seamless chain of associates who link activities along the entire supply chain throughout a network of information exchange nodes at the intra- and inter-business levels. This network can include activists engaged in product and component design, demand forecasting and planning, inventory control, production and delivery logistics (Bell 2000).

Buying, Purchasing, Partnership Sourcing and Strategic Procurement

At the lowest level, acquisitions are made by buyers when they place orders. Goods and services in this context are known, stable and understood. The risks are low. Examples of buying include buying a newspaper on the way to work, a faucet[2] washer from a hardware store, lunch at a local restaurant or commissioning a haircut at the barbers or hairdressers. Little is required in the way of formal contract. The laws of contract still apply, even when no words are spoken.

---

2   In British English, a faucet is a tap.

Reaching for the money or a credit card to pay is the sign that an agreement has been reached. Statutory rights for consumers remain intact.

The next level of acquisitions is purchasing. The budgets are significantly larger because typically the need is to fulfil the parts or services needs that have been categorized as 'buy' rather than 'make'. Purchasing is most often via contracts at a business to business level. Price is a key determinant in purchasing rather than cost. Purchasing agents may have some idea of the costs, but this is not the core emphasis of the contract. The aim is to spend the least amount possible of the annual purchase spend budget.

The duration of the contract can be significantly extended – usually six months or more. Purchasers may be involved in placing orders by the month and providing forecast data of future periods to suppliers. If the goods are relatively mature and the supplier is reliable, order placement can be handed-off to materials management, who use computer-based programs, including materials requirements planning (MRP), to calculate net requirements. Materials planners then confirm orders based on the plan. This type of planning can easily cause batches to be produced. Batches inherently create longer than expected lead times due to the queue and wait times prior to and post processing. The number of goods queuing and waiting is the number in the batch minus the number being processed on the machine. Batch and queue is a mass production based organization of work. This now is considered inefficient in well organized supply chains.

The next level of acquisitions is partnership sourcing (Ark Conferences 1994; Butterworth 1996; CBI and Arthur D. Little 1995; Dyer and Ouchi 1993; Ellram 1991; Greene 1991; Hoskins 1993; Lehtinen 1996; MacBeth and Ferguson 1994). The role of the acquisitions agent changes towards relationships and performance enhancement rather than purely order placement. Fewer suppliers are involved in order to spend more time with each to develop the relationship, trust and focus on enhancing performance. The fewer suppliers compete for future business based on their capacity to produce low cost goods. Partnership sourcing tries to make long-term use of existing local suppliers.

The highest level of acquisitions currently identified is strategic procurement (Lamming 1993). Procurement looks to develop long-term networks of high performance suppliers and service providers. Procurement recognizes that competitive advantage is no longer company versus company, but rather is highly competitive supply chain versus supply chain. The strategic aspect implies long-termism, that is a commitment by each organization to the enterprise. Motivation to compete is the key stress in the relationship. Just-in-time may be the core operating principle in the assembler, first- and lower-tier suppliers. The objective is to eliminate all types of wastes by careful design and improvement of the product and the processes that produce them.

Strategic procurement will identify on a global basis the best in class and work towards inviting and setting up a transplant to supply goods and services where no suitable local suppliers exist. Significant investments in infrastructure will need to be made. The setting up of the Nissan Motor Company assembly plant in Sunderland, UK is a significant example. Nissan bought the land at agricultural prices. They carved up the area, taking sufficient area for their plant, finished goods buffer area and car parking for employees. The rest of the space was sold at industrial rates to its key supplier transplants that would be located within minutes of the plant. The difference between industrial and agricultural land rates was a significant motivation to locate at that site. The 'profit' from this land sale virtually covered the cost of constructing and commissioning the assembly plant.

The Purchasing Manager

According to the Canadian National Occupational Classification system:

> Purchasing manager's plans, organize, direct, control and evaluate the activities of a purchasing department and develop and implement the purchasing policies of a business or institution. They are employed throughout the public and private sectors.[3]

The Canadian National Occupational Classification (NOC) provides titles used, they include: contract manager, director, procurement operations director of purchasing, food purchasing manager, manager – purchasing contracts, material manager and purchasing manager.

In an international context, those who are responsible for purchasing seldom place orders. They are in fact project coordinators who provide a service for product creation teams and production management. Product creators define what components are required and typically the materials and processes used to create them. From this specification, purchasing managers must find, select and approve suppliers who are capable of producing the parts to *quality*, at an appropriate *cost*, have sufficient capacity and can *deliver* to schedules.

Historically, suppliers 'made to drawing'. In today's context, that is not sufficient to be competitive. Two other criteria were recognized by Nissan Motor Company – *design* and *management*. If a supplier can only provide material conversion and delivery services at acceptable cost, they will never become true partners. As suppliers make the parts, they are considered to be the experts in what they do. Product designers and parts makers must work in harmony. It is pointless to have design specify characteristics on parts that are difficult and costly to produce. Minor modifications recommended by suppliers can significantly reduce processing time, scrap rates, special orders or basic raw materials, etc. The supplier must be able to recommend solutions, define process parameters for designers, rapidly create 'soft' tools for prototype or preproduction runs and quickly identify and debug designs.

Supplier's management must be able to work closely with their customer. An appropriate culture must be created based on shared values and common objectives that are measured using understood and agreed measures.

International purchasing managers can spend up to 80 per cent of their careers outside their home country. They have to be able to cope with different cultures and supplier behaviours. Examples include: in Latin countries the ubiquitous '*mañana, mañana*' – meaning 'later, later' or 'tomorrow, tomorrow'; in Japan, it is customary to say 'Yes' when a Japanese is trying to, understand, or understands, what is being said. This can lead to significant confusion as the following dialogue suggests (Magee 2003):

Fr: We think we need to close a plant.
Jpn: Yes.
Fr: Jobs will be lost.
Jpn: Yes.
Fr: We have no choice. It must be done.
Jpn: Yes.

The Japanese manager is now ready to digest what has been said and to think about a response. The French manager is now ready to take action.

---

3 The Canadian National Occupational Classification for purchasing managers weblink is http://www23.hrdc-drhc.gc.ca/2001/e/groups/0113.shtml. The general site index is found at http://www23.hrdc-drhc.gc.ca/2001/e/groups/index.shtml.

As a result, Renault, a French company in France, and Nissan, a Japanese company headquartered in Japan, both took English as the language of business. This meant massive expenditure on courses. This was to force both to use a second language in order to become more direct and verbally brutal rather than the indirect, non-frank dialogue that is sprinkled with courteous requests and sayings. Japanese would say 'Give it to me' in English. When speaking Japanese, the same individuals would use 'Please do so'. Japanese managers were told that speaking English would open up opportunities not available to non-English speakers. A 40-word French-English-Japanese company dictionary was created and shared with employees at all levels. Low level administrative workers still use Japanese. The higher up the hierarchy, the more English and French can be heard. A mixture of all three languages can be heard. For each employee, the words meant *record profit*.

Key Performance Metrics

How does an organization effectively measure the contribution made by buying, purchasing, partnership sourcing or strategic procurement? Nissan's QCDDM (quality, cost, delivery, design and management) can provide measure of specific aspects, yield rate in terms of parts per million defects, bottom line spend reduction for price, percentage on-time and correct deliveries, number of designs per year, number of days lost due to conflict (between workers and management).

Measuring how many quotes have been reviewed is a tactical metric. It measures activity, not achievement. Perception is a key determinant of what type of metric to use. Van Weele (2005, pp. 251–2) identifies management can perceive purchasing as operational, administrative activity; as a commercial activity; as part of an integrated logistics network; and as a strategic business area.

None of those metrics really look at performance or motivate team spirit and the need to improve. Each of them also is measured *a posteriori* – after the event (Likierman 2005).

On-time ramp-up for new products forces design, purchasing and operations to work together, to ensure all activities are coordinated, quality is sufficient to ensure materials flow and that customers receive their orders when they request, rather than when the manufacture promises to deliver. The loss of sales that results from late and slow ramp-up is calculable. Typically, one month late equals 30 per cent reduction in net profit from the launch. More than three months late, the risk of obsolescence can simply wipe out any hope of breaking even, let alone the cost of the stock in the pipeline that has been bought by suppliers on behalf of the assembler.

Field failure rate as a percentage and mean time to failure enable engineers to determine the probability a unit will fail at a given age or after a given amount of use. Trade customers and retailers may set stringent criteria in this respect. If they are not achieved, the retailer may claw back revenue from future invoices to cover their administrative costs and punitive damages due to 'loss of face'.

Suppliers should be assessed not just-*on*-time delivery, but also on response time between order and delivery. It is imperative that suppliers deliver the right goods to the destination. In one instance, a supplier sent Ford's parts to Nissan and Nissan's to Ford. An investigation was mounted to design a process to prevent this happening again. Supplier discipline to follow the procedure should have been sufficient. In the end, it did happen a second time:

The first time, shame on you. The second time, shame on me.

Sourcing Strategies

Single, sole, dual or multi-sourcing are strategies (Carter and Narasimhan 1996) used by procurement functions to ensure their businesses obtain appropriate quality, low purchase price and reliable deliveries (Baily et al. 1994). Such strategies emphasize long-term, profitable orders to suppliers. In return for these assurances, suppliers are required to be involved in new product creation processes (Barkan 1992), designing optimum manufacturing layouts and coordinating logistics.

Sole sourcing indicates the supplier has a monopoly supply agreement or is a technology or product leader and is the only supplier available. Sole sourcing is useful if the supplier has clear cost and technological leadership over its competitors and if they have sufficient global capacity. On occasion, such suppliers are located in only one site, for example as a result of a unique source of raw materials, or due to the intense capital investment required to set up facilities.

The dual sourcing strategy is an effort to limit the number of suppliers to two, and consequently the costs of maintaining relationships are also reduced as a result of focus on process capable suppliers. Also, there may be volume or capacity constraints at suppliers that determine that two sets of tooling are required. Dual sourcing is an ideal method of gathering benchmarking data on key performance indicators.

Single sourcing relies on obtaining a single part code number from a single supplier. Typically, volume requirements from a family parts or product group are allocated part code by part code to only one supplier.

Multi-sourcing is the approach taken when parts are commodities or made to common specifications such as international standards that are adopted on a country by country basis. This approach allows the buyer to acquire parts at the most competitive price and forces each competitor to achieve this.

Newlands (2003a, 2003b) concluded that suppliers need to be aware of their customers' strategic procurement policies for various products and take account of these policies when estimating the profit they might expect when participating in sole, single, dual and multi-sourcing environments. Product creation processes can be as profitable as low-volume production runs. Since investment can be significant, it may be more profitable for a company to focus on designing components, prototyping, pre-production runs, and process optimization. Their aim may therefore be to develop and transfer knowledge on a consultative basis.

On the basis of improving performance, large purchasing organizations are either compelled to buy from minority suppliers or seek to aid relatively small and specialized suppliers to become potential partners who can achieve the required capabilities and performance. Purchasing agents must manage their own activities and ensure the adequate development or creation of existing or new suppliers.

Conclusions

Purchasing managers must be generalist managers, capable of working with managers in their own business and their suppliers. It is insufficient today to merely order goods. Materials management specialists control stock and order accordingly.

Purchasing managers must deal effectively with quality, cost, delivery, product and process design, environment, plant efficiency, product changes, ethics and corporate responsibility, social and economic impacts of their decisions, corporate governance, knowledge transfer, ramp-up and ramp-down planning, training and improvement programmes, performance metrics, short-term problems and long-term strategies, evolving client needs and less money in their annual spend budgets.

The role of a purchasing manager is to decide with whom to work, what emphasis to put on the business to business relationships they manage with suppliers, how to behave and what they should prioritize for themselves.

References

Argyris, C. (1993), *Knowledge for Action: A Guide to Overcoming Barriers to Organisational Change* (San Francisco: Jossey-Bass).

Ark Conferences (1994), 'Partnership Sourcing: The Strategic Option', 30 November, London.

Baily, P. and Farmer, D. (1982), *Materials Management Handbook* (Aldershot: Gower Publishing).

Baily, P., Farmer, D., Jessop, D. and Jones, D. (1994), Purchasing Principles and Management, 7th edn (London: Pitman Publishing).

Barkan, P. (1992), 'Productivity in the Process of Product Development – An Engineering Perspective', in Susman, G. (ed.) *Integrating Design and Manufacturing for Competitive Advantage* (New York: Oxford University Press), pp. 56–68.

Bell, C. (2000), 'Supply Chain Integration – The Future', *Control* April, pp. 17–19.

Bevan, J. (1988), 'The Road to Co-makership', *Purchasing and Supply Management* October, pp. 30–33.

Brookes, N. and Backhouse, C. (1997), 'Variety and Concurrent Engineering', *Manufacturing Engineer* April, pp. 72–5.

Butterworth, C. (1996), 'Supplier-driven Partnerships', *European Journal of Purchasing and Supply Management* 2(4), pp. 169–72.

Carter, J. and Narasimhan, R. (1996), 'Purchasing and Supply Management: Future Directions and Trends,' *International Journal of Purchasing and Materials Management*, pp. 2–12.

CBI and Arthur D. Little (1995), *Partnership Sourcing and British Industry: A CBI/Arthur D. Little Survey* (London: Confederation of British Industry).

Cusumano, M. and Nobeoka, K. (1998), *Thinking Beyond Lean: How Multi-project Management is Transforming Product Development at Toyota and Other Companies* (New York: The Free Press).

Deans, K. and Rajagopal, S. (1991), 'Co-makership: A Worthwhile Word', *Purchasing and Supply Management* March, pp. 15–17.

Dobler, D. and Burt, D. (1996), *Purchasing and Materials Management*, 6th edn (New York: McGraw Hill).

Dyer, J. and Ouchi, W. (1993), 'Japanese-Style Partnerships: Giving Companies a Competitive Edge', *Sloan Management Review* (Fall), pp. 51–63.

Ellram, L. (1991), 'A Managerial Guideline for the Development and Implementation of Purchasing and Partnerships', *International Journal of Purchasing and Materials Management* March.

Gerstner, Louis V. Jr (2002), *Who Says Elephants Can't Dance? Inside IBM's Historic Turnaround* (New York: HarperBusiness).

Greene, D. (1991), 'Developing Supplier and Customer Partnerships for Improved Quality', in *Proceedings of the Fall Meeting on Council of Logistics Management, 29 September* 2(2), pp. 39–51.

Håkansson, H. (1982), *International Marketing and Purchasing of Industrial Goods* (Chichester: John Wiley and Sons).

Hoskins, C. (1993), 'Supplier Partnerships Power Up Production', *Machinery and Production Engineering* 17 September, pp. 48–9.

Janis, J. (1972), *Victims of Groupthink* (Boston: Houghton Mifflin).

Janis, J. (1982), *Groupthink*, 2nd edn (Boston: Houghton Mifflin).

Kolb, D., Rubin, I. and McIntyre, J. (1979), *Organization Psychology: An Experimental Approach* (Englewood Cliffs, NJ: Prentice-Hall Inc.).

Lamming, R. (1993), *Beyond Partnership – Strategies for Innovation and Lean Supply* (London: Prentice Hall International).

Lehtinen, U. (1996), 'Partnerships among Finnish Manufacturers', *European Journal of Purchasing and Supply Management* 2(4), pp. 161–7.

Likierman, A. (2005), 'Measurably Better, Manufacturing and Engineering Menu', Supplychain management.com http://www.Supplymanagement.co.uk/EDIT/SM_featuredchapters_item. asp?id=13287.

MacBeth, D. and Ferguson, N. (1994), *Partnership Sourcing: An Integrated Supply Chain Approach* (London: Pitman Publishing – Financial Times Series).

Magee, D. (2003), *Turnaround: How Carlos Ghosn Rescued Nissan* (New York: HarperCollins).

Medhat, S. and Bell, M. (eds) (1996), *Managing Technology and Processes in the Next Millennium*, CEEDA '96, 3rd International Conference, Bournemouth University, Poole, UK, 18–19 January.

Merli, G. (1991), *Co-makership: The New Supply Strategy for Manufacturers* (Cambridge, MA:Productivity Press).

Newlands, D. (2003a), 'Breakeven Analysis: Part 1 – Current Opinion', *Control* 29(7), http://www.littoralis.info/iom/topics.htm.

Newlands, D. (2003b), 'Breakeven Analysis: Part 2 – Results from Modern Purchasing Environments Non Recurring Expenditures Associated With Product Creation Projects', *Control* 29(8), http://www.littoralis.info/iom/htm/iom20031201.527319.htm.

Nutt, C. (1991), 'Limiting the Cost of External Services', *Purchasing and Supply Management* September, pp. 15–18.

Partnership Sourcing Ltd (1992), *Partnership Sourcing* (London: DTI).

Reck, R. and Long, B. (1988), 'Purchasing: A Competitive Weapon', *Journal of Purchasing and Materials Management* (Fall), pp. 2–8.

Sheth, J. (1973), 'A Model of Industrial Buyer Behaviour', *Journal of Marketing* 37(4), pp. 50–56.

Slack, N., Chambers, S., Harland, C., Harrison, A. and Johnston, R. (1998), *Operations Management* (London: Pitman).

Stannack, P. and Scheuing, E. (1996), *The Language of Supplier Performance*, National Association of Purchasing Management, Proceedings of the 1996 NAPM Annual Academic Conference, Portland, USA, 21–23 March, pp. 27–39.

Susman, G. (ed.) (1992), *Integrating Design and Manufacturing for Competitive Advantage* (New York and Oxford: Oxford University Press).

Van Weele, Arjan J. (2005), *Purchasing and Supply Chain Management: Analysis, Strategy, Planning and Practice*, 4th edn (London: Thomson Learning).

Webster, F. and Wind, Y. (1972a), *Organisational Buyer Behaviour* (Englewood Cliffs, NJ: Prentice Hall).

Webster, F. and Wind, Y. (1972b), 'A General Model for Understanding Organisational Buyer Behaviour', Journal of Marketing 36(2), pp. 12–19.

Chapter 10

Reverse Logistics

Isabel Fernández

Introduction

To create sustainable development, our present generation must not take resources that will be detrimental to future generations. We must learn to use the resources wisely. Each material must be used sparingly, many times over, and eventually made into other things: reduce, re-use and recycle. The working life of a good can be extended as a result of preventative maintenance. Parts that are expected to break can be replaced prior to the anticipated malfunction. Goods in poor condition may be serviced, repaired when damaged, or rebuilt to refurbish and extend their useful life. Cruise ships serve for many decades. The fittings in cabins are frequently replaced to maintain it as 'ship shape'. Safety specific equipment are checked and replaced when necessary. Certificates of conformance with safety and health criteria ensure vehicles are in adequate condition to serve for a defined period – typically one or two years.

Eventually the value of the good and the cost of repairing it are uneconomic. At the end of a product's useful working life parts can be cannibalized to keep other serviceable goods running. Materials can be salvaged that then may be recycled.

This chapter introduces key aspects related to reverse logistics (RL). This field has been coined as 'the last frontier for companies to cut down costs'. ISO 14000 states that organizations do not need to contribute to going green if it is not profitable to do so.

Relevant non-economic drivers are issues companies may seek as a result of adopting RL practices include: improved corporate image, compliance with stringent environmental legislation, supply of information and control of entry barriers. These also may be the result of efficient returns management. Given the listed advantages, a question arises: why have only a few companies successfully implemented RL? The answer strongly relates to certain problems posed by the specific complicating returns characteristics that are explained in this chapter.

Product Value Recovery

Recovery of products has been carried out for eons. Splinters from stone tools in the Stone Age were used for arrowheads, local coins from conquered cities were melted down to produce new coins in the Roman era, etc. However, only recently has literature analysed reverse logistics from a managerial perspective. Early work in this field (Terry 1869; Beckley and Logan 1948; Giultinian and Nwokoye 1975; Ginter and Starling 1978) mainly emphasized distribution configuration. Subsequently, scope and importance increased so that today recovery and Reverse Logistics are considered essential dimensions of an integrated corporate strategy.

These evolving changes are likely to stem from several simultaneously occurring situations:

1. there is significant concern on the subject of environmental matters and sustainable development from both institutions and individuals;
2. economic necessity identified by primarily shrinking margins, has led to an increasing awareness of the importance that reverse logistics issues have with respect to market competitive propositions;
3. standard technologies and products make service-related considerations key differentiating factors (Botter and Fortuin 200; Lele and Karmarkar 1983; Pfohl and Ester 1999; Porter 1998) with which to reinforce the competitive position of a company in the market (Emerson and Grimm 1996; Sterling and Lambert 1989). RL offers the possibility of simultaneously meeting the challenges posed by actual market and social scenarios.

Definition

RL is a relatively new field. In the last two decades the subject has received growing attention. This is perhaps due to its rapidly growing importance. According to the majority of RL authors, the ultimate aim should be to recapture value that otherwise would be lost to society. The reverse logistics concept has not yet been sharply defined. Consequently, some aspects may differ from one definition to another such as, the inclusion or not of the waste management within its scope (see Fernández 2004 for a more detailed discussion).

Reverse logistics has been defined as *the process of planning, implementing and controlling backwards flows of raw materials, in-process inventory, packaging and finished goods, from a manufacturing, distribution or use point, to a point of recovery or point of proper disposal* (The European Working Group on Reverse Logistics (RevLog) 2004).

Importance of Returns

In spite of the emerging nature of this discipline, the following statistics may serve to give an impression of the economic importance and the benefits from planning, implementing and controlling reverse logistics activities:

*   return rates in the Spanish editor sector on average are 41.17 per cent, clothes 19 per cent and electric and electronic equipment 10–12 per cent (Soto 2005);
*   efficient management of the reverse process can reduce up to 10 per cent from companies' total annual logistics costs (Minahan 1998);
*   companies involved in recovery activities may attain savings between 40 per cent and 60 per cent of the completely new product production costs, while reprocessing incurs around 20 per cent of energy requirements of raw materials (Dowlatshahi 2000);
    *   The department of transportation in Pennsylvania saved more than $250,000 in just one district by using retread tyres. American Airlines saved over $100,000 by converting to 100 per cent recycled paper (Biddle 1993);
    *   Estèe Lauder was able to evaluate 24 per cent more returned products, redistribute 150 per cent more of its returns and save approximately $500,000 annual labour costs after building its own reverse logistics systems (Caldwell 1999);

- the IKEA corporation turned a loss from its waste disposal processing of US$36,000 p.a. into a profit of US$5,000 through its campaign 'trash is cash' which was based on a 'sort at source' policy then sold waste parts and materials (Enarsson 1998).

Reverse logistics is perceived as being increasingly important because these programmes facilitate and manage returned goods (returns). In 1996, the Supply Chain Council (SCC), 'a not-for-profit organization originally founded by 69 member companies, developed the SCOR (Supply Chain Operations References) model that has become a key supply chain evaluation tool'. Although initially this model included four business processes (plan, source, make and deliver), 'five years later it was modified to include a fifth business process: return' (Supply Chain Council 2001).

This SCOR model is not unique in considering returns management as an additional variable of the good supply chain performance. Thus, in 1994, executives from a group of multinational companies, later to become the Global Supply Chain Forum (GSCF), 'developed a definition of supply chain management embracing eight processes' (Cooper et al. 1997; Lambert et al. 1998). Customer relationship management (CRM) and demand management or product development processes similarly pay attention to returns management received processes.

Reasons Why Companies Become Involved in Reverse Logistics

Economic Appeal

The economic appeal from efficient RL practices stems from a variety of sources.

a) Three ways of reducing corporate costs through:
   - Firstly, returns offer a significant opportunity to recover value (both added and material value). The components and materials obtained from returns may become perfect substitutes for virgin materials that otherwise would be acquired from markets. This recovery practice is usual in Rank Xerox photocopy machines, Mercedes and Ford end-of-life (EOL) vehicles. The recovery aspect is particularly relevant when (as at the time of writing) raw material prices rise spectacularly, in many cases reaching record levels (the price of steel increased in 2004 to historic figures with the annual average up 80 per cent; coal made an annual average increase of 73 per cent, from $27/ton in 2002 to $80 in late 2004; gold surpassed the symbolic level of $450 per ounce, reaching its highest price in 16 years; silver exceeded the increase in price of gold; aluminium approached the 1990 price highs with an annual average increase of 20 per cent in 2004).

   Returns facilitate value recovery and reduce the working capital needed to reprocess these materials. Recovery may take place more than once. The products may be treated differently each time via various recovery processes. According to Ayres et al. (1997), 'a typical structural optical component in Rank Xerox has at least four lives, first as a part of a module in a new machine, then as the same part in a remanufactured machine, third in a remanufactured module of a remanufactured machine and finally as recyclable material. Which part of this cannibalization is in operation depends on the state of the parts and the economic viability of raising the attractiveness of the goods and their functional performance. Several strategies beginning with 're' are identifiable: reduce, reprocess, re-use, repair, rebuild, refurbish, replace, recycle. The aerospace and commercial vehicle sectors (particularly London Route Master red buses) make use of traceability to track all components throughout the working life of the type of aircraft or vehicle. Patent manufacture can allow users to acquire goods made in the same factory on the same machine as original equipment to be bought at much lower prices because the parts are not sold in brand owner packaging from branded spares outlets.

- The second source of cost reduction is intimately related to the scarcity of landfills. In recent years landfill taxes have increased considerably. In the USA these taxes rise roughly 10 per cent each year (Johnson and Wang 1995), 'well beyond inflation'. Given these macro-economic pressures, it is little wonder that the traditional manufacturing idea coined as 'from cradle to grave' has been replaced by the more recent one 'from cradle to reincarnation'. In countries such as Germany, The Netherlands or Scandinavia, disposal of residues from manufacturing processes represents 2 per cent of direct manufacturing costs in laser printers, 3 per cent in the automotive industry and 12.5 per cent for fridges and refrigerators (Ayres et al. 1997). Reverse logistics offers companies the opportunity to divert old goods away from landfills and to reduce total production costs.

- Thirdly, increased concerns about recovery activities, reverse logistics and their beneficial influence on the environment should not be neglected as a means of avoiding fines and penalties. With the ever-stringent legislation, the charges may amount to significant levels of annual operating budgets. In spite of achieving 99.6 per cent of its applicable environmental requirements, Kodak faced a $358,551 payout in 2003 because they did not comply with several points.

b) Recovery systems similarly may generate income to support after-sales business activities. In the USA there are 73,000 companies are devoted to remanufacturing activities. They have a total turnover of $53 billion and an average profit margin of over 20 per cent (Lund 1996). Components and materials obtained from returns broadens the market and provides new opportunities in certain segments. The success of remanufactured products may be such that they pose a serious threat to their corresponding new original equipment that is produced and marketed by the brand owner.

c) Returns have an impact on the organization's expected profitability, more so if back flows were not foreseen in the company planning. Returns usually do not belong to the core business and hence this issue typically keeps a low profile within the organization. When returns start they are taken as an exceptional cost of being in the business. Returns from customers have been estimated to be responsible for decreasing retailers' profitability by 4.3 per cent and manufacturers 3.8 per cent. These figures stem from devaluation of returns as a consequence of the delay in the reverse chain, delay in getting cash from the customers, repacking, etc. Therefore, putting in place effective and adequate return management systems will affect directly on the final profitability level. Typically this is achieved by streamlining processes and reducing the 'exception driven effect'.

Ammons et al. (1997) provide an illustrative example from the carpet sector on the above-discussed economic appeal. Annual production was estimated in $10–12 billion, 70 per cent of which was aimed at the substitution of used carpets. This meant every year $7.5 billion went to landfills. Assuming a conservative disposal tax of $60/ton, the disposal total costs were about $64 million; transportation costs to the landfill location were a bit lower (the average trip was estimated as 32km and the rate $0.05/ton and km). The recovery of the fibres contained in carpets would negate the previously-described costs. It would also re-obtain the value of the fibres, estimated in $2 billion (30 times the disposal costs). This study concludes that savings provided by recovery for certain products may be significant. Other examples are given by Geyer and Jackson (2004).

Environmental Pressure

Environment protection is becoming an issue of compulsory compliance. Many countries require their companies to act and apply generic or specific processes to achieve defined conformance criteria. The number of laws passed is increasing that aim to prevent or limit the impact of both industrial activity and consumption on the environment.

A category of products that is expanding in our current way of living is consumer electrical and electronic goods. Wastes from these products (WEEE, Waste of Electric and Electronic Equipment) are drawing serious attention from environmental regulations.

European Union Directive 2002/96/CE requires the manufacturers to take full responsibility for collection, treatment, recovery and disposal of WEEE coming from households. These wastes are estimated between 6.5 and 7.5 million tons per year in Europe. These estimates represent 4 per cent (in mass) of total urban wastes. The Directive's main objectives are:

1. to prevent the generation of WEEE;
2. to foster recovery activities in order to diminished the need for disposal and thus improve environmental management.

'Producer responsibility' implies that the producer is accountable and empowered to set in motion and sustain the means required to selectively collect wastes and have adequate environmental management. The producer may fulfil obligations by establishing a brand operated and owned system or jointly by partnering with other parties that may include distributors, importers, etc.

Table 10.1   Scope and treatment rates: Art. 7 of the WEEE Directive

Rates of WEEE treatment to fulfill by 31 December		
Description	**Minimal rates by average weight**	
	Recovery	**Re-use and recycling***
Large household equipment, selling machines	80%	75%
TI and telecommunication equipment,	75%	65%
Other consumer equipment		
Lighting systems	70%	50%
Electric and electronic tools (large industrial equipment not included),		
Toys, leisure and sport equipment,		
Small household equipment,		
Control and measuring systems		

*   Re-use is referred to components, materials and substances. Re-using the whole equipment is not considered within the recovery goals, although the number of re-used apparatus will be recorded.

Packaging material represents a range of products that are already regulated. The Packaging Waste Directive passed into law by the European Parliament in December 1994. The principal aim of this legislation is 'preventing the packaging wastes produced by industries, retail, offices, shops, services and domiciles' (Directive 94/62/EC). Its objective was to provide a legislative framework to encourage EU member states to recover, re-use and recycle a minimum amount of these types of residue. In addition, each member state had to assure that adequate systems were implemented to physically recover the residue from the consumers and that databases were established to supervise the process.

The previous two examples are only a small sample of the products that will be reviewed with respect to the environment for mandatory environmental acts that require suitable management. The existence of such regulations exerts an external and unavoidable pressure on companies to implement reverse logistics practices.

By contrast, note that environmentalism and logistics are closely related and influence each another. Since one of the impacts of the environmentalism on logistics management is to broaden the scope of logistics from the perspective of forward logistics to reverse logistics, return goods handling emerges as one of the three factors most impacting logistics functions Murphy et al. 1994).

Environmental issues must be considered carefully when logistics are redesigned; for example, the facility location, sourcing of materials, transport means, etc. (Wu and Dunn 1995). Murphy and Poist (2003) assert that logisticians are best able to influence and/or manage environmental issues dealing with pollution, the conservation of resources and congestion.

The Competitive Weapon to Attract and Keep Customers

To retain customers in the scenario where markets are turbulent, as they are at the time of writing, has become as important as the conversion of prospects into clients. Returns offer a unique opportunity to gain customers' loyalty and to support the economic viability of the company.

King and Mackinnon (2002) surveyed different managerial practices related to such aspects as the personnel, philanthropy, local communities and environment. Participating organizations were evaluated from the perspective of their influence on the intention of the consumers to invest in, work for or use the company's products. The factors with the most influence were identified as becoming a leader in the development of a sustainable business and the increasing use of recyclable materials.

Ottoman (1998) estimated customers' loyalty to companies that have an environmental image and found that this translated into increased sales of between 5–15 per cent. This is approximately $75 million. The image projected by a company to customers is crucial, as it is the perception of added value as a consequence of these practices. Some companies are fully conscious of it as, for example, when consumers began to use Kodak's single-use cameras and the mass media reported the concerns of environmental stakeholders regarding the waste such 'use and throw' cameras implied. Kodak and Fuji Film subsequently launched a collection programme. As a result, more than 90 per cent of the throw-away cameras are recycled. The result was the inversion of an initially poor environmental image of the product category. The mass media, similarly, has portrayed Hewlett Packard as a protagonist of investment in recycling infrastructure. IBM Europe and Xerox have elaborated how their recovery activities have reinforced their brand image.

Magretta (1997) suggests, by extension, that increasingly the benefits are obtained in purchasing and in service. Rather than selling products, it is not unusual for some companies to move to selling complementary environmental sustainability services. For example, after considering the disposal costs British Telecom decided to 'rent' to its suppliers the lubricating oil its fleet of vehicles was using so that suppliers could take charge of the oil collection and treatment after the use.

Service quality today has an immediate effect on the market success of the company (Cohen et al. 1997). Returns have been revealed as one of the still untapped and promising opportunities to increase income and to consolidate client loyalty. Wood (2001) states that liberal returns policies favour volume backflows and that subsequent sales increases shall contribute to a clear positive net effect.

Section Summary

Reverse logistics can provide a competitive advantage due to the somewhat sporadic or scanty adoption and implementation. RL activities can offer organizations an opportunity to develop a differentiated strategy when compared to what competitors do. Improved service levels or reduced cycle times may be realized thanks to an effective RL implementation. The result is likely to be a larger market share or new market niches.

Other Reasons

1. Shortening of the product life cycle: due to rapid technological improvements, product life cycles have notably shortened. The computer industry is one such industry where the pace of technological change renders fully functional equipment obsolete at an incredibly fast rate. New designs rush to the market at incredible speeds, inducing the consumers to increase purchase frequency. While it is obvious that the consumers benefit from a wider range of products and of enhanced performance levels, this shortening trend inevitably causes the increase of unsold products, the increment of returns and of packaging materials, and the generation of more wastes (Tan and Kumar 2003). The reduction of the product life cycle causes a growing number of computers to become obsolete – very often even before being sold – and therefore the volume of both flows and wastes that enter in the reverse logistics pipeline, as well as their management costs, increase (Giutini and Andel 1995a).

2. Channel cleaning: RL can also be used as a means of freeing customers from obsolete or low rotation products; in this way, the investment held up in such inventories can to be utilized to purchase of new products (Andel 1997).

3. New distribution channels: the role played in recent years by online distribution is undeniable, mainly due to boost that the internet can give to impulse purchases. Consumers are provided with simpler and quicker ways of buying products. However, direct channels are also characterized by a high rate of returned products (see Figure 10.1), 'perhaps because the goods are damaged in transit or simply because they do not meet customer expectations'. According to Forrester Research (http://www.forrester.com/rb/consumertechno.jsp), 'in 1999 the value of returned goods previously bought online was $600 million, and the handling cost $468 million. Four years later, in 2003, the value of returned goods had multiplied by 20, reaching the figure of $11.5 trillion, with a proportional handling cost of $9 trillion.'

4. Valuable source of information: returns – in particular commercial returns – contain a rich amount of information as much on the product as on the marketing used to put it on the market. They also bring a great deal of information on consumers. The opportunities

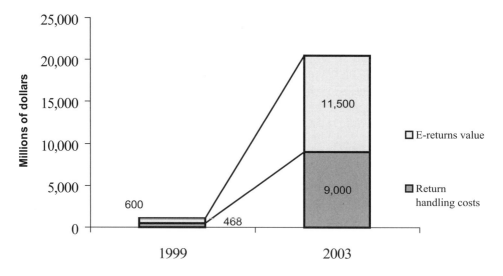

Figure 10.1   Total costs of e-returns, 1999–2003

Source: Forrester Research, http://www.forrester.com/rb/consumertechno.jsp.

given by this kind of information (more knowledge about the real performance of the product, the clarity of the instructions for use, product defects or consumers' expectations) is not always appreciated and grasped by retailers and merchants.

5. Brand protection: this usually refers to producers or salespersons who do not want to lose their brand image or the benefits that that brand image yield in the main distribution market (called 'channel A') by means of uncontrolled sales of their products in secondary markets or of channel B. These uncontrolled sales would imply, in most cases, a product image degradation (think, for example, of designer clothes unsold in their fashion period). RL activities guarantee the brand protection by returning the product to the producer, demarking the product, avoiding at the same time abuse from some consumers or building up barriers to competitors' entry.

Recovery Activities

In this section value recovery activities that justify the existence of efficient RL processes and activities will be presented. They will be ordered (as shown in Figure 10.2) according to the disassembly level required by each one. Thus, the section begins with 're-use' – the option that demands no disassembly – and ends with 'recycling', where disassembly is total.

Incineration and landfill, although depicted in Figure 10.2, are not considered as proper value recovery options (although they are placed after the recycling option, both options might take place at any time within the supply chain).

*   Re-use: apart from some cleaning or minor maintenance, neither materials, nor parts are replaced. The product is put into available usable stock 'as is'.
*   Repair: implies restoring failed products to 'working order', though possibly with a loss of quality.

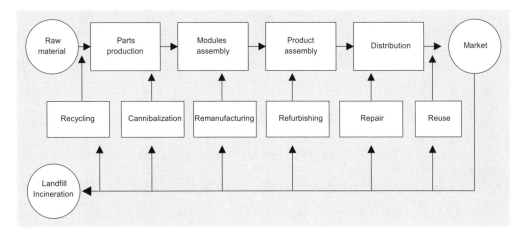

Figure 10.2   Value recovery activities

Source: Adapted from Thierry et al. 1995 by Rudi et al. 2000.

- Refurbishing: its purpose is to bring used products up to specified quality and, eventually, technologically upgrading them by replacing outdated modules. Lund asserts remanufacturing is an 'industrial process in which worn-out products are restored to like-new condition. Through a series of industrial processes in a factory environment, a discarded product is completely disassembled. Usable parts are cleaned, refurbished and put into inventory. Then the new product is reassembled from the old and, where necessary, new parts to product a unit fully equivalent – and sometimes superior – in performance and expected lifetime to the original new product' (Lund 1983, p. 19). Lund seems to focus only on discarded products. Guide et al. (1997) contend that a product does not have to be discarded to be a candidate for remanufacture.
- Cannibalization: implies selectively disassembling and recovering a limited set of reusable parts from used products or components, which may be either re-used in repairing, refurbishing, or remanufacturing other products and components or sold as spare parts.
- Recycling: denotes recovery of strictly material constituents of products (metal, paper, glass, etc.).

Challenges to Reverse Logistics Implementations

Reverse logistics has been considered as the reverse version of the traditional logistics. This view of perhaps the most recent sub-field within the logistics reveals that to be quite naïve. Decisions about the implementation of efficient reverse logistics processes pose a series of difficult challenges for companies. Although some corporations have already succeeded in adopting the required practices, they are still few in number even in worldwide terms. Reasons behind may be found within the company scope (see Guide et al., 2000 for a more detailed explanation):

a) uncertainty about time, quantity, variety and condition of returns, all of which information is required for adequately planning and organizing the company's resources;

b) imbalance between what a company wants to recover from the returns and what is supplied, causing inventory management problems and extra disposal costs;
c) loss of original packaging, implying not only loss of essential information for handling or tracking, but also increasing risks of damaging in transport and storing;
d) increase in number of (information and products) flows.

Problems may also be found in the supply chain context.

1. Cross-border transports: for example, waste transport through borders is strictly regulated by different countries. These laws (above all, those with global scope) may pose important constraints on companies, where cost-effective criteria or resources availability would have suggested centralized waste management plants in only one country. Another example can be found in countries where the recovery decision has been so strongly made that it jeopardizes the availability of the same process to neighbour countries by either acquiring all the recoverable returns or saturating the market by selling the reprocessed products. Nowadays, China heavily recycles metals imported from all over the world to meet the demand of its flourishing economy. By doing so, a scarcity has been detected in certain domestic markets, where prices have risen acutely (three times since 2003 (McGill 2005)).
2. Conflicts bewteen different objectives in the supply chain: for instance: a) remanufacturing companies that pose serious competition to OEM; b) retailers who send back products to distributors or manufacturers to get rid of the returns burden and pass the task to the upstream members, incurring costs that could be avoided; and c) empty containers which are not properly washed and cleaned, a situation that may alter the quality of future cargo causing risks for human or animal health.
3. Micro-internalization of macro-externalities.

Conclusions

Returns may represent a real headache, above all when considered as an afterthought. However, a) returns happen in daily businesses (and always have, for one or reason another) and b) they symbolize a kind of failure from which the company may learn and improve. The tools described in this section help in this path. Some of them imply working in the forward supply chain so that the chance of returns happening is diminished to the maximum extent. A second group of tools relates to the reverse supply chain. Obviously, each company should make an effort in choosing the ones that best fit its particular situation, since aspects such as the characteristics of tje product, industry or customers strongly influence on the final result.

1. The ideal for any company would be to have zero returns. To achieve this goal certain measures can be taken:
   – developing control procedures in the forward chain with direct influence on the reason for returning the product. A distributor of toner cartridge for printers adopted the procedure of asking customers the printer model so as to check the suitability of the cartridge ordered. Online buyers are often given the possibility of checking the whole shopping list to avoid unwanted duplications;
   – in a survey commanded by Phillips, 75 per cent of customers admitted to having returned products in which they had found no fault. This rate is not as unusual as it might seem (in HP the rate of 'defective not defective products' is estimated at

80 per cent of total returns). Reasons may be lack of appropriate information at the point of sale or difficulties in use, among others. Improvement in instructions manuals, free service phone calls or more extreme measures such as demanding an amount of money when returning the product (some online retailers charge up to 15 per cent of the purchase price) may deter certain customers from abusing liberal return policies.

 – establishing the so-called 'sero returns programmes', according to which two parties (manufacturer and wholesaler, for example) agree to forbid returns from the downstream to the upstream member once the products have been ordered. In recognition of the potential problems caused to the downstream member (such as management and disposal), 'the upstream member concedes a rebate (around 3 or 4 per cent) on the sales.

2. If returns cannot be avoided, the company can be prepared to deal with them by:

 – paying attention to the life cycle of a product from a marketing perspective, that is, recognizing the stage of sales (introduction, growth, maturity, decline) into which the product could be categorized. By doing so, the company can more easily forecast return volumes or condition, consequently reducing the management complexity introduced by the uncertainty inherent to return processes;

 – foreseeing future needs derived from recovery handling and reprocessing by paying attention to them in the early stages of product development;

 – implementing a cost system, so that costs related to returns are readily at hand and decisions on alternative return and recovery options can be made.

3. To improve efficiency in the reverse logistics and recovery processes, the company would need to:

 – decide which reverse logistics network design best meet its strategic and operational goals. Issues within this heading range from deciding between implementing RL activities in-house or outsource them; from adopting a decentralized design so that 'pre-ponement' can be applied or a centralized network where returns could be consolidated and from where being deviated to their appropriate recovery destinations (Blackburn et al. 2004);

 – foster cooperation when possible and strategically convenient. One example of this cooperation may be found in different countries where manufacturers in one sector, together with distributors and importers, have created integrated systems to offer a solution to their specific returns and/or waste;

 – implement good information technologies to track returns, resulting in turn not only to a better service to the company's customers but also valuable information to feed back into the whole system (product design, material quality, market acceptance, repeating abuse customers, etc.).

References

Ammons J., Realff, M. and Newton, D. (1997), 'Reverse Production System Design and Operation for Carpet Recycling', Working Paper, Georgia Institute of Technology, Atlanta.

Andel, T. (1997), 'Reverse Logistics: A Second Chance to Profit, Whether Through Refurbishing or Recycling, Companies are Finding Profit in Returned Products', *Transportation and Distribution* 38(7), pp. 61–4.

Ayres, R., Ferrer, G. and van Leynseele, T. (1997), 'Eco-efficiency, Asset Recovery and Remanufacturing', *European Management Journal* 15(5), pp. 557–74.

Beckley, D. and Logan, W. (1948), *The Retail Salesperson at Work* (New York: Gregg Publishing).

Biddle, D. (1993), 'Recycling for Profit: The New Green Business Frontier', *Harvard Business Review* 71(6), pp. 145–56.

Blackburn, J.D., Guide, V.D.R. Jr, Souza, G.C. and van Wassenhove, L.N. (2004), 'Reverse Supply Chains for Commercial Returns', *California Management Review* 46(2), pp. 6–22.

Botter, R. and Fortuin, L. (2000), 'Stocking Strategy for Service Parts – A Case Study', *International Journal of Operations and Production Management*, 20(6), pp. 656–74.

Caldwell, B. (1999), 'Reverse Logistics', *Information Week* April, http://www.informationweek.com/729/logistics.htm.

Cohen, M., Zheng, Y. and Agrawal, V. (1997), 'Service Parts Logistics: A Benchmark Analysis', *IIE Transactions* 29(8), pp. 627–39.

Cooper, M.C., Lambert, D.M. and Pagh, J.D. (1997), 'Supply Chain Management: More than a New Name for Logistics', *International Journal of Logistics Management* 8(1), pp. 1–14.

Dowlatshahi, S. (2000), 'Developing a Theory of Reverse Logistics', *Interfaces* 30(3), pp. 143–55.

Emerson, C. and Grimm, C. (1996), 'Logistics and Marketing Components of Customer Service: An Empirical Test of the Mentzer, Gomes and Krapfel Model', *International Journal of Physical Distribution and Logistics Management* 26(8), pp. 29–42.

Enarsson, L. (1998), 'Evaluation of Suppliers: How to Consider the Environment', *International Journal of Physical Distribution and Logistics Management* 28(1), pp. 5–17.

Fernández, I. (2004), 'Reverse Logistics Implementation in Manufacturing Companies', PhD dissertation, University of Vaasa, Finland.

Geyer, R. and Jackson, T. (2004), 'Supply Loops and Their Constraints: The Industrial Ecology of Recycling and Re-use', *California Management Review* 46(2), pp. 55–73.

Giuntini, R. and Andel, T. (1995a), 'Advance with Reverse Logistics: Part 1', *Transportation and Distribution* 36(2), pp. 73–5.

Giultinian, J. and Nwokoye, N. (1975), 'Developing Distribution Channels and Systems in the Emerging Recycling Industries', *International Journal of Physical Distribution* 6(1), pp. 28–38.

Ginter, P. and Starling, J. (1978), 'Reverse Distribution Channels for Recycling', *California Management Review* 20(3), pp. 73–82.

Guide, D., Srivastava, R. and Spencer, M. (1997), 'An Evaluation of Capacity Planning Techniques in a Remanufacturing Environment', *International Journal of Production Research* 35(1), pp. 67–82.

Guide, V.D.R. Jr, Jayaraman, V., Srivastava, R. and Benton, W. (2000), 'Supply-chain Management for Recoverable Manufacturing Systems', *Interfaces* 30(3), pp. 125–42.

Johnson, M. and Wang, M. (1995), 'Planning Product Disassembly for Material Recovery Opportunities', *International Journal of Production Research* 33(1), pp. 3119–42.

King, D.S. and Mackinnon, A. (2002), 'Who Cares? Community Perceptions in the Marketing of Corporate Citizenship', in Andriof, J., Waddock, S., Husted, B. and Rahman, S.S. (eds) *Unfolding Stakeholder Thinking* (London: Greenleaf Publishing).

Lambert, D.M., Cooper, M.C. and Pagh, J.D. (1998), 'Supply Chain Management: Implementation Issues and Research Opportunities', *The International Journal of Logistics Management* 9(2), pp. 1–19.

Lele, M. and Karmarkar, U. (1983), 'Good Product Support is Smart Marketing', *Harvard Business Review* 61(6), pp. 124–32.

Lund, R. (1983), 'Remanufacturing, United States Experience and Implications for Development Nations', MIT Centre for Policy Alternatives Report, CPA/83–17, Cambridge, MA.

Lund, R. (1996), 'The Remanufacturing Industry: Hidden Giant', Boston University Study funded by Argonne National Laboratory.

Magretta, J. (1997), 'Growth through Global Sustainability', *Harvard Business Review* January–February, pp. 79–88.

McGill, J. (2005), 'Materias primas: ¿obsesión especulativa o verdadera escasez?' [Raw Materials: Speculative Obsession or True Scarcity?], *ABC Journal* February, pp. 34–5.

Minahan, T. (1998), 'Manufacturers Take Aim at End of the Supply Chain', *Purchasing* 124(6), pp. 111–12.

Murphy, P. and Poist, R. (2003), 'Green Perspectives and Practices: A "Comparative Logistics" Study', *Supply Chain Management: An International Journal* 8(2), pp. 122–31.

Murphy, P., Poist, R. and Braunschwieg, R. (1994), 'Management of Environmental Issues in Logistics: Current Status and Future Potential', *Transportation Journal* 34(1), pp. 48–56.

Ottoman, J. (1998), 'Waste Not: Green Strategies Key to Efficient Products', *Marketing News* 32, pp. 12–13.

Pfohl, H. and Ester, B. (1999), 'Benchmarking for Spare Parts Logistics', *Benchmarking: An International Journal* 6(1), pp. 22–39.

Porter, M. (1998), *Competitive Strategy: Techniques for Analysing Industries and Competitors* (New York: Free Press).

Rudi, N., Pyke, D. and Sporsheim, P. (2000), 'Product Recovery at the Norwegian National Insurance Administration', *Interfaces* 30(3), pp. 166–79.

Soto, J.P. (2005), 'Devoluciones: ¿dolor de cabeza u oportunidad?' [Returns: Headache or Opportunity?], *Logicel* 51, pp. 20–21.

Sterling, J. and Lambert, D. (1989), 'Customer Service Research: Past, Present and Future', *International Journal of Physical Distribution and Logistics Management* 19(2), pp. 3–23.

Supply Chain Council (2001), *Supply Chain Operations Reference Model: Overview of SCOR Version 5.0* (Washington, DC: Supply Chain Council, Inc.).

Tan, A. and Kumar, A. (2003), 'Reverse Logistics Operations in the Asia-Pacific Region Conducted by Singapore Based Companies: An Empirical Study', *Conradi Research Review* 2(1), pp. 25–48.

Terry, S.H. (1869), *The Retailer's Manual* (Newark, NJ: Jennings Bros; repr. 1967, Guinn, NY: B. Earl Puckett Fund for Retail Education).

Thierry, M., Salomon, M., Nunnen, J. and Wassenhove, L. (1995), 'Strategic Issues in Product Recovery Management', *California Management Review* 37(2), pp. 114–35.

Wood, S. (2001), 'Remote Purchase Environments: The Influence of Return Policy Leniency on Two-stage Decision Processes', *Journal of Marketing Research* 38(2), pp. 157–69.

Wu, H. and Dunn, S. (1995), 'Environmentally Responsible Logistics Systems', *International Journal of Physical Distribution and Logistics Management* 25(2), pp. 20–38.

DIMENSION 4
Regional and Country Specific Differences

Chapter 11

Human Resource Management's Relationship to Company Performance

Nada Zupan

Introduction

Competitive forces in the international business environment are pushing companies to constantly develop their sources of sustainable competitive advantage. Employees' competencies and the speed at which these competencies can be transformed into high performance are crucial for long-term company success. Hence many companies focus on enhancing the relationship between people and company performance through human resource management (HRM) systems and practices. The aim of this chapter is to investigate this link between HRM and company performance. The chapter explores how companies can make this relationship stronger and thereby contribute to long-term competitiveness and success. The discussion starts with why and how people can be an important source of sustainable competitive advantage. The main HRM approaches used by companies to transform HR potential into high performance are explained. HR best practices and strategic HRM as a means to build competitive advantage through people are elaborated. Some new issues in the HRM–company performance relationship are discussed and the chapter ends with some concluding remarks.

People as Source of Competitive Advantage

Today there is a widespread agreement that people are the most important source of competitiveness in contemporary firms. When other resources such as capital and technology are more readily available to firms, people – with their knowledge and the ability to apply knowledge to create innovative solutions – become the key competitive factor. Wright et al. (1994) use five main concepts from a resource-based view of the firm to argue that human resources meet all sustained competitive advantage criteria:

1. Human resources *add value* through creative utilization of knowledge and energy towards achieving company goals. Because HR supply and demand are not homogenous in terms of knowledge, skills and abilities (KSA), differences are easily found in the abilities of companies to create value from individuals' contributions. The whole utility analysis research supports this argument and also provides methods for estimating this value.
2. Job complexity, globalization and fast changing environments demand highly competent workforces. However, high-quality human resources are relatively *rare* because skills and abilities are binomially distributed in the population and those firms that have the ability to attract the best talent are gaining human capital at the expense of others.
3. HR performance benchmarks practices are very *hard to imitate* because they reflect the company's unique history. Casual ambiguity and social complexity make it difficult to

identify precisely the sources of competitive advantage and then duplicate activities, methods and relevant components of the HR pool. Company-specific circumstances, in particular the leader's behaviour and drivers to survive and win, may provide opportunities to do similar things, even if the stated justifications and metaphors in place that motivate and create superior performance may be similar to textbook cases. Today's travel and communication infrastructure are making it easier to move and relocate. However, employees' *mobility is still not perfect* due to transaction costs that occur when moving from one employment situation to another. Due to their social knitting and behavioural patterns, some cultures and societies are somewhat averse to workforce mobility.

4. Although there are some substitutes in the short run (e.g., automation), until now HR have been non-substitutable in terms of human ability to creatively generate and use knowledge. People are one of the few firm resources that have the potential to avoid becoming obsolete. They are transferable across a variety of technologies, products and markets.

As soon as we agree that HR passes the test of sustainable competitive advantage, we need to consider two important concerns. Firstly, if a company can not extract high performance from HR over the long run people will remain *only a potential source* of sustained competitive advantage. The second concern is the limited control over creative and enthusiastic people.

People as Potential Sources of Sustained Competitive Advantage

Sports teams, such as the English soccer squad, demonstrate that it is not enough to put together excellent individuals and just expect that their high potential will yield high results. Their performance needs to be managed, from building their commitment to common goals and achieving individual targets. They need to have all of the relevant resources (e.g., knowledge, information, equipment, working environment, to name just a few) and have in place systems to reduce uncertainty and facilitate cooperation and goal achievement.

The simple performance model presented in Figure 11.1 shows four basic components of high performance. All sustained high performance starts with the right goals and with a management team that is able to get lower levels of the organization to work towards these. Traditional paradigms suggest that management's primary role then is to communicate company goals engage employees at all levels, making every employee aware of how he or she can contribute to the attainment of company goals. With the right goals, high performance then depends on capabilities, motivation, and resources and working conditions, available to employees. The Japanese *hoshin kanri* approach relies on individuals, at all levels, identifying what they can offer and do to achieve the company's goals.

The multiplication sign combining the three components suggests that as soon as one is missing, the resulting performance will be zero. None of these components are substitutable in such a way that one could be replaced by the other. Rather, if one of them is not properly developed the result will be suboptimal performance and underutilization of other two components. For example, highly motivated and capable employees without proper information may never solve complex problems effectively. Because of their skills and motivation, they might eventually find all the information needed. They would, however, have wasted time and other resources that could have been put to better use on value-adding activities.

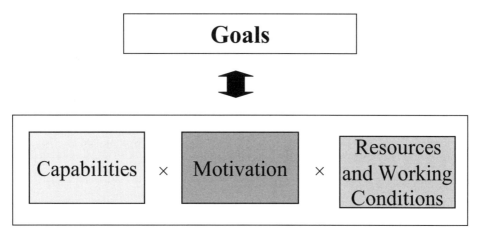

Figure 11.1   Model of high performance

When highly skilled employees have all needed resources available to them yet lack motivation to pursue goals, they will underutilize all resources, including their knowledge and skills. Most unfortunate, however, is the situation when highly motivated people have all the resources, but because they lack specific knowledge and skills, they may make wrong or dangerous decisions, may execute work poorly and may do more damage than positively contributing to results. Managers should be aware that, should any of the three components be poorly developed, this will diminish current and future performance. Frustration and dissatisfaction may decrease motivation to work and acquire new skills. Such a negative spiral of performance then becomes very difficult to reverse.

During the author's research, when discussing this model and its components of high performance with managers, they expressed most concern about the ability of companies to build high levels of motivation. They concluded that external motivation is less effective than internally generated enthusiasm, while at the same time internal motivation is more difficult to manage. Managers and HR specialists have limited opportunities to affect internal motivation because it largely depends on each individual themselves, with all their values, interests, personal goals and preferences. Nevertheless, to achieve sustained high performance managers need to develop all three components of the model, constantly monitoring their presence and acting immediately when they perceive imbalance or weaknesses of any component.

Limited Control Over People

The second important concern with regard to people as a source of competitive advantage stems from a limited control over people by the company. Even though a company may use many techniques and processes to fully engage employees into pursuing common goals, it is ultimately at employees' discretion how much effort they are willing to commit and what kind of behaviour will choose to engage in when dealing with others.

If an individual decides to leave there is very little a company can do. Even if the company chooses to enforce employment contract provisions to make the employee stay for a certain period of time (provided that such provisions are in the contract), the employee can in response lower their input and in extreme cases also opt for misbehaviour such as sabotage or, perhaps worse, corporate espionage.

Ricardo Semler (2003) suggests that, for his company at least, yesterday's strategy is as much use as an out of date horoscope prediction. This is because at his company they re-discuss hot topics without pinning themselves down to one strategy that would be obsolete in a month or two. Many companies treat ex-employees as *persona non grata*. In other words, the employees and the company have no further contact with them. Semlar suggests that employees need to have some time away in other companies to learn how good it actually is at Semco. For that reason, the door is always open to ex-employees to return. They bring new experiences, stories, lessons to learn and are remotivated. The cost of induction is minimized also, because they are fully aware of the company's culture, values and systems.

Unfortunately, the employees who usually want to leave the company are not the same ones the company would like to let go. It is those with most valuable capabilities who are targeted by other companies or are themselves searching for better opportunities and easily find them if they are not satisfied with their current employer. That is why it is essential that companies don't just build transactional employment relationships but rather relational ones (Figure 11.2) through which both employer and employee establish long-term high commitment relationships and consideration for the best interests of both.[1] Relational type employment relationships are more likely to succeed in satisfying employee needs and thus indirectly strengthen ties between employees and the company.

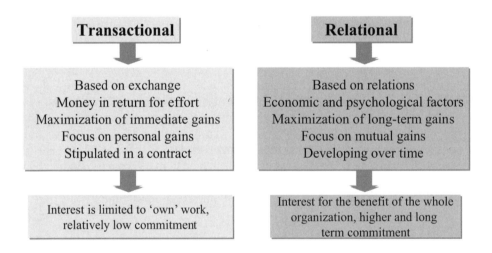

Figure 11.2   Types of employment relationships

Generally speaking, the question of how to retain the best employees is becoming increasingly important. The term 'talent war' reflects the current situation in the knowledge work labour market. Companies are using various strategies and methods to attract the best employees because they know they can build competitive advantage if they win the best talent over their competitors and, even more importantly, if they retain the best employees and thus take full advantage of all investment put in to developing employees within an organization. The only way to raise the likelihood that employees will turn down offers when approached by

---

1   For more about relational employment relationships see Rousseau (1996).

other employers is to provide an environment where they can get what they want; in strategic management terminology, it is important to maintain *employer-employee fit*. Hence the way in which companies manage implicit and psychological contracts that can be described as a set of beliefs, evaluations and assumptions held by employees with regard to their employment relationship is very important. The way employees perceive the fulfilment of the psychological contract by the employer plays an important role in employee outcomes such as satisfaction, commitment and performance. The underlying logic is that when employees feel that the company fulfils their expectations and treats them fairly, they are likely to be willing to put more effort into achieving company goals. Similarly, when employees feel that their psychological contract is breached or violated, they are more likely to use measures to lower their efforts or as a final step even leave the company.[2]

Our discussion so far has shown that people can be a source of competitive advantage. The process of transforming their potential into high performance is not an easy one and has to be properly managed. This also is the reason why human resource management has become an important business function that exists to enhance employee performance and ensure constant development of human resources in line with business needs. To strengthen the HR–company performance link, human resource management has to answer three key questions:

- How can and should the best employees be found?
- How should their performance be managed?
- How can to the company retain its best employees?

Figure 11.3 shows many HRM activities that can respond to these three challenges. However, just designing the relevant tools and methods by HR departments is far from sufficient.

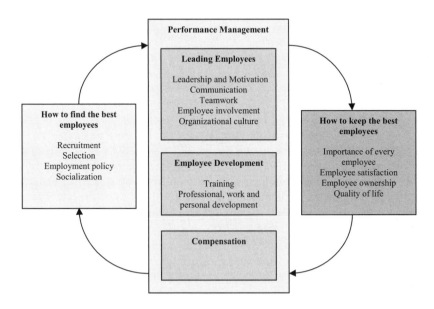

Figure 11.3   Main HRM issues in gaining competitive advantage through people

---

2   For more on the concept of psychological contracts and the effects of breach and violation see Rousseau (1995) and Robinson and Morrison (2000).

HR has the prime responsibility for managing human resources. Since most of the implementation may be lead by line managers, it is crucial that these methods and tools are used effectively by managers at all levels of the organization. Ulrich (1997) asserted that the role of HR managers and specialists needs to be transformed into a change agent which is more like a strategic business partner as well as employee champion. The aim of these facilitators is to help employees fulfil their potential and career aspirations (of course, within company needs). Although the role of a field expert, capable of designing HR systems, tools and methods, is important, only the ability to make effective implementation adds to building competitive advantage through people.

Different Approaches to Establishing HRM – Company Performance Link

Since companies operate in different environments and use different business strategies, observers can find different approaches to the practice of human resource management. HRM literature on theory and practices of companies in different parts of the world distinguishes two main HRM dimensions. The *first dimension* pertains to the *focus of HRM processes*. There is a variety of systems on the continuum from *result focused (hard approaches)* to *people focused (soft approaches)*. In extreme hard approaches cases, companies get results by exploiting HR (including underpayment, poor working conditions, child labour, etc.). In some transitional and developing economies such as China, India and Brazil, examples can be found of situations where companies compete based on low prices, in the context of high supply of cheap labour and poorly developed industrial relations systems. As soon as there is a shortage of skilled labour or trade unions increase the power of employees, companies have to take into account employee rights and interests, something that was observed in new member states of European Union (those joining in May 2005) all of whom underwent transition from socialism to market economy structures (e.g., Slovenia, Czech Republic, Poland). Because low-cost strategies depend on continuous improvement processes, employee involvement becomes important as a source of ideas and as a driver for high performance and companies need to search for balance between economic results and a people focus.

On the other hand, when companies depend on employee knowledge and creativity, soft approaches to HRM are more appropriate. Companies are more likely to take into account employees' need to be developed in order to raise performance and to offer proper returns for employee engagement in both financial and quality of working life terms. Employers strive to achieve high levels of employee satisfaction while assuring sustained high performance levels. When employees are the main stakeholders (e.g., through employee ownership) in extreme cases it may also happen that the focus on results is very low and employees allocate resources with regard to their personal rather than the company's best interests and through this even damage the business in the long run. Ricardo Semler (2003) suggests that employees will not do anything that is not in their own best interests. They will contribute to projects and business activities far more if they feel free to do so rather than compelled to comply with fixed performance measures. The two key questions are should individuals work on their own to set up a new project, and should they work on potentially new business ideas as quasi entrepreneurs? To answer the first question, individuals should continually ask who will verify I worked here today? The second question may be a matter of strategic flexibility and tolerance. If the business is focused on a single theme, such as vehicle manufacture or petroleum product refining, any potential business development outside these areas may not be encouraged during work time.

The *second dimension* where differences may be found relates to the issue of *universality versus contingency*.[3] The key question is whether companies believe in the universal power of HR best practices that can be found through benchmarking and reports in various publications (e.g., books and magazines presenting case studies), or whether they believe that it is better to develop bespoke HR strategies and activities that are contingent on their external and internal HR environment and business focus. Best practices or universal approaches to HRM have the advantage that they are basically adopting methods that have proven to be successful. This approach may be less time consuming and a good approach for smaller companies with low internal level of HR expertise. There may be distinct introductory cost such as consultancy, conferences, new recruits that bring specific needed skills and experience. The key to success in applying a universal approach is first how well the company chooses relevant best practices and then how well they are implemented. Details of implementation requirements are given in Chapter 30 by Newlands in this volume.

It is not easy to effectively transfer HRM practices across cultures because of casual ambiguity, social complexity and unique historical conditions as well as cultural differences which are very important scenario-specific contexts. Singing company songs and mass recreation during breaks were not well accepted by American employees. The simple imitation of what others are doing may not yield desired results. What has worked in one company may have completely different (sometimes even negative) effects in another one. These hard lessons were learned by some American companies, for example, when they were caught by surprise when Japanese *keiretsu* competitiveness surged.

Other examples are found in high-power distance cultures (regard for authority) such as China, Russia, India, etc. Empowerment, high-involvement employee practices and participative leadership may be ineffective because managers are expected to know what to do and how best it should be done. In this context, the employee's role is to execute assigned tasks. Elaborating on the effects of national culture on HRM is beyond the scope of this chapter. Readers interested in these effects will find information on cross-cultural management in, for example, Hofstede (2001), Trompenaars and Hampden-Turner (2000) and Warner and Joynt (2002).

The contingency approach advocates developing HRM strategies that fit the business situation and reflect the current state and future HR needs. With the contingency approach it is the fit between HRM and business strategy that is most significant. In order to achieve proper fit we need high levels of HRM expertise and strategic positioning of HRM function as well as more time and resources compared to best practices approach. That is the reason why we may find this strategic approach either in large corporations that have developed a good home-grown base of HRM knowledge, or in medium and small companies that depend heavily on HR as a source of competitiveness (e.g., knowledge-intensive high-tech companies) and use external HRM expertise delivered by consultants to build strategic HRM.

It is important to note that there is no one best way to approach HRM and so it may be useful for companies to find their most suitable position in the HRM approaches matrix shown in Figure 11.4 and then develop HRM accordingly.

Positioning along the two dimensions will depend on company business philosophy, strategy, goals and key success factors relevant to HRM. Of course, both external and internal environment play and important role in determining which approach is best suited to specific situations.

It is important to choose what appears to be the best fit for the situation and work hard on implementing the approach effectively. The best approach available may not be perfect. By contemplating implications of a chosen approach, the company can predict possible weaknesses and search to find or develop means to eliminate or control possible negative outcomes.

---

3   Additional discussion on this dimension can be found in Purcell (1999).

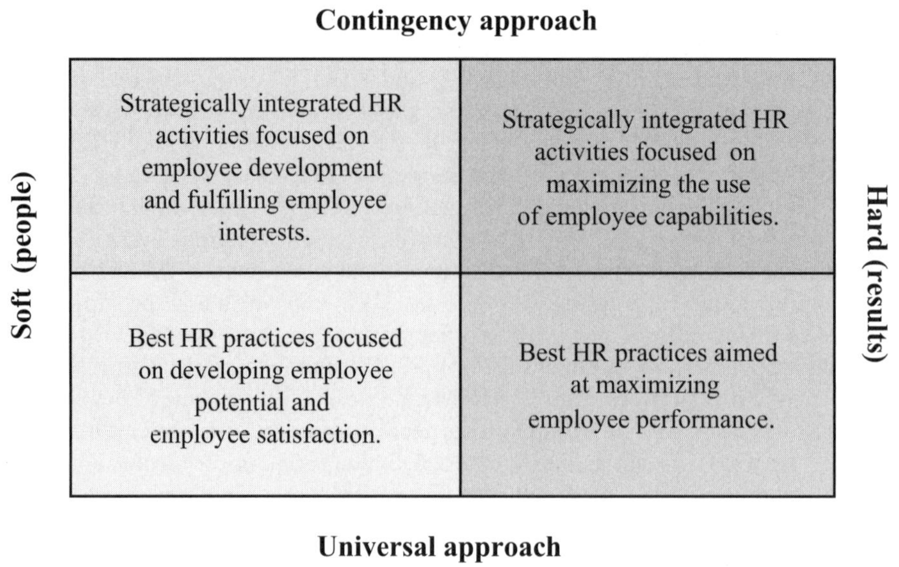

Contingency approach

Strategically integrated HR activities focused on employee development and fulfilling employee interests.	Strategically integrated HR activities focused on maximizing the use of employee capabilities.
Best HR practices focused on developing employee potential and employee satisfaction.	Best HR practices aimed at maximizing employee performance.

Soft (people) — Hard (results)

Universal approach

Figure 11.4   HRM approaches matrix

HRM Best Practices

The best way to identify HRM best practices is through benchmarking what successful companies are doing. The most often referenced work on HRM best practices are by Pfeffer's (1994, 1998). In his studies we find reports of high-performing organizations, conducted over several years. In Europe, CRANET research network produces comparative analysis of HRM in European countries, including the analysis of HRM practices.[4] Other sources are multiple case studies and periodical benchmarking reports of HRM professional associations and consulting companies. Based on these various sources, some of the HRM best practices most frequently reported are presented here:

- *Selective employment*: there is little doubt that most companies want to find the best employees. However, competing to attract the best talent today is very demanding. Companies have to build a good employer reputation as a result of developing their HRM activities. Recruitment and selection methods must be carefully designed and complied with in order to identify the best talent and employee-employer fit. With regard to the latter, increasing attention is being paid to matching employee values with those of the organization. Although the best companies always are open to highly talented employees, they also use flexible employment arrangements in order to buffer variations in demand for both employee numbers and, more importantly, the competencies required to satisfy customer orders.
- *Diversity management*: diversity, in terms of culture, knowledge and experience, can contribute abilities to innovate and respond better to anticipated future customer needs. There are two important elements to diversity management: internationalization creating culturally diverse workforces and an aging workforce in most developed countries creating

---

4 CRANET reports can be found in Brewster et al. (2000, 2004).

circumstances where diverse age groups (e.g., generations X and Y), with their own specific behavioural patterns, coexist and work. In this context, successful companies install diversity management programmes which aim to develop equal opportunities and the involvement of different employee groups. The aim is to increase awareness and sensitivity for diversity, as well as create processes, procedures and venues to manage potential conflicts and unacceptable behaviour.

- *Developing competencies*: as work performed increases in complexity and variability, job analysis and job description, which were the bases for making HRM decisions in traditional organizations, become less effective. These are being replaced by competency models that study the best performing employees. In so doing, companies try to identify key competencies (a combination of knowledge, skills, abilities and behaviours) that are relevant to sustained peak performance and then develop these systematically in their employees. Organizations are now aligning their key abilities and capabilities to the core competence of the company and translating this core competence into performance targets for teams and individual specialists.

- *Extensive training and knowledge management*: since knowledge has become the key to success in most high-performing companies, they offer extensive training opportunities. Training is predominantly action-based or makes use of problem-solving techniques. This reduces the gap between knowledge and initial experience gained on courses and the active knowledge retained over a period of time that is used in employee's everyday work. Investing heavily in knowledge acquisition and transfer requires an efficient corporate learning function. Good corporate training and education programmes depend on knowledge management processes that acquire, create, share and use knowledge creatively. The aim is to convert tacit into explicit knowledge. Explicit knowledge is the amount of data, information and routines that are recorded and remain at the company facilities after everyone goes home at night. This includes lecture materials and instruction manuals. Many successful companies have developed a true 'learning organization' where learning becomes a way of life and a constant source of knowledge creation and innovation. Seminars may be delivered by any employee on any subject. This facilitates creative exchanges and provides other perspectives and debate. The subtle nature of this process means that participants move away from face-to-face confrontation where people are the issue, to situations where ideas and concepts are discussed in a mature manner. In effect, this supports the organization's conflict management processes and negotiation becomes a tacitly acquired skill. See Chapter 5 by Holtom in this volume.

- *Extensive communication*: understanding the company's mission, vision, values, goals and business operations shapes the way employees behave and develop their commitment. Sharing information is a key to good decision-making and problem solving. Information technology is pervasive, communicating and sharing of data and ideas has become easier than ever and new e-communication techniques are widely used. Most of the best companies, however, still pay a lot of attention to personal, two-way communication, because it improves understanding (mostly through immediate feedback and dialogue) and also builds relationships between the people participating in the communication.

- *Performance management*: the aim of performance management systems (PMS) goes beyond simple performance appraisals that focus on identifying employee strengths and weaknesses. PMS builds on management by objectives through not only stipulating what needs to be achieved (i.e., setting objectives) but also finding the ways in which work can be undertaken most effectively and efficiently. Modern PMS approaches depend on employee involvement to reduce resistance and increase acceptance of goals and plans because they have contributed to setting expectations. Frequently responsibility for the performance appraisal initiatives is put into employees' hands. This requires managers to act as coaches in order to help employees reach their full potential. The fundamental perspective taken by managers in terms of performance and contribution is 'the higher you go, the higher I go too'. Managers thus have to understand the role of facilitator, to make it easier for others to achieve their own defined form and level of success.

- *Competitive compensation packages*: in order to attract and retain the best talent, companies need to offer competitive compensation packages. Most successful companies don't compete with base salaries but rather with offering good incentive packages (including long-term incentives such as stock options or shares in ownership) and by expanding the definition of compensation to include all returns to employees, such as status, recognition, quality of life, etc. Pay for performance is an important component of compensation and programmes such as success-or goal-sharing are designed to link pay with individual, group and company level performance. They thereby channel employee behaviour and actions towards achieving company goals.

- *Providing job security*: a high level of job security, like life-long employment, is a real challenge in today's unpredictable and fast-changing business world. By contrast, low levels of job security make employees averse to taking risks and implementing innovations because they may fear possible consequences of making mistakes, specifically losing their jobs. Companies are trying to answer the challenge of job security through building the employability of employees and thus assuring indirect job security. Highly employable people will have little difficulty finding another job, even when their current employer can no longer offer employment. Because developing employability poses some risk, employers may lose some employees through their transfer to competitors or other industries, or by their becoming self-employed contractors. Some employees may return after some years gaining experience in other organizations and be remotivated and full of ideas for improvement projects. Out of principle, others may simply never wish to return to a former employer. Provided that HRM manages a retention processes and motivators effectively, raising employees' employability could be an effective solution.

The whole point of building competitiveness through a best practices approach is *not* to simply find isolated, simple and fast solutions. A company wanting to use best HRM practices needs to start by selecting the most relevant organizations to benchmark and then examine their operations more deeply to understand the interconnectedness of the various practices they use. Unless organizations take into account the scenario and location specific circumstances, best practices can only be a source of ideas that will need a unique project plan and cooperation from the workforce to implement similar activities in the company. As Fitz-Enz (1997) correctly warns that organizations can not expect to find miraculous solutions and enlightenment about the future from simply studying current or historic best practices.

Best practices rest on a set of basic beliefs, traits and operating systems that are only found deep in an organization's psyche, values, knowledge and operational philosophy. Rather than fixating on a single practice, companies should focus on adding value in everything they do. They should build long-term commitment, proactive organizational culture, partnering with people inside and outside the organization, particularly with suppliers and corporate customers. They should collaborate across functions and processes. Constant improvement can be achieved only through nurturing competitive passion. This is based on two necessary elements: target-based product and service-oriented innovation and balancing risk with potential rewards.

HRM Strategy

Contingency approaches to HRM strive to establish the best possible fit between HRM and business strategy (vertical integration) and, at the same time, integration of all HRM activities (horizontal integration).[5] Vertical integration aims to ensure that HRM is able to respond to business challenges and contribute to developing core competencies. Horizontal integration is needed in order to standardize the use of particularly effective and efficient HRM practices by linking these with other existing activities. For example, if knowledge sharing is an important practice, companies need to take into account employees' aptitude for sharing knowledge when recruiting and reviewing internal candidates for promotion. They thus need to create knowledge-sharing criteria for use in promotion and allocating rewards, and organize training sessions for employees to become comfortable with knowledge sharing. Part of this can be effective writing and presentation skills. Horizontal integration can be achieved through developing 'HR practice bundles'.[6] These are a set of practices designed that the ideal candidate or employee would be skilled in that are pertinent to different HR activities (such as staffing, training and development, compensation, employee relation), that aim to develop a specific competency skill set or achieving a specific goal.

The best way to achieve vertical and horizontal integration of HRM is the result of a structured HRM strategy (see Figure 11.5). Firstly, organizations need to review the company vision, values and goals and identify key success factors to achieve them from an HR point of view. They then need to elaborate on those key success factors and specify all key HR capabilities needed for successful execution of the business strategy.

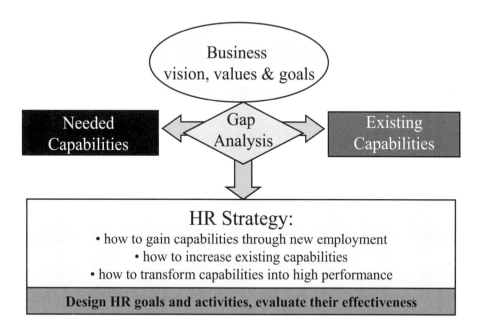

Figure 11.5   HR strategy formulation

---

5   For more discussion on vertical and horizontal integration see Snell et al. (2001) and Mabey and Salaman (1995).

6   The term 'HR bundles' was first used by MacDuffey (1995).

Next, the company needs to compare existing capabilities with those required and identify gaps between the two. A thorough HR analysis should provide necessary information for identifying this gap, focusing both on numbers (e.g., employee demographics) and on the assessment of existing knowledge, skills and abilities, together with employee attitudes and behaviour. Such an analysis is a good basis for designing HR strategic goals referring to closing the gap between existing and needed capabilities. Finally, specific activities and programmes can be prepared in order to achieve HR strategic goals.

An alternate approach is to review the amount of paid or unpaid overtime currently being undertaken. Calculations should be made of how many employees it will require to reduce the overtime to zero. Some slack time should be included for existing staff in order to recruit, facilitate training, and take time out to review longer term strategic needs and direction. Key questions to ask are: Is the new number of employees realistic? Are they affordable? Will they be needed over the longer term? The strategic analysis described above may be easier to undertake once the recruitment is underway, and pressure to 'firefight' managerial problems has eased.

Although designing a quality HRM strategy is important and not always easy, there will be little effect if we don't then assure an effective implementation. To achieve this, HRM needs a good power base such as strategic positioning of the HRM function, HR knowledge embedded in all HR actors, a good reputable HR department, effective HR information system and stakeholders' support for HRM. All HRM actors need to have significant involvement: HR specialists, managers at all levels (from top to line managers) and also trade unions and other employee representatives. With the process of HRM devolution (pushing decision-making and implementation of HR activities down to the line management) that is observed in Europe (see Brewster et al. 2004), special attention needs to be given to providing line mangers with sufficient knowledge and support to use HRM tools effectively.

Although there is good research evidence that strategic HRM approaches contribute to company performance, one of the major concerns is the issue of flexibility. If companies can achieve strong vertical and horizontal integration of HRM, this may decrease their ability to adapt quickly to changes in the business environment.[7] Changing one element of an integrated system in reality requires changes in all other parts. Problems with flexibility can be controlled effectively through increased resource flexibility (e.g., broad skill-sets and empowerment) or coordination flexibility (e.g., contingency workers, customized/innovative systems). It is imperative that HRM strategy is not treated as a once-in-a-decade project that might be reviewed every five years. HRM strategies have to be constantly evaluated to assess how well they still fit with the business strategy and how effectively tactics respond to everyday business challenges. If the answers are not satisfactory, some of its elements overall or the entire HRM strategy will need to be changed accordingly.

New HRM Issues: Strengthening the Company Performance Relationship

Changes in the business environment and support of information technology encourage conditions where knowledge is the most critical competitive asset a company can hold and is a vital source of superior performance in the knowledge economy. Unlike material resources, knowledge tends to increase than decrease with use – it stimulates new ideas and facilitates the creation of new knowledge. Knowledge actually increases for both the source and recipient side of knowledge transfer (McEvily and Chakravarthy 2002). Much of a company's knowledge, particularly its tacit knowledge, resides in its human capital, that is, in people and their

---

7　For more on the issue of fit and flexibility see Wright and Snell (1998).

capabilities. Human capital, however, is not owned by the organization; rather it is 'rented' on a daily basis and can appreciate in value. Therefore, additional challenges for HRM arise, such as how to build human capital and keep it in the company, by retaining employees with high individual human capital and through sharing of knowledge and managing tacit knowledge.

Social Capital

Traditional HRM has been focused on the individual and the formal relationship with the organization. Today, knowledge sharing occurs mostly through informal social networks. Since it can facilitate effective development and use of human capital, HRM should effectively manage social capital. Social capital can be broadly defined as the goodwill available to individuals and groups (Adler and Kwon 2002). Its source lies in the structure and content of the actor's social relations, while its effects derive from the information, influence and solidarity available to the actor. Youndt and Snell's (2004) study of various forms of intellectual capital and their impact on performance suggested that social capital was by far the strongest predictor of performance. Also, social capital may enable organizations to utilize their knowledge base more efficiently by leveraging it across the entire organization and thereby reducing redundancies, effort duplication and ultimately organizational costs.

The success of strategic HRM in the knowledge economy depends on its ability to harness the potential hidden in the informal social architecture, including tacit knowledge, informal learning and informal relationships. HRM can contribute to effectively managing social relationships as essential intangibles both inside and outside the organization and thus contribute by developing company social capital.[8] HRM needs to foster an environment that is conducive to relationships, to map strategically the relevant ones, to develop ongoing relationships with current and former employees, and improve relationships across value chain members.

Employee Classifications and Configurations of HR Practices to Manage Them

Traditionally, employees have been classified in several groups according to the individual's various characteristics. In practice, the most frequently used grouping variables for individuals have been demographic variables such as gender, age, tenure and education, organizational characteristics such as job position and functional expertise and hierarchical level or employment status variables such as employment mode, type of work (e.g., managerial/non-managerial), union membership and pay level.

Today, individual knowledge or individual human capital characteristics as criteria for classifying employees have become more relevant. Elaborating on this issue, Lepak and Snell (2002) classified employees based on human capital value and, according to this classification, identified employees with high human capital uniqueness and high strategic value of human capital. Core knowledge workers, for example, are very valuable to the company and therefore merit attention. To manage these core employees, companies should design commitment-based HR configurations that focus on relational relationships that include intensive training and development, empowerment, participation in decision-making, employment security and knowledge-based pay programmes.

Those rare core knowledge workers in the labour market with the highest levels of knowledge and skills are sometimes referred to as gold-collar employees because of their high value to

---

8   For more on HRM roles in building relationships see Lengnick-Hall and Lengnick-Hall (2003).

the company. The problem is that they are loyal mostly to their career rather than to a single employer. They would easily relocate to pursue better career opportunities (see Holland et al. 2000). They view their careers less in terms of financial gain and more through their professional and personal development when dealing with challenging work situations or creating something new and valuable. For them, even commitment-based configuration may not be sufficient. Companies then have to individualize employment relationships in order to accommodate their needs and interests as much as economically viable and possible. Another problem may then occur: awarding higher status to and accordingly different treatment of some employees can result in widespread inequality and may create conflict situations. HRM thus needs to find a fine balance between awarding somebody a special status in order to keep valuable resources in the company and assuring equal opportunities to others to achieve that special status.

Conclusions

To conclude, there are five test criteria for sustainable competitive advantage. HRM will remain or become an even more important means of achieving high performance and long-term competitiveness. The challenges for HRM professionals, as well as for managers responsible for managing people, are abundant and they are becoming increasingly more difficult to meet.

The power of knowledge workers, who own the most important company resource (i.e., knowledge), is increasing. Consequently, the traditional contractual control over HR decreases and companies have to build relational employment associations with retained service providers and portfolio workers. Because the customer base of HRM professionals is becoming more diverse in terms of different levels of strategic value and uniqueness, so HRM needs to develop different configurations and practices in order to create and sustain peak performance.

Under these circumstances, a strategic approach to HRM seems to be more appropriate than simply identifying and copying a correct combination of best practices. This requires significant HRM power in order to design high-quality HRM strategy and then implement the tactics effectively.

HRM's knowledge base needs to be constantly renewed, with managers (especially line managers) becoming competent HR actors and with HRM professionals who act as strategic partners and change agents. Only in this way will employees behave as desired, which, in turn, is likely to produce anticipated HRM outcomes.

References

Adler, P.S. and Kwon, S.W. (2002), 'Social Capital: Prospects for a New Concept', *Academy of Management Review* 27, pp. 17–40.

Brewster, C., Mayrhofer, W. and Morley, M. (2000), *New Challenges for European Human Resource Management* (London: Macmillan Press).

Brewster, C., Mayrhofer, W. and Morley, M. (2004), *Human Resource Management in Europe: Evidence of Convergence?* (Oxford: Elsevier).

Fitz-enz, J. (1997), 'The Truth about Best Practices: What They Are and How to Apply Them', *Human Resource Management 36*, pp. 97–103.

Hofstede, G. (2001), *Cultures's Consequences: Comparing Values, Behaviors, Institutions and Organizations Across Nations* (Thousand Oaks, CA: Sage Publications).

Holland, J.P., Hecker, R., Steen J. (2000), 'Human Resource Strategies and Organizational Structures for Managing Gold-collar Workers', *Journal of European Industrial Training* 26, pp. 72–80.

Lengnick-Hall, M.L. and Lengnick-Hall, C.A. (2003), 'HR's Role in Building Relationship Networks', *Academy of Management Executive* 17, pp. 53–66.

Lepak, D.P. and Snell, S.A. (2002), 'Examining the Human Resource Architecture: The Relationship among Human Capital, Employment, and Human Resource Configurations', *Journal of Management* 28, pp. 517–43.

Mabey, C. and Salaman, G. (1995), *Strategic Human Resource Management* (London: Blackwell Publishers).

MacDuffey, J.P. (1995), 'Human Resource Boundles and Manufacturing Performance: Organizational Logic and Flexible Production Systems in the World Auto Industry', *Industrial and Labor Relations Review* 48, pp. 197–221.

McEvily, S.K. and Chakravarthy, B. (2002), 'The Persistence of Knowledge-based Advantage: An Empirical Test for Product Performance and Technological Knowledge', *Strategic Management Journal* 23, pp. 285–305.

Pfeffer, J. (1994), *Competitive Advantage Through People* (Boston: Harvard Business School Press).

Pfeffer, J. (1998), *The Human Equation: Building Profits by Putting People First* (Boston: Harvard Business School Press).

Purcell, J. (1999), 'Best Practice and Best Fit: Chimera or Cul-de-Sac?', *Human Resource Management Journal* 9(3), pp. 26–41.

Robinson, S.L. and Morrison, E.M. (2000), 'The Development of Psychological Contract Breach and Violation: A Longitudinal Study', *Journal of Organizational Behavior* 22(3), pp. 525–46.

Rousseau, D. (1995), *Psychological Contracts in Organizations* (San Francisco: Sage Publications).

Rousseau, D. (1996), 'Changing the Deal While Keeping the People', *Academy of Management Executive* 10(1), pp. 50–59.

Semler, R. (2003), *The Seven Day Weekend* (London: Arrow Books, Random House).

Snell, S.A., Shadur, M.A. and Wright, P.M. (2001), 'Human Resource Strategy: The Era of Our Ways', in Hitt, M., Freeman, R.E. and Harrison, J.E. (eds) *Handbook of Strategic Management* (Malden, MA: Blackwell), pp. 627–49.

Trompenaars, F. and Hampden-Turner, C. (2000), *Riding the Waves of Culture* (London: Nicholas Brealey Publishing).

Ulrich, D. (1997), *Human Resource Champions: The Next Agenda for Adding Value and Delivering Results* (Boston: Harvard Business School Press).

Warner, M. and Joynt P. (eds) (2002), *Managing Across Cultures: Issues and Perspectives* (London: Thomson Learning).

Wright, P.M. and Snell, S.A. (1998), 'Toward a Unifying Framework for Exploring Fit and Flexibility in Strategic Human Resource Management', *Academy of Management Review* 23, pp. 756–72.

Wright, P.M., McMahan, G.C. and Williams, A. (1994), 'Human Resources and Sustained Competitive Advantage: A Resource Based Perspective', *International Journal of Human Resource Management* 5(2), pp. 245–63.

Youndt, M.A. and Snell, S.A. (2004), 'Human Resource Configurations, Intellectual Capital, and Organizational Performance', *Journal of Managerial Issues* 16, pp. 337–61.

Chapter 12

International Human Resource Management

Hedley Malloch

In the literature, international human resource management (IHRM) has three meanings :

1. the study of human resource management (HRM) in the multinational corporation (MNC);
2. comparisons of HRM practices across different cultures;
3. national studies of HRM in particular countries, for example, Japan, France (Sparrow et al. 2004).

Whilst recognizing that any MNC-focused explanation of IHRM must take account of the different cultural and national contexts in which it operates, this chapter takes as its framework the first of these.

Introduction

While IHRM as an academic subject is relatively new, as a management practice it has a much longer history. Egyptian pyramids and other monuments were constructed by peoples drawn from many regions under their influence. The Roman Army drew its soldiers from the four corners of their empire. Many large medieval projects, such as the construction of the great European cathedrals, drew on an itinerant multinational workforce. Selecting staff, managing performance and reward systems was a problem for the great merchant traders of the seventeenth century. Early cities tended to grow around commodity markets. The many canals that crisscross Europe that are still in use are evidence of the multinational trade and comparatively efficient transport. Jones (1996, p. 14) pointed out that many of today's European blue-chip firms such as Nestlé, Bayer and Siemens were well established as international operations before World War I. For many of these European firms such as Philips and Lever, internationalizing operations did not necessarily mean an internationally mobile workforce. Products and markets in household goods and food were constrained by local tastes and national regulation; they were firms that operated in many different national markets without any particular need to manage across borders. They were multinational rather than global and staffed accordingly (Bartlett and Ghosal 2000).

International human resource management (IHRM) rose to prominence on the back of what has been described as the 'global drive of US firms after the Second World War, that gave birth to the multinationals as we know them today' (Evan et al. 2002, p. 14). This drive was facilitated by international post-war reconstruction efforts such as the Marshall Plan and the progressive dismantling of barriers to trade and investment. During the 1960s the 180 largest US MNCs on average acquired six new foreign subsidiaries each (Vaupel and Curhan 1973). Yet at this time the US MNCs such as Ford, Procter and Gamble and General Electric differed from their European counterparts in two interconnected key respects. First, their products were more homogenous; differences between national product markets were much less important for them than they were for their European counterparts. Economies of scale and scope were therefore important, with an ensuing need to duplicate US administrative and manufacturing operations. The second respect was the belief that US management ideas and techniques were transferable across businesses (Goold and Luchs 1993) and national boundaries.

> All too often 'internationalization' is seen as something domestically reared mangers 'do' to other parts of their firm, whilst having no relevance to them.

Given these beliefs, the international deployment of US managers to their newly acquired subsidiaries in Europe or elsewhere was seen as the natural HR policy to service these strategic decisions. Their deployment was made easier by the declining cost of faster international travel; the cheaper and quicker methods of communication based on telex, computers and more reliable telephones. Selection decisions were mainly based on technical achievement. Motivating managers to accept such expatriate assignments largely was seen as a question of providing big financial incentives and support for the expatriate managers and their families. Such compensation packages tended to be both expensive and complicated, often requiring a detailed knowledge of different national tax and social security regimes. It was appropriate therefore that many of the first IHRM specialists had a background in compensation management.

The huge cost of supporting expatriate management was brought sharply into focus by 'expatriate failure'. This phenomenon graphically was described by Evans et al. (2002, p. 15) as 'the technically capable executive sent out to run a foreign subsidiary brought back prematurely as a borderline alcoholic, having run the affiliate into the ground'. Academic research by Tung (1981, 1982, 1984) seemed to confirm this view, and much serious academic interest in IHRM can be traced back to these ground-breaking studies of the problems of expatriate adjustment. Similarly, senior managers of multinationals, prompted both by the cost of expatriate failure and the block it posed to corporate growth, began to pay more attention to the problems of managing the globally mobile workforce.

During the 1980s expatriate failure was only one of many challenges. The dominant assumption was that internationalization should be led using the management style, techniques and culture practised by managers in a Head Office in the US.

What is IHRM and How Does it Differ from HRM?

Domestic HRM embraces the following activities (Dowling and Welch 2004):

- human resource planning;
- staffing policies and practices (deployment strategies, recruitment, selection and orientation);
- performance management;
- human resource development;
- reward management (compensation and benefits);
- employee relations.

IHRM includes all the activities listed above, but differs from domestic HRM in at least five respects:

1. IHRM includes some additional activities not found in domestic HRM such as repatriation.
2. Many HR activities become much more complex when placed in an international rather than a domestic context. When the MNC hires or deploys staff outside of its home country base, then the IHRM manager needs to be familiar with immigration regulations, work permits and health procedures. Similarly, reward management means that the IHRM manager must be knowledgeable about different tax regimes and social security systems.
3. Staff moving abroad will often be accompanied by their families; this means that the IHRM manager will become involved in decisions about housing, schooling and other family care issues, an involvement in the employees' personal life that otherwise would be regarded as an unwarranted intrusion in domestic HRM in this context is seen as an invaluable aid in the context of IHRM.
4. All HRM activities are overlain by the different cultural contexts in which they have to operate. For example, definitions of human resource development differ markedly between cultures with respect to 'formability', or the extent to which skills can be acquired. There are marked national differences in definitions of the competent manager. Germany and France favour knowledge evidenced by academic qualifications; whereas the Anglo-Saxon tradition has been for skills acquired by experience.
5. IHRM is a much riskier process than its domestic counterpart. It is easier to make mistakes and more expensive to correct them. For example, bad staffing decisions can mean premature and costly repatriation and can have disastrous consequences for the firm, the employee and his or her family.

Staffing Philosophies

The main explanatory framework used in the IHRM literature is based on Perlmutter's (2000) seminal work on the evolution of the MNC. Perlmutter's framework is based on 'recipes' (Spender 1989) or mental models of the organizational world held by the senior executives of MNCs that they use to help them set strategies, manage production, marketing, decision-making – in fact all areas of corporate life, including HRM. He claimed it was possible to identify four different mental models: ethnocentric, polycentric, geocentric and regio-centric. These provided the philosophical structure within which major IHRM strategies and policies were enacted.

Ethnocentric   An ethnocentric policy strongly favours appointing parent-country nationals (PCNs) to senior management posts in subsidiaries abroad. This can reflect a number of motives and assumptions including:

- A desire to appoint managers who already have a good working knowledge of company policies, procedures and corporate culture. Examples include Japanese, European and US chemical, petroleum, aviation, auto and electronics companies.
- To simplify communications. This is especially important in MNCs where the national language of the parent company. English is used as the working language in many MNCs. The language used between senior managers to aid understanding and speed up dialogue may not be widespread, for example, Nokia and Finland.
- A perceived lack of talent by the parent company in its foreign subsidiaries.
- A PCN employee may be seen as more loyal

Environmental factors can sustain an ethnocentric policy as, for example, where a firm has competitive strategy based low-cost, standardized commodity goods where national differences are not important. Fatehi (1996) argues that the policy can be justified where the enterprise has to take a firm line against political threats coming from the government of the home country.

The disadvantages of an ethnocentric policy cited by Harzing (2004) and Rodrigues (1997) include:

- the difficulties experienced by PCNs in adapting to a different language, culture and environment;
- the high cost selecting, training and deploying staff and their families abroad; and
- the family adjustment problems of staff's children and lack of employment opportunities for partners.

Mead (2004) highlighted family matters, especially children's schooling, as the main concern for families going overseas. Tung (1982) rated the spouse's inability to adjust as the biggest single for expatriate failure amongst European firms, though much less important for Japanese firms.

However, care is needed in interpreting this research. Spouses, children, failure to master local languages and to adapt to local cultures can be convenient excuses for the incompetent manager to save face and return home with his or her personal reputation intact.

Polycentric　A polycentric staffing policy favours the appointment of host country nationals (HCN) rather than PCN to key positions in their subsidiaries. Companies who have followed this policy include Shell, Quantas, Dupont, Philips, TNT and AT&T. HCNs are seldom transferred to the headquarters of the parent company. Polycentricism supports a policy of minimum parent company interference in the management of the subsidiary. It is often found in companies operating in product markets where there are significant national differences due to legal reasons, technical standards or consumer preferences; and in companies who have moved beyond the preliminary phases of internationalization.

According to Harzing (2004, p. 254) and Dowling and Welch (2004, p. 60) the advantages of polycentricism include:

- a management cadre in the subsidiary familiar with the language(s) and the national, cultural and competitive environment;
- substantially reduced costs across all points of the employment process. This can enable premiums to be paid to attract very high quality local staff (ibid.);
- improved career ladders for local nationals may increase their motivation;
- HCN can be more acceptable to the host country government;
- it avoids the disruptions to business incurred by the sudden departure of a PCN and the arrival of his replacement.

Disadvantages include:

- difficulty in aligning the goals and activities of the subsidiary and parent company;
- HCNs may have difficulties in communicating with PCNs, head office, customers and suppliers;
- HCN managers may be difficult to move to another location or appointment;
- HCN may lack the perspective of those employed at head office.

A comparison of ethnocentric and polycentric preferences invites the question of who is employed in the MNC – expatriates or locals? Research by Harzing (2001) into the background of the managing directors of subsidiaries reveals some interesting national and sectoral variations in the answer to this question. Japanese companies appear to be highly dependent on the use of PCNs with over three-quarters of Japanese companies employing Japanese managing directors of their overseas subsidiaries. On the other hand, Scandinavian countries were all below the average figure of 40.8 per cent, with Denmark having the lowest proportion of 18.2 per cent. Swedish companies (34.2 per cent) have a reputation for expansion based on internationalization, even though they appear to have achieved this without an over-reliance on a PCN staffing policy.

By industry Harzing's data show that PCNs are important in banking and banking services (76.1 per cent) security and commodity broking (84.8 per cent), motor vehicles and parts (62.2 per cent) and telecommunications equipment (53.2 per cent). However, the figures are relatively low in industries such as food and related products (25.8 per cent) and pharmaceuticals (25.0 per cent), both industries where national regulations and local tastes are important. The employment of PCNs varies markedly with function; more are found in managing director positions than in any other function. Only 17.2 per cent of finance directors were PCNs. The figure for marketing directors was 10.1 per cent and for personnel directors the proportion it was a meagre 2.2 per cent. Harzing also draws attention to the presence of important regional variations: European MNCs employ more TCNs than Japanese companies.

These figures could show important differences in national mind-sets and corporate strategy. On the other hand they could simply reflect variations in the supply of international managers; that is, it is easier for a Danish company to find a Swede (or other Scandinavian) to head up a Swedish subsidiary, than it is for a Japanese MNC to find local managers to staff a newly acquired Russian subsidiary. Country attractiveness can change and this can influence the ability of the MNC to service a subsidiary with PCNs or TCNs. Amoco reported that West African countries in which upwards of 30 per cent of the population are HIV positive have a dramatically reduced appeal to potential expatriates (Roberts et al. 1998).

Geocentric In this model the MNC appoints managers on the basis of skill and ability rather than nationality. Managers may be PCNs, HCNs or from a third country – third country nationals (TCNs). PCNs, HCNs and TCNs can be found anywhere in the MNC and working in any position. This policy of appointing the best people is commonly found in MNCs for whom integrated worldwide operations are important and who see themselves as a networked federation of businesses rather than a global monolith or a balkanized multinational enterprise. Electrolux and Coca-Cola are often regarded as good examples of geocentric organizations. Coca-Cola operates in more than 195 countries and TCNs make up the majority of international service employees and they have a strong presence in Coca-Cola's divisional offices based in the US. It is in the geocentric MNC that TCNs are most likely to be found.

The main advantages of this approach are:

- it enables the MNC to develop a multinational cadre of senior managers responsive to the various foreign socio-cultural, political and cultural environments in which the MNC must operate. This facilitates the development of a global perspective;
- it develops a pool of internationally mobile managers who can be deployed throughout the global operation;

- it can support cooperation, resource sharing and knowledge transfer within the MNC;
- to the extent that geocentricism relies on HCNs and TCNs rather than PCNs, it can be considerably cheaper than either an ethnocentric or polycentric approach.

The disadvantages of the geocentricism include:

- The costs and difficulties associated with the employment of both PCNs and TCNs, in particular employment restrictions and immigration controls imposed by the host county governments that appreciate the logic of hiring PCNs, applaud the appointment of HCNs and may resent the employment of TCNs. TCNs in this context may be heavily taxed, either directly or indirectly, and cost of living may be artificially higher than for PCNs because of the lack of low cost housing.
- The increased complexity of managing compensation. It follows that the greater the number of nationalities employed, the more difficult it becomes to operate a uniform international pay structure.
- Since international deployment of managers is central to the creation of geocentric organization, subsidiaries may be required to surrender control of managerial appointments to the centre, leading to real feelings of loss of autonomy and independence. Honeywell in the UK had 11 senior managers in 4 years during the 1980s. Each one had been tasked with specific improvements and changes. The result was a form of 'fad surfing' and implementation fatigue because the employees had to change emphasis to the 'flavour of the month'. This approach typically leads to remissions – reverting back to old ways of doing things once the boss left. The loss of independence also leads to a greater level of Taylorism, where managers give instructions and dictate rather than facilitate and promote self-reliance.

For many writers (Bartlett and Ghosal 2004), geocentricism represents an ideal model for the MNC. It is the foundation on which a trans-national firm can be built, a type of MNC that seeks to combine the efficiencies offered by operations on a global scale with local responsiveness and worldwide learning. These strong internal linkages, a geocentric mindset and the international deployment of highly competent managers are required to bind the transnational MNC. However, the evidence suggests that the managerial and organizational practices of MNCs lag someway behind this ideal. For example, in Harzing's study (2001) only 5 per cent of the positions were taken by TCNs, a number so small that Harzing did not feel it was necessary to discuss TCNs any detail. This suggests that companies like Coca-Cola and Electrolux are very much the exception rather than the rule.

The research by Roberts, Kossek and Ozeki (1998) suggests that such a conclusion may be premature. Their analysis is based on interviews with 24 senior international HR professionals employed in eight, mature, blue-chip MNC organizations including Amoco, Dow Chemicals, Merck, General Motors and Marks and Spencer. All respondents reported that their organizations were moving away from the traditional expatriate assignments in some highly innovative ways. They identified four global HR strategies:

1. the aspatial careerist;
2. the awareness-building assignment;
3. SWAT teams;
4. virtual solutions.

All four have a strong geocentric orientation.

The aspatial careerist has a borderless career and is globally orientated, mobile, loyal and prepared to accept long-term overseas assignments. Like a PCN, they focus more on improving the company performance than country culture and are chosen for their tacit and implicit knowledge of how the company operates. The chief difference between them and the traditional PCN expatriate is that they can be drawn from anywhere in the organization: the MNC recognizes that detailed knowledge of the company does not reside exclusively in the head office. Because of the cost of employing them, there are relatively few of aspatial careerists. They do, however, have an influence out of all proportion to their numbers.

The awareness building assignment is typically short term (between 3–12 months) and is given to high potential technically oriented employees early in their careers. Their aims are developmental: to produce a global perspective through a process of network building and cross-cultural immersion, and to improve technical know how through plant and cross-functional training. Due to the short length of such assignments, families are not expected to relocate. Frequent and planned trips home have to be budgeted to visit family. Work can be scheduled during the trips to add value and hence off-set the additional costs. The researchers reported that these assignments were frequently used on HCNs as a way of broadening their perspective.

SWAT teams are mobile teams of experts deployed to troubleshoot problems. They are nomadic and are used as internal consultants. They can be found in any part of the MNC. Their main role is transfer technical skills and processes. SWAT teams are composed on an 'as needed' basis. The amount of time they spend on overseas assignments is typically less than three months.

Virtual solutions embrace a collection of electronic information technologies including the Internet, intranets, video-conferencing, email, expert systems, databases, electronic noticeboards and forums. Virtual solutions are seen as low cost and enable managers to decouple real and virtual time. They are seen as particularly suitable for employees who for many reasons (family, work permit problems, health) may be difficult to rotate internationally. Together with awareness building assignment, virtual solutions can have the greatest potential for global HR strategies

Each of these four strategies is geocentric in their orientation, and each is hard to fit in to Perlmutter's (2000) model. Technology can render redundant physical expatriation as the sole means of implementing any of Perlmutter's four typologies. Further, their presence enables us to qualify Harzing's (2001) findings. An Australian engineer helping a colleague in Delhi over the MNC's intranet will not show up in the headcount of the Indian subsidiary. Neither may the employee posted there as part of an awareness building assignment, or the SWAT team working in the same plant. Their short stay may mean that neither shows up in any headcount; they may not even be classified as 'employed' in the conventional sense of the word. Finally, as the evidence relating to aspatial careerist shows, numbers employed is not necessarily a good measure of the strategic importance of the geocentric employee.

Regio-centricism Regio-centricism often is described as a halfway house between a polycentric and ethnocentric approach on the one hand; and a geocentric approach on the other. Managers can be deployed outside their countries only within a certain region,, for example, Europe or the Far East. The context 'regions' are defined by the organizational structure of the MNC rather than geographically. In this approach a UK manager could be transferred to France, or an Argentinean manger could be moved to Peru. Transfers across regions would be rare. The advantages of this approach are:

- the regional headquarters can become a forum for HCNs and PCNs to meet and exchange requirements;
- it can be a transition stage to the development of a geocentric organization, or back to an ethnocentric firm if that is required;
- it enables some responsiveness to local conditions.

The disadvantages include the emergence of a regional mentality that can be every bit as obstinate and obstructive to the MNC's strategic objectives as a national one. Both regio-centricism and geocentricism assume the existence of a global human resource information system to identify and locate talent in the MNC.

The Ethnocentric, Polycentric, Geocentric and Regio-centric Typology of Staffing Policies: A Critical View

The strength of Perlmutter's typology is that it draws attention both to the importance of management mindsets in the process of internationalization and to what defines an international business. Sales-based criteria dominate definitions of internationalization. The most widely cited categorization of internationalization is Stopford and Dunning's (1972) foreign subsidiaries' sales as a percentage of total sales (Sparrow et al. 2004, p. 42). This approach suggests that the international business is one that has an internationally acceptable product range.

Sales are not, however, a measure of 'mindset', a psychological rather than an economic phenomenon. As well as sales, we would expect any form of internationalism to show in the degree of internationalization of other functions such as operations and finance. The number of PCNs, TCNs and HCNs employed in a workforce as a whole rather than just in the ranks of senior management should be taken into account. We also would expect to see decisions about policies and strategies being made by a cadre of international management.

The process of internationalization does not occur evenly in the firm. Organization functions internationalize at differing rates (Malbright 1995; Yip 1992) and to different degrees (Harzing 2001). The last part of the firm to internationalize, typically, is the mindset of senior management. Decisions they make can be international in character, but the backgrounds of the mangers that produced them may be quite. All too often 'internationalization' is seen as something domestically reared mangers 'do' to other parts of their firm, whilst having no relevance to them.

While it is useful to think of Perlmutter's models as concepts and as a way of thinking about the different ways in which the MNC could operate, they have limitations. First, they are ideal types; it is doubtful if any MNC operates as a pure version of any of these models. Second, they only deal with the firms' view of the staffing problem; they are all essentially models of demand – what employers want from their international managers. The ability of the labour market, either internal or external, to meet these demands is not considered. For any staffing policy to be implemented, labour demand and supply have to meet at some point. There is a view (Robinson 1978) that firms should have formal policies with respect to staffing by PCNs, HCNs, and TCNs and persist with them; otherwise ethnocentrisms will emerge by default.

Such a view ignores the realities of HR decision-making. Matching demand and supply at the level of implementation can be a messy process. This can result when operating in a context of severe time pressures, lack of information, a high degree of strategic urgency and personal agendas. In these circumstances, carefully thought out staffing models of the Perlmutter typology, linked to some formal corporate strategy can be abandoned in favour of something fast and cheap that can be made to work. Much HRM work is of an ad hoc, reactive 'fire-fighting' nature, rather than concerned with carefully considered strategies and policies, and IHRM is no exception. Indeed, decisions to employ PCNs and TCNs can be forced on the firm by host government legislation, or by the fact that the attractiveness of foreign locations to PCNs or TCNs can change worsen rapidly for reasons outside the control of the MNC. Ethnic and tribal conflicts, AIDS particularly in Africa, and the current political and military instability in many Gulf countries are cases in point. In Mintzberg's (1979) terminology, planned strategies may be abandoned in favour of something that is forced and emergent. If the company has to employ PCNs, well drilled evacuation procedures and security personnel may be put in place. As a last resort, expert negotiators may be deployed if events such as hostage taking occur and to prevent situations from escalating.

Recruitment and Selection of Staff for International Assignments

In this section we shall examine the recruitment processes, the selection criteria, selection methods and processes used in selecting staff for international assignments, together with some common issues, notably female participation in international assignments and the management of the expatriate's family.

Recruitment Recruitment has moved to the fore, in part as the result of an intensifying battle now taking place amongst the MNCs to obtain the services of talented individuals. Each is attempting to secure the brightest and the best for their increasingly knowledge-based businesses. The supply of talent has diminished: demographic changes have led to a 15 per cent fall in the number of 35–45 year olds (Tulgan 2001). Talent has become more mobile and less attracted to the idea of a full-time lifelong career. For many MNCs, the problem of how to attract and retain talent has been to redefine the recruitment process as one of brand management. For example Diageo have redefined potential and actual employees as 'consumers,' with recruits tempted by a 'value proposition' (Sparrow et al. 2004, pp. 122–4). Shell have renamed part of their recruitment process as 'the Talent Pipeline', with a 'Center of Excellence Co-ordinator' whose remit is to develop best recruitment practices for 'on-boarding' the top 5 per cent of university graduates (ibid., pp. 126–7).

Most leading MNCs have now harnessed the power of the Internet to recruit globally.[1] Candidates seek information about vacancies, make applications and are notified of the outcome via the Internet. This process drastically reduces the time between a candidate seeing a job vacancy and being notified of the result. Potentially bio-data approaches can be used to screen applicants. Questionnaires can assess the candidates' fit with company culture and values. In practice, however, few companies have a clear idea of the competencies they require or of how to assess the fit between personality and culture.

Selection criteria It is easy to generate long lists of essential requirements for the successful expatriate. According to Dowling and Welsh (2004) the six most frequently used selection criteria used for filling international positions are:

1. technical ability (proven track record of sustained peak performance);
2. cross-cultural suitability (culture clash, direct and indirect, negotiating styles);

---

1   This directly mirrors the 'direct marketing' approaches described by Lyons, Chapter 17 in this volume.

3. family requirements (stability, international schools, life style, homesick);
4. country/cultural requirements (fit, shock, adjustment, acceptance);
5. fluency in appropriate languages and an aptitude to learn them;
6. MNC requirements (performance enhancement projects, turn arounds, growth).

The weight given to each will vary on the type of assignment. If we use Roberts et al.'s (1998) classification, technical ability will figure highly for those posted on SWAT assignments. Aspatial careerists appear to be chosen for their cross-cultural suitability. MNC requirements in the form of development and succession planning drive awareness building assignments. Family requirements or country/cultural requirements may act negatively to cast some otherwise suitable candidates as part of a virtual solution.

Technical ability   This is the most commonly used criterion, despite the fact than in many cases technical knowledge may not transfer and can be strongly influenced by culture. There are a number of reasons for its popularity. It is easily measurable. Appointing someone who is technically incompetent can be disastrous whereas transferring an employee who is at least technically competent will usually forestall immediate failure on the job. It minimizes the personal risk of the selector who takes the decision. The expatriate may be working some distance from Head Office and have to work on problems without access to backup and assistance (Harzing 2004). The dominance of this criterion could reflect a tacitly accepted model of management skills in which cross-cultural skills are assumed to be universal.

Managing Performance

The effective expatriate manager is required to develop significant skills. In a nutshell these are concerned with working in and managing a business environment that is very different to that to which he or she may be accustomed. This will require different planning skills, the ability to find and implement different techniques, and being more flexible in dealing with people and systems. They will foster these skills in a subsidiary where they potentially have much more influence on their unit's performance than in a unit in their home country. Such processes in the domestic organization are difficult enough. When the context is that of the expatriate manager in the MNC, processes acquire additional layers of complexity in the form of time, distance, culture, ambiguity, language, and more numerous and sometimes surprising stakeholders.
Performance management in the MNC has a number of related aspects. These are:

* the organizational context;
* who appraises the expatriate's performance;
* the factors influencing the expatriate's performance.

The Organizational Context

By definition the global environment of the MNC is more complex and volatile than that of the national context confronting the domestic firm. Factors such as volatility of exchange rates, national rules affecting profit reporting and its repatriation, terrorism, new diseases such as Severe Acute Respiratory Syndrome (SARS), the collapse of political regimes, the dismantling of trade barriers and the emergence of new competitor nations such as India and China, all have major implications for the global strategies of the MNC, their subsidiaries and hence for the performance measures of the expatriate managers working within them. Political clashes between governments can also affect business performance. The sales of French firms in Turkey fell as a result of the passing of a law in France making it an offence to deny the Armenian massacres in 1915. The goals of the subsidiaries and the activities of their expatriate managers need to be tailored to accommodate these changes as they impact on local conditions. Difficulties inevitably arise when expatriate managers are forced to implement MNC strategies, which they see as being no longer relevant to their local operation.

Clearly these problems can be ameliorated if there is some subsidiary involvement in setting the MNC's corporate strategy, but it is doubtful if they can ever be completely avoided. The global strategies of an MNC based on standardization through economies of scale and scope may be remarkably intolerant of any request for local discretion to accommodate the domestic peculiarities of the subsidiary. Similarly the expatriate manager may spend considerable amounts of time and ingenuity solving problems in his or her subsidiary, real difficulties, which are not recognized as such in the headquarters of the MNC. Strikes are a good example. The MNC with a home base in Germany or the US will probably have evolved its domestic employee relations in completely different legal and social contexts when compared with its foreign subsidiaries. In the country of the parent company, bargaining may take place at company, national or regional level. Strikes over issues arising from sections of the workforce at, or within a plant may not be seen as issues that need to be managed in the MNC Headquarters. Yet for the expatriate manager working in a Latin country such as Mexico or Peru, stoppages of work may be an everyday reality. The ability to manage them may be scarcely recognized at the MNC's head office.

Similarly there may be considerable variations in output per head or other key indicators of performance. The reasons behind these may not be understood in head office. For example factory output in Islamic countries usually falls during Ramadan, the period of daytime fasting leading to fatigue due to diminished blood sugar levels. Accidents and outbreaks of indiscipline can also rise for the same reason.

Harmonizing expectations about the performance of the expatriate manager in the subsidiary may be further complicated by distance. The falling cost of international communications and the rise of new methods such as email, teleconferencing and cell phones can lead to over-reliance on these substitutes for direct contact between the MNC and its expatriate manager. Direct supervision, in the form of face-to-face contact does have a place in any performance management strategy in order that both parties have a good appreciation of the viability of performance standards, the real extent to which they are being met, and working out jointly agreed plans for remedial action. Research indicates that such direct contact is rare. Many expatriates report irregular contact with the home office, and often it was not with their immediate superior. Further, bosses rarely initiate direct contact with the expatriate more than twice a year (Oddou and Mendenhall 2000, p. 216).

The collapse of Barings' Bank is a spectacular example of what can happen when the MNC becomes too reliant on indirect supervision of key employees in its subsidiaries. In this case Barings' General Manager in the Singapore office of Barings, the oldest bank in the United Kingdom, was allowed to run up massive debts in what was, in effect, an uncontrolled gambling spree on the Asian stock markets. Nick Leeson (http://www.nickleeson.com/) lost over £300 million and ruined the bank. Lack of supervision was among the factors contributing to this disaster that led to over 20 members of Barings' senior staff resigning or being sacked, and to Barings being sold to ING, the Dutch bankers, for £1. The Bank of England Report into the affair concluded that it is important for Head Office managers to make frequent visits to overseas offices in order to gain a sufficient understanding and feel for the business. Only then will they be able to ask the right questions and gather the right information (Bank of England 1995; http://www.nickleeson.com/).

Who Appraises the Expatriate's Performance?

Ideally those involved in appraising expatriate's performance should include the host country management, the home office and the manager him or herself. Research suggests that the dominant party in the process is usually the home office, in the form of the HR department, or the expatriate's superior manager. Often the home office of the MNC uses the criteria and paperwork of the home country system to appraise the expatriate's performance.

Appraisal of the expatriate by the home office can be difficult. Faced with many of the problems of distance mentioned earlier, home office managers may fall back on simple, objective and highly-visible measures of performance such as profits, market share and output. They may be unaware that these measures can be influenced by a wide range of factors outside of the control of the expatriate. This problem can be confounded by the ethnocentricity of those performing the appraisals at head office, relatively few of whom may have worked abroad. One study (Black et al. 1999) reports that only 28 per cent of human resources managers, key custodians of the performance appraisal systems in the US firms, had themselves worked abroad on international assignments. Given this lack of international awareness in the head offices of many MNCs at first glance it is surprising to find that the head office was the preferred place of assessment for many expatriates. Yet head office is where key decisions are made regarding promotions. Keeping performance assessment at head office is a valuable strategy by which the expatriate can keep his name in front of senior managers responsible for succession planning.

Harmonizing expectations amongst these different groups of stakeholders is vital to success. Local managers in the host country may have rather different definitions as to what constitutes successful job performance to managers in the head office of the MNC. Much organizationally required behaviour of the typical Anglo-Saxon manager, such as participation and delegation may not be valued in high-power distance countries such as France or India. Here a participatory management style may be viewed as an indication of weakness.

On the other hand there are clear dangers when the expatriate manager identifies too closely with the cultural norms host country. This is frequently expressed by the term 'going native'. Overall if there is a clash between behaviours demanded by the organization and those of the local culture, then those of the organization tend to win. The expatriate manager may be more familiar and comfortable with the behaviours demanded by the head office of his MNC than those of his local workplace.

This wide range of considerations and often conflicting goals, personal and corporate agendas suggests that MNCs should consider using '180°' or '360°' performance appraisal systems. The manager provides feedback to the expatriate by comparing evidence against objective. For the 360°, colleagues that have been directly aided or affected by the expatriate provide feedback on the value add they have received (hence perceived and appreciated). Together with personal responses from all of the participants, comparisons are made against the ideal profile of a candidate for the position. Deltas are identified and 'to do' or 'self improvement' projects are set up to enhance performance and overcome deficiencies.

Different perspectives of the expatriate's performance need to be formally incorporated into the process. This means that the MNC has to take into account the views of former expatriates familiar with the local culture. Similarly, the view of Evans et al. (2002, p. 130) is that 'only those who can observe the manager can judge him'. This implies that there must be some involvement from those local managers working with the expatriate, assuming that local managers are able and motivated to become involved.

The Factors Influencing the Expatriate's Performance

Oddou and Mendenhall (2000, p. 217) identified three types of variable influencing the expatriate's performance:

1. technical job know-how;
2. the expatriate's ability to adjust to a new culture; and
3. personal adjustment to culture.

Technical job know-how is regarded as absolutely critical. Failings in plant, systems and know-how are often the reasons why many managers are asked by their home office to relocate overseas. Of itself, technical knowledge is never sufficient for successful job performance. It has long been recognized that effective performance on the job in any organization depends upon the manager's ability to manage both the technical and social aspects of the organization (Trist et al. 1963). When work is performed internationally, this process becomes even more problematic. There are three reasons for this.

1. The expatriate manager is more likely to be unfamiliar with the important cultural variables in the host country and how they impact on local working customs and practices. For example, US managers working in the UK construction industry need to show sympathy with the custom of the local workforce to take a day off work when a worker is accidentally killed.
2. Unless the technical processes and product are identical, the expatriate will have to learn about what is currently done and made. Significant differences may exist in automation and equipment, layout, demand profiles, specifications and performance characteristics or measures. These must be understood then compared with the parent organization to determine which is more appropriate and if any hybridization or switching from one system to another is required. Introducing change to improve performance and profitability is one of the most challenging tasks to be faced. Specific human skills are required that pure technical competence doesn't cover. The expatriate will need to overcome resistance and set expectations. They will need to be effective negotiators, facilitators, coaches, trainers and educators.
3. The second reason is more subtle. Technical job know-how itself is not culturally neutral; technical knowledge is construed by the society that produces it. Good technical skills are not objectively defined. Technically speaking there are numerous ways of performing any task and the 'best way' is usually socially rather than technically defined. The following example demonstrates this.

An English Apprentice in France

Peter is 18 and English. He studied engineering at his local technical college and was a good student. When offered a place as an Apprentice technician working as a sheet-metal fabricator for a Motorola plant near Toulouse he jumped at the chance. Like all French apprentices Peter is required to study at nights and weekends in a Centre de Formation d' Apprenti (CAF). He described his early experiences in the CAF:

> It was traumatic. In England I was good at Engineering Drawing. Here in France I don't know anything. In England I was taught to draw using projection lines; to draw one part of a drawing from another. In England the projection lines are shown on the drawing; it's a way showing that your workings are correct. The French don't do this; they erase all projection lines; it's regarded as very bad form to show them; the French want something which looks neat. The French make drawings with side elevations, front elevations and plans in different positions on the paper to those taught in the UK. Neither is wrong; it's a question of different conventions. Then there are the calculations. In England I was taught one method for long division; in France they use another, which I don't understand. Both give the right answer, but I am told my method is wrong. I have been told that I cannot even write numbers properly because I use a decimal point where the French use a comma. It destroys your morale and confidence completely. (Author's own research)

The ability to adjust to a new culture is critical. The expatriate must be sufficiently at ease in his or her new surroundings to be able to integrate sufficiently in order to function socially. Language skills are therefore important. It has long been known that careful selection and training can substantially reduce expatriate failure (Holmes and Piker 1980), yet most expatriates are selected on the basis of their technical rather than cultural skills. This heightens the importance of pre-departure cultural and language training. Historically, however, many MNCs and especially those based in the US, have been reluctant to provide these (Baker 1984; Felman 1989; Tung 1982) due to senior management's perception that such training was neither necessary nor cost-effective. There is some evidence that the situation has improved since the 1980s with more than three-quarters of US-based MNCs offering pre-departure training (Dowling and Welch 2004). Attendance at pre-departure training usually is voluntary in many organizations and training tends to be short, listing specific nuances and 'show stoppers', together with 'be prepared for …', 'I did this and it worked' and horror stories.

His or her family influences the expatriate's personal adjustment to the culture. An important decision for both the firm and the expatriate is whether or not his or her family will accompany the expatriate. The inability of the expatriate's family to adjust to their new environment is often cited as the biggest single reason for the premature recall of the expatriate. There is a debate in the literature as the exact extent of the problem, but there is little doubt that a move abroad poses many problems for the expatriate and his or her family. The management of family issues such as schooling, housing, and health become much more complex and demand more time than they would in the home country. For example, in France foreign consulates are forbidden by the French government to supply expatriate workers with lists of medical specialists who can speak the expatriate's language. While the expatriate manager may have been carefully selected for his ability to work in a different culture and trained in languages and cross-cultural awareness, his or her family typically may have been excluded from these processes and will therefore be less prepared to manage culture shock.

An increasing problem is that of finding appropriate employment for the spouse of the expatriate. Talent tends to marry talent and finding an equivalent job for a professionally qualified, specialized and highly-trained spouse in the expatriate's home country can be impossible. Reasons include: differences in the structure of national labour markets, lack of international recognition of professional and academic qualifications, lack of language skills, and the spouse's physical removal from his or her social and professional networks. There may be problems with work permits: these may be issued only for the expatriate with none granted to the spouse. In France, dependent spouses may not work. Non-EU citizens must apply for residence permits each year for five years prior to being granted a ten-year permit. Getting into the local social security system and other official services can be rather tedious. In the UK, most documents such as passports and car licences can be obtained by post. In France and most of Europe, applications must be made in person.

Company policies can help. Many MNCs now have 'family friendly' policies and procedures to help embed the spouse in the host country. These include a job placement for the spouse in another MNC, or with one of its suppliers, job hunting assistance where the MNC provides help with employment search for the spouse by payment of job agency fees, career counselling, assistance with work permits; and help with career development and professional support by paying fees for training courses, professional associations, and language courses. An increasing number of MNCs are now supplying these types of support, providing further evidence of a growing awareness that support of the expatriate's family is a way of supporting the expatriate manager's performance.

Compensation Management

The objectives of any compensation system in any organization are to attract, retain and motivate competent staff, especially those who are the source of sustainable competitive advantage. These are not different for the MNC wishing to employ expatriates abroad. Yet as with the other functions of international human resource management, achievement of these objectives is complicated by the fact that the problem is overlain with international differences in salary levels, equity issues, cost of living differences, much wider range of allowances, different tax regimes and bonuses. A further issue for the MNC is the size of the expatriate's total compensation bill, estimated at two to four times of the expatriate's salary (Roberts et al. 2002). The size and complexity of managing expatriate compensation, combined with its considerable potential for generating dissatisfaction, means that it has become a sub-specialism of IHRM.

Managing compensation should:

* address issues of company strategy; and
* take into account the different types of international assignment and employees required to service them.

Earlier we drew attention to Roberts, Kossek and Ozeki's (1998) distinction between different types of international assignment: aspatial careerist, awareness building assignment, virtual solution and SWAT team. This is one of many typologies of the expatiate assignment to be found in the literature. Another example is Sparrow, Brewster and Harris' (2004, p. 139) description of four types of international assignment: long-term assignments, short-term assignments, international commuters and frequent flyers. This diversity means there is no universal approach to managing compensation in a MNC. Compensation strategies will be selected based upon the stage of evolution of the MNC's international strategy and the types of employees it requires to implement them. For example, in the early stages of the evolution of the company's strategy it may prefer to settle the expatriate's compensation on a case-by-case basis through individual negotiation. As they grow the company's overseas activities, they experience greater international mobility from a steadily increasing workforce it will require a more systematic approach to the problem. The companies will need to learn from past experiences by gathering 'lessons to learn' and debriefing their 'returning hero'.

Factors Influencing Expatriate Pay

These include cost of living, hardship, currency fluctuations, healthcare costs, housing, taxation, support for the expatriate's family (education and elderly care). These factors vary in importance over time, between regions and with the type of international employee. For example healthcare is a primary and growing concern for many expatriates due to the globalization of diseases and a growing awareness of travel induced illness such as stress and deep-vein thrombosis (DVT). Hardship embraces factors such as isolation, lack of cultural facilities, political concerns and crime. These vary with the assignment and the employee: the young graduate trainee management consultant posted to Chicago as part of an awareness-building assignment is not in the same category of hardship as an engineer on a trouble-shooting assignment in the Nigerian oilfields. Indeed, as increasing numbers of people accept international assignments as part of a career development plan, the concept of 'hardship' becomes less relevant. Hardship varies with time: fear of kidnapping in countries like Peru, Palestine, Afghanistan and Iraq varies with the changing political stability of the country. Nevertheless are some enduring features of hardship in any expatriate assignment irrespective of its location and timing such as separation from family and friends.

The Make-Up of Expatriate Pay

Basic pay   This is the principal component of the expatriate's pay. It is important because it is the largest element and it is used to calculate premiums, allowances and other benefits. Complexities arise because decisions have to be made about whether it is based on the basic pay in head office, the host country, or some global system; where it is paid, and in countries with unstable exchange rates, the currency in which it is to be paid. Inflation can be a primary consideration. In Zimbabwe at the time of writing inflation is running at 2.2 million per cent p.a. What can be bought with the money is another consideration. Shortages of basics and staples may incur long waits in queues. The company may need to consider shipping in necessities and other optional items.

Allowances   These are numerous and reflect the expatriate's local working conditions. In many MNC schemes the largest allowance is the cost-of-living allowance (COLA). These make up the difference in living costs between the expatriate's home and host country. Family support costs; travel and local transport and the costs of relocation are usually included. Hardship payments are included here, but there is growing tendency for these to decline especially when the posting is made to an economically developed country. For one of the editors of this volume, he received an allowance of £10,000 p.a. pro-rata. This was on the proviso that he 'not to learn the local languages and hence force the locals to speak English'.

Performance-related pay   These payments are linked to successful completion of the expatriate assignment. They can include participation in stock options or profit sharing. This may not be within the legal framework of the host county.

Benefits   This is perhaps the most complex area. Decisions have to be made about whether to transfer the expatriate employee into the health and social security systems of the host country, or to maintain them in the expatriate's home county. Often there is no choice: work permits may be issued on condition that the expatriate becomes a member of the host country system. Healthcare is a major issue as expatriates, like any traveller, are vulnerable to illness.

The options available to the expatriate and his employer will be influenced by the standard of health care in the host country; its availability and the coverage offered to dependents (Frazee 1997). Other benefits typically include flight costs home or to a holiday destination for leave, and leave allowances.

One major recent study of expatriates' perception of their compensation packages cited the overall level of pay, the inadequacy of data on costs in the host country, exposure to currency rate fluctuations, social security payments to the host country and family-related issues. Positives included lower rates of tax, car allowances and the presence of a company policy on compensation that enable the expatriate to negotiate a deal (Suutari and Tornikoski 2001).

Expatriate Compensation Systems

MNCs have developed a number of generic compensation systems to manage expatriate pay. None of them are ideal; all present the MNC and its employees with advantages and disadvantage. In choosing between them, the MNC needs to consider the cost and fairness of the scheme, irrespective of the assignment. The expatriate's nationality, or the location of the assignment are further considerations. Like any compensation system, the expatriate's compensation should be transparent and easy to manage (Evans et al. 2002). Yet whilst there are on paper many systems – Reynolds (1995) identifies ten – in practice the choice appears to be much more limited. The most popular system is the balance-sheet approach.

The balance-sheet approach This aims to give the expatriate a standard of living equal to that he or she would enjoy if they were employed in the home country, irrespective of the location of the assignment. Typically, the expatriate's home country salary is divided into four elements: goods and services, housing, taxes and savings. Home and host country expenditures on each element are compared and the MNC pays the expatriate the increased costs, if any, incurred by living in the host country. Apparently simple in concept, the balance-sheet approach is very difficult to implement and the problems increase the more international the workforce and the business becomes. For example, where is the expatriate's home country? For the aspatial careerist the home country may be somewhere in which he or she has not resided for several years. The balance-sheet approach in a MNC managed along ethnocentric lines may be easy to run with a handful of senior managers visiting overseas locations for periods of a few years before returning to their home country. Here 'home' is a simple concept, and calculations of housing costs are both meaningful and easy to calculate. They are less relevant for expatriates sent abroad for short-periods where they do not settle in the host country for any length of time.

Similarly, as a MNC moves away from a simple ethnocentric model of internationalization and adopts geocentric or polycentric forms then home country locations are more likely to be staffed by an mixture of PCN, HCN and TCN employees, all of whom are performing the same role, but come from different home countries with widely differing living costs and taxation systems. The result can be great differences in compensation packages for staff employed on the same type of work in the host country. No matter how rational this may appear to the manager of the MNCs international compensation scheme, paying staff different amounts for performing the same job can be disastrous for morale, commitment and motivation. One solution to this problem is to standardize the home base by giving all expatriates a nominal 'home country' of the head office of the MNC. This equalizes pay in the host country office, but can make it difficult to repatriate TCNs from the host country to their country of origin. Some MNCs adopt an intermediate approach: the expatriate's real home is used to calculate the cost of goods and services, whilst housing allowances are based on the housing costs in the MNCs home country.

From a strategic IHRM approach, the balance-sheet approach can create problems. It is hard to create a shared corporate culture in an office when expatriates are paid to import the living standards and spending patterns of life in the head office's country, when living standards in the home country may be quite low. Further, the balance-sheet approach has implications for performance management since it means that a large chunk of compensation is guaranteed. In these circumstances there may be motivation problems stemming from lack of a clear link between effort and reward. The balance-sheet approach can also become difficult to administer; as the expatriate's compensation package needs to be recalculated every time social security, tax and exchange rates change.

Neither is it clear that the balance-sheet approach adequately compensates dual-career couples for lost revenue or capital appreciation caused by an overseas posting. The loss of the spouse's income is an example of the former, if he or she chooses to accompany the expatriate abroad. The expatriate may be similarly penalized with respect to capital gains. Should the expatriate's international assignment require them to change tax regimes from the home country to that the host, then he may find his liability for capital gains of various types (e.g., inheritance taxes, investments) is adversely affected.

As an immigrant, they may find they are not allowed to vote in national or presidential elections. They may be eligible to vote in their original constituency for up to 20 years after becoming an ex-pat. US citizens have to declare income tax to the US authorities even if they live outside the US. They face being invoiced the difference if taxes in the host country are lower than in the US!

Recent Developments in Expatriate Compensation Management

Faced with these problems many MNCs are looking to alternatives to the balance-sheet approach when constructing compensation package. As part of this trend many MNCs are differentiating their compensation systems. For example, many MNCs are regionalizing global compensation policies; that is developing separate packages tailored to the needs of specific regions such as the European Union. Other MNCs are fragmenting their systems around particular groups of employees. The financial needs of the aspatial careerist are different to those of the member of the SWAT team or the young manager on an awareness building assignment. A balance sheet approach may work for an aspatial careerist; a lump sum may suit the short-term needs of the SWAT team, whilst the young manager honing his or her skills abroad might be fitted into local pay schemes. Finally, a manager who is working on a virtual solution international assignment may not require any additional compensation. This rationale leads to the creation of separate global systems of expatriate compensation patterned around different groups of the global workforce. A SWAT team member may be paid directly by the host nation. They may have to have a visa in their passport, and declare revenues to both governments. Nicolas Sarkozy, the French President, introduced various pieces of legislation to try to track earnings that otherwise would not be declared.

A differentiated approach to expatriate compensation management reaches its most developed form in a cafeteria system, which allows the expatriate some opportunity to tailor his or her compensation package to their individual circumstances. For example, some expatriates may prefer to spend money on their children's education whilst for others caring for elders may be the main family concern. This recognizes that all employees are different and that is the failure of compensation systems to manage these differences. This can create many discontents. It should be stressed that compensation is only one factor in employees' decisions to work abroad, or to participate in a team of people who are paid different amounts for the same work. Non-financial rewards include learning opportunities, improved career opportunities and access to social networks, and the many opportunities for cultural and personal development afforded to those who work abroad or at home in multicultural teams. Where these opportunities are not recognized, international assignments will always be a chore, and working in a multicultural team will be seen as another problem to manage. While these perceptions persist, no amount of fiddling with the compensation system will produce a motivated and dedicated cadre of expatriates.

Conclusions

This chapter has identified why each MNC is different. Their different strategies for internationalism are associated with different staffing policies. In turn these give rise to different approaches to recruitment and selection, performance management and compensation management. Their employees are different, too. Their tasks, aspirations, the stage in their career cycles and their involvement with the MNC's mission of internationalization vary. Therefore the job of the international human resource manager is not to implement the one best way of managing the expatriate workforce. Rather it is to achieve some consistency between the demands of the organization and the needs of the workforce while recognizing that a uniform approach for all expatriates is neither possible, nor desirable. This will require considerable skill, judgement and discretion on the part of the international human resource manager; and the expatriate employee must tolerate such ambiguity.

Referemces

Baker, J.C. (1984), 'Foreign Language and Departure Training in US Multinational Firms', *Personnel Administration* 29, pp. 68–70.

Bank of England (1995), *Report of the Banking Supervison Inquiry into the Circumstances of the Collapse at Barings* (London: Bank of England).

Bartlett, C.A. and Ghosal, S. (2000), *Transnational Management: Text, Cases and Readings in Cross-Border Management* (Singapore: McGraw-Hill).

Black, J.S., Gregersen, H.B., Mendehall, M.E. and Stroh, L.K. (1999), *Globalizing People Through International Assignment* (Reading, MA: Addison-Wesley).

Dowling, P.J. and Welch, D.E. (2004), *International Human Resource Management: Managing People in a Multinational Context* (Cincinnati, OH: South-West Publishing).

Evans, P., Pucik, V. and Barsoux, J.-L. (2002), *The Global Challenge: Frameworks for International Human Resource Management* (New York: McGraw-Hill).

Fatehi, K. (1996), *International Management: A Cross-cultural Approach* (Englewood Cliffs, NJ: Prentice-Hall).

Feldman, D. (1989), 'Relocation Practices', *Personnel* 66(2), pp. 22–5.

Frazee, V. (1997), 'It's Inevitable: Managed Care is Going Global', *Global Workforce* 76, pp. 18–23.

Goold, M. and Luchs, K. (1993), 'Why Diversify? Four Decades of Managerial Thinking', *The Academy of Management Executive* 7(3), pp. 7–25.

Harzing, A.-W. (2001), 'Who's in Charge: an Empirical Study of Executive Staffing Practices in Foreign Subsidiaries', *Human Resource Management* 40, pp. 139–58.

Harzing, A.-W. (2004), 'Composing an International Staff', in Harzing, A.-W. and Russeveldt, J.V. (eds) *International Human Resource Management*, 2nd edn (Thousand Oaks, CA: Sage Publications).

Holmes, W. and Piker, F. (1980), 'Expatriate Failure: Prevention Rather Than Cure', *Personnel Management* 12, pp. 30–33.

Jones, G. (1996), *The Evolution of International Business* (London: Routledge).

Malbright, T. (1995), 'Globalization of an Ethnographic Firm', *Strategic Management Journal* 16, pp. 119–41.

Mead, R. (2004), *International Management: Cross-Cultural Dimensions* (Oxford: Blackwell).

Mintzberg, H. (1979), *The Structuring of Organizations* (Englewood Cliffs, NJ: Prentice-Hall).

Oddou, G. amd Mendenhall, M. (2000), 'Expatriate Performance Appraisal: Problems and Solutions', in Oddou, G. and Mendenhall, M. (eds) *Readings and Cases in International Human Resource Management* (London: South-Western College Publishing).

Perlmutter, H.V. (2000), 'The Tortuous Evolution of the Multinational Corporation', in Bartlett, C.A. and Ghosal, S. (eds) *Transnational Management: Text, Cases and Readings in Cross-Border Management* (Singapore: McGraw-Hill).

Reynolds, C. (1995), *Compensating Globally Mobile Employees* (Scottsdale, AZ: American Compensation Association).

Roberts, K., Kossek, E. and Ozeki, C. (1998), 'Managing the Global Workforce: Challenges and Strategies', *Academy of Management Executive* 12, pp. 93–119.

Robinson, R.D. (1978), *International Business Management: A Guide to Decison Making* (Hinsdale, IL: Dryden).

Rodrigues, C.A. (1997), 'Developing Expatriates' Cross-cultural Sensitivity: Cultures Where "Your Culture's OK" is Really not OK', *Journal of Management Development* 16, pp. 690–702.

Sparrow, P., Brewster, C. and Harris, H. (2004), *Globalizing Human Resource Mangement* (London: Routledge).

Spender, J.-C. (1989), *Industry Recipes : An Enquiry into the Nature and Sources of Managerial Judgement* (New York: Blackwell).

Stopford, J.M. and Wells, L.T. (1972), *Managing the Multinational Enterprise* (New York: Basic Books).

Suutari, V. and Tornikoski, C. (2001), 'The Challenge of Expatriate Compensation: The Sources of Satisfaction and Dissatisfaction amongst Expatriates', *International Journal of Human Resource Management* 12, pp. 389–404.

Tulgan, B. (2001), *Winning the Talent Wars* (New York: Norton).

Tung, R.L. (1981), The Selection and Training of Personnel for Overseas Assignments', *Columbia Journal of World Business* 16, pp. 68–78.

Tung, R.L. (1982), 'Selection and Training Procedures of US, European and Japanese Multinationals', *California Management Review* 25, pp. 55–71.

Tung, R.L. (1984), 'Human Resource Planning in Japanese Multinationals: A Model for US Firms?', *Journal of International Business Studies* 15, pp. 139–49.

Vaupel, J.W. and Curhan, J.P. (1973), *The World's Largest Multinational Enterprises* (Cambridge, MA: Harvard University Press).

Yip, G.S. (1992), *Total Global Strategy* (Englewood Cliffs, NJ: Prentice-Hall).

Chapter 13
Employment Relations in a Global Networked Economy

Sandra Jones

Introduction

This chapter presents an overview of various forms that the employment relationship may take, the different perspectives from which to analyse and assess these relationships and the various cultural factors that affect the employment relationship. The information draws on explanations and practice of industrial relations, human resource management, knowledge management, conflict management and social justice. In so doing, the interrelated issues of social justice and the future role of unions in relation to the employment relationship as business globalizes are explored.

The Employment Relationship

As the world economy becomes more technologically linked, knowledge becomes the competitive advantage of business. Employment relations, through which people develop an affinity with an organization, becomes more central to organizational strategy, especially when recognition is given to knowledge that resides within employees' heads.

Developing and implementing a 'best practice' employment relations is not as easily achieved as are more traditional 'process' concepts that lend themselves to quantitative and qualitative 'measurable' and descriptive cause and effect (input-output) analysis. Despite research efforts to identify a single form of business process engineering appropriate for the employment relationship (such as the balanced score card (Kaplan and Norton 1992)), no one 'best practice' methodology for the employment relationship has emerged. Instead what is evidenced is that each organization must adopt its own approach that is appropriate for it's needs. This requires organizations to:

1. decide upon an appropriate form for the employment relationship;
2. identify the principal perspective from which the employment relationship is viewed by the organization;
3. consider the cultural environment (internal and external) within which the organization is working.

The first section of this chapter explores these factors.

Employment Relationship Forms

The particular form of employment relationship chosen by an organization is dependent on a number of factors: its purpose, the approach it has adopted to fulfil that purpose, the decision-making structure in place and the ideology management have about the roles managers and employees play.

Employment Relationship as Industrial Relations

The oldest form of employment relations, shown in Figure 13.1, is referred to as the systems model of industrial relations (Dunlop 1958). It characterizes the traditional approach to industrial relations of many 'developed' countries such the United Kingdom (Millward et al. 1992; Legge 1995), Australia (Morehead et al. 1995) and many European countries from the early 1900s to the 1980s as their manufacturing sectors grew (Ferner and Hyman 1999). As a result, the model is often associated with mass production techniques in which employees are functionally divided based on their level, type of skills and knowledge. Management is centralized and hierarchical and there are low levels of trust between employers and employees.

This model focuses on three principal actors, employers, unions (representing employees) and the government. Rules and regulations that govern actor's relationships within the broader economic, social, cultural and political environment in which they operate are taken into account. Descriptions of these interrelationships are static (viewed at a single point in time), within national boundaries in which conflict is negotiated and legislated in specific 'events'. Although this static model has been updated and developed into a more strategic interrelationship in the 1980s (Clegg 1979; Flanders 1965; Kochan et al. 1984), the principles remain basically the same.

This model assumes that employers (representing owners of physical capital) make all decisions about what to business to be in and how, why and where they will produce goods and services. Employers identify the form of decision-making (the managerial team) that will occur within the organization together with the size and composition of the workforce. Employers and employer bodies determine the industrial process and the employment conditions appropriate to that particular process.

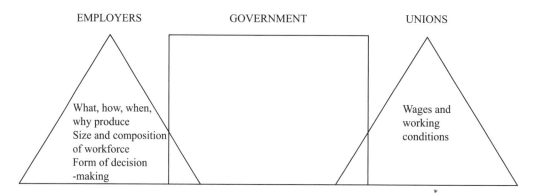

Figure 13.1   Industrial relations model

Government legislation is the only formal limitation to the power of the employers. Laws have been passed relating to employment issues such as child labour, occupational health and safety, minimum wages and equal employment opportunities. Informal limitations on the power of employers also exists, through trade unions which, as representatives of collectives of employees, bargain with employers on issues concerning wages and working conditions. Kochan (2000) states that 'unions focus on improving the economic dimensions of work; employers ... *take* ... primary responsibility for shaping the workplace culture and designing and coordinating work to achieve maximum productivity and quality'.

This 'pluralist' model recognizes many stakeholders who have competing views and interests, with no stakeholder having a dominant position. In seeking to avoid conflict, the government passes legislation that provides structures and processes for conciliation.

Employment Relationship as Human Resource Management

A second form of the employment relationship, presented in Figure 13.2, is often referred to as human resource management (HRM) (Guest 1987, 1989, 1995; Sisson 1993; Storey 1992; Legge 1995). The model emerged in the United States (Kaufman 1992; Katz and Wheeler 2004) in the 1940s–1950s, with many more countries (such as the UK (Edwards et al. 1999; Marchington et al. 2004) and Australia (Peetz 2005), moving towards such an approach towards the end of the twentieth century). It is associated with mass production techniques but with an emphasis on increasing trust between employers and employees.

The model focuses on individual employees rather than unions. It establishes a human resource function responsible for implementing government legislation and for addressing the 'hierarchy of needs' (Maslow 1954) of individual employees. The aim is to increase the trust employees in their employer and in doing so to increase employee motivation to the organization and reduce employee commitment to unions and.

This 'unitarist' model assumes that employers and employees work together in harmony towards a common goal. HRM practitioners work with line managers to ensure that the management view is accepted as *the* legitimate source of power and authority, conflict is reduced and activity that may reduce the organizations' primary activity, such as work to rule, strikes and other industrial action, is minimized.

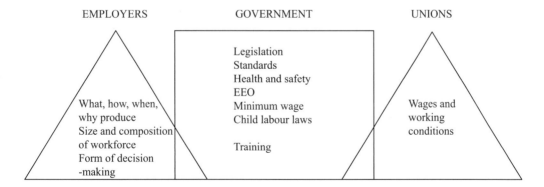

| EMPLOYERS | GOVERNMENT | UNIONS |

What, how, when, why produce
Size and composition of workforce
Form of decision-making

Legislation
Standards
Health and safety
EEO
Minimum wage
Child labour laws

Training

Wages and working conditions

Figure 13.2 Human resource model

Employment Relationship as Partnerships

The third form of the employment relationship (Figure 13.3) changes the nature of the interaction between the three parties. This form typically is referred to as a mutual gains (Cohen-Rosenthal and Burton 1993; Kochan and Osterman 1994) or partnership model (Bacon and Storey 2000). Many different forms of this model have been developed (Ferner and Hyman 1999). In Germany (Jacobi et al. 1999), it formed the basis of the development of 'Works Councils' which later became the basis of the European Works Council approach. In the 1970s, Scandinavian countries, particularly Sweden (Kjellberg 1999; Kochan et al. 1994; Hammarstrom et al. 2004) and Norway (Dolvik and Stokke 1999), used the model as underpinning to move toward a more socially conscious approach. In Japan (Kuwahara 1993, 2004) during the 1970s elements of the model were recognizable as a mixture of 'enterprise unionism' and Total Quality Management through quality improvement circles that assisted the development of 'productive manufacturing'. In the UK it became part of the 'partnership' movement of the 1990s. The model was the foundation which underpinned the Australian 'Accord' (Carney 1988; Curtain and Mathews 1990) between the government and unions in the 1980s.

Rather than focus on a separation of roles and conflict between employers and employees (through unions), the focus is on a partnership approach in which consultation between employers, employees and unions is the basis of agreement on wages and working conditions. This takes into account employers' needs to operate a profitable enterprise, and, at the same time, employees' need to receive adequate wages and working conditions.

This partnering approach focuses less on different (and competing) needs of employers and employees and more on potential mutual gains that benefit both. Consultation may involve all individuals, such as quality circles (Watanabe 1991, team briefs (Rayner 1993), or collectives of employees through elected union representatives (generally through consultative committees and negotiations on behalf of members (Jones 2000).

This model often is associated with lean production techniques (Dertouzos et al. 1989; Womack et al. 1990) in which employees are functionally flexible, based on their type and level of skills and knowledge. Management is team-based and emphasizes developing trust between employers and employees.

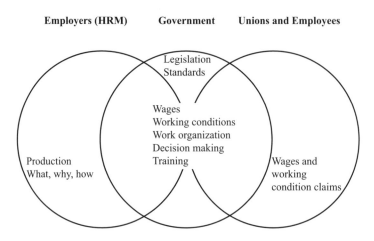

Figure 13.3   Mutual gains/partnership model

Employment Relationship as Networks

A fourth form of the employment relationship is presented in Figure 13.4. This represents a dynamic framework that is capable of emerging and changing over time and space (Jones 2004). It is illustrated in the 'intellectual capital' approaches, such as the Swedish Scandia Navigator model (Petersson 1988; Edvinsson and Malone 1997), which recognizes the contribution of organizational capital, customer and human capital. In so doing, the Scandia Navigator approach pays equal attention to intangible assets (human, intellectual, social capital) and tangible assets (financial capital).

The model recognizes a plethora of actors who interact on a global basis and may include: unions, social movement groups, employers (both single country and globally based, global not-for-profit agencies, and national and international government and semi-government agencies. Employment relations issues are influenced by a large number of issues and are raised at global rather than national or local site levels.

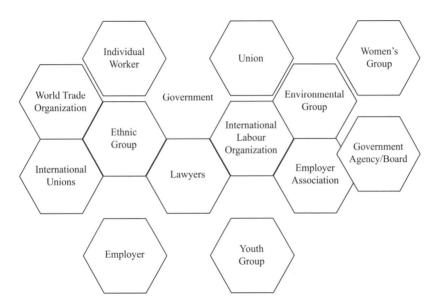

Figure 13.4   Network framework

The network framework recognizes the individual as a multi-collective actor (e.g., an employee, as well as a unionist, and a member of a social, environmental, political group) who is involved in a network of relationships that can affect the employment relationship. A principal benefit of this approach is a greater potential to share knowledge, particularly of sensitive data such as differing wages and employment conditions.

The network recognizes a plurality of views that are likely to change over time and place. This is because coalitions vary between individuals as members of many collectives. It is an emergent framework for 'intelligent organizations' in which employees are valued for their 'human capital' based on their knowledge, skills and personal (tacit) information (Baker 2000; McElroy 2002; Tymon and Stumpt 2003). This requires a collaborative 'leadership' in which the employment relationship is viewed as a collaborative partnership rather than dependent on a management-control approach. Trust forms the basis of the employment relationship and human resource practitioners are 'stewards' rather than managers (Lengnick-Hall and Lengnick-Hall 2003).

The network is behind organizational encouragement of communities of practice as forums in which social capital is developed as people share their 'passion' and knowledge on particular issues (Hildreth and Kimble 2004; Jones 2004; Wenger et al. 2002). The model is not confined to organizations. It is part of the newer models of union activity (Kelly 1998). Examples of 'social movement unionism' (Rose 1998; McVeigh 1996; Devinatz 1995; Fitzgerald 1991; Fitzgerald and Simmons 1991) and 'community unionism' (Brecher and Costello 1990; Tufts 1996) are evidence of the unions' growing acceptance of network frameworks (Jones 2002).

In summary, organizations may choose from an array of employment relations forms. These are:

- individual (employee) to collective (union) relationships;
- centralized managerial decision-making process to partnership approaches;
- static models that identify established actors and rules governing the employment relationship;
- dynamic frameworks that enable identification of networks between different actors over time and place.

A strategic organizational task is to decide which employment relationship is appropriate at varying times and places. This decision will be influenced by:

- the extent to which the organization is prepared to have managers solely, or employees jointly, engage in organizational decision-making;
- the degree of legitimacy afforded the views of different groups within the organization;
- the degree of satisfaction of employees with their employment conditions.

Frames through which to Perceive the Employment Relationship

The second important influence upon the organizational choice of an employment relationship is the perspective through which the organization views itself. Bolman and Deal (1997) identify five frames (or windows on the world) that they assert act as a series of filters through which organizations filter enormous amounts of information to help managers make decisions and order. These are:

1. structural;
2. human resource;
3. political;
4. cultural or symbolic; and
5. values frames.

The Structural Frame

The structural frame assumes that organizations exist to achieve established goals and objectives. They are assumed to work best when rationality prevails over personal preferences and external pressures. The focus of attention is on designing structures an organization's including goals, technology and an environment to fit current and anticipated scenarios. Organizations that view their employment relations through the structural frame focus on establishing:

- clearly identified tasks for employees' skill levels;
- appropriate forms of coordination and control to ensure that individuals and units work together to accomplish organizational goals;
- rational decision-making processes that produce the right decisions (either managers alone, or managers and employees through an agreed formal processes);
- performance evaluation that is formal and has rewards or penalties to control performance;
- conflict resolution mechanisms that are based on agreed (formal) rules, procedures and standards.

In summary, from a structural perspective, the employment relationship is regarded as having a role in the social architecture in which structure is attuned to task, technology and environment. This frame perspective suggests that the role of employees is to understand and work within the accepted structure.

The Human Resource Frame

The human resource frame assumes that organizations exist as a symbiotic relationship in which mutual needs are serviced. For example, employees provide organizations with ideas, energy and talent; organizations in return provide employees with careers, salaries and opportunities. The focus of attention is on designing employment relationships that are mutually advantageous. Organizations that view their employment relations through the human resource frame focus on establishing:

- consultative decision-making processes that are based on accepted process 'ground rules' that promote participation and produce commitment;
- balance between human needs and formal roles;
- evaluation systems facilitate performance improvement that help enlarge and enrich individuals' roles;
- conflict resolution based on individuals confronting and negotiating differences.

In summary, from a human resource perspective, the employment relationship requires empowered workers in order to align organizational and human needs.

The Political Frame

The political frame assumes that organizations are coalitions of various stakeholders (individuals and interest groups) that have different values, beliefs, information, interests and perceptions of reality. As a result of scarce resources, allocative choices potentially give rise to conflict and the use of personal or positional power to attract resources. Bargaining, negotiation and jockeying for position are used to attract resources. Organizations that view their employment relations through the political frame focus on establishing:

- internal 'spaces' that give stakeholders opportunities to discuss conflicting issues that need to be resolved;
- decision-making activities that are open to anyone to gain and exercise power as individuals or members of new coalitions;
- evaluating performance of stakeholders to try to increase power and influence;

- resolving conflict through bargaining and negotiating.

The political perspective suggests individual employees need to have power associated with their position. Connotations of this power are status, personality, knowledge and patronage. Alternatively, they need to have a powerful (collective) advocate, in order to balance the employment relationship.

The Symbolic Frame

The symbolic frame assumes organizations need to pay greater attention to the meaning behind activities as events have ambiguities and multiple meanings and innuendos. These interpretations stem from different frames people use to interpret experiences. Uncertain realities tend to demean rational analysis. This frame recognizes that people create symbols, myths, rituals, ceremonies and stories to resolve confusion, increase predictability and provide direction and anchor hope and faith. Organizations that view their employment relations through the symbolic frame focus on:

- creating and interpreting rituals to confirm values and provide opportunities to negotiate shared meaning. Japanese companies for instance insist employees undertake group exercises and sing the corporation's song prior to starting work. Western companies such as Xerox and Microsoft encourage workers to take a break from work and play team based games.
- evaluating performance through playing a role in a shared ritual.
- conflict resolution through developing shared values and meanings.

From the symbolic perspective, employment relations is regarded as establishing a process through which the creation of shared meaning is developed, subtle interrelationships occur and actions are appreciated.

The Values Frame

The values frame assumes that organizations consider ethical values are promoted within their organization in both words and deeds. The values perspective of employment relations is about establishing ethical working conditions that support and protect employees against exploitation and injustice.

The globalization of business has introduced new challenges to corporate conduct relating to ethical business. Organizations are expected to operate based on sound environmental sustainability propositions and recognize stakeholders needs. Organizations that view their employment relations through the value frame focus on developing approaches that adopt processes and instil social justice, equal opportunity, protect health and safety and provide career development opportunities. They aim to minimize exploitation (e.g., child labour) and maximize human rights.

Organizations can use the questions presented in Table 13.1 to identify the appropriate frame for their needs and encourage the inclusion of other frames. Table 13.1 suggests which frames can be used when answering certain questions.

Table 13.1   Questions with 'yes' and 'no' frames

Question	Frame to use if answer is 'yes'	Frame to use if answer is 'no'
Are individual commitment and motivation essential to success?	Human resource, symbolic structural	Political
Is the technical quality of the decision important?	Structural	Human resource, political, symbolic
Are there high levels of ambiguity and uncertainty?	Political, symbolic	Structural, human resource
Are you working from the bottom up?	Political	Structural, human resource, symbolic
Are there high levels of emotion being shown by the workforce?	Symbolic, human resource	Structural, political

Failure to choose an appropriate frame could mean the organization finds itself the subject of a global negative reaction from which it will be difficult to recover. For example, Nike faced massive negative customer reaction when its global employment practices in less developed countries were publicized. Individuals working within organizations also need to reflect on the degree to which their personal values (frame) are in harmony with that of the organization if they are to stay motivated within a trusted environment.

Cultural Influences on the Employment Relationship

Culture has been defined as the means by which people communicate, perpetuate and develop their knowledge and attitudes towards life. Culture is mental software (Hofstede 1994, p. 5). It is used to distinguish members of one group or category of people from another.

- Culture has been described as the customary or traditional way of thinking, unique configurations of norms, values and beliefs, ways groups behave, common assumed understanding of meanings, shared expectations and beliefs, widely repeated patterns how activities are done in specific locations and under specific conditions (Trompenaars and Hampden-Turner 2000).

Hofstede's (1980) global cultural study identified four (later five) dimensions of culture. It is possible to extrapolate how these dimensions may affect the employment relationships as follows:

- power-distance, or the extent of inequality accepted in a culture. This can affect attitudes to equal employment opportunity, to consultation and to the importance of equality in power relations between employers and employees;
- individualism and collectivism, or the extent of ties between members of a culture. This can affect attitudes to individual as opposed to collective (e.g., unionized) employees;
- masculinity and femininity, or the degree to which culture is influenced by gender. This can affect attitudes to equal employment opportunity based on gender;

- uncertainty avoidance, or the degree to which a specific culture is able to accept uncertainty. This can affect the degree of adherence to rules and regulations governing the employment relationship;
- long-term and short-term orientation. This can affect the degree to which an organization are willing to focus on supportive human resource relationships.

As organizations it is increasingly important to globalize and establish transplants and facilities in various countries. Corporations often send expatriate managers to establish and/ or manage the organization on an ongoing basis. It is important that organizations employ a culturally diverse workforce to identify the various cultural dimensions that influence the employment relationship (vertically between employers and employees and horizontally between employee peers).

In summary, varying cultural dimensions influence the form of the employment relationship adopted by organizations, and create challenges for organizations that employ a diverse workforce or that operate globally in a variety of cultures. When designing an employment relations strategy, organizations need to take cultures into account.

This first section of this chapter presented three factors that organizations need to be consider when designing an employment relations strategy. Emphasis has been placed on the need to decide the form the employment relationship should take that best suits the organizational need and employees. In each case, organizations should identify the dominant frame through which it views itself. Organizations need to address each of these issues in order to design an effective employment relations strategy.

The second section discusses implications of globalization on international employment relations, particularly with regard to social justice issues and union activity.

Global Union Activity and Social Justice

Since technology transcends geographical boundaries, as organizations globalize, significant change has occurred to work. Many Western 'developed' countries are reducing their manufacturing industry base and replacing it with a growing service sector heavily dependent on 'knowledge workers' (Cordata 1998). These often non-unionized labour forces accept wages and working conditions different from those of the traditional (unionized) manufacturing workforce. This has resulted in the rise of more part-time and casual work replacing full-time positions. Short-time and flexible employment has begun to replace long-term and stable employment. As a consequence, the level of unionization of the workforce has declined.

The decline in union membership is a worldwide phenomenon. Countries with a strongly unionized tradition, such as the UK and Australian, now record levels of unionism below 30 per cent, down from a previous high of around 50 per cent of the workforce. This has led to unions adopting new (economic) models that offer employees new services rather than the old social and political interests. It also led to new coalitions between unions and social movement groups. For example in Canada, Bellemare (2000) identified a coalition between a Public Transport Users Group and Union in Montreal, while Jones (2002) presented a case study of union-community activity in the Australian waterfront dispute of 1998.

At the same time that manufacturing industry and unionization are declining in Western countries, manufacturing plants and service facilities, such as call centres (Frenkel et al. 1998), are increasing in less developed countries such as China and India. Although unionism exists in many of these countries, strong competition for jobs is leading to a lowering of wages and employment conditions, with concomitant concern about global social justice issues in the employment relationship Park and Leggett 2004). Concern is being expressed that conditions of employment that would not be tolerated in organizations based in developed countries exist in the offshore plants of the same organizations. This is leading to discussion of the need for an employment relations strategy that has a global perspective.

Examples of union global activity include the 2001 the International Trade Union Advisory Council (TUAC) decision that unions must unite if the 'digital divide' is not to further contribute to the 'social divide'. The plan that was developed included:

- developing closer links between unions internationally;
- developing education campaigns for union leaders;
- seeking to secure national government commitments to the universal Declaration of Human Rights and International Labour Office (ILO) Conventions dealing with social justice and freedom of association;
- encouraging international financial institutions (such as the International Monetary Fund and the World Bank) to examine the social effects of their policies, and lobbying the World Trade Organization (WTO) to establish a working group of forum on labour standards and trade agreements;
- taking action through national trade union bodies to establish improved labour standards in multinational enterprises through framework agreements.

Examples of social justice campaigns that have been developed include:

- campaigns to provide social security support in less developed countries (for example money, education, medical aid);
- campaigns to support women in less developed countries start community enterprises;
- adoption of ILO Declaration of the Fundamental Right to work, including a ban on child and bonded labour;
- debate in the WTO over whether to introduce a social clause into the WTO framework.

It is clear that the globalization of organizations produces a new array of challenges for employment relations including new 'ethical' issues associated with social justice of a globally employed workforce emerge. Both employers and global collectives of employees and other social movements need to develop and use Corporate Codes of Conduct that apply to employee relations. These codes may include:

- national government commitment (accompanied by legislations to implement) ILO Conventions;
- social clauses in trade agreements;
- voluntary and negotiated corporate or sectoral codes of conduct;
- a commitment to developing relationships with local communities to create jobs;
- integrating human rights issues (including appropriate wage payments, compensation and health and safety) into the broader conduct of business;
- establishing 'ethical' supply chains between the final provider of goods and services to customers and their intermediate suppliers to ensure appropriate wages and working conditions have been paid at each stage.

Conclusions

This chapter presents an overview of forms that the employment relationship may take, the different perspectives through which it may be assessed and the different cultural factors that can affect the employment relationship. Decisions organizations need to take in regard to the appropriate employment relationship to facilitate achieving aims are outlined. The interrelated issues of social justice and the future role of unions in relation to the employment relationship as business globalizes are explored.

The central argument presented in this chapter is that there is no one 'best practice' model of employment relations. Instead, each organization needs to consider its own goals and values, together with the goals and values of its workforce and the local community in order to establish an appropriate employment relations strategy. As organizations globalize they need to pay special interest in consideration issues of global social justice and how these can be maintained and improved. This requires all parties, organizations, employees, unions and other supra national bodies to consider how best to support the employee relationship at both macro and local levels.

References

Bacon, N. and Storey, J (2000), 'New Employee Relations Strategies in Britain: Towards Individualism or Partnership?', *British Journal of Industrial Relations* 38(3), pp. 407–27.

Baker, W. (2000), *Achieving Success through Social Capital: Tapping the Hidden Resources in your Personnel and Business Networks* (San Francisco, CA: Jossey-Bass).

Bellemare, G. (2000), 'End Users: Actors in the Industrial Relations System?', *British Journal of Industrial Relations* 38(3), pp. 383–405.

Bolman, L. and Deal, T. (1997), *Reframing Organizations* (San Francisco, CA: Jossey-Bass).

Brecher, J. and Costello, T. (eds) (1990), *Building Bridges: the Emerging Grassroots Coalition of Labor and Community* (New York: Monthly Review).

Carney, S. (1988), *Australia in Accord* (Sydney: Sun).

Clegg, H. (1979), *The Changing System of Industrial Relations in Great Britain* (London: Blackwell).

Cohen-Rosenthal, E. and Burton, C.E. (1993), *Mutual Gains* (Ithaca, NY: ILR Press).

Cordata, J. (1998), *Rise of the Knowledge Worker* (Woburn, MA: Butterworth-Heinemann).

Curtain, R. and Mathews, J. (1990), 'Two Models of Award Restructuring in Australia', *Labour and Industry* 3(1), pp. 58–75.

Dertouzos, M., Lester, R. and Solow, R. (1989), *Made in America: Regaining the Productive Edge* (New York: Harper Perennial).

Devinatz, V.G. (1995), 'Wayne Kennedy, AFGE Local 2816 and Community Unionism: A New Conception of Public-Sector Unionism', *Journal of Collective Negotiations in the Public Sector* 24(2), pp. 121–32.

Dolvik, J. and Stokke, T. (1999), 'Norway: The Revival of Centralized Concertation' in Ferner, A. and Hyman, R. (eds) *Changing Industrial Relations in Europe* (Oxford: Blackwell Business), pp. 118–45.

Dunlop, J. (1958), *Industrial Relations Systems* (New York: Holt).

Edvinsson, L. and Malone, M. (1997), *Intellectual Capital: Realizing your Company's True Value by Finding its Hidden Brainpower* (New York: Harper Business).

Edwards, P., Hall, M., Hyman, R., Marginson, P., Sisson, K., Waddington, J. and Winchester, D. (1999), 'Great Britain: Still Muddling Through' in Ferner, A. and Hyman, R. (eds) *Changing Industrial Relations in Europe* (Oxford: Blackwell Business), pp. 1–54.

Ferner, A. and Hyman, R. (eds) (1999), *Changing Industrial Relations in Europe* (Oxford: Blackwell Business).

Fitzgerald, J. (1991), 'Class as Community: The New Dynamics of Social Change', *Environment and Planning D: Society and Space* 9, pp. 117–28.

Fitzgerald, J. and Simmons, L. (1991), 'From Consumption to Production: Labour Participation in Grass-Roots Movements in Pitsburgh and Hartford', *Urban Affairs Quarterly* 26(4), pp. 512–531.

Flanders, A. (1965), *Industrial Relations, What is Wrong with the System?* (London: Faber and Faber).

Frenkel, S., Tam, M., Korczynski, M. and Shire, K. (1998), 'Beyond Bureaucracy? Work Organization in Call Centres', *International Journal of Human Resource Management* 9(6), pp. 857–979.

Guest, D. (1987), 'Human Resource Management and Industrial Relations', *Journal of Management Studies* 24(5), pp. 503–21.

Guest, D. (1989), 'Human Resource Management: Its Implications for Industrial Relations' in Storey, J. (ed.) *New Perspectives on Human Resource Management* (London: Routledge), pp. 11–55.

Guest, D. (1995), 'Human Resource Management, Trade Unions and Industrial Relations, in Storey, J. (ed.) *Human Resource Management: A Critical Text* (London: Routledge), pp. 110–41.

Hammarstrom, O., Huzzard, T. and Nilsson, T. (2004), 'Employment Relations in Sweden', in Bamber, G., Lansbury, R. and Wailes, N. (eds) *International and Comparative Industrial Relations* (Sydney: Allen and Unwin), pp. 254–76.

Hildreth, P. and Kimble, C. (eds) (2004), *Knowledge Networks, Innovation through Communities of Practice* (Hershey, PA: Idea Group).

Hofstede, G. (1994), *Culture's Consequences: International Differences in Work-Related Values* (London: Sage, reprint).

Jacobi, O., Keller, B. and Muller-Jentsch, W. (1999), 'Germany: Facing New Challenges' in Ferner, A. and Hyman, R. (eds) *Changing Industrial Relations in Europe* (Oxford: Blackwell Business), pp. 190–238.

Jones, S. (2000), 'Workplace Reform and Workforce Participation', unpublished PhD.

Jones, S. (2002), 'A Woman's Place is on the Picket Line', *Employee Relations* 24(2), pp. 151–66.

Jones, S. (2004), 'Towards a Theory of Industrial Relations for a Knowledge Economy', *Industrielle Beiziehungen* 11(1/2), pp. 15–26.

Kaplan, R. and Norton, D. (1992), 'The Balanced Scorecard: Measures that Drive Performance', *Harvard Business Review* January–February, pp. 36–66.

Katz, H. and Wheeler, H. (2004), 'Employment Relations in the United States' in Bamber, G., Lansbury, R. and Wailes, N. (eds) *International and Comparative Industrial Relations*, (Crows Nest, NSW: Allen & Unwin), pp. 67–90.

Kaufman, B. (1992), *Industrial Relations in the USA* (Ithaca, NY: ILR Press).

Kelly, J. (1998), *Rethinking Industrial Relations – Mobilization, Collectivism and Long Waves* (London: Routledge).

Kjellberg, A. (1999), 'Sweden: Restoring the Model' in Ferner, A. and Hyman, R. (eds) *Changing Industrial Relations in Europe* (Oxford: Blackwell Business), pp. 74–117.

Kochan, T. (2000), 'Building a New Social Contract at Work: A Call to Action', Presidential Address to the 52nd Annual meeting of the Industrial Relations Research Association, MIT Institute for Work and Employment Research, Boston.

Kochan, T. and Osterman, P. (1994), *The Mutual Gains Enterprise* (Cambridge, MA: Harvard Business School).

Kochan, T., Katz, H. and McKersie, R. (1994), *The Transformation of American Industrial Relations* (New York: ILR Press).

Kuwahara, Y. (1993), 'Industrial Relations in Japan' in Bamber, G., Lansbury, R. and Wailes, N. (eds) *International and Comparative Industrial Relations: Globalisation and the Developed Market Economies* (Sydney: Allen and Unwin), pp. 249–74.

Kuwahara, Y. (2004), 'Industrial Relations in Japan' in Bamber, G., Lansbury, R. and Wailes, N. (eds) *International and Comparative Industrial Relations: Globalisation and the Developed Market Economies* (Sydney: Allen and Unwin), pp. 277–305

Legge, K. (1995), *Human Resource Management* (London: Macmillan Business).

Lengnick-Hall, H. and Lengnick-Hall, M. (2003), *HRM in the Knowledge Economy* (San Francisco, CA: Bennett-Koehler).

Marchington, M., Goodman, J. and Berridge, J. (2004), 'Employment Relations in Britain' in Bamber, G., Lansbury, R. and Wailes, N. (eds) *International and Comparative Industrial Relations*, (Crows Nest, NSW: Allen & Unwin), pp. 36–66.

Maslow, A. (1954), *Motivation and Personality* (New York: Harper Row).

McElroy, M. (2002), 'Social Innovation Capital', *Journal of Intellectual Capital* 3(1), pp. 30–39.

McVeigh, R. (1996), 'Structural Influences on Popular Support for Social Movement Activity', *Social Movements, Conflict and Change* 19, pp. 247–71.

Millward, N., Stevens, M., Smart, D. and Howes, W. (1992), *Workplace Industrial Relations in Transition* (Aldershot: Gower).

Morehead, A., Steele, M., Alexander, M., Stephen, K. and Duffin, I. (1995), *Changes at the Workplace: The 1995 Australian Workplace Industrial Relations Survey* (South Melbourne: Addison Wesley Longman).

Park, Y.-B. and Leggett, C. (2004), 'Employment Relations in the Republic of Korea' in Bamber, G., Lansbury, R. and Wailes, N. (eds) *International and Comparative Industrial Relations*, (Crows Nest, NSW: Allen & Unwin), pp. 306–28.

Peetz, D. (2005), *Brave New Workplace* (Sydney: Allen and Unwin).

Petersson, L-E. (1998), 'Intellectual Capital: The Future Innovative Enterprise', Intellectual Capital Prototype Report, Skandia (President and CEO), Sweden.

Rayner, S. (1993), *Recreating the Workplace: The Pathway to High Performance Work Systems* (Essex Junction, VT: Oliver Wright).

Rose, M. (1998), 'From the Field to the Picket Line' in Blee, K. (ed.), *No Middle Ground: Women and Radical Protest* (New York: New York University Press), pp. 225–50.

Sisson, K. (1993), 'In Search of HRM', *British Journal of Industrial Relations* 31(2), pp. 201–19.

Storey, J. (1992), *Developments in the Management of Human Resource Management* (London: Blackwell).

Trompenaars, A. and Hampden-Turner, C. (2000), *Riding the Waves of Culture* (London: Nicholas Breasley Publishing).

Tufts, W. (1996), 'Changing Unionism in Canada and the Changing Spatiality of Labour Organization Models', MA thesis, Kingston, Ontario, Canada: Queen's University.

Tymon, W. and Stumpf, S (2003), 'Social Capital in the Success of Knowledge Workers', *Career Development International* 8(1), pp. 12–20.

Watanabe, S. (1991), 'The Japanese Quality Control Circle: Why it Works', *International Labour Review* 13(1), pp. 57–78.

Wenger, E., McDermott, R. and Snyder, W. (2002), *Cultivating Communities of Practice* (Cambridge, MA: Harvard Business School Press).

Womack, J.P., Jones, J.T. and Ross, D. (1990), *The Machine that Change the World* (New York: Macmillan).

Chapter 14

Human Resources Management Practices within Japanese Companies

Peter Firkola

> Japanese and American management styles are 95 percent the same – and different in all important aspects.
>
> Soichiro Honda, Founder of Honda Motors (quoted in Jackson and Tomioka 2004)

Introduction

This chapter introduces key aspects of management practices in Japanese companies. Japanese management will first be discussed from a historical and cultural perspective. The main characteristics of traditional personnel management practices will then be looked at. Finally, recent trends and changes in these management practices will be examined.

In order to work in Japan or do business with Japanese companies, it is important to have an understanding of Japanese management practices. While often seen as unique and mysterious in other countries, during the 1970s and 1980s the personnel practices of Japanese companies came to be seen as one of the keys to the Japanese economic success. In the 1990s, when the Japanese economy went into recession, these same personnel practices were seen as a large part of the problem. Much has been written about the demise of these traditional Japanese management practices. As well, foreign media often place too much emphasis on special cases such as Nissan Motors. Thus, one can get a distorted picture of what is happening in most Japanese companies.

This chapter aims to help readers understand management practices in Japanese companies. It begins with a review of the origins of Japanese management, followed by a discussion examining key characteristics of traditional management practices. The final section will explain how management practices have been changing over the past decade as a result of changes in Japanese society, the Japanese economy and the global economy.

Japanese Management

'Japanese management' refers to management practices that are characteristic of Japanese companies and different from non-Japanese companies (Craig 2002). This chapter will focus on personnel (human resources) management practices within Japanese companies. Although it is only one part of the company management system, personnel practices provide insight into understanding the overall management system and the changes Japanese companies are facing. Personnel management also offers a window onto understanding the history and culture of the country.

Conflicting Theories about the Origin of Japanese Management

There are two theories on the origins of Japanese management. One theory states that history and culture are of little importance and that most of the current Japanese management system has developed over the past 60 years (Kono 1988). This theory asserts that much of the changes in the Japanese economy occurred in episodic phases, such as the rapid industrialization at the beginning of the Meiji period (1867–1910) and, in particular, after World War II when American management practices were introduced into Japan and adapted by Japanese companies. This post-war evolution theory claims that most business practices developed after World War II and have little to do with pre-modern Japan.

The second theory argues that history and culture are important (Odaka 1993). This continuity theory asserts that modern practices are based on the practices and values of pre-modern Japan. There are many explanations about the historical and cultural roots of Japanese management. Some of the possible roots and their characteristics related to Japanese business practices include Confucian philosophy (respect for elders, loyalty and harmony), Buddhism (humility, work ethic and working for collective good), Bushido (obligation, duty and honour) and rice farming villages (paternalism and collective behaviour).

Both theories provide valid arguments and the truth lies somewhere in between (Tsutsui 1988). Certain management practices are more recent than others yet culture and history are also important in understanding modern Japanese business. Rice farming village communities in pre-modern Japan, for example, provide insights into the origins of many key characteristics of modern business practices such as paternalism and collective behaviour.

Rice Farming Villages in Pre-Modern Japan

Business historians such as Odaka (1993) believe that the rice farming villages during the Edo period (1602–1860) provided the foundation for the behaviour and values of the modern Japanese company. Unwritten rules and values were shared by the members of these villages. As well, lifelong membership, age-based roles and collective behavioural norms were important characteristics of these communities. These three characteristics are seen as predecessors to modern Japanese management practices.

Lifelong Membership

During the Edo period, there was little chance to travel outside one's village. This limited mobility meant that individuals born in these villages often spent their entire lives there. The fortunes of all of the villagers were tied together throughout their life, thus members of a village shared a common fate with one another. In this environment, the best way to ensure prosperity for oneself was to dedicate one's life to the prosperity of the village. This is a possible origin of the modern practice of lifetime employment.

Age-based Roles

In these communities, one's age and experience determined one's role and status. Much of the learning was done by apprenticeship and emphasis was put on learning correct behaviours, etiquettes and work ethic. Younger members of the village started by watching and learning from older village members. They would then be allowed to work under supervision and, finally, to work unsupervised on their own. Based on their age and experience, members took on more important roles in the village. The leaders of the village were the male elders who were primarily responsible for much of the decision-making. This is a possible origin of seniority practices in modern companies.

Collective Behaviour

The practice of wet rice farming required an emphasis on group work. The villagers were taught to put the collective needs of the village before their own individual needs. This emphasis was important to maintain harmony and avoid direct conflict with other village members. Villagers were dependent on the village for all of their needs, including housing. Thus there was a symbiosis between the security which the community offered and the loyalty to the village which was required in return. These values of collective behavioural norms are remain important today in contemporary corporations, for example, in union and management relations.

How are the practices of rice farming villages connected to modern management practices? One explanation is that these practices were adapted by merchant houses during this period. Merchant houses had codes of conduct that contained specific rules regarding lifetime employment, seniority and collective behaviour (Sakudo 1978). They also used an apprenticeship system in which there was a correlation between age, experience, knowledge and skill. Young men who joined these merchant houses would spend years in training, slowly moving up in position. In some cases, they started their own business with the support of their merchant house employer.

These practices were adapted by business organizations in the late nineteenth century when Japan was industrialized and urbanized. At that time, Japan attempted to catch up with industrialized Western countries and transferred back the Western technologies useful to build their economy. In order to prevent the labour problems found in the West, many emerging businesses tried to model the characteristics of the merchant houses and the rice farming villages (Odaka 1993). By doing so, Japanese organizations created a structure that prevented worker alienation and promoted worker cooperation.[1]

Contemporary Japanese companies share many of the same values and behavioural norms of pre-modern rice farming communities. The three characteristics of lifelong membership, age-based roles and collective behaviour are the predecessors of traditional Japanese management practices. In the next section, these traditional management practices are examined.

Traditional Japanese Management

Pillars of Japanese Management

The economic environment in which traditional management practices were cultivated is important. During the post-war period of the 1950s to the 1970s, Japan was rebuilt and its economy grew rapidly (Hsu 1999). Japanese companies were trying to catch up with their Western counterparts. Workers dedicated themselves to their companies. The education system implemented after the war helped create an educated workforce. It was at this time that Japanese

---

1 This is often referred to using the German word *Gemeinschaft* (community organization), in which a group of individuals are bound together by mutual affection and sentiment as opposed to only contractual obligations and the organization is seen as a community such as a family.

companies reintegrated three key management practices – lifetime employment, seniority and enterprise unions – into a company's overall personnel system. These three practices were identified first by Abegglen (1958) in his book in the late 1950s. Each of these practices will be examined, along with their advantages and disadvantages.

Lifetime Employment

Lifetime employment refers to the practice of shielding important workers' right to work without the risk of redundancy and signified commitment to workers that their contributions are wanted. The company in effect offers employees to remain with the company throughout their working life. Lifetime employment was not unique to Japan and has been practiced in other countries, particularly in government and military organizations. Unlike other countries, however, lifetime employment in Japan was widespread throughout most organizations, in particular, large companies. The lifetime employment agreement was unwritten and there was no written contract guaranteeing that the individual could stay with that company until retirement (Kono and Clegg 2001).

Not all workers received lifetime employment, however. It was limited to male university and high-school graduates in large companies, meaning that roughly 30 per cent of the workforce had lifetime employment (Bird 2002). Female workers were mainly hired as part-time contingency workers and were encouraged to leave the company after they were married.

Lifetime employment was integrated into the company through recruitment, training and transfer practices. For university graduates and certain high school graduates this meant joining a company after graduation and working with that same company until about age 55. Students would be recruited during their final year of university or high school. The recruit agreed to take on general employment rather than being hired for a specific job in that company. Young Japanese customarily looked for a company and by inference a *keiretsu* rather than a job. Recruitment was thus a bilateral exchange of commitment: the recruit agreed to join the company and the company assumed the obligation of looking after him for as long as possible.

After joining the company, recruits spent a number of months receiving general training. During this time the emphasis was not on learning specific skills but rather on learning about the company and the way to work and behave in the company. These new workers would then be placed in a section of the company without being given any choice, and spent the next few years learning from senior workers in that section.

Every three to five years, workers were transferred to different sections which were often located in different parts of the country. Rather than staying in one particular functional area such transfers tended to be of a general naturec with workers moving across functions, for example from marketing to accounting (Sasaki 1990). For many employees cross-functional transfers would continue into their 30s and 40s. Employees were given little choice with regard to transfers and it was clear that transfer decisions were based on company needs. Such recruitment, training and transfer practices relied on a trade-off between job security and loyalty (Chen 2004). The implicit understandings between workers and companies in Japan remain one of the core underlying principles of business management.

Seniority

Seniority refers to a system in that determined promotion and wages based on the number of years in the company. Length of service was correlated directly to increased experience and accumulated knowledge. The seniority system was based specifically on the number of the years in the company and not on the worker's age. This acted as a deterrent to changing jobs late in a career. Promotion and wages scales combined seniority, length of service and merit. Personnel practices such as training and promotion were based on the seniority system.

Learning consisted mainly of on-the-job training and based on mentoring by senior workers. Employees would start out just by watching others do the job. They would then do the job while supervised and finally be able to do it on their own unsupervised. Thus, employees would have to depend on their supervisor and other senior workers for their training. In part due to the seniority system, older workers would share their knowledge with younger workers as they did not have to worry about being skipped over by younger workers.

Promotions were seniority-based and tended to be slow and limited in the early years of a career. The first promotion often did not take place until a worker was in his 30s. Early in their careers, workers rose through the company at about the same pace as members of their cohort. Moving together with members of the same cohort built cooperation among these workers. Once this period was over, some employees were promoted faster than others.

Although there promotion or wage differences early in their careers were absent, other ways of rewarding talented young workers could be used. For example, talented young workers would be matched with good supervisors to develop their skills, or they could be transferred to prime company locations, such as the head office where they could network with key players that would be important to their future advancement.

Enterprise Unions

Japanese enterprise unions had characteristics that distinguished them from unions in other countries. These unions where comprised of full-time company employees, both blue- and white-collar workers who were below the level of section chief. Part-time workers, upper-middle managers and higher were not part of the union. Employees belonged to enterprise unions were single company unions, as opposed to trade unions. This mechanism avoided 'them and us' differentiation based on occupation or job category.

Unions met with management to discuss collective agreements and convened to discuss the company's business strategies (Hagiwara 2002). These bodies were more cooperative than confrontational with management. The leaders were company employees transferred into the union for a number of years. Taking on these leadership positions frequently led to future management positions. Companies often provided the unions with office space. Because of this cooperative and close relationship, it has been questioned whether Japanese enterprise unions were really independent and represented the workers best interests.

The main role of the enterprise union was the spring wage campaign (known as *Shunto*). During this season, unions negotiate their members' monthly wage increases for the next year. The enterprise unions tried to obtain increases based on industry federation guidelines that set targets for wage increases. Companies made an effort to adhere to these industry guidelines. Unions exerted pressure for wage increases yet avoided striking or making demands that would impair the company. It was believed that enterprise unions and the company had an interdependent relationship that linked the fate of the union to the company.

Advantages and Disadvantages of Traditional Management Practices

Traditional management practices benefited both the company and the employees (Reischauer 1988). From the company's perspective, the system supported economic growth and was cost efficient. As long as the company kept growing, more lower-cost younger workers could be hired. Ideally this would create a workforce whose base was made up of young recruits. Based on seniority, these younger workers were the lowest paid, so labour costs were kept under control. This, in turn, led to economic growth in the company.

The system deterred workers from leaving their companies even if they were unhappy with their jobs. If a worker took another job, he would lose his seniority. And, since employees did not often leave the company, the company did not have to spend extra time and money retraining replacements. This lack of mobility also meant that companies kept talented workers, which made it easier to carry out long-term staff planning. These practice were very cost efficient for companies. Workers were motivated to ensure the long-term success of their companies and encouraged cooperation among workers, particularly those of the same age group. As a result of the long-term commitment made by the company, bonds created between the worker and the company increased worker loyalty and encouraged favourable labour relations.

There were many advantages for workers, the most important being job security. As long as employees worked hard, they had a secure job in the company. Because these practices encouraged cooperation and teamwork, a satisfying working environment evolved. Another advantage was that seniority-based wage increases matched a worker's stage in life. Salaries escalated roughly in relation to increasing lifestyle costs such as getting married, having and raising children and buying a home. The company also provided many social welfare benefits such as housing.

For companies, the main disadvantage was that the system is inefficient if a company is not growing. When a company stopped growing, it hired fewer recruits. As the average age of employees increased, labour costs increased. Due to lifetime employment commitments, companies could not easily reduce the now apparent burden of older and more expensive workers. If this lack of growth continued, companies faced the problem of having principally too many older workers. This system only worked well in strong economic environments; during a downturn, companies could not adjust quickly.

There also were disadvantages for workers in this system. For example, workers could become over-dependent on the company given that seniority and a lack of specialized skills made it difficult to leave a company if a worker was unhappy in his job. Workers had to make many personal sacrifices. They often had to work overtime, which limited time spent with their families.

Recent Trends in Japanese Management

Changes in Traditional Japanese Management System

Over the last decade, Japanese companies have been forced to change their management system. The traditional management system worked well in the decades after the war and was the envy of many countries in the 1970s and 1980s. But by the 1990s, this management system was seen as ineffective or dysfunctional. Some of the factors that forced companies to make changes to their management system included:

- a maturing economy: slowing growth, deregulation, service-based economy;
- recession: collapse of bubble economy, declining in sales and profits;
- corporate demographics: too many workers, increasing labour costs;
- changes in Japanese society: affluent society, aging society;

- global economy: appreciation of the Yen, increased competition from abroad;
- information technology: speed of communication, volume of information.

All of these factors led to a changing economic environment where Japanese companies forced operate. These companies and their workers were faced with many challenges (detailed in the box below). In particular, these changes led to declining profits and to growing concerns about having too many workers. Companies were forced to cut costs, in particular, labour costs. This in turn led to decreased worker morale. Companies used many methods to decrease labour costs, including moving their production facilities abroad. This led many companies to reassess the traditional management practices of lifetime employment, seniority and enterprise unions.

Company (personnel management) and worker-related issues in Japan 1990s included:

- Dealing with over employment
- Increasing white-collar productivity
- Developing an effective evaluation system
- Developing motivated and creative younger workers
- Transferring knowledge from older retiring workers to younger workers
- Increasing number of non-regular employees in the workforce
- Concerns about young Japanese not interested in working full-time
- Widening income gap between full-time and part-time workers
- Creating more diversity (female and non-Japanese workers) in workforce
- Increasing emphasis on the employees responsibility for their own careers
- Concerns about employee's mental health caused by work-related stress that leads to depression due to changes in company

---

Changes to Lifetime Employment

Although much has been placed on the demise of lifetime employment, many companies tried to preserve this practice (Emmot 2005). Companies used various strategies in order to reduce their labour costs:

1. decrease in salaries: workers took salary, bonus and allowance cuts and reduced overtime pay;
2. natural attrition: fewer new graduates hired;
3. voluntary early retirement: workers encouraged to retire a few years early;
4. secondment: workers transferred to another company, usually a subsidiary company;
5. increase in non-regular workers: hired more part-time or contract employees.

Many companies made restructuring announcements in the late 1990s. During this period, for example, Sony announced 17,000 job cuts, Hitachi, 20,000; Toshiba, 19,000; Fujitsu, 16,000; NEC, 19,000; and Panasonic, 3,000 (Kunii 1999; *The Economist* 2001; *The Japan Times* 2004). The Panasonic job cuts were surprising because the founder of Panasonic was often referred to as the father of lifetime employment as a key company principle. Those job cut announcements gave the impression that most companies were abandoning the lifetime employment system. In reality, many of the company's carried out the job cuts using voluntary early retirement, reducing new hires, natural attrition and secondment rather than dismissing workers. In many cases, Japanese companies did not follow through on their announcements (*The Economist* 2002).

The main method many companies used to deal with hard economic times was to increase the number of non-regular workers and decrease the number of regular workers (MHLW 2003). These part-time or contract workers did just as many hours and, in many cases, the same jobs as full-time workers. The only difference was that their wages and benefits were much less and they were not covered by the lifetime employment system. This created a two-tier employment system in most companies.

A last resort for cutting labour costs was restructuring which relied on laying off or firing employees. In the 1990s and in the early 2000s, however, most Japanese companies remained hesitant about doing this. In one survey conducted in November 2001, 100 large Japanese companies were asked about their personnel reduction methods. Not one of the companies said that they had dismissed workers (Asahi Shimbun Survey 2001). In another survey of employees conducted in 2003 about their company's cost-cutting policy, 24.8 per cent of the workers stated that their company had laid off full-time workers in one way or another (Daiichi Seimei Research Institute 2003).

Recent surveys indicate that companies and workers are still in favour of lifetime employment. In a survey of workers in 2001, 76 per cent of the workers still wanted to keep the lifetime employment system: 33.2 per cent of workers thought it was a good system and 43 per cent thought it was good on balance (MHLW 2003). The number of younger people in favour of this practice was fewer than older workers. In 2003, a survey asked full-time workers if they would like to work for one company for their entire working life: 44.1 per cent said they would and 26.5 per cent said they weren't sure (JIL 2003). This number was lower for younger workers, especially for those under 30. Those wanting to change companies cited reasons such as wanting to find a better job match and the high physical and time demands of their current job.

Many companies continue believe that the merits of lifetime employment outweigh the demerits. The merits these companies cited included maintaining worker loyalty, long-term investment in employee education and having a stable workforce. The drawbacks cited included talented workers finding the system unfair, the difficulty in making speedy adjustments to its labour force and the prospect of an aging workforce over the long term (Economic Planning Agency 1998).

In a company survey in 2003, 76 per cent of the companies thought they would maintain this system in some form: 36.1 per cent responded that the lifetime employment system would continue in its current form and 40 percent thought that partial modification was unavoidable but that the system would continue to be used (JIL 2003). Only 5.2 per cent of companies responded that their company no longer used a lifetime employment system. These findings are similar to the same survey carried out in 1999. Thus, it appears that most companies have not changed their way of thinking about lifetime employment and that most companies and workers still value this practice.

From Seniority- to Merit-based Systems

Survey data indicate that large companies are placing less emphasis on seniority and more on merit based on performance in determining promotion and wages. One survey on pay determinants indicated an increasing emphasis on job content, ability and performance, and a decreasing emphasis of seniority (MHLW 2001). Larger differences in promotion and pay among same-age workers are now more common and are more common within the first 10 years of employment with the company. Thus, most companies have shifted away from seniority and have focused more on merit when making wage and promotion decisions.

The shift from seniority- to merit-based on performance is not as simple as it seems. Surveys indicate that workers are dissatisfied with the new merit-based systems. According to one survey, almost 90 per cent of companies were having problems with their performance rating system. Some of the problems included insufficient training about evaluation, ratings not reflected in wages and promotion, difficulty evaluating different kinds of workers and unclear rating standards (MHLW 2002).

There are many ways to get around using a merit-based system in companies where workers do not support it. In one company, managers were forced to evaluate and rank subordinate employees in one of three categories, placing one-third of employees in each category. Individual wage increases for the following year would be based on these ranks. In reality those receiving the lowest rank were promised the following year they would receive the highest rank and their wage increases would balance out.[2]

There is even doubt as to whether this type of merit-based system functions properly in Japan because of the problems with introducing systems that emphasize merit (Takahashi 2004). Recently, merit-based systems have been used to justify salary cuts and reduce labour costs in companies with a large numbers of older workers. It was managers that complained the merit-based systems are time consuming, ineffective and limit employee motivation. Many companies are finding that implementing a mainly merit-based system is easier said than done.

The Decline of Enterprise Unions

Over the past few years, the role of unions in Japan has been declining. A number of companies announced that they would not negotiate with unions and would not increase basic monthly wages. In 2003, Toyota announced that it would no longer negotiate monthly wage increases with its union and that it would base all salary increases on performance. Surprisingly, the union accepted these conditions even though Toyota was the most profitable company in Japan at that time (*Kyodo News* 2003). These annual pay raises have been a key part of the seniority-based salary system – another sign companies are moving away from seniority-based wages.

Though most company unions negotiate a yearly spring wage, many companies no longer adhere to industry guidelines. In recent years, there has been a growing gap in wage increases among companies in the same industry based on the companies' performances (*Nihon Keizai Shimbun* 2006). Also, unions have indicated that they may shift their focus away from wage increases and focus more on other areas such as job security and expanding membership in order to include part-time and contract workers. What role Japanese enterprise unions will play in this changing economic environment is unclear.

Company Examples of Changing Personnel Practices

The following examples show how some major Japanese companies changed their personnel practices to deal with the changing economic environment of the 1990s.

---

2   Discussion with Japanese company employees, August 2005.

Nissan Motors

Nissan is one of the world's largest capacity auto makers and has a long history. In the 1990s, the company encountered many difficulties in the changing economic environment and fell on hard times. Some of the major problems it faced were a loss in its market share over ten years, being unprofitable for eight straight years, having a debt of $20 billion, low employee morale and no new product development.[3]

In 1999, Nissan entered into a partnership with Renault, a French car company. As part of the agreement with Renault, Carlos Ghosn would take over as CEO. Shortly after he took on this position, he made it clear to the employees that if they did not agree to making drastic changes, the company would go bankrupt and they would be out of work. To bring about these changes, Ghosn introduced a revival plan that emphasized performance and productivity. Two key elements of the plan were to motivate employees by stating a clear vision for the company and developing a fair appraisal system for promotions and wage rewards.

As part of the revival plan, the seniority system was discarded. Ghosn deemed this system to be counterproductive and had to be eliminated (Ghosn and Ries 2004). The new pay scheme was to be based on merit based promotion. The incentive system put into place established clear goals for employees at the beginning of each year. This approach attempted to limit the subjective evaluation of each employee's contribution. Part of the salary also was tied to company performance. Age and seniority no longer are determining factors though contribute to evaluating an individual's performance against the expected performance of a senior skilled and motivated practitioner.

Ghosn agreed with the idea of lifetime employment and believed that a company needed to show loyalty to its employees in order to receive their loyalty (ibid.). He thought that only companies with high levels of performance could guarantee lifetime employment and thus, it was a worthy goal to aim for. In Nissan's case, every effort was made to protect employees' job security. When a factory was closed, transfers were arranged for workers to other factories and help was provided to find new jobs. Employees willing to be transferred were guaranteed their jobs.

When the revival plan was announced, every effort was made to win the union's cooperation. After discussions with the union, the union accepted these changes. Even as other companies were freezing basic wages and limiting annual increases, Nissan agreed to all the union's demands to increase wages.

Canon

Canon, a leading world-wide company known for its electronic products such as cameras, printers and copiers, went through difficult times in the early 1990s. Some of its product divisions such as computers were unprofitable and losing market share. In 1997, a new president, Fujio Mitarai, took over the company. Having worked in Canon's US operations for over 20 years, he tried to combine the best parts of Eastern and Western management by combining a Western focus on profit with traditional Japanese values.

Mitarai believed that the seniority system didn't work even if the company could be revitalized by combining lifetime employment with a competitive salary system. He attempted to keep the good parts of the Japanese system while eliminating the inefficient elements Mitarai 2002). In 2002, Mitarai set up a system that promised lifetime employment and eliminated

---

3   Speech by Carlos Ghosn, Nissan CEO at Tokyo University, November 2003.

the yearly wage increases and seniority-based allowances. The new wage system was based on performance and a contribution based salary component was expanded both for managers and all workers in the company.

In Canon, lifetime employment was referred to as long-term employment (Mitarai 2005. In this system, after joining the company, employees could gradually accumulate skills and focus on long-term career plans that chart out employee training and performance targets over a number of years. Thus, the employee could grow and prosper with the company over the long term.

Canon has become one of Japan's most profitable companies.

Japan Airlines

Japan Airlines (JAL) was founded in 1951 with government support. In 1987, the government sold its remaining stake in the company and JAL became fully privatized. JAL faced many challenges in the 1990s such as deregulation that led to increased competition and price cutting, and a decline in its revenues. In 2005, JAL recorded a large loss in contrast to its main rival ANA, which recorded a large profit (Rusling 2006). A series of safety problems also have tarnished the company's image.

JAL attempted to deal with these problems by decreasing its labour costs. In the 1990s, JAL carried out massive cost-cutting activities to reduce its full-time workforce and mainly hired contract employees (Ujimoto 2002). A recent round of cost-cutting required 6,000 jobs cuts by 2008. However, specific ways to downsize the workforce have yet to be determined (*Nikkei Weekly* 2006a). The plan to cut wages has encountered opposition from JAL's labour unions. Unlike most Japanese companies that have only one union, JAL has nine unions. This makes it difficult to get all groups to reach an agreement.

JAL implemented few substantive changes over the years. As a former government-supported organization, JAL's corporate culture resisted making changes to the personnel system. One newspaper editorial stated 'JAL appears to be reluctant to embark on needed radical changes, especially in its corporate culture' (*Nikkei Weekly* 2006b). JAL resisted change and attempted to maintain most of the traditional management system.

Summary of Recent Changes in Japanese Companies

Some companies have adapted their personnel policies to deal with the changing economic environment while other companies have tried to maintain much of the traditional management system. Most Japanese companies tried to maintain the lifetime employment system while shifting emphasis, in varying degrees, from a seniority-based to a merit-based system when determining promotion and wages. The influence of unions has been declining, prompting companies to rethink the annual wage increase negotiation process.

Most companies in Japan now fall somewhere on a continuum between Japan Airlines and Canon. Most large manufacturing companies are closer to Canon and have made meaningful changes to their personnel policies. Japan Airlines is representative of the public sector, many service companies and other non-manufacturing sectors with traditional corporate cultures which have had difficulty dealing with the changing economic environment and which have resisted making meaningful changes. Nissan was able to turn around successfully and is considered to be a special case. Many companies have tried to imitate the Nissan model with limited degrees of success.

Conclusions

What can be learned from Japanese management? Japanese management offers opportunities to compare and contrast local workplace cultural issues, personnel management and provides useful examples related to the issue of change management. Successful Japanese companies provide clues to future management trends in Japan.

The above company examples indicate that the management of personnel should take into account local workplace culture, as in the cases of Canon and Nissan. Canon's president Mitarai sums this up by saying that 'there may be global standards as far as financial management and other scientific skills are concerned, but personnel management is local. I never considered it outdated to take good care of our employees' (Mitarai 2006). In the Nissan case, workplace traditions were respected. Ghosn believes that the Japanese workplace culture has many unique strengths and that it is important understand any management system in its context rather than to judging it to be either good or bad. Japanese companies have tried to take local culture into account in their local business practices when they expand abroad. It is necessary to consider what works in the society in which the company is based.

These cases demonstrate examples of change management. Canon and Nissan both illustrate organizations that made changes while maintaining the stronger aspects of the older traditional system. Nissan's Ghosn strived to respect and maintain Japanese workplace traditions and only eliminated those parts of the system that were wasteful and unproductive. Canon's Mitarai tried to combine the best parts of Japanese and Western management practices. The Canon and Nissan cases also show the importance of good leadership in bringing about successful change.

Much is still debated on how the Japanese management system will continue to change and what Japanese management will look like in the future. Japanese management systems such as seniority, appear to be shifting from a traditional Japanese approach to a more global style of management. By contrast, Abegglen (2004), who first referred to the three key traditional Japanese management characteristics, observes that in the early twenty-first century many parts of the Japanese management system, such as lifetime employment, remain.

Japanese Management

Successful Japanese companies demonstrate that they can make necessary changes to deal with a changing economic environment while maintaining the stronger aspects of the traditional management system.

References

Abegglen, J.C. (1958), *The Japanese Factory: Aspects of its Social Organization* (Glencoe, IL: Free Press).

Abegglen, J.C. (2004), '21st Century Japanese Management', Nihon Keizai Shimbun (in Japanese), Tokyo.

Asahi Shimbun Survey (2001), 'Collapsing Japanese-style Employment', *Asahi Shimbun* (in Japanese), 8 November, p. 20.

Bird, A. (2002), 'Permanent Employee' in Bird, A. (ed.) *Encyclopaedia of Japanese Business and Management* (London: Routledge).

Chen, M. (2004), *Asian Management Systems: Chinese, Japanese and Korean Styles of Business* (London: Thomson Learning).

Craig, T. (2002), 'Nihonteki Keiei' in Bird, A. (ed.) *Encyclopaedia of Japanese Business and Management* (London: Routledge).

Daiichi Seimei Research Institute (2003), *A Survey of Future Lifestyles* (in Japanese) (Tokyo: Daiichi Seimei Research Institute).

Economic Planning Agency (1998), *A Survey of Corporate Behaviour* (in Japanese) (Tokyo: Economic Planning Agency).

The Economist (2001), 'Layoffs with No Sign of Revival', *The Economist* online edition, 30 August.

The Economist (2002), 'Japanese Corporate Restructuring: Uncut', *The Economist* online edition, 18 July.

Emmot, B. (2005), 'Survey of Japan: The Sun Also Rises', *The Economist* 8 October, pp. 3–6.

Ghosn, C. and Ries, P. (2004), *Shift: Inside Nissan's Historic Revival* (New York: Currency).

Hagiwara, S. (2002), 'Enterprise Unions' in Bird, A. (ed.) *Encyclopaedia of Japanese Business and Management* (London: Routledge).

Hsu, R. (ed.) (1999), *The MIT Encyclopedia of the Japanese Economy*, 2nd edn (Cambridge, MA: MIT Press).

Jackson, K. and Tomioka, M. (2004), *The Changing Face of Japanese Management* (London: Routledge)

Japan Institute of Labour (JIL) (2003), *Survey on Personnel Administration Strategy of Companies and Workers' Consciousness about Employment* (in Japanese) (Tokyo: Japan Institute of Labour).

The Japan Times (2004), 'Matsushita to Cut Jobs Despite Return to Profit', *The Japan Times* online edition, 21 June.

Kono, T. (1988), *Corporate Culture Under Evolution* (Tokyo: Kodansha).

Kono, T. and Clegg, T. (2001), *Trends in Japanese Management: Continuing Strengths, Current Problems, and Changing Priorities* (New York: St Martins Press).

Kunii, I. (1999), 'Sony's Shakeup', *Business Week* 22 March, pp. 24–5.

Kyodo News (2003), 'Spring Wage Talks Going the Way of the Dinosaur?', *The Japan Times* 4 March, p. 3.

Nihon Keizai Shimbun (2006), 'Strategic Allocation in Next Generation of Wage Increases' (in Japanese), *Nihon Keizai Shimbun* 16 March, p. 3.

Nikkei Weekly (2006a), 'JAL Offers Murky Plan to Halt Descent', *Nikkei Weekly* 6 March, p. 5.

Nikkei Weekly (2006b), 'Safety Record Tops List for JAL's New Boss', *Nikkei Weekly*, 6 March, p. 28.

Ministry of Health, Labour and Welfare (MHLW) (2001), *Survey on Working Conditions, Ministry of Health, Labour and Welfare* (in Japanese) (Tokyo: MHLW).

Ministry of Health, Labour and Welfare (MHLW) (2002), *Survey on Employment Management, Ministry of Health, Labour and Welfare* (in Japanese) (Tokyo: MHLW).

Ministry of Health, Labour and Welfare (MHLW) (2003), *White Paper on the Labour Economy: Economic and Social Change and Diversification of Working Styles* (in Japanese) (Tokyo: MHLW).

Mitarai, F. (2002), 'How East Meets West at Canon', *BusinessWeek* online, 13 July.

Mitarai, F. (2005), 'Japanese-style Management Makes Most of Workforce' (in Japanese), *Nikkei Business* 3 January, pp. 62–3.

Mitarai, F. (2006), 'Mitarai: Competition will Rest on Labor', *Nikkei Weekly* 6 February, 11.

Odaka, K. (1993), 'The Source of Japanese Management' in Durlabhji, S. and Marks, N. (eds) *Japanese Business: Cultural Perspectives* (New York: State University of New York Press).

Reischauer, E.O. (1988), *The Japanese Today* (Tokyo: Tuttle).

Rusling, M. (2006), 'Japan Airlines Losing Altitude', *Asia Times* online, 1 March.

Sakudo, Y. (1978), *Showa-Kyoho no Keiei* [Management in the Showa-Kyoho Period] (Tokyo: Diamond-sha).

Sasaki, N. (1990), *Management and Industrial Structure in Japan*, 2nd edn (Oxford: Pergamon).

Takahashi, N. (2004), 'Making the Most of Japanese Seniority System' (in Japanese), *Nihon Keizai Shimbun*, 9 June, p. 27.

Tsutsui, W.M. (1988), *Manufacturing Ideology: Scientific Management in Twentieth-Century Japan* (Princeton, NJ: Princeton University Press).

Ujimoto, V. (2002), 'Japan Airlines' in Bird, A. (ed.) *Encyclopaedia of Japanese Business and Management* (London: Routledge).

DIMENSION 5
Marketing and Sales

Chapter 15
Doing Business in Western Europe[1]

Simon A. Mercado

Introduction

It is unsurprising that marketers attach such strategic importance to the West European market-place. The region's consumers, and there are some 400 million of them, are amongst the world's most affluent with per capita income at around $30,000 purchasing power parity (PPP). Consumption levels in Western Europe are amongst the highest in the world with sizeable markets for consumer durables and other categories of goods. The bulk of the region sits within the borders of the European Union (EU), which is itself the world's largest international trading bloc.

The present chapter assesses the conditions for doing business in this theatre and looks to some of the strategic choices to be made by firms as they seek to expand and/or succeed in the region. Analysis is complicated by the fact that business firms often view the West European market as an integral part of a larger regional (European) economy. In truth, Western Europe can almost be labeled as 'old' Europe and the 'new' Europe as a wider pan-European constellation of states and economies extending deep into Central and Eastern Europe.

Most of the region is associated directly or indirectly with the Single European Market (SEM), which provides for the free movement of goods, services, capital and labour on a regional scale.

Of the 20 West European economies subject to analysis here, 17 are members of the European Union (EU) and its Single Market.[2] These are: Austria, Belgium, Cyprus, Denmark, Finland, France, Germany, Greece, Ireland, Italy, Luxembourg, Malta, the Netherlands, Portugal, Spain, Sweden and the United Kingdom. The remaining three enjoy association with the SEM through membership of the European Free Trade Association (EFTA).[3] Switzerland's status as an EFTA economy ensures that it participates in the single market for goods. Norway and Iceland are more closely tied to the EU countries through the wider terms of the European Economic Area (EEA) Agreement.[4]

---

1   Extracts of this chapter are drawn directly from the author's forthcoming edition of *European Business*, printed by Pearson's Education Limited (2007, 5e). All such extracts are reproduced with permission.

2   Analysis focuses on the 20 primary West European economies (the WE20). The region's micro states and principalities, including Monaco, Andorra and Liechtenstein, are omitted from examination here and are excluded from data sets and presentations. Readers should be conscious of their exclusion.

3   The Association's goal is to remove all mutual import duties, quotas and other obstacles to trade in industrial products between members and to uphold liberal, non-discriminatory practices in trade. Switzerland, Iceland, Finland and Liechtenstein are all members. A cooperation agreement EFTA and the European Community (now EU) provides for a free trade area in industrial goods.

4   The EEA Treaty was signed between the European Community and most of the EFTA countries in 1991. The agreement amounted to their acceptance of the fundamental principles of the Community's Internal Market regime, namely free movement of goods, services, people and capital. In 1992, Switzerland

Since the 'completion' of the Single European Market (SEM) in 1992, the West European business environment has been truly transformed. The SEM itself delivers a high level of economic and financial integration through the elimination of internal customs barriers and a reduction in fiscal, administrative and technical barriers to cross-border trade and investment. This has enhanced opportunities for cross-market sales, strategy and operations. An attaching process of standards harmonization has increased the scope for standardization in sales and production strategies. Though cross-market standardization strategies rest ultimately with the market and its tolerance for uniform solutions, they are facilitated by progress to a commonly accepted set of principles, practices or requirements that goods or services must meet to be marketed within a particular jurisdiction. The EU's push to harmonized standards has reduced the number and variety of local standards in Europe which tend to require changes in designs and/or service features.

However, though the West European economies are united by the SEM and in most cases by EU membership, they are far from being a homogenous group. Cultural, linguistic, regulatory and market-based differences continue to restrict the scope for standardized products and marketing. Any understanding of business and marketing here must rest with account of these differences and with appreciation of their operational and psychological effects. Even as part of the completion of the Internal Market, we have witnessed the preference of Member States for national-level tax setting, local regulations on health and safety, and other local rules and controls. Harmonization has also been around minimum or essential requirements in relation to a variety of product features and work-related situations. It has rarely provided for uniform rules or measures.

A Region of Difference

A characterization of the West European business environment today highlights an environment subject to rapid change. Evolution in legal, socio-cultural, macroeconomic and political frameworks has accompanied dramatic developments in the competitive realm, including the regionalization of market and economic structures, rapid growth in emerging markets, and the globalization of technology, production and communication. The West European nations are central to an emerging pan-European economy in which national economies are increasingly connected, in which firms are often present in each other's back-yards, in which national policies are often coordinated, and in which business rules and regulations are widely harmonized.

A 'Single' Market

Central to this process is the SEM and the advancing project of *European Union* (EU). With the '1992 Programme' and new enlargement rounds behind it, the EU is now firmly established as the hub of a new European economy in which restrictions on the free flow of goods and services are now much reduced and in which national governments are cooperating ever more extensively in developing common policies and regimes that flank the SEM. In the EU context at least, the trend towards supranational authority and regulation continues with extension

---

declared its intention not to join the European Economic Area. EFTA members participating in the EEA do not adhere to the EU's common external tariff nor to the rules and requirements of the EU's common agricultural and fisheries policies.

from traditional concentrations such as mutual trade and standards harmonization into new and varied territory. For example, progress has been made towards a European company statute (see previously), a Community Trade Mark system and Community-wide patent scheme. Evolving regimes on services trade and e-commerce have emerged as a response to heightened links and interdependence between member countries and alongside new global frameworks such as the General Agreement on Trade in Services (GATS). Currency union (for many) and the liberalization of cross-border capital movements as a part of the Internal Market Program, also demonstrate deep financial and capital interdependencies. *EMU* alone introduced a single-currency regime in 12 West European states for over 300 million citizens.[5] All of this has offered a strengthened framework for pan-European trade and exchange and a stimulus towards corporate concentration and restructuring.

The effects and consequences of the SEM are well documented, as are those relating to EMU which has also had a trade barrier reducing effect. As a consequence of the rules and policies establishing the Single European Market, businesses can more easily trade across national borders, invest in other Member States and establish themselves internationally under the cover of more harmonized laws and standards. Firms are better able to exploit their diversity and the diversity of consumer tastes and demands by competing in each other's markets and across internal borders. Not only has the elimination of mutual tariffs and non-tariff barriers aided their efforts to sell abroad but the principle of freedom of establishment now ensures their right to set up branches or subsidiaries anywhere in the Union and to do so on the basis of equal treatment. Within the context of a large 'barrier-free' market they can achieve economies of scale and location, make foreign acquisitions with fewer constraints and/or procure the supply of parts and materials from across the region, in some cases without foreign exchange rate risk exposure. At a different level, most West European citizens are free to move around to live, shop and work anywhere in the EEA and are able to profit from an increased choice of goods.

Harmonized Standards

Although the Internal Market is neither perfect nor complete, its evidence and development has led to an altered perception of the European economy as a more integrated and dynamic trading area in which a common set of marketing programs and processes stands chance of success. Very few multinational corporations operating in the region will limit themselves to only a single country and many will look to achieve economies of scale and scope by treating the region as a homogenous market (Chen and Wong 2003; Chung 2005). Contributing to this has been the harmonization of technical and product standards among the EU/EEA states. For a range of industrial product groups the effort has been to stipulate minimum essential health and safety requirements in the form of a 'new approach' Directive and to mandate European standards bodies to set common or 'harmonized' standards in accordance with the terms of the directive(s) applying.[6] These then offer a route to compliance. There are near 50 industrial product areas where such directives apply. Examples include those appliances burning gaseous fuels (Directive 90/396/EEC) and industrial machinery (Directive 98/37/EEC). This approach is closely linked with the CE

---

5   Slovenia is the thirteenth EU Member State to have adopted the euro. As such, EMU is no longer a West European phenomenon or construct. The UK and Denmark have special derogations that exempt them from participation. Sweden rejected the euro in a national referendum in 2003. Iceland, Norway and Switzerland retain their own national currencies as fully independent economies.

6   Examples of European standards bodies include: the European Committee for Standardisation (CEN), the European Committee for Electrotechnical Standardisation (CENELEC) and the European Telecommunications Standards Institute (ETSI).

marking scheme (Directive 93/68/EEC). Products manufactured in compliance with harmonized standards and bearing an EU conformity symbol (CE marking), benefit from a presumption of conformity with the corresponding essential requirements of any and all relevant new approach directives. For this reason, the CE marking has been described as a type of European passport for industrial products allowing them to be placed legally on the market in any country within the European Economic Area (Delaney and van de Zande 2000; Tricker 2000).[7]

Of course, not all products are the subject of EU harmonization initiatives. In fact the majority of products marketed in the EU/EEA are not directly regulated at the Directive-level but by Member State laws. In theory – and according to the principle of mutual recognition-any product that can be legally marketed in one Member State can be legally marketed in another Member State even if the detail of domestic regulation differs. This principle has been derived from ECJ case law and is generally traced back to the 1979 Cassis de Dijon ruling.[8] However, the reality is that national governments are free to ban any product for which they can legitimately assert an environmental, health or safety risk and for that purpose can invoke health and safety protections in national law. Under such conditional terms, there remains much potential for argument and confusion over the mutual recognition principle and some opportunity for national authorities to protect domestic producers in the name of public interest. In recent years, Denmark has banned imports of certain beers from other Member States on environmental grounds (where these beers were not available in reusable beer bottles) and French authorities have blocked the sale of certain high-energy drinks including Red Bull citing concerns over high taurine content levels.

A 'Common' Currency

Monetary Union (achieved in 1999) has eradicated intra-zone currency transaction costs and foreign exchange risk exposure for participating economies, enabling reductions in hedging costs and activity. Marketing activities in Europe have also been greatly influenced. First, the increase in price transparency between different countries that arises from a common currency has ensured that prices for the same product in different countries are now transparently comparable in terms of a common unit, the euro. Retailers charging higher prices for identical goods (e.g., branded goods) in their home market may lose sales to those in other markets as consumers make simple price comparisons. Producers with control over distribution and price levels face pressures to justify price differentials, perhaps through emphasis of product and/or service differentiation. As a general rule, the pressure of price comparability will be to move prices towards the lowest market level under the competition effect. In this context, producers and retailers will need to consider their position and competitiveness and assess the impact of any price adjustments on their margins.

---

7   Affixed by either the manufacturer or in cases of high product risk by an authorized representative, the marking (CE) appears on the product itself, its packaging or in the documentation attaching to the product.

8   This ruling concerned a French liqueur made from blackcurrants which was deemed by German authorities to have too low an alcoholic content for retail in the German market as an alcoholic beverage. The ECJ decided otherwise and laid down that if a product has satisfied the requirement of one country then its import into another should not ordinarily be restricted (Case 120/78 *Rewe-Zentrale v Bundesmonopolvwerwaltung fur Branntwein* [1979] ECR 649). This has become the general rule and investment in the MR principle means that EU authorities do not have to waste time defining common standards for all product categories.

The early evidence suggests that the transparency and comparability of prices across the euro area is tending to discourage differential pricing strategies on the part of single businesses with a presence in different euro markets. The technology company Apple has already moved to harmonize euro area prices including value added tax. Other companies such as Beiersdorf AG, Schwarzkopf & Henkel GmbH and DHL, are pursuing a policy of price alignment, setting more harmonized prices within narrow ranges. These and other companies are using narrow price corridors or 'band-widths' in order to retain flexibility on pricing whilst fighting the threat of arbitrageurs and parallel imports (see Kohler and Bacher, 2003). The arrival of the euro has also raised other issues in connection with pricing. For example, important questions arise as to the definition of price points and to the management of price conversions at point of changeover.

It is also now much simpler to work with international suppliers across the region. Apart from the easier comparison of supply costs, exchanges and transactions are now often concluded in the same monetary unit and FOREX complications avoided. This raises the prospect of real business savings. A similar effect applies to the credit market, with enterprises now able to borrow from outside their home countries without incurring the risk of exchange rate exposure. The implied competition should produce improvements in service and better finance deals for businesses and consumers. EMU also favours the development of new financing methods such as euro-bonds. Businesses within the euro area and previously operating in different corporate currencies (i.e., currencies used for bookkeeping and reporting) are now able to record and to compare all accounting values, margins, costs, expenditures etc. in one common currency. Apart from the reduced complexity that this implies, such transparency may greatly assist in processes of internal planning and benchmarking.

On balance, EMU has had similar trade and investment barrier reducing effects to the Internal Market Programme and has further encouraged operators to develop regional strategies in such areas as pricing and procurement.

Shared Challenges

For these reasons and more, (Western) Europe is a *region of difference*. Distinctive in terms of its development, history and culture from other global regions (e.g., Asia and North America), it is hall-marked by deep processes of economic and political integration and formal community structures that are a reflection of and contribution to high levels of economic and financial interdependence. Three major developments at regional level – customs union cooperation, standards harmonization, currency union and the reduction of fiscal barriers – establish Europe as a unique theatre characterized by intensive trade and FDI links. Despite the EFTA-EU 'fracture', the WE20 are at the heart of these processes and face other challenges together. For example, most of the grouping find themselves at the high end of a global cost-spectrum that has resulted in higher rates of import penetration from emerging markets and new divisions of labour. Pressures are less obvious for the Iberian and Mediterranean states but are acute elsewhere. Across industry in Western Europe, R&D, design and high-end manufacturing activities are being retained in the west but assembly work and low-end manufacturing activities shifted eastwards where wage rates and unit labour costs are significantly lower (Marin 2005). The result is new regional and/or global production networks in industries like automotives that evidence the capacity for West European firms to realize scale and location economies but also a change in regional production and employment patterns. Many of these economies are also burdened by sizeable public deficits, impediments to business creation, weak productivity growth, high energy costs, and heavy pressures on pension and healthcare spending (IMF 2006).

A Region of Differences

None of this is to suggest that the West European region or Europe as a whole has become a homogenized, denationalized theatre, devoid of variety or national preferences. Nothing could be further from the truth. Europe *is* and remains a mix of cultures, polities and economies. Though managing in Europe is about managing the Single Market and processes of standards harmonization, it is simultaneously about managing difference and heterogeneity across the region and consistent pressures for local responsiveness. National environments are simultaneously a reflection of local histories and events as well as emerging regional and global developments. As such, there are elements of similarity and convergence that are supportive of cross-market standardization strategies but elements of difference and heterogeneity that represent an impediment to the adoption of such strategies. This point is underscored in the succeeding section of analysis that seeks to profile key elements of culture and political economy in Western Europe as relevant to business operations.[9]

Economic Systems and Culture

The West European states provide example of *free-market capitalist systems*, meaning that most economic activity is located in the private sector with prices set under market forces and governments limiting their intervention in the marketplace. Technically however, all of the WE20 are 'mixed economies' in the sense that they are characterized by active public and private sectors. In specific cases, that is, the UK and Denmark, over 90 per cent of national economic output is directly attributable to the private sector, a trend encouraged by sustained efforts at privatization. In other cases, traditional cultures of state ownership or interventionism contribute to larger public sectors, to significant public shareholdings, and to patronage of 'state champions'. Although the last two decades in Western Europe have seen a wave of privatizations and moves away from public ownership control, some state champions have remained under full or effective public ownership including strategically important oil and power companies. Even where privatization has applied, tranche-based sales have been pursued in order to slow down the process of wholesale transfer and/or to ensure that state authorities retain significant holdings. Several governments have been drawn to retain or purchase significant shares in private or privatized firms either for investment purposes or in order to influence the strategic direction of an organization and/or sector. In the Netherlands for example, a strongly liberal case, the state government continues to hold a sizeable minority stake in the partly privatized telecommunications company, Royal KPN. In the case of logistics company TNT, the Dutch government took all of 17 years to fully privatize its former postal and telecommunications monopoly, completing the process only in late 2006. In Spain, state authorities continue to hold ownership shares in the privatized businesses of Telefonica (telecoms), Tabacalera (tobacco) and Repsol (oil). These and rival EU states have used legal codes and decrees to protect what are seen by some as 'golden shares' giving power over the decisions of private companies and potentially posing obstacle to foreign acquisition.

---

9   The notion of *political economy* rests with a view that the political, economic and legal systems of a country are not independent of one another and interplay to influence the direction of state economics as well as the benefits, costs and risks associated with doing business in a country. Students of political economy draw on political science, law and economics in order to understand how the lego-political environment and the economies of states influence each other. In the European context, notions of regional political economy are supported by economic, legal and political linkages, although significant differences in business frameworks persist.

The scope and scale of state intervention in the WE20 is in truth quite variable. Contrast is often drawn between the UK's Anglo-Saxon model of market economy with its emphasis on private sector competition and limited public ownership and rival forms of European capitalism. Albert (1993) contrasts the strongly market-oriented model of the UK with what he calls the 'Rhenish' system, in which the role of the market is circumscribed by state and societal forces. The system is most readily associated with post-war Germany but its influence is evident throughout many neighbouring states including Austria and Switzerland. This system of organized or managed capitalism has been traditionally linked with long-term cooperation between big corporations, hausbanks, public and parapublic institutions. Notions of the 'Interventionsstaat' are indicative of a record of strategic state intervention which varies from paternalistic control of national champions to the promotion of national export activity through public export credit guarantees. Though the German state exercises more limited influence than in the French system of indicative planning, it is markedly more 'statist' in orientation than its British counterpart (see Busch, 2005). This is also true of rival capitalist sub-systems in Europe, including Nordic, Latin, French and Italian examples (see Schmidt, 2002; Amable, 2003; and Sapir, 2005).

Development and Progress

The previous section highlighted differences between national economic cultures in Western Europe. Our grouping is also characterized by variations in levels of wealth and development and by asymmetries in terms of economic performance and growth. Table 15.1 evidences considerable variations in the scale and scope of national economies as measured by – gross domestic product (GDP). GDP measures the net output or value added of an economy by measuring goods and services purchased with money. Germany, France, Italy and the UK are the region's largest economies. Spain, with its growing population (now 44 million) is another regional heavyweight. Its overall economic contribution has been significant in recent years touching €100,000 m in 2006. The majority of the West European economies are much smaller both in terms of value added and national population totals.

GDP per capita levels vary considerably. These rates can be calculated by dividing the value of all final goods and services produced within a nation over the national population, normally for the same year. It is possible to advance from a nominal measure of per capita GDP based on the above rule to a different measure based on purchasing power parity. The attempt here is to equalize, as best as possible, the purchasing power of incomes in different countries so as to provide a more meaningful measure of relative wealth and development. A purchasing power parity exchange rate equalizes the purchasing power of different currencies in their home countries for a given basket of goods. On this basis, most of the Southern economies have 'real' per capita income levels towards the lower end of the regional scale. Spain and Italy provide some exception to this rule (see Table 15.2). The full range for the WE20 in 2005 was $65,900 (Luxembourg) to $18,100 (Malta) with a weighted average at around $30,000 (CIA World Fact Book 2006). Of course the very lowest income levels in Europe (PPP) apply in the peripheral Eastern and South-Eastern European economies.

Amongst the West European states, Italy and Germany have been delivering some of the lowest rates of growth in recent years (see Table 15.3). More robust growth has been witnessed in Luxembourg, Ireland and Greece and amongst the EFTA group. At time of writing (January 2007), economic activity in Western Europe is strengthening, with real GDP growth accelerating driven by strong domestic demand and investment. Contributing to this pick-up is improvement in Germany's own economic performance, where labour market reform and corporate restructuring may now be paying dividends. More generally, a combination of stable

Table 15.1   National population and gross domestic product (GDP) in the WE20, 2006

Member State	Population (m)	Gross domestic product (€1,000 m, current market prices)
Austria	8.3	256.5
Belgium	10.5	313.0
Cyprus	0.8	14.32
Denmark	5.4	221.4
Finland	5.2	167.4
France	6.3	1781.0
Germany	82.5	2308.0
Greece	11.1	194.8
Ireland	4.2	173.8
Italy	58.8	1473
Luxembourg	0.46	32.3
Malta	0.41	4.769
Netherlands	16.3	529.2
Portugal	10.6	152.5
Spain	43.8	977
Sweden	9.1	304.3
United Kingdom	60.5	1890.0
		(US$1,000 m, current market prices)
Iceland	0.3	16.1
Norway	4.6	332.4
Switzerland	7.5	382.4

Sources: European Commission 2006 (for EU-17); IMF 2006 (for Iceland, Switzerland and Norway). Data compilation and tabulation with permission of S. Mercado.

monetary policy, wage moderation, low inflation and interest rates is creating the conditions for improved performance. Nonetheless, there are a number of uncertainties to the outlook. According to The IMF, West European states remain heavily exposed to the possibility of sharp currency appreciation that could undercut exports and investment as well as to heavy pressure on social spending as a consequence of ageing populations (IMF 2006).

Further contrasts can be drawn with respect to fiscal positions, growth rates and relative performance in such areas as price stability, loan rates, foreign trade and investment. Full comparisons of this nature are beyond the scope of this chapter but below we highlight the situation relating to tax differentials.

National Tax Regimes and Differences

Variations in national tax rates are a major issue for buyers and sellers alike. Although EU Member States have agreed to set standard sales-tax (VAT) rates within an agreed band or 'corridor' (15–25 per cent) this is a relatively rare example of tax rate coordination. Banding

Table 15.2   Gross domestic product per capita in the WE20 ($PPP), 2005

Member State	Gross domestic product per capita ($PPP, est. 2005)
Austria	32,500
Belgium	31,100
Cyprus	21,600
Denmark	34,800
Finland	31,000
France	29,600
Germany	30,100
Greece	22,300
Ireland	41,100
Italy	28,700
Luxembourg	65, 900
Malta	19,700
Netherlands	30,300
Portugal	19,000
Spain	25,600
Sweden	29,800
United Kingdom	30,100
Iceland	38,100
Norway	47,800
Switzerland	33,600

Source: CIA World Factbook 2006. Data compilation and tabulation with permission of S. Mercado.

itself implies differences in national rates, exaggerated by the existence of reduced and super-reduced rates for specific product lines (see Table 15.4). It is only really in the area of VAT and with respect to minimum duty rates for petrol, cigarettes and alcohol, that tax and duty differentials are influenced by decisions taken at EU-level. Outside of these areas and in relation to nearly all forms of direct taxation, the EEA countries remain free to determine their own tax rates and bases. In personal taxation (taxation on personal income), environmental taxation and taxation on corporate earnings, EU authorities enjoy no direct authority and national authorities determine headline (and effective) rates. As a result, a purported 'Single Market' is actually characterized by a series of differential tax rates and regimes.

Corporation tax is an area of particular note. Differences in statutory rates are considerable (see Table 15.5). For example, the main corporate tax rate in Spain (35 per cent) is nearly three times as high as the rate applying in Ireland (12.5 per cent). However, headline rates can be misleading and the activity that the tax is levied on is just as important. The overall trend in the EU is towards lower corporation tax, with the low-tax policies of the new Member States and resulting tax competition encouraging adjustments throughout 'old' Europe. Though not everybody is concerned with this fact – tax competition of this nature may promote convergence and a downward movement in applied rates – unilateral and strategic tax setting in the context

Table 15.3   GDP growth rates (year-on-year) in the WE20, 1996–2006

Member State	1996–2000 average	2001	2002	2003	2004	2005	2006
Austria	2.9	0.8	0.9	1.1	2.4	2.0	3.1
Belgium	2.7	0.8	1.5	1.0	3.0	1.1	2.7
Cyprus	3.8	4.1	2.1	1.9	3.9	3.8	3.8
Denmark	2.9	0.7	0.5	0.7	1.9	3.0	3.0
Finland	4.8	2.6	1.6	1.8	3.5	2.9	4.9
France	2.8	1.9	1.0	1.1	2.3	1.2	2.2
Germany	2.0	1.2	0.0	-0.2	1.2	0.9	2.4
Greece	3.4	5.1	3.8	4.8	4.7	3.7	3.8
Ireland	10.4	5.8	6.0	4.3	4.3	5.5	5.3
Italy	1.9	1.8	0.3	0.0	1.1	0.0	1.7
Luxembourg	6.1	2.5	3.8	1.3	3.6	4.0	5.5
Malta	4.6	−0.4	2.2	−2.4	0.0	2.2	2.3
Netherlands	4.0	1.9	0.1	0.3	2.0	1.5	3.0
Portugal	4.1	2.0	0.8	−1.1	1.2	0.4	1.2
Spain	4.1	3.6	2.7	3.0	3.2	3.5	3.8
Sweden	3.2	1.1	2.0	1.7	3.7	2.7	4.0
United Kingdom	3.2	2.4	2.1	2.7	3.3	1.9	2.7
Iceland	–	–	–	–	5.2	5.8	4.9
Norway	–	–	–	–	2.9	3.1	3.3
Switzerland	–	–	–	–	1.7	0.8	1.8

Source: European Commission, Statistical Appendix of European Economy, Autumn 2006 (for
EU17); IMF 2006 (for Iceland, Switzerland and Norway). Data compilation and tabulation
with permission of S. Mercado.

of a customs union arrangement can mean a potentially harmful tax race to the bottom. There
are many obstacles to the institution of a VAT-style 'floor-and-corridor' type approach and
Britain and Ireland have repeatedly rejected calls for an EU minimum company tax standard.
Recent Commission communications have concentrated on the notion of a universal tax base
for corporate profits rather than on the standardization of rates.

  Business in Western Europe is thus complicated by evidence of significant tax differentials
that influence price considerations, investment decisions and operations. One consequence of
the absence of uniform rates is a complex VAT payments and collection system. In the EEA
context at least, a final destination principle applies for commercial importers and traders
(taxable parties). These pay VAT at the home country rate on imports from other Member
States. It should be noted that most purchases by private individuals are treated differently. EU
rules allow for VAT and excise duty on products acquired by private individuals to be charged
in the Member State of purchase as long as these are for personal use (personal consumption
or gift). If private individuals bring in goods for resale, or for any payment, even payment in

Table 15.4   Applied VAT rates (%) in the WE20, as at 1 January 2006

Member State	Super Reduced Rate	Reduced Rate	Standard Rate
Austria	–	10	20
Belgium	0/1	6/12	21
Cyprus	–	5	15
Denmark	0	–	25
Finland	0	8/17	22
France	2.1	5.5	19.6
Germany	–	7	16
Greece	4	8	18
Ireland	0	13.5/4.5	21
Italy	4	10	20
Luxembourg	3	12/6	15
Malta	–	5	18
Netherlands	–	6	19
Portugal	–	5/12	21
Spain	4	7	16
Sweden	–	6/12	25
United Kingdom	0	5	17.5
Iceland	0	14	24.5
Norway	8	12	24
Switzerland	2.4	3.6	7.6

Source: Federation of International Trade Associations. Data compilation and tabulation with
permission of S. Mercado.

kind, they are regarded as being for a commercial purpose and the final destination principle
applies.[10]

For as long as they exist, many businesses will look to exploit differences in national tax
regimes within Europe, picking the regimes that suit them best and benefiting from competition
between different tax authorities. But it is doubtful whether business groups unite in belief
that such differences are good for them or for the Internal Market itself. Small businesses
may lack the capacity to engage in 'tax shopping' and attractions apart, multi-state businesses
face a significant downside in terms of complying with a multiplicity of national tax systems.
Indeed many multinational companies would welcome reforms in company tax law and the

---

10 Some exceptions apply here including the private purchase of motor cars, where VAT is levied in
the country of destination. In the case of cigarettes and alcohol, the tax and duty paid in the Member
State of purchase is the only tax and duty paid as long as the purchase is for 'own use' and is directly
transported by the buyer. It is this rule, and the evidence of significant duty differentials, that promotes
booze cruises from the UK to France and from Finland to Estonia along with a sizeable black-market
trade in cigarettes and alcohol.

Table 15.5   Corporation tax rates (%) in the WE20, as at 1 January 2006

Member State	Main Corporate Tax Rate
Austria	25
Belgium	34
Cyprus	15
Denmark	28
Finland	26
France	33.33
Germany	25
Greece	29
Ireland	12.5
Italy	33
Luxembourg	22
Malta	35
Netherlands	29
Portugal	25
Spain	35
Sweden	28
United Kingdom	30
Iceland	18
Norway	28
Switzerland	8.5

Source: Federation of International Trade Associations. Data compilation and tabulation with permission of S. Mercado.

harmonization of rates and/or bases. Benefits would range from reduced compliance costs to potential reductions in aggregate tax liability through such practices as 'offsetting'.

Political Systems and Culture

Western Europe's political systems have both similarities and differences. As functioning democracies they offer a mix of elected government, multi-party competition, pluralism and political freedoms for individuals and groups. Freedoms of expression, speech and association are generally underscored by independent media although public broadcasting remains a strong tradition. Beyond this, political frameworks divide between constitutional monarchies (as in the cases of Spain and the UK) and constitutional republics. Varying degrees of centralization also apply and some systems, like Germany's, are 'federal' by definition implying a formal division of powers between central and regional governments. Different political philosophies also compete for authority in national and regional assemblies with conservative (neoliberal), social democratic, socialist and green parties all in evidence throughout the region. Populist nationalist parties have proved influential in France and Austria. A result here is a diverse set of national governments based on different political principles and platforms. Many West European states have coalition governments consisting of more than one political party such as Sweden's governing Alliance for Sweden (centre-right). Such trends are echoed in Central and Eastern Europe where a number of fragile coalitions are in evidence, some involving populist parties of left or right.

As such, Western Europe offers a patch-work of national political systems, parties and administrations, inclined to generate a complex and varied set of national government regulations. Variations in national regulations and policies (like standards) can be a barrier to the adoption of standardized pan-European business and marketing strategies (Boddewyn and Grosse 1995). Multinationals can anticipate different forms of treatment with respect to their acquisitions, investment support, taxation (see subsequently), as well as in levels and forms of sovereign interference pertaining to employment and the environment. Fortunately, levels of political risk are low across the region and such major threats as expropriation and nationalization are negligible.

Legal Systems and Frameworks

In the legal field, different national systems continue to set the West Europeans apart from one another. Most have civil legal systems which set out a comprehensive system of rules, usually codified, that are applied and interpreted by judges. The French civil code (indebted to the country's Napoleonic period) and the German civil code are good examples. In civil law countries, legislation is seen as the primary source of law. Courts base their judgements primarily on the provisions of codes and statutes. In contrast, UK and Irish systems are based heavily on case law, with legal judgements established through interpretation of former cases and judicial precedent. These systems are referred to as common law systems.

Throughout Europe too, there are differences in the (legal) form of business organization, with businesses organized around different legal forms of ownership and control. In Ireland for example, limited companies must be fully registered (or incorporated) under the Companies Act and must have at least two directors and no more than 50 shareholders. These rules are different to those applying in the UK for the formation of private limited companies. In Germany, the most popular form of private limited company, the Gesellschaft mit beschrankter Haftung (GmbH), must have a minimum share capital of €25,000, a higher rate than in other West European countries. In the UK context, there is a minimum share capital for public limited companies (plcs) of £50,000. In Germany, the main publicly listed corporation is the Aktiengesellschaft (AG), in France, the Société Anonyme (SA). Minimum share capital requirements again vary.

The legal environment in Western Europe is further distinguished by the fact that economic actors confront a legal maze in which national codes and EU codes exist in complex relationship to one another and rarely in a state of autonomy. In areas like competition, employment, consumer protection and the environment, there is evidence of a multi-tiered order, in which legal codes are a mix of European level regulation (statute law), influenced national provision (where national law is shaped by EU-level codes), and independent national provision. Variance in regional codes within state boundaries can add another layer of complexity.

EU law is composed of three principal forms: primary law established through treaty provision, secondary law arising from institutional acts such as Regulations and Directives, and case-law extending from the judgements of the European courts. Although some EU law is statutory and direct in its effect in Member States, much is in the Directive category where the general principle is not to fully standardize legislation but to foster degrees of harmonization with toleration of workable differences in law. Directives also require transposition into national law by national authorities. As such, there is a lack of uniformity to many elements of law in Europe (even where the EU has the power to legislate) and inconsistent application of EU codes in member countries. Illustration can be provided here by reference to divergent rules on toy advertising via public television. Whilst advertising during children's programming slots is restricted in Greece and Sweden there are no such restrictions in most other parts of Western Europe. EU level advertising laws concern largely misleading and comparative advertising and do not extend into such areas, which remain under the control of national authorities.

Cultural Differences

Culture is essentially about people and the way in which they behave as a result of their background and group affiliation. It is about shared systems of meaning within and across groups including those at national level. Van Maanen and Schein (1979) are led to define culture as 'values, beliefs and expectations that members of specific social groups come to share', and Hofstede (1991) refers to 'the collective programming of the mind, which distinguishes one group or category of people from another'.

A number of studies highlight that the cultural environments of West European states are fairly diverse. At the most elemental level, language is an immediate factor of difference. Across the WE20 there are over a dozen official languages and a plethora of regional forms and dialects. In countries such as Belgium, several languages exist at the same time, in this case Flemish, French and German. While it does not necessarily follow that language differences create insurmountable difficulties, they do at least impact upon the process of communication in business, for example, in brand identification, marketing communications, negotiations and labeling. They also add cost. Though translation is achievable and generally straightforward, literal translations and/or weak command of local language, have led to many business blunders. This was certainly the case in General Motors' promotion of the 'Nova' brand name in Spain. When spoken in Spanish, this sounded like '*no va*', meaning 'it doesn't go'. Firms must look to ensure that the translation of a word or phrase into the local language has the desired meaning and does not communicate something unintended. Some people argue that it is impossible to understand other cultures without comprehending the medium through which that culture is perpetuated. In this respect, musicality, intonation, phraseology serve as secondary communication signals which can be lost or misunderstood.

Along the many *dimensions of culture*, the West European states have been shown to vary from one another in meaningful fashion. Anglo (e.g., the UK and Ireland) and Germanic countries (e.g., Germany, Austria and Switzerland) are revealed to be low context,[11] individualist,[12]

---

11 In low-context cultures, words used by speakers explicitly convey the speaker's message to the listener and the mass of information attaching to communications is found in the explicit transmission. Managers look for a body of detailed, explicitly coded information when they make decisions or evaluate a new enterprise. In short, and in direct opposition to managers in high-context cultures, they feel the need for 'contexting' or for the filling in of background information. From a managerial point of view, this tends to mean that in low context cultures much emphasis is placed on formal documentation, legal agreement, and fact-oriented communication (see Hall 1976).

12 Hofstede's individualism rating relates to the degree to which people in a culture prefer to act as individuals rather than as members of groups. At the high end of the scale are those (individualist) societies where ties between individuals are very loose and where individuals have a high sense of independence and self-responsibility. In organizational settings, individualists value freedom to make their own decisions and/or to adopt their own approach to the job. In addition, members of individualistic societies place

neutral and achievement-oriented.[13] This takes the form of explicit communication, devolved management systems, professional detachment, and a performance oriented work-culture. Most are regarded as competitive or masculine cultures with a relatively short-term orientation. Nordic countries (e.g., Denmark, Norway and Sweden) are generally associated with low power distance and more feminine values.[14] This takes the form of teamwork, consensual decision-making and an emphasis on trust and relationship-building. Latin countries (e.g., Spain, Portugal and Italy) are seen to be marked by high power distance, a more collectivist orientation, and high uncertainty avoidance[15] This takes the form of steep organizational hierarchies, centralized decision-making and an emphasis on group interest and achievement. Beyond apparent national differences, one can also see differences within countries. As stressed by Lane et al. (1997, p. 31):

> Culture is not monolithic or uniformly manifested in a country. Not all people will react the same way, but rather certain reactions will be found statistically more often in a particular society. Because of the existence of subcultures, cultural homogeneity within any country cannot be assumed. Within larger cultures, there are pockets of smaller cultures that can be identified as holding different dominant values.

Such differences may frustrate attempts to impose common organizational procedures, management practices and/or uniform marketing solutions. Standardized cross-market strategies are more likely to succeed in homogenous cultural contexts. Despite associations between certain clusters of countries (e.g., Germany, Switzerland and Austria), Western Europe does not provide a high level of cultural uniformity (see Boddewyn and Grosse 1995; Chung 2005). This brings us directly to a series of final strategic and marketing considerations focused on MNE choices for the West European marketplace.

---

an emphasis on personal liberties and on having sufficient time for personal or family life (Hofstede 1991).

13 Neutral cultures are characterized by controlled and subdued displays of emotion outside of the private sphere. They provide contrast with affective cultures which are more expressive and emotional. In achievement oriented cultures, status is accorded to people on the basis of their achievements and ability rather than by virtue of class, background or seniority (see Trompenaars 1997).

14 Hofstede's power distance rating indicates the extent to which a society expects and accepts inequalities between its people, and an unequal distribution of power and responsibility within its institutions and organizations. Countries with a high score (large power distance) are those which feature broad differences between individuals in terms of power, status and wealth, whose institutions are characterized by formal hierarchies, and whose populations consider a high degree of inequality as normal. In such societies, authority is largely centralized and subordinates are cautious about challenging or questioning the decisions and authority of their superiors. Low power distance cultures are more egalitarian and are associated with flatter management systems and consensual decision-making. Feminine societies promote harmonious relations in the workplace (between men and women, managers and their employees) and place a strong emphasis on social partnership and gender equality. By contrast, the more masculine a society the more it values assertiveness and materialism (see Hofstede 1991).

15 Hofstede's uncertainty avoidance measure relates to the extent to which countries and their institutions establish formal rules and fixed patterns of operation as a means of enhancing security and of avoiding ambiguity and doubt. High uncertainty avoidance societies are marked by a strong preference for structured over unstructured situations (see Hofstede 1991).

Strategic and Marketing Considerations – A Final Round

Throughout much of this chapter we have concentrated on the integration of markets in Western Europe and the strengthening of legal and political linkages between national economies. In a true sense, these trends are but a part of a wider process of globalization that has taken character and form in the internationalization of production and competition and in the emergence of global-scale markets and undertakings. It is clear that the formation of the SEM and EMU have created conditions for more integrated business management in the European context. At the same time however, we have stressed obstacles to the standardization of business and marketing strategies arising from enduring differences in economics, politics, law, language, culture and technology, plus caveats in both SEM and EMU regimes. Where then does this leave us in terms of an understanding of business strategy for our region of investigation and how have multinational enterprises approached the region in terns of their strategies and structures?

Multinational Strategy and the West European Context

It is widely viewed that a multinational enterprise's business strategy is influenced by its external environment and that in this regard, firms are subject to quite different pressures. For instance, where national or regional markets are diverse and globalization drivers weak, companies are seen to face pressures to be locally responsive and to deliver different or adapted products globally. Localization demands may extend from differences in consumer taste, political and legal factors, competitive dynamics, and distribution/retail structures, all of which can vary between countries. Others face pressures to globally integrate and to deliver quality products globally. Such pressures arise where globalization drivers are strong and market conditions uniform (see Prahalad and Doz 1987; Yip 1992).[16]

All organizations face this twin-set of pressures but it is often the case that one set of pressures is dominant in a given industry. For example, pressures for local responsiveness are high in food and beverages markets where tastes and preferences are diverse but weak in the golf-equipment market, where globally standardized clubs and balls are the dominant retail product. Many complex markets, like financial services and pharmaceuticals, are characterized by a combined pressure-set, with further complexity arising from evidence of regional standards and integration as attested to in this chapter.

With these points as guidance, it is possible to identify five broad 'international' strategies for the West European context as adopted by MNEs. These are not to be confused with choices over establishment modes (market entry modes), market share enhancement strategies, or with what Porter describes as competitive strategy tools (e.g., cost leadership, focus and/or differentiation). These are important strategic considerations in their own right and whilst there are associations between such choices and the orientations that follow, each would require a form of examination beyond the scope of this chapter.

---

16 This choice is sometimes characterized as a choice between external flexibility (localization) and internal efficiency (global integration) given the tendency for localization strategies to equate with responsiveness at cost and global strategies to deliver cost efficiency through economies of scale and scope.

(Integrated) Global strategy

One possibility for the West European market is to service it is a function of an attempt to achieve a coherent *global strategy*. In this case or scenario, there is no distinguishable strategy for the region, merely regional evidence of a wider strategy defined and executed on the global level. In a global strategy, the focus is on internal efficiency through global integration. Standardized goods are produced for sale around the world and firms enjoy economies of scale through global-scale manufacturing. Economies of scale contribute to lower costs and cost advantage in competition. Typically, strategic decisions are centralized and value-creation activities concentrated in a few key locations. Product modification is avoided and product branding global. Minor modifications in marketing/labeling are tolerated and accepted in light of language differences and voltage requirements but emphasis falls on uniform messaging and campaigns. Because of high global integration pressures, country subsidiaries enjoy little or no strategic autonomy. The effort is to ensure central control and global consistency in production, product image and quality (see Prahalad and Doz, 1987; Bartlett and Ghoshal 1989). Companies like Titleist (the golf ball manufacturer) and Intel (the chip manufacturer) provide good examples with their globally standardized products, brands and marketing campaigns.

Companies of this nature benefit from lower costs arising from standardization and as such, the global strategy is a popular response to an environment characterized by high global integration, but low local responsiveness pressures. The attraction and feasibility of a global strategy is lost however where legal, cultural and economic conditions are heterogeneous and globalization drivers weak. As noted previously, Western Europe does not provide a high level of cultural uniformity (see Boddewyn and Grosse 1995; Chung 2005) and the roll-out of global cross-market standardization strategies is also impeded by regulatory and administrative barriers as witnessed in such industries as financial services and pharmaceuticals. In other fields, such as media, publishing, food and beverages, there is little or no homogeneity at regional level let alone at global level. In the European context at least, globally standardized cross-market strategies may be difficult to realize and alternative approaches will often need to be found.

Glocal Strategy

One alternative strategy is the *glocal* or global-local strategy, in which global corporations modify globally branded products and services to particular local circumstances paying heed to local differences in taste, culture and/or regulation. A glocal strategic approach rests with the notion of a tailored global product or service and suggests a consciousness that not everything can be sold the same way around the world without some adaptation. This understanding necessitates some decentralization with local teams and managers enabled to localize the product and/or marketing communication wherever necessary. For example, McDonalds has found success in Europe (and worldwide) by retaining the core architecture of its fast-food restaurant concept but making adjustments to menu features in response to local tastes and preferences, for example, beer on its menu in France and smoked salmon in Norway. The attempt is to maintain an appropriate balance between global homogenization and local customization. The 'glocal' approach is applicable to marketing, management and production centred strategies (see Svensson 2001; Maynard 2003).[17]

---

17 Elements of the glocal strategy are consistent with Bartlett and Ghoshal's (1989) concept of 'international' strategy but the term is deliberately rejected here.

Country Specific Strategy

Though many companies pursue success in Europe through *global* or *glocal* strategies which deliver major cost advantages, others look to a quite different approach. A *country-specific* strategy is built around differences at national level and a choice to deliver the maximum degree of local responsiveness. In this case, focus is on external flexibility through a high degree of local responsiveness and on providing a strategic response to deep and significant *local* differences in culture, consumer behaviour, national regulation, etc. Many products and services are developed (and branded) locally. Those with transnational character and identity are frequently modified in order to meet local preferences or at least marketed in a locally responsive fashion. Nestlé's flagship coffee – Nescafé – provides a case in point. This popular product is blended and coloured differently for specific European markets with quite different coffee-drinking preferences. In the marketing domain, campaigns are defined and executed locally.

The business model is highly decentralized and strategic decisions are taken by local subsidiaries and business units in order to enable the adaptation of products and/or services to demands and requirements at national level. Local subsidiaries are treated as autonomous entities, with limited direction or control from the multi-national headquarters or from other strategic business centres. On a country-by-country basis, core value creation activities are dispersed and duplicated in order to ensure localized production and marketing, including the development of local product and brands. This is equivalent to what others have labeled 'multi-domestic' strategy.

The attraction of such a strategy in the European context has been progressively weakened through the processes of integration and convergence highlighted in this chapter. The integration of markets and technical standards in Europe has encouraged a number of merchandise goods manufacturers to move way from a pre-1992 business model based on high (local) responsiveness to a more integrated approach. This is less the case with commercial services providers where caveats in the Internal Market regime continue to incline companies to tailor their service-based products at this level. The high cost structure associated with country specific strategies has generally proved burdensome and manufacturing companies traditionally associated with the approach have looked to achieve savings and efficiencies through a measure of centralization and integration. In the Nestlé case, moves have been made away from a traditional multi-domestic model towards brand integration and the centralization of acquisitions decisions, financial controls, research and development. This has applied in other cases too including Philips and Unilever.

(Integrated) Regional Strategy

A *regionally integrated* strategy offers some of the benefits of the globally-integrated approach (economies of scale, etc.) and some of the advantages of locally responsive strategy. In this approach, decision-making authority is regionally-centred, product developed around harmonized or convergent European standards, and investment made in pan-European marketing solutions. The European market place is treated as being relatively homogenous and the firm is structured so as to manage the regional environment as a distinct theatre. This typically involves the establishment of a European HQ. A good example is provided by copier and camera firm Canon, which has settled on a regional model in which regional sales, marketing and distribution functions are under the control and direction of Canon Europe. Canon originally developed its presence in Europe through a number of stand-alone businesses but has recently looked to operate on a truly pan-regional basis, implementing common policies, sharing best practice, improving operational efficiencies and achieving economies of scale across its European units. This strategy encompasses a pan-European branding policy, *You Can*.

Like the *glocal* strategy considered previously, a *regional* strategy is one example of a 'multi-focal' or intermediate strategy (Prahalad and Doz 1987) in which the aim is to attain both responsiveness and integration advantages.

Country-cluster Strategy

Another example of an intermediate strategy is provided by the *country-cluster* approach. Here again, some of the benefits of localized strategy are combined with some of the benefits of a more integrated or 'global' approach. The emphasis is on identifying transnational clusters of markets and consumers that can be serviced jointly by common products or services, realizing localization at a different level to that achieved in the case of other strategies (glocal, country-specific, and regional). Work by Malhotra et al. (1998), VanderMerwe (1993) and Kale (1995) as example, has identified various West European clusters including Nordic, Anglo-Saxon, Central (Lutheran) and Mediterranean groups. The broad conclusion of these researchers is that whilst standardized cross-market strategies may fail at European level they enjoy a chance of success at this level given cultural (and linguistic) similarities between specific groups of countries.

One company to have had some success with this approach is MTV. MTV began its international expansion by airing programs similar to those broadcast in the US. However, it soon realized that the audience in various regions, including European regions, preferred localized content, which included music videos and documentary features. By the late 1990s, its approach to Europe was based on the launch of separate channels for distinct country clusters, such as the UK and Ireland. Although pan-European programming is evident and programs are generally adapted from American originals, these channels offer a localized content and format within the framework of a global product concept and brand.

Conclusions

European business organizations and non-European multinationals alike are responding to the regionalization of governance and market competition in Europe and are striving to find competitive positions and business models that will facilitate success in an increasingly integrated theatre. In this context, we can anticipate that different firms will adopt different strategies in/for Europe, including those focused on the WE20 or some part of it. The reason for this is that whilst Europe's integration encourages integrated responses at regional and/or global level, the relative weight and character of integration-responsiveness pressures in specific industries in Europe is quite variable. Though forces of globalization and regional integration have touched upon all business sectors in Europe (Western Europe included), firms in Europe must typically navigate a series of differences between market units that have their root in different political, economic, legal and cultural traditions. As such, hybrid or multi-focal strategies are often employed, with firms seeking to reconcile pressures for integration and (local) responsiveness. Amongst these, the *glocal*, (integrated) *regional* and *country-cluster* strategies appear to have a future in the WE context, though their evidence and performance requires empirical investigation.

In the final analysis, Western Europe is both a *region of difference* (of unification and interdependence) and a *region of differences*. Whatever the force and pace of regionalization, the differences that dominate the region continue to require respect, consideration and response at the strategic level. Those new to Europe or seeking to expand inside the region must not make the mistake of believing Europe to be a homogenous market, not even in its western sphere.

References

Albert, M. (1993), *Capitalism against Capitalism* (London: Whurr).

Amable, B. (2003), *The Diversity of Modern Capitalism* (Oxford: Oxford University Press).

Bartlett, C.A. and Ghoshal, S. (1989), *Managing Across Borders: The Transnational Solution* (Boston: Harvard Business School Press).

Boddewyn, J.J. and Grosse, R. (1995), 'American Marketing in the European Union: Standardisation's Uneven Progress (1973–1993)', *European Journal of Marketing* 29(12), pp. 23–42.

Busch, A. (2005), 'Globalization and National Varieties of Capitalism: The Contested Viability of the German Model', *German Politics* 14(2), pp. 125–39.

Chen, I.S.N. and Wong, V. (2003), 'Successful Strategies of Newly Industrialised East Asian Firms in Europe', *European Journal of Marketing* 37(1/2), pp. 275–97.

Chung, H.F.L. (2005), 'An Investigation of Crossmarket Standardisation Strategies: Experiences in the European Union', *European Journal of Marketing* 39(11/12), pp. 1345–71.

Central Intelligence Agency (CIA) (2006), *World Fact Book 2006* (Washington, DC: CIA).

Delaney, H. and van de Zende, R. (eds) (2000), *A Guide to EU Standards and Conformity Assessment* (Gaithersburg, MD: National Institute of Standards and Technology).

European Commission (2006), *Statistical Appendix of European Economy, Autumn 2006* (Luxembourg: Office for Official Publications of the European Community).

Hall, E.T. (1976), *Beyond Culture: The Hidden Dimension* (New York: Anchor Press-Doubleday).

Hofstede, G. (1991), *Cultures and Organizations: Software of the Mind* (New York: McGraw-Hill).

International Monetary Fund (IMF) (2006), 'World Economic and Financial Surveys', *World Economic Outlook*, September 2006.

Kale, S.H. (1995), 'Grouping Euroconsumers: A Culture-based Clustering Approach', *Journal of International Marketing* 3(3), pp. 35–48.

Kohler, R. and Bacher, M.R (2003), 'Euro Pricing – Why a Corridor Approach Makes Sense', *European Business Forum* 13(Spring).

Lane, W., DiStefano, J. and Maznevski, M.L. (1997), *International Management Behaviour*, 3rd end (London: Blackwell).

Malhotry, N.K. et al. (1998), 'Heterogeneity of Regional Trading Blocs and Global Marketing Strategies', *International Marketing Review* 15(6), pp. 476–506.

Marin, D. (2005), 'A New International Division of Labor in Europe: Outsourcing and Offshoring to Eastern Europe', *University of Munich Discussion Papers* 17, http://epub.ub.uni-muenchen.de.

Maynard, M. (2003), 'From Global to Glocal: How Gillette's SensorExcel Accommodates to Japan', *Keio Communication Review* 25, pp. 57–75.

Prahalad, C.K. and Doz, Y.L. (1987), *The Multinational Mission: Balancing Local Demands and Global Vision* (New York: The Free Press).

Sapir, A. (2005), 'Globalization and the Reform of European Social Models', Bruegel Policy Brief 2005/01.

Schmidt, V.A. (2002), *The Futures of European Capitalism* (Oxford: Oxford University Press).

Svensson, G. (2001), '"Glocalization" of Business Activities: A "Glocal Strategy" Approach', *Management Decision* 39(1), pp. 6–18.

Tricker, R. (2000), *CE Conformity Marking and the New Approach Directives* (London: Butterworth Heinemann).

Trompenaars, A. and Hampden-Turner, C. (2000), *Riding the Waves of Culture* (London: Nicholas Breasley Publishing).

VanderMerwe, S. (1993), 'A Framework for Constructing European Networks', *European Management Journal* 11(1).

Yip, G.S. (1992), *Total Global Strategy, Managing for Worldwide Competitive Advantage* (Englewood Cliffs, NJ: Prentice Hall).

Chapter 16

Doing Business in NAFTA

Coral R. Snodgrass

Introduction

The North American Free Trade Agreement (NAFTA) went into effect on 1 January 1994. It is an agreement among the three countries of Canada, The United States and Mexico to eliminate all internal tariffs and thus facilitate the free flow of goods and services across their shared borders over a 15 year period. NAFTA created an internal market of over 400 million potential consumers, of whom 300 million reside in the most affluent country in the world. The agreement covers the movement of an almost unlimited supply of goods, natural resources, services and investment capital. This massive, vibrant, rich and varied market can be considered both a business person's dream and a marketer's worst nightmare. In order to successfully operate in the North American market, marketers must understand why NAFTA was created by the agreement (especially in contrast with the European Union) and how the three markets of Canada, the United States and Mexico can be imagined as one big market or multiple, potentially lucrative market segments.

The Foundations of NAFTA

There are generally three reasons given for the development of NAFTA and the attempts of the three governments to solidify their market (Nevaer 2004). The first is historical. NAFTA is in many ways the logical conclusion of a series of trade agreements between Canada and the United States. The second is opportunistic. The first hints of the possibility of forming some type of North American marketplace that would include Mexico was announced in a speech by President Jimmy Carter in February, 1977 shortly after oil was discovered in Mexico (Abbot and Moran 2002). The third motivation for the formation of the North American market was a reaction against the successful 1992 integration of Europe into an economic powerhouse.

Canada and the United States

Canada and the United States historically have had a somewhat uneasy political relationship while sustaining a vibrant trading relationship. As long ago as 1854, the two countries entered into a short-term free trade agreement for grain, coal, livestock, timber and fish (ibid.). With over US$2 billion in goods and services crossing the Canada-US border everyday,[1] this trading relationship is now the largest bilateral trade relationship in the world. This massive flow of goods dwarfs other trading relationships. The amount of trade that flows across one single crossing – the Ambassador Bridge between Detroit, Michigan and Windsor, Ontario – is greater than all the trade between Germany and France and more than all the US exports to Japan.

---

1   Unless otherwise noted, all figures are denominated in US dollars.

Just one US chain of hardware stores, The Home Depot, does more trade with Ontario than the United States does with France (DFAIT 2005). In fact, Canada exports 87 per cent of its merchandise trade to the United States and, in turn, it is the largest market for US goods. In addition to merchandise trade, the amount of trade in energy between Canada and the United States is unparalleled. Canada supplies 100 per cent of all US imports of electricity and 94 per cent of natural gas. In addition, Canada is the largest supplier of oil, crude oil and uranium to the United States.

Forty per cent of the trade between Canada and the United States is intra-firm trade resulting from manufacturing companies moving components back and forth across the border to and from the production processes that contribute to their products (DFAIT 2004). This is especially the case for the automobile industry located in the manufacturing sectors around the Great Lakes. It is not unusual for subcomponents in the auto industry to cross the border up to six times before final assembly. The reason that so much cross-border activity has developed in the auto industry is that trade in auto parts has been 'free' since the signing of the Auto Pact in 1965. This has allowed the development of highly integrated, just-in-time assembly processes to be designed with an assumed 'borderless' perspective. Consequently, even when the Canada-US Free Trade Agreement talks began in the 1980s, much of the critical trade between Canada and the United States was already free, repetitive and guaranteed.

President Ronald Reagan and Prime Minister Brian Mulroney began discussions on free trade in early 1985. The Canada-US Free Trade Agreement (CUSFTA) went into effect less than four years later on 1 January 1989. At the time, this type of agreement was unique because it also included trade in services. In addition, CUSFTA provided included dispute resolutions processes that were carried over to the NAFTA accord. On the US side of the border, the talks and the trade agreement were almost a non-issue. On the Canadian side of the border, the outcry was overwhelming. Canadians already were feeling the threat of the economic power of their southern neighbour. There was concern that CUSFTA had bargained away their sovereignty. This was especially the case with culturally specific service industry sectors. Many outspoken Canadians believed their airwaves, TV broadcasts and movie choices would become completely 'American'. This concern resurfaced during the NAFTA negotiations.

Despite these concerns on the part of Canadians, CUSFTA did not drain the economic and cultural vitality out of Canada. There were, however, some negative effects. As an example, it did eliminate the need for US firms to maintain Canadian branded 'satellite' plants and administrative centres since it was no longer necessary to maintain a Canadian identity to do business there. Both governments considered CUSFTA a success and by April 1990 – just four months after CUSFTA took effect – talks with Mexico about a free trade agreement began.

Mexico and the United States

As chequered as the political history between Canada and the United States has been, their relationship is quite peaceful compared with Mexican-US history. This relationship is coloured by the history of Mexico's history with Spain. As a Spanish colony, Mexico suffered centuries of exploration, exploitation and foreign domination (Folsom and Folsom 1996). The Conquistadores crossed Mexico. As they went they built alliances with powerful tribes, destroyed villages and towns and drove less powerful indigenous groups to the brink of extinction. Having established Spain's control over Mexico, the 'conquerors' began a process of draining natural resources, especially silver and agricultural produce, out of Mexico and into Spain. The Spanish domination and exploitation of Mexico was bloody, iron fisted and absolute.

In addition to the Spanish military and the dominant indigenous tribes, The Catholic Church arrived and imposed their control over Mexico. The Church completed the set of change agents necessary to establish a social hierarchy of powerful elites who controlled all aspects of Mexican development. Even the Declaration of Independence in 1821 did not rid the country of Spanish control. However, after that date, Mexico officially was free from Spain. The military, Church and dominant tribal trinity ruled Mexico for over 200 years. Today this legacy has not fully died away. When President Salinas began negotiations for NAFTA, 12 per cent of the GDP of Mexico was controlled by 25 families (ibid.).

In 1841, the United States invaded. The War of North American Invasion – as the Mexicans refer to what Americans call the Mexican-American War – ended in 1848 with the signing of the Treaty of Guadalupe Hildalgo. As part of that treaty, Mexico had to cede territory that included California, Arizona, New Mexico, Utah, Nevada and Colorado. This was a loss that Mexico has not forgotten. It also is part of the reason that there is a popular expression in Mexico, 'Poor Mexico – so close to the United States and so far from God'.

As a result of its painful colonial past and the rapacious tendencies of its northern neighbour, Mexico undertook a protectionist economic position that relied on import substitution and the support of inefficient domestic producers. Decades of these government policies led to inflation and a lack of real economic development. Investing capital in the peso was risky. Another carry over from their colonial past led to the development of state owned industries dominated by the political and social elites. By the 1970s, Mexico's economy was fragile, unemployment was growing and the degree of income inequality was a major social issue. In 1976, oil was discovered.

When the massive reserves of oil were discovered, there was some hope that oil revenues could buy Mexico's way out of trouble. Unfortunately, world oil prices began to fall in the early 1980's. Once again, Mexico faced economic turmoil. It was then, as the United States and Canada were beginning their talks on free trade, that the first rumblings of including Mexico in some sort of agreement were being heard. It would be at least 15 years before NAFTA came into effect. It already was clear that the United States would have to address the economic upheavals occurring on their southern border.

To be sure, Mexico was very different from the two other North American countries. Whereas the United States and Canada had similarly robust industrialised economies with measures such as gross domestic product (GDP) per capita comparably strong, Mexico in the early 1980's was a developing economy with GDP per capita at less than one sixth the rates of The United States. However, as the Spanish had discovered centuries before, Mexico was rich in natural resources and had millions of people willing to work for what, by comparison, might be thought of as 'slave wages'. As the discussion of a possible North American Free Trade Agreement began to develop, these resources, especially oil, were deemed to be a very good fit with the manufacturing, agricultural and natural resources of Canada and the United States – especially as the foundation of the development of a North American Market that could compete against the developing combined market in the European Union.

NAFTA and the European Union

With the exception of the aforementioned invasion of Mexico by the United States in the 1840s and the Canadian march across the United States during the war of 1812 when they burned down Buffalo, NY and Washington DC, the relationships among and between Canada, the United States and Mexico have not been marked by centuries of war and mutual destruction. This is in part due to the relatively recent settlement and development of infrastructure by peoples that were eager to breakaway from their European heritage and be able to practice religious freedoms not permitted or accepted at home. The history in Europe is quite different.

Prior to 1945, Europe had not known an extended period of peace since the Pax Romana of the first and second centuries AD. With the notable exception of Great Britain, however, in the 60 years since the end of the war, Europe has been at peace. During the twentieth century, Britain experienced just one year of peace when no military action was undertaken by its armed services.

Peace was one of the goals of the early developers of the concept of a united Europe. If Europe was to be at peace, it would be best realised by building an economically interdependent market place wherein no one country would have sufficient armaments necessary to launch an offensive war. The heads of government started tangible negotiations over coal and steel. To date, the EU has advanced to a united market wherein goods, services, capital and people can move freely among 25 member nations (with some restrictions and exceptions). Internal national borders within Europe are to a great degree disappearing. Citizens of the member countries have European citizenship giving them access to jobs and education. Because the member nations retain their national identity and language, workers must still learn their host country language(s) – Belgium, Luxembourg, Switzerland, Wales and Finland all are officially bi- or multilingual countries. The Euro has simplified financial transactions and makes moving from one country to another (with the exception of the United Kingdom, Denmark and Sweden). This is much easier for tourists and business people alike. The political imperative to bring an end to war today has resulted in an integrated market of 450 million potential consumers. Turkey, a predominantly Muslim nation, with a larger population than either Germany or France, is in talks to become a member. North African nations such as Algeria, Tunisia and Morocco have not been invited to become part of the EU.

This development of the European Union is completely different in the goals of the integration and the future of the market structure from North America. This is critical for marketers to understand because on the surface, Europe and North America look like two highly integrated, vibrant markets. On the surface, they are. But fundamentally, these two market places have to be understood and approached very differently.

It is certainly the case that one of the reasons that North American business people were very supportive of NAFTA and lobbied hard for its passage was their concern over what is happening in Europe. They saw:

- a market where internal borders were no longer an obstacle to the movement of goods;
- European government agencies designing industrial standards that would be in force across all firms within the Union;
- European manufacturers rationalizing their production processes across a broad geographic region.

All of this integration appeared to be leading to the development of a unified marketplace. However, reports in the business press warned that as Europe integrated all aspects of its market, they would throw up a wall around it. 'Fortress Europe', as it was named, was presented to North American business people as an impenetrable, protected place in which they would not be allowed to participate. The fear was that the businesses that built their strength in this unified market would become the dominant global players across all world markets. Thus if North American businesses were to be able to compete against these European behemoths, they would also need a unified and integrated market.

Marketing Insights Drawn from the Historical Foundations of NAFTA

The history of the development of NAFTA provides marketing students with some important insights that can be used to begin to develop a strategy for doing business in and with the nations of North America. Included among these insights are the following:

1. The bilateral trading relationship between Canada and the United States is massive and unmatched anywhere in the world. Since 87 per cent of Canada's merchandise trade goes to the United States, the health of this relationship is critical to the economy of Canada. However, Canada does feel the burden of this dependency and has some concerns about how to maintain their sovereignty in the face of it. An opportunity exists for non-US firms to build trade relationships with Canadian firms to help off set this dependency.
2. Mexico has a long history of being exploited by other countries, one of which is the United States. The loss of vast expanses of their territory to the United States in 1848 still is a painful memory. There is little interest in losing even more self control. In order to off set their dependence on NAFTA trade, Mexico has entered into 11 other free trade agreements, including ones with the European Free Trade Area, Japan and the Central American countries. An opportunity exists for non-US firms to build on these free trade agreements and establish relationships with Mexican firms.
3. The growing economic and political strength of a United Europe is seen as a competitive threat to North American business. This is especially the case in the United States. It might be a good idea for European businesses marketing in the United States to try to look 'less European'. On the other hand, Canadian and Mexican firms might find the possibility of working with European firms to be a source of competitive strength against any perceived economic dominance by the United States. This provides an opportunity for non-US firms, especially those with ethnic and linguistics ties to Canada and Mexico, such as French and Spanish firms.

Differences between North America and the European Union

While it can be stated that NAFTA was developed in part as a response to the perceived competitive threat of the European Union, it should not also be concluded that North America resembles the European Union. There are three aspects that are radically different and that need to be clearly understood: borders, the free movement of people and monetary units.

Border Security

First of all, it is absolutely not the case that internal national borders in North America are disappearing, nor will they soon. There was a time when the 5500 mile border between Canada and the United States was quite open. Under CUSFTA, the aim was to make the border even more transparent. However, the terrorist attacks of 11 September 2001 have changed all that. If anything, the borders in North America are becoming even more difficult to cross. That this represents a permanent shift in US policy concerning her borders was succinctly summed up by then US Ambassador to Canada, Paul Cellucci, who said that security would 'trump' trade (Thompson 2003). By saying this, Ambassador Cellucci made it very clear that the United States will not compromise on issues of national security even if that imperils their largest trading relationship with Canada and their third largest relationship with Mexico.

When the terrorism alert levels rise in the United States, the borders either close or movement across them becomes very slow. As an example, in December 2003 the terrorism alert went to Code Orange. The resulting tail-backs at the Peace and the Lewiston-Queenston Bridges were reported to be worse than those in the days immediately following the 9/11 attacks when the tail-back of trucks trying to enter the United States from Canada on the Peace Bridge reached over 10 km (Tan 2003).

To be sure, the costs of increased border security for business are substantial. When movement of traffic on the bridges between the United States and Canada slowed after 9/11, many just-in-time production lines in the auto industry had to close. Within one week after the attacks, Ford Motor Company had to close five assembly plants in the United States because they could not receive the engines and drive train parts from their Canadian suppliers. It is estimated that it cost Ford $1 million per hour per plant (Canadian Trucking Alliance 2003). In order to try to make the border more open to the flow of 'safe' trade, Canada and the United States designed a Smart Border Action Plan that outlined 32 points for border management. However, costs of compliance with the present border management programmes are estimated to exceed $10 billion annually (Ontario Trucking Alliance 2004).

The Free Movement of People

The problem that keeps the borders closed at the southern border of the United States is the flow of illegal immigrants. Estimates are that at least one million illegal immigrants cross the Mexican border into the United States every year (*The Economist* 2005a). To try to control this influx, the federal government and border state governments instituted programmes such as 'Operation Hold the Line' in El Paso, Texas (ibid.). However, such programs make the border difficult to cross even for legal visitors. This can be quite costly. As an example, Mexican shoppers are credited with increasing retail sales in just four areas along the Texas border to over $20 billion in 2005 (Chozick 2006). However, as has been stated, 'security will trump trade.' These healthy retail numbers certainly will be negatively impacted if the United States government continues along its present path to make the borders non-traversable.

One important piece of this new approach by the United States government is the present plan to require all individuals (including US citizens) entering the United States to have either a passport or one of the propsed identification cards by the beginning of 2008 (Turner 2006). The costs of a US passport are $97.00. Costs for one of the other identification cards are estimated to be approximately half of that. At present, passports are not required to cross from either Canada or Mexico into the United States. In that regard, North America did resemble the European Union. However, as the countries of Europe minimise the barriers of national borders to the movement of people, at least one government in North America is working very hard to strengthen them.

A Single Currency

Arguably, one of the great successes of the European Union has been the almost painless adoption of a single currency for all of the member states who chose to participate. This has helped to strengthen European business and facilitated multi-country tourism. This is not happening in any way in North America. There is little interest on the part of Canada in giving up their dollar. In fact, the Canadian dollar has strengthened considerably against the US dollar in recent years, going from approximately US$1 = CAN$1.70 in 2004 to US$1 = CAN$1.14 in 2006. The Mexican peso has stabilized at approximately US$1 = MEX$11 over the same time period. Consequently neither Canada nor Mexico feel compelled to give up any of their sovereignty to the United States on currency. Even if the *de facto* currency of many North American business transactions is the US dollar, there is no movement towards a single currency.

Marketing Insights from a Comparison with the European Union

1. North American borders are not disappearing. In point of fact, the United States is attempting to make them more difficult to cross despite massive amounts of trade crossing these borders. There is a market opportunity for firms that can provide the technological infrastructure that distinguishes 'safe' from 'unsafe' goods and people. There is a huge growth industry in the 'intelligent design' of border crossings.
2. The costs of lost productivity due to border security and the costs of compliance with existing border security measures are substantial. Firms choosing to do business in North America have to give very careful consideration to facilities location. Any cost saving that may result from producing in a low wage country, such as Mexico, and selling into a high income country, such as Canada, may quickly be lost because of shipment delays or paperwork costs.
3. Canada, the United States and Mexico have three different currencies and will continue to do so. The potential impact on repatriated funds resulting from currency fluctuations must be calculated into the costs of doing business. Recent changes in the Canada-US exchange rates have shown substantial movements. The US and Mexican currencies have maintained a fairly stable relationship in recent years.

The Creation of the North American Market

When NAFTA went into effect in 1994, the intention was to implement the elimination of internal tariffs within North America on a staggered schedule over a 15-year period. In fact, the implementation has progressed so smoothly that at this point virtually all trade across the borders is tariff free. However, there are some critical exemptions to the list of items that could cross freely. Mexico would not negotiate away control of its petroleum and petro-chemical industry. The Constitution of Mexico declares that these are state owned. Canada continued to be concerned about control of its cultural industries just as they had been during the negotiations of the CUSFTA. Thus they insisted that they have the right to ban any materials or services that might somehow damage their cultural identity. The United States would not give up their price supports (subsidies) for farmers. Because agriculture is so important to all three nations, there is also a series of bilateral agreements protecting specified crops.

NAFTA has a few interesting features that set it apart from other free trade agreements. First of all, it combines three very different nations – different in terms of size, geographical features, population, language, culture and perhaps most importantly, economic strength. Secondly, it provides protections for the movement of capital across the borders to support investment. Under NAFTA, cross-border investors have the right to be treated as local citizens without any of the penalties and restrictions previously imposed on non-citizens. NAFTA is also unique because it was the first multilateral agreement that included protections for intellectual property. Further, although they were too contentious to be part of the main body of the agreement, both labour rights and environmental protection were included in a series of parallel agreements.

The one aspect of NAFTA that has proved to be the most difficult to manage is the interpretation and application of the 'Rules of Origin'. Simply stated, goods that are sourced 100 per cent within NAFTA are eligible to travel across the borders duty free. If a good is made up of a number of component parts, each and every part's history must be traced back to its original source. If the part has not originated in a NAFTA country, it cannot be considered eligible for free trade. However, if that part has been transformed within a NAFTA country such that it actually is changed from one category of the Harmonized System of Tariffs to another (e.g., tomatoes into tomato paste), it may have been sufficiently transformed to make it NAFTA eligible. In either case, the 'regional value' of the good must be greater than 60 per cent (62.5 per cent in the case of autos) for the good to be NAFTA eligible. As can be imagined, this can be a nightmare for any firm attempting to take advantage of the free trade treatment available under NAFTA. The number of pages covering 'Rules of Origin' runs into the hundreds. It is no wonder that many cross-border managers believe it was easier to move goods across the borders before NAFTA.

Another aspect of NAFTA that is not unique but it is vitally important are the dispute resolution mechanisms developed to manage the relationships. A series of trinational panels have been established to try to resolve the conflicts. Although their decisions should be binding, they certainly do not seem to be the final word. As an example, the United States has long complained that Canada subsidizes its softwood lumber industry and that this negatively impacts US producers. In retaliation for this, the US imposed import duties on Canadian softwood coming into the United States. The dispute resolution panel that was formed to decide on this case determined that Canadian exports had not harmed the US producers and instructed the US to lift the import duties. The United States has so far chosen to ignore the finding and has not lifted the import duties (*The Economist* 2005c).

The size of the NAFTA market is enormous. As of 2004, the value of the GDP was $11 trillion.[2] This represents approximately one-third of world GDP. However, this wealth is not evenly spread across the three nations. The allocations of this GDP are Canada = 6 per cent, US = 89 per cent andMexico = 5 per cent. The number of potential consumers in this market is also quite large. The total population of the NAFTA market exceeds 440 million. Again, these people are not evenly spread across the three nations. The percentages of total population are: Canada = 7 per cent, US = 69 per cent and Mexico = 24 per cent. The resulting GDP per capita allocations are: Canada = $23, 400, US = $36,200 and Mexico = $6,300

When a comparison is made using Purchasing Power Parity, the differences are diminished somewhat. However, it is clear that there are substantial differences in how the wealth and the consuming populations are spread out over this market.

The importance of NAFTA to the national economies is also skewed. The trade-to-GDP ratios are: Canada = 80 per cent, US = 25 per cent and Mexico = 60 per cent.

These differences become even more startling when the differences in imports and exports are considered. The US exports less than 10 per cent of its GDP. It is predominantly an importing nation that continuously runs huge trade deficits. Additionally, only 30 per cent of US exports are to other NAFTA countries. By comparison, 80 per cent of Canadian and Mexican exports are to other NAFTA countries, predominantly the United States. However, according the figures from the US Department of Commerce, US trade with its NAFTA partners has been continuously increasing (US ITC 2005). This is not meant to imply that Canada, the United States and Mexico are coalescing into 'Fortress North America'. It does, however, indicate

---

2   All trade figures in this section are derived from DFAIT 2004.

that there is a healthy, cross-border market place with a tremendous amount of commercial activity occurring.

Marketing Insights from the Creation of the North American Market

1. NAFTA created a huge market but it also created a bureaucracy to oversee the movement of trade across the borders. The 'Rules of Origin' requirements make it absolutely necessary that any company moving a product across those borders keep very clear records of the sourcing history of all component parts.
2. NAFTA created trinational panels to oversee the resolution of disputes over questions of NAFTA-eligibility. However, the United States does not always abide by these rulings.
3. The total size and wealth of North America make this a market that should not be ignored. However, the population and the wealth are not spread evenly across the three nations, making it important that marketers look at each country separately in order to develop new opportunities.

The Three Markets of North America

Given the complexities of North America, marketers are faced with a daunting task in the development of marketing strategies. Marketers need to search for market opportunities and find niches to develop. It is a massive market with lots of changes and lots of dangers. Start where? One useful approach is to look at each of the three marketplaces separately. In order to discern potential opportunities, marketers can scan economic reports and the business press. In the following discussion, government reports and business chapters are used to begin the development of marketing strategies. This provides a useful model for marketing students trying to understand how to market in North America.

Canada

The Canadian market is approximately one-tenth the size of that in the United States. However, it is also a wealthy population. And whereas Canada is a vast country, the majority of this wealthy population lives in the three metropolitan areas of Toronto, Montreal and Vancouver. The Canadian market is not generally described in the same dynamic terms as is its southern neighbour's, and there definitely are important trends that can lead to lucrative opportunities. A recent analysis of Canada in the business press indicated that it is a country characterized by high numbers of immigrants, substantial differences and tensions between the provinces, touchy relationships with the United States, and declining levels of productivity and investment (*The Economist* 2005c). These differences can form the basis of a marketing plan for Canada. As an example, immigration figures are approximately 250,000 people per year. Considering that the total population of Canada is about 33 million, this is a large proportion of the population. In fact, over half of the populations of Toronto and Vancouver are immigrants. Many of the immigrants are highly educated and skilled workers from Asia. This represents an opportunity to provide goods and services to this segment with controllable distribution costs since the geographic spread is confined. Thus restaurants, non-English news services, grocery stores and book stores can be lucrative investments. There is also tension between the provinces in Canada.

At the time of writing, Quebec is once again making noises about separating from Canada. Even if Quebec does not separate politically from the rest of Canada, it is certainly separating culturally. French is the official first language of the province. Quebeckers often identify more closely with France than with Canada. This also provides an interesting marketing opportunity for firms that can provide goods and services that address this cultural divide. As an example, French-language movies, books, magazines and music would be well received. Travel services to French-speaking resort areas could be very popular.

The tense relationships with the United States can provide yet another marketing opportunity. Canadians are sensitive to their dependence on the US market. Building trading relationships with countries other than the US is an important priority. This is yet another possible marketing opportunity and another way to find entry points into the lucrative Canadian market.

The United States

The United States is a large, wealthy, populous country which represents the largest consumer market in the world. It is not, however, a homogeneous marketplace. It is not easy to 'make sense' of the US market or to easily discern market niches. Marketing students can make use of the business press to begin to structure their understanding of this market. One recent analysis describes the United States as a country with four characteristics that capture the present dynamics of the country (*The Economist* 2005b). They are: the willingness to move, immigration, equality of opportunity (especially for education) and the willingness to volunteer and join groups. Each of these can be the basis of a marketing plan for accessing the US market. As an example, the article states that, 'Between 1995 and 2000, almost half of all Americans have changed address, more (often far more) than in any European country' (p. 6). This represents a tremendous opportunity for any firm that sells household items or packing equipment, recycle used clothes and small electronics, provide relocation services or trailing-spouse employment placements. Openness to immigration is another characteristic. The number of foreign-born citizens in the United States increased by over 10 million over the last 10 years. The vast majority of these immigrants are Hispanic. Projections by the US Census Bureau are that by the year 2030, 20 per cent of the US population will be Hispanic. By the year 2050, this is expected to have increased to 25 per cent. This represents a tremendous marketing opportunity. Some marketers have already noted that 'If you want to be successful, you must have a marketing and sales effort among Hispanic consumers' (Jordan 2006). These approaches to understanding the dynamism of the US market provide important starting points to discover market opportunities.

Mexico

To assume that, because Mexico has a weaker economy than either the United States or Canada, there are no market opportunities would be a mistake. Under NAFTA, the Mexican economy is expanding rapidly. Between 1993 and 2003, GDP increased 50 per cent. US government figures estimate that GDP per capita will approach $10,000 in Purchasing Power Parity (US Government 2006). The number of households comprising the middle class in Mexico (those with incomes between $7,200 and $50,000) has increased to 10 million families or 40 per cent of all Mexican households (Smith 2006). These families are taking out mortgages, buying homes and furnishing those homes. The impact of these improvements in consumer power is already being noticed by marketers. In a magazine chapter, an analyst at a Mexico City think tank is quoted as saying 'Who's buying all those 37-inch TVs at Sam's Club? The middle class'. The same chapter also reported that 140,768 tickets for two rock concerts sold out in less than five hours, even with prices running as high as $220. Sales of cars and small trucks reached record levels in 2005. In addition to changes in the consumer market, there are also increasing changes in the industries that were historically controlled by monopolies or operated by the state. This is especially the case in the industries that build and strengthen the infrastructure of Mexico: railroads, telecommunications, seaports, airports, and energy distribution. This represents a tremendous opportunity for engineering firms, construction companies, logistics hauliers and telecommunications experts. The changing dynamics of the Mexican market make this an attractive place to do business. Since Mexico is a Spanish-speaking country with cultural and ethnic ties back to Spain, this makes them especially attractive to Spanish companies.

Marketing Insights from an Examination of the Three Markets

1. Canada is smaller than the US in terms of population, yet it also is very wealthy. The population of Canada is concentrated in three metropolitan areas with high immigrant populations (in the case of Toronto and Vancouver) and a French speaking population in Montreal. Targeting these ethnic groups can be one way of approaching the Canadian market.
2. The United States represents a very large, wealthy, dynamic market that presents opportunities for virtually any good or service. Certain trends, especially the degree of mobility, the increases in the Hispanic populations and the value placed on higher education, can be used as the starting point for developing marketing plans.
3. Economically Mexico is the weakest of the NAFTA countries, with a history of government monopolies controlling key aspects of economic development. However, the middle class in Mexico is growing rapidly and they are spending their income. In addition, the government recently opened up competition in industries that will provide the infrastructure for future economic growth. Both of these developments in Mexico provide very attractive opportunities for marketers.

Conclusions

When NAFTA came into effect in 1994, it stimulated the development of one of the most wealthy, productive and diverse markets in the world. Although much of the production and consumption that takes place in this market is carried out among the three nations of North America, they also provide one of the most open, accessible and profitable market places in the world for importing and transplant firms from any other nation. The market may seem like a marketer's nightmare in its complexities, transformations and heterogeneity. It is absolutely a marketer's dream in its vibrancy, its dynamism and the population's willingness to spend money.

References

Abbott, J.D. and Moran, R.T. (2002), *Uniting North American Business* (London: Butterworth Heinemann).

Chozick, A. (2006), 'Thanks to Mexican Shoppers, Retail Boom on Texas Border', *Wall Street Journal*, 3 March.

Department of Foreign Affairs and International Trade Canada (DFAIT) (2004), 'NAFTA @ 10: A Preliminary Report', http://www.dfait-maeci.gc.ca/eet/pdf/NAFTA@10-2003-en.pdf.

Department of Foreign Affairs and International Trade Canada (2005), *Canada World View* 24, Winter.

The Economist (2005a), 'Dreaming of the Other Side of the Wire', 12 March.

The Economist (2005b), 'Degrees of Separation: A Survey of America', 16 July.

The Economist (2005c), 'Peace, Order and Rocky Government: A Survey of Canada', 3 December.

Folsom, R.H. and Folsom, W.D. (1996), *Understanding NAFTA and its International Business Implications* (Albany, NY: Matthew Bender).

Jordan, M. (2006), '?Cerveza, Si o No?', *Wall Street Journal*, 29 March.

Nevaer, L. (2004), *NAFTA's Second Decade* (Mason, OH: Thompson).

Ontario Trucking Association (2004), 'Ontario Prebudget Consultation to the House of Commons Standing Committee on Finance and Economic Affairs', Ottawa, Ontario.

Smith, G. (2006), 'Piggybanks Full of Pesos', *BusinessWeek*, 13 March.

Tan, S. (2003), 'Bridge Back Ups Called the Worst Ever', *Buffalo News*, 30 December.

Thompson, J.H. (2003), 'Playing by the New Washington Rules: The US-Canada Relationship 1994–2003', *American Review of Canadian Studies* 33(1), pp. 5–26.

Turner, D.L. (2006), 'White House Advances Border ID Plan', *Buffalo News*, 18 January.

US Government (2006), 'The World Factbook: Mexico', *Stat-USA*, 10 January.

US International Trade Commission (US ITC) (2005), *The Year in Trade 2004*, USITC Publication #3779, July.

Chapter 17
Direct Marketing – A Global Perspective

Tim Lyons

Before talking about what direct marketing (DM) is, it might be worth reflecting on the bigger picture of actually what marketing itself is and how DM possibly fits into this bigger picture.

Introduction

There are many schools of thought as to how one might actually define marketing. There are the traditional 'needs and wants' devotees. There are those who see it as an exercise in value exchange amongst interested parties. There also are those who consider marketing to be a resource allocation issue (Gabbot 2004). Whatever the case, within this ever-sprawling definition of marketing sits the world of direct marketing or 'DM'.

DM reflects the paradigm that emphasizes needs, wants, value-exchange and resource allocation. It also has something unique to offer. DM is traditionally grouped under the 'marketing communication' heading. The reality is that it is so much more than this narrow definition would suggest. DM, in fact, is typically more of a marketing hybrid – it is not a sub-element of one of the 4 Ps like advertising or public relations. Realistically, DM is a very comprehensive marketing philosophy in its own right. It is the 4 Ps *and* it is market positioning *and* it is segmentation *and* targeting. In essence, DM extends the limits put on traditional marketing to include much more. In a world of cash starved marketing departments and increasing accountability from board level for brand and marketing managers, DM is a way forward and a point of difference. This is not just rhetoric – evidence suggests there is an ever-increasing movement in marketing budgets to reallocate this marketing communication mode.[1]

The aims of this chapter are to debate DM's relevance and to review what direct marketing is and how it fits in with the global marketing environment. To do so, we must first look at a simple definition of direct marketing and how it might work in practice.

The Essential Ingredients of Direct Marketing

Before charging off into the world of 'global direct marketing' let's take the time to reflect on what defines and makes up direct marketing:

> Direct marketing is the interactive use of advertising media to stimulate an immediate behaviour modification in such a way that this behaviour can be tracked, recorded, analysed, and stored on a database for future retrieval. (Stone and Jacobs 2001)

---

1   http://www.createivematch.co.uk, last accessed August 2007.

Stone and Jacob's definition above is very typical of many in the field and reflects the duality of direct marketing – to be both interactive in nature and a form of communication. The result of our world continuing to be technology-heavy and increasingly user friendly, interaction globally is becoming increasingly frequent, personalized and focused on individuals rather than segments and niches.

Direct marketing is all about interactivity. Today, marketing has to be more than just advertising media or even communication in general. It is about 'connections' and while these can be transmission based they can also extend beyond the world of communication to other elements of marketing like pricing, positioning, product development, etc. For a company like Manage China, DM is more than a core communication strategy – it is an holistic solution to the customer acquisition and maintenance problems they face.

Manage China

In 2006 a small management consultancy in Hangzhou, China, staffed by two Australians, one French and two Chinese workers, was challenged to build its base of new customers and so sought a way to reach its target audience of 'foreigners'. 'Manage China' (http://www. managechina.com) is a consultancy that specializes in assisting those new to business in China with managing those operational issues that foreigners in China often find so difficult to manage by themselves. The challenge for this group was to reach an incredibly disparate group of potential customers, from across the globe, who didn't fit within any conventional marketing wisdom of segmentation or targeting. Furthermore, they had to do it in such a way as to create dialogue and not incur a high cost in so doing. This 'I want my cake and to eat it too' challenge seemed perfectly suited to direct marketing.

In the case of Manage China's customer relationship management challenge, the internet became effectively the 'advertising media' that Stone and Jacobs were talking about in their definition. While the internet obviously has so many more uses than this, in the case of Manage China, they did not underestimate the ability of the web as a medium to communicate to a wide potential client base. The information rich website of Manage China included a blog (more of this later) and opportunities on each page for interested parties to register either their details, additional comments or both. Manage China ran a customer relationship management tool to complement the website called 'Daylite' (http://www.marketcircle.com/daylite/) so they could reach out to customers, respond to customer enquiries and incorporate all dialogue in a customer tracking program that integrated with their email, contact lists and calendars. All information is shared via a database that distributes updates to the Manage China staff either at their desk or remotely, when they travel, on a virtual private network. This is not a one-way communication stream – it is real time interactivity. This was maximizing resources, meeting customer needs/wants and exchanging real value between Manage China and its customers or potential customers. This is an example of how direct marketing is likely to proceed during the twenty-first century.

The Impact of the Global Environment on Direct Marketing

Direct marketing can take many forms. While the internet-based marketing that Manage China undertake is one form, there are also numerous others:

- Direct mail – the most traditional of all DM forms, where mail is sent out to a named person or organization with a message that requires a reply and thus a dialogue begins between respondent and company.
- SMS marketing – texts are sent to recipients who can either respond to the sender or forward the message to others, thus increasing the reach of such a campaign. This is a type of what is called 'viral marketing campaign' in that the spreading of the message could grow exponentially, much the same way a virus might spread.
- Sales promotion – there are many examples. Perhaps the most classic are competitions that require a reply from the respondent. A dialogue between company and customer is created this way.
- Email marketing – this medium is becoming increasingly frustrated by those who send bulk unsolicited emails (called spam) and so making genuine efforts to reach customers via email more difficult. Due to a growing cynicism about such email campaigns, email marketers are being forced to behave more responsibly and allow customers to 'opt in' or 'opt out' of the correspondence is one such development. Despite the growth of spam, DM is still a very effective mechanism for targeting customers.
- Direct response TV or radio – where a message is delivered over traditional broadcast media but a telephone number links the audience to a telemarketing room where they may register interest or make a purchase. Satellite and cable subscribers may 'press the red button' to access data, offers, participate in quizzes, request samples or order goods. Increasingly, these services are being offered on formats direct to palm pilots and other mobile devices.

What one considers to be direct marketing really is only limited by one's imagination, available configurable technologies and the definition discussed earlier. Today, television and radio have become direct marketing tools. Twenty years ago, no one thought of television as an interactive medium and so didn't perceive and create strategies to use this conduit as a direct marketing mode. Once identified, 'Infomercials' developed where customers were shown an '0800' (i.e., free call) number on the TV screen or over the airwaves and suddenly there was interactivity; databases of customer information are now compiled and dialogue takes place between customer and company.

These examples have reviewed some of the direct marketing methods that currently exist. These reflect on what has come before by way of the countless direct marketing solutions. This chapter changes focus and now considers the way forward, the impact that global marketing environment has had on direct marketing (or vice versa for that matter) and then concludes with the five biggest emerging direct marketing strategies that are a consequence of this global environment. Let's start by reviewing the growing global nature of direct marketing on company, industry and country.

The Impact of the Global Environment on Direct Marketing

The scalability of direct marketing perhaps is one of its most underrated yet impressive qualities. Small, medium and large companies alike can start a campaign for under $10 and extend this to the many millions of dollars, depending on objectives and resources. This is not to suggest that it is a cheaper way of undertaking marketing – perhaps just a more accessible way. For companies, it is about thinking in a different paradigm to the traditional '4 Ps of marketing'. One such way is using the 'space' provided by information, communication, distribution and transactions (ICDT) model (Angehrn 1997). Although initially proposed as a method for

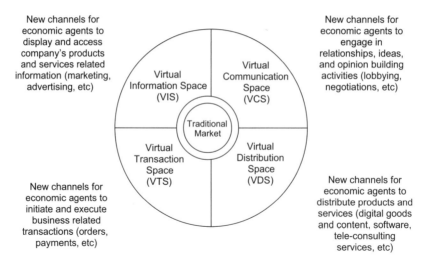

Figure 17.1   The impact of the global environment on direct marketing – company

Source: Angehrn 1997.

explaining mature internet strategies, it also serves as a pretty good proxy for direct marketing in a global environment.

- *I (information space)* – online options such as YouTube and Myspace provide environments for multinational corporations to be presented to prospective clients side-by-side micro sized enterprises. In this environment, they try to forge links with energized individuals that make up complex global organisms that loosely are call 'communities'. Other information spaces that dovetail direct marketing include sales promotions (both in the paper-based world and in the online world) and so too does the world of telemarketing and all it has to offer – sales, customer service, product information, etc. near-free voice of internet protocol (VOIP) systems such as Skype (http://www.skype.com) are set to revolutionize the way businesses inform and are informed by customers on a global basis. Imagine your customer service agents Skype address is embedded in the company's website. This enables instantaneous contact with customers looking for help or looking to buy a new product or service from your business's portfolio of companies and brands.
- *C (communication space)* – if we consider the oldest and perhaps most fundamental form of direct marketing to be direct sales, then we can see how this medium could be set for a renaissance given the contemporary global direct marketing environment. Long since thought over-cooked due to its low-volume contact/high-cost per customer approach, the use of the much-maligned salesperson has much to offer in the new global world of direct marketing. They are hooked up to consumers at one end and company databases at the other by devices such as Blackberrys (http://www.blackberry.com), Treos (http://www.palm.com) and a variety of other PDAs (personal digital assistants). Again, the internet provides the humble salesperson with the ability to project the face of the organization they represent and the not-so-simple telephone has been transformed into an email, internet, data and voice communication tool for the salesperson on the go.

- *D (distribution space)* – while the initial two elements reinforce the notion that DM might be exclusively about communication, this element demonstrates just how far the reach of direct marketing can extend. Do you remember the last time you walked into a store to pick up a CD, DVD or piece of software? The whole face of distribution has changed with the introduction of web based systems such as peer-to-peer networking and the omnipresent bit torrent. While this distribution revolution has its roots in the digital age, its impact is felt on a much broader level. Small companies in Lebanon are distributing French media content; Japanese speakers in Dalian, China are able to service customers in Osaka, Japan due to a technology called packet switching which vastly reduces telecommunication costs.

- *T (transaction space)* – the global direct marketing revolution is not confined to the internet. With the introduction of digital television and digital radio on a global basis, we are witnessing the ability of traditional mediums to emulate what the internet does best – reach market niches the size of one individual or client. Just-in-time manufacturers such as Dell Computer assemble products one at a time, even if the client requires larger volumes. This strategy minimizes the amount of time the product has to wait for the remainder of a batch to be produced. Consequently stock is significantly reduced. JIT producers only make to orders, never to stock. They do not want to be busy for busy's sake. They are busy because the customer wants something. In Dell's case, they have the money in the bank before they start to make the goods. This also helps their cash flow because they have few debtors.

Customers now watch programmes they load into their Tivos (http://www.tivo.com); they interact with screens, generate their own personal wide angle view, answer questions on quizzes that are the result of databases maintained about them and communicate with telemarketing operators when they are ready to purchase the product or service that has been ultimately customized for them.

Some companies have benefited from the opportunities that have come their way via the new direct marketing world. Others have let the world slide by. Having said this, while opportunities present themselves to all forms of business, firms are not always in control of their own destiny. Often the impact of change is felt at industry level and the organization is left to adapt to such change.

The Impact of the Global Environment on Direct Marketing – Industry

Industry change is impacted by global direct marketing at two levels. The first is where existing industries themselves are altered as a consequence of such change and the second is where new industries emerge and traditional ones disappear. The second relates to the emergence of an industry. Older traditional business brands may transition to offer other goods, services and niches

The very nature of industries, of which direct response television (DRTV programmes which are often called 'infomercials') is an example, is in a state of constant evolution.

The DRTV industry is in a constant state of flux. Once upon a time the products, TV commercial production and broadcast of these commercials only took place in a single country. Today, the products are being manufactured in China, the commercials themselves may be produced by New Zealanders in the Philippines (http://www.creativenations.com) and the shows are then broadcast on 1,000 TV channels in 100+ countries globally. Add to the mix one more important consideration. Now, infomercial providers can consider being narrowcasters rather than broadcasters. Traditionally, they always have relied upon a very broad and economically inefficient spraying of their message balanced by a narrow management of it through telephone rooms and management of the data via sophisticated databases. Now they can carefully target the delivery method and the message due to the breakthrough narrow reach (virtually one to one) that digital television has the ability to deliver. The result – a different message sent to everyone and a different dialogue with everyone when they contact the company via the phone room, a Skype service that appears on the television screen or an SMS message via their phone.

The second example is customer service and the emergence of an industry from what was once just a service. In the beginning, if your product didn't work, you took it back and got a refund. Today, if you ring the company you bought your product from, including Hewlett Packard and many other companies, the call is redirected to people at UPS (http://www.ups.com). Someone working for UPS in a city in India answers the phone on their client company's behalf and asks how they can help. Through a clever combination of telemarketing and basing themselves in the country of purchase, UPS have enabled many companies to outsource the troublesome customer service and product repair aspects of their business and left it in UPS's capable hands. If you purchase the product in France, an Indian will speak to you on a dedicated UPS telephone line to India and seek to identify exactly what your problem is. UPS will then access the German designed customer relationship management system, see the order, then proceed to pick up your Japanese brand/Chinese-made computer and take it to their French workshop for repair. Where once this marketing support activity was a one-way street for the customer (a request for repair), it is now a very efficient supply chain process that is outsourced to a third party. As these marketing activities move from being a cost business bears to becoming a superb direct marketing process, the result was the creation of a new industry.

The Impact of the Global Environment on Direct Marketing – Country

Consider this: in India every year, over 100,000 tax returns are processed for US citizens. This number is growing steadily (Friedman 2005, p. 14).

Accounting firms all over the Western world are sending their basic compliance work overseas to countries with cheaper labour. Customers can go online in the ultimate direct marketing experience with companies they have never seen and lodge their private financial details for their tax return, resting easy in the knowledge it will be done efficiently, cheaply and securely. What many of them don't know is that it will be done cheaply and efficiently – outside the US.

How does this marketing activity affect those customers in the US? How does it affect US workers who no longer have a job? While it would seem to be a boon for the Indians, how does it affect the Bangalore community when another doctor or lawyer is lured by the big dollars of telemarketing and compliance work and leaves medicine or the law behind?

Consider this: the internet is watching. Not actually the internet, but people who sit the other side of that screen. The law varies from country to country but the internet is the ultimate legal flattener. How do you stop someone in Portugal, who is protected by very detailed privacy legislation, from being spied on by someone who operates a website in Barbados, where the privacy laws are not so onerous? Civil libertarians are up in arms if Chinese authorities seek to limit content on websites or monitor search engines. What alternatives are there – zero censorship, partial access or site content replacement? The technology is there to provide supervision for children on the net. How realistic is it to expect to manage home use and the person creating and sending undesirable messages and images? With the advent of broadband wireless application protocols for mobile phones, data once collected from base stations across the border can be re-sent across the nation to any service subscriber. Satellite footprints spill over into other countries. Anyone with a dish and decoder can easily pick up transmissions and record, duplicate and disseminate data. Text and audio services piggyback on video signals in highly compressed formats. This enables many other information formats and content to be distributed via the same infrastructure. Given these alternatives, insightful, innovative and determined individuals and organizations will find a way to circumvent controlled information channels.

Society, morality, laws, ethics and so many other dimensions of our world are being changed by the global growth in direct marketing. It is not just about the internet and its reach. The issues can revolve around any aspect of direct marketing. For instance how telemarketing services might be managed out of developing countries? What about push marketing activities using unsolicited mail that turns up in your in-box or your letterbox that has been generated by global direct mail databases?

What about the direct marketing firm that takes the three-stage approach of:

1. customer profiling and matching of offers to profiles;
2. satellites tracking your physical movements via GPS;
3. messages sent via the 3G phone you have in your pocket to tell you of the latest big sale or to rush in before an offer closes.

Big Brother is watching, make no mistake: the fabric of sovereign countries is changing as a consequence.

The Big Developments in Direct Marketing Due to the Global Environment

There are so many things going on in the world of direct marketing at a global level that it would be impossible to list them all here. Rather than do so many things an injustice, we will concentrate on four big developments that currently are happening and consider how the direct marketing landscape is changing as a consequence of these elements. They are:

- the world of wireless and telephony;
- email/messenger service;
- all-things web: spotlight – the world of blogs, RSS and communities;
- search engine marketing.

Convergence – the All-purpose Device

You see them everywhere. They sit in airports, Starbucks, the corner bar, the sandwich shop and the licensed grocer. Today's business person seems almost physically attached to their ubiquitous laptop, PDA and mobile phone. The day of the paper-based diary and the portable files or briefcase seem numbered. The wireless office has arrived and, perhaps even more importantly, all of these devices seem destined to become one.

So how does this convergent technology affect us as direct marketers?

The very nature of these mobile devices already provides numerous opportunities for direct marketers. The convergence of such devices into one device will only extend the marketers reach further. Already we have access to the internet, email and messaging via our mobile phones. Maybe it is a PDA becoming a phone (Treo, available from http://www.palm.com), a phone becoming a PDA (Nokia E61, http://www.nokia.com) or a music machine morphing and becoming truly smart (iPhone, http://www.apple.com). Whatever the case, the mutual destinies of these devices seem inextricably linked. We now email on our phones, message each other on our PDAs and call from our iPods and laptops. The direct marketer has the ability to reach each individual with a tailored message in almost any communication format that suits and on one device.

The mobile office warrior sits at the coffee shop while on a business trip overseas and receives an email from a campaign that she has previously agreed to opt in to. She knows that this campaign has nothing to do with anyone else's judgement about which segment of whichever market she might or might not belong to. This is something she chose to belong to. Based on this choice, in combination with previous behaviour, she is now being asked if she would like to make a purchase. She checks the balance of cash left on her work 'smart card' telephone and decides, as she is overseas, it would be better and more secure to use her American Express card instead. She keys in the card number and password where the short message asks her to and she sends the request away. At the same time UPS receive a request to deliver to a pre-determined address at her workplace back in her home city. They issue a receipt via short message service (SMS) and the amount is added to her credit card balance. Upon receiving the receipt she then sends another message to the server at work, notifying the accounting program that she has made another commercial business purchase and the category it should be filed in is 'stationery'.

She then goes back to her coffee, safe in the knowledge that the purchase she has made is secure, that it will be delivered where she wants it to be delivered and that the transaction has been properly documented. She receives an email on her PDA asking if she is happy with her purchase and telling her that, should there be any problems, she can reach the customer service representative via a safe Skype connection.

Wirelessly. Effortlessly. Globally.

Email/Messenger Service

Five years ago, email was the most important weapon a direct marketer could have in their arsenal. With the rise of spam and increased privacy laws globally, some marketers began to question the effectiveness of email marketing. Then, some of the functionality of emailing began to increase and internet service providers became better at managing the flow of spam, and email marketing was reborn. Today it remains the pre-eminent marketing device on the web. The simple fact is, it was one of the earliest elements of the web, it is used more than the web and it can be accessed in so many ways that it is potentially more intrusive than the web.

The use of email marketing has real implications for international direct marketers in that it has the ability to reach a global audience from one central location. For this reason alone it remains perhaps one of the most significant mechanisms for reaching customers on a global basis that the marketer can employ.

One of the fundamental advantages of direct marketing over other forms of marketing is the use of 'testing'. Trying different approaches, until one works, seems counter-intuitive from a marketing perspective. From a DM perspective it is fundamental. In this way, email marketing is perfectly suited with its low cost per impact.

One of the foundations of DM is maintaining a database and the very nature of email marketing is a great fit. Profiles of clients from all over the globe built through the contact that email marketing generates a database that provides a very real advantage to marketers.

Pricing, sourcing or product development can build transient competitive advantages at best whereas the intricate web of customer relationships developed through an email/database offer the possibility for seriously sustainable advantage.

The advantage that email provides is only further extended through the network of relationships and contact points (now visual as well as written and audio) that messenger services such as MSN or latter day services such as Skype (http://www.skype.com) provide. Imagine how much further we can extend the customer-company connection by providing a toll-free number service on our global website to customers from any country. Imagine further adding voice and video capacity from a customer service perspective. None of this is a fairy tale – all of it is currently possible with a service such as Skype. Skype facilitates and enables the ultimate global DM step by reducing the impact of time zones through incorporating a voicemail service, accessible from either phone or laptop.

Email and messaging services deliver the ultimate DM capture-retention solution that any size business can access.

All-things Web: Spotlight – The World of Blogs, RSS and Communities

The corporate website is now morphing into the corporate blog site. A blog is a 'web log' – a record of something that is kept by the 'blog master' but that can be also added to, over time, by others that the blog master allows to. On many blogs, this access is carte blanche with the result that almost anyone can add to the blog site. In a world where we are trying to get two-way traffic with customers, the blog has a great deal of appeal on so many levels – none the least of which is this interactive nature it has.

Further adding to its appeal is the RSS capabilities that it possesses. RSS (Really Simple Syndication) is provided via a number of services but the most popular one is 'Atom'. The content that is created on the blog can be broken up into a series of separate 'stories' that can then be represented by a single URL – which can be hosted on other websites, blogs, sent as part of the body of an email, etc. 'Taking feeds' from websites in the form of RSS and providing RSS feeds to other websites are now a fundamental part of the way we can share information on the web. Websites in Australia, blogs in New York and mobile office workers in France all remain in the loop via RSS. From a direct marketing perspective it provides on of the most fundamental of the direct market building blocks – a reason to maintain constant contact with both customers and prospective customers. In a world where customers are constantly bombarded with messages, it was always very difficult to maintain such contact. The RSS feed eliminates this through a sense of connection and common interest. Customers request for feeds from company and the ability to place the feeds from customer's blogs on company blogs or websites based on RSS technology has changed the very nature of 'marketing dialogue'.

Both the blog and the RSS feed are evidence of a much wider phenomenon that goes to the heart of global direct marketing and that is the concept of an online community. Blogs tend to build a spirit of involvement that culminates in community – regardless of where any of the parties are located. With the spirit of community in mind, it will be interesting to see what technology emerges next.

Search Engine Marketing

In our earlier case study example we talked about Manage China and the way it used a contemporary approach to direct marketing to achieve its communication goals. Search Engine Optimization is one of the fastest growing direct marketing industries to emerge in the last five years. The potential for businesses across the planet using this direct marketing approached is almost without limits. In fact, there is no other form of marketing activity that can deliver the types of returns that SEO does for such a negligible outlay.

If you are fortunate enough to have a URL that 'points' to your site (e.g., http://www.cars.com) or a well known company name like Coke that allows people to guess your URL (e.g., http://www.coke.com) then that's fine. For the other 98 per cent of businesses, things are not so easy on the internet. When searching Google, the highest number of any search term was for the term 'homepage' (2,520,000,000 at 7 January 2007). While not every search term has such a high number of results it does bear testimony to the sheer volume of information out there. Consequently, if you don't have a strategy for getting noticed on Google, DMOZ, Yahoo or MSN (i.e., 'The Big 4'), or any other search engine for that matter, then you simply won't rate on a search.

If reaching out across the globe with your brand is important to you, then search engine optimization (SEO) should also be important to you. If you are trying to reach out with limited resources, as many SMEs do, it should be even more important.

Being listed in the first two pages of the Big 4 search engines is vital to the success of any business trying to make any sort of connection. Eighty-five per cent of all web searching starts with a search engine. Ninety per cent of all searching stops after the first two pages of the search are viewed. Eighty per cent of all traffic origination is driven to other search engines (e.g., Yahoo provides results for Altavista) by the Big 4. For a growing Indian company, being found in South Africa, linking to sites in Romania and coming first on Google Dubai for the search term could be very important. It could define their business and could end up doubling or tripling business or catapulting their business into the commercial stratosphere.

Conclusions

After undertaking an extensive search engine optimization campaign, Manage China reflected on the global reach they, as a small company, were able to exert. They were able to interact with over 600 prospects in the first 12 months of implementing the system, convert better than 50 per cent of these prospects into real customers and encourage 25 per cent of the prospects into becoming repeat buy customers (Pan 2007). The results far exceeded any expectations they might have had before undertaking their programme. The key to the programme was to maximize what limited resources they had to achieve the best possible outcome a business their size could hope for. The centrepiece of their activity was the use of search engine optimization, but several other global DM techniques were used also (blogs and RSS, for example). The net effect was immediate. Their message stretched across the globe, reaching customers in places as far away as France, Germany and the US. They built a database of future prospects, developed the multinational client base the campaign had produced and generally increased their reach across the globe. They did all of this to a point they never previously thought possible. In the end, they became the definitive global direct marketer.

In reaching out through their website and attracting recognition through search engines like Google, this little consulting company in Hangzhou, China came to look like a Goliath to its Greek, American, German and Australian clients.

References

Angehrn, A. (1997), 'Designing Mature Internet Business Strategies: The ICDT Model', *European Management Journal* 15(4), pp. 361–9.

Friedman, T. (2005), *The World is Flat* (London: Penguin/Allen Lane).

Gabbott, M. (ed.) (2004), *Introduction to Marketing* (Harlow: Pearson Prentice Hall).

Pan, J. (2007), Interview, Marketing Manager, Manage China, January.

Stone, B. and Jacobs, R. (2001), *Successful Direct Marketing Methods*, 7th edn (New York: McGraw Hill Professional).

Chapter 18

Retail Merchandising and Sales Promotions

Mayo de Juan Vigaray and Beyza Gültekin

Introduction

This chapter examines the value of the merchandising philosophy, describes how retail store's image is conveyed to consumers by recognizing the importance of *retail* and *lifestyle* merchandising in encouraging people to spend and enjoy more time shopping. The chapter covers, among other things, descriptions of store atmosphere and customer service. Promotional activities are reviewed as an integrated process, while placing more emphasis on the description, investigation and identification of the sales promotion tools and their objectives. The reader will be made aware of intriguing aspects of the retail merchandising and sales promotions plan.

Monday, Tuesday, Wednesday … One week, two weeks, three weeks … 1 February, 2 February … 3 March, 1999, 2001 … 2009! Days, weeks, months, even years pass by and many of us do not realize how and why time passes so quickly. Every day most of us get up in the morning, get ready, go to work and just do not pay attention to the day we are living and even more: *enjoying*. Most of us have lots of work, meetings, duties and emails. We send emails to everybody in the world – to someone in Australia, in France or even more to colleagues who are next to us in the office. Then, we have a quick lunch and afterwards we continue working. We go home and then… one more day has passed. Welcome to the twenty-first century.

What defines time periods? Is it perhaps birthdays? Not exactly, since there is usually a time when we decide that we would prefer our birthday to become just another day when we are not aware of our age, one of those days where we have meetings, duties and emails to manage.

Folk law suggests that 'Department Stores have "invented" St Valentine's, Mother's Day, Father's Day … in order to make us buy gifts and spend our money, even more money than we should', as shown in Table 18.1. People complain they have to buy a little gift for a loved one. The great availability and variety held in department stores, hypermarkets or speciality stores may make us realize that a 'special day' looms, for example, 14 February. Instead of being upset as a result of having one more errand to add to our daily routine, we should appreciate retailers' implicit warnings about how fast time passes. To become aware of this, however, it is very likely that we will have to become routine shoppers.

Retailers remind us with the aim of making us appreciate the 'compulsory pauses'. By paying attention to these messages, we attenuate our usual behaviour and appreciate giving the gift to our loved ones.

We all need to buy groceries. Many times a year this is done quite parsimoniously and unimaginatively. We also need to buy new clothes as a result of putting on weight, dieting, or just wanting to follow a fashion. Although some of us complain and argue that 'a gift does not show how much we love our mum and that we could buy something for her any other day' (although most of the time it is unlikely we will do so), we do buy her a present. Hearing 'I love you mum' is a treat. Mother also is expecting something else from us. Individuals have to perform task-involved shopping as well enjoying recreational shopping.

Table 18.1 International Mother's and Father's Day dates used by retailers to remind consumers that time passes

	Canada	Cuba	Greece	Italy	Mexico	Spain	Thailand	Turkey	USA
Father's Day	1st Sunday of June	3rd Sunday of June	16 June	19 March	2nd Sunday of June	19 March	5 December	3rd Sunday of June	2nd Sunday of May
Mother's Day	2nd Sunday of May	2nd Sunday of May	2nd Sunday of May	1st Sunday of May	10 May	1st Sunday of May	12 August	2nd Sunday of May	2nd Sunday of June

Going shopping to a pleasant and well-organized store can be a major source of relaxation and fun as well as a household chore (Bailey and Areni 2006). Whether consumers need groceries, apparel, or a gift for somebody else, they need to shop. People have many alternatives that are conveniently situated, including the options of electronic retailing, catalogues, direct mail, direct selling, television home shopping and vending machines. Both store-based (bricks-and-mortar stores) and non-store-based retailers (especially the internet) provide individuals with opportunities to acquire what they need or desire when they want it and where they prefer. Although the option of buying electronics, cookies or shoes using the internet is available 24 hours a day, 7 days a week, online sales remain a small fraction of total sales and firms continue to expand their online presence. Despite these improvements, the absence of sensory experience leads some consumers to avoid online clothes shopping because they cannot try on garments and touch the goods. Williams, Slama and Rogers (1985) identified the fact that consumers enjoy going shopping and bricks-and-mortar retailers continue to be the preferred choice for consumers.

Store-specific Characteristics

Store-specific characteristics including merchandise, comparable pricing, value for money, location, atmosphere and customer service influence consumer's evaluations and choices. This perhaps is an overly narrow focus. Perceptions that a prospective customer (known as a 'prospect') develops towards a specific offer by a retail outlet or chain also can be affected by the *retailer's promotion mix*, the *impressions that others express in relation to a store* (personal contacts such as friends and family, or impersonal sources such as the media) and by the *type of retailer*.

Store image is an important attribute of consumers' decision-making processes as they select and visit particular stores (Hartman and Spiro 2005). Retailers take great care to design the specific characteristics of their stores in order to attract their target market.

All Spaniards each year wait eagerly for 'la Fiesta of San Fermín' on 7 July. Ernest Hemingway described the event which now internationally is one of Spain's most well known events.

The opening of an IKEA store was similarly festive. On its first day of trading, more than 20,000 people visited the store before 6 p.m. A queue started to form at 5 a.m. in anticipation of the doors opening! (http://spainforvisitors.com, accessed March 2007)

This chapter now focuses on the concept of 'store image'. It reviews retail merchandising and sales promotions tools that retailers rely on to create the intended perceived image and to succeed in their retailing strategy.

Store Image and Mental Library

Image constitutes one of the most important elements of the consumer's shopping process. In his seminal study, Martineau (1958) first defined store image as 'the way in which the store is defined in the shopper's mind, partly by its functional qualities and partly by an aura of psychological attributes'. In 1958, Martineau could not have guessed how important this concept was going to become for retailers in future decades, especially in the twenty-first century.

Retail environments are changing more rapidly than ever before. Today increased competitive pressure is experienced by every sector. Increases in the number of retailers result in competition from both domestic and foreign companies. A significant concern as customers become more sophisticated is that, as their experiences as consumers lead them to become more demanding, their expectations also become higher. Consequently, retailers today must differentiate themselves in order to meet the needs of their customers better than their competitors can.

Tough and continuously evolving competition among retailers makes store image fundamental to achieving their objectives. To preserve and enhance their position in the market, retailers can use store image as a strategic tool (Steenkamp and Wedel 1991), which has a positive effect on retailers' profitability and store performance. Research suggests that a favourable store image and pleasant shopping environment increase customers' intention to purchase a product (Grewal et al. 1998), help them stay longer (increases the duration of the store visit), encourage them to examine and buy more products and, as a result, to spend more money and time compared to what they had planned in advance (Kaltcheva and Weitz 2006).

Positive evaluations of image have been linked to the development of *store loyalty* (Sirgy and Samli 1985; Koo 2003). Store image also has implications for developing *differentiation*. If a retailer has a unique store image (i.e., it is *different*), then image becomes a valuable asset to generate further competitive advantages that will be more difficult for competitors to replicate. Through careful management of the store with precise combinations of store-specific characteristics and promotion mix, a retailer can achieve a clear, distinctive and consistent image or 'personality'. From these differences, consumers then will be able to distinguish the store without hesitation.

Arriving to a crossroads, Alice came across the Cheshire Cat. Here is the Alice's famous conversation with the Cheshire Cat (*Alice's Adventures in Wonderland* [Carroll 1989]):

Alice: Would you tell me, please, which way I ought to walk from here?
Cat: That depends a good deal on where you want to get to.
Alice: I don't much care where.
Cat: Then it doesn't matter which way you walk. (Quoted in Saunders et al. 2003)

Frequently, consumers may feel like 'Alice in Wonderland' when they do not have a particular store in mind in which to go shopping. If the store projects a clear, consistent and distinctive 'way' (image or 'personality') to potential customers, it is very likely that they will choose the 'right way' (the store) rather than 'any other ways' (the competitors).

With all their intrinsic characteristics, stores offer fertile opportunities to *differentiate* retailers from their competitors and *to create value* for consumers that is consistent with their needs, desires and, potentially most importantly, their lifestyles. Many retailers keep this mission in mind: spend a huge amount of money to create a favourable consumer impression. Pragmatists and sceptics may suggest this is a triumph of style over substance.

Several factors contribute greatly to the creation of the overall and distinguishing 'store image', which is very critical for the retailers. When designing the store retailers focus on:

- merchandising;
- store atmosphere (exterior and interior environmental attributes);
- promotions.

Store image relates to customer's overall impressions of a retail offer that are formed from the totality of physical or inferred interactions that relate to the retailer. Consequently, no matter how a customer perceives a store's *personality*, their perceptions are filtered by previous experiences recounted from memories. Their interpretations are influenced by how that perception is depicted by the store's promotion and by others through their comments and expressed points of view. While consumers keep going to the stores, store image becomes a subliminally important component in their decision to revisit the store. For instance, we asked a Belgian consumer who knew nothing about FNAC's[1] strategies, merchandise management or marketing policies, 'why did you buy your last book in FNAC?' He replied with an elaborate discourse about the 'store image' based on his perception: 'It's like a pleasant walk between books, music and technology. It is a store concept unique in Europe. You can watch a movie, listen to CDs, buy tickets or watch a live concert, also look up things in reference books, without any stress and, at the end, have a drink at the bar. It's *"a must see place to visit"* for people interested in culture and lifestyles. Prices are very competitive and the staff is polite and efficient. A good location for a cultural afternoon combining shopping, walking and learning ...!'

Many authors in the retail management literature use the metaphor of the theatre to expose the dynamics and issues of a store (Levy and Weitz 2004; Varley 2006). We will borrow this and go further. First, identify a type of entertainment people would like to enjoy. People who appreciate music want to go to a music hall or variety theatre and, for classical music, an opera house. People who have children may opt to see a puppet show. Street theatre festivals are prime attractions for people who love to enjoy a sunny and beautiful day. The festival held annually in Edinburgh Scotland, is particularly noteworthy. These shows offer distinguishing atmospheres, various locations and a great variety of actors. In addition, the spectators perceive them in diverse ways. Similarly, variety is noticeable in stores. Consumers have many options from which to choose, including hypermarkets, discount stores, category killers,[2] shopping centres or speciality stores. Consequently, retailers try their best to attract consumers.

---

1   Based in France, FNAC is the leading retailer of books, CDs, videos, technical products, music, consumer electronics and entertainment in France, Belgium, Spain and Portugal (http://www.fnac.com/, accessed 28 December 2007).

2   A category killer is a product, service, brand or company that has a distinct sustainable competitive advantage such that competing firms find it almost impossible to operate profitably in that industry, for example, eBay.

Retail Merchandising

Merchandise Management

The merchandising of a store or chain is one of the factors contributing to consumer's preferences for particular stores. Merchandising as a concept is composed of the quality, assortment (brand and product mix), styling and fashion of products and pricing.

The quality of the brands on offer can aid the image of the store. Aldi, for exampl,e retails budget goods. Auchan and Tesco, by comparison, are perceived as 'up market' but not necessarily premium goods; they are more likely to hold 'big ticket' items that are at least as expensive, if not more than Carrefour and Wal-Mart. Similarly, McDonald's sells CocaCola because McDonalds is the number one and so is the soft drink. Burger King is number two and sells Pepsi. In this way, as quality of merchandised goods increases, so too does store image. Association with strong brands can improve a store's image. Consumers who perceive brands positively are more likely to have a favourable image of the store. Similarly, a strong store image may be damaged by association with poorly perceived brands (Mazursky and Jacoby 1986; Chowdhury et al. 1998; Collins-Dodd and Lindley 2003; Cudmore 2000; Ghosh 1990; Thang and Tan 2003; Baker et al. 1994). Because of these factors, it is important that retailers' store image should be consistent with the brands they offer to the consumers.

Customer needs and wants can be fulfilled by the wide variety of offerings and surroundings. Hence there is a wealth of choice of both goods held in stock and services provided during peak and low seasons. Stores that are perceived as having superior merchandising are likely to be preferred by consumers. These trends increase the probability of repeat shopping visits to the same retailer.

Retailers' offerings should be up-to-date to attract consumers. Today, most shoppers purchase by following the trends and impatiently await latest deliveries and the start of special offers and promotions. Many retailers constantly have to change their offerings. If they don't make or package anything as value-added services, retailers typically must carry consumers' preferred brands.

Consumers' perceptions about prices are important for store image. For this reason pricing strategy should be consistent with image (Lindquist 1974–75; Dodds et al. 1991). Retailers may set their pricing at the low or high end of the market or somewhere between these, approaching the average. The goods sold may be ultra-heavily discounted below the cheapest competitors. Equally, perception may be that 'if it isn't expensive, it isn't any good'. 'Reassuringly expensive' has been the catchphrase of a certain premium lager. No matter which pricing strategy is chosen, to be a successful retailer it is important to provide good value for money in the consumer's mind. To prevent consumers from comparing prices in other stores, retailers can use several tactics such as product variety differentiation, premium and basic own label brands, or they may prepare bundles of co-packaged complementary goods exclusively for that retailer.

Consumers may however decide to 'downshift', by choosing less expensive yet comparable goods. The quality aspect may be emphasized – the more expensive is higher quality. Downshifters seek comparable goods one price bracket down from their habitual purchase. After taking the packaging off at home, would the rest of the family notice? If they don't, they have spent less and pocketed the difference. Studies on the *Tonight* programme with Trevor McDonald (http://www.itv.co.uk) have compared regular and downshift shopping. They determined average minimum savings of 30 per cent using this strategy.

Before purchasing a product, consumers usually think about the value of the product. What do they receive (quality, convenience, pleasant shopping experience) and at what cost in terms of effort, time, and money spent. Because of this, consumers' perceptions of price differ according to retailer type, store atmosphere and customer service.

Retailers who offer high-quality products to their customers want to transfer the same product at a lower price when compared to competitors to enhance their image. Since retailers offer many products to their customers, it is very difficult for consumers to evaluate objectively the price divergence among retailers. According to research (Corstjens and Corstjens 1995; Sirgy et al. 2000), even when Carrefour[3] had the competitive advantage concerning price, consumers were not able to perceive any subjective or tangible differences. The perception of the retailers' price level depends more on promotional efforts than the objective price. Hence, managing customer perceptions of price becomes crucial.

As the distance between two competing supermarkets increases, the number of products common to both stores increases and the price competition for those common products significantly decreases. However, higher end retailers can use *product overlap* strategically. With some overlap, retailers become able to influence consumers' perceptions of price fairness and they hope these perceptions carryover to those products that do not overlap (Gourville and Moon 2004). A similar strategy is to use loss leaders. These are goods that are sold at a given price determined by the producer and are typically associated with special offers. The goods may have '3 for the price of 2'-type promotions. Consumers may make marginal purchases of other goods while seeking out special offers. Equally, they make marginal purchases of special offers while making their regular grocery shop.

The aim of the following section is to assist in the creation of conducive marketing environments that encourage sales', whether of an MP4 player or a pair of Manolo Blahnik shoes,[4] by visually exciting, entertaining and tempting the 'target market.

Store Atmosphere: Exterior and Interior Environment Attributes

Store atmosphere is a complex and multifaceted concept. Due to numerous definitions in the literature, conclusively defining store atmosphere in a single phrase is problematic. It is labelled as 'atmospherics' (Kotler 1973–74), 'ambient conditions' (Bitner 1992) and 'store characteristics'. Kotler gave it the label 'atmospherics' to describe various *visual* (colour, brightness, size, shape) *aural* (volume, pitch) olfactory (scent, freshness) and *tactile* (softness, smoothness, temperature) dimensions of a store that can influence the purchase probabilities of consumers. He defined atmospherics as: '... the conscious designing of space to create certain effects in buyers. More specifically, atmospherics is an effort to design buying environments to produce specific emotional effects in the buyer that enhance his purchase probability'.

Store atmospherics include all the tangible and intangible aspects that make up a store's environment. These include the layout, fixtures, customer service, décor and displays, lighting, scents, music and customer service. Each attribute of what is called 'retail store atmospherics' combines to create 'vibes'. Feng shui experts similarly attempt to create harmony by optimizing each attribute against the other.

---

3   Carrefour is famous for inventing the concept of hypermarkets in 1963 in France, which are stores that offer a wide range of food and non-food products at very attractive prices and whose shelves stock an average of 70,000 items. Hypermarkets' floor areas range from 5,000m² to over 20,000m² and their catchment areas are very large.

4   Manolo Blahnik is a famous Spanish shoe designer. With fans such as Madonna, Sarah Jessica Parker, Patti Labelle, Faye Dunaway and Winona Ryder, Blahnik has caused a virtual frenzy within the shoe world

Although the atmospherics concept is described by researchers from various perspectives, certain major variables are common to the different descriptions. The underlying precept of this term is 'what is in the mind of the customer'. It is the individual's perception of each cue that is provided both separately and collectively within the store and, perhaps also more overtly, by the site location, its environment and personnel (Davies and Ward 2002).

Theatres create an atmosphere for the audience. They set out to achieve it with good viewing for the audience, theatrical style lighting (steplights, spotlights), stage settings with curtain backdrops, front curtains that hide the screen before the play starts and the bulkheads that run in an arch along the sides. Stores similarly design their establishments to create a particular atmosphere.

Furniture and accessories stores are like a theatre where the walls, ceiling and floor represent the *stage*. IKEA are particularly noted for creating settings that resemble what they consider to be ideal aspirations for a family to live in. Emphasis is placed on the lighting, fixtures and signage, representing the *set*, the staff become *actors*, the merchandise is a *show* and the customers are the *spectators*. Subsequently, in a well-planned atmosphere, *merchandise* becomes more attractive to customers and they can enjoy the in-store show as much as they can appreciate a performance in a theatre. Retail managers must grasp a simple truth: shoppers are there to look at the merchandise and buy, not only to admire the store design.

Store atmosphere focuses on the basis of stimulation – creating consumer pleasure via the senses. Stores with favourable atmospheres are more likely to increase consumer preference. It validates the relationship between the emotive response of consumers and the physical aspects of stores. A pleasing store atmosphere – one that offers comfort and gratifications that stimulate consumers' visual, audio, olfactory and kinaesthetic senses and create a sense of wellbeing in the store – enhances the quality of their visit. This in turn increases consumer preferences and probability of their revisiting the store with a specific goal of purchasing goods that have been imagined as fitting in their own home environment. Thang and Tan (2003; see also Espinoza et al. 2004) assert that if the store atmosphere inspires positive effects such as pleasure, consumers' willingness to buy is more likely to increase. For some consumers the motivation to shop includes a desire to obtain sensory stimulation from the store itself and to affiliate themselves with various reference groups (Westbrook and Black 1985). Shoppers motivated to visit certain stores and buy certain products that raise their own sense of prestige value may place greater emphasis on store atmosphere.

The Physical Exterior

In life it is obvious that you will never have a second chance at creating a 'first impression'. The façade is outside the store and is the first phase of the shopping expedition. Consumers rely on their first impression of the store front. The store front should be eye-catching, inviting and imply the type of merchandise offered inside. If it is not well presented, the rest of the process may not be important for consumers. The right location, a captivating store façade and the surrounding area are significant plus points. For instance, Imaginarium, a toy store, entices both adults and children with two differently sized doors. Their aim is to use the exterior to create a different impression of the store for both groups.

Location

Location is another factor that attracts shoppers to stores. Two key questions are: is the store on the high street where there is plenty of passing trade? Is it out of town on a trading estate?

Good accessibility means ease of transportation coupled with a short travel time to the store. Retail sites that are near a bus interchange or mass rapid transit stations are likely to enjoy more exposure and draw greater traffic volume from 'passing trade' than stores that are not easily accessible. Despite the difficulty of accessibility or parking, there are stores that consumers still prefer simply because of their unique merchandise, atmosphere or customer service. Some customers make a special trip specifically because they know they can get what they want and know where to get it. Choice of goods on offer may be a secondary issue because they have specific needs and know what they want to satisfy them.

> 'Lotte Department Store' is in Daegu Station, South Korea. It has 12 levels and covers 750,000 square feet (228,600 square metres) of retail space over a subway station. The store's architectural design includes a pedestrian plaza surrounding the store; attached there are five levels of parking, two of which have direct access to subway transportation. With its strategic location, the shopping centre has reinforced its position as the leading retailer in South Korea. (http://www.visualstore.com, accessed December 2007)

'Just over the border' into another country can be a very interesting experience. The same brand retailer may offer significantly different ranges and prices may vary according to the wealth of the nation. Zara is of particular note in this context. Equally, other commodities such as cigarettes may have different national governmental duties. People living in Northern Ireland frequently travel over the border to Eire to buy petrol at a much lower price. Two hundred cigarettes in France costs around €50. Just over the border in Belgium they are €38. CocaCola in the US uses sweeteners to combat obesity while in Mexico they are sugary. US citizens can order Mexican-sourced Coke.

Marques and Brands

Brands are signs that may be familiar, famous and attract attention. They may be a physical projection of the *store name* which reflects the style and level of the store. Store names transfer a remarkable amount of information to consumers. The name 'Harrods' in the United Kingdom (in Knightsbridge, London and also some major international airports such as Heathrow), 'Loewe' in Spain, 'Tiffany & Co.' in the United States and 'Beymen' in Turkey evoke images of high quality merchandise, luxurious store atmospheres and high levels of customer service.

Store names are important marketing tools. Store branding demarcates organizational boundaries where ever the store operates. 'El Corte Ingles' in Spain, 'Boyner' in Turkey, 'Harrods of Knightsbridge', 'Debenhams' and 'House of Fraser' in The United Kingdom, 'Printemps' in France, 'El Corte Ingles' in Spain and 'Saks Fifth Avenue' in the United States are successful department stores that transfer their name and image to their customers. When the store name is well known and recognized by consumers, store image positively benefits from its reputation. This reputation becomes more influential when relying on the type of shopping, for example, the purchase is task-involved, for personal consumption or as gifts (Grewat et al. 1998; Thang and Tan 2003).

Window Displays

Window displays are akin to advertising in helping to create and maintain an overall image of the retailer in consumers' minds. Many retailers' communication strategies rely on their store window display. These serve as advertising and sales promotion media for retailers in the same way as a theatre uses its large posters on the façade of the building. Consumers use window displays as a key source of information in making purchasing and shopping decisions. For instance, in the retail category 'clothing', the role of window displays is likely, *a priori*, to be a pervasive and significant one.

Window displays are ubiquitous as well as a prominent element of retail strategies. By virtue of their location at the entrance of a point of sale, window displays can also directly induce consumers to enter a store to make specific purchases. The influence of window displays, particularly relative to other marketing actions, is likely to depend on various characteristics of the consumer, the product category, the retail context and the shopping task (i.e., shopping goal, planned versus unplanned task) (Sen et al. 2002).

Large consumer durable goods retailers typically change their displays four to eight times per year in line with seasonal and specific date themes. Their store front window may stretch for many tens or even hundreds of metres. A small bakery, by comparison, will change their store display several times per day. Early in the morning, they may sell prepared sandwiches and breakfast pastries. By late morning they may change over to lunch menus – 'hot and cold filled', 'light bite' type pastries such as toasted sandwiches and Cornish pastics. These will be complemented with fruit, prepared dairy and other deserts, cream cakes such as eclairs and perhaps coffee. In the early afternoon the range changes again, ready for afternoon tea – teacakes, scones and biscuits. The primary difference between stores such as Harrods and a bakery is whether goods in the window are sold from the window. Bakery goods are explicitly for sale, stock must be turned over rapidly, at least before the close of the store that day. The consumer doesn't need to read from a list near escalators on which floor to find types of goods and then go and find them. They simply ask for what they want and pay immediately prior to gaining the benefits. Excessive packaging used to store, protect and advertise big ticket items also is not required. A paper bag or cardboard box may used; the goods may even simply be placed on a napkin.

The Physical Interior

The interior design must be comfortable; to put the shopper in the proper buying mood and provide a setting that enhances the experience without distracting from the merchandise. Traditional branding focused solely on visual stimulation may be insufficient for today's sophisticated consumers. The importance of using all the senses (visual, audio, olfactory, touch and taste) in retail environments is increasing constantly. Victoria's Secret, a lingerie store, is constantly renovating the interior of its stores and creating a pleasant atmosphere. Fulberg (2003) reported that 'customers can be encouraged and motivated to make purchases by certain types of music or scents'.

Sounds

Music has been shown to affect consumers' responses to retail environments, typically in a positive manner (Baker et al. 1992; Morin et al. 2007). Music communicates to people's hearts and minds and serves as a powerful influence on emotions (Fulberg 2003; Garlin and Owen

2006). By association with previous memories and experiences, music encourages pleasant memories by transporting them to places in their minds where they would like to be.

Music is versatile. It has the ability to relax and invigorate. Love songs set the mood in a candle-lit restaurant. Up tempo tunes provide the perfect note for 'power lunches' and for combatting reticence and laziness, to become energized for a work out in a gym. Classical and ambient music invite consumers to linger in up-scale boutiques. It communicates 'distinction' the moment one walks into a consulting office and relaxes patients visiting the dentist. Music communicates at both conscious and subconscious levels. The emotional meaning of music can be communicated independently of age, gender, education or other individual characteristics.

Certain hypermarkets use loudspeaker systems. A salesperson communicates to those lucky enough to be shopping right now. They relate with excitement the latest developments and 'must see, must buy now' offers that are 'going fast'. The constant bombardment and loud volume may, however, demotivate individuals who find the noise oppressive.

Retailers may differentiate themselves from competitors even if they offer very similar categories of products, establishing distinct music zones within their establishment to create varying atmospheres. These subtle messages may appeal to customers and satisfy their purchase experience needs better than those of their competitors.

Music similarly has the ability to affect perception and behaviour among employees. Playing music may increase or reduce stress and affect confidence levels. This may facilitate employees to solicit customer feedback or they might become greatly annoyed with repetitive music, change the music to appeal to their own preferences without management's consent, become more productive with up-tempo music and become more easily distracted from some cognitive tasks (Areni 2003).

Scent

Store environment research (Spangenberg et al. 1996) has identified that various individual environmental elements such as scent affect consumer responses (Spangenberg et al. 2005). Researchers (Fiore 2000) found, via experiment, that fragrancing which was pleasant but inappropriate to the display did not improve subjects' reactions to the product. However, adding a fragrance that was both appropriate and pleasant improved subjects' expressed attitude toward the product and statistically, both their intention to purchase it and the maximum price they were willing to pay increased.

Shopping experiences can create either positive or negative effects on a person's behaviour. Scent and sound are ways to help retailers increase consumers' positive evaluations about store and satisfaction.

Colour

Colour affects moods and tends to manifest itself in the choices made. Store environment research (Bellizi et al. 1983) evaluated environmental elements, such as how colours affect consumer responses (Chebat and Morrin 2007). Consumers react more favourably to 'cool' store interior shades. For example, consumers prefer a blue interior: relatively greater shopping and purchase intentions occur with a blue décor as opposed to orange-based backgrounds (Babin et al. 2003).

Although academic researchers evaluate colour mostly as an in-store environment control variable, merchandise assortment colour coordination also is important. Taking items' colour into consideration in arrangements opens the way to 'cross-selling', which in turn can help customers buy items that can go together (Kerfoot et al. 2003).

Lighting

'Lights, camera, action' – the phrase used when filming – emphasizes the importance of lighting as the starting point of recording a movie scene. The same three attributes require consideration when the lights in the theatre are switched off and attention is turned to the stage (one of the clearest examples is the Famous Black Theatre in Prague (Davies and Ward 2002)).[5]

If a store resembles a theatre, success is inextricably linked to the lighting. For example, jewellery stores have spotlights trained on highly polished and clean goods in order that they sparkle. In normal light they don't seem so precious.

Using appropriate lighting to merchandise increases visibility and can make stores seem more inviting. Lighting must take attention away from the rest of the stores in the street and make the customers interested enough to stop and look at the store itself. Merchandise, store layout and competitors are other elements that drive illumination decisions. It is better to highlight merchandise with a light which is the same colour as the item itself. Candlelight makes a restaurant look inviting and evokes romance.

Appropriate lighting in the store creates an atmosphere for shopping. Improper use of coloured lighting is risky since it can change the colour of the merchandise. For example, blue light on a yellow dress is likely to make it look different from its daylight colour. This may result in misleading the customer, with consequences such as frustration and lost sales.

When creating a good lighting system, consistency with the image should be taken into account. Store image will decide which light is appropriate. Since this is an ongoing process, to sustain a distinctive position and minimize capital outlay, flexible lighting systems should be adopted that can change with the market, seasons, events and goods.

Lighting levels for boutiques and art galleries is generally very low. Restaurants and exclusive speciality shops also use low lighting levels; department stores, speciality chains typically use average levels; for supermarkets, discount stores, fairly high turnover and warehouse operations, high wattage lighting is used. Several light sources (e.g., fluorescent, incandescent, fibre-optic, high intensity discharge, neon and halogen) are used for various purposes (Diamond and Diamond 2004). Lighting is considered ordered (well arranged and neat) when the light is dispersed proportionally to the layout of the space; it is considered coherent (consistent) when modelling or shading is consistent across a space (Jay 2002).

Crowd

Various theories have been proposed to account for crowding and all approaches contribute something to a consumer's perception (Ergolu et al. 2006). Firstly, the crowding concept is not defined accurately. Two measures have been used interchangeably: one assesses how crowded people feel and the other how crowded people rate the environment to be. Hence, people may rate a setting as crowded but not describe themselves as feeling crowded (Dion 1999).

Crowding implies a relational characteristic between the person and the environment in which they are embedded. Crowding is determined by two appraisal processes: primary evaluation, which deals with whether something of relevance to a person's well-being happened or not, and a secondary evaluation that evaluates perceived control over the situation. Task-oriented

---

5   For example, see http://www.imagetheatre.cz/index_e.asp, accessed 11 December 2007.

shoppers look for space efficiency. For them, it is necessary to facilitate circulation and to space out counters. By contrast, to satisfy recreational shoppers, stores can make efforts to offer different activities (e.g., children' playgrounds in a hypermarket, a coffee area in a book shop) or thematic areas.

Layout and Displays

Store layout is significant to the customer's perception and evaluation of retail outlets. From a customer's perspective, store layouts include the ease of locating desired merchandise and the ease of moving around in the store. Wide aisles and slopes enable mothers to navigate with prams, pushchairs and baby buggies. In-store escalators and mobility lifts can be retrofitted to buildings that weren't designed with them. Typical layout styles are a grid store, racetrack, free form and spine. Each has an effect on the ease of finding merchandise within the store and in moving through the aisles and racks of merchandise. Merchandise display and layout factors tend to focus on in-store location and the shopping route to positively affect consumers' propensity to browse. In addition, attitudes toward visual product presentations influence browsing and purchasing behaviour in the store. A positive attitude leads to more browsing and purchasing, whereas a negative attitude towards the visual product presentation results in an immediate exit from the store (Kerfoot et al. 2003).

Effective merchandise displays guide and coordinate shoppers' merchandise selection (Khakimdjanovaa and Park 2005). Point-of-purchase displays (POP) can be either gondolas, straight and circular racks, or cut cases which are useful for showing the merchandise properly.

For clothing, retailers use shelving, folded piles and mounting clothes on hangers and mannequins to display and present merchandise. The aim is to influence consumers' evaluations of the coordinated selection of garments. Generally, display styles can influence purchase intention. Customers may be reluctant to disturb folded items. The consequence of this is that a garment displayed on mannequin is perceived more favourably compared to folded garments. Frequent maintenance is required to maintain the display appearance as ordered, abundant and minimize the time that the products could be assessed as untidy and thus number of viewings.

Customer Service

Customer service refers to identifiable service activities undertaken by retailers in conjunction with the basic products it sells. Customer service starts with personal greetings between individual shoppers and high-calibre sales people. Some stores, including larger Adidas outlets, use radio transmitter and receiver sets to alert sales staff to potential clients as well as to criminals aiming to steal items. Each Adidas employee is specifically required and trained to greet every store visitor. Greeting styles are based on politeness, willingness and offers of assistance, advice about merchandise and guidance around the store. Customer service goes beyond store personnel. Company staff represent the corporation and the brand. They enact the business objective to strengthen store-to-consumer relationships. They aim to increase consumers' pleasure of shopping experience in the store and encourage repeat visits (Oliver 1999).

In-store support services include rest areas, shopping carts, baby strollers, child-care areas, nappy-changing areas, play areas for children, clean washrooms, facilities for customers with special needs (e.g., wheelchairs), language service, cloakrooms (for checking coats, bags and packages), special order and product search desks, credit acceptance and gift wrapping. These are provided to reduce or eliminate any potential dissatisfaction. In this way stores hope that the following elements of customer service will increase the consumers' pleasure and indirectly increase the duration of visit: extended store hours, mail and phone orders, personal shoppers, parking and, of course, the amount of time shoppers spend in checkout lines. Consumers do not always go to retail stores with the purpose of acquiring specific merchandise. Sometimes shopping treated as a recreational activity whose value is identified by the level of service in the store.

Post-transaction services include customer reward programmes, tax refunds, delivery of merchandise to consumers' homes, installation, repair services, offering warranties ,exchanges or refunds for defects and complaints handling: all are tools that can differentiate a store from its rivals.

Tansaş is one of Turkey's largest supermarket chains. To enhance customer satisfaction, they open checkouts in less than three minutes following a request to a manager. Customers have come to expect this level of service. They do not want to queue because tills are closed. After the request a count down timer is used. If tills do not open in three minutes, Tansaş guarantees to discount 20TL (around €13) off the total price of the customer's shopping items. (http://www.tansas.com.tr/kampanya.html, accessed December 2007)

Success in today's retail world is knowledge driven. Retailers must know their customers and react positively to complaints. Such feedback is invaluable in helping retailers to know their customer requirements better and to identify expectations and perceived service levels. This data gives the retailer a chance to put measures in place to correct outstanding issues and consequently increase customer satisfaction (Berman and Evans 2001). A complaint is often the clue needed to nudge retailers to run their business better. Retailers should create an atmosphere and a communication route for customers to complain and express their dissatisfaction. 'If you like our store, tell others. If you don't like it, tell us!' Retailers can be proactive instead of waiting for complaints, by asking customers periodically, via surveys, to identify their perceptions about the service they received. Employees are or should be 'the eyes and ears' of the retailer. They can get immediate feedback from customers about their service expectations and problems and can inform managers accordingly (Levy and Weitz 2004). Another method is using 'mystery shoppers' who are hired to take the on role of 'expert customers'. After their visit they fill out questionnaires and create reflective journals with recommendations on how to improve the service level.

Many retailers make use of *rewarding services* that aim to build loyalty with clients because they want to create and sustain long-lasting relationships and repeat business. Stores can reward customers with merchandise, travel, gift certificates for partner stores and business alliance partner, or extras from the company. Other variants of this include: sending off for special offers, newsletters and member events. Knowing the customers by name and understanding their needs, wants and concerns is an alternative method to making them feel unique, special and appreciated. The Aston Martin sales executive in Australia knows the name, address, purchase history with competitor products and Aston's and spending power of his prospects.

> The problem hyper- and supermarket type retailers have with knowing customers' names is 'how many times do you go to a checkout and meet the same till operator?' They can get around this by swiping the credit card first and reading the name from their computer screens. This will also avoid the problem of cards being rejected because the supermarket can interrogate the bank and till up to the credit limit.
>
> At the local grocer or newspaper stand the attendant may use 'sir' or 'madam', 'governor' or some other nickname in order to address the 'punter' in either a respectful or friendly manner.

Effective customer service aims to create customers who come back again; positive word-of-mouth communication informs and brings in new customers (Levy and Weitz 2004).

Promotion

A retailer's promotion mix comprises advertising, sales promotions, personal selling and public relations. These components need to be managed from an understanding of 'gestalt' (Houston 1993) and must be integrated not only with each other but with the retailer's other managerial decision areas such as merchandising, store atmosphere and customer service. A retailer uses promotions to increase the probability of patronage by encouraging repeat visits and creating awareness about the store and the activities that take place in the environment. These include promotions that inform consumers about the retailer's offerings that are designed and stocked on the customer's behalf to meet their needs and desires. A well-developed promotional strategy should be able to attract new consumers and initiate planned special excursions to the store because the disseminated information creates value in customer's minds (Thang and Tan 2003).

Sales promotions tend to be relatively short-term oriented activities and an action-focused marketing event whose purpose is to have a direct impact on the behaviour of the customers, such as an extra incentive to buy (Laroche et al. 2001). Sales might have sprung from the focus on 'increasing sales volume' or informing customers about the ongoing discounts. Many retailers, such as hyper- and supermarkets, have many product lines that are not much different from the competitors. In addition to introducing private-label brands, enhancing store atmosphere and offering improved service relative to its competitors, a retailer can stand out from this competition by sales promotions.

Berman and Evans (2001) identified sales promotion techniques including:

- *Discounts*, that is, reductions to a brand's recommended retail price shown on the packaging. To show discounts, posters can be used that may be handwritten, as if this has just happened because the store manager wanted to give his customers a break (rather than give the message of a corporate cynical ploy). The offer can be printed in a brochure and/or declared loudly over the store speaker system. Numerous empirical studies have found that discount prices lead to a reliable increase in perceptions of value (Darke and Chung 2005). Limited shelflife goods may be offered with heavy discounts to move *end of day*, *out of date* or *obsolete inventory* (Voss and Seiders 2003).
- *Coupons* are distributed as print media, direct mail, packages or POP displays with different outcomes. Clothing retailers use these kinds of promotions to push merchandise that competitors also offer.

- *Frequent shopper programmes* provide points or discounts depending on the amount spent in a given period in the store. Another alternative is to offer *gifts* that are given with each purchase as shown in the following example.

David McConnell was once a bookseller specializing in Shakespeare's works. Faced with dropping revenues, McConnell tried to boost his business by distributing free perfume with every sale. He soon found, however, that his customers were more interested in perfume than they were in literature. McConnell promptly started another business (the California Perfume Company) – this he later renamed in honour of the river which flows through Shakespeare's hometown, Stratford-upon-Avon. Avon now is one of the largest direct-selling companies in the world. (http://www.anecdotage.com/index.php?aid=9893, accessed March 2006)

Other promotion tactics include *in-store contests*, where customers complete a game, a puzzle or create a slogan and winning depends on performance compared to the criteria and *sweepstakes*, which resemble contests but participants merely fill out an application form and the winner is picked at random. Filling out some application forms requires skill. *Samples* are free trial version given to customers. Products show their real performance by *demonstrations* such as cleaning up floors, mixing foods, and so on. In-store demonstrations can offer free samples of merchandise to build excitement in the store and stimulate purchases. A retailer can thank current customers when bringing in new customers by offering *referral gifts*. *Shopping bags* can be 'walking billboards' that are an opportunity for retailers. *Special events* include activities such as fashion shows, book signings, cooking demonstrations or autograph sessions and interviews with celebrities. All of these draw customers into the store and encourage impulse purchases.

Retailer: be careful! Do not design sales promotions that are too complex for consumers to comprehend since they go to the store looking for real advantages of sales promotions, not to work on mathematical exercises. A supermarket was showing this offer to the clients: *a pack of three cans of sauce, one for free, with the reimbursement of a pack if you buy two identical products, with a coupon of €0.60 increased discount of 25% if the happy buyer owns the card of the store.*

It seems a very perplexed commercial policy. (http:/www.gs2i.fr/fineprint/pdffactory.htm, accessed December 2007)

Conclusion

Retailers are exposed to a competitive international marketplace as well as globally accessible online retailing. Consequently, it is becoming increasingly difficult for a retailer to differentiate themselves from competitors. Retail store characteristics such as colour, lighting, customer service and sales promotions have effects on the buying decision-making process.

Customers' many decisions relevant to purchasing a product are described in this chapter. Recommendations are made on how to provide potential customers with their desired shopping experience and benefits.

There are times when the purpose of going shopping is just to buy simple supplies such as a loaf of bread, but consumers may return without the intended item and also be carrying a basket of other goods that were selected in the store. By contrast, there are times when without an intention to buy, people come home 'as usual' with an item they 'just had to buy'.

References

Areni, C.S. (2003), 'Examining Managers' Theories of How Atmospheric Music Affects Perception, Behaviour and Financial Performance', *Journal of Retailing and Consumer Services* 10(5), pp. 263–74.

Babin, B.J., Hardesty, D.M. and Suter, T.A. (2003), 'Color and Shopping Intentions: The Intervening Effect of Price Fairness and Perceived Affect', *Journal of Business Research* 56, pp. 541–51.

Bailey, N. and Areni, C. (2006), 'When a Few Minutes Sound like a Lifetime: Does Atmospheric Music Expand or Contract Perceived Time?', *Journal of Retailing* 82(3), pp. 189–202.

Baker, J., Dhruv, G. and Parasuraman, A. (1994), 'The Influence of Store Environment on Quality Inferences and Store Image', *Journal of the Academy of Marketing Science* 22(4), pp. 328–39.

Baker, J., Grewal, D. and Levy, M. (1992), 'An Experimental Approach to Making Recall Store Environmental Decisions', *Journal of Retailing* 68 (Winter), pp. 445–60.

Bellizi, J.A., Crowley, A.E. and Hasty, R.W. (1983), 'The Effects of Color in Store Design', *Journal of Retailing* 59, pp. 21–45.

Berman, B. and Evans, J.R. (2001), *Retail Management A Strategic Approach*, 8th edn (Upper Saddle River, NJ: Prentice Hall).

Bitner, M.J. (1992), 'Servicescapes: The Impact of Physical Surroundings on Employee Responses', *Journal of Marketing* 56 (April), pp. 57–71.

Carroll, L. (1989), *Alice's Adventures in Wonderland* (London, Hutchinson).

Chebat, J.-C. and Morrin, M (2007), 'Colors and Cultures: Exploring the Effects of Mall Décor on Consumer Perceptions', *Journal of Business Research* 60, pp. 189–96.

Chowdhury, J., Reardon, J. and Srivastava, R. (1998), 'Alternative Modes of Measuring Store Image: An Emprical Assessment of Structured versus Unstructured Measures', *Journal of Marketing Theory and Practice* (Spring), pp. 72–86

Collins-Dodd, C. and Lindley, T. (2003), 'Store Brands and Retail Differentiation: The Influence of Store Image and Store Brand Attitude on Store Own Brand Perceptions', *Journal of Retailing and Consumer Services* 10(6), pp. 345–52.

Corstjens, J. and Corstjens M. (1995), *Store Wars: The Battle for Mindspace and Shelfspace* (New York: John Wiley & Sons).

Cudmore, B.A. (2000), 'The Effect of Store Image, Package and Price Similarity on Consumer Perceptions of Store Brand Quality', unpublished doctoral dissertation, South Carolina University.

Darke, P.R. and Chung, C.M.Y. (2005), 'Effects of Pricing and Promotion on Consumer Perceptions: It Depends on How You Frame it', *Journal of Retailing* 81(1), pp. 35–47.

Davies, B. and Ward, P. (2002), *Managing Retail Consumption* (New York: John Wiley & Sons).

Diamond, J. and Diamond, E. (2004), *Contemporary Visual Merchandising Environmental Design*, 3rd edn (Upper Saddle River, NJ: Prentice Hall).

Dion, D. (1999), 'A Theoretical and Empirical Study of Retail Crowding', *European Advances in Consumer Research* 4, pp. 1–7.

Dodds, W. B., Monroe, K.B. and Grewal, D. (1991), 'Effects of Price, Brand and Store Information on Buyers' Product Evaluations', *Journal of Marketing Research*, pp. 314–18.

Eroglu, S.A., Machleit, K. and Barr, T. (2006), 'Perceived Retail Crowding and Shopping Satisfaction: The Role of Shopping Values', *Journal of Business Research* 59(5), pp. 535–48.

Espinoza, F., Liberali, G. and D'Angelo, A.C. (2004), *Testing the Influence of Retail Atmosphere on Store Choice Criteria, Perceived Value and Patronage Intentions*, American Marketing Association, Conference Proceedings, Chicago, 15, pp. 120–26.

Fiore, A.M. (2000), 'Effects of a Product Display and Environmental Fragrancing on Approach Responses and Pleasurable Experiences', *Psychology and Marketing* 17(1), pp. 27–54.

Fulberg, P. (2003), 'Using Sonic Branding in the Retail Environment – An Easy and Effective Way to Create Consumer Brand Loyalty while Enhancing the In-Store Experience', *InformDesign*, http://www.informedesign.umn.edu/Rs_detail.aspx?rsId=1694.

Garlin, F.V. and Owen, K. (2006), 'Setting the Tone with the Tune: A Meta-Analytic Review of the Effects of Background Music in Retail Settings', *Journal of Business Research* 59, pp. 755–64.

Ghosh, A. (1990), *Retail Management* (Forth Worth, TX: The Dryden Press).

Gourville, J.T. and Moon, Y. (2004), 'Managing Price Expectations through Product Overlap', *Journal of Retailing* 80, pp. 23–35.

Grewal, D., Krishnan, R., Baker J. and Borin, N. (1998), 'The Effect of Store Name, Brand Name and Price Discounts on Consumers' Evaluations and Purchase Intentions', *Journal of Retailing* 74(3), pp. 331–52.

Hartman, K.B. and Spiro, R.L. (2005), 'Recapturing Store Image in Customer-Based Store Equity: A Construct Conceptualization', *Journal of Business Research* 58, pp. 1112–20.

Houston, G. (1993), *Being and Belonging, Group, Intergroup and Gestalt* (Chichester: John Wiley & Sons).

Jay, P. (2002), Subjective Criteria for Lighting Design', *Lighting Research and Technology* 34(2), pp. 87–99.

Kaltcheva V.D. and Weitz, B. (2006), 'When Should a Retailer Create an Exciting Store Environment', *Journal of Marketing* 70 (January), pp. 107–18.

Kerfoot, S., Davies, B. and Ward, P. (2003), 'Visual Merchandising and the Creation of Discernible Retail Brands', *International Journal of Retail and Distribution Management* 31(3), pp. 143–52.

Khakimdjanovaa, L. and Park, J. (2005), 'Online Visual Merchandising Practice of Apparel e-Merchants', *Journal of Retailing and Consumer Services* 12, pp. 307–18.

Koo, D-M. (2003), 'Inter-Relationships among Store Images, Store Satisfaction, and Store Loyalty among Korea Discount Retail Patrons', *Asia Pacific Journal of Marketing and Logistics* 15(4), pp. 42–71.

Kotler, P. (1973–74), 'Atmospherics as a Marketing Tool', *Journal of Retailing* 49 (Winter), pp. 48–61.

Laroche, M., Pons, F., Zgolli, N. and Kim, C. (2001), 'Consumers Use of Price Promotions: A Model and its Potential Moderators', *Journal of Retailing and Consumer Services* 8, pp. 251–60.

Levy, M. and Weitz, B. (2004), *Retailing Management* (New York: McGraw Hill).

Lindquist, J.D. (1974–75), 'Meaning of Image', *Journal of Retailing* 50(4), pp. 29–39.

Martineau, P. (1958), 'The Personality of the Retail Store', *Harvard Business Review* 336, pp. 47–55.

Mazursky, D. and Jacoby, J. (1986), 'Exploring the Development of Store Images', *Journal of Retailing* 62(2), pp. 145–65.

Morin, S., Dubé, L. and Chebat, J.-C. (2007), 'The Role of Pleasant Music in the Dual Model of Environmental Perception', *Journal of Retailing* 83(1), pp. 115–30.

Oliver, R.L, (1999), 'Whence Consumer Loyalty?', *Journal of Marketing* 63, pp. 33–44.

Saunders, M., Lewis, P. and Thomhill A. (2003), *Research Methods for Business Students*, 3rd edn (Madrid: Prentice Hall).

Sen, S., Block, L.G. and Chandran, S. (2002), 'Window Displays and Consumer Shopping Decisions', *Journal of Retailing and Consumer Services* 9, pp. 277–90.

Sirgy, J.M. and Samli, C.A. (1985), 'A Path-Analytic Model of Store Loyalty Involving Self-Concept, Store Image, Geographic Loyalty, and Socioeconomic Status', *Academy of Marketing Science* 13, pp. 265–91.

Sirgy, M.J., Grewal, D. and Mangleburg, T. (2000), 'Retail Environment, Self-Congruity, and Retail Patronage: An Integrative Model and a Research Agenda', *Journal of Business Research* 49, pp. 127–138.

Spangenberg, E.R., Crowley, A.E. and Henderson, P.W. (1996), 'Improving the Store Environment: Do Olfactory Cues Affect Evaluations and Behaviour?', *Journal of Marketing* 60, pp. 67–80.

Spangenberg, E.R., Grohmann, B. and Sprott, D.E. (2005), 'It's Beginning to Smell (and Sound) a Lot like Christmas: The Interactive Effects of Ambient Scent and Music in a Retail Setting', *Journal of Business Research* 58(11), pp. 1583–9.

Steenkamp, J.B. and Wedel, M.E. (1991), 'The Contribution of Store Image Characteristics to Store-Type Choice', *Journal of Retailing* 53(2), pp. 300–20.

Thang, D.C.L. and Tan, B.L.B. (2003), 'Linking Consumer Perception to Preference of Retail Stores: An Empirical Assessment of the Multi-Attributes of Store Image', *Journal of Retailing and Consumer Services* 10(4), pp. 193–200.

Varley, R. (2006), Retail Product Management,.

Voss, G.B. and Seiders, K. (2003), 'Exploring the Effect of Retail Sector and Firm Characteristics on Retail Price Promotion Strategy', *Journal of Retailing*, pp. 37–52.

Westbrook, R.A. and Black, W.C. (1985), 'A Motivation-Based Shopper Typology', *Journal of Retailing* 61(1), pp. 78–103.

Williams, T., Slama, M. and Rogers, J. (1985), 'Behavioral Characteristics of the Recreational Shopper and Implications for Retail Management', *Journal of the Academy of Marketing Science* 13, pp. 307–16.

Chapter 19

Services Marketing: An Overview and Relational Approach of the B2B Setting

Ruben Chumpitaz and Nicholas G. Paparoidamis

The objective of this chapter is twofold. First, to shed light in the theory underlying the concepts of service quality, customer satisfaction, service recovery and loyalty, and second to bring into focus the business-to-business (B2B) field, presenting the theoretical grounds upon which the relationship marketing focused concepts of relationship quality, relationship satisfaction, trust and commitment are developed.

Introduction

Undoubtedly, during the last decade, successful business firms have started paying particular attention to service delivery in their effort to implement strategies that will lead to competitive advantage, a loyal customer base, and stable long-term financial and non-financial performance. The literature acknowledges that well-designed customer service programmes affect important factors related to managerial strategic objectives such as customer satisfaction and retention, profits and increased market share and revenue (Reichheld and Sasser 1990; Rust and Zahorik 1993; Anderson et al. 1994; Anderson et al. 1997; Johnston 1995b).

The Western world has experienced a boom in post-industrial service sectors for over two decades. This is not the situation in all parts of the world. In industrialized countries, the value created by the service sector as a percentage of GDP relating to prices rose from 53 per cent in 1960 to 66 per cent in 1995 (Gronroos 2001). In the European Union, GDP rose from 47 per cent to 68 per cent and in the USA from 57 per cent to 72 per cent, and it keeps rising (Griffiths 2000). For a long time, however, the service sector has accounted for over 50 per cent of gross national product and total employment in developed countries. In several countries, this percentage is much closer to 100 than 50.

The advent of relationship marketing and the increasing competition that characterizes markets over the last 30 years have placed consumer satisfaction and related research constructs at the heart of the services literature. Particular attention has been given to the conceptualization and measurement of the consumer satisfaction variable. This has become a central issue in modern marketing theory and practice as a principal indicator of marketing performance (Babin and Griffin 1998; Walker 1995). Service failures and mistakes, similarly, can occur in every business setting even in the best-run companies, thus complaining customers and advancing complaint management are the prompt modern business to take advantage of opportunities that are subsequently identified and they use these to set new product and performance agendas (Boshoff 1997, 1999). Complaint management strategies focus on customer complaints triggered by service failures. Service recovery is a tool firms may use to seek out dissatisfaction created from service episodes below customer expectations (Johnston 1995a).

Service encounters are at the heart of the services literature. This term refers to the interaction between service employees and customers, and influencing customers' evaluations of service offerings (Bitner et al. 1990). Management and evaluation of service encounters are an important part of the research stream in this area. Recent studies have highlighted the importance of employees-customers interactions in formulating service quality perceptions, satisfaction and loyalty attitudes, although the nature and direction of those relationships remain unclear.

Numerous studies in the business-to-consumer environment have tried to clarify, conceptualize and measure those related variables. This is done because researchers recognize the importance of studying and understanding them and how these relate to behavioural intentions and loyalty (LaBarbera and Mazursky 1983). In a business-to-business context this is rather rare, with very few studies trying to fill this vacuum of understanding concerning the existence of service quality dimensions and their influence on industrial satisfaction and behavioural intentions (Schellhas et al. 1999; Parasuraman 1998).

Service Quality

The conceptualization, operationalization and measurement of service quality is one of the most debated and controversial topics in the services marketing field (Lapierre et al. 1996). As services are intangible, consumers tend to homogenize quality assessment criteria subjectively. Perceived service quality has been referred to as elusive (Parasuraman et al. 1985) and research relating to this construct is still considered unresolved (Carhuana et al. 2000). Many researchers have suggested that perceived quality stems from comparing expectations against perceived performance (Parasuraman et al. 1988) and that differences then may affect behavioural intentions. Perceived quality is defined as a consumer's appraisal of a product's overall excellence or superiority (Zeithaml 1988) Quality can be viewed as an attitude towards a product or service (Parasuraman et al. 1988). Perceived quality therefore can be considered as a variable that might be added to models explaining behavioural intentions.

Early concepts of perceived service quality were founded on the disconfirmation paradigm (Parasuraman et al. 1985) employed by Oliver (1980) in order to define customer satisfaction. Oliver (1993) distinguished between the meanings of quality and satisfaction firstly by pointing out that the dimensions underlying quality judgements are rather specific, whether they are cues or attributes (Bolton and Drew 1994). Satisfaction judgements, however, can be made based on any attribute or benefit whether or not it is related to quality. Similarly, quality expectations can be based on ideals or excellence perceptions. A large number of non-quality issues, including needs equity or fairness, help in the formation of satisfaction judgements. Furthermore, quality perceptions do not require experience with the service or provider while satisfaction comes after the actual product or service experience.

In the literature, there has been considerable progress on how service quality perceptions should be measured (Parasuraman et al. 1985, 1988, 1991, 1994; Teas 1993). Little has been put forward to explain what exactly should be measured. Researchers generally have adopted three broader conceptual paradigms (frameworks). The first, proposed by Grönroos (1982, 1984), defines the dimensions of service quality in global terms as being functional and technical. The second, proposed by Parasuraman, Zeithaml and Berry (1988), identifies service quality dimensions using terms that describe service encounter characteristics (i.e., reliability, responsiveness, empathy, assurances and tangibles). The third, proposed by Rust and Oliver (2000), considers overall perception of service quality as based on the customer's evaluation of three dimensions service encounters: the customer – employee interaction, the service environment and the service outcome. Although all three paradigms dominate the literature, it is not clear which is the most appropriate to use. Moreover, although it is generally accepted that perceptions of service quality are based on multiple dimensions, there is no general agreement on the nature or content of these features (Brady and Cronin 2001; Rust and Oliver 1994). A call for empirical research that will examine the 'dimensionality' of the service quality construct (Parasuraman et al. 1994) has yet to be successfully addressed.

Consumer Satisfaction

A review of the specific literature provides evidence concerning the lack of an agreed definition for consumer satisfaction. This poses serious conceptualization, operationalization and measurement problems for researchers (Babin and Griffin 1998; Woodruff and Gardial 1996). The ongoing debate around the nature of the construct as a process or an outcome is only part of its definitional puzzle. The majority of researchers define consumer satisfaction as an evaluative response concerning the outcome of a particular service encounter (Fornell 1992; Cronin and Taylor 1995) and portray this response as either a cognitive or an affective proposition (Bolton and Drew 1991). On the other hand, given the lack of a clear definition, different research models use transaction-specific or overall assessments of consumer satisfaction (Parasuraman et al. 1994; Rust and Oliver 1994; Teas 1993). The 'transaction-specific' models define consumer satisfaction as an emotional reaction following a consumption-specific disconfirmation experience on the base attitude level (Oliver 1981). At the second level, consumer satisfaction is defined as an overall assessment referring to the consumers' overall dis/satisfaction with the organization based on overall service experiences, differentiating consumer satisfaction from perceived quality (Anderson and Fornell 1994). The various competing theories of consumer satisfaction measurement promote different response standards.

SERVQUAL and the expectancy-disconfirmation paradigms are the dominant measurement frameworks. These measurement approaches, involve customers in a continuous state of comparison between current product and service performance levels with prior expectations. The pre-consumption comparison standards (conceptualization of expectations), are principal components of these models. They, have received growing criticism. Various researchers proposed sets of alternative standards and drivers of satisfaction, including ideal performance levels, needs and wants congruency (Spreng et al. 1995) and consumption-related feelings and emotions (Oliver 1993). From a pragmatic standpoint, consumers follow different satisfaction processes when evaluating different kinds of products or services using various standards depending on factors related to levels of involvement or experience with the specific product or service (Churchill and Surprenant 1982). Prior research provides inadequate evidence concerning the usage of pre-purchase expectations in post-purchase evaluations. Some researchers argue that although expectations may help a consumer proceed with their purchasing decision. The impact on the post-purchase evaluation process, however, is unequivocal (Westbrook and Reilly 1983).

Overall satisfaction models assume information from all previous experiences with the service provider are taken into account. Overall satisfaction may be viewed as a function of all previous transactions – specific satisfactions (Parasuraman et al. 1994; Teas 1993). Overall satisfaction may be based on many transactions or just a few, depending on the number of times the consumer has used a particular provider. In essence, overall satisfaction is an aggregation of all previous transactions – specific evaluations and is updated after each specific transaction much like expectations of overall service quality are updated after each transaction (Boulding et al. 1993).

Memory selectivity may also play a key role. Customers may remember the 'good experiences' and omit average or slightly unsavoury memories. The effect of time on perceptions should not be underestimated. Cognitive dissonance mechanisms may be evident.

In general, transaction-specific satisfaction may not be perfectly correlated with overall satisfaction since service quality is likely to vary from experience to experience, causing varying levels of transaction-specific satisfaction. Overall satisfaction, on the other hand, can be viewed as a moving average that is relatively stable and more similar to an overall attitude (Parasuraman et al. 1994). For example, a consumer may have a dissatisfying experience because of lost baggage on a single airline flight (low transaction-specific satisfaction) yet still be satisfied with the airline (overall satisfaction) due to multiple previous satisfactory encounters.

Previous research has tended to measure satisfaction either on a transaction-specific level (Bitner 1990; Oliver and Swan 1989) or on an overall level (Anderson and Fornell 1994; Cronin and Taylor 1992) , though not both ways together. Thus it remains unclear whether the two types of satisfaction can be empirically distinguished from one another when measured at the same time using the same scale. Furthermore, previous research provides little empirical support concerning which type of satisfaction is a better predictor of future intentions.

Service Recovery

Over the years, service recovery has been defined as the actions a service provider takes in response to service failure (Gronroos 1982) and the attempt by an organization to offset the negative impact of a failure or breakdown putting the situation right (Zemke and Schaaf 1990; Berry and Parasuraman 1991). More recently, Johnston (1995a) defined service recovery as the actions of a service provider to mitigate and/or repair the damage to a customer's perception resulting from the provider's failure to deliver a service as designed.

Although the importance of implementing service recovery strategies has been widely acknowledged in the literature, there is little evidence of such practice. Armistead and Clark (1994) found that the potential of using service recovery techniques in order to win and keep customers had been overlooked. Instead, in the case of service failure companies come out with promises that the system has been changed for the future (Armistead and Clark 1994) These types of exhortation tend to leave customers with mixed feelings concerning the company's service provision and negatively colours expectations (Johnston 1995a). It is this disconfirmation of customers' prior expectations, caused by service failures affecting levels of customer satisfaction (Berry and Parasuraman 1991), that leads to customer defection (Reichheld 1996a, 1996b) and negative word-of-mouth messages. Such actions can escalate to threaten the long-term survival of firms; especially those that depend heavily on services' provision (Boshoff 1999).

Despite the fact that few companies have clear recovery strategies ready to be implemented in the service-failure scenario (Bitner et al. 1994), it has been empirically proved that it is possible for dissatisfied customers to return to a state of satisfaction after effective failure responses Such actions can affect both the degree of exhibited loyalty (Brown et al. 1996; Boshoff 1997; Boshoff and Leong 1998) and improve the service quality (Berry and Parasuraman 1991; Bailey 1994). Successful recovery policies can lead to loyal customers and transform them into advocates for the firm. They may, if situation arises, promote positive service by word-of-mouth because the experience was outstanding (Barlow and Moller 1996). In the same context, McCollough and Bharadwaj (1992) introduced the term 'recovery paradox', referring to the way in which recovered customers show greater levels of satisfaction and re-purchase intention compared to customers who have not experienced failure episodes.

Firms respond by implementing different service recovery strategies when they find to complaints, failures or dissatisfied customers (Grönroos 1988). Such strategies include:

* an apology acknowledging the occurrence of a failure;
* assistance and explanation of the different reasons that resulted in the failure;
* radical reviews of training, quality control, performance measures, learning mechanisms; induction procedures, cultural values, outsourcing and staffing;
* compensation in non-monetary forms; and
* compensation in terms of monetary reimbursements and vouchers.

Flying on business, one of the editors of this volume paid to be upgraded from Coach to Business Class. Within minutes, the airline officials were asking if he would mind being downgraded to Coach Class. Objecting, he was the last one to board the plane. To his surprise, he had been further upgraded to Upper Class on the Virgin Atlantic flight to Tokyo. Upper Class toilets are exclusively for them: Business Class travellers share with economy. Taking Business Class back to London, he decided would be prepared to travel with this company again provided long-haul flights of more than six hours were in Business Class.

Budget can cancel early flights at short notice in order to delay passengers to a later departure. Their key performance indicator is yield – the percentage of seats occupied. They will cancel one of two flights to the same destination in order to increase yield and hence not incur landing charges for planes that aren't carrying many passengers. Scheduled national carrier airlines typically overbook internal flights. If passengers don't turn up, they can hop onto the next flight or travel via another hub to their destination. Passengers whose ultimate destination is the airport where they will touch down are invited to step forward and are induced to take latter departures with extra air miles and vouchers to spend when booking further flights. Passengers with onward flight connections are not invited to step forward. Although the flights may be reserved as full, some passengers wait on standby, hoping to get a ticket.

One of the editors of this volume reported that in late December 2007, Speed Ferries 'Speed One' was crossing between Boulogne-sur-Mer in Northern France and the port of Dover in heavy seas. The boat lurched and the force cracked the aluminium hull. Passengers booked on the boat were informed via email addresses they had registered when they reserved their tickets that the boat was out of commission. Speed Ferries only has one boat and hence the company was running no services while the crack was being welded and patched. The company offered to offset the ticket price against another crossing in the next six months or reimburse the fare within two weeks.

Standing on the dock on a cold windy December day, the young staff put on a brave face and had an apologetic tone. Speed Ferries staff suggested passengers wait until the next day when services would be resumed, or book with a roll-on, roll-off ferry competitor in the next wharf (Dover) or the next town (Calais is about 30 minutes drive from their Boulogne jetty). The original crossing fare was €68, pre-booked several weeks in advance. The spot purchase price for immediate embarkation was £85 (approximately €126). The ability to get home on the same day and save parking meter and bed and breakfast costs was worth the extra cost. It saved a day and we could relax.

Speed Ferries phrase painted on the stern of their ship is 'fight the pirates'. They are deliberately cheaper than competitors crossing the English Channel. Having only one boat, the number of crossings per day is limited. The number of passengers on board is limited by the vehicles stored on the car deck. As a result they seldom have more than half the seats on board taken. Although the crossing is faster (50 minutes) than normal ferries (90 minutes), there are no hot cooked meals served on board.

Ticket availability, the price, showing children's television videos, having play areas and rapid crossing times are the key repeat purchase motivators. Speed Ferries had issued an email to all passengers. Not having gone online over the Christmas holidays in order to read emails, the cancellation had been unexpected. However, they are the cheapest operator. The town they leave from in France has excellent restaurants. Speed Ferries make a profit. Not liking profiteering or apparent price fixing by competitors, despite not knowing about this particular cancellation in advance, the editor involved will continue to book future crossings with this operator.

Elements that Can drive a Successful Recovery Programme

In their study in a retail context Kelley et al. (1993) found discounts, correction and management intervention in the recovery process to be particularly effective and that apologies and refunds have less significant impacts. Johnston's (1995b) study of different service industry settings identified empathy, information and action as three very important elements of successful service recovery. He states that staff involved in the service recovery episode need to show concern for the customer and points out the necessity for:

- solving problems with customers and suppliers participation;
- information provision concerning the problem that caused failure; and
- action from a dedicated team.

Whilst there is some uncertainty over precisely what are the elements that drive successful service recovery programmes, most research findings agree that an apology alone is relatively ineffective (Goodwin and Ross 1992). A simple notice that states 'broken, sorry for the delay' can be infuriating.

When booking airline tickets online, would-be passengers have to toggle a notice to confirm they have read the small print of the conditions and terms of travel. Turning up to an airport to book in a minor who is under a minimum age, who is also being accompanied by another minor and trying to book excessive baggage or prohibited items can mean the carrier turns the would-be traveller away because they are in breach of the conditions they had signed up to.

Loyalty

The importance of brand loyalty has been widely recognized in the marketing literature (Oliver 1999; Samuelsen and Sandvik 1997). Reichheld (1996a, 1996b) studied the economic impact of loyalty. Examples across 14 industries showed net profit increases about 5 per cent as a result of customer retention. Aaker (1991) discussed the role of loyalty in the brand equity process and specifically noted that brand loyalty reduced marketing costs. The relative costs of customer retention are substantially less than those needed to win new clients (Fornell and Wernerfelt 1987). Generating positive word-of-mouth and greater resistance to competitors' brands is important (Oliver 1999; Dick and Basu 1994).

Despite the clear managerial relevance of brand loyalty, conceptual and empirical issues remain unclear (Chaudhuri and Holbrook 2001; Lau and Lee 1999; Oliver 1999; Fournier and Yao 1997). More specifically, various definitions and measurement techniques exist in the literature. Early research efforts focused on behavioural aspects related to brand loyalty constructed as a subset of repeat purchasing and intention to re-purchase. Oliver (1999, p. 34) defines brand loyalty as: 'a deeply held commitment to re-buy or re-patronize a preferred product/service consistently in the future, thereby causing repetitive same-brand or same brand-set purchasing, despite situational influences and marketing efforts having the potential to cause switching behavior'. This definition emphasizes on behavioural and attitudinal aspects of brand loyalty (Aaker 1991; Assael 1998; Day 1969; Oliver 1999; Tucker 1964). Behavioural loyalty consists of motivated repeated purchasing of the brand. In particular cultures, repeat purchasing by contrast is based on obligation in Japan as a result of their *keiretsu* environment. In the West, repeat purchasing can be the result of preferring the familiar, comfortable and known. It's 'better the Devil you know than the Devil you don't'. Other contexts demand some affiliation to a legal (conformist), subversive or radical grouping.

Group identity can be created as a result of purchasing core goods and ancillary paraphernalia. Harley Davidson motorcycles are a core example. Harley makes more money out of selling franchised branded goods associated with the brand than they do from the motorcycle itself. Harley, in effect, sell the dream of a lifestyle; freedom from 'the rat race', independence and allegiance to a higher cause.

Attitudinal brand loyalty includes a degree of dispositional commitment in terms of some unique value associated with the brand. The attitude behind the purchase is important due to its power to drive behaviour. While brand-loyal behaviour is partly determined by situational factors (i.e., availability), attitudes are more enduring.

Academic research is continually engaged in refining various models of customer loyalty (Samuelson and Sandvik 1977; Oliver 1999) Much less attention has been paid to integrating loyalty into potential cause and effect relationships with other concepts of the marketing theory. The aim is to construct models that are tested empirically (Dick and Basu 1994; Oliver 1999). In an effort to understand loyalty, marketing theorists follow two directions:

1. The behavioural approach looks strictly at the repeated purchasing behaviour that may be somehow biased (Tucker 1964). The main measuring variables include items like proportion of purchase, sequence of purchase, and probability of purchase.
2. The stochastic approach of the measurement of loyalty is based on the customer's purchasing history. No cognitive elements were incorporated to explain the underlying buying motives in general and future actions in particular. No other loyal behavioural actions such as price tolerance, poor service experience tolerance, complaint reporting behaviour or word of mouth were integrated (Samuelson and Sandvik 1977).

Since there always are always customers who are forced to buy the same brand repeatedly or use the same distribution channel, Day (1969) argued that it is important to concentrate on the behavioural aspect of loyalty. An attitudinal perspective allows us to gain a better understanding of loyal behaviour. Investigating customer's mental, emotional and knowledge structures, which act as mediators between stimuli and responses, helps the firm to plan attempts to influence consumers' behaviour more effectively. Jacoby and Kyner (1973) advocated a six-point definition of brand loyalty, which they claimed to be attitudinally based. The study supported a multidimensional examination of the attitudinal dimension of loyalty similar to the recent three-dimensional loyalty concept proposed by de Ruyter, Wetzels, and Bloemer (1998) and Oliver (1999), which includes affective and cognitive aspects. These types of propositions also cover behavioural components.

The B2B Context

Over the past 15 years, a major shift has occurred in the ways industrial companies deal with their customers and suppliers (Christopher et al. 1991; Ellram 1995; Han et al. 1993; O'Neal 1989). Such changes have come about as companies recognize that sustainable competitive advantage in the global economy increasingly requires businesses to become trusted participants in various networks or sets of strategic alliances (Morgan and Hunt 1994; Ganesan 1994). Relationship marketing has emerged as an exciting area of marketing activity that focuses on building long-term relationships with customers and other parties. As Grönroos (1993) observed:

> ... establishing a relationship, for example with a customer, can be divided into two parts: to *attract* the customer and to *build the relationship* with that customer so that the economic goals of that relationship are achieved.

Customers expect performance, quality, low costs, reliable and accurate service, contemporary design and innovative solutions. They also seek to minimize negative interactions, reduce and manage conflict, raise harmony and satisfy needs with a minimum of 'fire fighting'. Suppliers are nominally the experts in what they do. Customers have needs and the purchasing power. Customers may know more about the product or service than do supplier personnel. If customers need responsiveness, a key determinant of successful repeat purchasing becomes how rigid and predetermined is the service or product offering from the supplier.

The fundamental principles upon which relationship marketing is based are mutual value creation, trust and commitment. The greater the level of customer satisfaction with the relationship (not just the product or service), the greater the likelihood that the customer will be loyal to the company providing that service or the product. The objective of relationship marketing is to achieve high levels of customer satisfaction through collaboration of the parties involved (Payne et al. 1995).

There is general agreement in the literature that the quality of the relationship between involved parties is an important determinant of the permanence and intensity of the relationship and the consequent success of relationship-marketing practices. Although academics recognize the importance of relationship-marketing practices (Berry 1995; Goff et al. 1997), there is little empirical evidence regarding the nature and extent of the impact of relationship-marketing *tactics* on relationship-quality outcomes (Gwinner et al. 1998).

Much of the literature on assessment of service quality has focused on end-consumers, rather than on business customers. There is a lack of compelling research into evaluative criteria and processes used by firms in forming service-quality perceptions (Parasuraman 1998). To date, in business-to-business contexts the term 'customer service' remains undefined and relatively unexplored. This lack of definition has produced unresolved issues with respect to understanding, modelling and measuring service-quality perceptions and their impact on business satisfaction and loyalty formation (Parasuraman 1998; Schellhase et al. 1999).

Relationship Quality

Drawing on the above literature review, 'relationship quality' can be seen as a relationship outcome and an overall means of assessing the strength of a relationship between two firms (Garbarino and Johnson 1999; Smith 1998). There is, as yet, no clear consensus in the literature on the set of dimensions that comprise the construct of 'relationship quality' (Dorsch et al. 1998; Kumar et al. 1995). The importance of *relationship satisfaction* and *trust* as indicators of the higher-order construct of relationship *quality* has been stressed by various authors (Crosby et al. 1990; Dwyer et al. 1987). Other researchers have added *relationship commitment* as a dimension of relationship quality (Hennig-Thurau and Klee 1997; Leuthesser 1997; Dorsch et al. 1998). In the same context, de Wulf, Schroder and Iacobucci (2001) assumed that better relationship quality is accompanied by greater satisfaction, trust, and commitment. Crosby, Evans and Cowles (1990) and de Wulf et al. (2001) point out that, although these three attitudinal dimensions are distinct and that consumers tend to 'lump' them together (Crosby ct al. 1990; de Wulf et al. 2001).

Relationship Satisfaction

One of the most critical elements in B2B markets, and particularly a service market such as the advertising industry, is the development of client relationships. The complexity of the products and services and the long-term nature of business relationships in the advertising industry mean that effective and satisfactory business relationships are of the greatest importance in the marketing of advertising services.

According to the principles of relationship marketing, successful business relationships enhance client satisfaction and thus enhance the performance of firms. In the past, relationship satisfaction has been proposed as a prerequisite for relationship quality. Crosby and Stevens (1987) identified three levels of relationship satisfaction: (i) interactions with personnel; (ii) core service; and (iii) the organization. In their study of insurance customers, Crosby and Stevens (1987) also found that all three levels contribute to overall satisfaction with the relationship. In a business context, relationship satisfaction has been defined as a positive affective state resulting from a firm's appraisal of all aspects of its working relationship with another firm (Anderson and Narus 1990; Ganesan 1994; Dwyer and Oh 1987; Dwyer et al. 1987).

Satisfaction with the relationship is important. Satisfaction *per se* does not automatically lead to re-purchase. Some studies have investigated the relationship between service quality and consumer satisfaction, although they have highlighted the antecedent role of consumer satisfaction in perceptions of service quality (Bolton and Drew 1991; Boulding et al. 1993). Most findings, however, support the opposite cause-and-effect relationship (Anderson et al. 1994; Cronin and Taylor 1992; Dick and Basu 1994). In contrast to a more rational outcome, de Wulf, Schroder and Iacobucci (2001) assert that relationship satisfaction can be conceptualized as an affective state (Smith and Barclay 1997). A number of studies posited relationship satisfaction as a cumulative affect developed over the course of a relationship, rather than as the outcome of a specific transaction (Anderson et al. 1997). Those studies use relationship satisfaction as an overall (global) relationship assessment in an effort to avoid overlaps between perceptions of service quality and relationships.

Commitment

Relationship commitment exists when a partner believes the relationship is important enough to warrant maximum efforts to maintain that relationship over the long-term.

Moorman, Zaltman and Deshpande (1992) defined relationship commitment as an enduring desire to maintain a valued relationship. Commitment is critically important as a basis of organizational buying behaviour and thus can lead to important outcomes such as decreased customer turnover (Porter et al. 1974) and higher motivation (Farrell and Rusbult 1981). Commitment is positively related to loyalty and repeat purchases. Because relationship performance is critical to re-purchase decisions in a relational exchange, business loyalty is similar to relationship commitment (Morgan and Hunt 1994). Anderson and Weitz (1992) asserted manufacturer–distributor commitment is necessary when they adopt a long-term orientation toward relationships. They proposed that mutual commitment results in 'channel members' working together to serve the needs of end-customers more effectively. Such synergy and symbiosis then increases mutual profitability beyond what either member could achieve by operating independently.

Trust

Ganesan (1994) found that long-term orientation is affected by the extent to which customers and vendors trust their 'channel partners'. Each partner's ability to provide positive outcomes to the other helps determine the amount of unilateral and bilateral commitment to the relationship. Trust is therefore a major determinant of relationship commitment (Morgan and Hunt, 1994), and exists when there is confidence in a partner's reliability and integrity.

Moorman et al. (1992) defined trust as a willingness to rely on an exchange partner in whom one has confidence. More specifically, Anderson and Narus (1990) defined trust in manufacturer–distributor relationships as a firm's belief that another company will perform actions that will result in positive outcomes and that the other company will not take unexpected actions that result in negative outcomes for the firm. This type of trust also can be present horizontally between cartel participants. Similarly, Ganesan (1994) proposed that a key component of trust is the extent to which the customer believes that the vendor has intentions and motives beneficial to the customer and is concerned with creating positive customer outcomes. In a business-to-business environment, suppliers can be assessed relating to how many improvement suggestions they make per year per employee. These suggestions can refer to internal activities, changes recommended to customers' activities and interactions. Suppliers are trusted, empowered and expected to make changes to improve their operational performance. They do not need to seek permission. If they wish to change the product or service, however, their ideas must be submitted and evaluated. Suppliers who are perceived as being concerned with positive customer outcomes will therefore be trusted to a greater extent than suppliers who appear interested only in their own welfare. Part of the trust relates to the ability of a company to respond to the emerging needs of the customer and the market. If the supplier is customer-oriented, they will probably streamline their activities and only undertake value-adding activities. They also are likely to avoid unresponsive burdens, organizational infighting and optimizing stand-alone processes at the expense of overall efficiency and effectiveness.

Suppliers equally must trust their customer to tell the truth, be accurate relating to their requirements, pay promptly for goods and services provided and keep suppliers informed of future plans. Suppliers' trust in customers can be increased if customers issue a decree that they intend to work with suppliers over extended periods of time, and not switch to lower price suppliers. Customers commit to spending a certain amount of money with a supplier. This enables suppliers to invest in plant and facilities on the understanding they will not lose the contract providing they contribute to improving quality, reducing costs, making delivery more reliable, help design products and services and want to work together to manage a better and mutually profitable future.

Morgan and Hunt (1994) summarize these concepts. Commitment and trust together encourage marketers to: (i) work towards preserving relationship investments by cooperating with exchange partners; (ii) resist attractive short-term alternatives in favour of the long-term expected benefits of staying with existing partners; and (iii) view potentially high-risk actions more favourably because they believe that their partners will not act opportunistically.

Conclusions

The central purpose of this chapter has been to explore the theoretical grounds of the core concepts of services marketing. The literature pertaining to service quality, customer satisfaction and service recovery have been presented, together with findings indicating their antecedent role on business loyalty.

This chapter focused on the business-to-business context and explored the relational variables that play a critical strategic role in the effort of modern enterprises to improve their service offering into today's highly competitive business environments. Research in this field is attempting to clarify and model the outstanding issues.

References

Aaker, D.A. (1991), *Managing Brand Equity* (New York: The Free Press).

Anderson, E. and Weitz, B. (1992), 'The Use of Pledges to Build and Sustain Commitment in Distribution Channels', *Journal of Marketing Research* 29 (February), pp. 18–34.

Anderson, E.W. and Fornell, C. (1994), 'Customer Satisfaction Prospectus', in Rust, R.T. and Oliver, R.L. (eds) *Service Quality: New Directions in Theory and Practice* (Thousand Oaks, CA: Sage), pp. 241–68.

Anderson, E.W., Fornell, C. and Lehmann, D.R. (1994), 'Customer Satisfaction, Market Share, and Profitability', *Journal of Marketing* 58, pp. 53–66.

Anderson, E.W., Fornell, C. and Rust, R.T. (1997), 'Customer Satisfaction, Productivity, and Profitability: Differences between Goods and Services', *Marketing Science* 16(2), pp. 129–45.

Anderson, J.C. and Narus, J.A. (1990), 'A Model of Distributor Firm and Manufacturer Firm Working Partnerships', *Journal of Marketing* 54 (January), pp. 42–58.

Assael, H. (1998), *Consumer Behaviour and Marketing Action* (Cincinnati, OH: South-Western).

Babakus, E. and Boller, G.W. (1992), 'An Empirical Assessment of the SERVQUAL Scale', *Journal of Business Research* 24(3), pp. 253–68.

Babin, B.J. and Griffin, M. (1998), 'The Nature of Satisfaction: An Updated Examination and Analysis', *Journal of Business Research* (41), pp. 127–36.

Bailey, D. (1994), 'Recovery from Customer Service Shortfalls', *Managing Service Quality* 4(6), pp. 25–8.

Barlow, J. and Moller, C. (1996), *A Complaint is a Gift* (San Francisco, CA: Berrett-Koehler).

Berry, L.L. (1995), *On Great Service – A Framework for Action* (New York: Free Press).

Berry, L.L. and Parasuraman, A. (1991), *Marketing Services: Competing Through Quality* (New York: Free Press).

Bitner M.J. (1990), 'Evaluating Service Encounters: The Effects of Physical Surrounding and Employee Responses', *Journal of Marketing* 54, pp. 69–82.

Bitner, M.J., Booms, B.H. and Mohr, L.A. (1994), 'Critical Service Encounters: The Employee's Viewpoint', *Journal of Marketing* 58 (October), pp. 95–106.

Bitner, M.J., Booms, B.H. and Tetreault, M.S. (1990), 'The Service Encounter: Diagnosing Favourable and Unfavourable Incidents', *Journal of Marketing* 54(1), pp. 71–84.

Bolton, R.N. and Drew, H.J. (1991), 'A Multistage Model of Customers' Assessments of Service Quality and Value', *Journal of Consumer Research* 17, pp. 375–84.

Bolton, R.N. and Drew, J.H. (1994), 'Linking Customer Satisfaction to Service Operations and Outcomes', in Rust, R.T. and Oliver, R.L. (eds) *Service Quality: New Directions in Theory and Practice* (Thousand Oaks, CA: Sage), pp. 173–200.

Boshoff, C.R. (1997), 'An Experimental Study of Service Recovery Options', *International Journal of Service Industry Management* 8(2), pp. 110–30.

Boshoff, C.R. (1999), 'RECOVSAT: An Instrument to Measure Satisfaction With Transaction-Specific Service Recovery', *Journal of Service Research* 1(3), pp. 236–49.

Boshoff, C. and Leong, J. (1998), 'Empowerment, Attribution and Apologising as Dimensions of Service Recovery: An Experimental Study', *International Journal of Service Industry Management* 9(1), pp. 24–47.

Boulding, W., Kalra, A., Staelin, R. and Zeithaml, V.A. (1993), 'A Dynamic Process Model of Service Quality: From Expectations to Behavioural Intentions', *Journal of Marketing Research* 30 (February), pp. 7–27.

Brady, M.K. and Cronin, J.J. Jr (2001), 'Some New Thoughts on Conceptualizing Perceived Service Quality: A Hierarchical Approach', *Journal of Marketing* 65, pp. 34–49.

Brown, S.W., Cowles, D.L. and Tuten, T. (1996), 'Service Recovery, its Value and Limitations as a Retail Strategy', *International Journal of Service Industry Management* 7(5), pp. 32–46.

Brown, T.J., Churchill, G.A. Jr and Peter, J.P. (1993), 'Improving the Measurement of Service Quality', *Journal of Retailing* 69(1), pp. 127–39.

Burton, S., Lichtenstein, D.R., Netemeyer, R.G. and Garretson, J.A. (1998), 'A Scale for Measuring Attitude toward Private Label Products and an Examination of its Psychological and Behavioural Correlates', *Journal of the Academy of Marketing Science* 26(4), pp. 293–306.

Carhuana, A., Erwing, M.T. and Ramaseshan, B. (2000), 'Assessment of the Three-column Format SERVQUAL: An Experimental Approach', *Journal of Business Research* 49(1), pp. 57–65.

Chaudhuri, A. and Holbrook, M.B. (2001), 'The Chain of Effects from Brand Trust and Brand Affect to Brand Performance: The Role of Brand Loyalty', *Journal of Marketing* 65 (April), pp. 81–93.

Christopher, M., Payne, A. and Ballantyne, M. (1991), *Relationship Marketing* (London: Heinemann).

Churchill, G.A. and Surprenant, C. (1982), 'An Investigation into the Determinants of Customer Satisfaction', *Journal of Marketing Research* 19(4), pp. 491–504.

Cronin, J.J. Jr and Taylor, S.A. (1992), 'Measuring Service Quality: A Re-examination and Extension', *Journal of Marketing* 56, pp. 55–68.

Crosby, L.A. and Stevens, N. (1987, 'Effects of Relationship Marketing on Relationship Satisfaction, Retention and Prices in the Life Insurance Industry', *Journal of Marketing Research* 24 (November), pp. 404–11.

Crosby, L.A., Evans, K.R. and Cowles, D. (1990), 'Relationship Quality in Services Selling: An Interpersonal Influence Perspective', *Journal of Marketing* 54(3), pp. 68–81.

Day, G.S. (1969), 'A Two-dimensional Concept of Brand Loyalty', *Journal of Advertising Research* 9(3), pp. 29–35.

De Ruyter, K., Wetzels, M. and Bloemer, J. (1998), 'On the Relationship between Perceived Service Quality, Service Loyalty and Switching Costs', *International Journal of Service Industry Management* 9(5), pp. 436–53.

De Wulf, K., Schroder, O.G. and Iacobucci, D. (2001), 'Investments in Consumer Relationships: A Cross-country and Cross-industry Exploration', *Journal of Marketing* 65, pp. 33–50.

Dick, A.S. and Basu, K. (1994), 'Customer Loyalty: Toward and Integrated Conceptual Framework', *Journal of the Academy of Marketing Science* 22(2), pp. 99–113.

Dorsch, M.J., Swanson, S.R. and Kelley, S.W. (1998), 'The Role of Relationship Quality in the Stratification of Vendors as Perceived by Customers', *Journal of the Academy of Marketing Science* 26(2), pp. 128–42.

Dwyer, F.R., Schurr, P.H. and Oh, S. (1987), 'Developing Buyer–Seller Relationships', *Journal of Marketing* 51, pp. 11–27.

Ellram, L.M. (1995), 'Partnering Pitfalls and Success Factors', *International Journal of Purchasing and Materials Management* 31, pp. 17–23.

Farrell, D. and Rusbult, C.E. (1981), 'Exchange Variables as Predictors of Job Satisfaction, Job Commitment, and Turnover: The Impact of Rewards, Costs, Alternatives, and Investments', *Organisational Behaviour and Human Decision Processes* 28(1), pp. 78–95.

Fornell, C. (1992), 'A National Satisfaction Barometer: The Swedish Experience', *Journal of Marketing* 56(1), pp. 1–21.

Fornell, C. and Wernerfelt, B. (1987), 'Defensive Marketing Strategy by Customer Complaint Management: A Theoretical Analysis', *Journal of Marketing Research* (24), pp. 337–46.

Fornell, C. and Wernerfelt, B. (1988), 'A Model for Customer Complaint Management', *Marketing Science* 7 (Summer), pp. 271–86.

Fournier, S. and Yao, J.L. (1997), 'Reviving Brand Loyalty: A Conceptualisation within the Framework of Consumer-brand Relationships', *International Journal of Research in Marketing* (14), pp. 451–72.

Ganesan, S. (1994), 'Determinants of Long-Term Orientation in Buyer–Seller Relationships', *Journal of Marketing* 58 (April), pp. 1–19.

Garbarino, E. and Johnson, M.S. (1999), 'The Different Roles of Satisfaction, Trust and Commitment in Customer Relationships', *Journal of Marketing* 63, pp. 70–87.

Geletkanycz, M.A. (1997), 'The Salience of Culture's Consequences: The Effects of Cultural Values on Top Executive Commitment to the Status Quo', *Strategic Management Journal* 18, pp. 615–34.

Goff, B.G., Boles, J.S., Bellenger, D.N. and Stojact, C. (1997), 'The Influence of Salesperson Selling Behaviors on Customer Satisfaction with Products', *Journal of Retailing* 73(2), pp. 171–83.

Goodwin, C. and Ross, I. (1992), 'Consumer Responses to Service Failures: Influence of Procedural and Interactional Fairness Perceptions', *Journal of Business Research* (25), pp. 149–63.

Griffiths, A. (2000), 'The Structure of all Industry and Services' in Blois, K. (ed.) *The Oxford Textbook of Marketing* (Oxford: Oxford University Press), pp. 69–102.

Grönroos, C. (1982), *Strategic Management and Marketing in the Service Sector* (Helsinki: Swedish School of Economics and Business Administration).

Grönroos, C. (1984), 'A Service Quality Model and its Marketing Implications', *European Journal of Marketing* 18, pp. 36–44.

Grönroos, C. (1993), 'Toward a Third Phase in Service Quality Research', in Swartz, T.A., Bowen, D.A. and Brown, S.W. (eds) *Advanced in Service Marketing and Management Volume 2* (Greenwich, CT: JAI Press), pp. 49–64.

Gronroos, C. (1994), 'Quo Vadis, Marketing? Towards a Relationship Marketing Paradigm', *Journal of Marketing Management* 10(4), pp. 347–60.

Gwinner, K.P., Gremler, D.D. and Bitner, M.J. (1998), 'Relational Benefits in Services Industries: The Customer's Perspective', *Journal of the Academy of Marketing Science* 26(2), pp. 101–14.

Han, S.L., Wilson, D.T. and Dant, S.P. (1993), 'Buyer–Supplier Relationships Today', *Industrial Marketing Management* 22, pp. 331–8.

Hennig, T.T. and Klee, A. (1997), 'The Impact of Customer Satisfaction and Relationship Quality on Customer Retention: A Critical Reassessment and Model Development', *Psychology & Marketing* 14(8), pp. 737–64.

Johnston, R. (1995), 'Service Failure and Recovery: Impact, Attributes and Process', *Advances in Services Marketing and Management: Research and Practice* 4, pp. 211–28.

Johnston, R. (1995), 'The Determinants of Service Quality: Satisfiers and Dissatisfiers', *International Journal of Service Industry Management* 6(5), pp. 53–71.

Kelley, S.W., Hoffman, K.D. and Davis, M.A. (1993), 'A Typology of Retail Failures and Recoveries', *Journal of Retailing* 69(4), pp. 429–52.

Kumar, N., Scheer, L.K. and Steenkamp, E.M. (1995), 'The Effects of Supplier Fairness on Vulnerable Sellers', *Journal of Marketing Research* 32(1), pp. 54–65.

LaBarbera, P.A. and Mazursky, D. (1983), 'A Longitudinal Assessment of Customer Satisfaction/Dissatisfaction: The Dynamic Aspect of the Cognitive Process', *Journal of Marketing Research* 20 (November), pp. 393–404.

Lapierre, J., Filiatrault, P. and Pierrien, J. (1996), 'Research on Service Quality Evaluation: Evolution and Methodological Issues', *Journal of Retailing of Consumer Services* 2, pp. 91–8.

Lau, G.T. and Lee, S.H. (1999), 'Consumers' Trust in a Brand and the Link to Brand', *Journal of Market Focused Management* (4), pp. 341–70.

Leuthesser, L. (1997), 'Supplier Relational Behaviour: An Empirical Assessment', *Industrial Marketing Management* 26(3), pp. 245–54.

McCollough, M.A. and Bharadwaj, S.G. (1992), 'The Recovery Paradox: An Examination of Customer Satisfaction in Relation to Disconfirmation, Service Quality, and Attribution-based Theories', in Allen, C.T. (ed.) *Marketing Theory and Applications* (Chicago, IL: American Marketing Association).

Moorman, C., Zaltman, G. and Deshpande, R. (1992), 'Relationships between Providers and Users of Market Research: The Dynamics of Trust Within and Between Organisations', *Journal of Marketing Research* 29 (August), pp. 314–28.

Morgan, R.M. and Hunt, S.D. (1994), 'The Commitment–Trust Theory of Relationship Marketing', *Journal of Marketing* 58 (July), pp. 20–38.

O'Neal, C.R. (1989), 'JIT Procurement and Relationship Marketing', *Industrial Marketing Management* 18, pp. 55–64.

Oliver, R.L. (1980), 'A Cognitive Model of the Antecedents and Consequences of Satisfaction Decisions', *Journal of Marketing Research* 17 (November), pp. 460–69.

Oliver, R.L. (1981), 'Measurement and Evaluation of Satisfaction Process in Retail Stores', *Journal of Retailing* 57(3), pp. 25–48.

Oliver, R.L. (1993), 'Cognitive, Affective, and Attribute bases of the Satisfaction Response', *Journal of Consumer Research* 20, pp. 418–30.

Oliver, R.L. (1997), *Satisfaction: On a Behavioral Perspective on the Consumer* (New York: McGraw-Hill).

Oliver, R.L. (1999), 'Whence Consumer Loyalty?', *Journal of Marketing* 63 (Special Issue), pp. 33–44.

Oliver, R.L. and Swan, J.E. (1989), 'Consumer Perceptions of Interpersonal Equity and Satisfaction in Transactions: A Field Survey Approach', *Journal of Marketing* 53(2), pp. 21–35.

Parasuraman, A. (1998), 'Customer Service in Business-to-Business Markets: An Agenda for Research', *Journal of Business and Industrial Marketing* 13(4/5), pp. 309–21.

Parasuraman, A., Berry, L.L. and Zeithaml, V.A. (1991), 'Refinement and Reassessment of the SERVQUAL Scale', *Journal of Retailing* 67, pp. 420–50.

Parasuraman, A., Zeithaml, V.A. and Berry, L.L. (1985), 'A Conceptual Model of Service Quality and its Implications for Future Research', *Journal of Marketing* 49(4), pp. 41–50.

Parasuraman, A., Zeithaml, V.A. and Berry, L.L. (1988), 'SERVQUAL: A Multiple-item Scale for Measuring Consumer Perceptions of Service Quality', *Journal of Retailing* 64(1), pp. 12–40.

Parasuraman, A., Zeithaml, V.A. and Berry, L.L. (1994), 'Reassessment of Expectations as a Comparison Standard in Measuring Service Quality: Implications for Further Research', *Journal of Marketing* 58(1), pp. 111–24.

Payne, A., Christopher, M., Clark, M. and Peck, H. (1995), *Relationship Marketing for Competitive Advantage* (Oxford: Butterworth-Heinernann).

Porter, L.W., Steers, R.M., Mowday, R.T. and Boulian, P.V. (1974), 'Organisational Commitment, Job Satisfaction and Turnover among Psychiatric Technicians', *Journal of Applied Psychology* 59(5), pp. 603–10.

Reichheld, F.F. (1996), 'Learning from Customer Defections', *Harvard Business Review* March–April, pp. 56–69.

Reichheld, F.F. (1996), *The Loyalty Effect* (Cambridge, MA: Harvard Business School Press.

Reichheld, F. F. and Sasser, W.E. (1990), 'Zero Defections: Quality Comes to Services', *Harvard Business Review* September–October, pp. 105–11.

Rust, R.T. and Oliver, R.L. (1994), 'Service Quality: Insights and Managerial Implications from the Frontier', in Rust, R.T. and Oliver, R.L. (eds) *Service Quality: New Directions in Theory and Practice* (Thousand Oaks, CA: Sage), pp. 1–19.

Rust, R.T. and Oliver, R.L. (2000), 'Should We Delight the Customer?', *Journal of the Academy of Marketing Science* 28(1), pp. 86–94.

Rust, R.T. and Zahorik, A.J. (1993), 'Customer Satisfaction, Customer Retention, and Market Share', *Journal of Retailing* 69(2), pp. 193–215.

Samuelson, B.M. and Sandvik, K. (1997), 'The Concept of Customer Loyalty', in Arnott, D., Bridgewater, S., Dibb, S., Doyle, P., Freeman, J., Melewar, T., Shaw, V., Simkin, L., Stern,

P., Wensley, R. and Wong, V. (eds) *Marketing: Progress, Prospects, Perspectives* (3). *EMAC Proceedings* (Warwick: Warwick Business School), pp. 1122–40.

Shellhase, R., Hardock, P. and Ohlwein, M. (1999), 'Customer Satisfaction in Business-to-Business Marketing: The Case of Retail Organizations and their Suppliers', *Journal of Business and Industrial Marketing* 14(5/6), pp. 416–32.

Smith, A.M. (1999), 'Some Problems when Adopting Churchill's Paradigm for the Development of Service Quality Measurement Scales', *Journal of Business Research* 46, pp. 109–20.

Smith, J.B. (1998), 'Buyer–Seller Relationships: Bonds, Relationship Management, and Sex-Type', *Canadian Journal of Administrative Sciences* 15(1), pp. 76–92.

Smith, J.B. and Barclay, D.W. (1997), 'The Effects of Organisational Differences and Trust on the Effectiveness of Selling Partner Relationships', *Journal of Marketing* 61(1), pp. 3–21.

Spreng, R.A., Harrell, G.D. and Mackoy, R.D. (1995), 'Service Recovery: Impact on Satisfaction and Intentions', *Journal of Services Marketing* 9(1), pp. 15–23.

Teas, R.K. (1993), 'Expectations, Performance Evaluation, and Consumer's Perceptions of Quality', *Journal of Marketing* 57(4), pp. 18–34.

Tucker, W.T. (1964), 'The Development of Brand Loyalty', *Journal of Marketing Research* 1 (August), pp. 32–5.

Walker, J.L. (1995), 'Service Encounter Satisfaction: Conceptualised', *Journal of Services Marketing* 9(1), pp. 5–14.

Westbrook, R.A. and Reilly, M.D. (1983), 'Value-percept Disparity: An Alternative to the Disconfirmation of Expectations Theory of Customer Satisfaction', in Bogozzi, P.R. and Tybouts, A. (eds) *Advances in Consumer Research, Volume 10* (Ann Arbor, MI: Association for Consumer Research), pp. 256–71.

Zeithaml V.A. (1988), 'Consumer Perceptions of Price, Quality, and Value: A Means-end Model and Synthesis of Evidence', *Journal of Marketing* 52(3), pp. 2–22.

Zeithaml, V.A. (2000), 'Service Quality, Profitability, and the Economic Worth of Customers: What We Know and What We Need to Learn', *Journal of the Academy of Marketing Science* 28(1), pp. 67–85.

Zemke, R. and Schaaf, R. (1990), *The Service Edge: 101 Companies that Profit from Customer Care* (New York: Plume Books).

Zins, A.H. (2001), 'Relative Attitudes and Commitment in Customer Loyalty Models. Some Experiences in the Commercial Airline Industry', *International Journal of Service and Industry Management* 12(3), pp. 269–94.

DIMENSION 6
Cost Management

Chapter 20
Strategic Cost Management

Roby B. Sawyers

Introduction

This chapter examines how companies use cost management methods and practices to help them reach their strategic goals and objectives. The chapter begins with a discussion of how companies create a competitive advantage using cost leadership, differentiation and focusing strategies. After discussing the unique sources of competitive advantage available to international/global companies, the chapter explains how companies can use value chain analysis and exploit internal and external linkages in order to reduce costs and strengthen a firm's competitive position. An in-depth review is made of how companies take advantage of external linkages using supply chain management and customer relationship management. The chapter discusses the concept of activity-based management (ABM) and how ABM is used by companies to help identify and eliminate non-value-added costs. The balanced scorecard is set in context to help focus management's attention on the company's long-term strategy. The chapter discusses managing and controlling quality costs and concludes with a discussion of target costing.

Companies have long been interested in managing (reducing) costs. However, rapid advances in information technology, improvements in manufacturing processes, an increased emphasis on both financial and non-financial measures of performance and the rise of global competition have made it both possible and necessary for companies to strategically manage costs. Put simply, strategic management is the process of formulating and implementing an organization's strategy. Strategic cost management is the process of using cost management methods and practices to help companies reach their strategic goals and objectives.

As more and more companies expand their operations into multiple countries, strategic cost management takes on even greater importance and provides a way for companies to coordinate their diverse operations, align their operations in different countries to their overall mission and successfully compete for customers in a global marketplace.

Strategy

Strategy refers to the policies, procedures and approaches to business that relate to the long-term success of a business. Strategy starts with an organization's mission or guiding principles. These are often very broad. For example, Toyota Motor Corp's seven guiding principles include 'dedicating ourselves to providing clean and safe products and to enhancing the quality of life everywhere through all our activities', 'creating and developing advanced technologies and providing outstanding products and services that fulfil the needs of customers worldwide', and 'working with business partners in research and creation to achieve stable, long-term growth and mutual benefits, while keeping ourselves open to new partnerships'.[1]

---

1   http://www.toyota.co.jp/en/vision/philosophy/.

Creating a Competitive Advantage

In competitive business environments, companies must make fundamental decisions with respect to how they position their products or services in the marketplace to ensure their long-term survival and growth. A key to achieving these aims is to gain competitive advantage. Historically, three general strategies for obtaining a competitive advantage have been identified:

1. cost leadership;
2. differentiation of products and services;
3. focusing on identifying market niches.

A company pursues a cost leadership strategy when its goal is to provide the same or better value to customers at a lower cost than its competitors. Cost leadership frequently results from productivity increases and the aggressive pursuit of cost reduction throughout the development, production, marketing and distribution process. Achieving cost leadership allows a company to earn higher profits than its competitors while selling products and services at the same, higher or lower prices. As a result, cost leadership is often accompanied by a large market share. Examples or companies that follow a cost leadership strategy include US companies Ford, Wal-Mart and Dell Computer, Ryanair in Ireland and the German discount retailer Aldi.

A product differentiation strategy focuses on distinguishing a product or service from those of its competitors. Product differentiation can result from unique design features, technological leadership, unique uses of products and attributes like quality, environmental impact and customer service. The combination of features and attributes are often described as a product's functionality. In the US, Apple Computer's focus on unique features and user friendliness is an example of a product differentiation strategy.

A focusing strategy involves selecting or emphasizing a market or customer segment in which to compete. Companies adopting a focusing strategy may choose only to compete in a certain geographic area or may target a product or service to a particular group based on age, gender, or income level. This strategy takes into consideration that some segments and some customers are more profitable than others.

In practice, many companies use a combination of strategies to create a competitive advantage and must compete on the basis of both cost and functionality. Strategic positioning is the process of selecting the optimal mix of these three general strategic approaches.

In '*Global Strategy: An Organizing Framework*' (1987), Ghoshal expands on these basic strategies and provides a framework for understanding the unique sources of competitive advantage available to international/global firms. These sources are:

*   national differences;
*   scale economies; and
*   scope economies.

National differences in such things as labour prices, the availability and proximity to raw materials, the availability of trained workers and the overall business climate in a country including the availability of tax incentives and other financial incentives allow companies to locate research, manufacturing or customer service functions in a country with a comparative advantage in providing the necessary inputs. Many US companies including most accountancy practices, Microsoft, HSBC, and Dell Computer operate customer service and product creation centres in India due to the availability of low-priced and highly skilled labour. For similar reasons, labour intensive production facilities for many US companies are located in Mexico where workforce hourly pay is cheaper than in the US.

Scale economies provide cost saving benefits and improved quality through the mass production of large volumes of product that result in the efficient use of equipment and other resources and lower costs.

In an international setting, economies of scale can be combined with national differences when manufacturing plants are designed to produce a component used in the final assembly of a product and that plant is then located in a country in order to take advantage of national differences in input costs.

On the other hand, scope economies come about when multiple products share equipment, production facilities, labour or other inputs. Companies with flexible manufacturing plants can make multiple products using the same equipment. When combined with just-in-time manufacturing techniques and computer aided design and manufacturing (CAD/CAM), this enables companies to compete using a product differentiation strategy based on product customization and short turn-around time. Global companies often enjoy scope economies as a result of manufacturing multiple products in a single plant and then marketing those products using shared resources. Further details relating to these arguments advocating lean supply are presented in 'Supply Chain Management', Chapter 8 by Macbeth and 'Supplier Development', Chapter 28 by Newlands. This volume suggests organizations should use this strategy for single variants or move away from this strategy for diverse product variants.

Nissan, Toyota and Honda utilize flexible assembly plants to make a large portion of their vehicles manufactured in North America. In contrast, only 32% of North American vehicles produced by DaimlerChrysler were made on flexible assembly lines in 2005. However, that is about to change as Chrysler has announced plans to retool two of its plants to make multiple car models. Savings come from standardizing the production process and more fully utilizing plant capacity. ('Chrysler Gains Edge by Giving New Flexibility to Its Factories', *Wall Street Journal*, 11 April 2006)

The choice of strategy is influenced by context. Ketels (n.d.) argues that in Europe the heterogeneous business environment faced by European companies doing business across the EU can serve as a source of competitive strength. While heterogeneity of the European market may make realizing economies of scale more difficult and may raise the costs of doing business, it may also lead to European companies developing more business specific strategies that are based on occupying defined market niches.

The Value Chain

Long-term success through the attainment of a competitive advantage requires managers understand an organization's value chain. As shown in Figure 20.1, the value chain is the set of activities that increase the value of an organization's products and services.

The value chain is based on activities performed within and outside an organization. They include activities such as research and development, product development, the acquisition of raw materials, production, marketing and distribution, and customer service (including post-sale customer service and the ultimate disposal of the product by customers). Companies typically

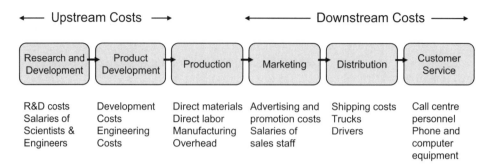

Figure 20.1   The value chain

are involved in only some parts of the value chain. The choice is a strategic decision that involves an analysis of the competition and whether the company can create a competitive advantage. Sometimes, companies that compete directly in the marketplace may be involved in different aspects of the same value chain. For example, Reebok and Nike compete directly in the highly competitive market for sports shoes. However, while Reebok designs and manufactures its shoes, Nike focuses on design and marketing elements of the value chain and leaves the actual manufacturing element of the value chain to other companies.

> In the aluminium industry, Norsk Hydro, a Norwegian company and Alcan, a Canadian company made very different strategic choices in the mid 1990s. While Alcan focused on one aspect of the value-chain (production) and chose to be a low-cost provider, Norsk Hydro used a combination of a differentiation/focusing strategy in which it targeted car manufacturers with an integrated, technologically advanced product. (Ketels n.d.)

Life-cycle Costs and the Value Chain

When deciding to compete based on a cost leadership strategy, it is important for companies to consider costs incurred throughout an organization's value chain. Life-cycle cost management emphasizes cost reduction throughout the value chain. Rather than focus simply on reducing the costs of manufacturing a product, life-cycle cost management focuses on reducing costs during research and development, product design and other pre-production activities as well as reducing post-sale costs related to providing repair services, warranties, etc. This is critical as a majority of a product's total costs are often incurred in pre-production activities.

Value-chain Analysis

Value-chain analysis requires an understanding of the differences between a company's structural, organizational and operational activities and the complex linkages and interrelationships among activities both within and external to an organization.

   Structural activities involve the fundamental decisions concerning a company related to the basic size and scope of its operations. For a manufacturing company, structural activities include such decisions as where to locate a factory and what types of technologies will be used to make products. Structural activities directly impact costs incurred by companies in the supply chain and affect the efficiency of organizational activities. Organizational activities are more detailed and include decisions related to how a company is organized and which suppliers are used. Operational activities involve the day-to-day activities undertaken as a product is manufactured or a service is provided and include processing customer orders, purchasing, receiving and inspecting parts or raw materials, moving materials, setting up equipment and manufacturing and assembly of products as well as packing and shipping products.

Internal linkages are relationships among activities that are performed within a firm's portion of the value chain. External linkages are relationships between a company's own value-chain activities and those of its suppliers and customers. In order to maintain a competitive advantage, an organization must be able to understand the relationship between these internal and external linkages and the costs that the company incurs and must take advantage of opportunities to exploit internal and external linkages in furthering the organization's strategy and maintaining a competitive advantage. Value-chain analysis involves identifying and taking advantage of internal and external linkages with the objective of strengthening a firm's strategic position.

Taking advantage of internal linkages often involves the redesign of products. For example, a company might identify the number of parts handled as a cost driver for several operational activities including material handling, receiving and inspecting, moving materials and assembly. In this case, redesigning the product using fewer parts and components that are used in other products can substantially reduce costs related to making and storing multiple stockkeeping units (SKUs).

Just-in-time manufacturing systems (JIT) can be used to exploit internal linkages. In many companies, the time and distance raw materials and finished products move in a factory are significant cost drivers. Utilizing a manufacturing cell structure in which each cell is a 'mini factory' reduces the handling and movement of materials and parts.

In a company employing a JIT manufacturing system, external linkages may be exploited by negotiating long-term contracts with a small number of suppliers, choosing suppliers located near the production facility, and by involving suppliers directly in the inventory management process. Establishing relationships with suppliers so that they deliver quality products in a timely manner is vital to the success of a JIT system. However, the relationship has to benefit both the buyer and the supplier. As such, contracts must be negotiated so that suppliers understand that their success is tied to the success of the buyer (see contributions on purchasing management, and supplier development by Newlands in this volume.)

The evolution of enterprise resource planning (ERP) systems and electronic data interchange (EDI) allows a company to place a great deal of the burden of inventory management and raw materials ordering in the hands of its suppliers, resulting in an evolution of supply-chain management from loosely coupled relationships into virtual organizations (O'Leary 2000).

Taking advantage of external linkages typically involves two primary strategies – supply chain management (see Chapter 8 by Macbeth in this volume) and customer relationship management.

Customer Relationship Management

The goal of customer relationship management (CRM) is to bring a company closer to its customers in order to serve them better. In *The One on One Manager*, Peppers and Rogers (1999) describe CRM as a four-step process:

1. identify your customers;
2. differentiate your customers;

3. interact with your customers;
4. customize your business to your customers.

One of the latest innovations in supply-chain management is the creation of supply-chain cities. Luen Thai Holdings Ltd. (a clothing maker that supplies products to Liz Claiborne and Ralph Lauren) built a huge complex in China where fashion designers from Liz Claiborne, technicians from fabric suppliers and engineers from button and garment manufacturers work together in one location. This group of companies drastically reduced the time it takes for new clothes to go from the concept stage to delivery to retail outlets. The new supply chain city also reduces costs by reducing the number of employees spread between the United States, Europe and Asia and by reducing shipping costs. ('Making the Labels for Less', *Wall Street Journal*, 13 August 2004)

TAL Apparel Ltd., a closely held Hong Kong clothing manufacturer, makes one in eight dress shirts sold in the United States and supplies clothes to a number of US companies including Land's End and J.C. Penney. TAL is much more than just a manufacturer. TAL collects point-of-sale data for Penney's shirts directly from its stores, decides how many and what styles, colours and sizes of shirts to make, and then ships the shirts directly to individual stores, all without the direct involvement of Penney.

　　The benefits Penney derive? Before working with TAL, Penney would hold up to six months of inventory in its warehouses and three months of inventory in its stores. Today, it holds virtually no inventory for some lines of clothing. ('Invisible Supplier Has Penney's Shirts all Buttoned Up', *Wall Street Journal*, 11 September 2003)

In September 2005, Ford Motor Company announced plans to revamp its $90 billion a year global purchasing program by offering larger, long-term contracts to a smaller group of suppliers, shrinking the number of world-wide suppliers from 2,500 to less than 1,000. Ford estimates that the company will save billions and suppliers will benefit through increased factory utilization. ('Ford Seeks Big Savings by Overhauling Supply System', *Wall Street Journal*, 29 September 2005)

　　Ford's US website however shows spending on suppliers owned by racial minorities and women significantly increased since the mid 1990s.

The use of CRM creates an interactive feedback loop from customers to companies, making it possible to more accurately and consistently forecast, manage and meet customer expectations.

　　CRM can highlight opportunities to take advantage of internal and external linkages. For example, customer surveys may indicate that customers are incurring significant costs related to disposing of a product due to the use of a hazardous material. The company might react by providing recycling opportunities to its customers or by redesigning the product to eliminate the use of a particular material. Such options may benefit the company by attracting new customers and may allow the company to charge a higher price if customers are willing to pay a higher price for the convenience of easy recycling or to help protect the natural environment. The use of enterprise resource planning (ERP) systems facilitates CRM by allowing customer information to be gathered, stored and easily accessed and shared. CRM allows organizations to focus sales efforts on what the customer values and to anticipate and react to customer needs.

> SAS (the world's largest privately held software company) uses a variety of tools including customer surveys to get a detailed picture of customer needs including suggestions for new software features, options, add-ons and capabilities. Results of the surveys are shared with the company's research and development division which implements over 85% of the suggestions. Most of SAS's new products are developed with direct involvement of one or more of its customers. (Peppers and Rogers 1999)

Activity-based Management and the Value Chain

Activity-based management (ABM) focuses on managing activities to reduce costs and make better decisions. As such it is critical to helping companies create and maintain a competitive advantage. Figure 20.2 shows ABM that has two dimensions – cost and process.

Activity-based cost management (ABCM) provides expenditure information relating to an organization's resources, activities and expense items. The objective of this analysis is to improve the accuracy of the organization's costing model. The process dimension provides information about the activities that are performed, why they are performed and how efficiently they are

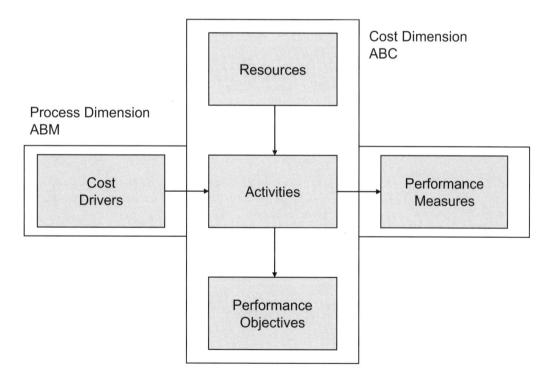

Figure 20.2   The cost and process dimensions of activity-based costing

performed. One of the benefits of ABCM is that it makes managers aware of exactly what causes costs to be incurred. Understanding the internal linkage between costs incurred and the number of different parts in a product focuses a company on simplifying product design. In the first ten years or so after implementing ABCM, Chrysler estimates that it saved hundreds of millions of dollars by simplifying product designs (Ness and Cucuzza 1995).

One of the goals of ABCM is to identify and eliminate activities and the associated costs that don't add value to goods and services. In today's competitive business environment, customers demand high-quality products and services and organizations that supply these products and services must strive to make sure that each activity adds value to the product or service in the mind of the customer.

However, not all activities create value. Non-value-added activities are those that can be eliminated without affecting the quality or performance of a product and are not necessary to meet the overall needs of the organization. Examples include the storage of materials and finished goods, moving materials from one place to another, idle time of employees while waiting for work, and so on. Likewise, packaging products (unless done for health or safety reasons or to make a product more appealing to a customer) might be considered non-value-added activities. Companies now consider quality inspections as a non-value-added activity. Successfully implemented quality improvement programmes usually result in extremely low numbers of defective products that rely on motivated operators to be responsible for the quality of the goods and services they produce rather than inspectors. These companies argue that if the products are designed correctly and production processes are monitored and controlled effectively, the quality of products will be ensured throughout the process. Consequently, inspections of finished products are redundant and do not add value to the product.

To be competitive, companies must strive to eliminate or to minimize non-value-added activities and the corresponding costs. The use of JIT production techniques can minimize non-value-added costs associated with inventory storage, product movements and other activities associated with ordering, receiving and handling inventory. Likewise, the implementation of total quality management (TQM) programmes significantly can reduce non-value-added costs associated with quality inspections, resolving customer complaints owing to defective or poor quality products, recalls, warranties and the like.

The Balanced Scorecard

Today's competitive business environment is characterized by rapidly changing technology, global competition and a focus on meeting and exceeding customer's expectations. In order to be successful companies are now using the balanced scorecard.

The balanced scorecard uses a set of financial and non-financial measures that relate to the overall strategy of the organization. By integrating financial and non-financial performance measures, the balanced scorecard helps keep management focused on all of a company's critical success factors, not just its financial ones, and helps to keep short-term operating performance in line with long-term strategy. Figure 20.3 shows that utilizing a balanced scorecard approach requires looking at performance from four different and related perspectives: financial, customer, internal business and learning and growth.

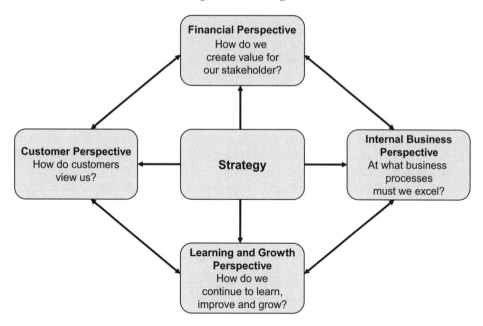

Figure 20.3   The balanced scorecard approach to performance measurement

Financial Perspective

While the primary goals of every profit-making enterprise are to satisfy clients and generate a profit, under the balanced scorecard approach financial performance is seen in the larger context of the company's overall goals and objectives relating to its customers and suppliers, internal processes and employees.

Customer Perspective

Critical success factors under this perspective include increasing the quality of products, reducing delivery time and increasing customer satisfaction.

Internal Business Perspective

The internal business perspective deals with objectives across the company's entire value chain from research and development to post-sale customer service. Critical success factors include productivity, manufacturing cycle efficiency, cycle time and throughput.

Learning and Growth Perspective

The learning and growth perspectives link critical success factors to create an environment that supports and allows the objectives of the other three perspectives to be achieved. Critical success factors include the efficient and effective use of employees, increasing the information systems capabilities of the company, and improving product innovation.

Measuring and Controlling Quality Costs

Over the last two decades, the demand by customers for quality has drastically changed the way companies do business. As a result, one of the critical success factors under the customer perspective of the balanced scorecard is improving the quality of products and services. From a customer perspective, improving quality leads to higher customer satisfaction and demand, increased sales and increases profitability. Quality is also related to the internal business perspective. From this perspective, quality measures focus on improving output yields, reducing defects in raw materials and finished products and reducing downtime owing to quality problems. These lead to lower costs.

Quality costs typically are classified into four general categories – prevention, appraisal, internal and external failure costs. Prevention costs are incurred to prevent product failures from occurring. These costs are incurred early in the value chain and include design and engineering costs as well as training, supervision and the costs of quality improvement projects. Most companies find that incurring prevention costs up front is less expensive in the long run than product failure costs.

Appraisal or detection costs are incurred in inspecting, identifying and isolating defective products before they reach the consumer. These include the costs of inspecting raw materials, testing products throughout the manufacturing process and final product testing and inspection. In general, it is more efficient to design quality into a product through prevention activities rather than to inspect quality into a product using appraisal activities.

If a product is defective or does not meet customer expectations, failure costs are incurred. Internal failure costs are incurred once the product is determined to be defective (through the appraisal process) before goods are sold to customers. Internal failure costs include costs incurred to rework defective units, scrap and spoilage. Internal failure costs include the downtime caused by quality problems, design changes and the costs of re-inspections and retesting.

External failure costs are incurred after a defective product is delivered to a customer. They include the costs of repairs made under warranty, the replacement of defective parts, product recalls, and liability costs arising from legal actions against the seller and eventually lost sales.

From a managerial perspective, the problem is improving the quality of products while at the same time reducing the costs of quality. Both external and internal failure costs can be reduced by paying more attention to quality issues early in the value chain. Products can be designed to emphasize quality and durability, suppliers can be certified, employees can be trained and the manufacturing process can be improved to increase quality throughout the value chain. In the short run, increasing expenditures related to prevention and appraisal can be a significant investment. However, in the long run companies typically find that quality failures are much more costly. As seen in Figure 20.4, the contemporary view of cost management is that total quality costs are minimized as quality improves and the percentage of output with defects is reduced.

Target Costing

With target costing, companies determine the volume of product to make, along with a desired price that will allow the company to capture a predetermined market share, and a target profit. The company then must engineer the costs of production in order to allow for the required profit. As mentioned earlier, companies must frequently compete both on cost and functionality.

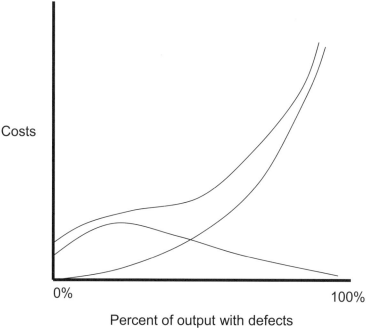

Costs

0%   100%

Percent of output with defects

Figure 20.4   Contemporary view of the costs of quality

In the summer of 1999, Coca-Cola faced one of the most serious crises in its history. A Coke bottling plant in Antwerp, Belgium failed to follow crucial quality control procedures, including receiving quality assurances from its suppliers and simply making sure that the carbon dioxide used to give Coke its fizz taste and maintain freshness. As a result, contaminated carbon dioxide was pumped in to the holding tanks at the bottling plant, resulting in bad smelling Coca-Cola and hundreds of sick consumers. In the aftermath, Coke products were recalled all over Europe.

Coca-Cola Enterprises, Inc. (the bottling company owned 40% by Coca-Cola) estimates that the problems resulted in a charge against earnings of more than $100 million. ('Anatomy of a Recall: How Coke's Controls Fizzled Out in Europe', *Wall Street Journal*, 29 June 1999 and 'Coca-Cola Enterprises Raises Estimate of Cost of Big Recall in Europe' *Wall Street Journal*, 13 July 1999)

Value engineering is used in target costing to analyse the trade-offs between product cost and product functionality. Value engineering includes the identification of key product attributes and features and customer preferences for those features, followed by an analysis of the cost of providing each of the important product' attributes. Value engineering may also include taking advantage of scope economies by developing products that share common platforms, parts or other resources. For details of this concept, see 'International Purchasing Management', Chapter 9 by Newlands, this volume.

Target costing is related closely to the concept of kaizen. Pioneered by Toyota in Japan, kaizen or continuous improvement refers to a system of improvement based on a series of gradual and often small improvements rather than major changes requiring very large investments. Kaizen takes the view that everyone is responsible for continuous improvement and consequently requires active participation by all of a company's employees (see 'HRM's Relationship to Company Performance', Chapter 11 by Zupan, this volume).

Kaizen focuses management's attention on continually improving a product while simultaneously reducing the costs of manufacturing a product through improving the productivity of manufacturing processes, implementing just-in-time manufacturing systems, implementing total quality management initiatives and identifying and reducing non-value-added activities.

Conclusions

Cost management is critical to profitability. Large corporate customers do not want price increases in line with inflation. They do not want the price to remain the same. What they demand is a year on year price reduction, typically of the order of 5 per cent per annum. To maintain their profitability, companies must reduce their costs by 5 per cent per year plus the rate of inflation. To increase the profitability, they must eliminate what is not necessary, do only what the customer wants and is willing to pay for, while being efficient, effective and disciplined in all aspects of its business plan. Businesses do not exist in a vacuum. If competitors are cutting costs and prices faster, and improving services and quality, customers may opt to re-source their needs from those companies better able to satisfy these requirements. To achieve a momentum, companies must initiate and support a learning organization structure, where people will not loose their jobs if the come up with ideas and suggestions that help the company compete. The company must strategically manage theirre tacit and explicit knowledge asset strategically (see 'Knowledge Management of Innovation and Technology', Chapter 24 by Jones and 'Tacit Knowledge and Implicit Learning', Chapter 25 by Dawes, both in this volume).

References

Ghoshal, S. (1987), 'Global Strategy: An Organizing Framework', *Strategic Management Journal* 8, pp. 425–40.

Ketels, C. (n.d.), 'Why the European Context Matters', *EBF Debates* 8, European Business Forum, http://www.ebfonline.com.

Ness, J.A. and Cucuzza, T.G. (1995), 'Tapping the Full Potential of ABC', *Harvard Business Review* 73(4), pp. 130–38.

O'Leary, D.E. (2000), 'Supply-Chain Processes and Relationships for Electronic Commerce', in Strader, T. and Whinston, A. (eds) *Handbook of Electronic Commerce* (Berlin: Springer Verlag), pp. 431–44.

Peppers, D. and Rogers, M. (1999), *The One to One Manager* (New York: Doubleday, Random House).

Chapter 21

Strategic Management of Not-for-Profit Organizations

Steve Molloy

This chapter provides an appraisal of the strategic decisions made by managers of organizations that do not exist with a primary goal of creating profits to survive.

Introduction

Not-for-profit organizations are an increasingly important segment of the international economy. In the US alone, the number of not-for-profit establishments increased from approximately 1 million different organizations in 1990 (Hodgkinson et al. 1992) to 1.2 million in 1997 (Independent Sector.org 2001). During the same period, revenue increased from approximately $100 billion to almost $665 billion. While there are variances from country to country, not-for-profits dominate some sectors, such as health, social services, education and the arts. In many countries, the sector is often aggregated to the household sector. This makes data analysis difficult (Hannig and Viet 2002). Research has indicated that not-for-profits account for 8 to 12 per cent of non-agricultural employment in many developed countries (Salamon et al. 1999). In a study of 37 countries in 2002, not-for-profit operating expenditures totalled $1.6 trillion (Salamon 2003).

In many markets, not-for-profits compete with for-profit organizations and public agencies. In virtually all markets, competition has increased, forcing not-for-profits to seek effective management techniques. While many not-for-profits have adopted some of the management techniques used by profit making concerns, there are (as will be shown later) significant differences between for-profit and not-for-profit organizations.

Primary Differentiators between Profit and Not-for-profit Establishments

The most obvious difference for not-for-profits is their tax and regulatory designation. In most countries, laws governing labour, contracts, securities, antitrust, etc., distinguish between for profit and not-for-profit organizations. Not-for-profits generally are treated more leniently. In most countries, not-for-profits are exempt from federal income and end of year surplus taxes, and are often exempt from regional and local taxes as well (*Harvard Law Review* 1992). Value-added taxes may be reclaimed for purchases and operating expenses. Sales prices also may be VAT exempt in certain categories and sectors. These tax and regulatory benefits often allow not-for-profits to pursue opportunities or activities that would not be viable for a for-profit organization.

In return for these tax and regulatory benefits, typically there are governmental limits on how the not-for-profit's revenues can be used or distributed. In for-profit organizations, any financial surplus (which would be called profits in profit-oriented organizations) can be distributed to the firm's owners, management, or employees after taxes have been deducted. Not-for-profit enterprises are constrained by law. They may not distribute any financial surplus to those in control of the organization.

Not-for-profits cannot have shareholders, or owners, the way a for-profit organization can. This raises several issues for a not-for-profit. Who owns the not-for-profit? How are senior management and employees motivated when management cannot give them an equity position? What is the appropriate governance structure?

There are other differences between for-profit organizations and not-for-profits. Not-for-profits tend to be very labour intensive and employ a large number of 'professionals'. With the exception of the higher education sector, not-for-profit's typically use, and may rely heavily upon, unpaid volunteers. Finally, to varying degrees, not-for-profits depend on revenue from non-client individuals, corporate philanthropy or groups for contributions to sustain their activities.

Advantages of Not-for-Profits – Three Theories

Why do not-for-profits exist? The traditional strategic management model would argue that not-for-profits possess distinct competencies and competitive advantages that allow them survive and thrive in certain markets. Three theories explain these advantages – contract failure, public failure and worker sorting.

Contract Failure

The traditional economic model is very market driven. Consumers are easily able to evaluate the quality of the products or services that they pay for and then use. Poor quality products or services will be avoided and thus forced out of the market. Consumers will favour and later demand higher quality products or services. These experiences are often then communicated to others in the market.

The products or services provided by not-for-profits often are complex and difficult to evaluate in terms of quality and effectiveness. The end user may not be the same as the person who is paying for the product or service. This creates an incentive to 'cheat'. It is relatively easy for an organization to provide much lower quality medical care to its 'customers' in Africa than they claim to be providing. This would save a significant amount of money for the organization, while the donors (often in other countries) would have no effective way to monitor and verify these claims. In these situations, the competitive advantage of not-for-profits is that they have greater reputation and trust than profit-oriented organizations. This is because the non-distribution constraint on not-for-profits results in fewer incentives to cheat. There are no surplus 'profits' for managers of the not-for-profit to appropriate.

Public Failure

Not-for-profits often have advantages over the public provision of goods or services. A not-for-profit may have lower labour costs due to fewer rules and less bureaucracy than in the public sector. Not-for-profits also may be able to charge fees for services that would be politically difficult to justify in the public sector (James 1987). Not-for-profits may specialize in public goods sectors that are controversial. They can appeal to fringe groups including religious sects, churches and ideologically routed associations. Examples would include religious or military education at the 'public school' level. Not-for-profits often work in tandem with the public sector and may receive a large proportion of their funding from the government.

Worker Sorting

The third source of competitive advantage is that not-for-profits often have strong ideologies. Because of this they may be able to attract committed activists or a motivated workforce. These workers are often motivated by non-economic factors, their 'cause' or 'calling', and are willing to give up premium salaries and benefits to reduce the load on the not-for-profit budget. Examples of this include those attracted to Greenpeace, Amnesty International and virtually all religions.

Mission

Given the above, the mission for a not-for-profit is very important. It is used to raise revenues (from donors or clients), attract staff, or highlight the failures of public or for-profit institutions.

There are three main roles of the mission statement. The first is to define the organization and set boundaries – both what the organization intends to be and what they specifically exclude from their mandate. The second role is to activate and mobilize both staff and donors. The third role is to aid in the process of evaluation of the organization. This last role is especially important given the absence of profits as an evaluation tool.

The founding entrepreneur typically determines the mission of the not-for-profit. This person's vision is imprinted on the new organization. Donors, staff and clients, as major stakeholders, are affected by the mission statement and should be considered. While long term in orientation, mission statements may need to be revised as the environment changes. Specific causes may be widened to encompass a broader remit. A wide scope of challenges may be refined to focus on core issues and themes. For example, the Tuberculosis Association became the Lung Association when a cure was found for tuberculosis.

Somewhat vague or generalized mission statements are more flexible, albeit less focused, and may provide less motivation for the stakeholder groups. A narrower mission statement provides greater focus and may become obsolete (Tuberculosis Association) or miss opportunities in the environment that do not fit within its narrow definition.

Industry Analysis

Before analyzing specific markets and industries, one must specify which industry the not-for-profit is in. For example, is Sesame Workshop (producer of *Sesame Street*) in the education industry, early childhood development industry, or entertainment industry? One way to answer this is to ask 'who, what and how'. Who (markets or market segments) are you targeting? What needs are being met? How are those needs being met? Once the industry or market has been identified, industry participants can be determined. Depending upon the industry definition used, Greenpeace, the Sierra Club and the World Wildlife Federation might all be placed within the environmental protection industry.

It is convenient to use a variation Michael Porter's (1980) model to analyse the industry.

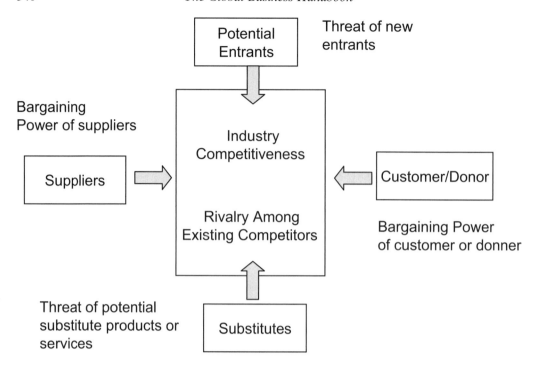

Figure 21.1   Competitive forces in industry

Rivalry among existing firms is predominantly a function of the size, number and characteristics of the firms in the industry. The attractiveness of a market will decrease as the number of competitors operating in that market increases. As diversity of competitors in an industry increases, the attractiveness of the industry also increases. However, often in not-for-profit activities there is increased cooperation among organizations. As there is an absence of a profit motive, organizations that share similar goals – whether it is saving children, helping the environment, or delivering aid during a disaster – are more likely to cooperate with one another if it will result in more effective attainment of their shared goals.

The potential threat of new entrants is a function of the entry barriers to the industry. Since reputation and trust are competitive advantages for not-for-profits, a good reputation typically is a significant barrier to entry. Distribution channels also can be significant barriers to entry. Exclusive access to churches or the workplace, for donations, can create significant entry barriers against new entrants. Scale economies can also deter new entrants. Large organizations may have scale economies with respect to lobbying, fundraising, operations or equipment. Government regulations may also limit new entrants. Hospitals must usually be certified by the government. The Red Cross is given a monopoly in many locations to collect blood. Asset specificity may increase the barriers to entry. The need for highly specialized assets that have no alternative use, such as a CAT scanner for a hospital, raises the risk for potential new entrants by raising exit costs.

The ready availability of suitable substitutes that satisfy needs and benefit society with similar provide services reduces the ability of an organization to attract clients or donors. While the Humane Society and the World Wildlife Federation have quite different missions, donors who are interested in animal welfare may be indifferent as to which they give to.

The bargaining power of the customer or donor will be a function of the percentage of total revenue that either provides. A private university gets a large percentage of its revenue from its client, the student, in the form of tuition. As such, the student will have a relatively stronger influence on the university. At a public university, the student pays a relatively small percentage of overall costs. Thus, the student's influence will be weak, while the influence of the major donors (government, alumni, etc.) will be relatively strong. Not-for-profits also run the risk of strong donors intruding on the organization's internal management.

Labour is typically one of the biggest suppliers to not-for-profits. Many employees are professionals, in limited supply (doctors, social workers, certified teachers, etc.) and there are no real substitutes. This increases their bargaining power. Also, strong employee commitments to professions may undermine their allegiance to the organization. In tight labour markets, there are fewer unemployed or underemployed and thus there are likely to be fewer volunteers.

After examining the forces affecting the industry, it is necessary to identify the key success factors. There usually are a limited number of factors that are critical to creating a success in the industry. There are two principal ways to do this. The first is to survey experts both inside and outside the industry. Special attention should be given to outsiders, as they are less likely to be biased or myopic in their views. The second approach is to look at market survivors and try to determine what made them successful. However, this method relies on historical data and only shows what was successful in the past. This approach does not necessarily indicate what may or may not work in the future.

Competition and Cooperation

For-profit motivated firms gauge the competition and winning in terms of the bottom line – profits. Profits dictate a for-profit firms' ability to continue uninterrupted and survive. They attract investment as a result of returns on investment and profitability. Profit therefore is one of their key performance indicators. Not-for-profits are different. They exist to serve. Any surplus is used to provide more services and goods for the needy. They often have transcending or higher esteem-based goals – that is, child welfare. As a result, they both compete and cooperate with one another. They may cooperate with one another to more effectively deliver children's aid programmes and compete with one another for donations.

Game theory can be used to analyse competition and cooperation between not-for-profits. The organizations are viewed as 'players' who can make moves and countermoves, with pay-offs at the end. The analogy of a chess game can be used. Competing players make moves and countermoves and try to anticipate their competitors' future actions. Each player tries to 'look ahead and reason back' (Dixit and Nalebuff 1991) – 'If I do X, then they will do Y'. To aid in the analysis, a number of quantitative decision-making tools can be used, including decision or game trees, sensitivity analysis and pay-off matrices.

Typically, under anti-trust laws, in for-profit organizations cooperation among competitors is illegal if these relationships and deals are cartel-like and limit free market economic activity. Cooperation among not-for-profits largely is expected. Since the not-for-profits often share common goals, cooperation, through synergy, helps the 'greater good'. Member organizations of the United Way cooperate with one another to reduce their fundraising expenses and ensure more money for their programmes. Not-for-profits may be under pressure from donors to cooperate to improve efficiency and effectiveness.

When in a cooperative arrangement, organizations need some way to guard against cheating by other members. Beyond the issue of shared values, there are other ways to promote cooperation. For example, if a group of not-for-profits decide to cooperate by forming a single, unified fundraising campaign, the members may internally monitor other organizations in the group to guard against 'cheating' members of the group that independently solicit donations. This is accomplished by having each member organization make a credible commitment to the centralized campaign by dismantling their individual fundraising operations.

If monitoring the activities of the member organizations is relatively easy and inexpensive, then the threat of eviction can be used to ensure cooperation.

Not-for-profits are often in competition with for-profit and public agencies. In these situations, each typically occupies a different niche and fills different needs. These differences are often based on socio-economic factors. In the daycare industry, for-profits are likely to cater to wealthier clients. Public agencies are likely to target the lower economic spectrum, while not-for-profits will be in the middle.

Human Resource Management in Not-for-Profit Organizations

Not-for-profits face unique issues with respect to human resource management. Not-for-profits are typically in service industries and have very high labour intensity. As there is a lack of clear ownership (they have no shareholders), employees and volunteers are the major stakeholders.

Attracting and motivating staff can be an issue. Not-for-profits often pay less than for-profits and are unable to offer other financial incentives, such as stock options. Not-for-profits, however, usually offer non-economic rewards such as flexibility and independence. The lower salary accepted by not-for-profit employees is a 'donation' of time – given because of the employees' commitment to the cause. Some employees working for not-for-profits may be less motivated because these organizations cannot offer strong economic incentives to perform.

Not-for-profits are often professional bureaucracies that have flat structures and employees operate with significant autonomy. When combined with the service nature of the not-for-profit, such a potentially chaotic environment can create difficulties to monitor and measure performance. Professionals may also look more to their profession for guidance rather than the organization. For doctors, the Hippocratic Oath takes precedence over the hospital's rules and regulations. An absence of clear effectiveness measures, difficulty in monitoring and commitment to professions creates limitations as to what can be used as rewards and punishments.

The flat structure and autonomy of professional bureaucracies results in decentralized decision-making. This may lead to suboptimization, with local or subunit issues dominating global or overall organizational goals. For example, that which is best for the Fine Arts Department may not be optimal for the university as a whole. The various parts of the decentralized organization must be trusted to make the right decision that contributes both to achieving and realizing both their individual and organizational goals. Adequate induction and coaching schemes must be in place to acculturate and develop employees.

The use of volunteers is an issue unique to not-for-profits. How does a not-for-profit attract, motivate, control and discipline employees who are not paid? Managers need to understand what motivates unpaid helpers to volunteer in the first place. There are two primary reasons why people give their support – investment and consumption (Menchik and Wesibrod 1987). Investment is the belief that volunteering will increase their skills and experiences and that this will be of benefit to them later in life. Consumption can be thought of as altruism – for the volunteer the reward is in obtaining the goals of the organization. Thus, volunteers have both altruistic and self-interested motivations and can be encouraged by appealing to both.

Board of Directors

The Board of Directors of a not-for-profit differs from that of a for-profit in a number of ways. The first is size. A for-profit board averages ten to 15 members, while a not-for-profit board averages 30 to 50 (Abzug 1994). The composition of not-for-profit boards also differs from that of a for-profit. The not-for-profit board typically consists entirely of outsiders, while for-profit boards are a mix of insiders and outside members. Not-for-profit boards typically have more dissension and conflict (Hirsch and Whistler 1979) and are more actively involved in operations (Unterman and Davis 1984) than their for-profit counterparts.

In a for-profit organization, the board has a statutory responsibility to protect the interests of the shareholders. There are no shareholders of a not-for-profit to protect. The board in a not-for-profit should protect the interests of donors, clients and the public. Recent scandals involving the Olympic Selection Committee and Olympic figure skating judges highlight this need. Such scandals threaten to tarnish the image of the Olympics (which would reduce the value to corporate sponsors), call into question the fairness of competitions (which would harm the athletes) and generally foster disillusionment among the public. The board of a not-for-profit also performs the role of a boundary spanner between managers and clients or publics. In this regard they may perform a political role.

Unlike for-profit boards, there is no market to discipline insiders on the board of a not-for-profit. While there are no profits to distribute, insiders can increase administrative costs in the form of salary increases. For this reason, profit boards are predominantly composed of outsiders, to protect against such self-interested behaviour.

Not-for-profit boards usually become more active than for-profit boards. This is a source of conflict and tension between the board and the management of the not-for-profit. This is exacerbated by the large size and internal conflict of the board itself. Conflict is often the result of the diversity of the board members and their different motivations for being on the board. Some may be on the board because they strongly believe in the 'cause'. Others are on the board for the social status it gives them.

The five primary tasks of the board of a not-for-profit are (Herman 1990):

1. select and evaluate the chief executive officer;
2. define and re-evaluate the mission of the organization;
3. develop a plan for the organization;
4. approve budgets;
5. help get resources.

These five tasks are a mix of strategic and operational activities.

There are four primary steps that can be taken to increase board effectiveness. The first is to ensure that there is a common vision among all members of the board. This is especially important given the risk of goal conflicts when an organization has multiple sponsors. The second step is the effective recruitment of board members. Members should be recruited for their technical abilities and experiences and their political, organizational, networking and interpersonal skills. It is important to maintain diversity on the board and not let it become inbred or homogeneous. Finally, while destructive conflict and infighting are bad, if managed properly healthy conflict and diversity of opinion are good for the organization.

Product Mix and Pricing

Product Mix

Both for-profit and not-for-profit organizations are similar with respect to their reasons for encouraging and sustaining diversification. Both are typically started with a focus on a single *core* activity. Over time, as the environment changes, both are motivated to change, or broaden, their product line in order to continue to meet their mission. Planned Parenthood initially focused on providing birth control information. As the environment changed and birth control became more readily available, they expanded their product line to include a whole range of family planning services.

As for-profit and not-for-profit organizations grow and develop, both look to diversification to take advantage of production and/or distribution complementarities. This is done to take advantage of economies of scope. Art museums often initially focus on exhibiting a particular type or period of art. Over time, these activities may be supplemented with the addition of film and lecture series to leverage their core capabilities in art collection and preservation.

Finally, both types of organizations use diversification to even out revenue flows. For not-for-profits this takes the form of cross subsidization – subsidized revenue losing activities are funded by surplus generating activities. Museums and art galleries typically cross-subsidize their collections and attractions with revenue collected from gift shop sales. Similarly, Sesame Workshop uses revenue generated from licensing its *Sesame Street* characters (everything from Tickle Me Elmo dolls to Sesame Street On Ice) to subsidize their core activity of creating children's educational programming.

For both for-profits and not-for-profits, unrelated diversification is generally not effective. Management gets into areas in which they have no experience or knowledge. The performance of the organization in such circumstances typically suffers.

A problem that is unique to not-for-profits is the need to balance the portfolio between ventures that contribute to the mission but have a negative net revenue and ventures that have a positive net revenue and do not contribute to achieving the mission of the organization. In this situation, not-for-profits run the risk of goal displacement. Resource contributing activities take precedence over mission oriented activities.

There are several cautions. The first is that, as revenue generating activities increase, there may be tax implications as these activities expand beyond the bounds of the not-for-profit's mandate. Revenue generating activities may require a different organizational strategy, structure and even type of personnel. Finally, performance of the not-for-profit's core activities often is difficult to measure and evaluate. The relatively easier to evaluate for-profit activities may crowd out the more difficult to measure core activities.

Pricing

Pricing presents unique issues for a not-for-profit. What the client or customer pays for a service typically has an insignificant relationship to the cost of providing the service. Private universities receive a significant proportion of their revenue from clients' fees, while aid organizations such as Oxfam and the Save the Children Fund receive no fees at all.

Pricing in a not-for-profit can be used to ration use. Free parks may get overused and consequently damaged. An entry fee, even if it is below the actual cost of providing the service, may be used to manage park attendance. The root causal phenomenon is that people often do not value things that are free and consequently will waste or abuse them. Many countries with free universal health care have found that clients waste this service by going to the hospital emergency room for non-emergency situations, such as a minor cut or a headache. This overloads the system and makes it difficult to provide proper care to legitimate emergency patients. Also, people are more likely to practice preventative care and try to live a healthy lifestyle if there is a cost involved for traditional health care.

Pricing can be used by a not-for-profit as a mechanism to determine which programmes or activities society values. Which programmes are customers willing to pay for?

For a not-for-profit, there are two basic situations in which fees are not charged. The first is in those situations when the cost of collecting the fee exceeds the benefits. The cost of erecting a fence and staffing a gate to control entry into a park may exceed the potential revenue generated from paid admissions. The second situation is when charging a fee is ideologically offensive. No fee is charged for blood or transplant organs.

Not-for-profit pricing decisions can use many of the same tools used by for-profit organizations to aid in this process. A break-even analysis can be done to determine volume/pricing issues. Activity-based cost accounting can be used to determine the cost of providing specific services. Elasticity of demand tools can be used to look at the effect of price on demand. Competition has to be considered in the pricing decision. A theatre company is in competition with a wide range of other for-profit and not-for-profit entertainment activities and must price itself accordingly. Finally, there is the psychological aspect of pricing. The price of a product or service can convey a number of images, including status, value, and quality.

Fundraising

Fundraising activities can be quite expensive and eventually follow the law of diminishing returns. Each additional euro spent on fundraising returns a smaller and smaller number of euros in donations. The question then becomes, when should one stop? From a theoretical standpoint, an organization should continue to spend on fundraising until marginal revenue equals marginal costs. If marginal revenue is greater than marginal costs – an additional euro in fundraising costs yields more than a euro in revenue – then keep spending on fundraising. As soon as marginal revenue is less than marginal costs – it costs more than one euro to raise one euro in donations – do not increase fund raising expenditure.

Most oversight groups look to averages as a way to evaluate the efficiency of not-for-profits. The maximum amount is generally considered to be 50–60 per cent. That is, fundraising costs should not exceed 50–60 per cent of donations raised. While the use of average costs is imperfect, it is easily measured, communicated to donors and understood by them. Benefactors want and expect that a large percentage of their donation will go to the cause and not be used for administrative expenses.

At the individual donor level, there are a number of observations to be made. For example, the profile of donations as a percentage of income is a U-shaped curve. As income rises, donations initially fall, and then begin to increase as income continues to rise.

Donations tend to increase with age, education and number of children and statistics suggest women tend to donate more than men.

Motives for individual giving tend to fall into one of two categories – 'paying your dues' or 'giving away your surplus'.

The concept of 'paying your dues' is firmly grounded in most cultures and can be found in the concept of 'tithing' in many religions. Many not-for-profits, such as the United Way, try to take advantage of this concept by suggesting donations tied to a percentage of your salary.

Buddy Holly is a noted example. The play based on his life story includes his specific request to have a percentage of his revenue paid directly to the church. Also, the reason giving goes up as families have more children is because the families feel compelled to support and pay their fair share of the activities their children are engaged in (this can range from not-for-profit athletic events to arts groups and the Scouting movement). The concept of 'paying your dues' is meant to reduce 'free riding' – gaining of benefits from society without paying for them. However, 'giving away the surplus' is very different from 'paying your dues'.

Not-for-profits need to understand their potential donors in much the same way that not for-profits need to know their customers. Not-for-profit fundraisers and managers need to know the demographics of potential donors as age and even marginal tax brackets can affect donations. Try to understand the psychographics of donors. What are their specific motives to donate? If they have a family member who died of cancer, they are more likely to give to the cancer fund. For wealthy donors, the motivation may be to provide a legacy – something with their name on it. Bill Gates of Microsoft has already given or pledged billions of dollars to the Bill and Melinda Gates Foundation which, among other things, tries to address tropical diseases in Africa.

Corporate giving is a self-interested form of 'paying your dues'. Many corporation board members view the organizations they control as guests, or members, of society. The board members' stated beliefs are that being a good corporate citizen means giving back to society – that is, paying their dues. However, corporations' directors cannot forget that they have a fiduciary responsibility to their shareholders and it is here that corporate self-interest arises. Corporate giving typically is done for one of three reasons:

1. Corporations may use giving to try to expand markets. Microsoft often donates software to not-for-profits. The hope is that the not-for-profit will then become a future Microsoft customer, buying upgrades and other Microsoft products.
2. Some companies use not-for-profits as a form of employee development by granting time off in order that employees may work with a not-for-profit. The employee may be exposed to greater challenges, more responsibility and different situations than they experience in their in the for-profit company. The hope is that the employee will develop new or improved skills from these experiences. Also, such experiences often lead to more loyal and motivated employees as they may feel positively toward their employers because they are making a difference.
3. Corporations usually target not-for-profits that have positive links to one or more of the corporation's important stakeholder groups. McDonald's sponsors Ronald McDonald House. This provides accommodation near major children's hospitals for families away from home while their child is in hospital. The market segment of young families with children is also the primary target market for McDonald's. Energy and lumber companies that may have tarnished environmental images often support environmental not-for-profits in an attempt to improve their image.

It is important for managers of for-profits to 'do the right thing' with their corporate giving. Obtaining some benefit from this for their shareholders is justification to continue to support the not-for-profit sector.

Competition and Cooperation for Funds

Due to the global increase in the number of not-for-profits, competition to attract donors has increased. Donors, no matter what cause they are interested in, face an increasingly large number of not-for-profits to choose from. Unlike for-profits, not-for-profits are allowed to cooperate with each other. The United Way is an example of cooperation to more effectively and efficiently raise funds for its member organizations. The downside of the United Way is that this cooperation takes away some of the discretion the donor has to choose the application and organization his or her donation will be used for. This also gives considerable power to the United Way bureaucracy as they decide which member organizations are in and which are out.

Some not-for-profits have outsourced the fundraising activity and have turned to professional fundraisers. Many government agencies have tried to limit the use of professional fundraisers because of their often excessive costs. In several cases, fundraising costs have exceeded 90 per cent of total funds raised, leaving less than 10 per cent of all money raised going to the not-for-profit.

Two ways in which a not-for-profit can compete for resources are the selection of a dynamic leader and the development of an *air of mystery*. Many not-for-profits select a high profile leader or spokesperson, often someone in the entertainment or sports industry, to attract media attention and donations. A common tactic is to establish a telethon or a celebrity sporting event to solicit donations. The second strategy is to develop a mystique. With their 'Rainbow Warrior' ships, the Peace Corps and Médecins sans Frontières (Doctors without Borders), Greenpeace have all developed 'mystique'. This helps them to attract volunteers and donations.

Not-for-profits face greater difficulty than for-profits in obtaining resources because the financial link between the service provider and the client is either weak or nonexistent. Doing an excellent job in meeting the needs of clients however does not ensure financial reward.

Managerial Control

For-profit organizations follow generally accepted accounting principals (GAP). Financial statements are regulated. This is to make them more easily understood by external reviewers. Budgets, either for planning or control, have an internal audience. In either case, the funds are *fungible*. This means that a euro or dollar is indistinguishable from any other euro or dollar, regardless of the donor.

The financial statements of not-for-profits are regulated, but the regulations are different than those of for-profits. As a result, not-for-profit financial statements are often confusing. Not-for-profit financial statements use different regulations. The use of fund accounting is different, setting up funds such as current, general capital, operating and endowment. Restrictions may have been placed by some donors on the use of donated funds, for example, a specific university scholarship. Both revenues and expenses are segregated by the use of funds and, as such, are not entirely fungible. Many people donated money to the International Red Cross with the provision that the donations specifically are used for tsunami relief in Asia.

Budgets are developed on an accrual (total cost to date) basis. They should be balanced, with respect to costs and revenue, and developed on a programme basis. Programme budgets allow each programme to be evaluated and in comparison to others for effectiveness and efficiency. Programme budgets also may highlight areas of cross-subsidization. This can lead to conflicts between programme managers within not-for-profits that have a positive revenue contribution and those that have a negative contribution, regardless of contribution to the core mission.

A variance analysis is performed as a control function. Differences between budgeted and actual performance are analysed to determine the cause and to suggest possible alternatives for addressing the variation. A variation between actual and budgeted revenue for a private university may be a function of variations in budgeted versus actual:

- number of students;
- mix of students – full or part time, graduate and undergraduate;
- price – tuition minus average student aid;
- cost of inputs – salaries, utilities;
- efficiency – average class size.

Programme Evaluation

Not-for-profits often face multiple goals and multiple constituencies. The separation between donors and clients also insulates the not-for-profit from the market. Consequently, for-profit organizations can find it difficult to evaluate programmes. Ultimately the bottom line measure is a surplus or deficit (this line is called *profit or loss* in for profit organizations).

Not-for-profits have mission-related goals. These must be considered their primary goals – their reason for existing. Not-for-profits face revenue generation goals. They need revenue to carry out their mission. As previously noted, revenue can come from a variety of sources, including governments, donors, fees from clients and profit making activities. These latter activities may be in conflict with their primary mission. Examples include user fees for universal health care and commercial, profit making activities for a church.

Efficiency and effectiveness are different measures. Efficiency involves minimizing inputs for a given level of outputs, while effectiveness measures the obtainment of goals. The two measures often conflict in not-for-profits. The most effective teaching in a university might require very small class sizes, even though this is very inefficient.

When programme evaluation is attempted, the not-for-profit's multiple constituencies create problems. With a lack of clear 'bottom line' results, each stakeholder group tries to assert their objectives on the not-for-profit. These multiple and often conflicting objectives make programme evaluation problematic.

The role of outsiders in evaluating programme effectiveness is accentuated. Not-for-profits often turn to outside accrediting agencies for evaluation and validation of programme effectiveness. Typically, such evaluations are either statistical or subjective in nature. Often not-for-profits are evaluated according to a model or formula or compared to similar organizations.

In situations where programme evaluation is extremely difficult to perform, for example, where ambiguous or conflicting operating objectives exist, not-for-profits instead often focus on efficiency measures. Inputs (resources) are measured and controlled rather than outputs (results). Because outcomes are not measured, rewards and penalties have little or no relation to performance. The not-for-profit runs the risk of becoming very bureaucratic, with rules and regulations generated to establish control.

Conclusions

Not-for-profits are significant and important components of the global economy. They operate in areas of human endeavour where for-profit and public organizations are ineffective. Many aspects of strategic management of for-profits can be applied to not-for-profits. However, there are a number of important differences, including the often weak influence of the client and ambiguous and difficult-to-measure performance objectives that create unique problems and which must be addressed. These issues require specific strategies not used by the for-profit sector.

References

Abzug, R. et al. (1994), 'Study of Non-profit Boards', Yale Program on Nonprofit Organizations, Yale University.

Dixit, A. and Nalebuff, B. (1991), *Thinking Strategically* (New York: W.W. Norton).

Hannig, C. and Viet, V. (2002), 'Publication of the Handbook on Non-profit Institutions in the System of National Accounts', United Nations Statistical Commission, document E/CN.3/2002/8/Add.1, March.

Harvard Law Review (1992), 'Developments in Law: Non-profit Corporations', 105, pp. 1578–699.

Herman, R. (1990), 'Methodological Issues in Studying the Effectiveness of Non-governmental and Non-profit Organisations', *Non-profit and Voluntary Sector Quarterly* 19, pp. 293–306.

Hirsch, P, and Whistler,T. (1979), 'Reforming the Corporate Board', University of Chicago working paper, September.

Hodgkinson, V., Weirzman, M.S., Toppe, C.M. and Noga, S.M. (1992), *Nonprofit Almanac, 1992–93* (San Francisco: Jossey Bass).

Independent Sector.org (2001), 'The Nonprofit Almanac in Brief – 2001' (Washington, DC: Independent Sector), http://www.independentsector.org.

James, E. (1987), 'The Non-profit Sector in Comparative Perspective', in Powell, W.W. (ed.) *The Nonprofit Sector* (New Haven, CT: Yale University Press).

Menchik, P. and Weisbrod, B. (1987), 'Volunteer Labor Supply', *Journal of Public Economics* 32, pp. 159–83.

Porter, M. (1980), *Competitive Strategy* (New York: Free Press).

Salamon, L. (2003), *UN Non-profit Handbook Project* (Baltimore, MD: Johns Hopkins Center for Civil Society Studies).

Salamon, L., Anheier, H.K., List, R., Toepler, S. and S. Wojciech Sokolowki and Associates (1999), *Global Civil Society: Dimensions of the Non-Profit Sector* (Baltimore, MD: Johns Hopkins Center for Civil Society Studies).

Unterman, I. and Davis, R. (1984), *Strategic Management of Not-for-Profit Organisations* (Boston, MA: Harvard Business School Press).

DIMENSION 7
Innovation and Quality

Chapter 22

The Quality Management Situation – An Introduction

Kevin Laframboise

Total quality management (TQM) is an international phenomenon. Its philosophical routes originated in the West. The Japanese subsequently developed techniques to implement the philosophies. Organizations in Western countries and other regions have since implemented these techniques to catch up. This chapter considers the history of the QM movement and a few of its major contributors by examining some of the different approaches to quality and looking at different measurements of quality assurance. It is through these initiatives that extended enterprises (Davis and Spekman 2004) and customers of the international supply chains can benefit from assured quality performance.

Introduction

Managing for quality is alive and well. Some might argue that quality management (QM) is rather faddish, that there have been many 'flavours of the month' over the past few decades and that it is now dead. To paraphrase Mark Twain: 'the report of its death is much exaggerated'.

New quality initiatives or approaches do not exist in a vacuum or start from point zero. There is a history to the quality movement and new approaches offer a different twist for good reason and represent an evolution in quality management thinking. While there have been different approaches over time, the fundamental principles still serve as the foundation. The QM philosophy has been consistent and today more than ever it remains important to seek quality and continuously pursue improvement.

Firms cannot survive if they fail to create and assure the quality of product or service that customers expect. The philosophy of managing for quality suggests that an individual or a firm succeeds best when there is a conscious effort to do the right thing in the right way, at the right time, that is, to be appropriately effective while being appropriately efficient. While a quality attitude at all times might start with an individual, business success requires that this attitude also exist at the organizational level. It may be said that individuals and firms need to have a quality attitude or 'quattitude'. This is because quality begins with personal attitudes and quality-focused individuals can exceed the expectations of whomever they deal with. While training, effort and personal initiatives can have a positive impact on success, a quality attitude can be contagious vis-à-vis the business, customers, family and friends. This concept relates strongly to unconditionally constructive behaviours defined by Fisher and Ury (1981) and Fisher and Brown (1988) which are embedded in negotiation. Holtom discusses these issues in Chapter 5, 'International Negotiation', in this volume. Although negotiation is an option, quality conformance to specification is a minimum compulsory requirement in order to qualify for the bidding process. Since quality has a positive impact on cost reduction, the benefits are both financial and also more subtle, intangible aspects such as learning, respect, determination to do better that stems from the positive feeling of succeeding, mutual understanding, proactive searching for further opportunities and higher reputation.

Quality Principles and the Supply Chain

For an organization that wants to identify with the quality philosophy, there are several principles to live by. It must first and foremost be focused on its customers. The aims are to satisfy needs and even to delight clients. All actions of the firm must be integrated towards these basic goals (Levy et al. 1995; Clark 1999: Logistics Management 2006). In order to be so focused, the organization must have strong, committed and capable leaders at all levels of the organization to guide this philosophy. These leaders must see to the participation of all their employees as associates in sharing the goals of a quality organization and being appropriately acknowledged for their involvement and contributions. The employees, as internal customers, must also be satisfied partners.

Regarding their responsibilities, these employees must cease to see themselves as just doing a job inside a particular function or department in the firm. Instead, they must perceive what they do as a step in a process, an internal value chain of actions that lead to the customer (Gardner 2004). Their superiors must see to the integration of information and the various functional activities into holistic systems.

Furthermore, there must be a structured and reasonable plan for measuring process improvement. This requires management to identify what can be measured, schedule measurement and analyse results and, where possible, to ensure that processes are continually improved. The consequence is that learning has taken place. This facilitates decision-making to be based on facts rather than gut feeling, intuition or whim. Finally, and equally importantly, the firm must also respect and appreciate the role of suppliers. As partners, suppliers also aim to achieve benefits without negatively affecting the other supply chain participants. Together thus they can forming an extended enterprise or network and thus create highly competitive supply chains end-to-end – from initial suppliers to end users (including the recycling of material back into the loop).

Today's focus on partner relationships in the supply chain provides goods and/or services to satisfy ever-increasingly demanding customers. The goal of quality performance should be a total supply chain philosophy. Each organizational participant in the chain must see the need for total quality for itself and for the chain collectively. Customer companies can anticipate that their remaining strategic suppliers and the focal firm itself will attain the highest possible performance and quality standards. This should help assuring assure the next partner in the chain (their customer) and ultimately the final customer (the user) will be delighted with the product (goods and/or services). Some will be competitors may who cut corners and might not necessarily follow the rules. Others might treat employees with less respect and assert control more than is necessary to the company's detriment. Faced with such challenges, only by being efficient and by controlling for quality of processes and products will a firm be able to keep its costs low (ASQ Quality Costs Committee 1999), win out in the long run over the less than noble competitor and survive profitably.

A Brief History of the Quality Movement

Quality as a work ethic has existed for centuries. Consider, for example, the long-standing ancient pyramids, the aqueduct system of the Romans, the artwork of the masters (sculptures, painting), stonework at Latin American monuments like Machu Picchu in Peru and the many masterful pieces of literature and engaging music. The creators of such quality left us a legacy of craftsmanship and perfection.

The quality movement can trace its origins to the skilled-craftsmanship and the guilds of medieval Europe. The craftsman-apprentice relationship initiated the notion of quality inspection (after which the guild inspector and the craftsman would leave their mark or symbol) since they wanted to assure both the quality of output and their reputation. The role of inspection was also created as a consequence of the Industrial Revolution and led to the development of separate quality departments. Additionally, the Industrial Revolution led to the factory system and specialized tasks to assure quality.

In the twentieth century, several individuals and organizations developed better ways of achieving excellence, for example, work simplification, the development of the assembly line, time-motion studies, statistical methods of the 1930s, computer-aided manufacturing and exciting information technologies of recent decades. Such contributions represent a continuing drive for improved effectiveness and improved efficiency. In World War I, around half of all the mortar rounds fired in the European theatre of operations did not explode. This required manufacturers to produce twice as much as required, and artillery to fire twice the number needed to achieve the desired impact on the enemy. More worryingly, mustard gas bombs failed to detonate. Even today, one of the most risky jobs in agriculture is to plough fields along the fighting front. Modern farmers may be driving their expensive tractors and break open a mustard gas bomb and they simply die at the steering wheel. World War II provided the opportunity to establish respect for standards for ammunition. There was too much stock of ammunition and demand was too great to examine each round for defects. As a result, statistical sampling methods were developed for quality inspection.

During twentieth century, productivity improvement evolved from a focus on manufacturing quality, to:

- improved product design;
- service quality; and
- excellence in performance.

This has created a drive for continuous and steady improvement (the Japanese term is *Kaizen*) in most production activities. Quantum leaps (order of magnitude) or stretch-goal improvements in other endeavours have often been accompanied by massive business process re-engineering initiatives (the Japanese term is *Kai Kaku*). Improvement which was promoted through quality awareness in manufacturing industries in the 1980s today similarly focuses on service industries, government, health care and education.

Quality Gurus

We must recognize some of the individuals who greatly influenced the quality movement. In the 1920s, *Walter Shewhart* recommended controlling processes, thus insisting not only on the quality of the finished product but that it should also be built into the processes that created it. More significantly, he recognized that processes produced measurable data which could be analysed. Thus began statistical quality control (SQC) and the control charts that followed. Two students of Shewhart, *W. Edwards Deming* and *Joseph Juran* made significant contributions to the quality movement.

After World War II, Japan evolved from a country focused on military production to one focused on products for civilian consumption. They were prohibited from rearming; however, they did supply trucks and other equipment to other nations, just as they had in World War I. Initially, their production was recognizably inferior. With time, Japan became noted for superior quality (e.g., electronics, appliances and automobiles). Rather than relying on reactive inspection, the Japanese improved productivity by using used a total -quality (TQ) approach to improve productivity that was proactive, focusing on process and people rather than relying on reactive inspection. Deming and Juran played significant roles in helping the Japanese quality movement to progress. Subsequently, these individuals were very influential in the development of a total quality management philosophy that has been adopted generally throughout the industrialized world, but particularly in the US.

Juran was an accomplished teacher of quality who suggested that improvement could be obtained gradually, one quality project at a time. He emphasized the need for top management involvement in the quality movement rather than limiting involvement to technicians. He also encouraged extensive training in quality. He wrote several textbooks and handbooks for quality control. He saw quality as 'fitness-for-use', that is, quality is tied to customer satisfaction or dissatisfaction with the product or service (Juran and Godfrey 1998).

Deming, a physicist, statistician, musician and poet, was also an outstanding teacher and author (Deming 1986; Mann 1985). He is recognized as the guru of quality and particularly statistical quality control. He taught the Japanese to rely on statistical control and his influence on business leaders in Japan was so great that he is recognized as a major reason for the Japanese turn-around in productivity. In 1951, the Japanese recognized him by naming their top quality award the Deming Prize.

Deming also stressed that management must take responsibility and lead quality. His often-cited 14 points succinctly sum up his philosophy of quality. These are:

1. create constancy of purpose for improvement of product and service;
2. adopt the new philosophy;
3. cease dependence on mass inspection;
4. end the practice of awarding business on price tag alone;
5. constantly and forever improve the system of production and service;
6. institute modern methods of training on the job;
7. institute modern methods of supervision;
8. drive out fear;
9. break down barriers between staff areas;
10. eliminate numerical goals for the workforce;
11. eliminate work standards and numerical quotas;
12. remove barriers that hinder the hourly worker;
13. institute a vigorous programme of education and training;
14. create a situation in top management that will push every day on the above points.

Deming is famous for a television show, *If Japan Can … Why Can't We?*. This show had a significant effect on the quality movement in the USA. By the 1970s, several North American and European industries began to fall behind Japanese industries in terms of quality and market share. In 1980, the show in which he and his philosophy played a central role caused American leadership, government and industry to sit up and take notice. Organizations began emphasizing not only statistical approaches but also the vital attitudes that contribute to creating and sustaining high performance the entire organization. These approaches became known as total quality management (TQM). Years later, the Malcolm Baldrige National Quality Award (MBNQA) was instituted as a response to both the show and the TQM movement. National awards and similar holistic programmes will be examined briefly later.

Other Gurus

Given the limited scope of this chapter, several others deserve at least a brief mention. *Armand Feigenbaum* was the originator of 'total quality control', a method of three steps to quality: quality leadership, modern quality technology, and organizational commitment.

Dr Kaoru Ishikawa offered a total quality viewpoint that incorporates company-wide quality control, an emphasis on the human side of quality, the use of tools such as the 'Ishikawa', 'fish-bone' or 'cause and effect' diagram and the use of the 'seven basic tools of quality', which are examined in the online accompanying text to this chapter.

Rather than attempt to control all the many variations during actual manufacture, *Dr Genichi Taguchi* argued for product designs that are robust or insensitive to variation in the manufacturing process. This represents the optimization of routines of product and process prior to manufacture rather than quality through inspection. For him quality means system design, parameter design and tolerance design.

Shigeo Shingo, author of 14 major books, is the pioneer of lean manufacturing. He is associated with just-in-time (JIT) manufacturing and the idea of the 'single minute exchange of dies' (SMED) system (at Toyota). The aim of SMED is to reduce set-up times from hours to minutes or even seconds. The processes should also include Poka-Yoke (a mistake proofing device and system).

Yoji Akao developed quality function deployment (QFD) as a to translate customers' expressed wants or needs into technical specifications of a product or service.

Philip Crosby is known for the concepts of 'Quality is Free' and 'Zero Defects'. His quality improvement process is based on the absolutes:

- quality is conformance to requirements;
- the system of quality is prevention;
- the performance standard is zero defect; and
- the measurement of quality is the price of non-conformance.

The CEOs of some major US corporations are also recognized for providing personal leadership in the quality movement. Examples include *Jack Welch* (General Electric's six sigma initiative (Evans and Lindsay 2005)), *Larry Bossidy* (Allied Signal), *Robert Galvin* (Motorola), *Sam Walton* (Wal-Mart) and *Horst Schultz* (Ritz-Carleton Hotel Company).

The twenty-first century is enjoying an evolving and maturing quality movement beyond the foundations laid by Deming, Juran and the early Japanese practitioners of quality. Some examples include the ISO 9000 series of quality management standards, which was revised to increase emphasis on customer satisfaction and the six sigma methodology to improve business processes and hence minimize defects and variations. This standard evolved into a widely adopted organizational approach. Sector-specific versions of ISO 9000 were developed for such industries as automotive (QS-9000), aerospace (AS9000) and telecommunications (TL 9000 and ISO/TS 16949) and for environmental management (ISO 14000). Quality is no longer just a manufacturing phenomenon: it now includes service industries, health care, education and government.

National and trading region (European) quality awards programmes have had significant effects on promoting the quality movement and motivating organizations to improve. These programmes came about in the 1980s just after the television programme mentioned above. The national awards programmes called for excellence in various categories and for measurement and demonstrated continuous improvement efforts. The prizes were awarded after voluntary submission, by competition and independent jury selection. Parallel systems also began with industry awards and regional awards (information about awards may be found at The Institute of Quality Assurance: http://www.iqa.org/mcr/index.shtml).

Examples of nations with such awards are:

- Britain (BQF) – http://www.quality-foundation.co.uk/;
- Canada (NQI) – http://www.NQI.com;
- Europe (EFQM) – http://www.efqm.org/Default.aspx?tabid=154;
- India (RGNQA) – http://www.bis.org.in/other/rgnqa_geninfo.htm;
- Japan (Deming Prize) – http://www.deming.org/demingprize/;
- Singapore – http://www.spring.gov.sg/Content/HomePage.aspx;
- USA – (MBNQA) http://www.quality.nist.gov/.

Assuring Quality in the Production Process

Quality assurance means providing a customer with a product (a material good or a service) of appropriate quality where the supplier determines the quality criteria, standards and measures, according to appropriate market research and its supplier's own design (off-the-shelf) or where the supplier and the customer mutually establish the expected quality (made-to-order).

The production process for goods and services is based on three elements – inputs, process, and outputs – with appropriate quality within each element. A process is defined as a group of activities that takes an input, adds value to it and provides an output. Whether a good is being manufactured or assembled or whether a service is being provided, different types of input are required for the production. From the perspective of the focal firm, the inputs include, for example, materials (raw or manufactured), machinery, or knowledge. There are usually several possible tiers of suppliers upstream from the focal firm. Quality is required by each of these because the product is only as good as the lowest quality component, system or control. The challenges associated with this are described by Newlands in Chapter 28 'Supplier Development', this volume.

The second production element, process, involves many possible aspects, including production, assembly and testing. Procedures and methods involved in goods manufacturing, assembly or service provision themselves must be based on quality principles and practices. Testing can be applied to the received material, to work-in-progress, to the methods and procedures used, or to the final product. Results may suggest possible areas or items for improvement. Machinery used in the production process must also be tested, maintained and, if necessary, repaired.

The third element, output, provides the finished product either to the consumer directly or to a distribution network for eventual delivery to the consumer. There is opportunity here for testing and improvement of logistics handling procedures and methods. Outputs are linked to consumer research, through design or redesign, quality of the product or the material and machinery that suppliers use to produce goods. The output is studied for data that suggest possible process and input improvements.

The production process can be described as a cycle flows of funding, information and goods and services (see Figure 22.1). Information, materials, or machinery are input into the production cycle where they are processed (value-added) before being output (or distributed) to customers. Goods and services flow downstream to the next customer in the chain. Information flows upstream from customers to suppliers through marketing research and design/redesign. Information also flows downstream in the form of details about the product and process. Information, as feedback, flows within the focal firm backwards through the process. If quality is to be assured then, at each step, opportunities must be provided to improve the cycle. Information about product or process must be seen as an opportunity to improve.

Further descriptions of the supply chain are provided by MacBeth, in Chapter 8, 'Supply Chain Management', this volume.

Defining Quality

Examining the production cycle provides us with an opportunity to define quality. There is no one single definition of quality because a different perspective or definition is possible from each of the various viewpoints within in the supply chain.

From the manufacture's perspective, quality is defined as a measure of its ability to respect specifications. This a manufacturing -based definition. At the design/redesign stage in the cycle, quality is defined as the ability to engineer value into the product, that is, meet specifications at the most efficient costs. This is a value-based definition of quality.

The final product would offer a number of attributes that a customer might find desirable. Considering the actual performance of the product as intended provides a user-based view from which we could define quality as *fitness for intended use*. Other attributes might provide a different definition. Examples include, various features and overall aesthetics (colour, weight, dimension, speed, etc.), or whether the product conforms to specifications, or the degree of

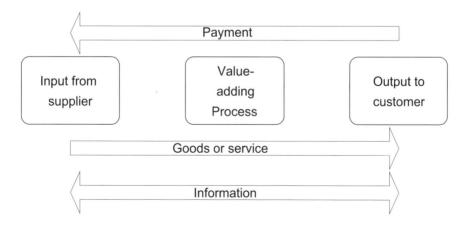

Figure 22.1   Supply chain process

reliability of the product, or how serviceable the product is when repair or maintenance is required. Thus, under these circumstances, the definition of quality would be from a product-based perspective.

More recent programmes of quality management tend to have a holistic slant. They focus on the big picture in order to involve the totality of aspects of a product and its delivery. Thus, the transcendent-view definition may be the most effective. This definition suggests that overall excellence, the sum of many views, would define quality as based on user-perceptions.

Process Management

Earlier in this chapter we described how production processes are comprised of three elements: input, process, and output. Here, the focus is on how firms manage these elements for quality improvement (see Figure 22.2).

A process is a string of linked activities related to these three input, process and output elements. The aim is to achieve a result that satisfies a customers (the firm or next person down the linor firm down the line). Since the string is repeated for each customer demand, if activities are studied and measured, quality improvement opportunities are provided. Since each activity is intended to add value to the process, making improvements to a process requires that, in addition to constantly improving activities that add value, it is necessary that non-value adding activities be modified or eliminated. This applies whether the string of activities is entirely in-house – within the firm – or includes activities undertaken by a supplier.

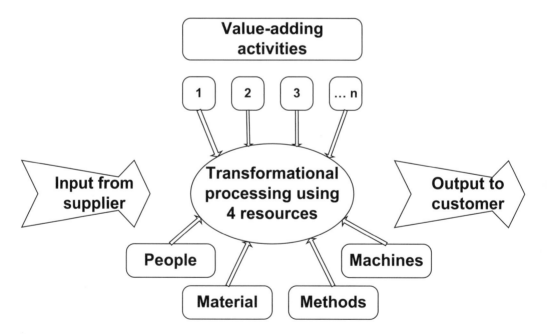

Figure 22.2   Process management

Quality as the Basis of Process Management and Supply Chain Performance

Process management includes inter-firm processes of the extended supply chain. Therefore, the concern for quality management must be a shared concern by all the partners in the chain. It serves little purpose if a focal firm has a quality philosophy but is working in isolation. If a full commitment towards quality by upstream or downstream firms in the supply chain is lacking, the good efforts of the focal firm regarding customer-focused quality are lost. Given that today competition is no longer firm versus firm but instead is a supply chain versus supply chain competitive phenomenon, quality management must be a shared supply chain concern, even if this requires a particular firm within the chain to take a leading role or exert a dominating presence upon the other firms regarding with respect to quality.

There are three main categories of processes within a firm: management, core business, and support.

Management Responsibilties

Management responsibilities include leadership, strategy development and implementation, overall management and direction of the firm. Management must ask important and probing questions. Answers may not be obvious. Techniques may not be available. Benchmarks of how well others are doing and what is possible may not be known. Uncertainty may be high. Education levels may be low. Management in such circumstances thus must:

- communicate the need to improve and compete;
- propose common vocabulary that everyone can use to effectively communicate;
- ask for ideas; recognise contributions, provide feedback and support implementations;
- demonstrate early successes using problem solving processes;
- facilitate learning;
- help develop tentative solutions even if these are not definitive answers;
- support workforces to produce their own solutions and provide resources – time, money, equipment and people in order realise changes (Evans and Lindsay 2005).

Such processes will be undertaken in-house first in order to gain experience with problem solving and continuous improvement. They will then identify the inputs that suppliers produce as goods or services to the firm. Suppliers then become the recipients of improvement and development programmes. See Newlands in Chapter 28 'Supplier Development', this volume.

Core Business Processes

Core business processes include research and design of product (goods and services), procurement of required material (raw, information, tools, etc.), market surveys, production, customer relationship management, etc. Firms are learning to retain core activities. They are focusing on the areas in which they are strong and becoming stronger at these. These strengths increase economies of scale and reduce costs because time, people and investment are reduced because of efficiencies and effectiveness. Firms are also learning to outsource activities that other firms, under their control, can do faster, cheaper and better than they themselves can. This is because outside contractors and key partners feel the competitive pressure to perform. Their business exists because they are better at certain tasks than other businesses. They specialize and maintain their competitive advantage because they are continuously seeking better, faster and cheaper ways of satisfying their clients. In so doing, they can reduce the price and thus sell more to more clients, while simultaneously increasing their margin, contribution and gross profit.

Few automotive producers in the world are happy to outsource design of the vehicle body styling. This is because vehicle assemblers are system integrators. The styling is the medium-term commitment to a customer-appreciated product type. Mistakes at this level can seriously reduce overall demand for branded goods. Few suppliers would be willing to take on that responsibility. Suppliers, however, tend to produce generic and bespoke parts and continually search for improvements. An engine is an engine. Does the customer really care which producer it came from, or if the brand owner produced it themselves? In some cases, yes. For instance, Ford created a relationship with Cosworth. Rolls Royce and Bentley used BMW engines. London Taxis International, who assemble the famous black London cab, used Nissan engines until the then Mayor of London Ken Livingstone decreed that Ford engines were cleaner and only those would be licensed. Such cases are, however, relatively rare.

Support Processes

Support processes are those that facilitate the core business processes. These include financial services, human resource and conflict resolution services, corporate travel and accommodation management, legal services, health provision and stakeholder care (paternalism), education and training – career management, outsourcing and partner network facilitation, performance appraisal and improvement facilitation, logistics and distribution, and information systems and technologies. Although the activities and resources of the core business processes are normally the focus of quality management initiatives, the other two categories should also 'think and act quality' in order to and enhance their value creation and value distribution activities when possible.

Process integration requires that the three sets of processes be aligned and, where necessary, controlled. Process integration is not required for organizational simplicity and managerial control for its own sake. Integration is a means of increasing the probability that successful outcomes are achieved and that results are of higher value than the effort and resources required to create them. Management, however, may have to accept that they have to empower employees. Management have to delegate and trust that their employees, suppliers and other stakeholders will make decisions in their own self-interest and that these area also in the interests of the organization and extended enterprise.

Tools for Managing Quality

We will explore different methods and tools that are useful for controlling for quality. Remember that a picture is worth a thousand words – so too are charts and diagrams. Such diagrams help make better decisions. There are several categories of such tools.

Causal Analysis

Cause analysis (CA) tools include cause and effect diagrams, also known as fish-bone or Ishikawa (see Figure 22.3). These diagrams depict the identified causes that led to a specific outcome. The result could be bad (a problem) or good (a solution). Causes could be peoples' actions or passivity, methods, material, or machines. This diagram provides a better understanding of the sources of an effect and an opportunity for improvement.

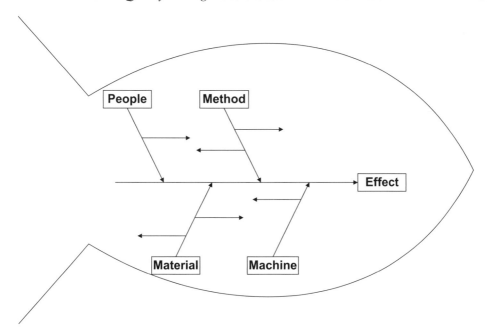

Figure 22.3   Cause and effect diagram

Another CA tool is the Pareto chart. This is based on a histogram sorted in descending order of the frequency of the identified items. This allows users to focus on the 20 per cent of items that cause 80 per cent of the problem. In the example below, to improve quality of service the firm would concentrate on solving problems of incomplete orders and stock inventory. Pareto diagrams enable management to prioritize managerial and other employees' attention on key 'show stopper' issues that can seriously impact on the viability of the business.

Figure 22.5 shows another CA tool, the scatter diagram (Figure 22.5), where variables are plotted against each other. These diagrams facilitate an understanding of the relationship between inputs and outputs. Relationships may be trends, statistical spread or stability. In this example there is a positive correlation with a possible outlier.

Potential Solution Identification and Creation

Idea generation (IG) tools include an element of brainstorming. This is where any participant can offer ideas without comment or criticism from the other participants. At the end of the brainstorming time period, the ideas are analysed, possibly using other tools like affinity diagrams. Affinity diagrams group ideas around an affinity key concept or relationship. Once ideas have been generated and classified, another IG tool – benchmarking – is used. The firm compares its ideas and outcomes against other similar firms or businesses that make use of the same inputs and have similar outputs or with comparable processes in non-competing businesses. In so doing, observations may lead to the generation of other ideas. These quality tools help assure competitiveness.

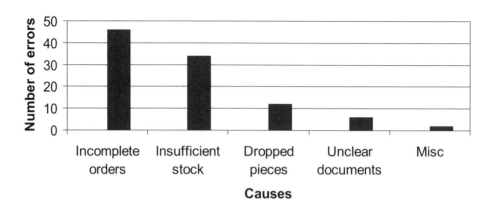

Figure 22.4   Pareto chart

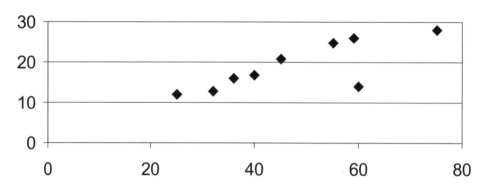

Figure 22.5   Scatter diagram

Process Analysis Tools

A third category of tools is called process analysis tools (PA). For example, consider that humans can be forgetful, may misunderstand directions, make simple errors in identifying something, may lack a needed skill, or be tired and absent minded. A simple way to prevent errors would be to use a 'Poka Yoke' (pronounced pok-ah-yoke-eh). This Japanese term describes an approach for fail-safe processes that usesing automatic devices or methods to avoid simple human error. For example, using a block-slotted screw head that constrains a screwdriver to prevent off-setting a hole on a wheel in order that it can be assembled only in one way. Batteries can be inserted incorrectly. Small 9-volt batteries have two different types of connector. They can only be inserted into the other type of connector. A 'Poka Yoke' tool makes an error either impossible or immediately identified. Machines can be equipped with cycle self-termination and report infrastructure. They will stop if an error is going to be made or has just been made. Because the machine will remain idle, alarms are fitted, a red, yellow and green light cluster similar to a road stop signal illuminated to show current status, and a master status control panel may be used to see at a glance the status of the entire facility. Employees will not be monitoring every machine constantly. They monitor for warnings (yellow lights) and faults (red – stopped). Employees will rush to the failed machine and determine what has gone wrong. They are empowered to make quick fixes to maintain production flow. Later, they will devote attention to finding the root cause and either eliminating it or preventing it from affecting the machine in the future. The aim of using total productive maintenance is to minimize downtime during production time. This type of environment requires employees to have two jobs – to do the work and to improve the work they do. Employees are expected to contribute ideas and not simply work to rule and do as they are told (as would happen in a Tayloristic environment).

Flow charts are another PA tool. They depicts the sequence of steps of a process, including who is involved, what materials are brought into the process, what decisions have to be made, how long queues and delays are, movements, inspection and storage. The anticipated value-added can be added together with actual cost. A target cost may be given and the objective is to identify how to make the process more efficient. In so doing, non-value added waste can be identified and eliminated (Levinson and Rerick 2002).

There is also a tool known as failure mode and effects analysis (FMEA). Here, a sequence of a process is analysed in order to identify what can go wrong. Three variables are assigned numeric values of between 1 and 10 – frequency, detection and consequence. If an error occurs frequently it receives 10. If it is extremely rare, it is assigned 1. If the error can be detected immediately and every time, it receives 1. If it is not detected and people would not be aware of it, it receives 10. If consequences lead to loss of life, property damage and catastrophies then it receives 10. If the customer would not notice, it receives 1. Multiplying these three factors together will produce results from 1 to 1,000. Companies typically reduce the result to below 125 by introducing safety measures and Poka Yoke to prevent the error. By careful design and retrofitting to existing processes, the aim is to correct the process before, rather than after, the process is put into operation or products are produced and sold. A histogram can also contribute to the FMEA analysis tool because it depicts the frequency distribution of items in a particular data set.

A fourth set of tools is for project management. One tool is the Gantt chart which shows progress of a project, what events are occurring and how long each event is taking. This facilitates comparisons with the original specifications of the project.

Another project tool is the PDCA cycle proposed by Deming. He argued that quality improvement had to be a continuous cycle of planning (P), doing (D), checking (C) and acting (A) on the issue at hand.

Each of these tools provides a picture of a situation, showing where improvement is possible, providing a better picture for controlling a process, or depicting the situation after quality improvement. However, the most common method for controlling process is to use statistical process control (SPC). A full description of SPC is provided on the Gower webpage to support this chapter.

Cost of Quality

Is it worth it? Many a company executive must have asked the question: 'Just what will it cost to institute a quality philosophy, including a quality program, in our company?' Crosby

(1979) said that 'quality is free'. Obviously there are costs involved and so the question must be answered. As we can observe, the total cost is not just the money spent on quality, but also the costs of not spending money on quality, that is, value that would have been gained if money were invested in a quality initiative and losses and waste did not occur.

There are definitely occasions where firms (manufacturing or service) waste money by not having quality instilled. There are many possible examples including inefficient movements (people walking or material being moved extra distances because of a lack of space and logistics planning); reworking any product part because it was not right the first time (including a need to respect warranties); correcting documents and forms; repeating orders already taken; re-entering data into a system (including redundant storage), etc. In other words, if the firm does not have to spend on redoing things or other waste areas because they did things properly the first time, the costs of quality is affected. The firm is making more money than it would if quality was not in place. Essentially, there are 'good' and 'bad' quality costs.

Regarding good quality costs, prevention costs include such examples as: quality improvement planning, teams and training; supplier and customer relationship consultation; supplier capability evaluation; and quality surveys. Good quality costs also include the designing of mechanisms and procedures for prevention of error and non-conformance. Appraisal costs include testing and inspecting material arriving from an up stream supplier (whether inside or outside the firm), in-process and final inspections, auditing products or services, calibration of tools and machinery.

Regarding bad quality costs, internal failure (before exit) includes scrap material, re-work, re-inspection, re-testing and any product part that is consequently scrapped. The most expensive costs are external costs because the product or service has exited the facility and possibly been delivered to the final customer. Examples include warranty claims, product recall, handling customer complaints and returns. The loss of image or market share is included with these costs.

So, how much does quality cost? The firm should add up the good costs and the bad costs. If the bad costs represent the greater value, the firm is losing; if the good costs are higher then the firm will reap benefits (greater reputation, sales, return on investment, etc.) that eventually could surpass their investment and quality will be free! Some financial analyses (Beecroft et al. 2003) show that investing €1 in good quality will return minimum €15 each year. Quality is not only free, it is 'profitable'.

Conclusions

If firms, and particularly individuals, develop 'quattitude' then extending the quality attitude among partners should produce mutual benefits. A quality-based supply chain partnership requires a clear mandate from committed senior managers of each firm in the chain; a quality culture in each firm that is supportive of associates as well as external partner needs; a flexible structure that allows partners to appreciate and adjust to the quality culture of the partner firms; and joint sharing of chairmanship of quality committees and a mutual exchange of documentation and learning.

This chapter has briefly touched on the large and exciting area of quality management. Within its limited scope, we have attempted to inspire you with a feel for the topic, a look at some of the many gurus and models of quality and examples of some simple problems that help quality managers to reach better decisions. If you wish to delve further into the topic, you are encouraged to join many students around the world who have become student-members (at a reasonable student rate) of the ASQ. The online accompanying text to this chapter, available at the Gower Publishing website (www.gowerpub.com) to accompany this volume, examines the seven quality tools.

References

ASQ Quality Costs Committee (1999), *Principles of Quality Costs: Principles, Implementation, and Use*, ed. Campanella, J. (Milwaukee, WI: ASQ Quality Press).

Beecroft, G.D., Duffy, G.L. and Moran, J.W. (2003), *The Executive Guide to Improvement and Change* (Milwaukee, WI: ASQ Quality Press).

Clark, T.J. (1999), *Success Through Quality: Support Guide for the Journey to Continuous Improvement* (Milwaukee, WI: ASQ Quality Press).

Crosby, P. (1979), *Quality is Free* (New York: McGraw-Hill).

Davis, E.W. and Spekman, R. (2004), *Extended Enterprise* (Upper Saddle River, NJ: Prentice Hall).

Deming, W.E. (1986), *Out of the Crisis* (Cambridge: Press Syndicate).

Evans, J.R. and Lindsay, W.M. (2005), *An Introduction to Six Sigma & Process Improvement* (Mason, OH: South-Western (Thomson Learning)).

Fisher, R. and Brown, R. (1988), *Getting Together: Building a Relationship that Gets to Yes* (Boston, MD: Houghton Mifflin Co.).

Fisher, R. and Ury, W. (1981), *Getting to Yes, Negotiating Agreement Without Giving In* (London: Hutchinson).

Gardner, R.A. (2004), *The Process-Focused Organization: A Transition Strategy for Success* (Milwaukee, WI: ASQ Quality Press).

Juran, J. and Godfrey, A. (1998), *Juran's Quality Handbook*, 5th edn (New York: McGraw-Hill Books).

Levy, P., Bessant, J., Sang, B. and Lamming, R. (1995), 'Developing integration through Total Quality Supply Chain Management', *Integrated Manufacturing Systems* 6(3), pp. 4–12.

Levinson, W.A. and Rerick, R.A. (2002), *Lean Enterprise: A Synergistic Approach to Minimizing Waste* (Milwaukee, WI: ASQ Quality Press).

Logistics Management (2006), 'Quest for Quality Winners: Logistics Providers at the Top of their Game', http://www.logisticsmgmt.com/chapter/CA6365022.html?nid=2721&rid=1285779121.

Mann, N. (1985), *The Keys to Excellence: The Deming Philosophy* (London: Mercury Books/ WH Allen & Co.).

Chapter 23
Technology and Innovation Management

David J. Newlands

Introduction

This chapter introduces elements of technology and innovation management. As most economies still need to maintain a manufacturing base, since economies can not easily exist exclusively as a service economy, it is the contention of this author that technology and innovation are prime drivers of the globalizing economy.

An examination is made of methods and implications across the whole organization, from operations through to strategy. By highlighting the role of technology and innovation in an integrated strategy for the firm, this chapter provides an integrated understanding of its subject matter as well as an appreciation of how organization-wide synergies can be achieved by managers.

Manufacturing has remained relatively constant as an employer of approximately the same number of people over the twentieth century. At the beginning of the industrial revolution, they went in search of jobs in factories. This migration primarily has seen the progressive reduction in workers on farms (Heizer and Render 2006). In developed nations, people have left the land and now only a small percentage of the population produce the food for the rest of society. Service industries and service activities are now the largest segment of vocations in many mature and newly industrialized nations. Professional managers appeared alongside owner-managers. The information technology age has enabled people to work not so much with their bodies as with their minds. Ideas are created and communicated at amazing speeds right around the world.

Knowledge workers of all kinds are specifying, analysing, simplifying, organizing, designing and reporting information. To make things happen, they plan what others will do: how, where and when. A large proportion of the knowledge service sector activity is likely to be repetitive, self-sustaining and of low value. The education services sectors give advice, propose recommendations, provide assistance and transfer established and well documented skills and techniques. They may recognize the dynamic nature of the business environment and hence train course participants to solve problems by first asking questions, identifying what they do not know or do not have. They may then set out a plan to answer those questions and accomplish or acquire what is needed achieve satisfactory solutions to identified needs.

Creativity is required in various professions. At least a proportion of knowledge workers, and perhaps to a lesser extent workers in manufacturing, are directly involved in creative pursuits. For nearly two centuries shopfloor workers were expected to clock in and leave their minds at the door, ready to start thinking when they left to go home or to the pub. The division of labour had manifested itself into those who think and those who do. The workforce in industrialized nations tends now to have a higher level of general and specialized vocational education. They no longer need to be herded like sheep and made to put in physical effort like mules walking in circles at a water pump. Leading companies have woken up to the fact that when they hire a body, they get a mind for free. These companies may use cognitive dissonance techniques to reward suggestions. They give small monetary rewards to employees for each idea that has merit.

Technical specialists' knowledge gained as a result of further and higher education can have a half life usefulness of only a few years. This is because their fields advance rapidly. If they do not take further courses and engage in lifelong learning, they will become less effective. Other solutions that have been developed and adopted will be missed because the specialists' awareness of the current state of the art is no longer accurate. After several years as a specialist, they may have to migrate to managing projects where they coordinate the efforts of new recruits and more recent graduates.

Designers must interpret customer requirements and translate them into product concepts, aesthetic and technical specifications. Designers will select technologies appropriate to satisfy customer requirements and production processes to be used.

Product creation project managers must ensure suitable technology solutions are available to be incorporated or selected by product designers. An imperative is that the right technology must be developed, purchased, franchised or reverse engineered from comparable solutions, to satisfy future expected trends and needs. Technologies must contribute to the creation of new products and be able to enhance existing offerings in order to extend their production life cycle.

Product development managers (PDM) must achieve a viable product by certain deadlines. Competitors want to release products that have unique selling propositions based on performance, weight, size, efficiency, speed, cost, reliability, functionality, etc. It is vital that specifications are released by Design that enable purchasing, suppliers, subcontractors, production, distribution and product launch specialists to coordinate their teams' activities. Even if the product isn't what the PDM may want as a finished product, the market will accept at a given price the good or service. Further development may be undertaken after a specification version has been frozen, to further enhance the solution. This strategy is not limited to physical variants. Software solution providers continuously identify further improvements and release downloadable upgrades as part of their post purchase product support services package.

Many multinational corporations produce and sell the same product, albeit with minor technical specification modifications, in many countries. Pringles Crisps are an example of this. The same standardized sizes of carton and equipment needed for packaging and product are exported all over the world. International corporations by contrast bespoke their products to country by country and even region by region needs. They may release further flavours, but the general shape, common materials used and processes necessary to make them are common. Coca-Cola modify the flavour and sweetness of their beverages in order to satisfy the mean local market preferences. Tour guides at Coca-Cola's museum in Atlanta, USA proudly proclaim they have 240 syrup formulae and packaging variants of their core cola.

These companies need to identify the point at which the variants are introduced. For Pringles and bottled or canned cola, this happens in the factory. Coca-Cola may also introduce variants after the sale has occurred. At fast food restaurants and cinemas, etc., they provide cups that are filled from drinks fountains that mix the selected syrup with fizzy water. Mobile phone producers have adopted similar strategies to ensure all products are common at the factory and the customer may snap on covers or download software variants through their devices wirelessly.

Innovation and Invention and Commercialization

Discovery is the recognition of a phenomenon, fact or realignment of ones' perception to generate an insight. Such insights may lead one to create a new paradigm.

Invention is discovery and unique one-off configurations. Most inventions will not be sold commercially. Pharmaceutical companies register many patents, yet only about one in a thousand compounds are converted to prescription and over-the-counter drugs. Honda Motor Manufacturing advertisements in the early years of this century have promoted their technical expertise. The basis of this level of achievement is the core question 'What if ...?' This approach implies they are open to new ideas, concepts, inventions and methods. Honda's motto is 'fuel efficient engines at an affordable price'. Honda produces motorbikes, cars and other vehicles as a means of commercializing their engine technologies. Honda also held the world fuel efficiency record in the early 1990s. At the time of writing, the fuel efficiency record stands at 5,385 km per litre (http://www.primidi.com/2005/07/05.html; see Chaper 30 'Change Management – Realizing the Transformation' by Newlands, this volume). Commercially-released vehicles now provide between 0.1 per cent and 1.0 per cent of performance that has been demonstrated from proven technologies.

Invention also is the integration of existing elements to create a device that does a function that is original and has not been replicated or copied. Some inventions remain as isolated unique examples of a particular technology. Other inventions are commercialized.

Innovation is not the same thing as invention or discovery. Innovation is the successful development and launch of new products and features (Smith 1995). It includes the processes of taking an invention, discovery or new technology and converting them into a viable commercial product that can be released for sale either at a business-to-business or business-to-consumer level. Some products are commercialized and become spectacular commercial failures. The Sinclair C5 is a classic example of this. Other goods have fewer fashion elements in their offering and hence become perennial favourites.

Innovation also can be seen in how products are assembled and how work is done. For instance, Henry Ford's moving assembly line changed expectations of consumers concerning price, quality and waiting time to have their orders satisfied. Both those innovations also changed the economics of producing goods.

McDonald's innovation was a more efficient and fast food delivery system to satisfy the demand for barbequed food without needing to own or set up a barbeque. These foods also are available at the restaurants, even in bad weather when picnic barbeques would be in appropriate. Complementary technologies have been used to enhance the delivery system including: the development of frozen French fries that are rapidly cooked, point-of-sale drinks fountains that produce flavour variants on demand, the application of *kanban* and other just-in-time techniques to fast food production, assembly and delivery systems.

The division of labour first identified by Adam Smith (1776) and embedded into mass production systems enabled far more to be produced with much less effort and cost. Similarly, just-in-time and lean manufacturing methods developed at Toyota further reduced resource requirements. These advances and their founding principles have been replicated initially in car assembly plants and now have extended into government, the private sector and service sectors. Both invention and innovation involve identifying needs and creating ideas prior to creating the object.

The company's values expressed in their mottos reflect their ability to develop solutions and their emphasis toward invention and innovation:

- IBM – Think
- Apple Macintosh – Think Differently
- Hewlett-Packard – Innovate
- Nike – Just do it.

When buying a product, the user is acquiring the entire collected creativity, ideas, attention to detail and care that has evolved over the history of the company and supply chain that produced the good or service. When purchasing a Mercedes car for example, one buys into a certain heritage and prestigious brand. Mercedes were the first car company to introduce driver airbags as standard. They also led with anti-locking brakes and crash cage strength enhancements.

Our Technology will be Junk

There is one truism that is increasingly relevant:

Today's pinnacle of technology is tomorrow's junk.

Products made today were designed in the past, sometimes many years ago. Manufacturers will continue to produce them while customers buy them. As demand drops for older specification goods, upgrade specification releases must be made to re-invigorate the sales rate. An alternative strategy is to co-package goods with other items. Each item alone may have limited value. Higher value is added because customers may buy gifts for others to use. Co-packaging is evident in school child geometry sets, sound system and entertainment systems that include CD, radio tuner, twin tape decks and graphic equalizers. In effect, a car has become a co-packaged product because optional extras such as headrest rear seat display units enable passengers to watch DVDs and play video games. Luxury cars' seats essentially are armchairs fitted into vehicles. When fitted with high quality sound systems, trim, fitted mobile phones, satellite navigation systems, anti-roll systems, heads-up night vision systems, airbags and other safety devices, drivers feel as comfortable and safe as they would at home. The technologist or innovator may not need to invent anything. Co-packaging specific combinations together may be all that is necessary to register international patents. An entrepreneur appearing on the BBC's *Dragon's Den* in 2007 had patented his idea. He had embedded a Game Boy type device into a soft stuffed toy. Completely different yet complementary items can be co-packaged. Cosmetic and cleansing products such as facial washes, soap, body milk, moisturizer, shampoo, conditioner, night creams and toners can be shrink-wrapped on top of a basket. Additional packaging materials may be used to keep the displayed items in position and make the volume of the goods appear larger.

Price Erosion

Significant price erosion is evident in many market segments – prices of goods decline over time. The price of a good reflects how long the good will serve the customer. Soft drinks are quite cheap, despite the materials perhaps taking several years and transnational logistics and processing in various countries, to be made and delivered to the point of sale (Womack and Jones 1996). Vehicles are quite expensive by comparison. One of the fastest price erosions for second-hand vehicles was the Opel/Vauxhall Astra. Owners trying to sell these cars second hand found that even after only eight months prices had dropped by around 60 per cent from showroom levels. Porsche, by contrast, tend to lose 5 per cent in the first year but by the end of the second year demand is higher and second-hand prices tend to rise above the original purchase price.

Generally, more expensive purchase prices are indicators of investment costs, early adopter premiums soon after launch, the total volume produced of a good (amortizing and fixed cost division methods), the price decay of second-hand goods, the durability and total life costs, and most importantly, the sum total of all the ideas the company has had (learning and cost decay curves) that are embedded into the product and processes to produce them. The price also reflects local taxation. Vehicle prices in the United Kingdom include new car registration tax, value-added tax, import duty, green tax and the annual road tax licence. Once each of these deductions has been taken into account, the company has a very tight revenue within which to design, purchase, produce, distribute and market the good.

Competitive pricing is typically in function with absorbing the conceptual and detail design costs of technology development, prototyping and pre-production runs. Early in the production life cycle, design will continue to improve the product. During the mature stage of a product's production cycle, emphasis typically changes to manufacturing and supply chain efficiency improvements. To sustain the manufacturing life cycle, design typically become involved again to find ways of enhancing the product without too much investment.

The purchase price of a good also took account of the length of time that a good or service will last and the value appreciated by the customer. Higher-priced cars were associated with a long service life. Historically, one would expect that cheaper cars would likely end up on the scrap heap much sooner. This assumption now doesn't hold true because all cars are built to much higher quality specifications. Computers can be upgraded because most of the operating circuits are modules that can be plugged into a motherboard. Laptop computers are more problematic to upgrade, however. Other price components include the satisfaction of stated and tacit needs. The cost of maintenance and use incurred during the service life may or may not be a consideration of the consumer when purchasing a consumer durable.

If the market changes unpredictably and those products are designed with unique components, manufacturing has to cover leftover stock as obsolescence costs, or store them in the hope that spares will be purchased after the warranty period elapses. If the company is crafty, they may have negotiated 'buy or return', or even better, 'free issue' materials contracts. Rover recognized that they owe their suppliers when they take goods from store to build, while Toyota will guarantee to pay precisely 120 days after the car has passed all routine quality testing procedures.

Process and Product Kaizen

Technology and innovation management must be examined within the context of total quality management. Many companies guarantee their employees they will never lose their jobs if they contribute to improving quality. They have two jobs: *do the work and improve the work done.* This reflects the need to:

- make product or provide service in order to raise revenue that keeps the organization viable; and
- enhance the product, service or processes used in order to keep pace with the benchmarks for competitive advantages set by customers, competitors or formal governmental watchdogs.

If the current state is managed as is, performance and customer satisfaction will likely reduce over time. *Kaizen* or continuous improvement requires 'total employment involvement' – the active participation of all direct employees, suppliers' personnel and others involved in the product, service, process or concept. The essence of JIT is a reliance on the willingness of workers to spot quality problems, which they consider to be opportunities, and have the authority and courage to halt production when necessary, group together people to analyse problems and implement a quick fix. A team comprised of the different functions in the business will be established to generate ideas for improvement, that will identify the route cause and eliminate this to prevent a similar problem reoccurring. Step-jumps in performance, known in Japanese as *kai kaku*, may be the result of going live with a new, adopted or revised technology.

Warren (1995) and Unipart (c.1995, p. 4, quotes in Taylor 1995) suggest that a company and its supply chain have to have a policy of continuous improvement and must develop to surpass competitors' performance to achieve success, as depicted by Figure 23.1.

Watson (1994) extends the model used by Warren and Unipart by suggesting that key performance metrics are improved on a project-by-project basis and as a result of implementing solutions derived from technology breakthroughs. The multiple project concepts proposed by Watson presumably allow networks of companies to prioritize management attention and investment opportunities. This has the effect of reducing perceived risk and companies then have the opportunity to apportion them to dependent, independent and intervening or extraneous variables.

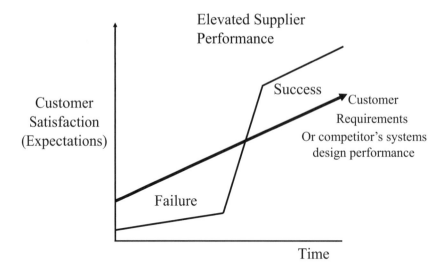

Figure 23.1   Key performance metric improvement over time – satisfaction, success and failure adapted (Warren, Unipart)

Greenfield (n.d.) builds on Watson's work by depicting performance improvements in a series of phases using curvilinear relationships based on Pareto's concept and the learning curve that anticipate initial gains will be rapid and then subsequently optimized over a settling in learning period (Figure 23.2). In effect, Greenfield alters the scale of the axes of the graph to absolute values rather than artificially designated ranges used in the Warren and Unipart model. This distinction in representation hypothetically is linked to improvement initiative fatigue due to a lack of understanding of an overall programme or framework for change.

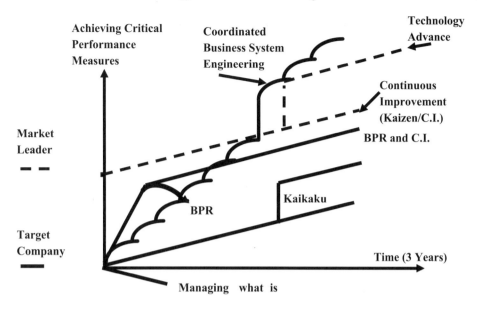

Figure 23.2   Greenfield's sequential curvilinear performance improvement model

Competitors will probably bring out comparable and increasingly attractive, newer product offerings. This can be predicted and financially beneficial if the company opts to co-invest with that competitor. In effect, they are competitors in the market with differentiated products and services, yet behind the scenes they collaborate and co-fund products for mutual benefit. In the automotive industry, Ford is the supreme example of such practices. They have bought rights to use components and co-invested in new technologies with various brand companies. Diesel and petrol engines (Peugeot), body crash cells (Fiat and Mercedes), hydrogen storage tanks (Mercedes), six speed automatic gear boxes (GM). Simultaneously, suppliers of many of the core systems are common to most assemblers. For example, Faurcia design and produce steering wheels, airbags and front bumper systems for most brands.

To remain ahead of competitors, technology and design leaders may sell their technologies to others (e.g., Intel) that will mass produce and compete on economies of scale, or sell to producers in lower cost countries for emerging markets. During the 1980s IBM funded RAM memory chip designs and bought from two producers. They provided non-recurring expenditure grants to each, alternating between them. Each time a project commenced, the challenge was to design and produce double the memory capacity of the competitor. Company A would receive an order to develop a 256k chip. Company A and B would both produce these once the design was ready. Company B would then develop a 512k chip. Both would then make this. Subsequently, the cycle would repeat when company A would receive an order to develop a 1024k (1 meg) chip and company B would follow with a 2048k chip, etc. IBM made money out of this strategy by having exclusive rights to sell computers and systems that had unique features, capacity, performance and capabilities. Other competitors would be allowed to sell similar products that had been de-tuned or did not have the same full functionality. As a result, IBM maintained a market perceived and benchmarkable product performance competitive advantage. IBM no longer make computers. They make more money out of selling memory systems to other assemblers. IBM have sold their PC assembly business to a Chinese consortium and now specialize in providing solutions. A customer may not receive any elements of the system that have been made by IBM. IBM's core competences are the ability to purchase high performance modules and they know how to integrate them. Given the 'plug and play' type infrastructure such as the USBII technologies, that is now commonplace, IBM's role seems to be under threat.

Some large producers will purchase small technology leading start-up enterprises in order to get technologies they neither have the skills nor time to develop (GM bought Lotus, learned, then sold the company).

Rather than just making what designers have created, manufacturing companies 'buy solutions'. These are product specifications and plans created by product development teams. Manufacturing companies want products they can make and customers that want to buy them. If the product isn't attractive to them, they are increasingly empowered to not accept to make a product because they are assessed on profitability, on-time product ramp-up and launch.

Technology Cycles

Osborn (1957) suggested that designers can use a number of strategies to evolve designs. The elements, which he called a generalized checklist, are:

- put parts to other uses;
- adapt other parts to serve an alternate requirement;
- modify, magnify (enlarge), minify (miniaturize), substitute (exchange for another lower cost, easier to produce, less dangerous, etc.), rearrange (re-sequence, make more ergonomically appropriate), reverse (opposite oriented, doing the unexpected), combine (fewer parts = less time to assemble, hence lower costs incurred and increased productivity).

Zara are famous for copying designer catwalk show display garments. They do this by rapidly replicating original creations and bringing these to market very quickly. These goods are produced in limited quantities. If they sell well, they are not reproduced. Instead, Zara exaggerate design attributes of the garment in line with Osborn's generalized checklist. Further exaggerations may take the modifications in a particular direction. Eventually, either the market or the designers will become predictable, passé and uninteresting. The result would be reduced sales prices. To avoid this scenario, Zara designers forcibly reject the trend they created and design further variants in other directions or inverse their trend. If this trend is successful, they will continue until they decide there is no more viable means of creating variants from the garment theme. At this point, they abandon the material or theme and go in search of new creative ideas to commercialize.

Zara compete because they produce close to the market. They produce limited quantities and never repeat. This creates rarity value. In addition, they make larger profits because they set the market. Mass producers of garments make many goods in China and other low cost countries. They miss the early introduction of goods and rapid product updates because they invest too heavily in standardized products that have to be discounted to sell of the remainder of the stock.

Figure 23.4 shows the consequences for followers in terms of being late to market. The description in the box on the next page applies to various consumer goods sectors. Certainly mobile phone industry leaders in Japan operate this way.

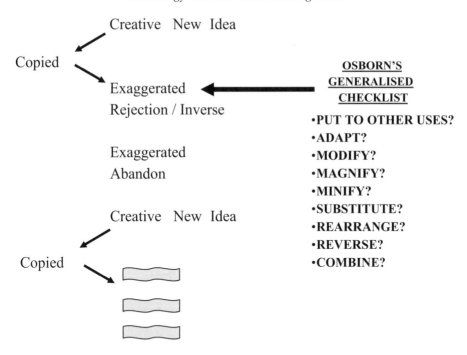

Figure 23.3   Copying designs

Design leaders define new products, verify they can make the functionality viable and can produce the goods (on prototype and pre-production assembly lines). They tool up production and order materials. Then they set product specifications and build up a stock at the point of sale (POS). It is only once a product is launched that copiers will 'get their hands on a copy' of the product in order to try to reverse engineer the good. If they are lucky, a 'me too' copier may get hold of the specifications that were devised around a fully developed product. By the time the copier has assimilated the specification, designed variants that do not impinge copy right and verified their production capabilities in order to make the goods and launch them, they are entering the market significantly behind the lead producer. They may benefit however from lower component prices because the suppliers will be actively reducing their costs.

The only way to reduce or eliminate being later to market than the lead organization is to be part of the 'consortium'. Ericsson made mobile phones. They were the world's largest producer. Consumers fell out of love with these. To survive, Ericsson subsequently joined forces with Sony, an organization that is part of the consortium of Japanese producers.

Technology Challengers

A technology challenger is a project to develop a viable solution that is beyond current capabilities. The aim may be to design and produce goods that, for example, may be smaller, faster, lighter, more powerful, easier to use, constructed of alternative or higher specification materials. The output of such a project would likely create a competitive advantage that would be difficult to replicate quickly. This increases the duration of the sales window when the company has a unique sales proposition.

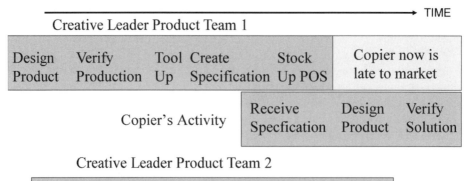

Figure 23.4   Design leadership

Business process re-engineering may provide significant improvements in performance. However, Champy (1995) and Hammer (1995) both conclude that few of the re-engineering projects they outlined in their joint work (Hammer and Champy 1993) achieve the performance expected by planners and business leaders. This is in part due to the top-down 'telling' – giving instructions and acting in a 'hard' psychological manner. Japanese management based on total employee involvement uses Hoshin Kanri to roll out strategic decisions, by encouraging voluntary contributions to the corporation's objectives. The question is 'what can we do to help' rather than 'you do this in the prescribed way'.

The Hoshin Kanri[1] management style is 'not to take the monkey'. If an employee comes in all hot and flustered, and lays their problem at a manager's door, managers can have a number of reactions. Stereotypical reactions are aggression, passivity or unconditionally constructive behaviour (Fisher and Ury 1981; Fisher and Brown 1988). For example they may:

- *Take the monkey* – immediately take charge, issue orders, make snap decisions, assign blame, define the solution, assign responsibilities and tell people in detail. The manager may find it difficult to relinquish control after the change has been made.
- *Analyse and procrastinate* – prepare a study, gather information, analyse, codify, categorize, prioritize, plan and then repeat these to be sure.
- *Facilitate the process* – Edgar Schein (1969, 1987) defined this as process consultation. The manager envisions a possible solution. They may explain the idea or give instructions after a period of consultation. An alternative and probably better approach requires the manager to ask simplistic questions that create the illusion they are dumb and expects

---

1   Good Hoshin Kanri websites include http://www.mcts.com/Hoshin-Kanri.htm, http://membres. lycos.fr/hconline/hoshin_us.htm and http://www.geocities.com/parthadeb/hosinkanri.html.

answers to the questions they ask. Ask employees to identify what is wrong, asking them what they would do about it if they could or were allowed to, giving permission and support to those employees to actually do what they have envisioned. At the end of the day, the manager has to trust that employees will do what is to their own personal advantage and to the benefit of the company. The eventual solution may not be the same as that envisioned by the manager. The solution however will be appropriate to the situation within which the employees perceive themselves. Employees may be aware of controlling influences and conditions that the manager doesn't know about.

The Management of Innovation and Technology

How a product is marketed depends on whether the company knows the name of the customer. Marketing data may be massaged to derive the lowest common denominator and this becomes the basis of a specification for a product, family of products or orders. The products may be produced to order, stocked in advance of expected demand, designed and engineered to order, or assembled from existing parts to make the specific combination selected by the client. Each strategy takes a different amount of time, stock, investment and inherent technology.

Knowing the client's name is important because this will give the solution providing company an idea of how specific the goods will be. Clients that want a known product that is held in stock will expect same day or immediate service and sale. End of line goods may have centralized stores and require a few hours or next day delivery. A client may have an account and require a product that is available 'off the shelf' or assembled rapidly from existing stock options. A small lead time is required for the configuration and assembly time. Clients with unique requirements may expect to wait for unique goods to be designed, materials to be purchased, tooling to be created, designs prototyped, tested, produced, delivered, installed and commissioned. They also may anticipate having to terminate using legacy infrastructure once they have been trained and are confident the new product or system operates flawlessly.

A key question to be answered is how long clients will wait. During the early 1990s, one tractor/excavator manufacturer in the UK took an average of 18 months to develop and integrate relatively minor design changes for an established product to meet a customer requests. Its principal competitor could do the same work and deliver the customized product within six weeks. Farmers could then use the product that was developed faster fully two harvests earlier. In this respect, time is a competitive advantage and can be the difference between an order qualifier – (the initial qualifications and experience audit that gives a client an idea of the competitive positioning of a supplier) and an order winner – (the difference that is a 'show stopper' that eliminates candidates or an over riding criteria that clinches the deal. *Concurrent or simultaneous engineering* is used to reduce the calendar time the client needs to wait to obtain the required good or service.

Key Questions

Companies must compete in a competitive environment. If other companies can convert their ideas into products faster, based on the same marketing data or survey samples, those businesses will win market share and be able to consolidate their position. In order to compete, technology development, design and innovation must happen over a shorter elapsed time in order to be more relevant, up to date and competitive.

Key questions that need to be answered of competitors' products, processes and technology include:

- Do they? (Do they do it, create it, design it, use it, make or buy it, lead or follow ….?)
- How do they do this?
- How good are they? What benefits to they provide? At what cost? How efficient is the operation? How satisfied are their customers?
- Why do they use these strategies? Are the strategies used uniformly for all of the company's product, components, modules and suppliers?
- Do we do the same? If not, why not? Should we continue doing or not doing this?
- Could we? What resources do we have or need that will allow us to do this? What effect would us doing this have on competitors, suppliers, customers, others? Could we use our competitors as service, product, component or process suppliers and yet still compete in the market?
- How good are we? Compared to them, to what we would like to be, today? How good do our customers perceive us to be?
- How could we do better? Asking suppliers and customers what we could do better to be a better supplier or customer to them.
- Why should we? What financial, time, competitive advantages to benefit from and drawbacks to be avoided are there?

Show Stoppers

A show stopper is any justification or limitation that has or hasn't been identified, that requires the company to withdraw from bidding, exit a market, stop producing a product, sell off a business unit, causes significant loss of market share, and brand-damaging loss of reputation. B2B customers may terminate contracts or simply no longer award work for subsequent versions.

The time lag between marketing finding out what the market segment wants at a given point of time and the launch of a product designed and made in accordance with those requirements can be a show stopper for design, production, distribution and shelf life at the point of sale. Competitor products and new product concepts may obviate the need to produce a good, or those new market segments do not exist yet and the company doesn't want to produce goods that are of lower value to the customer and hence revenue would be lower if they staid on track to make the original good.

Concurrent and Simultaneous Engineering

Concurrent engineering (CE) is development and preparation work that is undertaken by more than one functional department at the same time in a company. Simultaneous engineering is the same thing, done between supply chain partners. They may not know the final solution, however they know the general concept and approximate specification, size and shape, process choice and sequence required. The participants must want to work together, whether or not they are co-located. Data must be up to date and shared with those that need to know. Meetings must be held to assess progress, identify snags, deciding who shoulders specific responsibilities, who will be involved, what will be reported to whom and when, and who is to action items on 'to do lists'.

Traditional product development work is modelled as occurring sequentially (Figure 23.5). One project is finished before another functional project starts. The total elapsed time is longer than expected because show-stoppers require previous work to be revised, updated or scrapped and redone. Work is carried out in several functional disciplines simultaneously. No answers are definitive until the activities are completed and a solution is created. The total elapsed time is reduced because work is done at the same time in parallel, and show-stoppers are identified early and rectified or modified to compensate for new ideas and information.

Sequential product development relies on one team doing their work and then 'throwing it over the wall' to the next team. The solutions are supposed to be complete. The problem is the at work is done in isolation and with little input from those who will receive the information and have to do something with it. Eventually, there will be 'show stoppers' that require the job to go back to previous departments. This 'throwing over the wall' mentality lengthens the time taken to develop viable solutions.

It is insufficient that employees work in close proximity to colleagues. Philosophical problems with this approach are 'I told you so' or 'I knew it wouldn't work'. The employees have either sabotaged, or kept quiet and not raised their concerns. It is imperative that employees want to work together.

Concurrent engineering accepts ambiguity and working together at the same time on various projects. Employees do not have the answers. They agree to work together to define the questions and create or buy solutions. The total chronological time spent should be much reduced because, unlike in the traditional sequential product development model, solutions are agreed together near the end of the activity. This solution will remain in place until the next

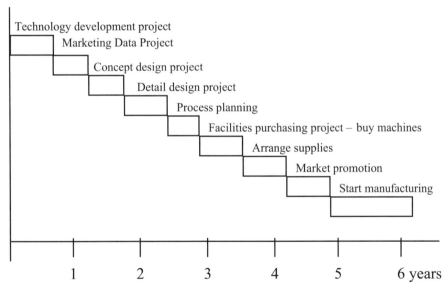

Core problem is slippage. Any of the project phases that take more time than planned means less time for other activities or the whole project will slip.
Work done by preceding projects may not be acceptable to subsequent projects and be rejected, or the problems may be 'show stoppers'.

Figure 23.5   Traditional product development

product variant is developed. The aim is to commercialize goods rapidly. If mistakes are made, learning occurs and improvements are made or planned for the future variants.

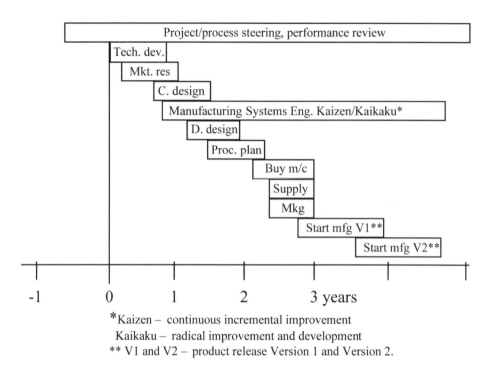

Figure 23.6   Concurrent engineering

Design Influence

The ability to influence design decreases the nearer the product development project gets to manufacture. The costs of changes to designs increases as plant is specified, bought and commissioned. Goods must be designed with 'updateability', serviceability and expandability in mind. For example, computer cases have not varied significantly, despite the major advances in computing power. Automobile skins, transmission and trim changes do not significantly alter the basic model, particularly components under the skin that are not appreciated by the client.

Wheelwright and Clark (1995) suggest that as a product design progresses to a point where it is viable for high volume production, the ability to radically change aspects and characteristics dramatically reduces. Effort to manage design and production activities seems to peek late in prototyping and early in pilot production, and then again serges during production ramp-up. By contrast, Japanese management seem to tend to focus on earlier design stages when there is a greater ability to influence the total cost of the production life cycle, particularly in basic research and technology knowledge generation, idea generation and early conceptual design.

Newlands and Steeple (2000) noted:

> Components that are used to make up vehicles are delivered to assemblers in relatively high-density containers. As such, the value density is increased for goods inbound to the assembly plant. As finished

goods, vehicles nominally have a lower value to volume ratio in comparison to electronic goods such as computers. Japanese vehicles tended to be available in a range of colours with two trim levels: basic and luxury. This variant policy allowed the assembler to avoid producing significant volumes of many intermediate grades of trim and options. By only having two trim levels, significant reductions in stocked parts can be achieved. Given common touch points, only one assembly method and fixing component can be used.

Component commonality permits assemblers to source components from any region and deliver them to their assembly facilities that are located in any other region. This procurement flexibility serves to reduce risks associated with none availability. Simultaneously this contributes to pressure to reduce unit prices due to multiple sources that are in direct competition for supply contracts.

Delorean Motor Company's DM-12 was in large part based on the Lotus Esprit chassis. [2] The engine and other elements were cobbled together from various suppliers of modules.

Corporations such as Nike do not manufacture the products that carry their name. They outsource all product delivery activities to subcontractors. This allows them to determine the optimum price and obtain sufficient volume capacity for fast moving consumer goods. Nike Corp. focuses on marketing, product design and supply chain management.

Distributed Contribution to Design

Design occurs at two levels: the product and the processes used to create the product.

A product can be designed in one place and marketed in completely different countries and regions. Such products may be mass produced, with a gross sales target of many millions of units. Regional variants may be included to take into account specific requirements or preferences. Alternatively design can take place at the point of sale and manufacturing responds by rapidly setting up production equipment to produce exactly what is required by the client in a job lot. Kitchens typically can be designed in the home on a personal computer, using measurements taken by the surveyor/consultant. An order is placed and signed by the home owner and the factory produces goods to an agreed specification. Kitchens and other household goods can also be specified in a DIY retail outlets, hard and soft furniture stores.

All businesses must answer the key question – what to make and what to buy in. Newlands (Chapter 9, this volume) reviews purchasing issues. Suppliers typically are given 100 per cent authority to change the logistics of what they do. They may not, however, modify the design or material specification of parts without prior consent from their corporate customer. Brand owners will assess the suggestion and issue design updates to all comparable suppliers. The supplier who suggested the idea will benefit from sharing the cost savings with the customer. Other suppliers will simply be told to make it in a different way with new materials and they will have to make it for a price given by their customer. In order to create higher margins, suppliers are therefore in competition with each other to propose suggestions to their customers. A key performance indicator (KPI) of this is 'number of suggestions per employee per year'. Suppliers with lower KPI ratings will probably not be awarded future work because their practices aren't improving sufficiently quickly to compete with suppliers who are learning and communicating their findings.

---

2   http://stason.org/TULARC/vehicles/lotus-cars/B5-Is-the-DeLorean-a-Lotus.html, accessed 1 February 2008.

Centralized Product Design and Supplier Authorized Modifications

If the product design work is centralized at the client's regional or global headquarters, suppliers are expected to submit proposals and await a response to authorize or decline the suggestion. The supplier may not receive an order for the modified product; however, they are regarded with greater esteem because they are providing suggestions, any one of which could lead to a breakthrough in productivity, cost reduction, quality improvement and other competitive advantages.

Suppliers are given *carte blanche* authority to create styles and make design changes only for certain products and components. Examples include car bumpers, exterior mirrors and vehicle body skirting parts, mobile phone 'snap on' printed or transferred patterns, named brand engines – for example Cosworth, specialized modules such as Lucas and Bosch alternators, computer memory and processor designers – IBM, Intel and AMD.

Car bodies are the intellectual copyright of the assembler. They provide 'black box' design information to their part suppliers, for example, the touch points for bumpers. Knowing that a given car base can be customized for given market segments, bumper suppliers are asked to design a set to fit the car in accordance with the stereotypical demands of that image of the client. Segments include first-time buyers, retirees, second car buyers for family use, business traveller and boy racers. Purchasing executives will then have to decide on an appropriate purchasing strategy – single, sole, dual or multi-sourcing. These purchasing strategies are defined in Newlands (Chapter 9, this volume).

Target Costs

Japanese companies tend to choose the volume they wish to produce, determine the amount of profit they intend to make and then engineer the total costs, in what has been termed target costing, in order that they produce the required profit.

If the buying company provides materials on a free-issue basis to its suppliers, the supplier is restricted to reducing fixed costs and variable costs associated with the conversion process. This consequently is a stimulus for flatter organizational structures and re-engineering value-adding processes. An alternative to these two options is to focus on creating value by providing consultative and product development services. The supplier then enters into the market searching for non-recurring expenditure contracts (NREs) from companies that are leading in terms of their innovative products and willingness to create niche markets Newlands 2003a, 2003b).

These companies have the choice of creating engineering solutions to reduce total costs. As volume rises, the choice of what type of technology is employed in the manufacturing system becomes more critical. Suppliers can also be commissioned to develop new process technologies and product variants that integrate functionality previously provided by separate components. These commissions typically are in the form of 'non-recurring expenditures'. These tend to be fixed prices payments to fulfil contracts to develop a component or technology.

Choosing Technology

New product concepts need to be envisioned. New niche markets may be identified that currently are not exploited. Brand-name producers will need to employ imaginative individuals who put themselves into the role of the customer and identify representational concepts for products.

Differences may be in how an existing product or technology is used, alternate and easier interfaces or ergonomics, more intuitive structures that reduce the need for technical training. Ergonomic keyboards for computers for example separate the keyboard and angle the keys the way the user holds their arms – with elbows out wide. The Windows-type environment originally conceived and prototyped by Xerox Corporation and commercialized by Microsoft on computers relieves the user of having to use code keys and text-based instructions. The mouse allows user to do many operations with just a right, double or left click.

Technology may be available off the shelf from a solution provider. It is more likely, however, that technology will be sourced from a number of vendors who provide elements of the required functionality. Designers may decide to integrate selected elements, such as computer chip wafer designs, in order to reduce the component count (reducing product assembly time and geometric size of the printed circuit board), increase reliability and performance. The challenges to achieving concept design specifications will need to be identified. These include size, weight, power consumption, speed, memory capacity, upgradeability and manufacturability.

Key Technology Choice Questions

Should the company create its own technology? What competitive advantages are there to be gained? What off-the-shelf technology already exists at competitors that is waiting either for the current product sales to decline before being introduced or wait for their competitors to commit to investing heavily to develop a technology that is already inferior to the off-the-shelf solution? What technology already is being sold at commercial rates business-to-business that will take some time to role out to business-to-consumer market segments? What is the technology development trajectory (direction and speed)? What solutions are competitors likely to develop? How widespread is the availability of given technologies? What new market segments could be created and expectations met with existing technology? How long will it take to specify, develop and validate technological solutions? What resources are there within the existing and virtual supply chain or supplier network that can be harnessed to make the project happen? How much investment will be required? What is the lead time to complete the project? What secrecy issues and levels of confidentiality are required? Which company will retain intellectual property rights? How easy will the new solution be to copy? These questions impact on how long it will take to clone, duplicate or create compatible like-for-like solutions. What commercial value is there to sell franchised versions of the technology solution?

Strategically key questions to commercialize the technology include:

* Do we understand what the customer wants? What are the current and future order qualifiers and order winners?
* Do we do everything? What are the current and future core competences of the business?
* What do we make? What do we buy? A subset question is: How can the company spread financial risks and initial capital costs?
* How dedicated should the facilities be? Should high technology solutions be included into the processes to produce the product as well as the product being made? Examples of this are using computers to design computers, and using robots to assemble robots.
* Where do we do things? Single site, dual or multiple locations? Which region, country and city should the activities occur in? What type and extent of risks and cost differentials are there inherent in each location?

- Should multiple brands be used with superficial modifications in order simultaneously to create niche roles and increase market share? PSA use Peugeot and Citroen brands. Nissan historically used old Toyota platforms. Since their alliance, Renault use the PSA platforms to create Renaults and Nissan models.
- What's first? Last? The correct sequence?
- What will happen to the cash flow during the project?
- Secrecy? Who needs to know? What do they need to know? When?
- Did we think of everything?
- Are we too confident of our own abilities?
- Do we have the experience necessary?
- Who can help?
- Do we have all the legal requirements sorted?
- Concerning corporate and individual procrastination: How good is the organization at expressing opinions and decision-making – yes, maybe or no?

To invest in technology, the company must envision the commercial requirements and demands into the future. Key questions to justify the investment and to obtain economies of scale and scope include:

- How many should we make? When and should we outsource to lower cost countries? What factors should be included in this decision?
- What price will the customer pay? Is the price stable? Will rarity value sustain a premium price? Will the price be pushed down by more competitive product offerings?
- What cost reduction possibilities are there? These may be found in the QCDDM acronym used by Nissan Motor Manufacturing – quality, cost, delivery, design and management.
- How many years will the company make derivative products in the same plant? Automotive assembly plants for instance typically remain operational for 70 to 90 years. Once established, plant layouts may determine how a product is put together.
- What radical changes might occur in the near to mid range strategic time horizon?

Product Life Cycles

Theoretical product life cycles have five described zones: an introduction or launch, ramp-up, maturity, decline and withdrawal. The theoretical model is a smooth extrapolation that may exist, though actual sales in various industries may vary significantly from the norm. General Motors had introduced product families and the customer appreciated variety in terms of colour, trim and engine options. Ford had a single product type that did not have any major revisions or styling updates, the Model T had an extensive product life cycle. A major problem when Ford changed to the next model was that the machines used were too specific to the Model T and hence many were replaced.

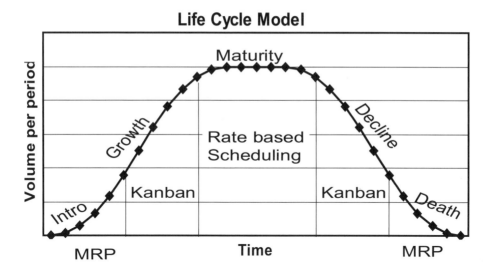

Figure 23.7   Theoretical product life cycle

The Model T was introduced and launched relatively in line with the theoretical profile. The decline and withdrawal similarly are similar. However, the Model T did not have a stable mature phase and sales varied significantly over the product manufacturing life cycle.

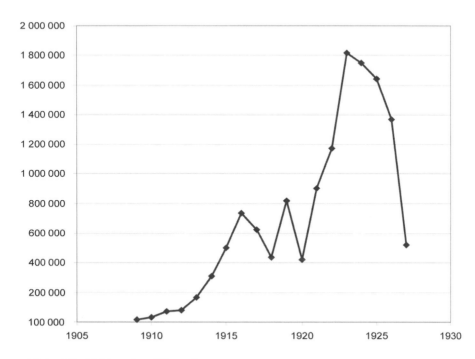

Figure 23.8   Model T product life cycle

Sources: Various annual accounts.

Typically, products are introduced together with a marketing campaign. The price can initially be high as business customers and early adopters are the first to get hold of what is new, higher performance and rare. As volumes rise, special offers may be made to win market share. An existing product made by the company might be replaced as this may be the only competition the product faces. The high price maximizes contribution to profit early in the manufacturing cycle. This contribution may be used to amortize tooling more quickly. More strategically, it is used to fund the completion of further technical improvements to the design and manufacturing processes.

During the early stages of a product life cycle, development emphasis is on improving product quality and introducing variants based on the platform. During the mature stage of the life cycle, emphasis tends to focus on making the manufacturing processes more efficient, flexible, higher quality, faster and reliable. In order to extend the sales life as much as possible, toward the end of the product life cycle, emphasis returns to the product. Stylistic changes may be made on external aesthetic panels, light clusters and trim in order to encourage customers to buy. Advertising campaigns may be run with two messages: to the owner of existing cars, they feel their car is still current, and secondly to potential customers to say this car has many satisfied owners, all the problems are ironed out and the quality of the product is much better than the earlier examples.

Technology Life Cycles

Components that are assembled into a product do not necessarily need to be replaced with new designs when the product offering is changed. New products can be introduced more quickly and at lower cost if many of the parts remain the same. To achieve this, design management must undertake a value analysis to determine which components will continue to perform their tasks and whether the customer appreciates them. Components that provide fashion or styling variants may be updated in order to refresh the appearance of the product. Under-the-skin mechanical or structural components may remain unchanged from model to model and from series to series since the customer doesn't care about, see or value these parts.

A key aim of technology creation projects is to ensure that technology, designs and specifications can be used in subsequent product designs that can be sold in other countries and regions. Three separate specifications were developed for second generation (digital) mobile phones. The USA had a mix of analogue and digital specifications. The US digital phone specification was GSM1900. Europe and many other countries adopted GSM900 and GSM1800 technologies. Nokia and Ericsson, both European handset producers, and Motorola, an American corporation, took significant market shares in this market. Japan adopted PDC – Personal Digital Communication protocol. The name later changed to Pacific Digital Communication in an attempt to encourage other countries to adopt the standard. By contrast, Japanese producers missed out on second generation mobile phone sales. Japanese producers were determined to take a leading role in future technology evolutions.

Nokia has 35–45 per cent of the world market for mobile phone handsets. Up until 2000, Nokia had 0.35 per cent of the Japanese handset market. Today, Nokia doesn't sell handsets in Japan. Instead, it buys technology from Japanese component suppliers and is part of the consortium that sets specifications for 'third generation' or '3G' wideband technologies.

When 3G became more proven, three separate specifications were proposed that developed on the regional preferences. Japanese producers and system operators came to market first. As a result, the Japanese version of 3G now dominates the global standards debate. To retake its lead as a handset producer, Ericsson joined Sony.

Platform Management

Platform management makes use of existing components to build products for other brands and thus avoids the necessity of a complete redesign and its associated costs. This strategy allows corporations to increase the brand mix and product offerings and simultaneously reduces the component cost, since tools and development costs are amortized over a higher volume of goods and over a longer time period. Fast food ingredients, computers, vehicle engines and body substructures are prime examples of this approach.

Food Platform Management

Pizzas and hamburgers are fast food examples. Pizzas all have a bread base and cheese. Most pizzas have tomato paste to moisten the palate, although sour cream can be used as an alternative. A price is given to the basic 'margarita' pizza. Factory-produced pizzas can have toppings added and can be covered in film to keep everything in place for distribution. Value can be delayed as much as possible. For example, restaurant-produced pizzas usually do not have toppings added until a customer orders from the menu. This creates added value to the customer and reduces the range of finished goods required to be held. Prices vary according to the type and quantity of added toppings.

McDonald's, Burger King and other hamburger type restaurants have a range from a simple burger in a bun to the top of the range Whopper with everything. The bread bun may differ inasmuch as whether there are sesame seeds or not and perhaps in the thickness. A middle section may be cut out and included as part of a layered sandwich. The hamburger itself is common from the basic burger bun through to the top of the range offering. Other complementary elements include zucchini, salad, sauces, rashers of bacon and slices of cheese. Packaging provides a visual indication of which variant is inside, keeps the product warm and, most significantly, can create a cognitive dissonance that justifies the price premium.

Computer Platform Management

Computer motherboards are designed to have full functionality. When customers specify what they require, the PCB is populated with basic functionality and specified optional extras. The cost differences are minimal. Costs are not incurred because the components are not used. Savings also are made as component mounting times are reduced.

There are about ten companies around the world that design computer motherboards. These companies can optimize their products to use components they commission to be developed. Other companies buy the motherboard designs and populate them with 'patent parts' that are produced under licence or do not have the original brand name on them.

IBM traditionally commissioned other companies to develop technologies on their behalf. This allowed IBM to offer unique features and specifications to its customers at a premium price. In order to maximize return on investment, the specifications would be 'dumbed down', reducing the features or limiting functionality. This strategy gave IBM a market sale window and performance lead over its competitors, even those that bought under licence technologies from IBM. After a given amount of time, typically six months, IBM would release an upgraded performance version that was comparable to the products IBM had been selling in the previous six months. By this time, IBM would have introduced a new variant or product that had specifications that would outperform competitors and provide better solutions for their clients.

IBM sold its personal computer business to the Chinese. Today, IBM is a consulting services provider that integrates products from other suppliers. They still make and sell hard drives and other memory devices. IBM makes more profit from these than it did from making complete computers.

Engine and Car Platform Management

Engine manufactures can use the same engine casting to make different capacity and fuel variants. A 1600cc petrol engine can be made into a 1400cc economy version, 1300cc high rpm performance model, 1800cc high torque and 1900cc diesel. Key variants are piston diameter, connecting rod length changes, smaller and larger crank shaft diameters, skimming material off the head to increase compression ratios, adding turbo chargers and fuel injection systems. All the variants can be made from the same casting and use the same production machines. Designs may be modified to follow the existing flow route in the workshop. The machines will be capable of working on all variants. Machining cycles are typically less than 30 seconds, with multiple activities occurring simultaneously. Just as with hamburgers, designers will take the most complex, complete variant and de-select attributes in order to create a descending range of specifications for goods. Prices are adjusted to compensate for reduced desirability.

Conventional four-stroke engines work on a suck, squeeze, bang, blow cycle. Pistons reciprocate up and down inside cylinders. Valves open and shut to allow in fuel and exhaust out. An air or air fuel mixture is sucked in as the piston moves down. The next stroke compresses the gases. A controlled explosion occurs as the fuel is injected and/or ignited. The piston is forced down creating motive forces to force the vehicle to move. Spent fuel exits via the exhaust valve.

Two-stroke valves do not have moving valves. The piston exposes ports on the sides of the cylinder. Piston movement creates sufficient positive and negative pressure variations to encourage air/fuel/lubricant mixtures from the carburettor via the crank case into the cylinder and out of the exhaust port.

A key problem of platform management is the long-term production of out-of-date technology that makes up a product. General Motors is frequently accused of this. Two- and four-stroke engines have been in existence for around 100 years. Typical fuel economy levels achieved by conventional road going cars or motor cycles are very low by comparison to the levels achieved under competition conditions. The fuel economy has remained almost static, neither getting worse nor significantly better. At the time of writing, the world fuel economy record is 5385 km/ltr of 98 octane petrol.[3]

Normal internal combustion engines are inefficient because they exhaust heat. Steam engines by comparison, recycle steam as hot water and reheat this to steam. About 4 per cent of the calorific value of fuel is converted to force to propel standard vehicles. This is compared to around 90 per cent efficiency for steam engines. Steam engines also force pistons in both directions, unlike engines that only force the piston when mixtures explode. The world record for hydrogen fuel cell vehicles is nearly 9000km/ltr. The author would suggest that when Toyota and GM roll out their fuel cell vehicles, they will achieve little more than 10km/lr, much the same as a standard engine car, but they will produce air and water and hence are 'cleaner'. The consumer, however, will probably still have to pay significant 'contributory tax' to government exchequers in order to keep the tax revenue high. An alternative to this proposed by Tony Blair's government is taxation on distance travelled!

---

3   World fuel economy records are reported in the *Guinness Book of World Records*. The competition is the Shell Eco Challenge.

Carlos Ghosn has stated Nissan will be ready when alternative power systems become common place. Nissan have paid Toyota £350million to obtain fuel cell technology in order to be a 'me too'. (http://www.auto-careers.org/Hybrid per cent20info.htm)

Nissan sales suffered because their products were considered by the general car buying public as being older technology. Consequently, to maintain sales Nissan discounted their cars to the extent that they effectively gave away $1000 on each unit. Carlos Ghosn sold non-core shares in order to release capital. This he invested in designing a new range of vehicles. (Magee 2003)

Floor Pan Example of Platform Management

The floor pan in a car is the large sheet of formed metal used to separate the passenger from the road underneath. The car side panels are welded to the floor pan, as well as seats, exhausts and suspension parts. This relatively high precision piece of metal constitutes about 17 per cent of the value of a monocoque[4] constructed car.

The floor pan, engine, gearbox and running gear used in Ford's Cortina Mark Four were used in the Sierra Mark One, Sierra Mark Two and Mondeo Mark One. This strategy of carrying-over components and systems the customer doesn't really care about, allowed Ford to amortize the tooling over an extended component life cycle. This type of commonality and carry-over strategy has become known as 'platform management'.

To commercialize products, it is vital that product development managers ensure that designers focus their creative energies on high value-adding activities. Designers must not be left alone to reinvent the wheel, introduce variants without significant justification but must standardize as much as possible on as few component variants as possible. For example, in 1998, Nokia mobile phones had over 400 types of screw on the product design database: many of those had been produced and sat in stores unused because there was no further demand for the design as the product production life-cycle had ended.

The Design Dilemma

There are product design houses that rely on wild ideas to create 'off-the-wall' solutions. These businesses find solutions by defining concepts, debugging the design and then finally setting specifications. In such businesses, knowledge and skills are predominantly intuitive. Semi flexible and bureaucratic businesses in contrast conduct their design activities in accordance with broad guidelines. More autocratic businesses develop their designs strictly according to

---

4   'A metal structure, such as an aircraft, in which the skin absorbs all or most of the stresses to which the body is subjected', http://dictionary.reference.com/search?q=monocoque. Monoque cars do not have a separate chassis that is still used to construct trucks, buses and Land Rover type off road vehicles. A chassis typically consists of two parallel beams that are deeper than they are wide. This structure provides a bending moment that is relatively rigid and does not require a solid girder. The vehicle weight thus is lower, and is strong enough to take heavy loads. The last chassis based car to be produced in the United Kingdom was the Triumph Herald.

design checklists. These types of organizations demand specifications are nearly set before detailed design and type testing. This type of business focuses on commercializing existing technology and tends to be risk averse in the product development phase.

Perfect product design from a functionality and aesthetic perspective may be a disaster from a production efficiency and effectiveness perspective. The formalized processes for influencing product characteristics during their development stages is now generically called 'design for manufacturing'. Design for manufacturing is the umbrella term used in the same way that quality is used to summarize many initiatives. As a specific subset of design for manufacturing, this chapter focuses on design of logistics and design of the product for logistics.

Design Rules: Guidelines for Efficient Logistics

When the market becomes mature, retail prices drop, hence costs must be reduced via clever design that makes manufacturing easy, low cost, high quality and fast. IBM, for example, reduced the price of their mainframe systems by 96 per cent during the 1990s. They also increased their profit and earnings per share (Gerstner 2003).

To achieve significant results, corporations must ask how they can make components easily, cheaply, quickly and to a high quality standard. If they buy these items, how many suppliers can they be bought from? Are they local?

Assemblers are predominantly system integrators. Their design rules focus on:

1. *common interfaces* – for example the touch and mounting points, and protocols used to synchronize technical systems;
2. *commonality and carry-over* – use of the same parts in many models in the family, and reuse of existing components and subassemblies in future products. These rules reduce the obsolescence risk and increase the probability that new products are developed on time;
3. improve after sales service, and ensuring that consumers are 'tied' to the business for *upgrade* and *wear parts*. Automobiles and many electronic goods have some kind of opportunity to upgrade trim or performance of functional parts. Vehicles and some consumer electronics products have wear parts. Examples from vehicles include filters, spark plugs, tires, brake pads, window wiper blades, and low cost exhausts. Electronic product examples include batteries, replaceable covers, rotating magnetic heads and drive belts.

There may be a danger of isolating the design and development activities undertaken in the parent organization from the day-to-day activities in production plants in far off countries. This can be avoided by producing standard interface modules that can be fitted in the same way in all assembly plants despite their location. It may be attractive to outsource some research and development to companies in the target market, especially at the component and modular levels.

Ford Motor Company introduced their World Car concept, where they design a vehicle in one place to suit the same market sector in all countries and regions. This strategy serves to reduce the amount of product development and harmonizes the expectations of the various regions based on the product's common industrial design. Minor changes in specification are nominally required for products to conform to regional or country specific regulations and requirements.

The fourth element of cost reduction is to reduce the number of components required. Electronic goods manufactures consolidate a number of wafers onto a single chip. This increases reliability, reduces components that need to be assembled (hence assemble them faster and increase productivity) and reduces costs of materials, labour and overhead apportionment.

Component Commonality, Carry-over and Obsolescence

The availability of high-end components made in all regions is a significant challenge for electronic consumer goods manufacturers. High-end technology electronic components, including chip scale packages, micro ball grid array ASICs and manufacturer-designed integrated-chips, are nominally only produced in limited locations. Silicon Valleys in the USA and Japan lead high-end module manufacture. Leading-edge components tend to be made in one or two places. Later, as technology becomes mature, industry standard chip sets such as Intel Pentium processors and various RAM memory devices are made under licence in many more locations.

There is little a company can do to reduce long component lead times except reduce the number of engineering change requests after the component has been verified.

Many generic electronic components tend to be the lowest cost surface mount components. Basic electronic components can be sourced from local and regional distributors, though these generally have additional handling overhead costs. Basic components have high commonality across product families and product lines. This contributes to lower the obsolescence risk and increases bulk order discounts.

Some manufacturers recognize an imperative to reduce the number of components or modules in a product. Others focus on balancing the production line and outsourcing more value-adding activities to suppliers. The imperative in that situation is to increase suppliers' capacity.

If a generic type or brand of electronic product becomes popular, volume demand becomes significant in a very short period of time. Historic examples are the wireless, transistor radios, televisions, battery operated wristwatches, computers, 'Sony Walkmans', Discmans, games consoles and mobile phones. In the rush to make and sell popular products, electronics producers increase annual volume output year on year for fast moving consumer electronic goods. This strategy allows the assembler to establish the brand in the global market. The strategy then drives suppliers to produce ever more standardized components and modules which in turn reduce the differentiation in the hardware between assemblers' brands. Consequently, there is a major push on software as a differentiator. The computer industry is synonymous with a variant of this – configurability.

Assemblers' production data management systems must be able to cope with the diversity created by the ability to produce significant product variety. Customer-defined product configuration ordering will then become achievable. Internet interfaces or point of sale requirement entry systems will be needed to service the customer in this mode of mass customization. The implications of this for small- to medium-sized companies are significant. Supplier visibility of actual sales will be needed to ensure that make to order and make to replenishment service levels are maintained at their optimum.

Automotive Examples of Platform Management

Ford bought Jaguar Motor Cars, Volvo, Land Rover and Aston Martin and created a luxury car division. The Jaguar XK shares the same platform as the Mondeo Mark Two onwards.[5] Recent Volvos have followed this strategy. Typically, around 60 per cent of the financial value of parts used to construct these three different brands are common. Customer-appreciated differences in styling, trim an accessories create value for the customer. These differences serve the corporate company car driver, executives, safety conscious family car owners and sustain niche market segments with a much lower corporate design and production cost structure that can fund new product and technology development.

Aston Martin[6] cars were hand built by skilled craftsmen using traditional panel beating techniques in Newport Pagnall, north of London. Ford acquired a 75 per cent stake in Aston Martin in 1987. In 1994 Ford bought the remaining shares. When Ford acquired Land Rover, they also bought the test track and historic vehicle centre at Gaydon, Warwickshire. Aston Martin subsequently moved to Gaydon. Many of the components are now borrowed from Ford's existing component range. The current Aston Martin Vantage was originally designed as a Jaguar. However, it was too heavy for this brand. Superficial trim and styling changes were made in order rapidly to create a viable product for Aston Martin.

Managing Research

New product concepts must be created. This allows producers to define new types of niches that do not yet exist and satisfy them first. The company enters a new niche it has created with innovations in products. It takes time for competitors to enter the niche. By this time, the leader has established a strong market niche presence. The company will be reaping significant profit margins from the premiums it can charge. Technology followers and companies late to the market force prices down. They can do this partly because technologies already exist and have been developed. The fixed costs and overheads required for basic research and technology development have not been incurred. Technology followers may be able to purchase goods, components and processes based on relatively recent specifications from suppliers that originated these developments.

Intel Corporation, for example, develops all improved specifications of processor for computers. They produce a limited quantity for prototypes and then exclusively produce chips for sale in latest specification equipment for business-to-business markets. Since businesses can budget and payback investments because they will be able to work harder, faster and hence incur lower development costs, these are a key primary market for latest developments. As technology becomes more mature, Intel licence the production of their chip designs to other fabricators. Volume competition rapidly reduces the price in order to sell older technologies in home computers, games equipment and other devices that require processing technologies.

Market Driven Innovation

Hammer and Champy (1993) described how existing and potential customers made requests to technology providers to create and sell products that:

---

5   Land Rover, Jaguar, Aston Martin and Volvo are all European produced brands. The luxury car market has been sustained by exports to North America. Recent currency exchange rate values have reduced American interest in these comparatively more expensive vehicles. Gasoline price rises at the pump are impacting on large inefficient engined vehicle sales. http://news.bbc.co.uk/1/hi/business/3659946.stm.

6   http://www.astonmartin.com/.

- did what they wanted;
- did it as fast as they wanted;
- are scaleable; and
- are ergonomically intuitive to use so that detailed technical training is not required.

The development of advanced hardware and compatible software enable solution providers to create bespoke products for their clients' unique requirements. Generic versions may be produced later that can be sold to a wider, less demanding client base. These generic versions may be customized either by the client or by specialist consultants.

Suppliers should be aligned to product assembler needs to create new or improved processes. Purchasing companies should include suppliers in their product creation programmes in order to ensure parts, components and materials are processed and sub-assembled in a manner that best suites the supplier facilities.

Off-the-shelf Technology Solutions

As a technology provider creates advanced technologies, these may not have an immediate solution or product that could be developed with these features. Scientific protocols for experiments usually require technicians to write up technical reports relating to methods, materials, equipment used and their discoveries. If no obvious application is evident, what has been learned should be archived in a relational database that will later allow others to search and select collections of basic research and combine these with existing product combinations. The aim of brand-owning organizations is to integrate solutions in attractive product proposals.

Conclusions

International managers must decide what they want to design, make in one or more locations, and sell in many populous regions around the world. It may be cheaper and strategically important to release technology in a predefined sequence of countries. The company may wish to duplicate infrastructure and tooling in low-cost countries. Their goods may be made under licence or franchise.

Some countries may exhibit significant competition. The company may choose to partner, or simply purchase goods technology and components for inclusion in their products destined for less developed and demanding markets.

The churn of technological specialists may be significant in certain disciplines where developments are frequently introduced. The company should prepare to train their employees or side shift them into roles of responsibility and project management.

References

Champy, J. (1995), *Re-engineering Management: The Mandate for New Leadership: Managing the Change to the Re-engineered Corporation* (London: HarperCollins Publishers).

Fisher, R. and Brown, R. (1988), *Getting Together: Building a Relationship that Gets to Yes* (Boston, MD: Houghton Mifflin Co.).

Fisher, R. and Ury, W. (1981), *Getting to Yes, Negotiating Agreement without Giving In* (London: Hutchinson.

Gerstner, L.A. (2003), *Who Says Elephants Can't Dance? How I Turned Around IBM* (New York: HarperBusiness).

Greenfield, C. (n.d.), Lecture notes for Manufacturing Strategy, School of Engineering, Coventry University.

Hammer, M. (1995), *The Re-engineering Revolution: The Handbook* (London: HarperCollins).

Hammer, M. and Champy, J. (1993), *Re-engineering the Corporation: A Manifesto for Business Revolution* (London: Nicholas Brealey Publishing Ltd).

Heizer, J. and Render, B. (2006), *Operations Management*, 8th edn (Upper Saddle River, NJ: Pearson).

Magee, D. (2003), *Turnaround: How Carlos Ghosn Rescued Nissan* (New York: HarperCollins Business Books).

Newlands, D. (2003a), 'Breakeven Analysis: Part 1 – Current Opinion', *Control, Institute of Operations Management* 29(7), http://www.littoralis.info/iom/topics.htm.

Newlands, D. (2003b), 'Breakeven Analysis: Part 2 – Results from Modern Purchasing Environments Non Recurring Expenditures Associated With Product Creation Projects', *Control, Institute of Operations Management* 29(8), http://www.littoralis.info/iom/htm/iom20031201.527319.htm.

Newlands, D. and Steeple, D. (2000), 'Logistics and Supply Chain Development: Part 1: Lessons from Japan: Automotive and Electronic Industries', *Control, Institute of Operations Management*, May, pp. 15–17, http://www.littoralis.info/iom/secure/assets/2000050115.pdf.

Osborn, A. (1957), *Applied Imagination – Principles and Practices of Creative Thinking* (New York: Charles Scribners Sons).

Schein, E. (1969), *Process Consultation: Its Role in Organization Development* (Reading, MA: Addison-Wesley Publishing Co.).

Smith, A. (1776), *The Wealth of Nations*, reprinted 1986 (London: Penguin).

Smith, G. (1995), *Managing to Succeed: Strategies and Systems for Manufacturing Businesses* (London: Prentice Hall International).

Taylor, T. (1995), 'How Can Customers and Suppliers Develop Trusting Partnerships for Enhanced Performance?', in Ashmore, S. (ed). *Supplier Development: Measuring, Developing and Improving Supplier Performance*, ICM Marketing Ltd. (International Communications for Management), The Cavendish Square Conference Centre, London, 11–12 December.

Unipart DCM (Demand Chain Management), (c. 1995), 'Ten(d)-to-Zero: The Programme: The Second Phase – Towards World Class', Unipart.

Warren, I. (1995), 'How Customers Select Key Performance Indicators Against Which Suppliers are to be Measured', in Ashmore, S. (ed.) *Supplier Development: Measuring, Developing and Improving Supplier Performance*, ICM Marketing Ltd (International Communications for Management), Cavendish Square Conference Centre, London, 11–12 December.

Watson, G. (1994), *Business Systems Engineering: Managing Breakthrough Changes for Productivity and Profit* (New York: John Wiley & Sons).

Wheelwright, S.C. and Clark, K.B. (1995), *Leading Product Development* (New York: The Free Press).

Womack, J. and Jones, D. (1996), *Lean Thinking: Banish Waste and Create Wealth in Your Corporation* (New York: Simon & Schuster).

Chapter 24
Managing Knowledge Strategically

Sandra Jones

Introduction

This chapter introduces the key issues presented by the knowledge era. The chapter explores challenges for business seeking to operate in a global economy as knowledge becomes recognized as *the* competitive advantage. The focus then shifts to the micro (organizational) level and explores challenges in developing a knowledge management strategy that integrates technology with people such that knowledge is both continually developed and shared.

Issues covered include the need to encourage:

- more participative roles for employees;
- more collaborative management and leadership approaches;
- recognition of the challenges presented by complex environments;
- new approaches to evaluating knowledge sharing.

Reflection has been described as a 'process of stepping back from an experience to ponder, carefully and persistently, its meaning to the self through the development of inferences' (Seibet and Daudelin 1999).

Reflection is an important tool to assist the management of knowledge as it encourages the reflector to recognize new knowledge gained from past events and to use this new knowledge to plan for the future.

This chapter presents the changes required within organizations that have recognized the importance of knowledge as their competitive advantage for the future. The focus is upon managers as knowledge developers, leading employees into the continual exploration and sharing of new knowledge. In this way, knowledge management (KM) is treated as an inclusive term that brings together industrial relations (IR), human resource management (HRM) and information technology (IT).

This chapter explores KM as an integrated strategy of people and IT, given the many forms, facets and characteristics of knowledge that require a plethora of ways to capture, transfer and share knowledge. It also discusses the need for a new leadership approach of a more participative employment relationship.

Finally, the chapter evaluates challenges for organizations to straddle the knowing-doing gap, with particular focus upon how to evaluate the development, transfer and sharing of knowledge.

This chapter commences by exploring the implications of the knowledge era for organizations that seek to operate in a global knowledge economy. It then focuses at the micro (organizational) level and explores challenges in developing a knowledge management strategy that integrates the role to be played by technology with that of people such that knowledge is both continually developed and shared within and between organizations.

Implications of the Knowledge Era for Organizations

The so-called 'Information Age' has reintroduced knowledge as the fundamental element of business success in an era that, it is claimed, is 'the ultimate step in the transformation of knowledge' (Allee 1997, p. 6). Focus on knowledge is not new although its form and effects have changed. Drucker (1998) identified three evolutionary epochs of knowledge, from the mid 1700s when the application of knowledge to capitalism and technology created the Industrial Revolution, through the post-World War II period when knowledge was systematically applied to technology to create the 'productivity revolution', to the current period when knowledge is applied to itself to create the 'management revolution'. Herzenberg, Alic and Wial (1998, p. 91) assert knowledge has 'untapped potential for performance gains'. However, they argue that, in the current epoch, the speed with which knowledge can be communicated has increased the potential for performance gains from knowledge development and sharing. Indeed, Tymon and Stumpf (2003) claimed that there had been more information produced in the last thirty years than during the previous 5,000 and that the information supply available doubled every five years.

Snowden (2002) extends this and argues that the knowledge era itself has gone through two generations and is currently entering a third. The first generation (prior to 1995) focused on timely information provision for decision support and in support of business process re-engineering (BPR). The second focused on tacit-explicit knowledge. The third generation, according to Snowden, requires a clear separation of context, narrative and content management and challenges the orthodoxy of scientific management. This does not simply involve adding new to existing knowledge. It is, instead, a fundamentall new way of thinking that sees knowledge as the major factor of production that recognizes the duality as both a stock and a flow.

The change is so fundamental that it questions the basic assumptions upon which both the social and natural sciences rest. For natural sciences, the challenge is how to grapple with a global knowledge world where simple Newtonian linear cause and effect relationships are being replaced by complex, sometimes chaotic situations where knowledge is both a stock and a flow whose path needs to be tracked through patterns rather than dyadic relationships. The change, it is argued, is as important as the emergence of quantum mechanics in which this duality is accepted. This leads Capra (1996) to emphasize relationships, interconnections and probabilities, rather than hard and solid material particles.

For business as a social science, the challenge is similarly dramatic. In seeking to replicate as far as possible Newtonian mechanics, business has to reconsider the nature of economics, accountancy and, indeed, the managerial decision-making foundation of bureaucratic organizations. Economics, once viewed as study of scarcity given the finite and limited nature of resources, now faces the inexhaustible resource of knowledge which is limited only by human creativity (Allee 2003). This reverses the law of diminishing returns, which asserts that costs per unit increase as demand exceeds supply of scarce resources. It also changes:

- the nature of markets – from commodity markets where resources are exchanged to value-added markets for knowledge;
- the primary economic goal of efficient production extracted for labour and machines – to a focus on developing human creativity to increase new knowledge;
- the focus on value chains of simple relationships to value networks of complex, interdependent and dynamic relationship.

In summary, a new economic theory is required that is based on an ideology that reverses the assumption that labour is a scarce, overworked resource and natural capital is abundant and unexploited. New assumptions are that 'people have become the abundant resource, while nature is becoming disturbingly scarce' (Hawken et al. 2002, p. 8). The resource-based view of economics (Wernerfelt 1984) may be of more assistance as it focuses on the internal strengths and weaknesses of the organization rather than measurable outputs like products, prices and market share.

Accountancy – traditionally focused on measuring costs of lagging variables such as return-on-physical assets, expenses, short-term debt through an easily identifiable accounts receivable-accounts payable process – requires new ways to measure knowledge through emerging, leading measures that recognize human and social capital as well as structural capital.

Social organization is also affected. Kelly (1998) claims that the world of intangibles (media, software and services) is replacing the world of the hard (atoms, objects, steel and oil). In stating this, he asserts that social organizations will change into 'an infinite variety of new shapes and sizes of social organization' (ibid., p. 6). More participative relationships will underpin these new social organizations. The 'networked economy is founded on technology, but can only be built on relationship … It starts with chips and ends with trust' (ibid., p. 123). Thus, there is need for a new theory of social relationships that has been built on networks of actors interacting in a chain, hub or all-channel patterned structure (Evan 1972; Nohria and Eccles 1992; Wellman and Berkowitz 1997). In this view, power and influence depend less on personal attributes and more on interpersonal relations, with individuals valued not for their 'human capital' but for their 'social capital', and the unit of analysis is less the individual and progressively more the network in which the individual is embedded (Ronfield and Arquilla 2001).

The implications of these changes for organizations are equally as far-reaching. Ellinor and Gerard (1998) link the new sciences (chaos theory, quantum physics and self-organizing systems) to work, in an approach that they argue moves us beyond the 'machine model' of organizations. They argue that organizations need to move from:

- a fragmented to a holistic approach;
- a focus on structure and tasks to relationships and processes;
- a reliance on power and control to shared leadership;
- top-down decision-making to shared meaning and consensus;
- competition to collaboration;
- self-mastery to collective mastery and leveraging diversity;
- linear thinking to systems thinking;
- one right answer to many right answers.

Instead of a focus on Adam Smith's (1776) 'division of labour', through which increased productivity is associated with separation of tasks into single repetitive activity, the network character of knowledge means that organizations grow more organically and chaotically than linearly and require more flexible structures and a more holistic approach in which systems thinking is used to understand phenomena (Capra 1996; Checkland and Holwell 1998).

Decision-making needs to be more inclusive, with employees empowered to participate in the development of a consensual approach in which shared meaning is maximized. In this environment management is less about planning, organizing and controlling and more about developing and maintaining good relationships and becoming insightful leaders.

Work needs to be restructured to enable employees to continually develop and share new knowledge, rather than be structured around the input of raw materials and/or the cost of financing output. Employees need to be encouraged to collectively share their knowledge rather than continue to see knowledge as an individual factor that provides power to the owner. This requires a more co-operative team working and collaborative work design. Finally, work needs to be seen as more flexible in terms of time and space as multiple time periods (across different time zones) in multiple places (across the globe) become a business reality.

In summary, governments and organizations need to develop a more global networked approach, described by Marceau (2000, p. 227) as an economy in which 'it is networks not entities that matter'.

Developing a Holistic Organizational Knowledge Strategy

Characteristics of Knowledge

The acknowledgment of knowledge as the competitive advantage for the future has led to the need to explore the many facets. Knowledge has a number of important characteristics that set it apart from other resources. Knowledge is:

- subjective – interpretation is heavily dependent on the individual's background and context in which it is used;
- transferable – it can be extracted from one context and placed in anther;
- embedded – it resides in a person and is not easily removed;
- self-reinforcing – it gains value the more it is distributed;
- perishable – it loses value over time and thus needs to be continually increased;
- spontaneous – its growth cannot be controlled or predicted.

Whilst the first generation of knowledge management focused on explicit knowledge as a single entity, the second recognized knowledge as a complex factor (Nonaka 1998; Nonaka and Takeushi 1995). Explicit knowledge is observable (facts and figures) and can be committed to some form of communication medium, gathered, recorded and shared. It is often content- and skills-based, answering question of 'knowing what' and 'knowing how'. Explicit knowledge can occur as either data (simple facts and figures often regarded as the key or building block of higher forms of to knowledge), as information (characterized as data endowed with relevance and purpose (Drucker 1998)), or as knowledge (defined as information combined with experience, context, interpretation and reflection (Davenport et al. 1998)).

Drucker (1998) presents knowledge as a continuum along which information is data endowed with relevance and purpose. Converting data into information thus requires knowledge. Davenport and Prusak (1998) support this view in their claim that data presents an observation of the state of the world. However, it has no inherent meaning and no judgement or interpretation to support a sustainable basis of action. Seely Brown (1999, p. xi) confirms this in his claim that 'a document does not contain knowledge; it contains information'.

Allee (1997, p. 110) describes data as 'consciousness of the environment that allows registering of input or variation' but states that it is neither synonymous with learning, nor capable of being recorded in other than the immediate point in time. This leads her to develop a more intricate, dynamic and staged knowledge archetype as follows:

- Data that becomes Information through linking and organizing with other data;

- Information that becomes Knowledge when it is analysed, linked to other information and compared;
- Knowledge operating in a larger social context that gives it Meaning, which encompasses archetypal patterns and forces, as well as our social and cultural biases and interpretations;
- Meaning that becomes embedded in the larger and more abstract realm of Philosophy, or the broad territory of assumptions, beliefs and theories about how things work;
- Philosophy and systemic thinking that is embedded in Wisdom, through perspectives of values;
- Wisdom that enfolds values and purposes and encompasses the totality of a worldview;
- Union that is an open, inclusive state of oneness enabled by the intellect that allows understanding and ability to change values in relation to the ultimate good (ibid., p. 62).

In this first generation of knowledge IT contributed significantly to the recording and sharing of explicit knowledge. However, the second generation of knowledge recognized the need for human intervention to turn data into information and knowledge. As Kelly (1998, p. 143) states 'it starts with chips and ends with trust'.

It was recognition of the existence of 'tacit' knowledge that dominated the second generation of knowledge. Tacit knowledge is not easily observable but usually deeply embedded, often unconsciously, within an individual. It is not easily accessed and requires a willingness by employees to share. It is often 'know-how' that is formed from experience, insights and intuition, and is a much more difficult form of knowledge to be either identified or expressed and documented. In an early discussion of tacit knowledge Polanyi (1958) identified tacit knowledge as being the result of subjective insights, intuitions and hunches that have become deeply embedded in the knower's cumulative perception and experiences. In so doing he discussed the difference between knowledge and 'knowing'. Tacit knowledge is hard to formalize (1962); it is often deeply embedded in subconscious action (Cohen and Bacdayan 1994; Schon 1995), it is less easily accessed, it requires a willingness by employees to share it and it is difficult to make explicit. Snowden (2002, p. 8) states that it is deeply rooted in action and implied in skills possessed by individuals, their experiences and intuition, their relationships and understanding. Nonaka (1998) states that creating new knowledge depends on tapping the tacit and often highly subjective insights, intuitions and hunches of individual employees and making these insights available for testing and use by the company as a whole. He developed a model to explain the movement of knowledge between tacit and explicit through socialization, externalization, combination and internalization (SECI model) (Nonaka and Takeushi 1995).

Thus knowledge cannot be regarded simply as a commodity that can be separated from the knower, negotiated, stored, protected and measured, but rather as a dynamic process that includes its sharing, creating, learning, applying and communicating (Sveiby 1997). It is shared through a social process that needs to be seen within a context. Tacit knowledge can become explicit knowledge, but only if people are willing to recognize and share it. Reflection is an important tool for turning knowledge into explicit knowledge.

In the third generation, recognition that knowledge exists in different types, dimensions, contexts and domains is becoming more important. Leonard-Barton (1995) identified four interdependent dimensions – employee knowledge and skills, physical and technical systems, managerial systems and values and norms. Each of these dimensions requires different strategies for ongoing development. Knowledge can be general or situation specific. Zack (1999) differentiated between six types and contexts of knowledge:

1. declarative;
2. procedural;
3. causal;
4. conditional;
5. relational; and
6. contributional.

Allee (1997) related these types of knowledge to domains that range in degree and type of skills required, from simple data (knowing what) to more skill-based application that involves more abstract reasoning (knowing why). Knowledge can be individual or part of a collective, with different cultures varying in the way they view knowledge. For example, she claims that Western cultures have traditionally focused on individual rather than collective knowledge development. Bourdieu (1985) and Portes (1998) both focus on the collective (social) rather the individual configuration of knowledge.

Integrating Information Technology and Human Resources

Viewed in all its dimensions, it becomes clear that knowledge needs to be carefully managed as both a technical concept and a cultural entity. While there is great potential for KM to contribute to innovation in the development of new products and services, competitive advantage can only be gained by creating, sharing and mobilizing knowledge effectively. In the second generation knowledge management was defined as a systematic processes by which an organization identifies, creates, captures, acquires, shares and leverages knowledge (Rumizen 2002).

It was argued that an effective organizational knowledge strategy must be able to first encourage employees to recognize their knowledge. Nonaka (1998, p. 24) stated that 'creating new knowledge … depends on tapping the tacit and often highly subjective insights, intuitions, and hunches, of individual employees and making these insights available for testing and use by the company as a whole'. Organizations also need to be able to encourage their employees to share their knowledge. Zack (1999, p. 125) stated that organizations needed to manage their 'intellectual resources and capabilities' better. Davenport and Prusak (1998) state that the way knowledge is managed within businesses can determine an organization's prospects of success. They argued that management needs to recognize the importance of developing a culture and practices that supports a holistic knowledge sharing.

Davenport (1997, p. 29) presented an integrated model of an 'information ecology' that had four key attributes:

1. the integration of diverse types of information;
2. recognition of evolutionary change;
3. emphasis on observation and description; and
4. focus on people and information behaviour.

The model recognized the importance of interaction between business, physical, and technological, elements in the organizational environment (strategy, staff, culture, politics, architecture and process) plus the two-way interaction between the internal organizational and the external environment.

It was claimed that before organizations can extend beyond a traditional focus on structural capital (the hard physical assets of an organization – land, buildings and equipment) and financial capital (financial balance sheets plus investments) they must recognize the existence of human capital (employees competencies, skills, abilities, know-how) and intellectual capital (the sum of an organizations' ideas, inventions, technologies, data skills, processes, creativity and publications).

Some organizations, such as Scandia (Edvinsson and Malone 1997), have developed intellectual capital models to more accurately reflect both tangible and intangible assets including social capital that come from people sharing knowledge through collaboration in communities and networks.

Snowden (2002) argues that the third generation of knowledge makes it even more difficult to 'manage' knowledge in a traditional linear cause and effect sense as communities become more complex. Complex systems require a focus on recognizing patterns of interactivity over time and space. He argues that in a complex domain we manage to recognize, disrupt, reinforce and seed the emergence of patterns and allow the interaction of identities to create coherence and meaning. Recognition of complex systems requires a totally new conception of organizational structures and models and managerial concepts.

Moving from Knowledge Management to Knowledge Leadership

Although management thinking evolved over the decades since the early 1900s it is still influenced by a Newtonian concept of linear cause and effect control for predictability and order. The development of management decision-making over employees engaged in task-based repetitive work (Taylor 1964), the emergence of total quality management (TQM) with its emphasis on removing wastage by identifying divergence from a linear relationship (Deming 1982) and the business process engineering movement (Hammer and Champy 1993) all assumed predictable, measurable processes governed by technology in which the employee is an adjunct to the technology.

The inability of these concepts to produce the desired outcomes for business by the 1990s led to a growing acknowledgment that complexity required different approaches. First is the need for a new approach to management-employee relations as it is recognized that employees hold the major factor of production in their heads. By early 2000 a survey of knowledge management by McKinsey and Co (Kluge et al. 2001) found that successful knowledge management depends on the creation of the right cultural context within the organization that encourages employees to continually develop and share their knowledge beyond simple IT solutions. It is argued that managers need to cultivate a knowledge 'pull' rather than manage a knowledge 'push'. Indeed, managers need to adapt a more strategic leadership approach in which they facilitate knowledge development and sharing by encouraging employees to develop and share their human capital through rewards and recognition that build strong relationships. As Wenger (2000, p. 18) stated: 'knowledge managers who think that their role is to manage knowledge had better think twice … Knowledge is not an object that can be managed from outside…It is an integral part of the life of communities – the people in the best position to take stewardship of it.' Communities of practice (CoPs) are an important way for leaders to develop the social capital within the organization.

Developing Social Capital through Communities of Practice

Tymon and Stumpf (2003) describe social capital (SC) as the stock of accumulated resources that can be accessed via these relationships and argued that it is not until people in a network become a resource that SC exists.

The term communities of practice (CoPs) was first coined in 1991 when Lave and Wenger (1991) and Brown and Duguid (2000) discussed the link between knowledge and practice-based organizational learning 'on-the-job', such as the 'journeyman' of 'master-servant' apprenticeship models. In recent years interest in CoPs as a source of networking to encourage knowledge sharing has increased (Snyder 1997). As Wenger, McDermott and Snyder state (2002, p. 6): 'it is not that CoPs themselves are new, but the need for organizations to become more intentional and systematic about "managing" knowledge.' CoPs are defined as 'groups of people who share a concern, a set of problems, or a passion about a topic, and who deepen their knowledge and expertise in this area by interacting on an ongoing basis' (ibid., p. 4).

Membership of CoPs is voluntary, with members self-selecting on the basis of their expertise and passion for a topic. Commitment to the CoP is developed from identification with the group and its expertise. CoPs are not structurally rigid, although they share a basic 'structure' with an identified domain of knowledge, a community of people who care about the domain, and the shared practice that they are developing to be effective in the domain. Boundaries of CoPs are fuzzy rather than clear, and each CoP evolves and ends organically.

More recently the growing acknowledgement of the importance of social capital has added a further layer of interest to the contribution that can be made by CoPs. A number of practical examples of the effectiveness of CoPs have emerged in the literature (Hildreth and Kimble 2004). First Lesser, Fontaine and Slusher (2000) and more recently Hildreth and Kimble (2004) have edited books that include a diverse range of positive case studies. In a study of 13 CoPs, Fontaine and Millen (2004, p. 5) undertook a survey which identified that CoPs have a number of benefits for individuals, community and the organization. Over 50 per cent of those surveyed stated that CoPs have positive impact on individual skills and know-how, job satisfaction and personal reputation, while close to 50 per cent agreed that there were positive advantages for personal productivity and sense of belonging. More than 70 per cent agreed that CoPs assist knowledge sharing, expertise and resources and collaboration, while more than 50 per cent stated that CoPs assist consensus and problem solving, community reputation per cent legitimacy and trust between members. Finally, more than 50 per cent agreed that CoPs contribute to organizational operational efficiency and save costs, and close to 40 per cent agreed that CoPs improve level and speed of service or sales.

More recently, the role of 'virtual' CoPs to counter problems of distance, space and time are being discussed. Apart from the usual advantages of enabling people to interact at different times and from different geographical sites, it is also claimed that the advantage of these online discussions is that they provides a written record of discussion, debate and emerging ideas (Hislop 2003; Ardichvili et al. 2003).

Thus, as shown in Figure 24.1, CoPs provide the potential to increase an organizations social capital and assist employee and organizations to develop knowledge such that it has meaning, provides a philosophy and wisdom and assists the organization to develop a holistic knowledge union as described by Allee (1997, p. 6).

Figure 24.1   Community of practice process

Evaluating a Holistic Knowledge Strategy

Business has traditionally measured tangible assets in quantitative input-output processes involving numbers, costs, volumes and price. This has been influenced by traditional scientific methodology that makes observations of experiments, takes measurements and compares results against predictions of mathematics. Arianrhod (2003) states that the natural world studied by physicists is full of quantifiable concepts, defined by just energy and mass, and even more basic concepts like time and distance, where the variables appear only to the power of 1. Measures of effectiveness are made by following simple rules of certainty, stability and predictability in linear relationships.

The knowledge era, particularly the current third generation, requires new ways of demonstrating change in intangible assets that have value to an organization yet have no physical existence. Some use can be made of mathematics for measuring physical displays of intangibles such as number of patents, copyright and trademarks. However, much knowledge transfer occurs more indirectly. Intellectual assets are created whenever human capital is committed to an explicit form, codified and defined. At this stage it no longer belongs to the individual. The Scandia Navigator Intellectual Capital model (Edvinsson and Malone 1997) mentioned earlier in this chapter identifies a number of key indicators that as well as relating to a financial focus, include customer, process, renewal and development and human focuses identified across time rather than at a single point

Sveiby (1997) uses a three-point framework of growth and renewal, efficiency and stability which he demonstrates in terms of business environment (external structure); organizational environment (internal structure) and people (individual competence).

Allee (2003) has developed a value network approach that identifies a number of intangible assets between the organization and the customer. Thus while the traditional simple economic model was limited to measurement of the flow of goods and services, the value network approach seeks to identify the flow of values associated with technology support, sense of community, personal responses, feedback leading to product development, customer loyalty and fee for service.

Allee uses five concepts to demonstrate value, asset development, efficiency of value conversion, utilization, stability and renewal. For example, human competence can be demonstrated by:

- asset development – years of experience, qualification, succession ratio;
- efficiency of value conversions – value added per expert employee, ratio of non-revenue creating employees;
- utilization – knowledge re-use, employee utilization;
- stability – turnover, percentage of novice to expert employees;
- renewal – percentage of diversity, time in training.

However, Snowden (2002) argues that identifying approaches to demonstrating knowledge effectiveness requires a totally new approach that recognizes that efficiency and effectiveness are not necessarily related, that what is needed in order to live in complex environment is the identification of connections, patterns and interactions and then action to stimulate positive and discourage negative patterns rather than a total focus on measuring points in time. Like Allee, he focuses on understanding knowledge flows as well as stocks and the development and use of different tools, practices and conceptual understanding of how to move between four spectrums that he identifies as known, knowable, complex and chaos spectrums.

Empirical Examples of Successful KM Strategies in Organizations

There have been a number of empirical studies of successful KM strategies, among which exist some important global comparisons. McKinsey's Kluge, Stein and Licht (2001) published the outcome of their global survey of knowledge management that highlighted a number of particular case studies including:

- Buckman Laboratories 'knowledge pull approach' through communication, participation and knowledge sharing;
- Oticon 'Spagetti' structure to replace a linear organizational structure;
- SAP's development of a user friendly software environment;
- Intel's development of a supportive team environment;
- Fuji Xerox's innovative use of a movie making environment to encourage creativity.

The effectiveness of communities of practice in assisting organizations to improve performance has also been demonstrated in recent international empirical case studies (Hildreth and Kimble 2004) . These examples include:

- the link between CoPs and business value is recognized by the American Productivity and Quality Centre;
- Saba Software linked customer communities into improving business value;
- Oresund Bridge identified the need for rich media for the effective establishment of a 'virtual' learning community of practice;
- Siemens used CoPs as a means to share and develop expertise.

The effective development of knowledge strategies in public sector organizations has also been documented in empirical case studies by the IBM Cynefin Centre (Callaghan 2004) and Jones and Lockwood (2006).

Conclusion

This chapter introduced the key issues presented by the knowledge era. It first explored the challenges for the macro environment and then focuses at the micro (organizational) level. In so doing it presented the many challenges facing organizations as they seek to develop a knowledge management strategy that can assist them to address the complex environment in which business functions. In keeping with what is presented as challenges in the chapter, no attempt is made to provide easy solutions. This is not possible in complex environments. Rather, the chapter combines reflection activities with content to assist the reader to respond to these challenges with 'questions' that will assist them to identify patterns, rather than with answers that will simply restrict the ability to respond appropriately to these challenges.

References

Allee, V. (1997), *The Knowledge Evolution* (Newtown, MA: Butterworth-Heinemann).

Allee, V. (2003), *The Future of Knowledge* (Newtown, MA: Butterworth-Heinemann).

Ardichvili, A., Page, V. and Wentling, T. (2003), 'Motivation and Barriers to Participation in Virtual Knowledge Sharing Teams', *Journal of Knowledge Management* 7(1), pp. 64–77.

Arianrhod, R. (2003), *Einstein's Heroes: Imagining the World through the Language of Mathematics* (St Lucia, Queensland: University of Queensland Press).

Bourdieu, P. (1985), 'The Forms of Capital', in Richardson, J.G. (ed.) *Handbook of Theory and Research for the Sociology of Education* (New York: Greenwood Press), pp. 241–58.

Brown, S.J. and Duguid, P. (2000), 'Organisational Learning and Communities of Practice: Towards a Unified View of Working, Learning and Innovation', in Lesser, E., Fontaine, M. and Slusher, J. (eds) *Knowledge and Communities* (Newtown, MA: Butterworth-Heinemann), pp. 99–122.

Callaghan, S. (2004), 'Cultivating a Public Sector Knowledge Management Community of Practice', in Hildreth, P. and Kimble, V. (2004), *Knowledge Networks: Innovation Through Communities of Practice* (Hershey, PA: Idea Group Publishing), pp. 267–81.

Capra, F. (1996), *The Web of Life* (New York: Bantam Doubleday).

Checkland, P. and Holwell, S. (1998), *Information, Systems and Information Systems* (Chichester: John Wiley and Sons).

Cohen, M. and Bacdayan, P. (1994), 'Organizational Routines are stored as Procedural Memory: Evidence from a Laboratory Study', *Organization Science* 5(4), pp. 554–68.

Davenport, T. (1997), *Information Ecology* (Oxford and New York: Oxford University Press).

Davenport, T. and Prusak, L. (1998), *Working Knowledge* (Boston, MA: Harvard Business School Press).

Davenport, T., de Long, D.W. and Beers, M.C. (1998), 'Successful Knowledge Management Projects', *MIT Sloan Management Review* 39(2), pp. 43–57.

Deming, W.E. (1982), *Quality, Productivity and Competitive Position* (Cambridge, MA: Massachusetts Institute of Technology, Centre for Advanced Engineering).

Drucker, P. (1998), 'The Coming of the New Organisation', *Harvard Business Review on Knowledge Management* Boston MA (reprint, first published 1997), pp. 2–23.

Edvinsson, L. and Malone, M. (1997), *Intellectual Capital: Realizing Your Company's True Value by Finding its Hidden Brainpower* (New York: HarperBusiness).

Ellinor, L. and Gerard, G. (1998), *Dialogue: Rediscover the Transforming Power of Conversation* (New York: John Wiley & Sons).

Evan, W. (1972), 'An Organizational-set Model of Interorganizational Relations', in Tuite, M., Chisholm, R. and Radnor, M. (eds) *Interorganizational Decision-making* (Chicago: Aldine), pp. 181–200.

Fontaine, M.F. and Millen, D.R. (2004), 'Understanding the Benefits and Impact of Communities of Practice', Hildreth, P. and Kimble, C. (eds) in *Knowledge Networks: Innovation through Communities of Practice* (Hershey, PA: Idea Group Publishing).

Hammer, M. and Champy, J. (1993), *Reengineering the Corporation: A Manifesto for Business Revolution* (New York: HarperBusiness).

Hawken, P., Lovins, A. and Lovins, H. (2002), 'Natural Capitalism: Creating the Next Industrial Revolution', http://natcap.org/sitepages/pid5.php, accessed 19 August 2002.

Herzenberg, S.A., Alic, J.A. and Wial, H. (1998), *New Rules for a New Economy* (Ithaca, NY: Cornell University Press).

Hildreth, P. and Kimble, C. (eds) (2004), *Knowledge Networks, Innovation through Communities of Practice* (Hershey, PA: Idea Group Publishing).

Hislop, D. (2003), 'The Complex Relations between Communities of Practice and the Implementation of Technological Innovations', *International Journal of Knowledge Management* 7(2), pp. 163–88.

Jones, S. and Lockwood, O. (2006), 'Communities of Practice: Leveraging Knowledge by Complementing Technology with Social Participative – An Australian Case Study', in Garson, D. (ed.) *Public Information and E-Governance: Managing the Virtual State* (Ontario: Jones and Bartlett), pp. 470–75.

Kelly, K. (1998), *New Rules for a New Economy* (New York: Penguin).

Kluge, J., Stein, W. and Licht, T. (2001), *Knowledge Unplugged* (Basingstoke: Palgrave).

Lave, J. and Wenger, E. (1991), *Situated Learning Legitimate Peripheral Participation* (Cambridge: Cambridge University Press).

Leonard-Barton, D. (1995), *Wellsprings of Knowledge: Building and Sustaining the Sources of Innovation* (Boston, MA: Harvard Business School Press).

Lesser, E. Fontaine, M. and Slusher, J. (eds) (2000), *Knowledge and Communities* (Newtown, MA: Butterworth-Heinemann), pp. 3–20.

Marceau, J. (2000), 'Australian Universities: A Contestable Future', in Coady, T. (ed.) *Why Universities Matter* (St Leonards, NSW: Allen & Unwin), pp. 214–34.

Nohria, N. and Eccles, R. (eds) (1992), *Networks and Organizations: Structure, Form and Action* (Boston, MA: Harvard Business School Press).

Nonaka I. (1998), 'The Knowledge-creating Company', Harvard Business Review on Knowledge Management, *Harvard Business Review*, Boston (reprint, first published 1997), pp. 24–44.

Nonaka, I. and Takeushi, H. (1995), *The Knowledge-Creating Company* (Oxford and New York: Oxford University Press).

Polanyi, M. (1958), *Personal Knowledge: Towards a Post-Critical Philosophy* (Chicago, IL: Chicago University Press).

Portes, A. (1998), 'Social Capital: Its Origins and Application in Modern Sociology', *Annual Review Sociology* 24, pp. 1–24.

Ronfeld, D. and Arquilla, J. (2001), 'What's Next for Networks and Netwars', in Ronfeldt, D. and Arquilla, J. (eds) *Networks and Netwars: The Future of Terror, Crime and Militancy* (Santa Monica, CA: RAND), pp. 311–61.

Rumizen, M. (2002), *Knowledge Management* (Madison, WI: Pearson).

Schon, D. (1995), *The Reflective Practitioners: How Professionals Think in Action* (Aldershot: Avebury).

Seely Brown, J. (1999), 'Foreword', in Ruggles, R. and Holthouse, D. (eds), *The Knowledge Advantage* (Dover, NH: Capstone).

Seibet, K. and Daudelin, M. (1999), *The Role of Reflection in Managerial Learning: Theory, Research and Practice* (Westport: CT Quorum).

Smith, A. (1776), *The Wealth of Nations*, reprinted 1986 (London: Penguin).

Snowden, D. (2002), 'Complex Acts of Knowing: Paradox and Descriptive Self Awareness', Special Issue of the *Journal of Knowledge Management* 6(2), pp. 1–13.

Snyder, W. (1997), 'Communities of Practice: Combining Organizational Learning and Strategy Insights to Create a Bridge to the 21st Century', paper delivered at the Academy of Management Conference, Boston, August.

Sveiby, K. (1997), 'The Intangible Asset Monitor', *Journal of Human Resource Costing and Accounting* 2(1), Spring, pp. 25–36.

Taylor, F.W. (1964), *Scientific Management* (reprint of the 1947 edition) (New York: Harper and Row).

Tymon, W. and Stumpf, S. (2003), 'Social Capital in the Success of Knowledge Workers', *Career Development International* 8(1), pp. 12–20.

Wellman, B. and Berkowitz, S. (1997), *Social Structures: A Networked Approach* (updated edn) (Greenwich, CT: JAI Press).

Wenger, E. (2000), 'Communities of Practice: The Key to Knowledge Strategy', in Lesser, E., Fontaine, M. and Slusher, J. (eds) *Knowledge and Communities* (Newtown, MA: Butterworth-Heinemann), pp. 3–20.

Wenger, E., McDermott, R. and Snyder, W. (2002), *Cultivating Communities of Practice* (Boston, MA: Harvard Business School Press).

Wernerfelt, B. (1984), 'A Resource-based View of the Firm', *Strategic Management Journal* 5, pp. 171–80.

Zack, M. (1999), 'Developing a Knowledge Strategy', *California Management Review* 41(3) Spring, pp. 125–45.

Chapter 25

Tacit Knowledge and Implicit Learning

Keith Dawes

> … there is nothing commonsensical about [knowledge]; we inevitably assume away the difficulties or find ourselves with a Russian doll in which there are more knowledge puzzles inside every set of answers.
>
> Spender (2005)

Introduction

Tacit knowledge is a difficult concept for many to acknowledge, let alone study. An early empiricist criticism of the study of mental processes was 'if they were not explicit then, by definition, they do not exist'. There have been many philosophical analyses of what constitutes conscious ideas and what unconscious ideas may be (Block et al. 1997). This chapter contributes to this shortfall by examining contributions to creating and identifying knowledge that then can be analysed, categorized, theorized, modelled, stored and retrieved.

Defining Tacit Knowledge

Many advances have been built upon the models proposed by Freud and Jung in the final years of the nineteenth century. Their models were based around situations and descriptions of individuals involved, that is, personified and animated to make the concepts more human and intuitively understandable. Descriptive ideas such as subconscious, preconscious and unconscious all have their place. However, within management literature they are not adopted uniformly.

A tight definition of tacit knowledge is not so difficult to construct; to begin with, *tacit knowledge is unspoken*: when it becomes explicit it is no longer tacit. A thought that readily comes to mind is:

> Wouldn't it be of great advantage to make all that is tacit explicit, so everyone can see what it is.

This is more an emotional pull to transfer everything from the abstract form to the concrete form. Piaget extensively researched this type of psychological mechanism (Gruber and Vonèche 1977).

Tacit knowledge itself is an abstract or theoretical construct, because it is true: once it is expounded it is no longer tacit. The nature of tacit knowledge is best accessed via the information processing studies in the psychological literature.

Conceptually we could say that there is an immense repository of knowledge stored away beyond the grasp of normal awareness. However, this knowledge informs our every action, thought and motivation and somehow stays out of awareness, like some friend and ally or, unfortunately, some destructive foe, whose influence we may follow blindly.

Tacit Knowledge and Memory

Anderson's (1976) model of information processing classifies the contents of memory into:

- *procedural* knowledge, the repertoire of skills, rules and strategies that operate on declarative knowledge in the course of perception, memory thought and action;
- *declarative* knowledge structures, the individual's fund of general and specific factual information. Declarative knowledge can be classified further as either *episodic* or *semantic* in nature (Tulving 1972).

Episodic memory is autobiographical in character and contains more or less explicit reference to the self as the agent or experiencer of some event. It is focused on the unique environmental and organism's context in which that event occurred. Semantic memory is the 'mental lexicon' of abstract knowledge, stored without reference to the circumstances in which it was acquired (Kihlstrom 1987, p. 1446).

Anderson conceives that memory is a network of 'locations' corresponding to events, concepts and so on. Each location is associated with several other locations, each of which is 'tagged' with information about:

- the spatiotemporal context in which the event occurred;
- the semantic and syntactical properties of the concept;
- properties of the words used to form the concept; and
- strength of memory trace.

Given these attributes, the inputs, retrieval and outputs of the recollection process require a search of associations that is guided by the presence of the tags.

Roediger (1990) argues against a spatial organization of memory. In describing phenomena associated with memory, he asserted that theorists such as Anderson model the mind as being like a geometric space in which memories are stored, just as objects are stored in physical space. He argues for a more dynamic, synthesized model of memory retrieval. Nevertheless, whether structure or function is the more appropriate way of conceptualizing memory, empirical evidence supports several memory systems.

Hilgard (1977) views memory as a dynamic and self-selecting phenomenon. Although he is clear that structural sequences exist, he is more interested in what happens to the input stimulus, based upon the presence of a wide variation in individual cognitive processes and existing memories. He proposes that there exist divisions or themes in the human mind: some that control and guide action and behaviour with conscious awareness and others that are out of consciousness. Other workers have sought to use scientific approaches to ground these ideas.

Schacter and Graf (1986) noticed that task performance may be affected by residual memories of prior experiences, even though those experiences are not accessible to conscious recall. This led them to defining a distinction between *explicit* and *implicit* memory. They used the descriptive terms implicit and explicit to distinguish between the forms of memory that are classified by priming effects and by individuals ability to recall and recognize using tests. Implicit memory occurs when test performance is facilitated without deliberate or conscious remembering of a study episode, whereas explicit memory occurs when test performance requires recollection of the study episode (ibid., p. 432).

Roediger (1990) notes that at one level the theories postulating memory systems and those emphasizing different component processes in explicit and implicit memory seem quite different. Defining what constitutes a memory system or a mode of processing requires theoretical subtlety and it would be rash to quickly assert, 'tacit memory is the same as implicit memory', on the basis that tacit is simply a form of memory that is not explicit.

Tacit Knowledge as a Component of the Unconscious

The term *tacit knowledge* comes from the writings of Michael Polanyi (1958). He described it as a philosophical term used to denote knowledge whose origins and general epistemic contents were simply not part of one's ordinary consciousness. The economist Friedrich von Hayek (1962) referred to a form of 'supra-conscious' that comprised deep rules and other rich mental representations that were simply not part of or available to one's ordinary conscious awareness.

During the latter part of the nineteenth century and then onwards into the modern era, there was considerable focus on the existence of *unconscious processes* within the human mind. It was not simply a reaction against the notion of 'rational man'. Being hypothesized in part was due to a clear recognition amongst thinkers, especially those concerned with philosophy, and its sub-branch psychology, that some systematic form of knowledge existed out of ordinary awareness. Freud wrote that Groddeck (1989) appeared to have been the first to propose unconscious processes, referring to them as 'the It'.

Tacit knowledge comes as required, generally when a problem or a series of issues needs to be resolved. We also know that it does not come to all of us, only to those who are prepared to 'expect the unexpected'.[1] Reber (1993) mused that tacit knowledge seemed to result from a form of 'osmosis'. The resulting awareness was the result of simply being immersed within an environment. Essentially 'this is the way we do things around here' is picked up by the individual and they adopt the same manner, tone and methods used by those in their surroundings. Understanding emerges magically over time. 'Sitting next to Nelly' is a recognized way of training that has now been superseded by formal training. This essentially is an uncontrolled cognitive development and behaviour modification

People say 'It just came to mind' or 'the answer (or idea) just came, I don't know how'.

Calming one's mind and using postures as cues to induce calm minds that then enable one to hear the quiet internal messages that are available may be a means of accessing solutions that otherwise would not become explicit.

There is a consensus that studying unconscious processes presents many difficulties. Such studies must determine what is conscious and unconscious. As Reber (ibid.) acknowledges, this is not merely a theoretical or an epistemological problem. It is '... first and foremost, a

---

1 Expect the unexpected. 'If you do not expect the unexpected, you will not find it.' Heraclitus *Fragments*, c.500 BC. Quoted by William Starbuck in his Preface to Baumard's *Tacit Knowledge in Organisations* (1996). This phrase epitomizes the realization that much of what the tacit guides arises from sources that often appear to be non-rational, oblique and of uncertain origins.

measurement problem' (ibid., p. 8). Reber warns that 'there are many methodological booby traps awaiting anyone who ventures to study unconscious processes' (ibid.).

Studies into Tacit Knowledge and Implicit Learning

One of the earliest studies conducted on learning without awareness was conducted by Thorndike and Rock (1934). In their association and four quadrants experiments, they attempted to bridge the divide between behavioural and cognitive approaches used to define the implicit rules and patterns of individual perception of which they previously were not aware. These were laboratory studies that introduced the notion of *learning without awareness* and *accidental learning*.

Reber (1993, p. 5) defines implicit learning as 'the acquisition of knowledge that takes place largely independently of conscious attempts to learn and largely in the absence of explicit knowledge about what was acquired'.

One of Reber's core assumptions is that implicit learning is a fundamental process that exists as a central medium within the *adaptive behavioural repertoire* of every complex organisms. If this is so, then it bodes well for senior managers, who are individuals with tremendous experiential databases and highly effective implementation skills.

Psychological Polarities

Human thinking shows a distinct penchant for categorizing and labelling everything that comes to our attention. Our strongest tendency is to identify differences between two entirely opposing concepts or things (dichotomies), such as yin and yang and then place related entities at the opposite ends of a continuum. This is in part due to Socrates, who suggested there is little between guilty and innocent, right or wrong, good or bad. This approach is ambiguous and individuals may not tolerate ambiguity or chaos.

Goschke (1997) notes that how we perceive, learn, think, and act are often grounded in the idea of opposition between two fundamentally different modes of mental functioning.

The dichotomies that have been followed during the history of psychology include:

Perceptive	v	Aperceptive
Analytic	v	Holistic
Rational	v	Experiential
Logical	v	Intuitive
Verbal	v	Imaginal
Symbolic	v	Subsymbolic
Figurative	v	Actual

Conscious	v	Unconscious
	←→	
Abstract	v	Specific
	←→	
Mindful	v	Automatic
	←→	
Declarative	v	Procedural
	←→	
Propositional	v	Analogue
	←→	

Epstein (1994) observes that, ever since Freud (1901) distinguished between primary and secondary mental processes in his book on the interpretation of dreams, the most fascinating dichotomy is the one between conscious and unconscious processes. Contemporary ideas about the unconscious seldom include those conceived by Freud. Epstein included the basic physiologically derived 'id' states, such as hunger, need to eliminate bodily wastes, sexual libido and aggression combined in a maelstrom of forbidden repressed wishes and unbearable emotional conflicts. Nowadays, authors speak of forms of information processing that occur automatically and outside awareness, but are not necessarily connected to the psychoanalytic terms used by Freud.

The Cognitive Unconscious

A closer study of the psychoanalytic theory of the dynamics of the mind reveals that there is a continuum between the fully conscious and the fully unconscious. The range can be divided into various levels of awareness, cognition and sensory data processing. The term 'preconscious' refers to ideas that currently aren't explicit. They may be capable of coming to conscious awareness, sometimes with minimal intensity of focus or sometimes with great focus, as achieved in meditative or hypnotic states. Even the most persistent unconscious memories[2] can be 'surfaced' in the psychoanalytic tradition by the techniques of dream analysis or 'screen memory' analysis. Both these require the strength of concentration of the individual concerned and frequently can only be made conscious through the subjective analyses of the psychoanalyst. As to the usefulness of these processes in surfacing memories, the jury is still out and it remains a question of doubt, even for Freud himself.

The Polarity Fallacy

Surfacing memories continues into modern discussion. Reber (1993) writes that it is one thing to say that there are distinctions between implicit and explicit processes and another entirely to conclude that they are processes of altogether different kinds. To say this is to fall prey to what he calls 'the polarity fallacy':

> ... we need to be careful not to treat implicit and explicit learning as though they were completely separate and independent processes; they should be viewed as interactive components or cooperative processes, processes that are engaged in what Mathews (1991) likes to call a 'synergistic' relationship. (Ibid., p. 23)

---

2   The 'subconscious' is Pierre Janet's term used to describe the pre-conscious together with the unconscious.

This caveat doesn't provide closure on the issue. Researchers have not decided upon the operational criteria that discern the presence or absence of knowledge let alone achieved consensus if tacit knowledge exists at all.

Polyani's distinction was a major catalyst for bringing back into vogue the return of the unconscious into human information processing psychology. Empirical findings demonstrated the existence of implicit learning, even when subjected to the functional phenomenon of hypnotic amnesia. Also, the study of brain injured patients and developments in brain imaging techniques have illustrated the existence of different neural structures associated with implicit and explicit learning (Schacter and Tulving 1994). Farah (1994) asserted that damage of a specific neural structure produces an impairment of a specific cognitive function. Despite these findings, and notwithstanding the ingenuity of these empirical designs, a clearer definition of unresolved and controversial theoretical issues is still needed.

Implicit Learning and Unconscious Knowledge

A major contribution has been put forward by Thomas Goschke (1997). He attempted to resolve theoretical issues by posing five major theoretical questions and then proceeding to provide answers, using his own work as well as the others' findings.

The questions posed were:

1. Does implicit learning actually lead to unconscious knowledge, and if so, how can (un)conscious knowledge be measured?
2. Does implicit learning require attention or is it automatic?
3. Does implicit learning lead to abstract knowledge?
4. What are the computational mechanisms underlying implicit learning?
5. Does implicit learning involve specific brain systems?

Before responding to these questions he presents an overview of implicit learning tasks and basic findings. Goschke focuses on four classes of tasks, which he terms *incidental concept learning, sequential contingency, simultaneous co-variation* and *dynamic system control* tasks to comment on the role that implicit learning takes in the formation of unconscious knowledge and the measurement of (un)conscious knowledge.

Incidental Concept Learning

Goschke cites Reber's (1989, 1993) study of artificial grammar learning. Subjects are asked to study a list of meaningless letter strings (e.g., XVCCMT) under some orienting tasks (such as judging their 'pleasantness', or committing the letter string to memory). The subjects were not told that the letter strings had been generated according to a finite state grammar.[3]

> ... such a grammar consists of a set of states (represented by numbered circles) which are connected by labelled arrows. Legal strings are generated by following a sequence of arrows from the start to the end state. Each time one passes from one state to another, the symbol on the connecting arrow is written. The set of strings that can be generated this way is called a language and the strings of this language are termed grammatical. (Ibid., p. 250)

---

3   All are Markovian systems that are finite-state. Markovian systems means that they generate strings of symbols in a left-to-right, non-hierarchical fashion (Reber 1993, p. 29).

Subjects were later asked to differentiate between grammatical and ungrammatical letter strings. They selected grammatical strings significantly higher than chance (60–70 per cent). Subjects are often unable to describe the underlying rules and sometimes indicated that they made their decisions on an intuitive basis. This implies '… an unconscious abstraction process which maps veridically the intrinsic structure of the environment' (Reber and Allen 1978, p. 191).

Sequential Contingency Tasks

In these tasks the order of the sequence of stimuli is determined by a fairly complex rule. The *serial reaction task* (Nissen and Bellemer 1987) asked subjects to observe while a stimulus is presented in one out of four possible locations arranged horizontally in a visual display. The subject has to press one of four response buttons that correspond to the location of the stimulus. Goschke (1997, p. 251) noted that:

> Performance increments in this task have been observed even for subjects who were not able to verbalise the sequence after training and who performed poorly in a cued recall test of the sequences.'

A clear indication from this study is that subjects can acquire procedural knowledge about sequential structures incidentally and without conscious awareness about the sequence.

Simultaneous Co-variance Tasks.

These are similar to sequential learning tasks. Goschke notes that the critical variables usually are chosen to be intuitively improbable in order to prevent subjects from becoming aware of it. Lewicki (1986) used hair length and personality notes as his stimuli and found subject's judgements were influenced by the differences, even though they were unaware of them.

Dynamic Systems Control

Computer simulations of fictitious workplace systems were provided to subjects. They are given feedback on one or more of the system variables which he/she were able to manipulate. They were then provided with sets of algorithms that mapped either previous or current states of the system. What fascinated Berry and Broadbent (1984) was the observation that subjects sometimes achieved high proficiency at controlling the system (indicated by their success in producing required outputs of the system) even though when tested they had little or no declarative knowledge of the rules that governed the system.

Summary

According to Goschke (1997, p. 253), common features of these four classes of tasks are:

1. subjects process stimuli is recognized or used as some kind of regularity, structure, contingency or co-variation;
2. at least two different dependent variables must be measured, one indicating that implicit knowledge has been acquired and the other indicating lack of conscious knowledge of the relevant regularity, contingency, or co-variation;

3. performance criteria that have been used as measures or indicators to judge grammatical compliance or category membership, response times and accuracy;
4. with respect to the measurement of explicit knowledge, an ongoing controversy exists whether *verbal reports* or *discriminative behaviour* and *forced choices* are better suited to infer the existence or non-existence of conscious knowledge.

Goschke (ibid., pp. 253–5) asks five central theoretical questions concerning intrinsic learning and tacit knowedge:

1. Does implicit learning lead to unconscious knowledge?
2. Does implicit learning occur automatically and without attention?
3. Does implicit learning lead to abstract knowledge?
4. What are the computational mechanisms underlying implicit learning?
5. What brain systems are involved in implicit learning?

Conceptions of Knowledge from the Ancient Greeks to the Present

A widely adopted paradigm within the scientific community is that 'knowledge' is a model of the real world. Positivist sciences define knowledge as a sound representation of the world, tested and validated against the real. It is objective in that the model, formulae or system interactions that are tested remain independent of people. Usually there is a strong attempt to control the environmental or situational conditions so that 'pure' knowledge can be gleaned from mere inference or even 'commonsense'. However, there appear to be sizeable gaps in the positivist definition of knowledge.

A number of alternate forms of knowledge become apparent, especially when time is taken to reflect on our experiences. Baumard (1999) postulated that experience itself tends to 'paper over' its own character, which is itself intuitive, tacit and unique. Nonaka (1994, p. 15) wrote that 'knowledge is a multifaceted concept with multilayered meanings' and noted that the history of philosophy since the time of the Ancient Greeks 'can be regarded as a never-ending search for the meaning of knowledge'.

The relevance of the work of Chomsky (1987) is especially important in this discussion. He favours the existence of deep inherent *a priori* logical and language structures. These imply deeper, anatomically preserved or encoded structures and layers to all of the modern mental processes.

Psychological Dichotomies

Here we review psychological discussion on knowledge. Research has distinguished explicit (objective) and tacit knowledge. Polanyi's work and his distinction between objective and tacit knowledge have become extremely influential. Polanyi (1958) argued that tacit knowledge' sorigins and essential epistemic contents simply were not part of one's ordinary consciousness. He classified human knowledge into two categories. Explicit or codified knowledge refers to knowledge that is transmittable in formal, systematic language, while tacit knowledge has a personal quality that makes it hard to formalize and communicate. Nonaka (1994, p. 16) specified that '… tacit knowledge is deeply rooted in action, commitment, and involvement in a specific context'. In Polanyi's own words, it 'indwells' in a comprehensive cognizance of the human mind and body. Spender (1996, p. 67) restated James' (1950) distinction between 'knowledge about' and 'knowledge of acquaintance'. There are two important aspects of tacit knowledge that contribute to this discussion: (i) it is gained experientially, private and incommunicable, and (ii) it is inseparable from the process of its creation and application and it has not yet been abstracted from practice (Spender 1996).

While positivistic knowledge has the character of being atomic and discrete, Csikszentmihalyi and Csikszentmihalyi (1988) describe tacit knowledge as being more like a 'state of flow', knowledge of which the actor was not explicitly conscious and which does not need to be fitted into or manipulated through a conscious decision-making process.

Forms of Knowledge of the Ancient Greeks

As has been indicated above, the Ancient Greek philosophers had developed a systematic approach to the different forms of knowledge. Both Spender (1993) and Detienne and Vernant (1978) reviewed the work of Plato,[4] who distinguishes between four forms of knowledge:

1. *epistêmê* (abstract generalization);
2. *technê* (capability, capacity to accomplish tasks);
3. *phronesis* (practical and social wisdom); and
4. *metis* (conjectural intelligence).

Epistêmê[5] refers to knowledge that is universal, shared and circulated, which we teach and preserve and what we commonly refer to as our heritage. It is knowledge about things. It is often referred to as 'theory'. *Technê*, on the other hand, is translated as either 'craft' or 'art'. As Parry (2003) observes:

> Outside of modern science, there is sometimes scepticism about the relevance of theory to practice because it is thought that theory is [generated remotely] from reality ... at the level of practice, concrete experience might be all we need. ... science, theory strives for a value-free view of reality.

A sensible balance is reached, however, by Lewin (1951), who once quipped that 'nothing is more practical than a good theory'.

Phronesis is the opposite of *epistêmê*. It is personal, singular and idiosyncratic; the result of experience and social practice. It cannot easily be shared. It has vivid meaning only to the person who has lived the experience. It is generated only through the 'intimacy of lived experience' (Baumard 1999). *Phronesis* is usually the result of trial and error. It stems from interaction in social or organizational settings and is very difficult to analyse or test. It especially is difficult for science to observe and evaluate *phronesis* because it is difficult to characterize and operationalize. *Phronesis*' intuitive content makes it difficult to study scientifically. To characterize this knowledge phenomenon from a scientific perspective requires a radical new paradigm (Kuhn 1970), one that abandons the scientific method and relies on more sociological concepts such as 'intersubjectivity' (Berger and Luckman 1966) or 'communities of practice' (Wenger 1998).

---

4   Plato thought of knowledge as justified true belief, an idea that has been rejected in current sociological thinking.

5   'Science' derives from the Latin *scientia*, which in turn translates the Greek *epistêmê*, from which English derives 'epistemology'. Strictly speaking, for the Greeks, for something to be studied it needed to be *epistêmê*.

Mètis, or conjectural knowledge is based on the question 'what if?' and is recognized by the lack of fact and presence of desire and statements such as 'I think...'. Gossip is a clear sign of dynamic *mètis* data transfer. *Mètis* is:

> ... furtive, discretionary and simultaneous, it spurns idealisations and established representations – it provides a contrast to abstract generalisations on every point. Where one is hierarchical, the other is organic, indivisible, encapsulated in action. Where one tends towards universality, the other chooses the ephemeral as its playing field (as it is only the tactical outcome that counts). Where one seeks truth, the other seeks results. (Baumard 1999, p. 45)

Mètis is like Prospero's Ariel, a personification of the wizard's shrewdness and cunning. Where *epistêmê* is steadfast and reliable, the result of a long maturation, *mètis* is unpredictable and intuitive. In short, where one can be analysed and singular, the other is multiple and tacit. Most importantly, conjectural knowledge is embodied in purposeful behaviour.

In his Paris Lectures in 1929, Husserl (1929) advised that *doing* science is an admirable human venture, but *to apply* science, a subset of human endeavour, to the totality of human experience and expression, is not logically coherent. The Ancient Greek analysis provides clear guidance, pointing the way for using forms of analysis that do not aim to impose scientific method onto forms of human expression that do not adhere to its requirements.

Nativist Arguments – Phylogeny and Implicit Learning

Chomsky and deep structures   Chomsky (1987) made the incontrovertible point that there is a fundamental organization to the physical development of the human body. We all make the assumption that the human species has a certain biological endowment. Each of us develops according to our inherited genetic programme, with a predefined sequence of change according to what occurs within our complex environment that has a direct impact on the organism. The result is interaction; an integrated series of bio-physiological systems. Each is mutually supportive according to a predetermined blueprint. Chomsky wrote:

> It is fortunate that we have such a refined and specific innate endowment. Were this not so, each individual would grow into some kind of amoeboid creature, merely reflecting external contingencies, utterly impoverished, and lacking the special structures that make ... human existence possible. (Ibid., p. 419)

There is an important corollary. The same factors that bring about this ordering principle also prevent many other possible developmental outcomes – options and possibilities are negated. This drastically limits the number of final state options that can be achieved in physical growth. Although the developmental biology sciences provide much knowledge, there is little known about how all of this happens. However, no one really doubts that there must be some kind of internal, innate mechanism afoot. This is obvious because there is '... a vast qualitative difference between the impoverished and unstructured environment on the one hand, and the highly specific and intricate structures that uniformly develop, on the other' (ibid, p. 420). Chomsky applies this analysis to the human mind. He says that we also find structures of great intricacy developing in a uniform way without the benefit of learning. Language is a case in point, but there are also other faculties:

> A 'capacity to deal with abstract properties of ... number(s) ... it seems, unique to humans'. (Ibid. p. 420)

This ability to spend time thinking about (concentrating on) numbers equations and other abstract properties, such as time, space, relationships or causes and effects highlight capacities that lie at the base of managerial endeavours. These are in essence, unlearned, and are based upon our biological endowment. As with physical systems, these mental systems develop epigenetically, that is, each successive development stage depends on what has been achieved before. Biological readiness is a necessary precursor for environmental influence to have any meaningful influence on these capacities. A sub-phenomenon is 'regression to the mean'. Intelligent people may have less intelligent progeny. Tall people may have shorter offspring.

Chomsky argued that a biological endowment provides the basis for a social existence in common with others. Even though we may have differing environmental histories, we nonetheless share capacities that support commonalities in practice. He extended far beyond nativist arguments when he wrote:

> We live in a world of shared understanding that extend(s) far beyond the limited experience that evokes cognitive structures in the mind. (Ibid p. 420)

Reber and implicit learning   Arthur Reber (1993) dedicated much of his research career to the study of implicit learning. He defined implicit learning as the acquisition of knowledge that takes place largely independently of conscious attempts to learn and largely in the absence of explicit knowledge about what was acquired. One of the core assumptions of Reber's work was his conviction that implicit learning is a 'fundamental "root" process, one that lies at the very heart of the adaptive behavioural repertoire of every complex organism' (ibid., p. 5). Drawing on the heuristic strength of Darwin's evolutionary theory, he asserted that implicit learning has phylogenetic precedence over learning with awareness. Reber had four 'Darwinian Postulates':

1. Consciousness and phenomenological awareness are recent arrivals, genetically speaking. This is in accord with Darwin's own proposition.[6] Consciousness and conscious control over action must have been built upon deeper, more primitive, processes and structures that functioned independently of awareness. On these grounds, it can be assumed that implicit processes operate independently of consciousness and are more primitive and basic than those that are dependent on consciousness and conscious control.
2. One of the standard heuristics in evolutionary theory is that genetically older and more primitive structures are more robust and resilient and less prone to disruption than newer strains. One would expect to see implicit cognitive structures show greater resistance to interference from neurological insult, functional disorder and hypnotic intervention.
3. Evolutionarily more ancient implicit functions of the cognitive unconscious should show a tighter distribution in the population than the more recently emerging explicit conscious functions. This implies that we would expect to find fewer individual differences between people when implicit processes are in use than when explicit processes are. The more successful an evolutionary adaptation, the less likely it will display variation. Also, as most of our educational programmes and theories of instruction are based on explicit,

---

6   Darwin considered conscious control an evolutionary failure, largely because of all the biases that come into being because of the very nature of individual and group consciousness.

overt paradigms we must expect, in our culture of inequalities, an increase in population variance on virtually any explicit cognitive function that we measure.

4. There should be a relationship between a phylogenetic point where a particular property evolved and the degree to which we are conscious of its form and content. That is, we would expect to find that the more primitive a function is shown to be, consciousness will be more fragmentary. Hence the reliability of hypnotic responses such as the ideomotor response is called into question.

It is surprising that an evolutionary heuristic is not used more frequently in modern psychology. It formed the basis for Piaget's cognitive theories (Gruber and Vonèche 1977), of Kohlberg's moral development (Kohlberg 1969) and even of Tuckman and Jensen's (1977) team development theory. Nonaka (1994) would argue that this is because we are in the 'knowledge society' and, as observed by Drucker (1967) and Toffler (1990), it is a time when forces of centrally controlled empiricism far outweighs local approaches.

Knowledge creation relies on the interaction of explicit and tacit knowledge. Polanyi's work was philosophical. Nonaka (1992) believed that it was possible to expand this idea along a more practical direction. Tacit knowledge involves both cognitive and technical elements. Cognitive elements centre on mental models that the human mind creates using such devices as diagrams, sketches, paradigms, beliefs and viewpoints that provide perspectives. These enable individuals to perceive and understand their world. Meanwhile, tacit knowledge also covers technical elements such as concrete know-how, crafts and skills that apply to specific contexts. The cognitive components of tacit knowledge are future oriented; that is 'what is' and 'what might be likely'. Nonaka (1994) also pointed out that the articulation of tacit perspectives is a kind of mobilization process; a key factor in the building of new knowledge.

Piaget and cognitive growth   The life work of Jean Piaget (Gruber and Vòneche 1977) is focused on the developmental sequencing of the logical cognitive structures. He was guided by the logical theory of Poincaré (ibid., p. 457), who maintained that the human mind is capable of some 42 logical operations, each dependent on more elemental, less complex logical elements. Piaget's genius was to realize that the growth of logical operations was epigenetic, that is, it is formed according to successive stages over a long time period, from concrete logical operations during the first few years of life, such as sequencing, correspondence and grouping, to the highly sophisticated logical forms of correlation, probability and regression analysis, which come much later in life and only to a relative few individuals. Piaget was clear that these logical structures were immanent and implicit, and only become explicit in the study of their forms, such as in the disciplines of mathematics and logic.

Bateson (1990) perceives communication between individuals as 'an analogue process' that aims to share tacit knowledge to build mutual understanding. This model involves what he terms 'parallel processing' of the complexities of current issues, as the different dimensions of a problem are processed simultaneously.

Intention, autonomy, and fluctuation   Polanyi (1958) noted that individuals are the prime movers in creating their world in accordance with their own perspectives. He noted that commitment underlies human knowledge-creating activities. Three factors were identified that contribute to the strength of this commitment: intention, autonomy and a certain level of environmental fluctuation (change) that may result from imperatives to survive, greed or others' dominating a situation.

Husserl's (1929) analysis of consciousness is instructive to those who wish to promote change. He denies the existence of conscious awareness *per se*, arguing that consciousness arises when individuals pay attention to an issue. Any form of consciousness is awareness of something: it arises, endures and disappears with a subject's commitment to an object. People may be more motivated to avoid the things they fear than to chase their dreams and obtain or become something they want.

Current ideas of empowerment and self-efficacy promote autonomy where only 'minimum critical specification' (Morgan 1986) is provided and monitored. Nonaka (1994) believes individual autonomy creates the environment where individuals motivate themselves to develop new knowledge. From work on emotional intelligence, Salovey and Meyer (1990) propose that self-motivation is based on deep emotional drives to achieve personal goals. Purpose serves as the basis of conceptualization while autonomy provides the freedom to absorb knowledge.

> Desperate need is the mother of innovation. Economic survival is the father.

Environmental fluctuations cause disruption to individuals' intentions. *Chaos* or dramatic and unpredicted discontinuity can generate new patterns of interaction between individuals and their environment that take into account ambiguity, redundancy, noise or randomness generated from the organization and its environment. 'Order without recursiveness' represents an order where the pattern is hard to predict in the beginning (Gleick 1987).

Knowledge conversion   Nonaka (1990) developed the idea of knowledge conversion. He traces the idea back to Anderson's ACT model (Anderson 1983), developed in cognitive psychology. This model is based on two concepts, 'declarative' and 'procedural' knowledge. Declarative knowledge (actual knowledge, according to Anderson) is expressed in the form of propositions and procedural knowledge (methodological knowledge) is used in such activities as playing the guitar or walking down stairs. In our discussion, the former might be considered as explicit knowledge. The latter is tacit knowledge. In this model Anderson hypothesizes that declarative knowledge has to be transformed into procedural knowledge in order for cognitive skills to develop. One might acknowledge that Anderson's hypothesis is a more sophisticated version of Ryle's (1949) classification of knowledge into knowing that something 'exists' and knowing 'how' it operates. Nonaka (1990) identifies one limitation of the ACT model – it says that knowledge transformation is unidirectional and only involves transfers from declarative to procedural knowledge, while anyone who has ever learned a new skill shall attest such transformations are bidirectional. He has developed the following transition sequence based on tacit-explicit interfaces.

1. From tacit to explicit. Articulation – this form of conversion occurs as the continual foundation of life. The way that tacit rules become recognized as internal regulations is a good example. That which is commonly known, and which we could call 'common knowledge', is gradually articulated into explicit knowledge
2. From explicit to explicit. Combination – the conversion of explicit knowledge into another form of explicit knowledge is a question of combination. Nonaka notes that 'individuals exchange and combine their knowledge through mechanisms such as

telephone conversations[7]. ... [Combinating existing] information can be facilitated by the selection, addition, grading, and categorisation of explicit knowledge' (1992, p. 13)

3. From explicit to tacit.

    The panoptic prison is circular, made up of open cells through which light passes in order to sharply outline the silhouettes of the prisoners. The warden is lodged in a tower at the centre of the circular building, which is fitted with blinds enabling him to 'see without being seen'. In this context, prisoners have explicit knowledge of the surveillance tower. They recognise the possibility that they are being watched at any given time, without it being possible to know whether the warden is really looking at them or at something else. The prisoners internalise this explicit knowledge, and turn it into tacit knowledge; they know tacitly that they may be watched at any time and accept the possibility. While the explicit expression of their knowledge amounts to a black tower at the centre of the building, their tacit knowledge has internalised the 'presence' of the warden within this obelisk. (Baumard 1999, pp. 25–6)

4. From tacit to tacit. Socialization – this mode of knowledge conversion allows us to pass tacit knowledge on:

    An individual can acquire tacit knowledge directly from another without the use of language. Artisans live with their masters from whom they learn their art not through language but through observation, imitation, and practice... Tacit knowledge conversion is based on the sharing of experience. (Nonaka 1992)

Modelling is a form of learning that is evident to us all. Rather than hypothesize an *'unconscious'* entity to account for such learning, we can rest assured that it is simply our implicit learning facility that has copied a schema and represented it according to what exists within the realm of our personal tacit knowledge.

Implications for International Managers

The author proposes 'Tacit Knowledge and Implicit Learning' programmes that combine theoretical and practical approaches to skill development. Particular emphasis placed on practical learning by applying grounded theory research techniques. During the week-long training events, participants actively are involved in personal and group development. They combine sharing web and library research, participate in actual research work and establish a collegiate mutually supportive work environment. They bring their own laptops and headsets to learn the technicalities required for digital transcription of interviews. They are guided in line-by-line analysis of transcripts and become adept at establishing precise, usable open codes. Adaptive team practices are established based on the clear understanding of the ongoing process of tacit-explicit interaction. Leonard and Swap's (2004) 'deep smarts' concepts provide two focuses: greater reliance on utilizing one's personal resources and the necessity of tapping into the resources of others. Ongoing individual challenges have the effect of fostering an atmosphere of success. Time must be given to allow groups to peer assess progress. Excellence is expected and it is materialized in the work done. The guiding philosophy of tacit knowledge awareness development programmes is unabashedly directed towards participants' success. The aim of training experiences is to enable participants' to transfer acquired skills to respective work places. Tacit knowledge training programmes facilitated by the author wrap up by using the *Explicit/Tacit Interface Technique*; this method was developed and is expounded by the author

---

7   Nonaka did not seek to delimit this exchange of knowledge here, he was mentioning this communication form in passing. Other forms include face-to-face discussions, group meetings, emails, bulletins, letters and so on.

to assist managers when they access their own tacit assumptions. Once identified, these may facilitate more successful problem solving, decision-making and personal and organizational strategy planning.

Conclusions

The study of tacit knowledge and implicit learning will eventually become part of mainstream management education. Claiming that some 85 per cent of an individual's mental resources are tacit and usually under-appreciated by managers in general, then one would hope that the immediate future will witness a tremendous surge in interest in tacit knowledge.

References

Anderson, J.R. (1976), *Language, Memory and Thought* (Hillsdale, NJ: Erlbaum).

Anderson, J.R. (1983), *The Architecture of Cognition* (Cambridge, MA: Harvard University Press).

Bateson, M.C. (1990), *Composing a Life* (New York: Plume).

Baumard, P. (1999), *Tacit Knowledge in Organisations* (London: Sage).

Berger, P.L. and Luckman, T. (1966), *The Social Construction of Reality* (Garden City, NY: Doubleday).

Berry, D.C. and Broadbent, D.E. (1984), 'On the Relationship between Task Performance and Associated Verbalisable Knowledge', *Quarterly Journal of Experimental Psychology* 36: pp. 209–31.

Block, N., Flanagan, O. and Guzeldere, G. (eds) (1997), *The Nature of Consciousness* (Cambridge, MA: MIT Press).

Chomsky, N. (1987), 'Language: Chomsky's Theory', in Gregory, R.L. (ed.) *The Oxford Companion to the Mind* (Oxford: Oxford University Press), pp. 419–21.

Csikszentmihalyi, M. and Csikszentmihalyi, I.S. (1988), *Optimal Experience: Psychological Studies of Flow in Consciousness* (Cambridge: Cambridge University Press).

Detienne, M. and Vernant, J.P. (1978), *Cunning Intelligence in Greek Culture and Society*, J. Lloyd (trans.) (Hassocks: Harvester Press).

Drucker, P. (1967), *The Effective Executive* (London: Heinemann).

Epstein, S. (1994), 'Integration of the Cognitive and the Psychodynamic Unconscious', *American Psychologist* 49, pp. 709–24.

Farah, M.J. (1994), 'Neuropsychological Inference with an Interactive Brain: A Critique of the "Locality" Assumption', *Behavioural and Brain Sciences* 17, pp. 43–104.

Freud, S. (1901), 'The Psychopathology of Everyday Life', in Strachey, J. (ed.) *The Standard Edition of the Complete Psychological Works of Sigmund Freud* (1981) (London: The Hogarth Press).

Gleick, J. (1987), *Chaos: Making a New Science* (New York: Vilroy).

Goschke, T. (1997), 'Implicit Learning and Unconscious Knowledge: Mental Representation, Computational Mechanisms, and Brain Structures', in Lamberts, K. and Shanks, D. (eds) *Knowledge, Concepts and Categories* (London: Psychology Press).

Graf, P. and Schacter, D.L. (1985), 'Implicit and Explicit Memory for New Associations in Normal and Amnesic Subjects', *Journal of Experimental Psychology: Learning, Memory and Cognition* 10, pp. 164–78.

Groddeck, G. (1989), *Exploring the Unconscious*, V.M.E. Collins (trans.) (Plymouth: Vision Press).

Gruber, H.E. and Vonèche, J.J. (1977), *The Essential Piaget* (London: Routledge & Kegan Paul).

Hayek, F.A. von (1962), 'Rules, Perception, and Intelligibility', *Proceedings of the British Academy* 48, pp. 321–44.

Hilgard, E.R. (1977), *Divided Consciousness: Multiple Controls in Human Thought and Action* (New York: Wiley-Interscience).

Husserl, E. (1929), *The Paris Lectures*, P. Koestenbaum (trans.) (1964) (The Hague: M. Nijhoff).

James, W. (1950), *The Principles of Psychology* (New York: Dover Publications, Inc.).

Kihlstrom, J.F. (1987), 'The Cognitive Unconscious', *Science*, pp. 1445–52.

Kohlberg, L. (1969), 'Stage and Sequence: The Cognitive Developmental Approach to Socialisation', in Goslin, D.A. (ed.) *Handbook of Socialization Theory and Research* (Chicago: Rand McNally), pp. 347–480.

Kuhn, T.S. (1970), *The Structure of Scientific Revolutions*, 2nd edn (Chicago: University of Chicago Press).

Leonard, D. and Swap, W. (2004), 'Deep Smarts', *Harvard Business Review* 82(9), pp. 88–97.

Lewicki, P. (1986), *Nonconscious Social Information Processing* (New York: Academic Press).

Lewin, K. (1951), *Field Theory on Social Sciences* (New York: Harper & Row).

Mathews, R.C. (1991), 'The Forgetting Algorithm: How Fragmentary Knowledge of Exemplars Can Yield Abstract Knowledge', *Journal of Experimental Psychology: General* 120, pp. 117–19.

Morgan, G. (1986), *Images of Organisation* (Beverley Hills, CA: Sage).

Nissen, M.J. and Bullemer, P. (1987), 'Attentional Requirements of Learning: Evidence from Performance Measures', *Cognitive Psychology* 19, pp. 1–32.

Nonaka, I. (1990), 'Managing Innovation as a Knowledge Creation Process', presentation at New York University, Stern School of Business, International Business Colloquium.

Nonaka, I. (1992), 'A Management Theory of Organisational Knowledge Creation', research paper.

Nonaka, I. (1994), 'A Dynamic Theory of Organisational Knowledge Creation', *Organisational Science* 5(1), pp. 14–37.

Parry, R. (2003), 'Epistêmê and Technê', *The Stanford Encyclopedia of Philosophy*, p. 1, http://plato.stanford.edu/entries/episteme-techne/.

Polanyi, M. (1958), *Personal Knowledge: Toward a Post-critical Philosophy* (Chicago: University of Chicago Press).

Reber, A.S. (1989), 'Implicit Learning and Tacit Knowledge', *Journal of Experimental Psychology: General* 3, pp. 219–35.

Reber, A.S. (1993), *Implicit Learning and Tacit Knowledge: An Essay on the Cognitive Unconscious* (New York: Oxford University Press).

Reber, A.S. and Allen, R. (1978), 'Analogic and Abstraction Strategies in Synthetic Grammar Learning: A Functionalist Interpretation', *Cognition* 6, pp. 189–221.

Roediger, H.L. III (1990), 'Implicit Memory: Retention without Remembering', *American Psychologist* 45(9), pp. 1043–56.

Ryle, G. (1949), *The Concept of Mind* (Chicago: University of Chicago Press).

Salovey, P. and Meyer, J.D. (1990), 'Emotional Intelligence', *Imagination, Cognition and Personality* 9, pp. 185–211.

Schacter, D.L. and Graf, P. (1986), 'Effects of Elaborative Processing on Implicit and Explicit Memory for New Associations', *Journal of Experimental Psychology, Learning, Memory, and Cognition* 12(3), pp. 432–44.

Schacter, D.L. and Tulving, E. (eds) (1994), *Memory Systems* (Cambridge, MA: MIT Press).

Spender, J.-C. (1993), 'Competitive Advantage from tacit Knowledge: Unpacking the Concept and its Strategic Implications', Proceedings of the Academy of Management Annual Meeting, Atlanta.

Spender, J.-C. (1996), 'Competitive Advantage from Tacit Knowledge? Unpacking the Concept and its Strategic Implications', in Mosingeon, B. and Edmondson, A. (eds) *Organizational Learning and Competitive Advantage* (London: Sage Publications), pp. 56–73.

Spender, J.-C. (2005), 'Speaking about Management Education: Some History of the Search for Legitimacy and the Ownership and Control of Management Knowledge', *Management Decision Incorporating Journal of Management History* 43(10), pp. 1282–92.

Thorndike, E.L. and Rock, R.T. Jr (1934), 'Learning without Awareness of What is being Learned or Intent to Learn It', *Journal of Experimental Psychology* 1, pp. 1–19.

Toffler, A. (1990), *The Third Wave* (New York: Batman Books).

Tuckman, B. and Jensen, M. (1977), 'Stages of Small Group Development', *Group and Organisational Studies* 2, pp. 419–27.

Tulving, E. (1972), 'Episodic and Semantic Memory', in Tulving, E. and Donaldson, W. (eds) *Organisation of Memory* (New York: Academic Press).

Wenger, E. (1998), *Communities of Practice: Learning, Meaning, Identity* (Cambridge: Cambridge University Press).

DIMENSION 8
Business Transformation

Chapter 26

Service Operations Management

Erkan Bayraktar

Introduction

This chapter introduces key issues of service operations management. Services are intangible and are provided and used at specific times because they can not be stored for later. Consumers may participate in the service provision as a co-producer. A service package includes supporting facilities, facilitating goods, information, explicit and implicit services. It is a bundle of goods and services. Topics covered in this chapter include delivery system and service encounters, location and servicescapes, capacity planning, quality and managing the information in service operations:

> As machine technology once changed an agricultural economy into an industrial economy, today's information technology is transforming our industrial economy into a service economy. (Fitzsimmons and Fitzsimmons 2006)

It is nearly impossible to go through a day without taking part in some kind of a service design. The most obvious services include hotels and guesthouses, hairdressing and using an automated teller machine (ATM). Other examples of a service that are taken granted are utilities, communication (inbound – cinema, TV, radio; and two way – telephone, internet), transportation, food. Today it is difficult to think of everyday life without these services. Services always have been a part of humanity – where there are people, they have demands that need to be met with services. The conceptual framework of services, in the form of a formalized business operation that are strictly disciplined, dates back no further than a couple of decades.

A service is a time-perishable, intangible experience or activity performed for a customer acting in the role of co-producer (Fitzsimmons and Fitzsimmons 2006). Distinctive characteristics of services include:

- In contrast to goods, services are intangible. The result of some services may be mostly an emotion, a feeling or an idea. There will be little physical evidence afterwards. This aspect of services can make it relatively easy or difficult for competitors to imitate. Consequently, only a few service innovations stay novel for long after they are introduced. To turn intangible experiences into tangibles, most service providers bundle the services with goods or vice versa. Examples of attempts to aid the memory after the completion of a service include pictures taken during a vacation or fairground attraction and promotional materials presented by service companies.
- Customers participate in the service process. They configure the services directly. A travel arrangement, a bank transaction and a waited table in a restaurant are services that require interaction with the customer. This increases the importance of the servicescapes and the role of service provider for the perception of the quality of the service from the customer's perspective

- Concurrent production and consumption of services is a common attribute in many service operations. Live performances and fast food restaurants are among the better examples of this simultaneity. It may be difficult for services to respond promptly to negative feedback relating to customers perceptions of quality and to rapid changes in demand.
- Unlike, goods, many services cannot be stored for future use. Examples include empty seats at the venue of a live performance, hotel room vacancies for a particular day can not used to satisfy excess demand the following day in order to match the demand with available capacity. Limited decoupling can be applicable by making customers wait and reserve in advance, though this may not be very attractive or convenient for customers. Notable exceptions to the storability issue are the on-demand or pre-recorded TV and films, music and computer software. Many software programs, videos and music files can be downloaded directly from the internet.

Governmental and infrastructure services such as transportation, communication, health care, banking, security, education and other utilities are very important to the development and sustainability of service industries. These infrastructure services are a prerequisite of being an industrial or service economy and to being part of a global service network.

In OECD economies, services sectors account for over 70 per cent of total employment (OECD, 2005). In 2000, this ratio reached 74.2 per cent in the USA. There is a quiet but stable shift from industrial- to service-based employment. Based on the share of the workforce employed in service industry, all highly industrialized countries have transformed into 'service economies' by the early part of this decade (Schettkat and Yocarini 2006). Ranging from very low and high levels of per capita income, there is a stable relationship between service/industry employment. With increasing GDP per capita, share of the service employment in the labour market increases. As the GDP increases so too does the share of service businesses. Figure 26.1 illustrates this relationship between different national income and service employment rates.

A recent yet influential shift has been in the globalization of services. This is due to the rapid technological advances in communication and transportation. As a result, certain services have been outsourced to locations where comparable highly skilled labour forces are available which operate at lower costs. Producers of designer clothes, for instance, only need to concentrate on the design and have partners in other activities from any part of the world to reach to their customers all over the world. Similarly, a fast food chain designs its products and services for almost anyone in the world. The OECD (2005) estimated the total number of jobs that potentially could be affected by domestic or global outsourcing is close to 20 per cent of employment in certain countries. A McKinsey Company Global Labour Market report (2005), projected that in 2008 there would be 1.46 billion service jobs worldwide. Of these, about 160 million jobs (11 per cent) could be performed regardless of location. These numbers emphasize the importance of services in our global economy.

Service Operations

Even though services have been an unavoidable part of normal life since very early civilizations began, in recent years they have excited growing interest. Many factors, some influential, have contributed to this. Technological developments have made productivity improvements in agriculture and manufacturing possible. More is produced with fewer resources and a smaller labour force. Mature economies are absorbing resources liberated in this way into the

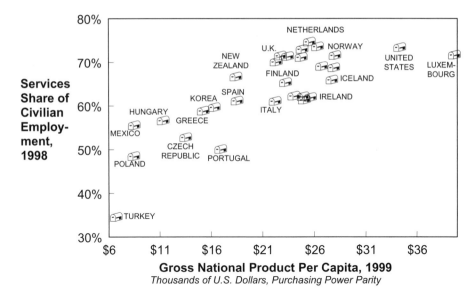

Figure 26.1   Relationship between services employment and national income

Source: Sauvé and Dihal 2002.

service sector. There also is significant pressure to reduce costs in services. Globalization and technological innovations increase global competition. Their influence is so pervasive that few local businesses are subject to solely local competition any longer.

Improved productivity and processes are essential to the sustainability of a business. Service operations management is used to identify the common characteristics of different functional services and focuses on operational issues dedicated directly for services.

Goods and services mostly go hand-in-hand and complement each other. In many situations, it is very difficult to identify a purely service or manufacturing industry. Even though a fast food restaurant can be considered as a pure service industry, the foods to be served are goods. In contrast, production of electronic appliances is pure manufacturing. The product warranties and after-sales maintenance form the after sales service provision. Goods and services are together and bundle-up to be presented to the customers in the market.

Service package is a term used to define a bundle of goods and services. A service package covers the following features (Fitzsimmons and Fitzsimmons 2006):

*   *Supporting facility*: the physical resources required to perform the services such as a hospital, movie theatre or computer server.
*   *Facilitating goods*: materials procured or consumed by customers such as hamburgers, medicine or movies.
*   *Information*: operational data provided by the customer to enable efficient service delivery. Examples include menus, employment/medical history, bus schedules.
*   *Explicit services*: readily observable outcome of the service, for example, smiling and feeling happy after a sitcom show, feeling better after a medical treatment, satisfaction following a quality meal.

- *Implicit services*: psychological benefits, such as an ego boost felt by the customer even if only vaguely as a result of service from a reputable company, the sense of security given by having a firewall installed on a computer network and a fully paid up insurance policy just in case a credit card is stolen or private medical treatment is needed.

Service operations deal with the design and management of service packages. Developing a sound service strategy is the first step in the service design where we define our target customers, differentiate our services from our competitors and position ourselves in the market. Service packages may be defined as a result of a new service strategy. Equally, the service strategy may be redesigned as a result of breakthrough technological developments in the core product (see Chapter 23 on technology management and Chapter 29, 'Supplier Development', both by Newlands, this volume). Location of our services, servicescapes, service encounter selection and service quality are key issues to design in the services. Once the service package is designed, managing the services is a further area where service operations management should be involved. Waiting theory and yield management are two tools with which to manage the demand and capacity available. In the following sections, these issues will be briefly explained and international issues affecting them are discussed.

Service Strategy

Strategic positioning relates to the decisions of the company as to how it will satisfy potential customers' needs. These decisions relating to service provision send a clear message by the firm to its customers about why they should prefer the firm. Michael Porter (1985) suggested three generic competitive strategies: cost leadership, differentiation and focus.

Cost Leadership Strategy

Managers focus on driving organization's costs down below the cost of its competitors. Organizations pursuing cost leadership strategy provide their services for less than their competitors and are still able to make a profit because of their lower costs. This strategy does not mean being the lowest cost service provider. It means competing based on the value for money spent by the customer. Some cost leadership approaches in services are as follows (Fitzsimmons and Fitzsimmons 2006):

- clustering customers to seek out low-cost ones;
- standardizing a custom service by delivering routine services at low cost;
- reducing the time spent to delivery the service;
- reducing network cost;
- taking service operations offline.

Differentiation

Efforts focus exclusively on how to distinguish the organization's services from those of competitors in some dimensions such as brand image, technology, customer service or features. The most important outcome of this strategy is the customer's perception of the service being unique. Some approaches to differentiate services are as follows (Fitzsimmons and Fitzsimmons 2006):

- making the intangible (service) tangible, reminding the customer about the services;
- customizing the standard product;
- reducing perceived risk;
- training personnel;
- ensuring quality standards and methods are adhered to.

Focus

This strategy 'cherry picks' a few market segments in which to serve. Both cost leadership and differentiation can be selected and applied in these market segments to satisfy customers' specific needs to a very high level.

The first step in strategy development is to create a vision statement and identify the organization's purpose. According to Heskett et al. (1997), strategic service vision has four elements:

- a focus on target market segments;
- a service concept is identified and elaborated;
- an operating strategy is developed;
- the chosen service delivery system is implemented.

Each of these elements should be supported by the others in a well developed service vision. *Target market segments* are a clear answer to the question 'who are the organization's customers'. The principal challenge and opportunity with the target market segment is not the identification of the market, rather it is the implementation of the concept. In service businesses, to be selective on behalf of customers and to elect to offer them some services rather than others has some problems in practice. Performance of the *service concept* typically is the reason customers prefer a particular organization. The service concept should be established from the customers' perspective and fulfil customers' wants and needs in such areas as cost, variability, response times, quality and flexibility. *Operating strategy* is related to how a service organization should be structured to implement the service concept. The most fragile elements of the strategy are identified to understand where to concentrate the most managerial attention. Quality measures must be established that affect performance criteria that customers value. The *service delivery system* relates to the design and specific decisions made by the organization about location, facility design and layout, procedures and job definitions, quality measures, personnel, equipment, adequate service capacity and technology. The customer's voice should be used to develop service concepts.

Fitzsimmons and Fitzsimmons (2006) state that in order to design a service system in line with the vision defined above, the following service design elements should be engineered:

- structural elements:
    - *delivery system*: identification of customer involvement in the service and establishment of front and back office;
    - *location*: selection of location based on targeted customers, competitors, and site characteristics;
    - *facility design*: aesthetics, layout;
    - *capacity planning*: deciding on the number of servers, capacity adjustment choices;
- managerial elements:
    - *service encounter*: type of culture to be created for service environment, employment policies and training, and level of empowerment;

— *quality*: measurement of customer perceptions and service guarantees;
— *managing capacity and demand*: decisions on how to meet the demand with available capacity and how to manage queues;
— *information*: data collection for use as a source of competitive advantage.

In the following sections, we will briefly explain those service elements.

Service Facility Location

Selection of facility location is one of the most important strategic decisions for services. Compared to manufacturing site selection, service facilities may encounter location-related decisions more frequently. Business growth, economic factors, shifts in the regional demographic characteristics and political turmoil may force the service businesses to reconsider location decisions. While the cost reduction through tax advantages and lower labour and transportation costs are top priorities in the decision of manufacturing facility locations, revenue generation potential is the main consideration in the selection process of the location of service facilities. Flexibility to adapt to the changing market conditions in the future, such as a new competitor in the market, regional economic turndowns and global economical, cultural and political atmosphere, should also be taken into account. Overwhelming presence in a particular region is a result of competitive positioning as in Seven-Eleven in Japan. It will increase the market awareness from a marketing perspective while helping to reduce cost of restocking and transportation. In some cases, being the first in the region and holding a prime location will dissuade competitors from investing in the region. It helps to create a natural barrier to entry. Fast food restaurants prefer to be located where the people tend to congregate, such as shopping malls and city centres. Hotels are located next to airports and main convention centres. In each of these cases, entrepreneurs want to have greater access to the demand and better control over their activities by locating near a market populace.

Various types of service organizations practice in a number of industries such as health care, solid-waste disposal, distribution, telecommunication, medical emergency, utilities and various others. Their needs will vary with respect to facility locations. It is reasonable to classify services into three groups for analysis (Metters et al. 2003): demand-sensitive services, delivered services and quasi-manufacturing services. Their main characteristics are shown briefly in Table 26.1.

Demand-sensitive Services

Location is very important to generate demand on those types of services. Grocery stores, gas stations, convenience stores, banks and restaurants are only a few examples of this group. Site-specific details will even need to be considered very carefully. Such in the gas station's location, being on the corner of main streets or intersection of highways has a prime impact on the business volume. Pharmacies may locate close to the main hospitals. Hotels are located either close to the main tourist attraction/business centres or major transport routes and hubs. Being close to residential areas, easy to access and the availability of parking spaces are required for convenience stores. The main challenge in this category is to forecast the location-specific demand. Intuition and judgement are the primary factors in the selection of locations, as well as factor rating and regression analysis (Metters et al. 2003).

Table 26.1 Facility location issues based on service types

Service type	Goal	Examples	Solution techniques	Characteristics of good location
Demand-sensitive services	Attract customers through location	Banks, restaurants, grocery stores	Informal judgement Factor rating Regression Geographical information systems (GIS)	Proximity to target market Proximity to destination points Proximity to competition Proximity to similar services Ease of access: availability of parking, traffic Visibility Room for expansion Ease of governmental regulation, taxes
Delivered services	Covering a geographic area	Public sector: fire protection, medical emergency Private sector: food delivery, saturation strategy	'Set covering' problem Establish service goal List potential sites or mathematically represent service area Determine demand from service area Determine relationship of sites to demand	Minimize costs of multiple sites that meet a service goal (e.g., everyone within a city boundary should be reached by ambulance within 15 minutes) Serve a maximum number of customers
Quasi-manufacturing services	Minimize logistics cost of a network	Warehouses, call centres	Heuristics Deterministic simulation Mixed integer linear programming Find followings: How many facilities Location of facilities Customer assignment to facilities Staffing/capacity of each facility	Logistics cost minimization of multi-echelon system Location decisions reviewed frequently

Delivered Services

Area coverage is the main characteristic of those types of service. Emergency ambulance and medical services, fire protection, some of the utility services, educational services in public sector, and food and parcel delivery, services using saturation strategies in the private sector are some applications of delivered services. Most of the time for delivered services, the number of service facilities and their locations to satisfy an adequate coverage based on pre-approved service levels should be identified simultaneously. Fire stations may be located according to an acceptable reach-time to the furthest point in their responsibility area. A pizza delivery service should be placed in such a location that delivering the pizza to the furthest customer in the region within an acceptable time should be guaranteed. In each of these examples, decision makers should maximize the coverage with respect to service levels while considering cannibalization effect of services if they are constructed to close to each other.

Quasi-manufacturing Services

There are many services functioning in a very similar way to manufacturing, such as distribution centres, warehouses and call centres. In contrast to the previously discussed service types, for quasi-manufacturing services location decisions will not be dominated only by the proximity of customers. For example, there is no need for call centres to be close to the customers as long as there is adequate telecommunication infrastructure. In fact, some other logistic costs become important here. In the US and Europe, many call centre jobs already have moved abroad. These are the services which will be the most affected by globalization. The number of service facilities and their locations, their capacity and serving region should be decided in order to minimize overall logistics cost for quasi-manufacturing services. This problem has the same characteristics with transportation problem in the literature, and can be modelled as a mix-integer linear program.

Geographic information systems (GIS) provide invaluable information especially for location-sensitive services. GIS helps to predict demand for services based on geographic databases as well as territory partitioning and vehicle routing. There are many GIS available on the market provided by many vendors such as ESRI (http://www.esri.com), Tactician (http://www.tactician.com), Intergraph, GDS, Strategic Mapping and Mapinfo.

Many service facility location problems are hierarchical in nature. For banking facilities, location of ATMs, branch offices, and main bank offices ideally should be located in a hierarchical manner. In health-care facility systems; location of local clinics, hospitals and regional hospitals should be decided based on the coverage and proximity to demand points and to each other. Excellent reviews of hierarchical facility location problems can be found in Jayaraman et al. (2003) and Şahin and Süral (2007).

Some services do not choose their location. Universities, for example, may be the beneficiaries of donated buildings. Examples of such buildings are Herstmonceux Castle, near Battle in Sussex, given to Queens University, and a building in central downtown Melbourne, Australia donated to the Royal Melbourne Institute of Technology Business School. A building may exist and be available. The opportunity cost of moving in and starting business versus waiting to find an ideal location can force pragmatic decisions.

Servicescapes and Facility Design

Servicescape is the environment in which the service is delivered and where the firm and the customer interact (Hult 2001). It is a complementary part of service concept and should be designed harmoniously with a service strategy. Servicescape has a strong influence on customer perception regarding the service and its quality. For self-service facilities, servicescape serves the customers to expose the service properly. In case of remote services, employee motivation, efficiency, and quality of work life can be achieved by proper design of servicescapes. See Chapter 18, 'Retail Merchandising and Sales Promotions', by de Juan Vigaray and Gültekin, this volume for detailed examples.

Service facility design and layout is an important part of service package. A proper service layout enables (Heizer et al. 2001):

- higher utilization of space, equipment, and people;
- improved flow of information, materials, or people;
- improved employee morale and safer working conditions;
- improved customer/client interaction;
- flexibility, designing for future.

> As a consumer I prefer Starbucks over Gloria Jeans. For me Starbucks has always been a place that *feels like home rather than a restaurant*. The *dark and heavy furniture* and the design of *the armchairs and sofas* gives the impression that I have stepped in the library or even a favourite spot in my or one of my relatives' houses. I feel as if I own a part of the interior. This feeling is also strengthened as once I pay for my coffee as I order and am served it rather quickly – usually under a minute – I am *not bothered by servers* wanting to take my order or dropping by later to add up my check. When I am through I simply walk out. Of course I enjoy the quality and range of the coffee at Starbucks on top of everything else I've described so far. I feel I get my money's worth at Starbucks. Finally, the one final yet very strong sense of feeling at home is evident as most of the employees at the counter make the *effort to learn and remember my name* as I walk in and out. In essence, Starbucks does a good job with the fundamentals of running a coffee shop as well as the seemingly small yet important details as well, contrasted with Gloria Jeans where there may be basically good coffee, but in the end that is it really, a moderate coffee house. (*Can Üsküdarlı* – customer's voice)

Service facility layouts are similar to manufacturing layout types. *Product-oriented layouts* in services resemble manufacturing assembly lines. In cafeterias, customers stand in line and pick up the food using a service line approach. Fast food restaurants can be a good example of product-family layouts. The back-office operations (kitchen) can permit all sorts of activities: frying, preparing different type of hamburgers and many drinks are at different workstations that are flexible enough to respond to customers' orders from a fixed variety menu. Movie theatres, concert halls, stadiums and gymnasiums can be considered as *fixed-location layouts*. For high utilization events, the so-called main attractions, all manner of facilities are used to deliver goods backstage and services such as electricity and moving platforms are provided for artistes to create the spectacle. In *process-oriented layouts*, similar processes are gathered within the same department. Materials or people flow between departments. Grocery and hardware stores, departmental stores and hospitals are organized based on product and/or service categories such as dairy products, bakeries, men's department, children's department, laboratories, x-ray machines and so on. Amusement parks are another example of process-oriented layouts. A common theme of all these examples is that customers may define the sequence of service activities to meet their needs and have some degree of freedom for customization.

Other than such a generalization, service layouts require some special consideration other than their manufacturing counterparts. For office workers, *office layouts* are important to facilitate the movement of information efficiently and in a timely manner. This requires an understanding of capacity and space requirements for information flow as well as decisions regarding environment and aesthetics.

Retail industry, having mainly process-oriented layouts, has special issues to resolve. In tje *retail layout* many products compete for limited shelf space to be able to respond to customer wants and needs. The main characteristics of retail layouts need to maximize product exposure to customers. Some rules of thumb for retail layouts are (Heizer et al. 2001):

- locate high-draw items around the periphery of the store;
- use prominent locations such as the first or last aisle for high-impulse and high-margin items;
- remove cross-over aisles that allow customers the opportunity to move between aisles;
- distribute what are known in the trade as 'power items' (items that may dominate a shopping trip) to both sides of an aisle, and disperse them to increase the viewing of other items;
- use aisle ends because they have a very high exposure rates.

Service Encounter

Services are in a process of transforming from a traditional service concept into an experience (Fitzsimmons and Fitzsimmons 2006). Experience-based services have distinctive memorable and personal service encounters over the time. Customer loyalty beyond just satisfaction is the main target of the service concept. The goal of Disney World (http://disneyworld.disney.go.com) is to transform a basic entertainment business in to a memorable life-time experience. Active participation of visitors to the shows is encouraged to really immerse to the environment. Their service concept is based on 'something for everyone' and 'choose your experience'.

The design of a service experience has the following principles to consider for service encounters (ibid.):

- the experience should have a central theme;
- positive cues are provided to harmonize perceptions;
- negative cues are eliminated;
- memorabilia are mixed in;
- all five senses are to be stimulated and engaged.

Service encounters are based on three components: service organization, contact personnel and the customer. Interaction among them shapes the particular service encounter. Service organizations determine the type of service encounter to reach to the target customers and must also consider the efficiency and effectiveness of their activities. Other than self-service, contact personnel directly engage customers based on an autonomy provided by the service organization. Rules, regulations and procedures are established to control the interface among the parties. The interaction between customer and contact personnel is quite important. When they develop a mutual understanding, the overall service satisfaction will be enhanced.

In the case of e-services the nature of service encounter will change quite a bit. Contact personnel will be replaced by a program which will interface with the customer directly. Expectations from e-services are much more than traditional service encounters. Continuous uninterrupted 24-hour, seven days a week service should be achieved. Since there is no limitation on the accessible area, e-services should be designed to serve a much larger group of people with multiple languages, dialects, religious and cultural characteristics.

Organizational culture is the collection of beliefs, expectations and traditions shared by the members and unique identity to hold people together. It is a significant enabler or drawback to effective and efficient service encounters. Without a radical change on the organizational culture, the service encounter cannot be changed positively. To provide a satisfactory service to the customer, the service organization may create a culture about the mean of customer satisfaction its staff capabilities. Alternatively, it may extend customers' expectations by setting an exceptionally ambitious high performance service. The organization then can develop its employees. Without a satisfied employee, it is very difficult to have a satisfactory service encounter.

Culture itself plays an important role in the service design as well as service encounter. It is surprising that service customers' satisfaction-seeking behaviours are not related to their cultural orientation, and culture is not related to effort or satisfaction level (Youngdahl et al. 2003). This emphasizes the validity of service operations management across the cultures.

Service Quality

Considering quality as a sign of customer satisfaction, service quality can be defined from many different perspectives. Engineering- or manufacturing-based definitions highlight the importance of defining a service's quality characteristics and define it as a conformance to specified characteristics. As long as service achieves the pre-specified conditions, it is of good quality. Quality may be defined by users' perspective as fitness for purpose as well. Both conforming to design characteristics and fitness to purpose of use are required for quality. A delicious meal may fulfil the requirements of the first definition. Serving it in a fine dining restaurant relates to the latter definition.

Service quality is even harder to define. A restaurant, café or hotel that may be ranked high by one group of people may not be considered in the same way by another. Individual's perception of a service based on the expectations is very important in service quality. Service quality can be defined as excessive expectations of service received when compared to desired expectations of the service (Fitzsimmons and Fitzsimmons 2006). This raises the issue of service perception to the attention of the service designer. This is something that is even harder to satisfy. As a result, it is very common to identify the determinants of service quality. They include:

- timeliness: promptness, acceptable waiting time for service, completion of service on time;
- completeness: fulfil all customer wants from a service;
- consistency: same level of service for all customers all the time;
- competence: having skills needed for service;
- courtesy: treatment by employees;
- communication: understanding the customer, empathy;

- credibility: sign of trust;
- accessibility and convenience: ease of obtaining service;
- accuracy: performed right every time;
- reliability: consistency of service performance, accuracy and dependency;
- responsiveness: reactions to unusual situations;
- security: service safety measures;
- tangibles: state of physical assets for service.

I am a classical Pizza Hut consumer over its perceived rival of Domino's Pizza as long as I'm dining outside. For me the *atmosphere and the taste of food* go hand in hand and I like the *small home-like atmosphere* of Pizza Hut and the *appetizers* I get to enjoy before the pizza arrives. I also believe the taste is superior to Domino's where I see the main difference as the *taste and consistency* of the dough. I am a classical thick pan eater as I like the feeling of fullness it provides. The same goes for the breadsticks that I enjoy which is a must for me. When I leave a Pizza Hut I feel *psychologically and physically satisfied*.

In contrast, I would order Domino's over Pizza Hut if I am home alone and feel like *ordering* in as opposed cooking myself or ordering something other than pizza. My expectation from a delivered pizza is not high. I am prepared that the pizza may not be very hot, tasty, or even the correct type I ordered. The main idea is that I am mostly *tight-pressed for time* and looking for a relatively *economical quick fix*. (*Can Üsküdarlı* – consumer's perception of service)

In general, services are labour intensive. From time to time this can be hard to stabilize. This creates a potential source for variability in service quality. Measuring and improving service, quality and design characteristics should be established. Taking consultancy services or entertainment business as a good example, what should be measured, how to measure, where and when to measure demonstrate a great deal of ambiguity. For a good quality consultancy, or show business, service personnel (consultants or showpeople) have a tremendous influence on the service quality. What is expected from service personnel in those cases may change from client to client, or from participant to participant. In case of unsatisfied participant of a show, entertainment cannot be replaced or repaired. Since time is perishable and intangible, many services engage with customer on a temporary basis and are irreversible.

Since many features of services are intangible and psychological, the measurement of service quality requires a special instrument other than products. SERVQUAL is a survey-based instrument used to measure five dimensions of services. It has 22 questions that are easy to adapt to many different service areas. The first set of questions attempts to identify the expectations of customers from the particular service. The second set is slightly modified in order to involve the specific service business, customer's perception of the particular service to be gathered. The final stage compares service perception with service expectations based on various dimensions of quality. Managers must choose which service areas should be improved and quality areas satisfactorily can be numerically measured. An electronic version of the survey can be accessed from http://www.businessadvantage.ndirect.co.uk/SERVQUAL.htm.

Service quality dimensions used in the SERVQUAL instrument are summarized below (Fitzsimmons and Fitzsimmons 2006; Metters et al. 2003):

- *reliability*: perform promised service dependably and accurately, for example, receive mail at same time each day;

- *responsiveness*: the willingness of employees to provide service and help customers promptly, for example, never waiting more than five minutes at the counter no matter what;
- *assurance*: the knowledge, competence and courtesy of service employees and their ability to convey trust and confidence, for example, being polite and demonstrating respect for customer;
- *empathy*: ability to be approachable, the caring and individual attention, for example, being a good listener;
- *tangibles*: physical facilities and facilitating goods of the service, for example, cleanliness, tidiness.

Quality in services as in many other fields requires the service organization to fully participate and collaborate. Total quality management principles equally are applicable to services. Leadership of top management and its direct involvement, continuous improvement, shared problem solving, and training for all employees are just a few issues to be addressed. Quality should be handled as the principal business strategy for services to ensure they both qualify for and win orders. All service employees should be made responsible as a result of empowerment for the quality of their activities.

Many techniques developed for quality of products are applicable for services as well. A short list of them is listed below:

- *Poka Yoke (fail-safing)*: getting rid of potential sources of problems before they crop up as a real problem, for example, setting the alarm clock for an important meeting, a buzzer on a grill to remind the cook;.
- *quality function deployment*: transforming the voice of customer into design characteristics, processes and quality plans;
- *Pareto analysis*: identifying the few most important route causes behind the many occurrences of service complaints, for example, 80 per cent of customer complaints are triggered by 20 per cent of the potential service failures such as poor personnel training and improper equipment usage;
- *flow charts*: graphical representation of the service processes – process mapping;
- *fish-bone diagram*: also called an Ishikawa diagram or cause-effect diagram. It represents all possible reasons for a service failure in the form of a fish-bone.

Whatever the preventive precautions we may undertake, sometimes it is inevitable to have to deal with service failures and dissatisfied customers. A *service recovery plan* should be designed to respond to a previously dissatisfied customer and try to turn them into a loyal one. A training programme for service employees and empowerment of the front-office personnel is essential for a proper service recovery programme. Employees should react to service failures as fast as is practicable. An immediate response is to listen to the complaints of customers closely. A response and plan of action should be developed quickly and expectations for recovery should be provided to the client and met.

Service recovery strategies may consist of three actions (Wong 2004):

- an apology;
- assistance to fix the problem;
- compensation by paying the cost of the problem.

Each of these strategies can yield some degree of improvement from the service assessment of customers. Their effectiveness is varying across cultures. In high power distance cultures such as Singapore, apology may be more effective than compensation, while compensation works better in low power distance and high individualism cultures.

Capacity Strategies and Yield Management

In service operations management, capacity management plays a vital role in ensuring the success of a service organization. Demand for the many services varies over time. Restaurants, for example, are faced with high demand during regular meal hours. Hotels located in holiday towns and on tourist routes typically are busy at the weekend and during the high seasons of summer and other school holidays. Building extra capacity that lies unused for the majority of off-season periods is a regular practice for services to avoid losing customers. Capacity can also be used as a strategic response tool to pre-empt the market. Having enough capacity in the long run for relatively small markets may dissuade competitors from setting up facilities that would directly compete for a limited market demand. Similarly, demand may increase if choice is offered that results in higher value at lower prices. Capacity may then be used.

Service capacity management is much more difficult than product management, where long-term forecasts for demand dominate investment decisions on whether to acquire machines and plant to raise capacity in order to build products. However, this approach is almost meaningless for services because they have to match their capacity to a daily, weekly and seasonal variability. For lunch a fine dining restaurant, if the demand cannot be handled properly, there is little value in knowing how many tables are available for the rest of the day. Since the service capacity is perishable, an empty table is a revenue opportunity that is lost forever. There is no possibility of taking the customer back in time to a period when the table was available. Decision makers should decide the service capacity by balancing the costs of keeping idle capacity versus the cost of losing customers or making them wait.

General service capacity strategies can be listed as follows (Metters et al. 2003):

- *provide*: keep enough capacity to fill the demand at all times. High-margin services may pick this strategy up;
- *chase*: capacity is adjusted as needed. Demand exceeds supply. Supply is increased only in response to proven excessive demand. This practice is very common;
- *influence demand to fit capacity*: capital-intensive services may follow this strategy since the change of capacity is quite expensive, if it is not impossible. Prices are raised when demand is high. Special price offers are used to drum up business when demand is slack;
- *control to maximize capacity utilization*: low-margin services with high demand and competing on cost bases may prefer this strategy. Bottleneck management techniques may be used to ensure capacity constrained activities are fully utilized.

Those strategies can be implemented with the help of the following policies related to the supply and demand of services:

- supply-related policies:
  - *work-shift scheduling*: assign personnel to the shifts based on dynamic demand predictions;

- *increasing customer participation*: a customer might participate in the service process. In self-service fast food restaurants, customers pick the order up and return trays to garbage bins;
- *adjustable (surge) capacity*: capacity available for short periods of time can be called in to assist. Typically this is done by shifting some of the facilities to the demanded areas, *cross-trained personnel* or making use of *part-timers*;
- *sharing capacity:* on a demand basis, underutilized capacities can be shared between departments and different service organizations. Scheduled flight airlines now code share. Using one aeroplane point to point with two or more carriers' passengers on board is a good example for these applications. They combine some of their routes with their competitors when demand is low;

- demand-related policies;
  - *partitioning demand:* demand is disaggregated into predictable and random components. Later, an attempt is made to schedule the random component to where predictable demand is low through appointments, such as doctors' visits;
  - *price incentives and promoting off-peak demand:* this is a very common approach to influence the demand for low seasons. Restaurants offer 'happy hours'. Hotels have special prices on high and low seasons. Utilities and telephone companies may set their prices differently based on the usage characteristics;
  - *develop complementary services:* to avoid the seasonality of many services, countercyclical services are introduced. Summer vacation centres/hotels offer spa or congress tourism on the rest of the year;
  - *using reservation systems and overbooking:* reservations help to reduce the tension for both supply and demand sides. Customers avoid the risk of waiting for unavailable services while service providers get data about the demand and pre-sell the service. In case of no-shows, a reasonable overbooking policy may help to increase expected revenues.

Yield Management

Services are perishable in nature. An empty seat on an aircraft or in a movie theatre, a car available to rent and a vacant room in a hotel are lost in time. However, the same available facilities can be quite attractive when the price is reduced for different market segments. Airlines, passenger and freight railway services, car rental agencies, cruise ships, hotels and medical facilities may benefit from the use of yield management systems. The service providers may consider that revenue at any price will maximize returns investment. The purpose of yield management may be summarized as selling as much capacity to a variety of customer segments at appropriate prices.

Ideal service characteristics that apply yield management systems are (Fitzsimmons and Fitzsimmons 2006):

- a fixed capacity over the short term, such as the number of seats available on an aircraft. Capacity may be fixed over the long term, such as in a concert hall;
- markets can be segmented into seasonal, regular, large family, student and other discount systems, peak user, early adopters, corporate travellers, cost conscious, whim and short notice users;
- excess underutilized and immediately available capacity that can be perceived as a perishable inventory such as a vacant hotel room, an empty concert seat;

- products sold in advance through reservation systems and pre-booking;
- uneven and seasonal fluctuating demand;
- instances where the additional (marginal) sales cost of selling extra use is low and where costs are high to change capacity, or it would take too much time to react;
- availability of systems that create, analyse and distribute accurate, detailed information.

Yield management systems typically use one of the following (Metters et al. 2003):

- Overbooking: this is a natural consequence of making more reservations than the available capacity in order to ensure idle capacity is reduced to zero because of people that do not show up. For service companies, how much to overbook is the question, based on the trade-off between stock out (having a customer with a reservation when insufficient capacity is available to provide the service) and overage costs (the cost of keeping the service facility idle). Overbooking is a common practice in the hotel and airline industries.
- Differential pricing to different customer groups: consumers are differentiated based on their actual willingness to pay. Price-sensitive customers may need to pay far in advance as compared to those who like to make a last minute decision. Cancellation options can be another criterion to discriminate between customers. Weekend vs. weekdays rates are quite commonly applied on hotels and recreational service operations. In Europe, Accor Hotels charge less at the weekends than during the working week. They charge a premium if special events are being run in the city that will result in higher utilization. This can be perceived as profiteering. By contrast, in Australia, Accor Hotels charge more at the weekends.
- Capacity allocation among customer groups: Another form of yield management is to bring in some restrictions on either duration of the price available or the number of customers who may use the service from available price. The main operational problem here for the service organization is to identify capacity assigned to low-margin business in anticipation of the high-margin business booking later.

Yield management is an intersection area of services marketing and operations management. Finding a good differentiation mechanism for yield management requires careful consideration of the market and previous history. Corporate policy will then become embedded in the contract's small print. Some commonly used yield management approaches are:

- single transaction for low volumes vs. ongoing global purchase volume agreements;
- limited numbers of special price tickets that 'grab headlines' and stimulate market responses;
- time of purchase/usage such as advanced/spot purchases and day-of-week/season;
- purchase restrictions such as no cancellation/change options and Saturday night stay for airlines;
- customer affiliation (corporate, contract user);
- duration of usage such as single night/weekly rate/weekend rate;
- service level such as all-inclusive vs. pay for extra.

Successful yield management depends on many parameters. Industry should be ready for such type of sensitivity on the customers. This is not always easy for the customer to accept. What are the consequences of a customer paying several times more for a service than the person next to him/her, or facing an overbooked hotel? Whatever the complimentary service offered, it may not counteract the customer's impression of the service organization.

Banks make accounts dormant as little as six months after no transaction has been made. Interest-bearing accounts then no longer attract interest. Cheque book current accounts can have agreed overdraft facilities removed if regular payments are not made into them.

Waiting Time Management

Waiting is an inevitable part of services. A queue is formed by customers waiting for the service. Most people spend quite a bit of time for waiting in traffic jams, for lunch, to pay to the cashier, or to get on buses. Waiting is principally a result of variations in arrival and service rates. When arrival rates are higher than service rates, an infinite length queue is formed because service capacity is too low. In this instance, there is plenty of demand available that may be 'mopped up' by competitors. From a managerial perspective, there is little to do other than increase service capacity. Management policies and strategies are essential only if the service rate is greater than arrival rates. Fluctuations in both of these rates are the main source of queues. The length of queue and waiting time are the result of how management values customer waiting time compared to the cost of lowering utility cost to server(s). Waiting line/queuing theory helps managers predict the average line length and waiting time as well as utilization rates for different service design characteristics.

The social and psychological perspectives of waiting are important in the management of waiting times. Other than increasing the service capacity, management should understand the customers' perception of waiting in different situations. Disney World is one of the places known to have many long queues. They manage waiting as an integral part of the entertainment experience. Arguments relating to psychological effects of waiting are (Metters et al. 2003; Nie 2000):

- perception is more important than reality;
- people think they have waited longer than they actually have. Unoccupied time feels longer than occupied time. Designing the line layout, adjusting the rate of line movement and filling waiting time with interesting activities can alter people's perception of waiting without actually reducing the actual waiting time. Mirrors in elevators and recorded music at call centres and in waiting rooms are examples of modified facilities that take into account this need;
- customer expectations based on service promises are aroused through advertising, personal selling and word of mouth. Realistic expectations can be set by the company;
- people tend to make a link between events and causes. If there is no explanation given, perceptions of waiting deteriorate:
  - unexplained waits feel longer;
  - anxiety makes waiting feel longer;
  - uncertain durations feel longer than known periods.
  Proper communication about the reasons of waiting is the right approach to take:
- pre-process waiting feels longer than in-process waiting;
- unfair waiting feels longer;
- the prior notice of expected waits can give customers the perception of control and reduce their stress level. In funfair environments, visitors can choose to visit other attractions and delay they time they join queues until they have reduced;

- cultural norms impact people's perceptions of waiting and service firms operating in different cultures should design their services accordingly. European-American perception of time considers it as a scarce resource and equates time to money. People under the influence of a procedural-traditional model do not consider time and money as related topics.

Waiting is particularly important when people are in pain or in need of medical attention. Healthcare groups typically have a charter of patients' rights and set expectations relating to delays prior to treatment. The Scottish Executive in the Regional Assembly lists ten golden rules they espouse as efficient and effective healthcare management (http://www.scotland.gov. uk/Publications/2003/09/18035/25475, accessed January 2008).

Conclusions

It is difficult to think of everyday life without services. Seventy per cent of total employment in OECD countries is in service sector. According to McKinsey Company Global Labour Market report (2005), 1.46 billion service jobs worldwide in 2008 are projected.

Services are time-perishable, intangible experiences. Customers may participate in the role of co-producer. Services are produced and consumed simultaneously. They cannot be kept for use later. Goods and services go mostly hand-in-hand and complement each other. Service package defines the bundle of goods and services and includes facilities, goods and information facilitating delivery of explicit and implicit services.

Strategic positioning of services refers to the reasons why the customers prefer the service organization. Three generic service strategies suggested by Michael Porter (1985) are cost leadership, differentiation and focus. A sound service strategy is derived from a service vision that defines target market segments, service concepts, operating strategies and service delivery systems. The target market segment classifies customers of the service organization into stereotypes. Service concepts are the reasons why customer should prefer a particular service provider. Operating strategy is related tp how service organization should be structured so that service delivery system – simply designing the interactions between front-and back-office applications – provides the service concept to the customers.

Service facility location decisions are so vital that location itself may be accountable for the overall success of business. Demand-sensitive services attract customers through their location. Delivered services select their facility location to maximize the number of customers they can serve in the geographical area covered. For the location of quasi-manufacturing services, minimizing the cost of overall logistic network is the main objective. In each of those service location decisions, geographical information systems (GIS) provide invaluable data to decision makers.

Servicescapes are the environment where the service provider delivers the service to the customer. Functionality of layout and ambient conditions, as well as artefacts and signs, are complementary part of service concept. Service encounters are the 'moments of truth' that define all activities especially intensive interactions between service organization, contact personnel and customer involved in the service delivery process. Organizational culture is very designative on service encounters.

Service quality relates to excessive perceptions of service received relative to expectations of service desired. It is very common to define the service quality with its dimensions such as timeliness, completeness, consistency, courtesy, credibility, accessibility, accuracy, reliability, responsiveness and security. In the measurement of service quality a survey tool called SERVQUAL instrument is commonly applied. Considering service failure and unsatisfied customer, service recovery should be designed carefully to create service loyalty.

Service capacity is related to the supply and demand for a service. Dynamic shiftwork scheduling, increased customer participation, adjustable capacity and sharing capacity with companion organizations are all attempts to adjust the service supply, while partitioning demand, price incentives, developing complementary services and using reservation systems as well as yield management strategies influence the demand side of services. Yield management is a scientific approach to sell the right capacity to the right customer at the right price. Overbooking, differential pricing to different customer groups and capacity-based discrimination among the customer groups are a few examples of yield management.

A sign of service capacity mismanagement is waiting in queues. In many instances, waiting is inevitable in the area of service operations. Waiting time management should be understood properly and the psychological and social consequences of waiting should be handled carefully.

References

Fitzsimmons, J.A. and Fitzsimmons, M.J. (2006), *Service Management: Operations, Strategy, Information Technology*, 5th edn (Singapore: McGraw-Hill).

Heizer, J. and Render, B. (2001), *Principles of Operations Management* (Englewood Cliffs, NJ: Prentice Hall).

Heskett, J.L., Sasser, W.E. and Schlesinger, L.A. (1997), *The Service Profit Chain* (New York: Free Press).

Hult, G. and Tomas, M. (2001), 'Additional Thoughts on International Services Marketing,' *Journal of Services Marketing* 15(1), pp. 5–10, http://globaledge.msu.edu/NewsAndViews/views/papers/0007.pdf.

Jayaraman, V., Gupta, R. and Pirkul, H. (2003), 'Selecting Hierarchical Facilities in a Service-Operations Environment', *European Journal of Operational Research* 147, pp. 613–28.

McKinsey Global Institute (2005), *The Emerging Global Labor Market: Part I –The Demand for Offshore Talent in Services*, http://www.mckinsey.com/mgi/publications/emerginggloballabormarket/.

Metters, R., King-Metters, K. and Pullman, M. (2003), *Successful Service Operations Management* (Ontario: South-Western).

Nie, W. (2000), 'Waiting: Integrating Social and Psychological perspectives in Operations Management', *Omega* 28, pp. 611–29.

OECD (2005), 'Growth in Services: Fostering Employment, Productivity and Innovation', meeting of the OECD Council at Ministerial Level, OECD, Paris, http://www.oecd.org/dataoecd/58/52/34749412.pdf.

Porter, M.E. (1985), *Competitive Strategy* (Boston, MA: Free Press).

Şahin, G. and Süral, H. (2007), 'A Review of Hierarchical Facility Location Models', *Computers and Operations Research* 34(8), pp. 2310–31, http://www.sciencedirect.com.

Sauvé, P. and Dihel, N. (2002), 'Services Liberalisation and Evolving Regulation: Trends and Outcomes in OECD Countries', Symposium on Assessment of Trade in Services, Geneva, 14–15 March, http://www.wto.org/English/tratop_e/ serv_e/symp_mar02_sauve.ppt.

Schettkat, R. and Yocarini, L. (2006), 'The Shift to Service Employment: A Review of the Literature', *Structural Change and Economic Dynamics* 17(2), pp. 127–47.

Wong, N.Y. (2004), 'The Role of Culture in the Perception of Service Recovery', *Journal of Business Research* 57, pp. 957–63.

Youngdahl, W.E., Kellogg, D.L., Nie, W. and Bowen, D.E. (2003), 'Revisiting Customer Participation in Service Encounters: Does Culture Matter?', *Journal of Operations Management* 21, pp. 109–20.

Chapter 27

International Transportation, Shipping and Logistics

Phil Scott

This chapter introduces all of the significant components of an integrated international logistics system and how to manage each activity and combine them in a strategic manner. The detailed analysis of the many different combinations of relationships available to managers is beyond the scope of this chapter. In this chapter we will be addressing the logistical channel. The logistical channel handles the physical flow of products and service.

What is Globalization?

Globalization is a trend that has affected most companies around the world. Even if your company does not trade with any other organization outside your own country's borders, it is very possible that your products may be purchased by a company who incorporates them into a product or be part of a portfolio of products, offered for export or to be distributed in countries other than where they were manufactured.

Unlike a multinational market, a global manufacturing policy requires a world perspective when developing a logistics strategy. Most goods and parts can be produced at distant locations and shipped wherever a market exists. The responsibilities of a particular production location are determined by existing conditions, and centralized managerial planning keeps company operations in line with overall goals.

Sharif-Zadeh stated that:

> The following complex and often conflicting trends and factors are leading many organizations to globalize their operations, whether that be manufacturing or just drawing together a portfolio of products:
>
> a) National markets newly opened or reopened to foreign goods and competition;
> b) Import restrictions and local content laws in many countries;
> c) Policies in many developing countries that make licensing of foreign companies contingent on their ability to develop export markets;
> d) Foreign domination of formerly strong domestic markets;
> e) Foreign firms use of multinational sourcing and manufacturing to gain cost and quality advantages;
> f) US firms entering foreign markets, often in competition with strong domestic and multinational firms;
> g) An increasingly global market place that supports common products, albeit with local difference and preferences.

To deliver these products and achieve customer satisfaction with these complex sources of supply and disparate markets, a new logistics approach is needed.

Logistics: What is it and Why is it Important?

Logistics describes the entire process of materials and products moving into, through, and out of the firm. The term logistics is sometimes used interchangeably with supply chain management. However, it is appropriate to understand the definitions of all the relevant terms used in logistics and distribution to eliminate any confusion.

The following definitions from the Council of Supply Chain Management Professionals (CSCMP) are widely accepted by logistics and supply chain managers.

Supply Chain Management/Logistics Management Definitions

CSCMP Definition of Supply Chain Management

Supply Chain Management encompasses the planning and management of all activities involved in sourcing and procurement, conversion, and all Logistics Management activities. Importantly, it also includes coordination and collaboration with channel partners, which can be suppliers, intermediaries, third-party service providers, and customers. In essence, Supply Chain Management integrates supply and demand management within and across companies.

Supply Chain Management – Boundaries and Relationships

Supply Chain Management is an integrating function with primary responsibility for linking major business functions and business processes within and across companies into a cohesive and high-performing business model. It includes all of the Logistics Management activities noted above, as well as manufacturing operations, and it drives coordination of processes and activities with and across marketing, sales, product design, finance and information technology.

CSCMP Definition of Logistics Management

Logistics Management is that part of Supply Chain Management that plans, implements, and controls the efficient, effective forward and reverse flow and storage of goods, services and related information between the point of origin and the point of consumption in order to meet customers' requirements.

Logistics Management – Boundaries and Relationships

Logistics Management activities typically include inbound and outbound transportation management, fleet management, warehousing, materials handling, order fulfilment, logistics network design, inventory management, supply/demand planning, and management of third party logistics services providers. To varying degrees, the logistics function also includes sourcing and procurement, production planning and scheduling, packaging and assembly, and customer service. It is involved in all levels of planning and execution – strategic, operational and tactical. Logistics Management is an integrating function, which coordinates and optimizes all logistics activities, as well as integrates logistics activities with other functions including marketing, sales manufacturing, finance and information technology. (© 2006 Council of Supply Chain Management Professionals)

Many practitioners cannot agree on a single definition for all the activities of logistics. The primary reason for the multitude of definitions and terminology is because, over the past few decades, logistics has become one of the most exciting and challenging operational areas of business. The primary reason for this attention is because the logistical functions performed by businesses and the public sector offer great potential for implementing best practices and cost savings. The following definitions will aid an understanding of logistics literature.

What are the Components or Activities of Logistics?

The activities of the logistics function within an organization are quite broad. The actual number and importance of the activities vary from one business to another. However, the following are typical activities performed by logistics managers:

1. Site location – this entails time and place utility for the goods or services provided by the firm. Such things as the number of warehouses, their site locations and plant locations are of major importance to the effective and efficient operation of the firm.
2. Transportation – the physical movement of materials, finished goods and works-in-process from supplier to the customer. This can be done by the business itself (private carrier) or by an outside transportation firm (public carrier).
3. Storage – this includes inventory management and warehousing of raw materials, works-in-process and finished goods. Inventory and storage generally account for a very high percentage of the logistical costs of an organization.
4. Packaging – this insures products are protected, while in transit, as well as, providing marketing functions to achieve a design that appeals to customers and functionality for the customer. There are large trade-offs between the transportation, storage, cost and convenience issues in packaging. Packaging may be discarded at the point of use. It must prevent damage to the product and be low cost. In business to business transactions, suppliers may charge extra for packaging, insurance and transport. Suppliers may levy a deposit on packaging in order to promote the return and hence re-use of such materials.
5. Materials handling – efficient warehousing and inventory handling equipment and systems used for the movement of the goods within the firm. Cross-docking may be undertaken as a value adding activity by a third party logistics services provider (3PL). Warehouses breakdown pallet loads and consignments from suppliers, select what is needed for picking, then reload onto trucks or containers for delivery to specific destinations. The remainder then may be stored to satisfy later demand. Defective goods may be returned to the distributor, or destroyed rather than return and repair. Credit notes are issued to reimburse the company for the purchase price. Transportation costs may be borne by either producer to distributor, dependent on the contract agreement.
6. Order management – this consists of all the activities necessary to complete customer orders. This can start with forecasting the inventory requirements to actual delivery in a satisfactory condition to the customer. Purchasing agents may focus on creating responsive suppliers in order to react fast to actual orders. This then avoids the inherent inaccuracies that occur as a result of forecasting. Some products depreciate rapidly. Hence minimum inventory reduces the stock holding costs. Inventory should be held at the lowest value state possible in order to minimize the customer specificity and investment in stock that may not be sold.

7. Production planning – managers determine the amount to be produced to satisfy customer demand, and the amount of raw materials necessary for this production. It also involves the efficient planning of production activities for optimum cost savings and service satisfaction.
8. Purchasing – purchasing objectives are based on having the right amount of materials (raw materials, works-in-progress, and component parts) at the right time, in the right place, in the right quantity and at the right cost for effective and efficient production.
9. Customer service – all activities that lead to customer satisfaction, by having the product available, in the form, at the right place on time and in quantities customers require. Dependable, reliable and cost effective logistics is now one of the primary competitive advantages sought by many firms.

This list of activities is important to the efficient logistics of the firm.

Supply Chains

In today's business environment, it is rare for a single company to develop all the technologies it requires, and design each part for their complete product from scratch, extract raw materials, develop processes to refine and produce materials, fabricate components, assemble sub-assembles, construct the final core product and ancillary peripherals, provide packaging materials and distribute, via whatever channel, to customers and industrial users. Figure 27.1 shows a typical schematic of a simplified supply chain. Henry Ford tried to do this via vertical integration and bureaucracy in order to produce the Model T.[1]

It is common practice today for companies to outsource non-core activities. Many times other companies, or suppliers can provide these activities better, faster, and cheaper, than the manufacturer (Christopher 1997) and do these more often (Gerstner 2002) than the company that needs the goods and services.[2]

Each firm may locate in widely different geographical regions. Physical distance between customer and supplier may be bridged with third parties acting as logistics service providers.

As a result, firms develop a supply chain that is comprised of its suppliers and customers. A supply chain is comprised of a set of interconnected firms. This supply chain should be viewed as a system of inter-related, typically autonomously managed, processes that influence the overall performance.

Information, materials and money are required to make supply chains work efficiently.

- Information relating to demand is sent from customers upstream to distributors, assemblers, suppliers and transport service providers.
- Companies add value to materials by assembling, configuring, co-packaging and customizing. This requires materials and goods to be transported from where the processes are located to the next process, company or to the client.
- Financing for the supply chain can be conducted in various ways. Work can be paid in arrears, at the time of purchase or in advance. Traditionally, suppliers give credit of 30 days from the time of dispatch or verified arrival of goods. Many large powerful buying organizations, such as Toyota, reimburse suppliers precisely 120 days after the good

---

1 For an in depth discussion of supply chain management see MacBeth, Chapter 8, this volume.

2 For a detailed discussion on outsourcing see Newlands, Chapter 9, 'International Purchasing Management', this volume.

has been assembled and verified to be of quality. The auto parts retailer Halfords pays suppliers 120 days after store-held goods are sold to consumers. Companies building to order, such as Dell Computer, can demand 100 per cent upfront payment of the total cost of a product before asking suppliers to build and deliver parts specifically to fulfil the order. Assemblers will arrange credit terms in advance for larger capital expense goods such as machine tools and vehicles.

SUPPLY CHAIN AS A TOTAL SYSTEM

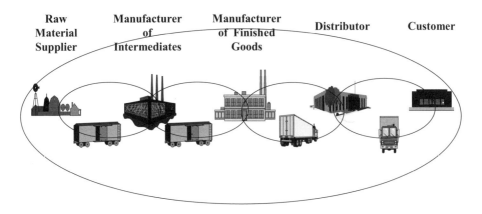

Figure 27.1   A schematic of a simplified supply chain as a total system

Source: Scott et al. 2003.

The Total-Cost Approach to Logistics

More and more businesses are placing emphasis on keeping goods moving and increasing velocity and yield of the supply chain flow, etc. When goods are in transit from one stage to another they are moving, however when they reach the facility and are stored, they are static and therefore judged to be losing value and costing money. Throughput, yield, turnover, speed and velocity are the buzz words. In truth, emphasis is on keeping lower levels of stock and undertaking more frequent deliveries. These goals are being pursued because 'trade-offs' are recognized between keeping higher levels of inventory and providing a more frequent delivery service. Small, high value goods may be transported by air half way round the world. The cost of holding stock on a ship, which takes weeks to arrive, ties up working capital. Depreciation of the sales price between departure and arrival can equal or exceed the profit made. If the time to transport is reduced, depreciation per unit is reduced. If the total amount of stock is reduced, this reduces the scale of the loss.

The cost implications of any distribution strategy must incorporate the 'total-costs' perspective in order to make the appropriate decision. Total cost is the concept that all expenditures necessary to perform logistical requirements must be considered and not each activity separately. The best-cost efficiency in one operational area may not result in the least total cost for the total logistical operation. From the perspective of the organization, the least total cost concept would be what best meets the service requirements of the customer and utilizes the least amount of company resources (money, time and people).

The prevailing managerial practice in many organizations is to focus attention on achieving the lowest possible cost for their specific functional area, with little or no attention devoted to the total costs. This practice is commonly referred to as suboptimization.

The concept of total cost analysis is also referred to as the systems approach to solving business problems. In Figure 27.1 firms should try to minimize the total cost, or all the costs associated in the large circle. When firms seek to minimize the costs in the individual functional areas, or the small circle, they are suboptimizing.

Systems Thinking

A useful definition of the systems approach is proposed by Colin Barrett (1971, p. 3):

> The systems approach to a problem involves not only a recognition of the individual importance of the various elements of which it is composed, but also an acknowledgment of their interrelationship. When field specialists concentrate restrictively on their own particular bailiwick, the more versatile systems people, in their capacity as generalists, seek the optimum of many of these individual operations in order to fulfil a broader objective.

The goal of the logistics manager is to identify the least-total-cost system design. This generally involves trade-offs. The minimal total-cost point for the system is typically not at the point of least cost for either transportation or inventory management. The transportation function and inventory management functions must be coordinated with all the other functions in logistics to approach the best possible combination so that the total system is operating at an optimum level. This is one of the primary reasons for the development of integrated logistics.

The example on the next page is taken from the journal *Distribution* in 1991. The chapter titled 'Casebook: Brooklyn Brewery', written by Ruriani (1991), gives a perspective on how the total-cost approach is used in international logistics.

What are the Significant Differences in a Company's Logistics Operations when they Go Global?

Globalization has changed the way many companies plan and operate. The following statement by Nabdan Nilekani, Chief Executive and co-founder of Infosys Technologies, illustrates the impact globalization is having on businesses today:

> Manufacturing has been at the forefront in exploiting the opportunities of globalization. Initially, manufacturers sourced and produced everything close to the customer. However, as costs of sea and air transport fell, it became possible to source components from those locations where they were most efficiently made and assemble goods close to the customer. As this approach matured and supply chains disaggregated, manufacturers moved from buying components elsewhere to outsourcing whole swathes of the manufacturing process to new partners around the globe. For example, Li & Fung, a Hong Kong-based clothes maker and distributor, has 7,500 business partners in 37 countries. Through this network of specialist suppliers, it is able to manufacture a wide range of apparel for its global customer base. (Nilekani 2006, pp. 154–5)

'Total Cost Provides Freshness', Dr. D.R. Castalano

Brooklyn Brewery currently distributes Brooklyn Lager and Brown Ale in the United States. Brooklyn Brewery has been in operation three years, and while it has not yet established a national presence in the United States, it is creating a niche market for itself in the $20 billion per year Japanese market.

Brooklyn Brewery had no immediate plans to export its beer to Japan until Keiji Miyamoto of Taiyo Resources Limited, an international subsidiary of Taiyo Oil Company, visited the brewery. Miyamoto believed that Japanese consumers would like the beer and convinced Brooklyn Brewery to meet with Hiroyo Trading Company to discuss marketing in Japan. Hiroyo Trading suggested that Brooklyn Brewery ship the beer by air to Japan and advertise its unique freshness for an import beer.

Not only is this an interesting marketing strategy, but it is also a unique logistical operation as no other breweries currently export beer by air to Japan because of the high costs. Brooklyn Brewery shipped its first case of Brooklyn Lager to Japan in December 1989 and used a variety of air carriers over the first few months. Eventually Emery Worldwide-Japan was selected as the sole air carrier for Brooklyn Brewery. Emery was chosen because of the value-added services it offered to Brooklyn Brewery. Emery takes delivery of the beer at its terminal at J.F.K. International Airport and arranges for transport on a commercial flight headed for Tokyo. Emery includes custom clearance through its Japanese custom brokers. These services help maintain the integrity of the product's freshness claim.

The freshness claim is achieved since the beer arrives direct to the customer from the brewery within the week it is manufactured. The average order cycle for beer shipped overseas is forty days. The freshness of the beer allows it to be priced at a premium, five times higher than beer shipped by sea. While Brooklyn Lager is an average-priced beer in the United States, in Japan it is a premium product and receives significantly higher margins.

The high price of the lager has not hindered sales of the beer in Japan. In 1988, its first year in Japan, Brooklyn Brewery achieved half a million dollars in sales. Sales increased to $1 million in 1989 and $1.3 million in 1990. The total export business accounts for 10 per cent of Brooklyn Brewery's total sales.

In the future, Brooklyn Brewery will change the packaging by shipping kegs instead of bottles to reduce airfreight costs. The keg weight is equivalent to bottled beer but will reduce the chance of damage due to broken glass. Kegs may require less protective packaging as well, which further reduces the cost of shipment. Exporting to other foreign countries is next on the horizon for Brooklyn Brewery. (Based on Castalano 1991)

The requirements placed on integrated logistics and distribution by these business practices are wide ranging. They include:

- Extending the supply chain to include other countries. This requires a balance between planning for distribution globally and thinking and optimizing locally. Within different regions of the world, that is, European, Japanese and Far East, companies must adopt various strategies and consider many distinct factors that are only appropriate to trading and operating in that part of the world.
- Ability to increase deliveries for simultaneous multi-country, multi-product launches, often require a variety of packaging and labelling requirements.
- Local taxation and transfer price regulations, that govern the value-adding that can be produced or incorporated within different countries and sometimes these, vary with the type of product. Indigenous producers may have to pay import duty and value-added tax on components. This then puts the price of the bill of materials up to a point where the assembler is uncompetitive in the home market, compared with completely assembled goods made in lower cost countries. This is one of the reasons television sets are no longer made in the United Kingdom.
- Semi-finished materials or work in progress is transferred throughout manufacturing organizations across national borders. Transferring semi-finished parts increases the packing density, and hence logistics efficiency of each delivery. Parts are stacked one inside another. This makes better use of the cargo space. Low-cost parts then are assembled rapidly into the finished product.
- Global resource management and balancing throughout structures of organizations.
- Differing levels of IT infrastructure throughout the world, and the need for integration wherever possible. Recognition and awareness of the constraints that a variety of communications capabilities places on the IT infrastructure.
- Monitoring and managing the changing logistics environment in many countries. A general trend that sees a movement toward a reduction in non-tariff barriers, administrative procedures, restrictions in inter-country transportation for all modes, coupled with increasing concentration of distribution and freight forwarding companies.

Integrated distribution operations for global manufacturers will now have to support rapidly changing marketing and manufacturing strategies, new product launches (standard goods for some products and country specific for others), and increased information linkage between manufacturing and distribution operations. Figure 27.2 illustrates how satellite communications can be used to support this information linkage required between manufacturers and distributors.

What are the Key Distribution Considerations for Management in the Globalization of the Firm?

Julekha Dash (1997, pp. 86–8) stated:

> Managers at multi-national corporations know from experience that going global involves more than pointing to a few regions on a map. For these companies, dealing with language barriers, customs, import/export regulations, and finding local trading partners are just a few of the complexities involved in doing business on a global scale. Before they sell or source abroad, companies first need to determine how to get their goods from point A to point B. This can be a far more trying task when

a shipment to a city is coming from an international location instead of one in your own country. The shipping process involves knowing the costs associated with overseas manufacturing, how long the goods take to deliver, what international trade regulations apply, and what bottlenecks might impede timely delivery.

A variety of solutions seeks to balance these differing pressures.

Networks – Infrastructure Development and Complexity

A global transport network is much more complex than a domestic network. The distances involved are greater, and typically there are more parties involved. Oceans separate most trading regions of the world; the major modes of global transport are road, ocean, river, canal and by air.

One of the first infrastructure improvements beyond ancient mud track roads were the principle highways laid down by the Romans. These linked settlements in direct lines and facilitated communication and information dissemination as well as the transfer of goods.

As loads became larger to satisfy growing demand from expanding urban populations, rivers and later canals were used to transport goods. A single horse then could move a barge boat laden with goods. Systems of locks needed to be created to maintain the level of water in the canals. This enabled bulk transported goods to travel vertically over land masses and thus avoid meandering along the course of natural rivers.

MODELING COSTS AND BENEFITS – MICRO SYSTEM

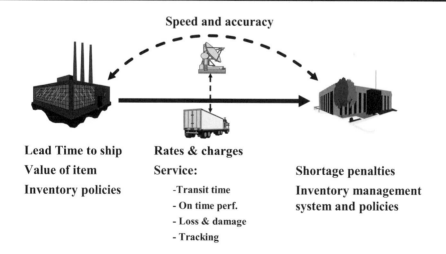

Figure 27.2   The use of satellite communications to support information linkages required between manufacturers and distributors

Source: Scott et al. 2003.

Land modes also carry significant amounts of freight between countries, particularly in Europe where land routes tend to be faster. Each region also has significant cultural differences, levels of economic development, degrees of infrastructure and local legislation that also must be taken into account as part of the multi-criteria decision-making that must be made when establishing and operating the logistics function. Each of these transport modes fulfils a specific role within the worldwide distribution network.

A major improvement in the efficient transport service industry was containerization. Instead of loading sacks of produce by hand into the hold of a ship, a container that is pre-loaded at the originating firm is simply moved by crane from vehicle to ship to barge. Goods in sacks then do not need to be removed from the hold at the destination. This minimizes re-handling. Such as strategy minimizes the time ships spend at docks and maximizes the value added activity of transporting across oceans and seas.

It is important to remember that the transport network in a country invariably reflects its prosperity and its level of economic development. Dubai, in the United Arab Emirates, is a modern example of this phenomenon. The city acts as a hub for aeroplane passengers, business negotiation, cross-docking and forwarding. Due to the level of capital investment normally required to initiate large scale transport projects, governments in general provide the infrastructure. Large transport air, road, sea and rail network projects are both costly and require a 'medium-' or 'long'-term perspective to be taken. This is in order that they not only serve the transportation needs of today but also the future.

In recent times we have seen a movement towards 'corporatizing' or privatizing some of these facilities, which is affecting the way in which some infrastructure is managed day-to-day. As transport can represent up to 10 per cent of GDP in Western countries, it is therefore vital that it is managed both effectively and efficiently on a macro and micro level.

Many companies now rely on logistics software – with specific features designed to meet import/export requirements – to track and trace the movement of goods around the world. Programs have been developed specifically to address the problems presented in order to streamline and integrate global logistics networks. Key problems are created, and solved, by these systems. The core issue is what is known as the Forrester Effect or the Bull Whip Effect. This has many specific causes.

Current Trends in Logistics Developed in Response to 'Globalization'

There are a variety of current trends that have occurred within logistics that are in some part as responses to, or facilitated by, the globalization of the trading and manufacturing environment. Some of these are:

- electronic commerce;
- postponement and customization;
- centralized regional distribution networks.

Electronic Commerce

Electronic commerce can be said, in some part, to have facilitated and improved the prospects for companies to trade in the disparate global environment. By default, having the means to communicate in a protocol, that does not require both parties to speak the same language, has enabled companies to overcome one of the major traditional regional barriers. Government authorities, freight forwarding companies and associated international transport carriers have embraced international standard bills of loading and associated electronic trading mediums that now facilitate the smooth transmission and transfer of all necessary import/export documentation. Simply put these developments have removed barriers, enabling new entrants to join the global manufacturing, procurement and distribution markets.

Postponement

Postponement principles are adopted because costs can be reduced by:

a) postponing changes in the form and identity of a product to the last possible point in the marketing process, and
b) postponing inventory location to the last possible point in time, since risk and uncertainty costs increase as the product becomes more differentiated. Postponement results in savings because it moves the point of differentiation – where product and packaging variants are introduced – nearer to the time and place of actual purchase, when demand is more easily forecast (Stock and Lambert 1993).

The 'time' and 'place' utility delivered by the logistics function is more difficult to manage and coordinate over the distances in a company operating within a global network. The principles of postponement are incorporated into the strategic plans of global firms, in part to minimize the risk and uncertainty costs.

Centralized Regional Distribution Networks

Centralized regional distribution centres are used within global organizations to reduce logistics costs by sorting products into economic storage quantities, in relatively undifferentiated states and strategically locate them within regions. Parts and service support centres also are located using these same principles. In doing so, the number of inventory locations for slower moving goods is minimized by utilizing improved communications links and quick response transport modes, that is, courier's services and air transport.

Distribution Strategies

There are many distribution strategies used within international logistics. One such strategy is just-in-time (JIT) delivery. The aim is to deliver goods to production lines or retail outlets in a timely manner to eliminate inventory. This strategy is now standard practice within the automotive industry. However, the principle, or variations of it, is spreading across other industries.

Other methods of achieving a higher throughput of goods through the pipeline include efficient consumer response (ECR) and quick response (QR) and vendor managed inventory (VMI). These trends focus on the speed of response to the customer, the emphasis being a demand driven, 'lean' inventory model. This in turn relies on the transportation function to become much more responsive, and in many cases causes the overall operation to be drastically reviewed and re-engineered. An example of this changing role of transportation is the use of 'milk-runs' to serve the JIT environment.

Cross-docking and Flow-through

The practice of cross-docking and flow-through type operations mean that goods being shipped are very time sensitive, given that many pallets may be 'store-ready' before their receipt at a distribution centre. With these methods of pre-picking, schedules are likely to be ready for sorting or immediate transport routing, again increasing the pressure on the transport link to deliver in a timely and reliable manner. This overall emphasis on consistency of service and speed has lead many organizations to produce information systems that link into the organization's planning mechanisms. The effective transport operation is now seen as the key to the successful implementation of these trends.

For a detailed discussion on transport logistics in the global economy see OECD (2002).

Channels of Distribution

Historically, channels of distribution have been described as neatly arranged alignments of independent businesses. The members of the channel typically were the manufacturers or suppliers, wholesalers or distributors, retailers, and consumers or industrial users. The purpose of this channel of members is the process of making the product or service available for use or consumption. They satisfy demand by supplying goods and services at the right time, place, quantity, quality, right condition and price that the end user demands. Bowersox and Cooper (1992) defined a channel of distribution as a system of relationships existing among businesses that participate in the process of buying and selling products and services. A wide variety of unique businesses and special service providers form a relationship identified as a distribution channel, one that competes with other channels for customer patronage.

The channels of distribution in a society are the direct reflection of its culture. In general sophistication of the distribution system is highly influenced by the particular component of economic development in a country. The higher the level of economic development, the more sophisticated a distribution system tends to become over time. This is because managers are motivated to find the most efficient and safe method to deliver products to final consumers.

Because of the wide variety of channel arrangements that exist, it is difficult to generalize the structure or alignment of channels across all industries. Typically members of the channel take ownership of the inventory of goods, but this is not always the case. In most agency relationships, the member does not take title to the goods, so ownership does change hands. However, members do assume varying degrees of risks associated with relationship in the channel. This risk may be financial or functional.

In addition to the primary or typical members of the distribution channel mentioned above, there are many less well-known members who play minor yet very necessary and important roles. They are called facilitators, or channel intermediaries. Intermediaries make the entire system function better. They are specialized firms that perform vital tasks and services important to the overall distribution process. For example, in international transactions, translators may be an important intermediary.

In some parts of the world, channels of distribution are simple and easy to use. However, in most of the world channels of distribution are multilayered, cumbersome and difficult to understand. The length of a channel of distribution is characterized by the number of levels and types of roles that people play as intermediaries in the channel. In general, the length of international channel of distribution tends to be much longer than domestic channels.

International logistical managers have a difficult task when they build an overseas distribution channel. They must select, motivate and control middle managers with whom they interact in the overseas market, as well as determining the most cost-effective channels of distribution. The selection of the type and mode of carrier will depend on the speed of the shipment and quantity of product needed to satisfy the customer.

In order to market its products successfully, a firm must select the appropriate channel structure, choose the intermediaries to be used and establish policies regarding channel members, and devise information and control systems to ensure performance objectives are met.

Customer Service Concept

James E. Morehouse of A.T. Kearney (Zigiaris 2000), when referring to the extended supply chain, stated that the goal of the extended enterprise was to do a better job of serving the ultimate consumer. He claimed that superior service leads to increased market share and this results in higher profits.

The benefits from effective global supply chain management can come in many ways. It could be a reduction in the total logistics costs through the elimination of unnecessary or non-value adding steps in moving product to market. Enhanced customer service that results from closer coordination among suppliers and vendors upstream and carriers, distributors, and customers downstream will result in improved market share. Higher profits will come from better customer service or lower costs. The one thing that is certain is that it will depend on the level of customer service provided.

If logistics is a flow, the objective and output is service delivered to customers. However, service is expensive. One firm found that increasingh on-time delivery from a 95 per cent rate to a 100 per cent rate tripled total logistics costs. Higher levels of service require tactics, such as:

- more inventory to reduce stock outs;
- more expensive transportation to improve speed and lessen damage; and
- double or triple checking of orders to ensure correctness.

A firm's goal should be to provide adequate customer service while controlling logistics costs. Customer service is now seen as an expense and as a strategic tool for increasing customer satisfaction and sales. A survey conducted by the 3M corporation (Lamb et al. 1998, p. 493) among 18,000 European customers in 16 countries revealed surprising agreement in all countries about the importance of customer service. Respondents stressed factors such as:

- condition of product delivered;
- on-time delivery;
- speed of delivery after order placement; and
- effective handling of problems as criteria they used in evaluating firms overall performance.

Customer service, as interpreted by the logistics manager, will have to include:

- time;
- dependability;
- communication; and
- convenience.

Time generally refers to lead time for an item, order cycle time, or replenishment time. Dependability is the consistency of replenishment. Consistent service allows planning (such as appropriate inventory levels), whereas inconsistencies create surprises. These lead to either over stocking or under stocking. Communication is a two-way link between buyer and seller that helps in monitoring service and anticipating future needs. The increased communication capability of transportation carriers (such as satellite communication systems) has enhanced the accuracy of tracing information and improved the ability of buyers to schedule shipments. Convenience in relation to the logistics manager means that there should be a minimum of effort on the part of the buyer in doing business with the seller. This relates to the ease of order making, convenient locations or outlets for the product, convenient order size requirements, and job-lot availability for all logistics services.

Cost/Revenue Trade-offs

The importance of customer service to the logistics manager should now be clear. However, logistics decision-making would be enhanced if you knew more precisely how much sales would change with known changes in logistics customer service levels.

There are some observations that can be made. When no customer service exists between a buyer and supplier, or when service is extremely poor, little or no sales are generated. Obviously, if a supplier provides no logistics service and the buyer does not provide it for himself, there is no way of overcoming the time and space gap between the two. That is, if you do not provide the service and the customer cannot provide the service for himself, you will make no sale. At this level there are no sales and no service.

As the service level is increased to that approximating the level offered by the competition, few sales can be gained. If you are offering the exact same service as the competition, and assuming price and quality are equal, you are now at the threshold of the relationship between customer service and sales. You are basically not in business before this point.

When a firm's level of service reaches this threshold, further customer service improvement relative to competition can show significant improvement in sales. As the service level offered increases, the level of sales continue to increase, however at a slower rate. This is known as diminishing returns. This relationship is illustrated in Figure 27.3. The level of customer service reaches a point of diminishing returns when the additional level of input of customer service returns a less than equal return in increased sales. This is the level at which most firms operate.

It is possible that service improvements can be carried to far, resulting in a decline in profits from the increase in the levels of service. An example is when it would triple logistics costs to increase the level of service from 95 per cent on time delivery, to 100 per cent on time delivery. The benefits from the increased sales from the improved service level would probably cost more than the benefit gained. However, if the customer demands 100 per cent on time delivery, the firm has no option but to offer this level of service, or lose the customer.

A significant task logistics managers undertake is to determine the right level of customer service that will result in the highest profit for the firm. Using existing management practices this is not easy. The optimal level is where the cost of the additional service is equal to profit brought in by the increase in sales. There are mathematical models developed for this purpose, however it is beyond the scope of this chapter to analyse these models. The development of these models is one of the fastest growing consulting businesses in the world. The increased use of information technology and the power of personal computers have made the use of these models affordable for even very small organizations.

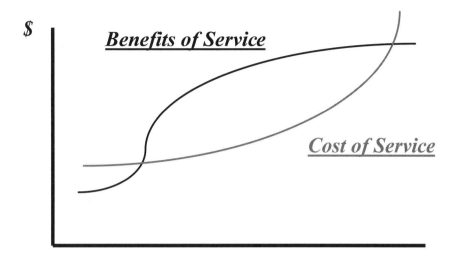

Level of Service Element

Figure 27.3   Costs and benefits model

A simple illustration can explain how these types of models work. Remember, this is a simple illustration and that most logistics problems require much more analysis. Assume your organization is operating currently at a 95 per cent level of customer service. Marketing has told you that must increase the level to 98 per cent to meet company objectives. Assume the costs of the most efficient logistics system for a 98 per cent service goal is $2 million higher than the existing systems' cost. If each dollar of additional sales yields a 25 per cent contribution to fixed costs and profit – that is, for each $1 in revenue, the company incurs 75 cents in out-of-pocket manufacturing, marketing and logistics costs – what additional sales volume will the company need to recover the increase in the logistics costs resulting from the increase in the service level to 98 per cent?

You can calculate the point at which the company would break even on the service improvement by dividing the $2 million increase in costs by the 25 per cent contribution margin. The company needs a sales volume increase of $8 million per year just to break even on the additional costs of the service plan. You can then estimate if this level of sales improvement is possible. If this $8 million increase is a major increase, say in the magnitude of 20 to 30 per cent, it is unlikely that sales can be increased to that level. However, if the increase is the 2 to 5 per cent level, this may be possible. One would have to take into consideration the competitive environment and the probability that competitors might match your service level increase.

Another simple method of determining the levels of customer service is known as the ABC method. The logic behind the ABC analysis approach is that some customers and products are more profitable than others. Thus a company should maintain higher levels of customer service for the most profitable customer-product combinations. A customer-product contribution matrix is developed that classifies customers and products according to their level of impact on the firms profit performance. The most profitable customer-product combinations receive the highest level of service. This is an over-simplified example; however, you should get the general idea.

What Should Be The Level of Customer Service?

The level of customer service offered to by the firm to the customer is critical to the success of the organization. Exactly what should this level of service be? The following discussion from Bowersox, Closs and Cooper (1986) addresses this question:

> To implement a basic service platform, it is necessary to specify the level of basic service commitment to all customers in terms of availability, operational performance, and reliability for all customers?
>
> The fundamental question – how much basic service should a logistical system provide – is not easy to answer. At the highest level of policy formation, the answer depends on a firms overall marketing strategy and relative emphasis placed on specific elements of the marketing mix (product, price, promotion, and place). If a firm seeks to differentiate its marketing offering on the basis of logistical competency, then high levels of basic service are essential. If the main competitive feature is price, then it is highly unlikely that a firm will be able or will desire to implement high-level logistical performance because of the need for cost control. Once again, the level of basic service to provide is a question of essential trade-offs and determination of the available competencies that will be most apt to influence consumer behaviour. Evidence suggests that logistical performance is increasingly becoming a critical competency.
>
> In terms of overall logistical performance, the basic customer service platform or program should be the level of support provided to all customers. It is important to stress that a firm should not deliberately violate its basic service program by offering or limiting it only to selected customers. Basic service is just what the name implies – a minimum level of support to all customers. The choice is not to provide lower basic service to marginally profitable customers. The critical decision is whether or not to do business with such customers. Once a customer' order is accepted, a firm is obligated to service the business in accordance with its basic service commitment. Anything less is clear discrimination. On the other hand, performance at a level above the basic service and provision of value-added services represent extra commitment justified by the unique business situation. This form of providing extra service is similar to adding options that are over and above the features of a base model automobile, such as a sunroof or leather interior. The expectation is that customers will pay for the extras. In the case of logistics, over-and-above service can be compensated by service up charges or the awarding of more business. The extreme level of service-based competency is when a supplier becomes a sole source provider of a product or service.

The discussion above suggests that the level of customer service provided is critical for logistics managers. The boxed text about Schneider National, Inc., in the United States, will illustrate how one firm has answered the question of the level of service to provide.

Global Issues in Logistics Customer Service

Customer service strategies for global logistics organizations must focus on such issues as:

*   convenience;
*   numbers of outlets;
*   direct versus indirect distribution;
*   location and scheduling.

One of the key factors influencing the selection of a global logistics provider is convenience. Therefore, firms must offer convenience.

An important objective for many global logistics firms is the number of distribution centres or warehouses to use or the number of distribution centres or warehouses to operate

'Zero Defect Service from a Carrier', Agis Saplukis

As a general trend, shippers are using fewer and fewer carriers in an attempt to increase quality, reduce costs, and develop closer working relations. Most shippers establish a core group of carriers that can meet strict quality standards as defined by the shipper's organization. By providing zero defect service, Schneider National, Inc. (SNI), the nation's largest truckload and specialized carrier group, is able to meet a wide range of quality standards. As such, SNI is considered by many shippers as a key candidate for participation in customized partnership arrangements.

SNI's corporate vision supports zero defect service by including commitment to the never-ending improvement of quality. SNI strives to surpass customer expectation and become the carrier of choice in the industry. One way SNI provides zero defect service is by utilizing a satellite tracking system. SNI has invested millions of dollars into this technology to align itself more closely with the customer as well as provide employees more time to work on continuous improvement. SNI uses the Qualcomm Star Serv system, a network that provides real-time, two-way communications between SNI and its drivers. One benefit of this system is that it allows vehicle to be tracked within a quarter mile of their current location every two hours.

The Star Serv network creates benefits for both the customer and SNI. Since data are more accurate and quickly received, shippers are now better able to manage in-transit inventories and make changes in service requirements. Furthermore, diversion strategies are simplified, allowing shippers to quickly change the destination of a shipment in transit. Access to real-time pickup and delivery confirmation has improved forecasting. Furthermore, potential problems are recognized faster, making immaculate recovery a possibility.

SNI's benefits include a reduction in voice communication costs and greater scheduling efficiency. Mangers' time is now more flexible since dispatching drivers is no longer their main concern. Managers can concentrate on improving operations and communicating with customers rather than scheduling drivers. In addition, equipment is better utilized to increase productivity. Perhaps most important, zero defect service has positioned SNI as a leader among the carriers, as a result of its reliable customer service and accurate delivery and information exchange. (Based on Saplukis 1992)

in a specific country or region. As a general rule, the intensity of these distribution centres or warehouse should meet, and not exceed, the target market's needs and preferences. Not having the distribution centres or warehouses close to the customers could result in lost business opportunities. Having too many may increase costs unnecessarily. Intensity of distribution may also depend on the image desired; having only a few distribution centres or warehouses may make service seem more selective.

The next decision is whether to provide distribution services directly to end users or indirectly through the use of transportation carriers that can provide fast and reliable service. The rapid growth of third party logistics providers has become a more acceptable option for shippers today. The range of activities performed by third party logistic providers typically expands beyond warehousing and transportation to include much broader functions. However, many firms use direct distribution so they can have more control of the service delivered. With the growth of more global third party logistics firms that specialize in these areas; many firms are shifting to more indirect service operations

The geographical location of the logistics provider use to clearly reveal the relationship between the carrier and its target market. The closer the location of the provider to the consumer, the more likely the relationship with the customer will be strong. The building of plants next to major customers is an example of this type strategy. The increase in the global footprint of the major third party providers, such as UPS, DHL and FedEx, demonstrates the marketing strategy and the logistics strategy for global organizations will be to provide a faster, more dependable and customer responsive capability. The selection of the distribution service in relation to the customer is a major logistic decision.

Where time-dependent service is critical, like JIT operations, scheduling is often the most important factor. In the customers opinion, when selecting a logistics service the schedule of delivery and reliability of the carrier, sometimes is a more important factor than the price. The service must fit the wants and needs of the target market.

Global Issues in Logistic Services

The selection of shipping and logistics service providers is a major part of global business. At present the United States is the world's largest exporter of logistic services. However, other countries, like Germany, the home of DHL, are entering the market and competition is increasing rapidly.

To be successful in the global marketplace, logistics firms must first determine the nature of their core service. Then the marketing and logistics services should be designed to take into account each country's cultural, technological, and political environment. The firm must determine the competitive advantage it can offer in the market place and the exact knowledge and experience advantage the firm possesses. Delivery services have great potential for globalization. United Parcel Service went global in 1996. It entered the market by first becoming a major sponsor of the 1996 Olympics. UPS's home office is in Atlanta, the home of the 1996 Olympic Games, so this presented an excellent opportunity. UPS's goal now is become the world's largest delivery service.

The logistics manager must be aware of the customers' wants and needs and do whatever is necessary to meet these wants and needs. The quality of the logistics operation will be determined by customer satisfaction. If customers are satisfied they will develop long-term relationships with the firm and long-term profitability will be assured.

Conclusions

The transport function is emerging in today's global trading environment to be capable of delivering important advantages and cost savings; if it is managed on an integrated level. Many of the international logistical trends are affecting transport planning and operation. Organizations have recognized how the smart use of logistic functions can leverage 'total costs' down. The pressure being brought to bear on this sometimes neglected area is now highlighting the necessity of managing it in a professional manner, with more emphasis than ever before on the relationship between costs and the value delivered by the transport function.

In terms of achieving customer satisfaction, it is important to take an overall view of the order management cycle, not only for external but internal customers. Adopting this holistic approach to order management will provide the focus for the whole organization to work together towards collective goals. The benefits for the company are gained by satisfying your customers in the 'long term', thus providing the company with a competitive advantage.

By successfully managing the international transport function and the order management cycle within the supply chain, many organizations are realizing the long term benefits that come with the capacity to fulfil customers increasingly demanding needs.

References

Barrett, C. (1971), 'The Machine and Its Parts', *Transportation and Distribution Management*, April.

Bowersox, D. and Closs, D. (1986), *Logistical Management: The Integrated Supply Chain Process* (New York: McGraw-Hill).

Bowersox, D.J. and Cooper, M.B. (1992), *Strategic Marketing Channel Management* (New York: McGraw-Hill).

Castalano, D.R. (1991), 'Casebook: Brooklyn Brewery', *Distribution*, January.

Christopher, M. (1997), *Logistics and Supply Chain Management: Strategies for Reducing Costs and Improving Services*, 2nd edn (London: Pitman Publishing).

Dash, J. (1997), 'Going Global with Logistics', *Software Magazine* 17(13), pp. 86–88.

Gerstner, L.V. Jr (2002), *Who Says Elephants Can't Dance? Inside IBM's Historic Turnaround* (New York: HarperBusiness).

Lamb, C.W., Hair, J.F. and McDaniel, C. (1998), *Marketing*, 4th edn (Cincinnatti, OH: Thompson South-western).

Nilekani, N. (2006), 'Competing on a Level Playing Field', Global Agenda.

OECD (2002), *Transport Logistics Shared Solutions to Common Challenges* (Paris: Organisation for Economic Cooperation and Development).

Saplukis, A. (1992), 'Computers Give Truckers an Edge', *New York Times National Edition*, 25 May.

Scott, P., Tract, J., Rishel, D. and Stenger, A.J. (2003), 'Managing Information in the Supply Chain to Enhance Customer Service and Build Relationship', *International Journal of Service Technology and Management* 4(4–6), pp. 532–48.

Stock, J.R. and Lambert, D. (1993), *Strategic Logistics Management* (New York: MacGraw-Hill).

Zigiaris. S. (2000), 'Supply Chain Management', http://www.adi.pt/docs/innoregio_supp_management.pdf.

Chapter 28
Supplier Development

David J. Newlands

Introduction

Products such as vehicles and computers are essentially sets of systems that have been integrated as part of brand name assembler's product development activities. In essence, such goods are co-packaged amalgamations of different technologies and modules produced by numerous companies other than the brand owner. Co-packaging of core technologies from different primary sources can add significant administrative costs and increase overheads to pay for the licensed manufacture of integrated goods. This is particularly important in electronics, where manufacture of wafers is carried out using semi-conductor technology from more than one vendor.

It is now rare for any single company to develop an entire product or own the complete supply chain necessary to design, produce, deliver, sell, service and dispose of goods. IBM had been successful using the in-house model when computers were large, expensive and technologies used were funded and controlled internally to develop and introduce solutions rapidly. Today, there are many niche businesses that have unique selling propositions and they compete on responsiveness, quality, cost, design expertise, service and product flexibility. Small business managers have autonomy because they are empowered to run their own business and the customer speaks to people in charge. Given significant proportions the values of finished consumer durables are attributed to bought-in parts, assemblers have recognized the importance of strategic supply chain management and their role in developing suppliers.

This chapter examines supplier development specific literature models and inhibitors to implementation are identified. Recruitment of suppliers to supplier development programmes is a significant challenge. Supplier development models have focused on the activities undertaken by purchasing staff. As with other intra- and inter-company improvement initiatives, the number of supplier development initiatives undertaken and the success rate are comparatively low.

Tacit and explicit knowledge, training, development and facilitating are core concepts significantly omitted from conventional supplier development literature. No single management system provides an holistic solution to modern market conditions.

Profitability and Optimization from Corporate Structures

Manufacturing firms create value by converting commodity raw materials into higher-value components and assembling modules and systems into finished goods. To continue making sufficient profit and thus survive, essentially companies must do this without incurring a higher total cost than the difference between the price paid for the materials and that paid by customers to obtain the goods (Smith 1995, p. 306). Competitive pressure and price versus demand force the recommended purchase price to be capped. Typically, the retail price of established product segments is externally determined by the market:

- There is a price that individuals will pay for the type of product and basic functionality.
- A premium may be achieved if product features extend this based on greater functionality, or potential clients have a subjective desire to own a brand or aspire to higher quality goods and standard of living.
- Premium prices may be charged because goods are available only from certain official outlets. Disney characters, for instance, command a premium in this manner.
- Prices erode as a result of competition in the market place between comparable products from various brands and because, newer, higher specification goods are made and introduced that reduce the attractiveness of older stock.
- Prices paid to suppliers for parts, modules and technology usually erode rapidly over the production life cycle because:
  1. Large business customers expect suppliers to reduce prices paid.
     - Customers do not want to increase prices paid just because of inflation (take last year's cost multiplied by 1+ the inflation percentage). Customers want to pay less next year than this year. Suppliers therefore have to find savings at least as fast as the rate of inflation plus the price reduction requested by customers. They must achieve this in order to maintain their profit margin. If they do not improve their processes or reduce their costs, suppliers will within several years find their profits are squeezed to zero. They then have the choice of leaving the industry, attempting to find other customers, learning to implement rapid improvement programmes, or going into liquidation. They may at this stage become targets for hostile takeovers, mergers and acquisitions.
  2. Development and infrastructure fixed costs are amortized quickly.
  3. Yield rates improve, reduce non-value-added wastes and improve productivity as production ramps up. These reduce the direct costs of production.
  4. As a result of the learning curve, experience gained, observations and process monitoring lead joint customer and production teams rapidly to identify potential savings that are realized as a result of constant attention to probing how to improve processes.
  5. First-tier suppliers pass on what they have learned from their customers to lower-tier suppliers. This forces second-tier suppliers to reduce their cost structure, find efficiencies and attempt to make a larger profit from falling revenues.

With increasing raw material, energy and labour costs, margins become squeezed over time. Searching for cost savings internally within the firm can only yield certain savings. There are more opportunities to make significantly larger savings in operations undertaken by suppliers on behalf of their customers.

Heizer and Render (2004) show two plants, one in Connecticut, USA; the other in Juarez, Mexico. With price per unit as the core objective, they show that at $70 wages per day in the US, if each employee on average produces 60 units that gives a cost of $1.17/unit. The Mexicans are paid $25/day and produce 20 units. This gives a cost of $1.25/unit. Business managers now can use re-engineering, benchmarking and kaizen/kaikaku SWAT teams to blitz working environments and make rapid improvements. In exchange for a 20 per cent pay rise, which is well above most inflation levels, Mexican workers would then receive $30/day. They would be expected to adopt the work practices used at the benchmark plant in Connecticut. Now producing 60 per day, with workers being paid $30, the unit cost would be $0.50 Henry Ford (1924) understood the importance of paying just that extra bit in exchange for significant productivity improvements. The extra money is easily funded from the changes. The extra wealth can turn employees into customers.

Manufacturing close to the market, within the trading region (NAFTA), and having a pipeline liability cost advantage over longer inbound logistics chains provides significant motivations to transfer knowledge, best practice and shut down highly productive plants. An example of this is Peugeot. They shut down their Ryton plant near Coventry, in the UK, even though it was very productive and had superior assembly quality.

Customer companies it seems, have the ability to affect the costs incurred in their suppliers by optimizing the structure and processes used to create goods they need. Customers may help suppliers to achieve, via ever increasing efficiency, the goal of providing low cost, high quality goods and services. Such customers have to keep in mind that suppliers also need to achieve a reasonable profit. The aim is to eliminate non-value-adding waste which increases cost without providing any recognizable benefit.

Mass Production and Lean Manufacturing – Business Paradigms

A paradigm is a model of how business is done. The first paradigm to change the standard of living and boost economies was mass production. This was based on Ford Motor Manufacturing's assembly system that was originally implemented at Ford's River Rouge plant to make the Model T. Economies of scale were created by vertically integrating Ford's supply chain infrastructure. The company owned most of the required facilities and plant within their various inbound supply chains to mass produce Ford branded goods.

The word 'mass' implies bulk or volume. To amass something is to have many – inferring inventory or stock. Mass production relies on spreading the set-up cost over a production run to produce stocks and work in progress in the most economic batch sizes rather than concentrating on the economics of the production system and processes themselves. Goods and services not directly made by the vertically integrated organization typically were bought on a commercial basis using adversarial purchasing practices to leverage down the unit price. Emphasis in this paradigm is on what is done and optimizing this. The early scientific management studies by Taylor (1947), for instance, focused on productivity.

In the 1990s, the rationale behind vertically integrated supply chains to achieve economies of scale was challenged in Western society by partnership sourcing (Partnership Sourcing Ltd 1992), the lean production concept (Lamming 1993), activity-based costing (Drury 1996) and economies-of-scope that are based on product family agility and variant flexibility (Dornier et al. 1998). The paradigm used by lean manufacturers is based on forming relationships with partner companies and optimizing supply chains by minimizing non-value-added waste. They focus on what isn't necessary and eliminate this in order to increase margins. Japanese supply chains, using the Toyota production system (Monden 1983), pioneered principles of systematic and continuous waste eradication in manufacturing.

Typically, the final assembler, or a strategic partner, synchronizes production of components and modules within the network of associated companies. Relationships between Toyota and its suppliers, according to Cusumano (1985), were initially based on indebtedness and obligation. Miyashita and Russell (1996) asserted that psychological relationships are a founding principle upon which the keiretsu were sustained and maintained their links. The combination of obligation, motivation and competitive pressure serves to motivate the clusters of organizations.

Miyashita and Russell (1996) also examined contemporary clusters, the six keiretsu, that coordinate more than 85 per cent of companies in Japan (Otabe 1991).[1] The six Japanese keiretsu are Mitsubishi, Mitsui, Sumitomo, Fuyo, Sanwa and DKB (First National Bank). Miyashita and Russell further established that each company in the keiretsu held a small equity stake in the other businesses within the network. Korean industry is structured in a similar manner with four Chaebol: Hyundai, Daewoo, Samsung and Lucky Goldstar Electronics.

The keiretsu model lies between the pure vertical integration of Fordist mass producers and the adversarial approach of competitive purchasing relations between non-equity-linked customers and suppliers. American and other Western corporations are reported to use the keiretsu concept (Dyer 1996; Burt and Doyle 1993). The concept does have its limitations, however, as Japanese corporations have been allowed to collapse and there are reports of keiretsu in difficulties (Bremmer et al. 1999).

Virtual vertical integration is derived from the keiretsu system. Virtual networks of companies group together in *ad hoc* clusters to fulfil the requirement for the production of various products on a project basis. The period that individual companies remain part of a virtual enterprise is largely dependent on that company's relative performance and improvements in manufacturing, managing the logistics flow and the rate and quality of its design innovation.

During the 1980s and 1990s, companies in the West made progress towards focusing on core competencies (Campbell and Sommers Luchs 1997). As a consequence, leading manufacturing companies abandoned the traditional concepts of attempting all design, manufacturing and distribution activities for their product. The result is that firms now emphasize two operational strategies:

1. focusing on in-house core competencies to maximize return on capital; and
2. the purchasing role in facilitating and co-ordinating activities undertaken by other focused enterprises.

Therefore, the facilitating task is the selection and development of suppliers for non-core value-adding activities that the company does not wish to retain in-house.

Assemblers' facilities in the 1990s typically accounted for less than 50 per cent of the value added in producing most consumer goods. Lysons (1989, p. 3) quoted a survey of 1,000 UK companies which indicates that the mean product cost breakdown was 39 per cent in-house value adding and 61 per cent expenditure on acquiring materials. It is accepted that the range for purchasing expenditure as a percentage of total product cost can be as low as 25 per cent for service-oriented companies and as high as 95 per cent for electronics surface mount subcontractors (Pritchard 1996), although the majority range between 60 to 85 per cent. The consensus is that the percentage of outsourced value added is generally increasing as a result of pressure to become more competitive (Ashmore 1995). Simultaneously, assemblers are attempting to reduce their supply base. This increases the time available to develop relationships with suppliers with the ultimate goal of improving the performance metrics for quality, cost, delivery reliability, design cycle time and management.

Outsourcing (Oates 1998) as a concept is in line with Adam Smith's (1776) 'division of labour'. This strategy increases the reliance of a business on its suppliers as progressively more value-adding is outsourced to a smaller supplier base. As a result, in Western societies the advocated model of industrial manufacturing changed significantly from adversarial price-based transactions to one of holistic supply performance incorporating non-financial metrics.

---

1   Characteristics of Japanese inter-company transfers by type quoted in Hines (1994, pp. 152–3).

The ongoing nature of business, compounded by the ability to catch up, suggests that:

- there is no single company, supply chain or technology that will be an outright winner; and
- any advantage(s) gained over competitors will be fleetingly short as commercial entities learn to embrace change.

The challenge that has spread to face all business sectors is how rapidly to achieve superior results and stay ahead of, or sufficiently differentiated from, the competition for sustained periods of time (Peters 1994). This has significant potential impact on the people side of the business, including communication and efficiency (Syrett and Lammiman 1997), unionization (Moody 1997), skill acquisition (Craig 1987; Reid and Barrington 1997; Johansen and Swigart 1995), conflict management (Thomas and Bennis 1972), career development (Mayo 1991) and inter-organizational training programmes.

Sources of Competitive Advantage

Porter (1985, p. 10) suggests the basis of competitive advantage is the value a company provides its customers. He further proposes (Porter 1990, p. 75) a choice between cost or differentiation and between a narrow or broad focus to achieve competitive advantage. The lower-cost producer creates an advantage over competitors if the customer perceives the product or service as comparable. Differentiation relies on creating truly unique attributes. The narrow manufacturer achieves success by focusing exclusively on market segment specific requirements. Porter (1980) also describes the changes in emphasis Japanese vehicle assemblers made:

> They initially penetrated foreign markets with inexpensive compact cars of adequate quality, and competed on the basis of lower labour costs. Even while their labour-cost advantage persisted, however, the Japanese companies were upgrading. They invested aggressively to build modern process technology, pioneering just-in-time production and a host of other quality and productivity practices. This led to better product quality, repair records, and customer satisfaction ratings than foreign rivals. Most recently, Japanese automakers have advanced to the vanguard of product technology and are introducing new, premium brand names.

Core to this rapid transformation has been 'the willingness to abandon what has long been successful [which] is found in all successful companies, not only those in Japan' (Nonaka and Takeuchi 1995, p. 5). Hammer (1990) recognized this in the phrase 'don't automate, obliterate.

Porter used the concept of *value chains* to separate customers', suppliers' and the company's functions that impact the total competitive advantage of a company. Nominally, competitive advantage is judged solely on potential customer's perceived value of a company's products and services, and their preference repeatedly to choose those. In effect, consumers buy products which they subjectively consider best fulfil their needs.

Businesses have sought competitive advantage internally within their business activities, externally at competitors and suppliers and by fulfilling customers' requirements. Various approaches to achieve competitive advantage include:

- division of labour and industrial engineering to increase productivity (Smith 1776);
- price-based purchasing (Baily and Farmer 1982);

- market-driven sales price used as a governor for manufacturing and distribution costs;
- cost-based purchasing and an emphasis on total acquisition costing (Biggs et al. 1990; Smytka and Clemens 1993; Ellram 1993);
- outsourcing production of mature and end-of-life products in order to focus on higher-margin new product development and launches;[2]
- just-in-time manufacturing and delivery to create low transportation and stock costs using smaller batch sizes, more frequent deliveries of made-to-order goods and reduced production lead times. Stable processes to manufacture high quality components are a requisite of just-in-time manufacturing. Quality was perceived as a strategic advantage for Japan over Western industry during the 1980s and 1990s (Sugimori et al. 1977; Schonberger and Ansari 1984; Voss 1988);
- creating broadly aesthetically appealing product designs and releasing frequent variants as a result of concurrent engineering;
- creating greater product and process availability (Blanchard 1992, pp. 80–81; Palmer 1999);
- integrating other products in co-assembled multifunctional consumer goods (Susman 1992);
- creating low volumes based on a backlog of orders of products;[3]
- focusing on calibrated and tested products set up to exact customer requirements;[4]
- focusing on products with performance that is based on calculated nominal response, where the processes are standardized and controlled by statistical sampling (Barnett 1992);
- creating high volumes of low-cost, high quality, standardized products for export or setting up transplant operations in the target region (Dunning 1977);
- creating networks of businesses based on partnership sourcing principles to reduce transaction costs (Black 1988).

Hayes and Wheelwright (1985, p. 40) identify cost, price, reliability, performance, dependability, 'peace of mind', service and flexibility as being enduring priority sources of competitive advantage.

Christopher (1997, p. 247) states that 'competitive advantage is increasingly a function of supply chain efficiency and effectiveness ... the greater the collaboration, at all levels, between supplier and customer, the greater the likelihood that an advantage can be gained'. Leading businesses apply techniques and lessons learned internally up their supply chains to suppliers and downstream through distribution channels. Competitive advantage in this context is achieved through manufacturing based on chains of enterprises focusing on continuously improving the rate at which costs are reduced while quality and value-added rises.

The effectiveness with which the Japanese adapted techniques and lessons learned up and down supply chains in Japan became a significant source of competitive advantage. Transplant assembly facilities and subcontractors in the West later made similar improvements. This implies

---

2   This project's second collaborating establishment's purchasing strategy, April 2000.

3   Statements made during presentation and factory tour by Reginald Freake, Manager – Focal point, Dell, Limerick plant, 16 February 2000.

4   Sales literature from Gervase Instruments Ltd., Hewitts Industrial Estate, Cranleigh, Surrey. Part of Spirax Sarco since 1990. All Gervase meters were calibrated using traceable systems back to national and international standards. This allowed the company to charge a premium since all meters were made to order and calibrated to suit the conditions specified (Womack et al. 1991, pp, 88–91).

that the performance standards achieved are not entirely related to a monocultured society, which Japan largely represents.

Techniques and practices to improve supply chain efficiency have been largely explored and adopted across manufacturing industries. It is likely that leading firms will need to monitor continuously their environments to identify new requirements, approaches and techniques in order to remain competitive. Rhodes (1996, pp. 264–7) highlights possibilities associated with alternative forms of response that could develop to create competitive advantage:

> Tomorrow's world will be different. It will not consist of high-tech ways of doing things we do in a low-tech way today. It will consist of an entirely new set of more-or-less compatible businesses and institutions, which variously compete and collaborate in a largely unmanaged, uncontrolled search for new ways of doing things. We and our organisations are engaged in an evolutionary process. If we know the outcome we would know the future; something we generally agree is impossible. It is thus imperative that we pay attention to where we are, what others are doing and, via the best strategic thinking we can muster, where we might go.
>
> Strategic awareness is crucial. When a significant change occurs somewhere around the globe, be it in manufacturing or wherever, we ought to know about it and be ready for it.

Awareness of the environment is considered a pre-requisite to world-class performance for the various criteria used to assess competitiveness.

World Class

Hayes and Wheelwright (1985) used the term 'World-class manufacturing' (WCM) to express the competitive advantage achieved by leading manufacturing organizations. Drivers of competition and critical practices necessary to fulfil the drivers that are used by world class manufacturers include:

- workforce development;
- development of technically competent management;
- competing through quality processes to produce high-value products;
- maintaining and stimulating the participation of the workforce;
- investing in state-of-the-art equipment and facilities.

During the 1990s, while corporations have focused on their core competencies, networks of focused, flexible and responsive enterprises have become the core theme of organizational search for competitive advantage. To satisfy demand for consumer goods in the global market, multinational corporations produce in regionalized production facilities – transplants. A core attribute of globalization is to strategically source components within the target market region and sell excess capacity to other regions.

To be competitive, companies are striving to become and remain world class (Kanter 1995). There is a consensus on the necessity for Western manufacturing businesses to re-organize their operations to compete on a global scale with world-class competitors (Womack et al. 1991; Hammer and Champy 1993). During the 1980s, many Western businesses sought competitive advantage through automation; for example, the use of robotics reduced operating costs by cutting work force numbers. Rank Xerox is typical of companies that invested in automation, for example, automated guided vehicles, to reduce direct labour (Zimmerman 1988). This type of automation became less popular during the 1990s and was replaced by faster and more flexible driver operated machines.

Japanese manufacturers have a strong presence as world-class competitors for automotive and electronic goods sectors (Schonberger 1982, 1987, 1990) and Schonberger (1982) described competitive advantages being used by Japanese manufacturing enterprises.

Just-in-time (JIT) manufacturing is a disciplined approach to improve productivity and eliminate waste (Voss 1988). Toyota Motor Manufacturing developed the Toyota Production System (Monden 1983) based on JIT principles, using kanban cards as cues to initiate manufacture of specified products in small batches. JIT is a demand-pull value-chain control and synchronization technique that relies on a small backlog of orders. Emphasis is placed on control of work done, rather than the Western emphasis on simulation using manufacturing resource planning (MRPII) information tools.

The JIT concept, combined with workers at Toyota who 'often worked one to two hours compulsory "work to finish" overtime at the end of each shift' (Williams et al. 1992), served to increase plant utilization to between 90 and 120 per cent of the plant's nominal capacity. This is in comparison to US manufacturers, which ranged between 60 and 90 per cent (ibid.).

Motorization

Motorization is the stage in the industrial development of a country when the nation acquires its own capability to produce vehicles. Motorization was used by a number of countries as a significant step toward becoming an industrialized society. Microelectronics has now made it possible for third world countries to bypass historical manufacturing and management evolutionary processes. By adopting advanced technologies and manufacturing practices, economic regional power has shifted with the emergence of newly industrialized countries (NICs) (James 1989). Large international businesses have stimulated the industrialization of low labour cost countries such as China, Mexico and the other Asian economies (Porter 1990).

Older industrialized countries (OICs) have had to adapt to the new business conditions. The performance levels of supply chains in OICs have had to improve toward world-class levels to compete with newly industrialized countries.

New manufacturing technologies and planning techniques have led to reengineered processes. Out-of-date infrastructure may remain on the fixed asset list for considerable periods of time after becoming obsolete. These are theoretically relatively straightforward to 'obliterate' (Hammer 1990), re-organize, upgrade, or re-arrange. It is also necessary to change facilitating organizational structures and approaches that supported the obsolete processes (Deming 1986). This is challenging within any business organization. Attempting significant improvements when the target elements are in other companies complicates the challenges. Since the 1960s, purchasing professionals have expanded their functions' scope to include the development of suppliers (Leenders 1965). Since some modern business operations are carried out on a global scale, cultural obstacles and value-sets also have significant impact (Hooper 1999).

Porter developed a generic 'value chain' model (Porter 1985), based on a business system concept developed by McKinsey & Company, which identified a company's basic direct and support activities. The model applies to a stand-alone company rather than a network of suppliers. Porter's model was built on the premise that there will be added value contributed to materials from left to right. By convention this reflects the flow of materials and goods from suppliers through to customers. The difference between total costs incurred and the price at which goods are sold to customers is depicted as the net profit margin. Revenue is the amount buyers are willing to pay for a product or service. In this context, revenue represents value that is quantified by a price system. A business is profitable when there is a surplus of cash from its activities. This occurs when the value it creates exceeds the total cost incurred from performing all the firms operations and indirect activity charges necessary to bring the product into being (Fletcher 1999) and to market them.

Lamming (1993, p. 90) interpreted Porter's value-adding model as a series of distinct stages or steps rather than interdependent continuous flow processes undertaken concurrently.

Hines produced an integrated materials value pipeline model that removes the boundaries between processes and focuses perception upstream from demand to supply, right to left (Hines 1994, p. 49). Based on the premise that companies exist to serve the needs of customers, Hines' model supports the perspective that supply chains ultimately must respond to customer demands. This argument proposes the rationale that assemblers are more sensitive to market requirements than upstream inbound supply chains and thus are in a position to lead the development of first and lower tier suppliers.

Hines' model attempts to avoid departmental and functional boundaries and focuses on team roles, co-operative planning and action by all the individuals involved in the network of businesses. The model depicts profit as a by-product of all the activities undertaken, rather than an end result. Primary and secondary activities are inverted in comparison to Porter's model. This is in line with two mental constructs: 1) the metaphor of an 'iceberg' whereby direct activities are more easily visible 'above the water line'; and 2) the philosophy that employees have two jobs, firstly, direct activities to add value to materials and goods required by customers and secondly, improving the job they do by undertaking work-related studies, learning about improvement techniques and participating in improvement projects.

Value-chain analysis is one of three themes that Shank and Govindarajan (1993, p. 54) hold as the basis for strategic cost management. They argued that strategic cost management concepts derive from an amalgamation of: 1) value-chain analysis: 2) strategic positioning analysis; and 3) cost driver analysis. Their value-chain concept highlights four cost control and profit improvement areas:

1. links with suppliers;
2. links with customers;
3. process linkages within the value-chain of a business unit;
4. links across business unit value-chains within the firm.

Optimizing customer and supplier linkages is core to optimizing life cycle costs, since this relates to the relationships between selling price and other costs incurred over the manufacturing life cycle and the working life of the product.

Supply Chain Competition

Supply chains are groups of companies linked together to service the tangible and intangible needs of the market. Competitive pressures recognized since the 1980s motivated companies to focus on their core competencies and outsource non-core services and manufacturing activities (Saunders 1997). Perspectives of competition altered from company-versus-company in adversarial trading environments to supply chain versus supply chain, each competing to win a share of the global market.

Supply chain development has been practitioner led (Ashmore 1995), particularly by automotive assembler companies in Japan and subsequently in other regions (Newman and

Rhee 1990). O'Laughlin, Cooper and Cabocel (1993) identified sources of competitive advantage from an holistic perspective, based on product development and integrated order fulfilment processes. They assert that, to be successful, firms should be capable of reliable delivery at reasonable prices. The price is a function of the business efficiency that result from investments in product and process design.

Application of the sources of competitive success model includes Warren's (1995) model shown in Figure 28.1. As a Production Purchasing Director, Warren highlighted that Rover Group recognized the need to improve and develop. The model identified that intangible attitudes and company culture form the gestalt background for tangible metrics which are the primary benchmarks of competitive advantage.

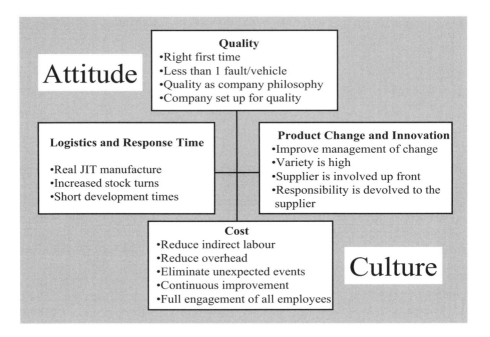

Figure 28.1   The need for change

Source: adapted from Warren 1995.

Watson suggested that companies need an effective change strategy to avoid the danger of making existing strategies too rigid, which increases the predictability of business' responses and allows competitors to generate effective counterstrategies (Watson 1994, p. 40).

Supply Chain Development and Improvement

Supply chain development focuses on increasing value-added as a result of business decisions to specialize in core activities; this is an extension of Smith's (1776) division of labour between interdependent business enterprises. Storck and Hill (2000) identified that the relationship dynamics between customer and supplier are similar to the relationship between satisfaction and dissatisfaction, and hygiene and motivators. They suggested that teams can concentrate on reconciling differences or trying to understand similarities.

Purchasing functions, in conjunction with cross-functional teams, are engaged in processes to identify performance improvement opportunities and most appropriate supply company partners, and to develop and deliver appropriate training. Partnership sourcing (Partnership Sourcing Ltd 1992) is promoted as an alternative to traditional adversarial purchasing practices based on price. Both partners' work together to achieve optimum commercial advantage, quality and cost for both themselves and to satisfy their end customer. Partners agree objectives and build relationships based on trust and open communication as well as providing assistance to accomplish shared benefits. Solutions are jointly developed, though funding for these projects may be required from the lead company as a non-recurring expenditure (NRE).

Supplier Development Concepts

> Japanese and American management is 95 per cent the same and differs in all important respects. (Takeo Fujisawa, co-founder of Honda Motor Company)

Each part of the supply chain focuses on its 'core business', based on the principles of 'division of labour' (Smith 1776) applied at individual employee and business levels. Conflicts can develop as a result of ownership of different types of businesses that are fundamentally incompatible. A significant issue is associated with limiting purchasing of goods from 'internal suppliers'. Recognized phenomena resulting from vertical integration are lack of competitive pressure reducing motivation to provide high quality goods and service classes and increased direct costs due in part to a normalization of wage rates (Womack et al. 1990).

Western businesses had a choice – either vertically integrate or approach negotiations based on unit price. This latter approach is based on adversarial trading practices. Negotiations of this type stroked purchasing agents' and sales representatives' ego states; purchasing achieved a reduction in expenditure and sales had formed a profitable contract, even though the supplier's engineering activities might cut corners actually to achieve the profit. Lamming (1993, p. 240) states that 'in lean supply the short-term expedients of irrational action by the customers towards the suppliers makes no sense'. By inference, then, customers had acted irrationally when using the adversarial paradigm.

In this context centralized purchasing enables businesses to leverage bargaining ability to achieve economies of scale (Biggs et al. 1990; Syson 1992, p. 21) by:

- consolidating quantities to obtain discounts or rebates;
- giving suppliers the option of pursuing contracts for most or all of the business' specific requirements;
- introducing the possibility that supplier overheads may be divided over longer production runs, thus reducing apportioned costs per unit, that allow the supplier to offer the customer a lower price or better service;
- enabling purchasing staff to specialize by commodity or category;
- potentially justifying specialist ancillary staff positions;
- possibly reduging administrative costs by processing fewer, larger value orders;
- enabling information technology support to automate most clerical data manipulations.

The Japanese approach differed to these paradigms, with government support that encouraged assemblers and suppliers to form long-term partnering relationships based on trust, information and commitment.

Cusumano (1985) described how Toyota avoided negative aspects of vertical integration by retaining commercial relationships with its suppliers based on keiretsu partnering relationships. Dyer and Ouchi (1993) are in agreement with Cusumano by recognizing the costs of acquiring suppliers or customers by vertically integrating are more than the cost of partnering:

> The disadvantages of acquisition include: paying a 30 percent to 40 percent acquisition premium; a tendency toward increased wages in the acquired firm since the larger firm, which usually does the acquiring, typically pays higher wages that are then transferred to the acquired company; and a loss of market discipline because a captive customer reduces the supplier's incentive to innovate and continuously improve. Indeed, ... the Japanese partnership structure creates substantial incentives for firms to improve continuously.

This section has examined specific supplier development literature and determined the limits of the state of the art. Supplier development models and inhibitors to implementation have been identified. Supplier development models have focused on the activities undertaken by purchasing staff. As with other intra- and inter-company improvement initiatives, the number of supplier development initiatives undertaken and the success rate are comparatively low. Further literature is reviewed from training, learning and facilitating fields. The section identified that supplier development models have focused on the first of three approaches: systematic, dynamic and a continuous improvement attitude. It concludes that the Honda BP approach used at TRW in Mexico most closely fits with the continuous improvement attitude by focusing on hygiene factors in the workplace to stimulate and sustain motivation to improve. This case supports the theoretical framework of a preconditioning programme. The section further concludes that supplier development is fundamentally a learning process undertaken by individuals working within groups and that existing conceptual models of supplier development focus on company to company level preparatory and monitoring activities undertaken by customer's purchasing staff.

Supplier Self-development and Customer-assisted Supplier Development

Assemblers from the auto and electronic sectors, together with retail chains are regarded by many observers as being the premier *Sources* of development programmes upon their supply chains. In order to achieve higher levels of business resource utilization, organizations target existing and potential suppliers and customers with development and/or improvement programmes. Assemblers deploying supplier development teams, aim to increase overall supply chain management (SCM) performance through development programmes and by stimulating improvements.

Assemblers facilitate their programmes by making available resources to develop and sustain better SCM relationships. They assist strategic suppliers with training in new tools, techniques and methodologies. This reduces stress involved in deciding which cure-all should be adopted, because the development programme is structured to enable the assembler to act as a mentor for its suppliers' development. They promote quality, benchmarking, insist upon continuous and/or annual cost, quality and delivery performance improvement targets and encourage lean initiatives.

Supplier Development and Partnership Sourcing

The term 'partnership' has legal connotations, hence some businesses prefer to use the term 'partnering' to define the paradigm supporting their activities. Partnership sourcing in this research is interpreted as a state of being – companies are partners, and is couched in specific cultural and behavioural ethos. Supplier development by contrast, is based on implementation – carrying out activities. This difference enables purchasing to operate in adversarial modes, while encouraging suppliers to develop and providing support services to achieve performance criteria – supplier development in a traditional purchasing environment. Partnership sourcing is a long-term state, while supplier development is a transition – a project managed transfer and implementation of knowledge, orders, skills and techniques. This implies the conversion or creation of long-term partnering relationships with suppliers focused around specific, relatively important purchased items. The term conversion is used since in some circumstances customer and supplier have already had long-term relationships based on adversarial or commercial interactions, and attempts are being made to alter the status to partnership.

Supplier Development – Survey Evidence

Watts and Hahn (1993) surveyed 81 suppliers to determine customer's emphasis and progress, concluding supplier development initiatives to be more widespread than they expected. Walker (1995) highlights Coopers and Lybrand's survey results listed below, showing supplier development ranked 7th, early supplier involvement 11th and supplier performance evaluation 13th overall on a prioritized scale.

1. Cost reduction activities.
2. Quality improvement initiatives.
3. Long-term contracting.
4. Reduction in the number of suppliers.
5. Longer-term supplier relationships.
6. Single sourcing.
7. *Supplier development programmes.*
8. Use of full service suppliers.
9. Cross-functional sourcing teams.
10. Corporate-wide consolation of purchasing.
11. *Early supplier design involvement.*
12. Buyer/seller consulting teams.
13. *Supplier performance evaluation.*
14. Cost-based pricing.

McGinnis and Vallopra (1998) emphasize early supplier involvement in new product introduction. The Oliver Wight ABCD Checklist by Souza (1993) emphasizes performance measurement as a means of gauging progress toward European quality award evaluation. Larson (1994) tested and confirmed the hypothesis that co-operation between customer and supplier would reduce total costs and enhance product quality based on 712 survey responses.

Monczka and Trent (1991) correlate the proportion of firms utilizing a sequence of elements to be achieve various levels of performance improvement.

1. Supply base optimization/total quality management.

2. Worldwide sourcing.
3. Longer-term contracting.
4. Longer-term relationships.
5. Formal supplier evaluation.
6. Cross-functional teams.
7. Early involvement.
8. Supplier certification.
9. Consulting teams.
10. Total cost.

Monczka and Trent's data suggested that fewer and fewer businesses achieved expected results because fewer and fewer implemented the project phases later in their list. It is interesting to note that these elements do not refer directly to training, development and education in order to enhance work performance and capabilities.

Edwards' (1996) profile of Ken Lewis highlighted that take-up of offers, given by customer companies to enhance business performance in partnering supplier development programmes, in the 1980s was unusually low. Lewis ascribed this resistance to change to 'The attitude of SMEs … they will not open their minds'.

Hines reported on a survey by Consigny (1994) examining automotive, electronic and machine tool supply chains from the perspective of supplier associations. This revealed a significant range of approaches and the extent to which Japanese lead companies coordinate supplier-associations. The study revealed that significant numbers of lower-tier suppliers in Japanese supply chains receive free-issue materials. This could lead to reduced supplier leverage and rewards based on conversion of materials and high process yield rates.

Monczka and Trent (1995, p. 13) collected 190 data sets via surveys between 1990 and 1993 and compared projected to actual results for current purchasing and materials management strategies. They state focus in the 1990s would emphasize core competencies and proprietary technologies, intense competition resulting in pressure to innovate and compete by continuously improving key performance results. Monczka and Trent also recognized that customer expectations rose faster than actual supplier performance improvement and that aggressive supply base reductions alone do not stimulate suppliers to enhance performance. They conclude that early supplier design involvement, direct supplier development and rewards for supplier performance enhancements can accelerate the rate of improvement.

An Arthur D. Little survey (CBI and Arthur D. Little 1995) indicated increasing commitment and trust in partnerships between customer and supplier. The findings indicated that buying companies were focusing on key supplier relationships, numbering typically ten or less, and that the key issue to facilitate more extensive implementation initiatives was provision of advice and knowledge about how to project manage the change process. Krause et al. and Handfield et al. (2000) supported this.

Krause (1996, 1997a) and Krause and Ellram (1997b, 1997c) surveyed literature and industrial supplier development practices. Krause and Ellram concluded from the literature that most supplier development activities were short-term, and targeted at improving suppliers' products and service performance in preference to enhancing their capabilities. From this set of data, practice seemed only to be fulfilling half of the sources of competitive advantage identified by O'Laughlin et al. (1993).

Supplier Development – Definitions, Conceptual, Observational and Prescriptive Approaches

Leenders' (1965) reported on various situations occurring in Canadian industry during the early 1960s. His definition for the basic concept used in that study was 'Supplier development is the creation of a new source of supply by the purchaser. … It is primarily directed toward the development of new sources of supply, rather than the furthering of relations between purchaser and existing suppliers'. Leenders divided his analysis by size of supplier. Assuming the customer size is constant, he states that:

> First, differences in supplier size require different supplier development considerations. Such aspects as the need for assistance, follow-up, and control tend to vary with differences in supplier size. Small suppliers tend to need far more assistance than larger suppliers do, for example. Second, the common concept of supplier development held by purchasing executives is that it is limited to small suppliers alone. It is true that the development of a small supplier may be more easily accomplished and yields highly rewarding results for both parties. This in no way refutes the need for the development of large supplier(s) … as well as small.

He points out that both types produced equally rewarding results. Leenders stated that:

> Supplier development implies a degree of executive involvement not normally encountered in supplier selection. For example, it frequently places a purchasing manager in a position where he must persuade a prospective supplier to accept an order.

General supplier development considerations outlined by Leenders to be necessary for successful activities include the:

- need for perseverance and planning;
- requirement of good faith by both companies;
- need for control and a gradual approach;
- probable existence of supplier internal management resistance;
- determination of price, supplier investment;
- make or buy decisions.

Hines' (1994) work on supplier associations in the Welsh Economic Development Regions contributed to the definition:

> Activities made by a customer to help improve the strategies, tools and techniques employed by suppliers to improve their competitive advantage, particularly by removing intra-company waste.

Hines stated that supplier development is a crucial element of the process of emulating performance benchmarks emanating from Japan.

Monczka, Trent and Callahan (1993) called for senior managerial action to reduce the number of suppliers in supply bases by a *natural selection process*. They explained that: 'By aggressively increasing supplier performance expectations, a buying firm expects supplier contributions to increase at an accelerated rate. Eventually, firms must maintain only those suppliers capable of satisfying higher performance expectation levels.' From this basis, Monczka and Trent (1995, p. 57) define *direct* and *indirect supplier development* as:

An aggressive approach for accelerating supplier capability improvement ... *providing additional business, capital, equipment, technology, or the assignment of support personnel to a supplier's facility directly linked to improvement of supplier capabilities.*

Indirect supplier development stresses *supplier encouragement, training, increased performance goals,* and *self-improvement.*

Krause and Ellram (1997b) defined supplier development more generally as:

Any effort of a buying firm with a supplier to increase its performance and/or capabilities and meet the buying firm's short and/or long-term supply needs.

Krause and Handfield (1999) updated Krause and Ellram's earlier definition from a unilateral initiative, to be a suitable definition for supplier associations:

Supplier development is a bilateral effort by both buying and supplying organisations to jointly improve the supplier's performance and/or capabilities in one or more of the following areas: cost, quality, delivery, time-to-market, technology, environmental responsibility, managerial capability and financial viability.

This definition is broader and may be interpreted to suit the situation. In recognizing that development may be bilateral, reciprocal and mutual, Southey and Newlands (1994) defined customer/supplier-development as:

The process of assisting existing customers and/or suppliers to develop and improve their overall capability, performance and versatility, whilst meeting and serving mutual needs and the customer in the most cost-effective and resource efficient manner.

Although there is some similarity between the definitions, there is still no single dominant methodology definition or interpretation of supplier development. The number of supplier development events highlights the need to investigate the assumptions and programmes of reported case studies.

Hahn, Watts and Kim (1990a) analysed Hyundai as a supplier development process case study and Galt and Dale (1991) provided one UK case study. Companies themselves are now making public their own case histories and practices, notably via internet sites.[5]

The interpretation of supplier development has extended in its use, particularly in the United States, toward lower-tier small to medium-sized enterprises managed by high potential minority groups,[6] demonstrated by the rise in spend on this size of supplier. This is a result of:

Public Law 100-656 that requires OEMs receiving government contracts in excess of $500,000 give preference to, or put good faith effort toward, setting aside as much as 20 percent of their subcontracts (or the priced bill of materials) for small, disadvantaged, and minority-owned businesses. Of this 20 percent, 5 percent is allocated for small disadvantaged businesses and 5 percent for businesses owned by women. (National Research Council 2000, p. 103)

---

5   BMW (c1999) Supplier Development at BMW, Bayernische Motoren Werk AG., Petrielrling 130, D-80788 Munich, Germany; Chrysler (1996) Supplier Development team focuses on coaching, September – October, Daimler Chrysler AG. Eppestrasse 225, 70546 Stuttgart, Germany.

6   Ford Motor Company, Minority Supplier Development, Ford Motor Company, One American Road, Dearborn, MI 48126; Westinghouse Savannah River Company, Procurement and Materials Management Department, Building 730-4B, Aiken, SC 29808.

The Ford Motor Company states they have the highest spend of any US company in this area,[7] represented by year in Figure 28.2. Other companies are offering supply chain management support services to manufacturing firms.[8] Ford provide action plans and standards of what they expect on their web site. Data from 2005 onward hasn't been released.

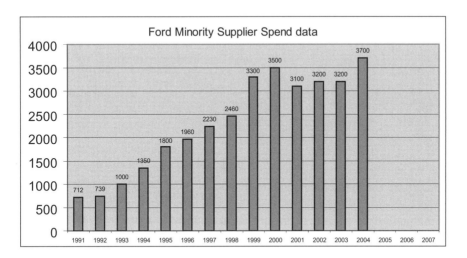

Figure 28.2   Ford Motor Company's expenditure on minority suppliers (1991–2004)

Source: Ford Motor Co.

Hahn, Watts and Kim (1990b) proposed a prescriptive process flow chart model, which depicts at a top-level customer's change agent activity emphasis. As the basis of benchmarking suppliers, the model suggests customers identify learning and improvement opportunities by comparing supplier's actual capabilities to a capabilities matrix. Their matrix forms a 'pick list' of desirable attributes associated with a world class supplier base.

Ellram (1991) proposed a five-phase model to develop and enhance partnerships with supplier:

Phase 1 – Preliminary phase
- Establish strategic need
- Form team
- Confirm top management support

Phase 2 – Identify potential partners
- Determine selection criteria
- Identify potential partners

Phase 3 – Screen and select
- Contact potential partners
- Evaluate partners
- Decision

---

7   Ford Motor Company, One American Road, Dearborn, MI 48126 (2000).
8   Everest Group Inc. Consultancy Group (2000).

Phase 4 – Establish relationship
- Document expectations/contacts
- Provide high attention level
- Give prompt feedback

Phase 5 – Evaluate relationship
- Continue at current level
- Expand/build relationship
- Reduce/dissolve interaction

Hines (1994, pp. 274–88) suggests a ten-point supplier development initiative implementation methodology developed from Camp's (1989) 'benchmarking methodology':

1. benchmark present competitive position;
2. select appropriate coordination and development tools;
3. gain internal acceptance and create cross-functional teams:
    - establish the management environment;
    - develop cross-functional team;
    - gain an understanding of the firm's requirements and those of its customers;
    - training the cross-functional team;
    - developing implementation plans;
4. select appropriate suppliers;
5. benchmark supplier position;
6. jointly target improvements;
7. focus coordination and development efforts;
8. undertake group activities:
    - yearly conferences;
    - series of seminars for senior management;
    - specific tools, techniques and strategies training or direct line staff;
    - news letter updates;
    - visits to demonstration companies;
    - social events to promote informal ties;
9. measure improvements;
10. refocus size of group and target areas. Once this has been completed, return to point 5. Benchmark supplier position.

These activity phases follow the Deming cycle (Deming 1986): plan, do, check and act. Hines' points 1–4 are concerned with pre-planning. Points 5–7 are concerned with planning. Point 8 is implementation (Do). Point 9 is check. Point 10 is act.

Lascelles and Dale (1990) identified key steps in a supplier development programme:

- establish and articulate programme objectives;
- set priorities for action;
- identify key suppliers as potential long-term partners;
- make plans to reduce the supplier base;
- communicate the programme objectives;
- methodology to key suppliers;
- assess the capability of suppliers to meet purchase requirements;

- engage in advanced quality planning with suppliers; formally recognize suppliers which achieve 'preferred' status;
- develop an on-going quality improvement relationship with suppliers based on a free exchange of information.

The last of their points is an imperative – *to do*, rather than a current state that *is*. The 'improvement relationship' raises the question of whether it is the same as an attitude for continuous improvement.

Briggs (1994) used a six-phase methodology for assessing business performance. The elements of the methodology are, however, relatively generic:

1. identify strengths and weaknesses of the current assessment process;
2. research alternative approaches currently being practised by industry;
3. brainstorm new ideas and potential alternative methods of approach to the assessment process;
4. select the 'best' approach for the business in context with the basic principles;
5. develop a draft procedure and benchmark the result both internally and externally;
6. amend the draft procedure and produce the final result.

Based on page 52 of Womack and Jones (1996), the following six steps are identifiable and applicable in-house and throughout the supply chain:

1. define value from the customer's perspective;
2. identify the entire value stream;
3. ignore the traditional boundaries of jobs, careers, functions or firms and work in cross functional teams;
4. focus on the actual target:
   - the specific design, order or product;
   - never let it out of your sight from beginning to end – in order to complete the task;
5. rethink specific work practices and tools to eliminate back flows, perhaps using 'from-to' analysis;
6. identify scrap and stoppages of all sorts so that the design, order and production of the specific product can proceed continuously and uninterrupted, though including appropriate product mix:
   - include cluster analysis, quality, concurrent engineering, simplified and unified customer liaison interface and pull, using appropriate shop and interplant layouts – cells and through the wall deliveries from adjacent suppliers.

Krause and Handfield (1999, pp. 8–9) proposed a four stage, 12-element flow chart based implementation strategy for supplier development initiatives. Krause and Handfield also highlight four active elements and seven project management elements listed below.

Active elements:

1. identify, assess and rationalize the supply base;
2. problem-solving development;
3. proactive development; and
4. integrative development.

Seven-stage process to implement supplier development initiatives:

1. identify critical commodities;
2. identify critical suppliers;
3. form a cross-functional team;
4. meet with supplier top management;
5. identify key projects;
6. define details of agreement;
7. monitor status and modify strategies.

Handfield et al. (2000) endorsed a two by two commodity portfolio matrix to categorize required materials by criticality and opportunity in order to infer which suppliers or processes should be prioritized for supplier development.

The models presented thus far reasonably follow Sheth's (1981) purchasing decision model. Each omits contingency protocols to manage potentially rapidly changing requirements. The models assume supplier cooperation and the customer's purchasing organization is leading the improvement and development process. A growing body of evidence suggests improvement initiatives do not achieve the stated objectives. This is, in part, due to implementation fatigue and resistance to change.

Improvement and Development Initiative Resistance and Fatigue

Handfield et al. (2000) enumerate inhibitors to implementation, progress and creating results. They state that only a few of supplier development initiatives achieved anything more than the first three of four stages of the seven project management elements. They specify four barriers to successful implementation arose:

1. during meetings between buyer and supplier management teams;
2. when defining key projects;
3. when defining agreement terms and determining metrics for success; and
4. when monitoring project status and subsequently modifying strategies.

The first and third of these remarkably resemble issues associated with the adversarial traditional trading paradigm that are based on win/lose negotiation strategies, what Handfield et al. (2000) call the 'bargain'. The second and forth relate to unsupportive management, lack of commitment or trust, availability of resources and target project over complexity. Lewis (quoted in Edwards 1996) concurs with Handfield et al. (2000) concerning the lack of voluntary suppliers taking up offers to be developed by their customers. The first and third points identified above can be associated to the philanthropic attitudes identified in Chapter 3.

To facilitate the management of conflict within the dyadic relationship between customer and supplier, Handfield et al. (ibid.) further highlighted the use of an ombudsman. The role is sponsored by the customer company to arbitrate, resolve conflict and reduce resistance to change by reassuring suppliers. The ombudsman uses interpersonal communication, for instance, using behavioural guidelines such as Fisher and Ury's (1981) and Fisher and Brown's (1988) 'unconditionally constructive strategy', to deal with the soft side of the business. This creates a triadic relationship. The psychological relationships are reminiscent of 'good cop/ bad cop' scenarios.

Purchasing and other specialists in a multifunction team represent customer company management when negotiating and introducing the concept of supplier development to supplier's senior management. In such circumstances, the participants would tend to divide into either technical or administrative management. The ratio of successful implementations of supplier development to offers could therefore be considered a purchasing and managerial performance indicator. Given the low take-up rate of supplier development, what are the route causes of this?

Given the cross-functional nature of the teams involved, a significant proportion of the supplier development team participants stem from technical backgrounds. For new participants, this is likely to be the first time they have been involved in a managerial level process. The transfer to a front line management position either is made as a temporary secondment out of necessity, or as a result of a conscious decision and commitment on the part of the individual. Bayton and Chapman (1972), Balderston (1978) and Badawy (1971) provided six categories representing reasons why engineers and scientists moved of their own volition into management positions:

- financial advancement;
- authority, responsibility, and leadership;
- power, influence, status, and prestige;
- advancement, achievement, and recognition;
- fear of technological obsolescence; and
- random circumstances.

Earlier research by Miner (1975) identified 35 potential causes of unsatisfactory performance from technical and administrative management relating to individuals, the job and work context. Badawy (1982) subsequently identified stereotypical causes of troublesome transition from technologist to manager:

- the nature of technical education;
- the nature of the organization's management systems and policies;
- technical competence as a criterion for promotion;
- the dual-ladder system;
- the nature of the management task;
- the nature of scientists and engineers as a group;
- bias towards objective measurement;
- paralysis by analysis;
- fear of loss of intimate contact with their fields;
- technologists as introverts;
- poor delegators;
- inadequate interpersonal skills.

Badawy additionally proposed seven mechanisms to ease the transition to management:

- identify managerial potential;
- employ better selection methods;
- make the dual ladder work;
- provide appropriate support, orientation, and coaching;
- reward managers for subordinate's development;

- provide training in the functions and skills of management;
- provide opportunities for management internships.

Status symbols and prestige associated with management's offices and other perks in hierarchical organizations are pointed to by Badawy relating to an 'index of success'. For Japanese management style influenced companies, these seem progressively to be replaced by open plan offices, company standard jacket and trouser suit work attire, and empowerment to entrepreneurially influence the business.

The relative inability of organizations promoting supplier development to secure co-operation and implement change programmes with their suppliers in part also can be ascribed to leadership. Lack of leadership, or in-appropriate leadership style, combined with reward structures, provides the basis for arguments proposed by Carlisle and Parker (1989) and Leenders and Blenkhorn (1988).

Bennis et al. (1994, p. 161) stated that, as a result of integrating processes, 'even if the total number of employees does not decrease, the increase in scale and acceleration of development will still mean a significant change in all management positions. Now all unsuitable appointments made in the past, all merely nominal functions, all those who have been shunted into sidings or 'kicked upstairs' into harmless positions will be revealed'. Fear of losing one's position in distinctly bureaucratic management hierarchies provides sufficient incentive to impede otherwise successful supplier development. Antithesis of this fear is proposed by Deming in his 14 points. Two tactical approaches to this are exemplified by Nissan's lifetime employment promise and Rover Group's 'job for as long as you want it' policy.

Womack and Jones (1996, p. 97) identified the crucial role of change agents that are 'the catalytic force ... generally (being) an outsider who breaks all the traditional rules, often in a moment of profound crisis'. Womack and Jones suggest the change agent will likely succeed provided the organization does not actively sabotage the efforts or ignore them due to 'organizational lassitude' in response to implementation fatigue or the empire-building efforts of technocrats. Two elements for success they suggest are that: 1) the change agent would be required to assume a beneficent despots (or kindly tyrant) style for approximately five years; and 2) a consensus amongst the participants that everyone will be treated fairly in the new system.

Beer, Eisenstat and Spector (1990) are critical of change programmes being overlaid on existing organizations that do not attend to fundamental processes or the fabric of the organization. Shapiro (1996) highlighted evidence suggesting frequent introductions of latest improvement or development initiatives, by senior management in a process she calls 'fad surfing', leads to implementation fatigue. Brandon and Morris (1997) recognized this phenomenon and offer a prescriptive solution in line with reengineering (Hammer 1995; Champy 1995) analysis to clarify tacit assumptions that form the barriers to implementation. In discussing fads Rhodes (1996) suggested that 'the problem is not the fad but the faddish approach: proceeding without a proper understanding of the implications, uncertainties or prerequisites. ... Any new idea must be evaluated for its suitability to context ... Companies cannot avoid having a strategy in the sense that, while they trade, they must be conscious to some extent. The challenge is for them, and us as individuals, to increase the level of consciousness'. Two elements of this consciousness seem apparent: awareness and perspective horizon.[9] The tenet behind the interpretations matrix complies with Rhodes' perspective that the ideas are evaluated for suitability within their context by identifying various levels of Target.

---

9   'Perspective horizons' is a term taken from Senge (1990).

'Honda BP' change agents at TRW in Mexico (Nelson et al. 1998) overcame similar reluctance and implementation fatigue in the Rocio example. The change agents actively listened. By rooting around in scrap piles for usable materials, they rapidly implemented quick fixes to employees' work station aesthetic 'hygiene problems' (Hertzberg 1966). This demonstration of responsiveness subtly altered the psychological contract between source and targets by ensuring the originator of ideas was identified and peer congratulated. This formed the primer for rapid spread of rumours by the informal network within the business and subsequently led to a reappraisal of the change agents by the targets. The net effect in the example was a cultural re-adjustment and renewed motivation to contribute ideas.

Schaffer and Thompson (1992) argued the merits of continuous incremental improvement, suggesting:

- material and process changes are introduced as they are required;
- that a Darwinian process based on empirical testing reveals what is effective;
- that frequent short-term success motivates; and that
- by undertaking analysis, diagnosis and managing change, employees develop the skills required to sustain the initiative.

Schaffer and Thompson summarized six reasons why activity centred change programmes fail and they promote result driven approaches:

1. activities are not linked to specific results;
2. a company-wide programme lacks focus and change would probably have happened without the initiative based on demand driven forces;
3. managers are accused of short-termism;
4. programme-driven measures confuse activity with results;
5. the initiatives are based on the principle 'one solution fits all' and are driven by external specialists or consultants rather than the operations manager;
6. lessons are not learned because the effort is based more on compliance to dogma than comparing performance to goals

They also identify four practical guidelines for implementing organizational improvement successfully:

- each organization should set short-term goals;
- periodically review progress to capture lessons to learn and reformulate strategies accordingly;
- discard inefficient processes and practices, and institutionalize the rest;
- identify crucial business challenges and create the context by sharing vision and direction for future change.

Combining the work of Kao (1991), Hampden-Turner (1990) and Stalk et al. (1992) provided the following general guidelines:

- aim for structural simplicity;
- clarify sources of competitive advantage (O'Laughlin et al. 1993);
- commission parts of the organization to identify and analyse the business environment for competitive advantages;
- ensure the efficiency of core processes;

- develop human resource management as the company gets bigger;
- develop the leadership style by adapting to the changing environment and organizational structure.

A significant piece of research focuses on the recipients of supplier development initiatives. The United States' National Research Council's (NRC) Committee on Supply Chain Integration (NRC 2000) identified characteristics of successful small and medium-sized manufacturing enterprises (SMEs). The committee suggested that SMEs should:

- choose customers carefully;
- react appropriately to salient events that can define success or failure;
- establish strategic alliances and partnerships with customers and suppliers;
- cater to customers' needs;
- focus on quality;
- treat employees as valuable assets;
- select and monitor manufacturing processes;
- use the internet for business communication and education;
- share information with supply chain partners.

The Committee on Supply Chain Integration argues that customer companies carefully select targets for supplier development based on performance metrics and recognize the inherent resistance demonstrated to proposed change. The committee 'emphasises that each SME must carefully assess its own circumstances in the rapidly changing business environment, identify gaps between supply chain requirements and its own capabilities, and find ways to fill the gaps'. They go on to state that, 'based on a thorough analysis, each participant (SME) should then develop an internal business case for participating in particular supply chains and decide, … the extent to which they will integrate with their customers and suppliers'. To use a metaphor, the committee suggested that one can lead a horse to water, but can't make it drink, and that the horse would find its own water if it wanted, though not necessarily that on offer by those that would wish to provide that opportunity.

The NRC's evidence that SMEs carefully choose their customers corroborates Leenders and Blenkhorn's and Carlisle and Parker's perspectives that customers have to sell themselves as worthy of receiving goods and services from their suppliers. This raises self-analysis questions such as *how good are we as customers?* and *are we easy to do business with?* Such an approach is suggestive of strategic level analysis using the Johari window (Luft 1961). The NRC report also provides balance to Handfield et al.'s (2000) remarks on the difficulties present in producing recognition, procedural and substantive agreements during the negotiation phases of a supplier development initiative.

Given that supplier development is designed to make the manufacture of saleable products more viable, it may be perceived as a value-adding activity. The principal objective is to create competitive advantage by raising performance levels through structured programmes. Performance improvement objectives include increasing quality and delivery reliability, reducing cost and new product development times (Nishiguchi 1994). A major issue for the designers and implementers of supplier development initiatives is long-term dependence on the source or change agent.

Many first-tier suppliers for automotive and electronic goods supply chains have subsequently served as facilitators of supplier development to lower-tier suppliers and raw material producers. These suppliers become showcase examples of performance levels and customer-focused operations that can be achieved. For this tiering to be successful, a contention is that it is necessary to create a climate in which the recipients of the training are motivated to participate in the formal events. The principal objective of any preconditioning sessions, therefore, should be to empower individuals and businesses to be able to develop autonomously by implementing agreed strategies and principles.

Even though the automotive and electronic goods sectors have pioneered cooperative supplier development, traditional/adversarial price-based contracting remains a valid purchasing practice for commodity items and goods manufactured by transferable technologies (Christopher 1997). This is especially evident at lower-tier levels where open competition for contracts remains the norm. The majority of the automotive assemblers are reducing their active supplier base to the minimum (KPMG Automotive Industry Group 1996). They select specific suppliers that have a long-term close strategic role to fulfil with the assembler-company and focus on their core competencies. A common objective amongst leading proponents of supplier development initiatives is the creation of competition for a bigger percentage of their business (Toffler 1971). Contrary to popular understanding, a high failure rate for supplier development is considered as a purchasing success since this justifies deselecting suppliers. Deselecting suppliers, though, also serves to increase the importance of relationships with successful suppliers (Morgan 1987; see also Hakansson 1987).

From OEM's perspective as the coordinator of the value-adding activities, they can specify: 1) from which suppliers' specific goods and services must be sourced; and 2) the price to be paid (Newlands and Southey 1994). This approach creates motivating forces in the interim suppliers to increase effectiveness and efficiency, since they are only paid for the conversion or sub-assembly procedures. It therefore becomes imperative for these companies to add value in other ways. Typically these are by providing value adding creative services, for example, design, modifications, prototyping, process technology research, lower tier supplier training and auditing or benchmarking (Pritchard, in Ashmore 1995).

The core objective of customer's supplier development initiatives is to reduce the unit price through cost reduction. This draws attention to the value-adding process. Key to increasing value add and reducing non-value-adding waste are simplicity, reliability, ease of maintenance, maximum flexibility, lowest possible lead time, responsiveness to volume ramp up and turn-down and superior quality.

Conventional supplier development tends to be the formalized strategy for implementation of improvement and development from one company to another in the supply chain. These initiatives are developed and implemented with the objective of improving the suppliers' capabilities and performance levels. In effect, the customer company is the source of knowledge, motivation and facilitating resources for the initial programme. All attributes and aspects of the supplier business are possible targets for review during the initial phase of supplier development.

The principal driver(s) behind the range of approaches to supplier development vary significantly (Medori 1998). Recognized drivers include:

- performance measurement and qualitative audit selection;
- strategic selection based on expenditure;
- supplier base reduction;
- cooperation and motivating input from suppliers;
- technological leadership;
- monopoly source leverage;
- quality kaizen (continuous improvement) and kaikaku (opportunities for stepped or very rapid bursts of improvement);
- costs – waste, failure and detection;

- delivery reliability and lead times;
- innovation;
- product features;
- volume capacity;
- speed of capacity ramp-up and turn down;
- flexibility – product changeovers and modular component designs;
- productivity;
- staffing level reductions;
- absenteeism reductions;
- coordination;
- long-term stability;
- environmentally 'green' manufacturing and recycling, particularly ISO14000.

Each principal driver contributes values, objectives, strategies, tactics and implementation initiatives to the customer-supplier relationship.

From the supplier development examples collected, no single driver or approach to supplier development has been found to be dominant. Total quality, however, is recognized by a significant majority of organizations. Only at the level of supply chain management (SCM) strategies and objectives, are there broad similarities between the recognized improvement and development paradigms. This is only possible due to the evolving nature of SCM. Ross (1998) proposes the following definition for SCM:

> Supply chain management is a continuously evolving management philosophy that seeks to unify the collective productive competencies and resources of the business functions found both within the enterprise and outside in the firm's allied business partners located along intersecting supply channels into a highly competitive, customer-enriching supply system focused on developing innovative solutions and synchronizing the flow of market place products, services, and information to create unique, individualized sources of customer value.

Supplier Development – Summary

Various definitions exist for supplier development. These vary to suit the objectives of supplier development and are relevant to the trading environment and the paradigms in operation within which the initiatives take place.

To date, there still remains only a small core of widely recognized data specifically referring to the subject of supplier development. A search of supplier development literature reveals pluralistic scope to develop suppliers:

- evaluating suppliers as a prerequisite to further supplier development activities (Giunipero 1990; Krause and Handfield 1999; Handfield et al. 2000);
- providing feedback on supplier performance (Lascelles and Dale 1989);
- selling the concept based on future benefits (Carlisle and Parker 1989; Leenders and Blenkhorn 1988; Monczka et al. 1993);
- greater information exchange through common interface platforms (Monczka and Carter 1988);
- performance and capability enhancements made possible by investing directly in the supplier in exchange for raised performance expectations (Monczka and Trent 1991);
- cultural and technological interchange by implementing tour of duty training and secondments (Newmand and Rhee 1990).

The basis of these studies distils into seven principal elements:

- identify and assess supplier's operations;
- providing incentives and inducements to improve performance;
- instigating competition among suppliers;
- the need to overcome resistance;
- working directly with suppliers, either through training or other activities;
- periodic performance assessment and audits;
- information technology infrastructure development and standard interfaces.

Due to contemporary customer assembler's supplier development emphasis on substantive results, the people issues will probably either be used as a selection criteria or will need to be addressed prior to the development team's arrival.

- Existing supplier development (SD) specific literature does not distinguish between training, development and education for engineers, technicians, craft workers, semi- or unskilled labour. For such categories, different levels of assistance and syllabus will also be required to suite the stage of career and achievement of staff (Thomas 1995). Contemporary supplier development models have tended to concentrate training on specific skills and techniques, transferred during supplier events designed to teach and stimulate both rapid cost savings and continuous improvements. SD-specific literature does not examine issues of preparing to teach (Gibbs and Habeshaw 1989), preparing to learn and change as a result of feedback, or skills required by the change agent (Egan 1988a, 1988b). Additionally, internal dynamics of the customer company, especially direct operations teamwork for productivity (Manz et al. 1997), and management styles (Wilson 2000) are absent. The surveyed literature does not identify any specific companies that are statistically shown to have a very effective procedural methodology that increases the rate of supplier participation and scope of development work.

In the next section of this chapter, focus shifts to the knowledge transfer and creation processes present during training and subsequent development and learning.

Supplier Development as a Learning Process: Converting Tacit to Explicit Knowledge and Competency

The conceptual issues relating to converting tacit knowledge to explicit knowledge are reviewed by Dawes in this volume (Chapter 25). Tacit knowledge relates to things known that are in people's heads and not recorded. Awareness is a key issue relating to identifying and recording tacit knowledge. This issue is one of the significantly understated elements of supplier development literature.

The discovery of what is known yet not utilized knowledge can provide paradigm shift and significant competitive advantage over competitors in the global economy. It is for this reason, that international businesses have aggressively outsourced work their skilled employees undertook to lower cost suppliers, contractors and countries. Supplier development initiatives rely on transferring techniques and philosophies that underpin the implemented solutions with an aim of creating self-sufficient and self-improving learning organizations. The current best practice may be the early goal, however, using the philosophies and continuously questioning

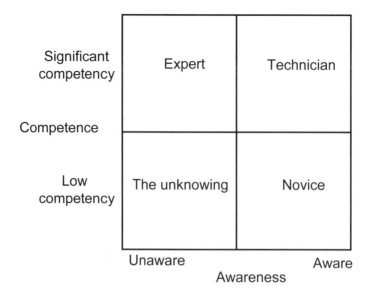

Figure 28.3   A 2×2 matrix of high and low awareness and competence.

'what is happening?' and asking 'what does the customer really want?' which can enable breakthroughs and paradigm shifts that would not otherwise have been possible.

The Expert

We may be aware that we have absolutely no idea about something or we may be completely oblivious to the issue and notion. Equally, we may be aware we know something. A true expert is proficient and makes it look easy. Primarily this is because they do not require to think each step through because it is so well practiced. As they learn, they may lose their ability to explain what it is they are doing. The best teachers are able practitioners who have taken the time to describe what they do, how it is done and how others could start to achieve similar levels of competence. The Japanese culture reveres the pursuit of excellence, turning the trivial into an art form.

The primary role of the expert is to perform tasks at a consistently high level of achievement. Their activities constitute a form of training or practice (doctors and dentists run their own practice, athletes train). An expert welder or machinist, for example, knows how to get the best out of their equipment. Only a poor worker blames their tools.

The secondary role of an expert is to transfer their knowledge and create competent co-workers (the term 'associates' is now used in many companies that include blue-collar and supplier employees). The associates may be in the same plant or elsewhere in the same or other trading regions. ISO9000 and other quality standards require the organization for whom the expert works to document the way they do their activities and to comply with the written procedures. This is in stark contrast to the 1920s when Henry Ford wrote his two books. Ford liked his employees to experiment and relied on them to adopt the most effective approach. Once adopted, this would have become the standard way of doing things. The key problem with this approach is that the reasons why a solution was devised are lost over time and it becomes 'the way we do things around here'. Similarly, there is a distinct lack of transferability except by detailed method study or 'sitting with Nelly' and 'monkey see, monkey do!'

The expert must start putting words to their activities. They have to define everything, even if it is obvious:

- What are the limits, ideal settings?
- Which have proved the best ways?
- What are the differences between experts – their personal preferences?
- What things they do to prepare?
- How do they measure themselves?
- How do they know it is right?

Fundamentally, experts have to question each activity for value, convenience, effort, waste and break down their work into identifiable and teachable (describe and show) elements.

The expert who assumes the role of a leader is required to either prepare themselves to teach or to develop a formal a course with learning objectives, prerequisites and a set of pedagogical materials and methods. The aim of these preparations is to raise novices up to technician levels.

The Unknowing

The unknowing are people that have no awareness or competency in a specific task. The state of unknowing is the result of little experience or a lack of interest and observation.

In most industrializing economies, people have migrated from rural villages to towns and cities in search of a better standard of living. Henry Ford made use of the masses by dividing work into simple repetitive tasks. He asserted that we (managers) should not concern ourselves unduly with this type of employee because they learn to tolerate the monotony in exchange for the certainty of knowing what tomorrow will bring – the same. Ford also pointed out that skilled people will not thrive in such circumstances and that they rely on variety, discovery and intellectual pursuits. These two types resonate with Theory X and Y.

The unknowing may be suspicious, fearful or apprehensive, motivated by purely selfish gain, unsure of their fit with the organization or even of the needs and mission of the company. The unknowing may be invited to learn with the aid of some kind of sales pitch and related literature. Equally, they may take the first step themselves and identify what it is they would like to learn.

International business leaders have come to understand that the key differentiation between developed economies and those that are rising is the leadership that stems from innovation and commercialization. With so many countries producing graduates and postgraduates, to retain the lead they must develop attractive and technologically advanced products that are made using superior processes.

The Novice

The novice has some idea of what is expected of them and what they are trying to achieve in terms of performance. Simple training over a few minutes up to a few days may be all that is necessary to acquire the competence to do work to a given quality level. For some physical tasks that require concentration and dexterity, such as welding, several weeks of constant practice may be required to raise the level of productivity to the standard where they are considered as qualified to operate and gain the regular productivity bonus.

Some individuals are recruited to remain novices over an extended period. Trainees and apprentices may work as specialists only once they have completed an extensive series of exercises, activities and courses. Tax advantages against the rest of the work force can be significant in various countries.

Certain countries have lost significant numbers of engineering and building oriented courses because other service sector studies have become popular. The managing director of the firm where I did my apprenticeship couldn't offer such courses any more because the colleges stopped offering them. Instead, they offer tourist guide and acting.

Apprentices typically will work to develop a good all-round skill set. Only once they have gained a general level of experience and skill to technician level, in all the areas will they select their specialism and invest their time in becoming an expert.

The Technician

Technicians have a certain amount of skill and an acceptable productivity. They rely most on their training, although they can be empowered to experiment and propose projects. With a given skill set, they are prime candidates to become area supervisors and plant managers later in their careers.

If there is a batch of technicians finishing their course every year from a company, competition for the best jobs and opportunities increases. Plant managers may choose who they want to join their group. Equally, the company may perceive that certain individuals are likely to outgrow the company and would look for other work or qualifications. With the best intentions, their managers may encourage them to leave and find other jobs and get other experiences. Some of these may come back to the company after a few years, having proven they are capable in the real world. Competitors and suppliers may actively poach technicians away with interesting jobs, promotion and higher salaries.

Training, Development and Learning

Brown et al. (1994) categorized training, development and learning by facilitator and time horizon. The classifications by Brown et al are focused on shop floor employees. Alternate focuses are self (Pedler et al. 1994), management (Nixon 1981), teams (Bicheno 1997) and the individual (Johansen and Swighart 1995; Wood 1988), regardless of organizational role (Handy 1993).

Bennis et al. (1994, p. 297) suggested four major approaches that can be used to develop individuals' understanding of their potential and how it could be applied to achieve full career and organizational growth:

1. direct mentoring between a manager-once-removed and the individual;
2. coaching to explore and understand all the subordinates' roles and highlight strengths and weaknesses;
3. imparting knowledge by teaching to individuals in lectures, seminars, discussion and practice;
4. training by using newly acquired knowledge on the job or in learning simulations to help individuals develop or enhance skills.

While partnership sourcing is regarded as organizational behaviour, supplier development by contrast provides agents of change with procedures and a curriculum of transferable competencies and skills. Interpersonal skills change agents likely would need are discussed by Fisher and Ury (1981) and Fisher and Brown (1988), who described philosophical attributes to guide an individual's behaviour during negotiations. This is complemented by Walther (1993) and Berry (1996, p. 180). Part of an individual's ability to manage is understanding one's personality (Crozier 2000), management styles (Blake and Mouton 1985; Wilson 2000) and learning styles (Honey and Mumford 1992, 1995).

Training

Occupational skill training initiatives can be categorized as:

- off-the-job training under full-time supervision in a special area away from production facilities, following properly designed syllabus;
- on-the-job training under supervision in a production area;
- semi-supervised on-the-job training by 'sitting with Nelly' (this is generally discredited as a training method);
- use of projects and departmental assignments;
- use of external training organizations. This includes supplier development staff training activities sponsored by customer organizations and training consultancies.

Training for occupational skill acquisition was boosted in the UK by the Industrial Training Act 1964, empowering training boards to charge a levy to firms based on either number of employees or the amount of pay role (HMSO 1964; Engineering Industry Training Board 1969). Participant firms received cash-back grants based on quantity and quality of training provided. The act had three main objectives:

- to ensure an adequate supply of properly trained men and women at all levels in industry;
- to secure an improvement in the quality efficiency of industrial training;
- to share the cost of training more evenly between firms.

Finnigan (1970, p. 11) identified line manager, training specialist and industrial representative roles of a training manager, and that training strategies are 'clearly called for and the form of strategy must be conditioned by:

- the organization;
- the line manager's attitude to training;
- the receptiveness of individuals to the need for training;
- external factors such as the ideas of co-operating academic institutions and industrial training boards;
- the training manager's own attitudes, hunches, fancies and prejudices (ibid.).

Brown et al. (1994) categorized training as a short-term provision of specific knowledge, usually provided by specialists, with the aim of rapidly achieving a foundation of common skills. Training is focused on supporting business strategies by providing appropriate input or conversion skills and techniques. Training needs analysis (TNA) is a process of comparison between desired characteristics and attributes of ideal candidates to fulfil a role and current abilities of available individuals (Armstrong 1977). This is somewhat reflected in by Hahn et al.'s Figure 4.3 (1990a). Once an initial TNA has been undertaken, management nominally determine an optimum sequence of standardized training packages delivered in seminars (Cayer 1990; Honey and Mumford 1996). Training is the application of knowledge, which can be cascaded down through a business and extended through supply chains by training trainers. Typically, this knowledge will be formatted for rapid understanding and assimilation (Eastburn, in Craig and Bittel 1987). Training provides specific job and people skills (Investors in People UK 1996), for which companies would reasonably expect significant returns on investment (Institute of Personnel and Development 1996).

Kirkpatrick (1987) is recognized by the Institute of Personnel and Development as a standard by which to assess training, development and learning. Kirkpatrick's evaluation criteria are:

- *reaction* (concern about mistakes made, feelings including apathy and excitement, situation-dependent reactions – alarmist; intellectual inquisitiveness; route cause driven and solution driven – isolated cause and effect, systemic analysis);
- *learning* (increased understanding, acquisition of skills, capabilities and experience);
- *job behaviour* (synchronization, efficiency, effectiveness);
- *organizational effects* (results, product and service popularity – increased sales, stability and predictability); and
- *ultimate value effects* (results, key performance indicators, competitive advantage, growth).

Kirkpatrick suggested paper-and-pencil tests before and after seminars, and assessing individuals feedback on intrinsic and extrinsic perceptions using forced agree/disagree questions. A significant conclusion reached by Kirkpatrick is that favourable reaction to programmes *does not assure* that learning has taken place. A grid can therefore be drawn to illustrate the value (in terms of completeness) versus reactions or quality of presentation to categorize and compare various initiatives. An alternate assessment tool for joint analysis between customer and supplier is the Gartner Group's[10] matrix evaluates completeness of vision against ability to execute.

Wickens (1997) depicted four sequential levels of ability used to grade Nissan employee's abilities and competencies. These levels of ability are related to quality and time, and therefore contribute to cost reduction, quality, efficiency and productivity. The matrix enables managers rapidly to identify who is qualified for which level of task – performing, training others or improving the process.

Code: Tasks can be performed:

- to the right quality;
- quality and in the standard time;
- quality, standard time, can train others;
- quality, standard time, train others and trouble shoot/improve the operation.

Development

Training relates to acquisition of defined techniques to fulfil a specified role. In this perspective, there is a metaphoric 'glass ceiling' that forms a boundary to the role. Roles are an extension

---

10 There are many examples in GartnerGroup literature, including Malik and Cushman (1996).

of scientific management, whereby perceived elements of a company having defined activities and purpose and whose interactions could be defined, formalized and standardized (Handy 1993). Development by contrast relates to job enrichment and expansion. Development implies iteration and expansion, progress and advancement. Targets for development include individuals, groups, subgroups and businesses (Wood 1988). Heirs and Farrell suggested that change agents, or sources of development are best served by introspective analysis in order to identify the current state and subsequently the requirements Targets must fulfil as a result of the initiative:

> The manager responsible for conducting decision-thinking performance – be that his own or that of his organisation – must therefore start with a sound and shrewd assessment of his own thinking abilities. Only if he knows his own thinking strengths and weaknesses can he start to build upon the former and, as far as possible, remedy or compensate for the latter. Only when he understands where his own talents lie can he look around for the indispensable talents that will balance and complement them. And only after he has assessed his own skills as a manager, motivator and assessor of other people's thinking efforts can he set about improving those skills. (Heirs and Farrell 1989, p. 163)

They related the 'not invented here' phenomenon to Japanese industrial emulation of Western industrial practices following cognitive behaviour modifications (Meichenbaum 1977), which were originally based on a national psyche which believed that all foreigners and extraneous methods were intrinsically inferior.

Learning

Henry Ford (1924) contended that learning occurred in the organization, so that experiments that had not worked in the past would be recalled by the collective memory. Ford assumed that the cumulative knowledge of all previous experiments would lead to an exhaustive list of what could not be done, leaving no discernible opportunities for examination. This perspective heralded learning organizations and organizational learning (Easterby-Smith et al. 1999). Ford advocated pro-rata compensation, stating:

> If an employer urges men to do their best, and the men learn after a while that their best does not bring any reward, then they naturally drop back into 'getting by'. But if they see the fruits of hard work in their pay envelope – proof that harder work means higher pay – then also they begin to learn that they are a part of the business, and that its success depends on them and their success depends on it. (Ford 1924, pp. 117–18)

Ford (ibid., p. 86) also advocated not writing down practices and experiments already undertaken. By contrast, the quality standard ISO9000 series accentuate explicit documentation of standard operating practices and QS9000 emphasizes quality tools and statistical process capability measurement to achieve significant yield based on product design tolerances.

Argyris and Schön (1978) developed single- and double-loop learning. Single-loop learning compares actual states of variables against governing variable limits and determines error. Double-loop learning adds a feedback loop to allow for the governing variables to change. In effect, double loop learning is the fourth level of Wickens' employee skills. Imai, Nonaka and Takeuchi (1985, quoted in Lamming 1993, pp. 101–2) stated:

> Everyone participating in the development process is engaged in learning, even outside suppliers. Learning also takes place across all phases of management and across functional boundaries. It is this kind of 'learning in breadth' that supports the dynamic process of product development among

Japanese companies. This learning emanating from the development process, in turn serves as the trigger to set total organisational learning in motion. In this sense, new product development is the particular device that fosters corporate-wide learning.

Learning at individual and organizational levels is linked with competitive advantage (Moingeon and Edmondson 1996), trust in intentions and competence (Argyris 1993), exploring individuals margins of freedom that form a source of uncertainty and games for colleagues, the organization and other enterprises in the supply chain (Crozier and Friedberg 1981, pp. 90, 286), through innovation (Nonaka and Takeuchi 1995) and improved management (Burgoyne and Reynolds 1997). The decision to learn occurs at different levels of organizations at different times (Esbroeck et al. 1997). Attitudes of people in the organizational scenario play a considerable part in the maintenance of individual's commitment to learn (Park 1994, 1995).

Stiglitz (1987) hypothesizes: 'Just as experience in production may increase one's productivity in producing, so experience in learning may increase one's productivity in learning. One learns to learn at least partly, in the process of learning itself.' Neural linguistic programming (NLP) categorizes individuals into three types: auditory, visual and kinaesthetic (Bandler and Grinder 1979; Alder 1994). In learning settings, it is advisable to match the medium to the recipient (O'Connor and Seymour 1994). Calder et al. (1995) identified deep and strategic level learning, and surface learning as being present in their sample of British industrial organizations and further education colleges. They identified that FE colleges focus on learner's potential and specific qualifications while in-company training focus on preparing and inducting employees into specific jobs and improving performance. In Calder's study, responding in-company courses did not normally use the concept of passing or failing.

Collis (1994) and Grant (1996) conclude that business strategists recognized the ability to learn faster or 'better' than competitors may alter the competitive advantage relationship between organization's goods and services.

Myers-Briggs Type Indicator (MBTI) is the source of a balanced strategy for work definition that uses all eight participant preferred styles: extroversion versus introversion, sensing versus intuition, thinking versus feeling and judging versus perceiving.[11] The strategy has seven steps:

1. *Define the problem* by using sensing perception to see it realistically. Avoid wishful thinking.
   Sensing Questions
   ° What are the facts?
   ° What exactly is the situation?
   ° What have you or others done?
   ° What are the bottom line realities?
   ° What are my resources?
2. *Consider all the possibilities* by using intuitive perception. Brainstorm. Don't leave out a possibility because it doesn't seem practical.
   Intuitive Questions
   ° What are all the possibilities?
   ° What might work?
   ° What other ways are there to look at this?
   ° What do the data imply?
   ° What are the connections to other issues or people?
   ° What are the patterns in the facts?

---

11 MBTI Analysis and Use Strategies, p. 29, http://www.cpp.com/detail/detailprod.asp?pc=157.

3. *Weigh the consequences of each course of action* by using thinking judgement. In a detached and impersonal way analyse the advantages and disadvantages of each alternative. Make a tentative decision about what will give the best results.
   Thinking Questions
   – What are the pros and cons of each option?
   – What are the logical consequences of each option?
   – Is this reasonable?
   – What are the consequences of not acting?
   – What impact would this have on my other priorities?
4. *Weigh the alternatives* looking at the impact on people by using feeling judgement. Use empathy to put yourself into the situation.
   Feeling Questions
   – How does each alternative fit with my values?
   – How will the people concerned be affected?
   – How will each option contribute to harmony?
   – How will I support people with this decision?
5. *Make a final decision*, consciously, on your best course of action. (Judging)
6. *Do it!* Act on your decision. (Avoids the danger of procrastination associated with 'perceiving'.)
7. Evaluate the *decision*. Was it a good one? Did you consider all the facts, possibilities, impacts, and consequences? If you are satisfied, keep on. If not, rework the steps. You may have new information; the situation may have changed; you may see consequences you didn't anticipate; or your values may have changed. (Perceiving)

This balanced strategy is also in line with Deming's plan, do, check and act cycle.

Group Facilitation

Heron (1993) provided guidance on preparation, delivery and evaluation of training materials based on joint content agreement with the client. By contrast, Chalmers (1996) focuses on what the trainer can achieve in isolation. Odiborne (1961) and Weaver and Farrel (1997) examined how managers facilitate change and work.

Sheal (1989) examined facilitators' roles and authority, charismatic presence and treating the learner in an holistic manner. Sheal identified an approach for transposing training centre practices to the workplace and related this to creation of individual and peer pressure to achieve results. Most significantly, Sheal advocated peer review audits within firms to set quality and performance targets. In this respect, Sheal's concept is autonomous, self-directed and sustainable supplier development.

To achieve 9,9 on the grid by Blake and Mouton (1969, 1985), one hypothesis proposed is to start with a facilitator who has achieved an emphasis on both tasks and people. External parties who are not exposed to the detail associated with the scenario under examination are likely to be able to act as a chairperson. This role makes use of a balanced scorecard to ensure both aspects are reviewed, analysed and assists in the decision-making process as an ombudsman or arbitrator. The facilitator will be able to identify the focus of concern of the principal protagonist groups. From the starting grid, the facilitator is likely to combine both concern for task and concern for people in defining a series of projects that form a programme of continuous improvement. Figure 28.4 depicts a facilitator changing perspective to assimilate a client's position on the grid. From there, each project is framed in a people oriented introduction to ensure recognition and procedural agreements. Only then, are substantive task oriented agreements reached and improvements implemented. This approach emphasizes attitude, appraisal of current performance, and subsequently improvement via systematic training (reversing Barrington's model – starting with people, then tasks, in a multi-project environment). This can have an impact on employee perspectives by creating 'implementation fatigue' identified by Shapiro (1996).

Kaplan (1996, p. xiv) identifies that development practitioners must have imagination, flexibility and the ability to work with ambiguity and contradiction; one which does not use rules, it relies on guidelines. Kaplan noted that contradiction stemmed from a situation where 'the people resisted change, yet were patently unhappy with their current state'. The ambiguity emanated from a perceived imperative to develop, while questioning the correctness of implementing and facilitating development on targets who were unwilling to accept the consequent changes.

The dominant model of supplier development is a based on a business-to-business teaching and learning contract to improve the supplier's capabilities by transferring techniques and concepts. Johnson (1986) perceived business success as emanating from employees rather than the structure of the company. Wood, Barrington and Johnson (1988) promoted an attitude of continuous development that is effective as the basis of skill and knowledge acquisition by individuals in a business environment.

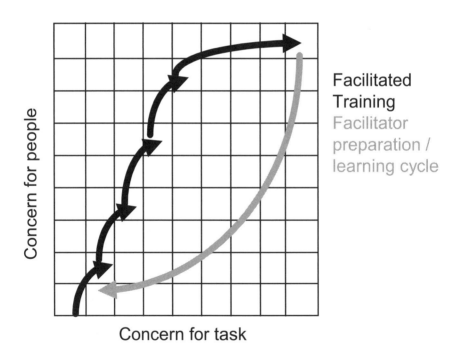

Figure 28.4   Overlay of hypothetical facilitating and facilitator preparation profiles on the managerial grid

Source: Adapted from Blake and Mouton (1969).

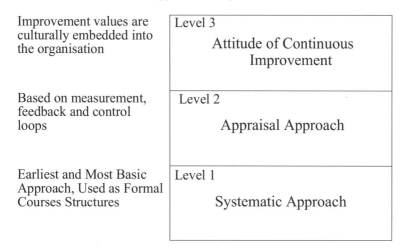

Improvement values are culturally embedded into the organisation	Level 3 Attitude of Continuous Improvement
Based on measurement, feedback and control loops	Level 2 Appraisal Approach
Earliest and Most Basic Approach, Used as Formal Courses Structures	Level 1 Systematic Approach

Figure 28.5   A depiction of Barrington's proposed hierarchy

As depicted in Figure 28.5, Barrington (1984) reviewed experiential learning (Kolb 1984), organizations' training packages and individuals' attempts to learn in a supply chain enhancement context. This analysis was in conjunction with Adair's leadership model which identified group tasks, group harmony and individual happiness. Qualitative descriptions were exclusively used to trace the evolution of training processes through three stages:

- The 'systematic approach' predominated in the 1950s. Managers define job descriptions – the activities undertaken and responsibilities. From this a job specification is created that details the skills and profile of the ideal candidate. Based on analysis leading to formal training plans that are implemented soon after new recruits join the organization. The underlying proposition is that employees will then be able to undertake the set of activities. The principal drawback of this method is that jobs and roles change over time due to external influences.
- The 'dynamic approach' uses employee appraisal interviews as the interface between business requirements, strategies and objectives and performance improvement plans tailored to the individual. This level was developed during the 1960s and uses appraisals as the basis of training needs and career development. This stemmed from the view that a workforce as a whole was no longer competent and static job descriptions and specifications could not keep pace with changing business requirements.
- An approach that adopts 'continuous development' as the *attitude* that leads to integrating work and learning opportunities was developed in the 1970s, following the fuel crises. The attitude stems from a philosophy that thinks positively about problems; viewing them as opportunities for learning. As Deming (1986) noted, this requires that fear is eliminated from the working environment and punitive punishments are abandoned in favour of reward for effort and innovation. Continuous development does not rely on a trainer or manager to push learning experiences on to employees. Individuals themselves identify learning needs and are provided opportunities to decide how best to meet and exploit them. Continuous development is not a defined process or clear set of techniques or tools; rather is a philosophy or commentary on how business and management has evolved:

- from stability to dynamism;
- from descriptions to objectives;
- from systemization to creativity;
- from management command to participative decision;
- from teaching to learning;
- from training alongside work to learning within it.

According to Barrington (1984), continuous development (CD) attitudes liberate individuals from a misguided dependence on an 'authority' that provides teaching and learning experiences. It allows workers to become self-reliant by providing tools and techniques that are widely applicable – employees might not know the answer. They are encouraged to ask: 'How can I find out?' This type of learning is pulled by the 'front-line personnel' – those directly undertaking current value-adding work for the customer. In this environment, managers become facilitators, providing employees with resources to undertake learning activities that are requisite to innovative solutions. The CD approach emphasizes the interrelationships between technical and personnel aspects of day to day operations, and also the need to develop in parallel the technology and competence of people.

Barrington combined five aspects of attitude into the sixth – continuous development:

1. *Continuous enquiry* is an attitude which accepts that few things are ever 100 per cent right or wrong, good or bad, and that there are always new links to be forged between the past and the future. It accepts that learning is not all of one kind and constantly searches for new meanings in any experience. It is *not* cynical about things that seem obvious, but is always ready to review them.
2. *Sensitivity* is an attitude that promotes links with whatever is happening around and about. It uses (and trusts) perceptive skills and faculties and values the outside world (including the people in it) as important and valuable simply by virtue of their existence. It does *not* imply kindness, or a wish to help or serve, but it is always ready to accept what is there without taking a judgemental 'praise or blame' view.
3. *Authority* is an attitude which assumes the right or duty to think strategically for others. It accepts that decisions must be made, and draws on past experience and current knowledge in making them. It does *not* necessarily impose those decisions on the world, but it is always ready to propose a line of action and to present it as the 'best possible'.
4. *Confidence* is an attitude that assumes success – either because the relevant decisions are 'the right ones' or because they are backed by such a level of commitment that the expected results are inevitable. It does not demand support from others, but it does assume that support will be forthcoming if it is needed.
5. Enthusiasm is an attitude that assumes that what is happening is worthwhile and enjoyable. It finds satisfaction in problems and successes alike; it creates ways to communicate that satisfaction to others. It does *not* always report accurately, but selects those aspects of experience that can be praised and ignores the rest.
6. Continuous development is an attitude that assumes 'progress' – in the sense of movement towards a superior future. It draws on and balances all the other attitudes mentioned: having collected information and treated it with respect, it takes a strategic decision and assumes success, enjoying the prospect and communicating it to others, but still looking for further new experiences to produce new information and start the cycle over again. (ibid., pp. 36–7)

Barrington argued that when reading the above six points, if the perception is formed that these are idealistic, the reader is not displaying *any* of those attitudes described.

Lamming (1993, ch. 6) followed the same logic used by Barrington, and thus provided a quasi-supportive approach, using data from 129 interviews, to make the assertion that a majority of the qualitatively described attributes of the phases must be achieved sequentially.

All supplier development initiatives identified in this literature review conform to the systematic approach, with exception of the Honda BP initiative described in Nelson, Mayo and Moody (1988), that emphasized quality circles to identify and correct workplace ergonomics and to stimulate ad hoc improvement suggestions. Honda BP approach used at TRW in Mexico most closely fits with the continuous improvement attitude by focusing on hygiene factors in the work place to stimulate and sustain motivation to improve. The Nelson, Mayo and Moody work does not contain a detailed process, though the TRW case supports the hypothesis of a preconditioning programme.

Summary of Training, Development and Learning

This section of the chapter reviewed elements of training, development, learning and approaches to their management. These are related to conventional supplier development. A balanced strategy based on the Myers-Briggs type indicator has been shown. Barrington's three stages were compared to a supplier development initiative.

Brown et al.'s training, development and learning model reflects the three levels highlighted by Barrington's hierarchy consisting of a systematic approach, an appraisal approach and an attitude to continuous improvement. These converge with Adair's leadership model, which identifies the individual, groups and the task.

It was noted during the preparation of this thesis that philanthropic attitudes found lacking in supply chain and supplier development literature were reflected by the highest level of effectiveness in Barrington's model. The quotation below by F.W. Taylor is indicative of the resentment or 'resistance' that is inherent in trying to attempt change within an organization. The difficulties are compounded by the fact that buyers and suppliers are separate businesses, all be it bonded together via contracts and social commitments.

> I was a young man in years but I give you my word I was a great deal older than I am now, what with the worry, meanness, and contemptibleness of the whole damn thing. It's a horrid life for any man to live not being able to look any workman in the face without seeing hostility there, and a feeling that every man around you is your virtual enemy. (Taylor 1947)

Conclusions

In contemporary supplier development literature and activity, there is a distinct lack of any consideration of learning styles, approaches to training and long-term development of individuals, subgroups or teams. Management must search specialized literature for guidance on implementation issues that are an essential part of relationships between facilitating agents from customer companies, supplier facilitating and coordinating staff,and direct process employees working to produce goods. This chapter concludes that procedural guidelines developed by Hahn et al. (1990a) and Handfield et al. (2000) apply predominantly to indirect preparatory activities by purchasing participants, and that guidelines for the implementation of training and learning events are most noticeable in supplier development literature by their absence. This is intriguing, since suppliers also are assessed on the human and managerial aspects of their businesses. This chapter concludes that direct supplier development activities correlate to learning, teaching and innovative interaction between the participants.

Supplier development training initiatives attempt to redress the shortfall of technical education in schools, colleges and universities. Given the supplier association system, such networks seem ideally suited to sponsor generic industrially oriented academic courses, such as the Jaguar Masters programme at Coventry University, and provide additional specialist learning opportunities for employees, especially on 'train the trainer' courses.

References

Alder, H. (1994), *NLP (Neuro Linguistic Programming): The New Art and Science of Getting What You Want* (London: Piatkus).

Argyris, C. (1993), *Knowledge for Action: A Guide to Overcoming Barriers to Organisational Change* (San Francisco: Jossey-Bass).

Argyris, C. and Schon, D. (1978), *Organizational Learning* (London: Addison-Wesley).

Armstrong, M. (1977), *A Handbook of Personnel Management Practice* (London: Kogan Page).

Ashmore, S. (ed.) (1995), *Supplier Development: Measuring, Developing and Improving Supplier Performance*, ICM Marketing Ltd (International Communications for Management), Cavendish Square Conference Centre, London, 11–12 December.

Badawy, M. (1971), 'Understanding Role Orientations of Scientists and Engineers', *The Personnel Journal* 50(6) June, pp. 449–55.

Badawy, M. (1982), *Developing Managerial Skills in Engineers and Scientists* (New York: Van Nostrand Reinhold).

Baily, P. and Farmer, D. (1982), *Materials Management Handbook* (Aldershot: Gower).

Balderston, J. (1978), 'Do You Really Want to be a Manager?', *Journal of the Society of Research Administrators* 9(4) Spring, pp. 36–42.

Bandler, R. and Grinder, J. (1979), *Frogs into Princes – Neuro Linguistic Programming* (Exeter: Eden Grove Editions).

Barnett, H. (1992), 'Getting the Measure of it!', *Purchasing and Supply Management*, September, pp. 34–7.

Barrington, H. (1984), *Learning About Management* (Maidenhead: McGraw-Hill).

Bayton, J. and Chapman, R. (1972), *Transformation of Scientists and Engineers into Managers* (Washington, DC: National Aeronautics and Space Administration (NASA)).

Beer, M., Eisenstat, R. and Spector, B. (1990), 'Why Change Programs Don't Produce Change', *Harvard Business Review* 68(6), pp. 158–66.

Bennis, W., Parikh, J. and Lessem, R. (1994), *Beyond Leadership: Balancing Economics, Ethics and Ecology* (Oxford: Basil Blackwell Ltd).

Berry, W. (1996), *Negotiating in the Age of Integrity: A Complete Guide to Negotiating Win/Win in Business and Life* (London: Nicholas Brealey).

Bicheno, J. (1997), 'Self Directed Work Teams: Opportunities and Pitfalls,' Institute of Operations Management, IOM Annual Conference.

Biggs, J., Thies, E. and Sisak, J. (1990), 'The Cost of Ordering', *Journal of Purchasing and Materials Management*, Summer, pp. 30–36.

Black, J.T. (1988), 'Cellular Manufacturing Systems', in Voss, C. (ed.) *Just-In-Time Manufacture* (Bedford: IFS Publications Ltd), pp. 27–49.

Blake, R. and Mouton, J. (1969), *Building a Dynamic Corporation through Grid Organization Development* (New York: Addison-Wesley).

Blake, R. and Mouton, J. (1985), *The Managerial Grid III: A New Look at the Classic that has Boosted Productivity and Profits for Thousands of Corporations World-wide* (London: Gulf Publishing Co.).

Blanchard, B. (1992), *Logistics Engineering and Management*, 4th Edn (Upper Saddle River, NJ: Prentice-Hall).

Brandon, J. and Morris, D. (1997), *Just Don't Do It! Challenging Assumptions in Business* (New York: McGraw-Hill).

Bremner, B., Thornton, E. and Kunii, I. (1999), 'Keiretsu', *Business Week*, 15 March, pp. 35–40.

Briggs, P. (1994), 'Vendor Assessment for Partners in Supply', *European Journal of Purchasing and Supply Management* 1(1), pp. 49–59.

Brown, A., Evans, K., Blackman, S. and Germon, S. (1994), *Key Workers: Technical and Training Mastery in the Workplace* (Bournemouth: Hyde Publications).

Burgoyne, J. and Reynolds, M. (1997), *Management Learning: Integrating Perspectives in Theory and Practice* (London: Sage Publications).

Burt, D. and Doyle, M. (1993), *The American Keiretsu: A Strategic Weapon for Global Competitiveness* (Homewood, IL: Business One Irwin).

Calder, J., McCollum, A., Morgan, A. and Thorpe, M. (1995), 'Learning Effectiveness of Open and Flexible Learning in Vocational Education', Research Management Branch, Employment Department, Moorfoot, Sheffield.

Camp, R. (1989), *Benchmarking: The Search for Industry Best Practices that Lead to Superior Performance* (New York: Quality Press).

Campbell, A. and Sommers Luchs, K. (eds) (1997), *Core Competency-based Strategy* (London: International Thomson Business Press).

Carlisle, J. and Parker, R. (1989), *Beyond Negotiation: Redeeming Customer-Supplier Relationships* (Chichester: John Wiley & Sons).

Cayer, S. (1990), 'Caterpillar's Quality Institute', *Purchasing*, 16 August, pp. 80–84.

CBI and Arthur D. Little (1995), *Partnership Sourcing and British Industry: A CBI/Arthur D. Little Survey* (London: Confederation of British Industry).

Chalmers, J. (1996), *Organising Effective Training: How to Plan and Run Successful Courses and Seminars* (Plymouth: How To Books).

Champy, J. (1995), *Re-engineering Management: The Mandate for New Leadership: Managing the Change to the Re-engineered Corporation* (London: HarperCollins Publishers).

Christopher, M. (1997), *Logistics and Supply Chain Management: Strategies for Reducing Costs and Improving Services*, 2nd edn (London: Pitman Publishing).

Collis, D. (1994), 'Research Note – How Valuable are Organisational Capabilities?', *Strategic Management Journal* 15, pp. 143–52.

Consigny, T. (1994), 'EC-Japan Industrial Cupertino Centre', in Hines, P. (ed.) *Creating World Class Suppliers: Unlocking Mutual Competitive Advantage* (London: Pitman Publishing – Financial Times Series), pp. 160–65.

Craig, R. and Bittel, L.R. (eds) (1987), *Training and Development Handbook*, 3rd edn: *A Guide to Human Resource Development* (New York: McGraw-Hill).

Crozier, G. (2000), *Personality* (London: Institute of Management/Hodder and Stoughton).

Crozier, M. and Friedberg, E. (1981), *L'acteur et le systeme* (Paris: Seuil).

Cusumano, M. (1985), *The Japanese Automobile Industry: Technology and Management at Nissan and Toyota* (Boston, MA: Harvard University Press).

Deming, W.E. (1986), *Out of the Crisis* (Cambridge: Cambridge University Press).

Dornier, P., Ernst, R., Fender, M. and Kouvelis, P. (1998), *Global Operations and Logistics: Text and Cases* (New York: John Wiley & Sons).

Drury, C. (1996), *Management and Cost Accounting*, 4th edn (London: Thomson Business Press).

Dunning, J.H. (1977), 'Trade, Location of Economic Activity and the MNE: A Search for an Eclectic Approach', in Ohlin, B., Hellelborn, P.O. and Wijkman, P.M. (eds) *The International Allocation of Economic Activity* (London: Macmillan), pp. 395–431.

Dyer, J. (1996), 'How Chrysler Created an American Keiretsu', *Harvard Business Review* July–August, pp. 42–54.

Dyer, J. and Ouchi, W. (1993), 'Japanese-Style Partnerships: Giving Companies a Competitive Edge', *Sloan Management Review* Fall, pp. 51–63.

Easterby-Smith, M., Burgoyne, J. and Araujo, L. (1999), *Organisational Learning and the Learning Organisation* (London: Sage Publications).

Edwards, N. (1996), 'Preaching the Faith', *Supply Management*, 12 December, pp. 26–8.

Egan, G. (1988a), *Change-Agent Skills A: Assessing and Designing Excellence* (San Diego, CA: University Associates, Inc.).

Egan, G. (1988b), *Change-Agent Skills B: Assessing and Designing Excellence* (San Diego, CA: University Associates, Inc.).

Ellram, L. (1991), 'A Managerial Guideline for the Development and Implementation of Purchasing and Partnerships', *International Journal of Purchasing and Materials Management* March.

Ellram, L. (1993), 'Total Cost of Ownership: Elements and Implementation', International *Journal of Purchasing and Materials Management* October, pp. 3–11.

Engineering Industry Training Board (1969), *Engineering Industry Training Board Report and Accounts 1967* (London: Engineering Industry Training Board).

Esbroeck, R., Butcher, V., Broonen, J. and Klaver, A. (eds) (1997), *Decision Making for Lifelong Learning* (Brussels: Fedora Vubpress).

Finnigan, J. (1970), *Industrial Training Management* (London: Business Books Ltd).

Fisher, R. and Brown, R. (1988), *Getting Together: Building a Relationship that Gets to Yes* (Boston, MD: Houghton Mifflin Co.).

Fisher, R. and Ury, W. (1981), *Getting to Yes, Negotiating Agreement Without Giving In* (London: Hutchinson).

Fletcher, K. (1999), 'The Evolution and Use of Communication and Information in Marketing', in Baker, M. (ed.) *The Marketing Book*, 4th edn (Oxford: Butterworth-Heinemann).

Ford, H. with Crowther, S. (1924), *Today and Tomorrow* (London: Heinemann).

Galt, J. and Dale, B. (1991), 'Supplier Development: A British Case Study', *International Journal of Purchasing Materials Management* January, pp. 16–22.

Gibbs, G. and Habeshaw, T. (1989), *Preparing to Teach: Interesting Ways to Teach: An Introduction to Effective Teaching in Higher Education* (Bristol: Technical and Educational Services Ltd).

Giunipero, L. (1990), 'Motivating and Monitoring JIT Supplier Performance', *Journal of Purchasing and Materials Management* Fall, pp. 19–24.

Grant, R. (1996), 'Prospering in Dynamically-competitive Environments – Organisational Capability as Knowledge Integration', *Organization Science* 7(4), pp. 375–87.

Hahn, C., Watts, C. and Kim, K. (1990a), 'Supplier Development Program at Hyundai Motor', *Journal of Marketing Research*, Spring, pp. 24–36.

Hahn, C., Watts, C. and Kim, K. (1990b), 'The Supplier Development Program: A Conceptual Model', *Journal of Purchasing and Materials Management* Spring, pp. 2–7.

Hakansson, H. (ed.) (1987), *Industrial Technological Development: A Natural Approach* (London: Croom Helm).

Hammer, M. (1990), 'Reengineering Work: Don't Automate, Obliterate', *Harvard Business Review* 68(4) July–August, pp. 104–12.

Hammer, M. (1995), *The Reengineering Revolution: The Handbook* (London: HarperCollins).

Hammer, M. and Champy, J. (1993), *Re-engineering the Corporation: A Manifesto for Business Revolution* (London: Nicholas Brealey Publishing Ltd).

Hampden-Turner, C. (1990), *Corporate Culture: From Vicious to Virtuous Circles* (London: Hutchinson).

Handfield, R., Krause, D., Scannell, T. and Monczka, R. (2000), 'Avoid the Pitfalls in Supplier Development', *Sloan Management Review* Winter, pp. 37–49.

Handy, C. (1993), *Understanding Organisations*, 4th edn (London: Penguin Books).

Hayes, R.H. and Wheelwright, S.C. (1985), *Restoring our Competitive Edge: Competing Through Manufacturing* (New York/Chichester: John Wiley & Sons).

Heirs, B. and Farrell, P. (1989), *The Professional Decision Thinker: Our New Management Priority* (London: Sidgwick and Jackson Ltd).

Heizer, J. and Render, B. (2004), *Operations Management*, 7th edn

Heron, J. (1993), *Group Facilitation: Theories and Models for Practice* (London: Kogan Page).

Hertzberg, F. (1966), *Work and the Nature of Man* (Cleveland, OH: World Publishing Company).

Hines, P. (1994), *Creating World Class Suppliers: Unlocking Mutual Competitive Advantage* (London: Pitman Publishing – Financial Times Series).

HMSO (1964), *Day Release* (London: HMSO).

Honey, P. and Mumford, A. (1992), *The Manual of Learning Styles* (Maidenhead: Peter Honey).

Honey, P. and Mumford, A. (1995), *Using Your Learning Styles*, 3rd edn (Maidenhead: Peter Honey).

Honey, P. and Mumford, A. (1996), *How to Manage Your Learning Environment* (Maidenhead: Peter Honey).

Hooper, M. (1999), 'Company Culture: The Relationship of Organisational Values to Business Excellence', Doctoral thesis, Coventry University.

Institute of Personnel and Development (1996), 'What Makes Training Pay?', *Issues in People Management* 11 (London: IPD), pp. 10–11.

Investors in People UK (1996), *An Introduction to Investors in People: Better People, Better Business* (London: Investors in People UK).

Imai, K., Nonaka, I. and Takeuchi, H. (1985), 'Managing the New Product Development Process: How Japanese Companies Learn and Unlearn', in Clark, K., Hayes, R. and Lorenz, C. (eds) *The Uneasy Alliance: Managing the Productivity-Technology Dilemma* (Cambridge, MA: Harvard Business School Press).

James, B.G. (1989), *The Trojan Horse: The Ultimate Japanese Challenge to Western Industry* (New York: Mercury Business Books).

Johansen, R. and Swighart, R. (1995), *Upsizing the Individual in the Downsized Organization: Managing in the Wake of Reengineering, Globalization and Overwhelming Technological Change* (London: Century Books).

Johnson, R. (1986), *Building Success through People* (London: Business Books).

Kanter, R.M. (1995), *World Class: Thriving Locally in the Global Economy* (New York: Simon & Schuster).

Kao, J. (1991), *The Entrepreneurial Organisation* (Englewood Cliffs, NJ: Prentice Hall).

Kaplan, A. (1996), *The Development Practitioners' Handbook* (London: Pluto Press).

Kirkpatrick, D. (1987), 'Evaluation', in Craig, R.L. and Bittel, L.R. (eds) *Training and Development Handbook*, 3rd edn: *A Guide to Human Resource Development* (New York: McGraw-Hill), pp. 301–19.

Kolb, D. (1984), *Experiential Learning: Experience as the Source of Learning and Development* (Englewood Cliffs, NJ: Prentice Hall).

KPMG Automotive Industry Group (1996), *Europe – the Battle Continues* (London: KPMG).

Krause, D. (1996), 'Success Factors in Supplier Development', NAPM 1996 International Conference, Portland, OR, 21–23 March, pp. 251–59.

Krause, D. (1997a), 'Supplier Development: Current Practices and Outcomes', *International Journal of Purchasing and Materials Management* 33(2) April, pp. 12–19.

Krause, D. and Ellram, L. (1997b), 'Success Factors in Supplier Development', *International Journal of Physical Distribution and Logistics Management* 27(1), pp. 39–52.

Krause, D. and Ellram, L. (1997c), 'Critical Elements of Supplier Development', *European Journals of Purchasing and Supply Management* 3(1), pp. 21–31.

Krause, D. and Handfield, R. (1999), *Developing a World-class Supply Base* (Tempe, AZ: Center for Advanced Purchasing Studies).

Lamming, R. (1993), *Beyond Partnership – Strategies for Innovation and Lean Supply* (London: Prentice Hall International).

Larson, P. (1994), 'Buyer-Supplier Co-operation, Product Quality and Total Costs', *International Journal of Physical Distribution and Logistics Management* 24(6), pp. 4–9.

Lascelles, D. and Dale, B. (1990), 'Examining the Barriers to Supplier Development', *International Journal of Quality and Reliability Management* 7(2), pp. 46–56.

Leenders, M. (1965), *Improving Purchasing Effectiveness through Supplier Development* (Cambridge, MA: Harvard Business School).

Leenders, M. and Blenkhorn, D. (1988), *Reverse Marketing: The New Buyer-Supplier Relationship* (London: Collier Macmillan Publishers).

Luft, J. (1961), 'The Johari Window', *Human Relations and Training News* 5, pp. 6–7.

Lysons, C. (1989), *Purchasing*, 2nd edn (London: Pitman).

Malik, W. and Cushman, A. (1996), 'Riding the Whirlwind: The Transformational Effects of Managing Distributed Systems,' GartnerGroup 26 September.

Manz, C., Neck, C., Mancuso, J. and Manz, K. (1997), *For Team Members Only: Making your Workplace Team Productive and Hassle-free* (New York: AMACOM).

Mayo, A. (1991), *Managing Careers: Strategies for Organisations* (London and Guildford: Institute of Personnel Management/Biddles).

McGinnis, M. and Vallopra, R. (1998), *Purchasing and Supplier Involvement: New Product Development and Production/Operations Process Development and Improvement* (Tempe, AZ: CAPS).

Medori, G.M.D. (1998), 'The Establishment of Non-Financial Performance Measures in Medium to Large Sized Organisations Consistent with World Class Manufacturing Objectives', Doctoral thesis, Coventry University.

Meichenbaum, D. (1977), *Cognitive-Behaviour Modification: An Integrative Approach* (New York: Plenum Press).

Miner, J. (1975), *The Challenge of Managing* (Philadelphia, PA: Saunders).

Miyashita, K. and Russell, D. (1996), *Keiretsu: Inside the Hidden Japanese Conglomerates* (London: McGraw-Hill).

Moingeon, B. and Edmondson, A. (eds) (1996), *Organizational Learning and Competitive Advantage* (London: Sage Publications).

Monczka, R. and Carter, J. (1988), 'Implementing Electronic Data Interchange', *Journal of Purchasing and Materials Management*, 25th Anniversary Edition, Summer, pp. 26–33.

Monczka, R. and Trent, R. (1991), 'Evolving Sourcing Strategies for the 1990s', *International Journal of Physical Distribution and Logistics Management* 21(5), pp. 4–12.

Monczka, R. and Trent, R. (1995), *Purchasing and Sourcing Strategy: Trends and Implications* (Tempe, AZ: CAPS).

Monczka, R., Trent, R. and Callahan, T. (1993), 'Supply Base Strategies to Maximise Supplier Performance', *International Journal of Physical Distribution and Logistics Management* 24(4), pp. 42–54.

Monden, Y. (1983), *Toyota Production System* (Atlanta, CA: Industrial Engineering and Management Press).

Moody, K. (1997), *Workers in a Lean World: Unions in the International Economy* (London: Verso).

Morgan, I. (1987), 'The Purchasing Revolution', *Mckinsey Quarterly* Spring, pp. 149–55.

National Research Council (2000), *Surviving Supply Chain Integration: Strategies for Small Manufacturers* (Washington, DC: National Academy Press).

Nelson, D., Mayo, R. and Moody, P. (1998), *Powered By Honda: Developing Excellence in the Global Enterprise* (New York: John Wiley & Sons).

Newlands, D. and Southey, P. (1994), 'Which Information System is the Most Advantageous? How Should OEMs Relate to Material Suppliers?', 3th Annual IPSERA Conference, Glamorgan, UK, 28–30 March.

Newman, R. and Rhee, K. (1990), 'A Case Study of NUMMI and its Suppliers', *International Journal of Purchasing and Materials Management* 26(4) Fall, pp. 15–20.

Nishiguchi, T. (1994), *Strategic Dualism: The Japanese Advantage* (New York: Oxford University Press).

Nixon, B. (ed.) (1981), *New Approaches to Management Development* (Aldershot: Gower).

Nonaka, I. and Takeuchi, H. (1995), *The Knowledge-Creating Company: How Japanese Companies Create the Dynamics of Innovation* (New York: Oxford University Press).

Oates, D. (1998), *Outsourcing and the Virtual Organisation: The Incredible Shrinking Company* (London: Century Books).

O'Connor, J. and Seymour, J. (1994), *Training with NLP: Neuro-Linguistic Programming* (London: HarperCollins).

Odiborne, G. (1961), *How Managers Make Things Happen* (Englewood Cliffs, NJ: Prentice Hall).

O'Laughlin K., Cooper J. and Cabocel E. (1993), *Reconfiguring European Logistics Systems* (Oak Brook, IL: Council of Logistics Management).

Otabe, A. (1991), Production Technologies of Japanese Subcontractors, Customer-Supplier Relationships Tour, EC-Japan Centre for Industrial Cupertino.

Palmer, A. (1999), 'The Marketing of Services', in Baker, M. (ed.) *The Marketing Book*, 4th edition (Oxford: Butterworth-Heinemann), pp. 667–92.

Park, A. (1994), 'Individual Commitment to Learning: Individual's Attitudes – Report on the Quantitative Survey', Research Management Branch, Employment Department, Moorfoot, Sheffield.

Partnership Sourcing Ltd. (1992), *Partnership Sourcing* (London: DTI).

Pedler, M., Burgoyne, J. and Boydell, T. (1994), *A Manager's Guide to Self-Development*, 3rd edn (Maidenhead: McGraw-Hill).

Peters, T. (1994), *The Tom Peters Seminar – Crazy Times Call for Crazy Organisations* (London: Macmillan).

Porter, M. (1980), *Competitive Strategy: Techniques for Analyzing Industries and Competitors* (New York: Free Press/Macmillan).

Porter, M. (1985), *Competitive Advantage: Creating and Sustaining Superior Performance* (New York: Free Press/Macmillan).

Porter, M. (1990), *The Competitive Advantage of Nations* (New York: Free Press/Macmillan).

Pritchard, J. (1996), 'How Can Suppliers Develop Themselves to Become "Preferred" Suppliers', in Ashmore, S. (ed.) *Supplier Development: Measuring, Developing and Improving Supplier Performance*, ICM Marketing Conference, London, UK, 11–12 December.

Reid, M. and Barrington, H. (1997), *Training Interventions: Managing Employee Development*, 5th edn (London: IPD).

Rhodes, D. (1996), 'Who Needs Strategy?', *Manufacturing Engineer, IEE* December, pp. 264–67.

Ross, D. (1998), *Competing Through Supply Chain Management: Creating Marketing Winning Strategies Through Supply Chain Partnerships* (New York: Chapman & Hall/International Thomson Publishing).

Saunders, M. (1997), *Strategic Purchasing and Supply Chain Management*, 2nd edn (London: Pitman Publishing).

Schaffer, R. and Thomson H. (1992), *Successful Change Programmes Begin with Results* (Cambridge, MA: Harvard Business School Press).

Schonberger, R. (1982), *Japanese Manufacturing Techniques: Nine Hidden Lessons in Simplicity* (New York: Free Press).

Schonberger, R. (1987), *World Class Manufacturing: The Lessons of Simplicity Applied* (New York: Free Press).

Schonberger, R. (1990), *Building a Chain of Customers: Linking Business Functions to Create the World Class Company* (London: Hutchinson Business Books Ltd).

Schonberger, R. and Ansari, A. (1984), '"Just-In-Time" Purchasing Can Improve Quality', *Journal of Purchasing and Materials Management* Spring, pp. 2–7.

Senge, P. (1990), *The Fifth Discipline, The Art and Practice of the Learning Organisation* (London: Century Press).

Shank, J. and Govindarajan, V. (1993), *Strategic Cost Management – The New Tool for Competitive Advantage* (New York: Free Press).

Shapiro, E. (1996), *Fad Surfing in the Boardroom: Reclaiming the Courage to Manage in the Age of Instant Answers* (Oxford: Capstone).

Sheal, P. (1989), *How to Develop and Present Staff Training Courses* (New York: Kogan Page/Nichols Publishing).

Sheth, J.N. (1981), 'Consumer Behaviour: Surpluses and Shortcomings', *Advances in Consumer Research* 9, Twelfth Annual Conference, Missouri, Association for Consumer Research, pp. 667–78

Smith, A. (1776), *The Wealth of Nations*, reprinted 1986 (London: Penguin).

Smith, G. (1995), *Managing to Succeed: Strategies and Systems for Manufacturing Businesses* (London: Prentice Hall International).

Smytka, D. and Clemens, M. (1993), 'Total Cost Supplier Selection Model: A Case Study', *International Journal of Purchasing and Materials Management* Winter, pp. 42–9.

Southey, P. and Newlands, D. (1994), 'Supply Networks: Can Customers Drive Supplier Improvements?', 10th IMP Annual Conference, Groningen, The Netherlands, 29 September–1 October.

Souza, S. (1993), *The Oliver Wight ABCD Checklist*, 4th edn (New York: John Wiley & Sons).

Stalk, G., Evans, P. and Shulman, L. (1992), 'Competing on Capabilities: The New Rules of Corporate Strategy', *Harvard Business Review* 70, pp. 57–69.

Stiglitz, J.E. (1987), Learning to Learn, Localized Learning and Technological Progress', in Dasgupta, P. and Stoneman (eds) *Economic Policy and Technological Performance* (Cambridge: Cambridge University Press).

Storck, J. and Hill, P. (2000), 'Knowledge Diffusion through "Strategic Communities"', *Sloan Management Review* 41(2), pp. 63–74.

Sugimori, Y., Kusnohi, K., Cho, F. and Uchikawa, S. (1977), 'Toyota Production System and Kanban System: Materialisation of Just-in-Time and Respect for Human System', *International Journal of Production Research* 15(6), pp. 553–64.

Susman, G. (1992), *Integrating Design and Manufacturing for Competitive Advantage* (New York and Oxford: Oxford University Press).

Syrett, M. and Lammiman, J. (1997), *From Leanness to Fitness: Developing Corporate Muscle: The Role of HR in Developing Corporate Muscle* (London: The Institute of Personnel and Development).

Syson, R. (1992), *Improving Purchase Performance* (London: Pitman Publishing).

Taylor, F. (1947), *Scientific Management* (New York: Harper Row).

Thomas, A. (1995), *Coaching for Staff Development* (Leicester: BPS Books).

Thomas, J. and Bennis, W. (eds) (1972), *Management of Change and Conflict* (Baltimore, MD: Penguin Books).

Toffler, A. (1971), *Future Shock* (London: Pan Books).

Voss, C. (ed.) (1988), *Just-in-Time Manufacture* (Bedford: IFS Publications Ltd),

Walker, P. (1995), 'How Can Suppliers Develop Themselves to Become "Preferred" Suppliers?', in Ashmore, S. (ed.) *Supplier Development: Measuring, Developing and Improving Supplier Performance*, ICM Marketing Ltd (International Communications for Management), Cavendish Square Conference Centre, London, 11–12 December.

Walther, G. (1993), *Say What You Mean and Get What You Want* (London: Judy Piatkus).

Warren, I. (1995), 'How Customers Select Key Performance Indicators Against Which Suppliers are to be Measured', in Ashmore, S. (ed.) *Supplier Development: Measuring, Developing and Improving Supplier Performance*, ICM Marketing Ltd (International Communications for Management), Cavendish Square Conference Centre, London, 11–12 December.

Watson, G.H. (1994), *Business Systems Engineering: Managing Breakthrough Changes for Productivity and Profit* (New York: John Wiley & Sons).

Watts, C. and Hahn, C. (1993), 'Supplier Development Programmes: An Empirical Analysis', *International Journal of Purchasing and Materials Management* 29(2), Spring, pp. 11–17.

Weaver, R. and Farrell, J. (1997), *Managers as Facilitators: A Practical Guide to Getting Work Done in a Changing Workplace* (San Francisco: Berrett-Koehler Publishers).

Wickens, P. (1997), *The Ascendant Organisation*, IOM National Conference Proceedings.

Williams, K., Haslam, C., Williams, J., Cutler, T., Adcroft, A. and Johal, S. (1992), 'Against Lean Production', *Economy and Society* 21(3), August, pp. 321–54.

Wilson, J. (2000), *Test Your Management Style, Institute of Management* (London: Hodder and Stoughton).

Womack, J. and Jones, D. (1996), *Lean Thinking: Banish Waste and Create Wealth in Your Corporation* (New York: Simon & Schuster).

Womack, J., Jones, D. and Roos, D. (1991), *The Machine that Changed the World* (New York: Rawson Associates).

Wood, S. (ed). (1988), *Continuous Improvement: The Path to Improved Performance* (London: IPD).

Wood, S., Barrington H. and Johnson R. (1988), 'An Introduction to Continuous Development', in Wood, S. (ed.) *Continuous Improvement: The Path to Improved Performance* (London: IPD).

Zimmermann, B. (1988), 'Rank Xerox', in Voss, C. (ed.) *Just-In-Time Manufacture* (Bedford: IFS Publications Ltd), pp, 251–80.

International Entrepreneurship: Developing Cross-cultural Entrepreneurial Competence

Olga Muzychenko

Introduction

Research Influencing suggests entrepreneurs increasingly search for opportunities in foreign countries (Austrade 2002). This is primarily due to the rise of global entrepreneurship that is reflected in the proliferation of small and medium size Enterprises that export goods and services and emergence of a new breed of entrepreneurial ventures, namely 'born globals' (ibid.; Hill 2005; Oviatt and McDougall 1995). Also, there is now a significant representation of ethnic/migrant entrepreneurs in the overall population of entrepreneurs in many Western countries and in Anglo-Saxon cluster in particular (Ram 2003; Collins et al. 1997).

This chapter explores the influence of the cross-cultural environment on the behaviour of international entrepreneurs and its effectiveness. The aim is to review the effects of growing cross-cultural and cross-border interaction on the content of entrepreneurial tasks and competencies.

International Entrepreneurship

Empirical Influencing (Acs 1992) has confirmed that changes in the global economy increase the prominence of entrepreneurship as a vehicle to maintain economic growth through innovation and job creation. In this era of globalization, the economic wellbeing of any country depends on the extent to which local companies are integrated in the international economy (Muzychenko and Saee 2003). Entrepreneurs increasingly transcend national borders in their quest to start up or grow their ventures and, thus, contribute to international competitiveness of the host national economy (McDougall and Oviatt 2000). These trends stem from:

- the shift toward a knowledge-based economy;
- increased fragmentation of the value chain;
- the proliferation of niche markets;
- the formation of global markets; and
- globalization of production.

There is a decrease in the cost of conducting business internationally due to:

- accessibility of information;
- reduced costs of transportation; and
- advanced communication technologies including e-commerce (Hill 2005).

Regional economic integration and proliferation of bilateral free trade agreements simplify access to regional markets (Aldrich and Martinez 2001).

Empirical Influencing by Austrade (2002) suggests that companies with an international scope of operations perform better than those that concentrate on serving domestic markets only. From the policy makers' perspective, it is notable that those companies that internationalize early appear to have high growth aspirations and overall are more likely to exhibit faster growth (Autio et al. 2000; Oviatt and McDougal 1995). As a consequence, they will therefore contribute earlier and more to the national economy. Maintaining a highly competitive national economy in a global context requires better integration of local businesses in global markets along with moving up the value chain through research commercialization and innovation.

Acceleration of international entrepreneurship and its significance from policy makers' perspectives led to the rise of research that reflect specific issues facing entrepreneurs as they expand their ventures internationally (Zahra et al. 2000). International entrepreneurship, as a field of study, focuses on 'the discovery, enactment, Evaluation and exploitation of opportunities across national borders to Create future goods and services' (McDougall and Oviatt 2003, p. 7) and is growing rapidly.

What do Entrepreneurs Do: Entrepreneurial Tasks

Entrepreneurs undertake purposeful tasks in order to take advantage of apparent, transitory and seldom obvious opportunities (Knight 1921). Writers on this subject consider opportunity identification, risk taking, team building (Brush et al. 2001) and resource alignment (Alvarez and Barney 2001; Brush et al. 2001; Bygrave 1997; Ireland et al. 2001; Timmons et al. 1994) as distinctive entrepreneurial tasks.

Opportunity Identification

Opportunity identification can be defined as an insight into the commercial value of an idea or turning an idea into a business concept (Bhave 1994; Hills and Shrader 1998). Opportunity identification is a process that consists of three stages:

- opportunity search/development;
- opportunity recognition; and
- opportunity evaluation (Lindsay and Craig 2002; Hills and Shrader 1998).

Why do some entrepreneurs recognize opportunities while others do not? One answer to this question is that cognitive processes play an important role in opportunity identification. There is something very different in entrepreneur's thinking, reasoning and information processing (Mitchell et al. 2004, 2000, 2002).

Cognitive research in the field of entrepreneurship provides insight into the thinking, reasoning and information-processing mechanisms behind discovery, evaluation and exploitation of opportunities (Baron 1998; Busenitz and Lau 1997; Forbes 1999; Gaglio 2004; de Konig 2003; Mitchell et al. 2000, 2002, 2004; Simon et al. 1999). Two major theories help explain how entrepreneurs think:

1. the theory of social cognition sees human behaviour as a function of interaction between person and environment (Fiske and Taylor 1984); and

2. information processing theory explains the mechanisms of cognition, that is, information acquisition, transformation, elaboration and use (Neisser 1967) and differences in cognitive processes of experts and non-experts (Glaser 1984).

According to information processing theory, experts' knowledge is arranged into particular structures, scripts or heuristics, which are acquired through cognitions that emerge from real-life experience (ibid.). It is the use of such structured knowledge that explains the performance of experts including entrepreneurs (Mitchell et al. 2000).

Essentially, entrepreneurship is a network activity (Birley 1984) and opportunity recognition occurs necessarily in a network context. De Koning (2003) argued that opportunity development, that is, developing initial opportunity ideas toward a business concept, is a socio-cognitive process. She identified four types of cognitive activity undertaken in different segments of entrepreneurs' social context and reliant on various networks:

- information scanning occurs thought networks of weak ties;
- information seeking – through the network of entrepreneurs and experts (a subset of network of weak ties);
- thinking – through talking within the inner circle network (people who are personally close to the entrepreneur); and
- assessing resources within the entrepreneur's action set (the network of strong ties, or a team behind business concept, built by entrepreneurs to pursue the opportunity).

Risk Taking

Risk taking is an essential entrepreneurial task. This is because entrepreneurs must act under conditions of uncertainty (Knight 1921; Yamada 2004). Some see risk taking as a generic entrepreneurial personality trait. The cognitive perspective on entrepreneurship suggests this is a behaviour and not a personality trait. Risk-taking behaviour is based on various cognitive scripts (knowledge structures) employed to evaluate and reduce the risks that the entrepreneur might face (Mitchell et al. 2000). Empirical Influencing shows that entrepreneurs tend to reduce their emphasis on apparent risk (Simon 1999) – in effect they ignore the danger signs and they have absolute confidence in their abilities to cope with eventualities. Barron suggested that an accurate risk assessment is one of the cognitive factors that successful entrepreneurs have to possess (Barron and Markman 2000). Risk evaluation by entrepreneurs requires the cognitive map as a point of reference in this process (Mitchell et al. 2004).

Risk evaluation is not a totally rational process. This is due to some natural human characteristics such as limited information-processing capacity, the quest to minimize cognitive effort and inclination to use cognitive 'short cuts' (Baron 1998, 2004; Stephan and Stephan 1996).

Entrepreneurs often act under conditions of information overload, lack of time to undertake advanced data analysis, concept novelty and environmental uncertainty, and hence they are subject to intense emotions and their cognitive processes are particularly susceptible to the use of cognitive 'short cuts' (Baron 1998). They also tend to mitigate risks through reliance on heuristics and biases rather than rational analysis (Aldrich and Martinez 2001; Busenitz and Barney 1997).

Heuristics are informal, intuitive cognitive frameworks that facilitate the discovery of quick solutions to problems (Nisbett and Ross 1980). Biases are predisposed judgements that stem from specific heuristics (Bazerman 1990).

Team Building

The importance of team building in the process of new venture creation is well documented. Evidence from entrepreneurship literature shows that individual entrepreneurs are much less likely to succeed than are teams (Brush et al. 2001; Timmons et al. 2004). Moreover, Timmons (ibid.) suggested that a team is prerequisite for creating a higher potential entrepreneurial company. Therefore, team building and teamwork are identified as one of the entrepreneur's essential skills (GEM Australia 2001). Successful entrepreneurs seek team members based on what the opportunity requires (Timmons et al. 1994) and ensure that the team can work together to produce a heterogeneous effort directed to achieve common objectives (Bounchen 2004).

Resource Alignment

Resource alignment and building a resource base from scratch is a challenging entrepreneurial task due to a lack of a venture reputation and absence of a track record (Brush et al. 2001). Resources needed to create new ventures are numerous and they can be categorized into six types:

1. human;
2. social;
3. financial;
4. physical;
5. technological; and
6. organizational (Greene and Brown 1997).

During the initial stages of organization creation, entrepreneurs seldom possess more than human (experience, education and reputation) and social (industry contacts) capital. Typically they have to leverage those to obtain the remaining resources.

The commercialization of entrepreneurial ideas requires distribution, manufacturing, marketing and other organizational resources that small entrepreneurial ventures often do not have (Alvarez and Barney 2001). To access critical resources without owning them entrepreneurial ventures can join networks of companies or enter into strategic alliances (Bygrave 1997; Ireland et al. 2001; Oviat and McDougall 1995).

How do Entrepreneurs Achieve Outcomes: Entrepreneurial Competencies

Competence is a multifaceted phenomenon that can be analysed from three angles:

1. inputs (antecedents);
2. process (behaviour); and
3. outcomes (achieving the accepted standard level) (Mole et al. 1993).

Which are the antecedents of competence or what predisposes a person to exhibit competent behaviour? One's personality traits, body of knowledge and a set of skills and abilities delineate predispositions. Bartlett and Ghoshal (1997) and Parry (1998) distinguish between internalized and externalized elements of competence. Internalized elements are 'deeply embedded personal characteristics … intrinsic parts of the individual's character and personality' (Barlett and Ghosal 1997, p. 104) and are very unlikely to be affected in any way by training. Externalized elements could be acquired through training and include knowledge, experience and understanding and skills and abilities.

Entrepreneurial competence is defined as the set of knowledge, skills and abilities that enables an entrepreneur to successfully perform the job role (Baum et al. 2001; Chandler and Hanks 1994; Man and Lau 2000; Man et al. 2002).

Chandler and Hanks (1994) differentiated between managerial competencies that entrepreneurs need to possess to capitalize on the opportunity and to ensure venture performance and competencies unique to entrepreneurs. Man et al. (2002) identified seven clusters of entrepreneurial competence and pertinent component behaviours. These clusters are:

1. opportunity: identifying, seeking and assessing opportunities;
2. relationship: building, keeping and using networks and relationships; building, keeping and using trust and confidence; exposing to the media; communicating; negotiating; managing conflicts; building consensus;
3. conceptual: thinking intuitively; viewing various dimensions of business from different angle; innovating; assessing risks;
4. organizing: planning; organizing resources and developing efficient systems and processes; leading; motivating; delegating; controlling;
5. strategic: setting and evaluating vision and goals; using resources and capabilities to develop opportunities into outcomes; making strategic change; achieving set goals; monitoring strategy implementation;
6. commitment: sustaining effort; exerting long term commitment to goals; devotion to work; commitment to staff; commitment to personal beliefs; values and goals; tolerating failure and persevering;
7. supporting competencies: learning; adapting; managing time; self-evaluation; leading balanced life; managing anxiety and stress; integrity.

The next section introduces the notion of culture as the context for entrepreneurial tasks and competencies.

Culture as the Context for Entrepreneurial Tasks and Competencies

Culture, Human Behaviour and Cognition

Culture is a difficult phenomenon to define. Kroeber and Kluckhohn (1985) found 164 definitions of culture in the literature. From a social perspective, culture can be seen as a system of values, beliefs and attitudes that are shared by the members of a society. Hofstede (1991) viewed culture as the collective programming of minds that distinguish members of one category of people from another.

The link between national culture and human behaviour interests anthropologists and sociologists alike. 'Cultural dimensions' theorists (Kluckholn and Strodbeck 1961; Hall 1976; Hofstede 1991; Hofstede and Bond 1984; Trompenaars 1993) perceive human behaviour as a function of culture. Although this Approach has been criticized for its limited view in explaining human behaviour by culturally-bound system of values, beliefs and attitudes, it provides a valuable insight into different dimensions of culture that have a direct effect on human behaviour, and how human behaviour varies depending on dominating cultural dimensions.

Hofstede (1980), for example, suggested five cultural dimensions delineate cultural differences between societies. These dimensions are:

- collectivism versus individualism – perception of an individual as an autonomous person or as a member of a social group/family;
- small versus large power distance – the perception of inequality in the society;
- strong versus weak uncertainty avoidance – the level of ambiguity tolerance;
- femininity versus masculinity – the perception of gender roles in the society;
- Confucian dynamism – long- versus short-term time orientation.

In his exploration of cultural dimensions, Hofstede (1991) established a link between national culture and variations in human behaviour, such as, communication, relationship building, networking and goal orientation.

Cross-cultural psychologists look at the human mind to explain how differences in human behaviour across cultures may affect one's sense-making mechanism and the effectiveness and appropriateness of one's behaviour. Our cognitive processes allow us to make sense of our environment fairly easily and to interact with others effectively as long as we deal with people whose behaviour is directed by the same set of cultural beliefs and values as our own. This is because the human mind is programmed by the system of cultural beliefs and values that are unique to the ethnic group and are subconsciously absorbed by individuals from a very early age (Samovar and Porter 1995). But what happens if one enters the culturally alien environment of a foreign country? Unfamiliar cultural territory can negatively affect an individual's affective and sense-making/cognitive mechanisms due to one's inability to accurately perceive and interpret the alien cultural environment and explain and predict the behaviour of people of different cultural background(s) (Kim 1988, 1991, 1995; Gudykunst 1991, 1993; Ruben 1976; Ruben and Kealey 1979; Saee 1999, 2004). Therefore, the appropriateness and effectiveness of one's behavioural responses are thrown into question.

Entrepreneurs who cross national boundaries in pursuit of business opportunities will face challenges in understanding what the effective and appropriate behaviours in the cultural environment different from their own are. They also will need to learn to extend the capacity of their cognitive system to deal with these challenges as a result of developing a coping mechanism.

The next section explores how entrepreneurial process may be affected, should an entrepreneur need to perform his/her tasks within a cross-cultural business environment and what challenges may be endemic to the process of international entrepreneurship as a result.

Opportunity Identification and Culture

Opportunity identification is grounded in entrepreneurs' perception and interpretation of the environment (Bird 1992; Baron 2004) with the entrepreneur integrated within his/her operating environment at the individual level (Bouchikhi 1993). It is legitimate to assume that the knowledge scripts – the foundation for an entrepreneur's perception and interpretation processes – are, to a larger or smaller extent, culturally specific. This is because they are based on one's personal experiences that took place in a particular cultural environment and, thus, a culturally alien environment will negatively affect the effectiveness of cognitive processes enacted in opportunity identification. Entrepreneur's networking that forms an important part in opportunity development varies across cultures (Drakopolou-Dodd and Patra 2002). This is further complicated by culturally determined behavioural differences in communication and relationship building (Hall 1976; Hofstede 1991; Saee 2004).

Thus, opportunity and relationship competencies developed in one's own cultural environment may not be sufficient for effective opportunity recognition in a culturally alien environment.

Risk Taking and Culture

Risk taking tends to be based on cognitive maps that have inherent biases and heuristics (Mitchell et al. 2004). However, biases and heuristics are grounded in an entrepreneur's cultural values (Busentiz and Lau 1997) and, therefore, their cognitive map may not be applicable across different cultural contexts.

Thus, conceptual competencies related to risk evaluation developed in one's own cultural environment may not be sufficient for effective risk evaluation in culturally alien environments.

Team Building and Culture

Whilst building a team, the entrepreneur may consciously choose , or be required by law, to have culturally diverse team members (partners) to provide the venture with a unique competitive edge, enhanced creativity potential, and knowledge of networks within foreign markets (Bounchen 2004; Groen et al. 2003). For example, Groen et al. (ibid.) argued that nations are often endowed with distinct competencies such as design of products (French and Italians), manufacturing (Germans) and marketing (Dutch and British). Culturally diverse entrepreneurial teams can help merge these different talents.

The creative power of cultural diversity has been acknowledged in the management literature (Adler 1997). Florida (2001, 2002, 2005) argues that openness to cultural diversity enhances the pool of potential new ideas and speeds up information and knowledge exchange.

Although cultural diversity brings numerous benefits, the literature on management of culturally diverse teams suggests that cultural differences may lead to increased ambiguity, complexity, confusion, anxiety, and conflict within the team due to cultural differences in people's behaviour and value system.

Thus, relationship and organizational competencies such as communication, negotiation, conflict management, consensus building, leadership, motivation, delegation and control competencies developed in one's own cultural environment may not be sufficient for effective team building in cross-cultural environment.

Resource Alignment and Culture

National borders do not delineate resource alignment by entrepreneurs. This is because differences in competitive advantage between countries and the low cost of conducting cross-border transactions opens new horizons for entrepreneurs as far as global search for procuring the best resources at the best prices is concerned (Oviatt and McDougall 1995). Further, in some instances entrepreneurs find it more appropriate to look for financing beyond the borders of their home country (ibid.). In addition, because of the resource constraints entrepreneurial ventures have to leverage resources externally through strategic alliances and networks. Culture has numerous affects on the participation of entrepreneurial ventures in networks and strategic alliances. Acceptance into the strategic alliance network depends on how well the entrepreneur is able to communicate his/her vision of the venture to the potential alliance partners (ibid.). Brush et al. (2001) identified five competencies considered most crucial for entrepreneurs in attracting resources:

1. social perception (accurate assessment of intentions and motives of others);
2. impression management (ability to induce positive reactions from others);
3. expressiveness (ability to express one's affective state clearly and generate enthusiasm in others);
4. persuasiveness (the ability to change others' behaviours or views); and
5. social adaptability (ability to feel comfortable in a wide range of social situations).

Networks and strategic alliances are increasingly becoming international in their reach and nature (Gluati et al. 2000; Hagedoorn and Duysters 1996). Entrepreneurs' thus have to be effective communicators with international alliance partners. The level of conflict and 'good will' depend on an understanding of counterparts' communication and management culture. Further, the preference for organizational forms of an alliance (equity ties versus flexible arrangements) is culturally determined (Steensma et al. 2000), and therefore understanding cultural preferences of potential alliance partners can assist in the process of partner selection and negotiation.

The author contends that organizing and relationship competencies developed in one's own cultural environment may not be sufficient for effective resource alignment in a cross-cultural environment.

The above discussion asserts that culture, as a variable, interjects with the content of entrepreneurial process and entrepreneurial competencies developed in one cultural environment. These competencies may not guarantee effective performance if the entrepreneur is to operate in a cross-cultural setting. This is because entrepreneurial venture performance is the function of congruence between the entrepreneur's competence and entrepreneurial tasks. Such congruence in a cross-cultural environment can be achieved by complementing entrepreneurial competencies by cross-cultural entrepreneurial competence. Its role in the interrelationship between culture, entrepreneurial competencies and entrepreneurial tasks is illustrated by the Figure 29.1.

The next section introduces the notion of cross-cultural entrepreneurial competence.

Cross-cultural Entrepreneurial Competence

A vast array of cross-cultural literature suggests that challenges inherent in cross-cultural interactions can be overcome through developing cross-cultural competence (Gudykunst 1993).

Being 'competent' means being able to achieve intended outcomes. Cross-cultural competence theorists look at outcomes across three dimensions (ibid.):

1. communication as a foundation of relationship building with individuals coming from different cultural background;
2. psychological adjustment to the new culture; and
3. doing well in one's job.

Therefore, international entrepreneurs need to develop cross-cultural communication competence, psychological adaptability competence and entrepreneurial tasks related cross-

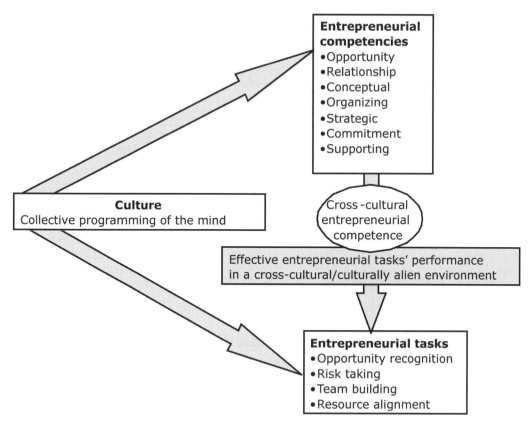

Figure 29.1 **Interrelationship between culture, entrepreneurial competencies and entrepreneurial tasks and the role of cross-cultural entrepreneurial competence**

cultural competence. Cross-cultural entrepreneurial competence can be defined as knowledge, skills and abilities that lead to appropriate and effective behaviour of the entrepreneur and, thus, effective entrepreneurial task performance in a cross-cultural environment. Its elements are depicted in Figure 29.2.

Psychologists, sociologists and anthropologists have contributed significantly to understanding the process of cross-cultural communication and psychological adaptation in the foreign environment. There is little doubt these two 'building blocks' or dimensions of cross-cultural professional competence can be applied universally across all professional fields. These two dimensions are now considered and then we attempt to complement this discussion by exploring how international entrepreneurs may generate competent responses in relation to task content and process specific issues affected by culture as a variable.

Almost everything that people do involves interacting with others. This interaction occurs through communication and building interpersonal relationships. Gudykunst (1991) and Spitzberg and Kupach (1984; see also Dodd 1998) argued that cross-cultural communication competence is about minimizing misunderstanding, while Lustig and Koester (1999) perceived appropriateness and effectiveness of one's behaviour as being a function of knowledge, behavioural skills and motivations.

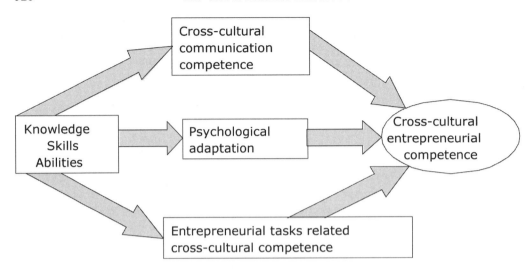

Figure 29.2   Cross-cultural entrepreneurial competence

Developing cross-cultural communication competence requires:

- culture general knowledge, or what is culture and what are its components (Lustig and Koester 1993);
- culture specific knowledge, or one's own and others' cultural attributes, including similarities and differences between the cultural groups (ibid.);
- knowledge of what is appropriate to do to have an effective communication outcome (ibid.; Ruben and Kealey 1979);
- understanding of dialectical perspective on multiple variables in cross-cultural communication such as power, personality, social class, etc. (Martin and Nakayma 1999);
- personal qualities such as empathy, respect, non-judgmentalness, openness (Saee 2004);
- ability to perform role behaviours (Saee 2004);
- interaction management (ibid.);
- ability to establish meaningful interpersonal relationships through understanding the feelings of others (ibid.);
- ability to work effectively with others (Walter et al., cited in Dodd 1993);
- ability to deal with different social customs (Gudykunst et al. 1977; Ruben and Kealey 1979).

Psychological Adaptability

Cross-cultural individual adaptability is considered in the literature through the focus on personal traits and attributes that help to generate internal psychological responses in the alien environment. The following abilities are associated with successful psychological adaptation in the new cultural environment through managing stress and reducing anxiety and uncertainty:

- being able to be mindful, to tolerate ambiguity and to calm ourselves (Gudykunst and Kim 1997);
- being able to explain and make accurate predictions of strangers' behaviour (Gudykunst 1991);
- being aware that stress, anxiety and uncertainty affect both sides of the intercultural encounter – the stranger and the host (Saee 1999);

According to Walters et al. (cited in Dodd 1998), adaptability to foreign cultural environment depends on flexibility, maturity, knowledge of host culture, language skills, non-judgemental attitude, patience, respect for culture, and appropriate social behaviour.

Cross-cultural communication and psychological adaptation are interrelated closely: successful psychological adaptation facilitates effective communication. Effective communication also can speed up the process of psychological adaptation (Gudykunst 1991).

Table 29.1   Task specific elements of cross-cultural entrepreneurial competence and corresponding competence clusters

The elements of cross-cultural entrepreneurial competence	Competence clusters
Ability to exert global vision by detaching oneself from business thinking delineated by a single country or culture (Oviatt and McDougall 1995; Johnson 2004)	Opportunity Strategic
Ability to use foreign investors in order to gain access to their networks and thus develop global vision by being exposed to international opportunities (Maula and Makela 2003)	Opportunity Relationship
Avoiding over-reliance on previous international business experience and minimizing the tendency to look for 'tried and true' solutions by exercising creativity and trial-and-error learning (George et al. 2004)	Conceptual Supporting
Understanding differences in networking behaviour across cultures and the ability to build and develop a cross-border network (Muzychenko 2006)	Relationship
Ability to Create Wealth by reconciling conflicting cultural values (Trompenaars and Hampden-Turner, 2000) and through 'intellectual internationalization' (Geursen and Dana 2001)	Opportunity Conceptual
Awareness of cultural differences in the behaviour of investors (Oviatt and McDougall 1995)	Relationship
Awareness and understanding of dominant entrepreneurial cognitive archetypes across cultures in order to better manage stakeholder relationships in cross-border alliances and partnerships (Mitchell et al. 2002)	Relationship
Awareness of the culturally determined preference for organizational forms of an alliance, such as equity ties versus flexible arrangements (Steensma et al. 2000)	Relationship Organizing
Understanding of cognitive biases strongly related to risk evaluation such as illusion of control and belief in the law of small numbers coupled with ability to take appropriate actions to overcome these biases (Keh et al. 2002)	Conceptual
Ability to establish moral legitimacy of the venture, that is, that the new venture conforms to the cultural norms and values of the society (Aldrich and Martinez 2001)	Opportunity Organizing
Understanding potential cross-cultural communication problems and conflicts that are likely to arise in the context of international expansion of entrepreneurial venture (Oviatt and McDougall 1995)	Relationship Organizing

Entrepreneurial Tasks Related Cross-cultural Competence

Although cross-cultural competence has been given considerable attention over the last twenty-five years or so, the field of study has been largely dominated by psychologists, sociologists and anthropologists who have contributed toward the understanding of process of cross-cultural communication and psychological adaptation in the foreign environment. There is little justification to doubt that the content of 'interpersonal relationships' and 'adaptability' dimensions of cross-cultural professional competence can be applied universally across all professional fields. To gain insights into effective professional task performance across cultures, an understanding of effective communication and successful psychological adaptation has to be complemented by exploring the effect of culture on task content and process (Hughes-Wiener 1986). In this chapter an initial conceptualization of the effect of cross-cultural environment on entrepreneurial tasks content and process has been provided. Table 29.1 summarizes influencing of task specific elements relevant to cross-cultural entrepreneurial competence and to which entrepreneurial competence cluster(s) they correspond.

Conclusions

The environment in which entrepreneurs create and grow new ventures is affected by globalization of the world economy. As a result of growth in international entrepreneurship and the rise of ethnic entrepreneurship major entrepreneurial tasks, namely opportunity recognition, risk-taking, team building and resource acquisition are now often performed in a cross-cultural business environment.

In this chapter we conceptualized the effect of cross-cultural environment on entrepreneurial tasks content and process. Meanwhile, entrepreneurial venture performance is the function of congruence between the entrepreneur's competence and entrepreneurial tasks. Such congruence in a cross-cultural environment can be achieved through developing cross-cultural entrepreneurial competence.

References

Acs, Z. (1992), 'Small Business Economics: A Global Perspective', *Challenge* 35, pp. 38–44.

Adler, N. (1997), International Dimensions of Organisational Behaviour, 3rd edn (Cincinnati, OH: South-Western College Publishing).

Aldrich, H. and Martinez, M. (2001), 'Many are Called, but Few are Chosen: An Evolutionary Perspective on the Study of Entrepreneurship', *Entrepreneurship Theory and Practice* Summer, pp. 41–56.

Alvarez, S. and Barney, J. (2001), 'How Entrepreneurial Firms can Benefit from Alliances with Large Partners', *Academy of Management Executive* February, pp. 139–48.

Austrade (2002), *Knowing and Growing the Exporter Community* (Canberra: Austrade).

Autio, E., Sapienza, H. and Almeida, J. (2000), 'Effects of Age of Entry, Knowledge Intensity, and Imitability on International Growth', *Academy of Management Journal* 43, pp. 909–92.

Baron, R.A. (1998), 'Cognitive Mechanisms in Entrepreneurship: Why and When Entrepreneurs Think Differently than Other People', *Journal of Business Venturing* 13, pp. 275–94.

Baron, R.A. (2004), 'The Cognitive Perspective: A Valuable Tool for Answering Entrepreneurship's Basic "Why" Questions', *Journal of Business Venturing* 19, pp. 221–39.

Baron, R. and Markman, G. (2000), 'Beyond Social Capital: How Social Skills can Enhance Entrepreneurs' Success', *Academy of Management Executive* 14(1), pp. 106–16.

Bartlett, C. and Ghoshal, S. (1997), 'The Myth of a Generic Manager: New Personal Competencies for New Management Roles', *California Management Review* 40(1), pp. 92–116.

Baum, J.R., Locke, E. and Smith, K. (2001), 'A Multidimensional Model of Venture Growth', *Academy of Management Journal* 44, 2, pp. 292–303.

Bazerman, M.H. (1990), *Judgement in Managerial Decision-making*, 2nd edn (New York: John Wiley and Sons).

Bhave, M.P. (1994), 'A Process Model of Entrepreneurial Venture Creation', *Journal of Business Venturing* 9, pp. 223–42.

Bird, B. (1992), 'The Operation of Intention in Time: The Emergence of the New Venture', *Entrepreneurship Theory and Practice* 17(1), pp. 11–20.

Birley, S. (1984), 'The Role of Networks in the Entrepreneurial Process', *Journal of Business Venturing* 1, pp. 107–17.

Bouchikhi, H. (1993), 'A Constructivist Framework for Understanding Entrepreneurship Performance', *Organisation Studies* 14(4), pp. 549–70.

Bounchen, R.B. (2004), 'Cultural Diversity in Entrepreneurial Teams: Finding of New Ventures in Germany', *Creativity and Innovation Management* 13(4), pp. 240–53.

Brush, C., Greene, P. and Hart, M. (2001), 'From Initial Idea to Unique Advantage: The Entrepreneurial Challenge of Constructing a Resource Base', *Academy of Management Executive* 15(1), pp. 64–78.

Busenitz, L. and Barney, J. (1997), 'Differences between Entrepreneurs and Managers in Large Organisations: Biases and Heuristics in Strategic Decision-making', *Journal of Business Venturing* 12, pp. 9–30.

Busenitz, L. and Lau, C. (1997), 'A Cross-cultural Cognitive Model of New Venture Creation', *Entrepreneurship Theory and Practice* Summer, pp. 25–39.

Bygrave, W. (ed.) (1997), *The Portable MBA in Entrepreneurship* (New York: John Wiley and Sons).

Chandler, G.N. and Hanks, S.H. (1994), 'Founder Competence, the Environment, and Venture Performance', *Entrepreneurship Theory and Practice*, Spring, pp. 77–89.

Collins, J., Sim, C., Zabbal, N., Dhungel, B. and Noel, G. (1997), *Training for Ethnic Small Business* (Sydney: TAFE NSW Multicultural Education Unit and UTS).

De Koning, A. (2003), 'Opportunity Development: A Socio-cognitive Perspective', in Katz, J.A. and Shepherd, D.A. (eds) *Advances in Entrepreneurship, Firm Emergence and Growth: Cognitive Approaches to Entrepreneurship Research*, Vol. 6 (Oxford: Elsevier), pp. 265–314.

Dodd, C. (1998), *Dynamics of Intercultural Communication*, 5th edn (New York: McGraw Hill).

Drakopolou-Dodd, S. and Patra, E. (2002), 'National Differences in Entrepreneurial Networking', *Entrepreneurship and Regional Development* 14, pp. 117–34.

Fiske, S.T. and Taylor, S.E. (1984), *Social Cognition* (Reading, MA: Addison-Wesley).

Florida, R. (2001), 'The Entrepreneurial Society', paper presented at the Conference on Entrepreneurship and Public Policy, Kennedy School of Government, Harvard University, 10 April.

Florida, R. (2002), *The Rise of the Creative Class* (New York: Basic Books).

Florida, R. (2005), 'Creativity and its Links to Wealth Creation', keynote address at CEDA seminar, Adelaide, 22 February.

Forbes, D.P. (1999), 'Cognitive Approaches to New Venture Creation', *International Journal of Management Reviews* 1(4), pp. 415–39.

Gaglio, C.M. (2004), 'The Role of Mental Simulations and Counterfactual Thinking in the Opportunity Identification Process', *Entrepreneurship Theory and Practice* Winter.

GEM Australia (2001), 'GEM Australia 2001 Report', http://www.swin.edu.au/hed/test/gem/archive.html.

Glaser, R. (1984), 'Education and Thinking', *American Psychologist* 39, pp. 93–104.

Greene, P. and Brown, T. (1997), 'Resource Needs and the Dynamic Capitalism Typology', *Journal of Business Venturing* 12(3), pp. 161–74.

Groen, A., Fayolle, A., and Ulijn, J. (2003), 'Teaching Diversity in Technology Entrepreneurship: Some Experiences from France and the Netherlands', *Internationalising Entrepreneurship Education and Training* conference proceedings.

George, G., Zahra, S., Autio, E. and Sapienza, H. (2004), 'By Leaps and Rebounds: Learning and Development of International Market Entry Capabilities in Start-ups', paper presented at the Academy of Management Conference.

Gudykunst, W.B. (1991), *Bridging Differences* (Newbury Park, CA: Sage).

Gudykunst, W.B. (1993), 'Toward a Theory of Effective Interpersonal and Intergroup Communication: An Anxiety/Uncertainty Management (AUM) Perspective', in Wiseman, R. and Koester, I. (eds) *Intercultural Communication Competence* (Newbury Park, CA: Sage), pp. 33–71.

Gudykunst, W.B. and Kim, Y.Y. (1997), *Communicating with Strangers*, 3rd edn (Boston, MA: McGraw Hill).

Gudykunst, W., Wiseman, R. and Hammer, M. (1977), 'Determinants of a Sojourner's Attitudinal Satisfaction', in Ruben, B. (ed.) *Communication Yearbook 1* (New Brunswick, NJ: Transaction).

Geursen, G.M. and Dana, L.-P. (2001), 'International Entrepreneurship: The Concept of Intellectual Internationalisation', *Journal of Enterprising Culture* 9(3), pp. 331–52.

Gulati, R., Nohria, N. and Zaheer, A. (2000), 'Strategic Networks', *Strategic Management Journal* (special issue), March, pp. 203–16.

Hagedoorn, J. and Duysters, G. (1996), 'Internationalisation of Corporate Technology through Strategic Partnering: An Empirical Investigation', *Research Policy* 25, pp. 1–12.

Hall, E.T. (1976), Beyond Culture (New York: Anchor Press).

Hill, C. (2005), *International Business: Competing in the Global Marketplace*, 5th edn (New York: McGraw-Hill Irwin).

Hills, G.E. and Shrader, R.C. (1998), 'Successful Entrepreneurs' Insights into Opportunity Recognition', in *Frontiers of Entrepreneurship Research* (Wellesley, MA: Babson College), pp. 30–43.

Hofstede, G. (1980), *Culture's Consequences: International Differences in Work-related Values* (Beverley Hills, CA: Sage).

Hofstede, G. (1991), *Cultures and Organisations: Software of the Mind* (London: McGraw Hill).

Hofstede, G. and Bond, M.H. (1984), 'Hofstede's Culture Dimensions: An Independent Validation using Rokeach's Value Survey', *Journal of Cross-Cultural Psychology* 15, pp. 417–33.

Hughes-Wiener, G. (1986), 'The "Learning How to Learn" Approach to Intercultural Orientation', *International Journal of Intercultural Relations* 10, pp. 485–505.

Ireland, R., Hitt, M., Camp, S.M. and Sexton, D.L. (2001), 'Integrating Entrepreneurship and Strategic Management Actions to Create Firm Wealth', *Academy of Management Executive* 15(1), pp. 49–63.

Johnson, J.E. (2004), 'Factors Influencing the Early Internationalisation of High-technology Start-ups: US and UK Evidence', *Journal of International Entrepreneurship* 2, pp. 139–54.

Keh, H.T., Foo, M.D. and Lim, B.C. (2002), 'Opportunity Evaluation under Risky Conditions: The Cognitive Processes of Entrepreneurs', *Entrepreneurship Theory and Practice* Winter, pp. 125–48.

Kim, Y.Y. (1988), *Communication and Cross-cultural Adaptation: An Integrative Theory* (Clevedon: Multilingual Matters).

Kim, Y.Y. (1991), 'Intercultural Communication Competence: A Systems-theoretic View', in Ting-Toomey, S. and Korzenny F. (eds) *Cross-cultural Interpersonal Communication* (Newbury Park, CA: Sage), pp. 259–75.

Kim, Y.Y. (1995), 'Cross-cultural Adaptation', in Wiseman, R. (ed.) *Intercultural Communication Theory* (Thousand Oaks, CA: Sage).

Kluckholn, C. and Strodbeck, F.L. (1961), *Variations in Value Orientations* (Evanston, IL: Row and Peterson).

Knight, F.H. (1921), Risk, Uncertainty and Profit (New York: Houghton Mifflin).

Kroeber, A.L. and Kluckhohn, F. (1985), *Culture: A Critical Review of Concepts and Definitions* (New York: Random House/Vintage Books).

Lindsay, N. and Craig, J. (2002), 'A Framework for Understanding Opportunity Recognition', *Journal of Private Equity*, Winter, pp. 13–24.

Lustig, M. and Koester, J. (1993), *Cross-cultural Competence: Interpersonal Communication across Cultures* (New York: HarperCollins).

Lustig, M.W. and Koester, J. (1999), *Intercultural Competence: Interpersonal Communication across Cultures* (New York: Longman).

Man, T.W.Y. and Lau, T. (2000), 'Entrepreneurial Competencies of SME Owner/Managers in the Hong Kong Services Sector: A Qualitative Analysis', *Journal of Enterprising Culture* 8(3), pp. 235–54.

Man, T. W.Y., Lau, T. and Chan, K.F. (2002), 'The Competitiveness of Small and Medium Enterprises: A Conceptualization with Focus on Entrepreneurial Competencies', *Journal of Business Venturing* 17, pp. 123–42.

Martin, J. and Nakayma, T. (1999), 'Thinking Dialectically about Culture and Communication', *Communication Theory* 9(1), 1–25.

Maula, M. and Makela, M. (2003), 'Cross-border Venture Capital', in Hyytinen, A. and Pajarinen, M. (eds) *Financial Systems and Firm Performance: Theoretical and Empirical Perspectives* (Helsinki: Taloustieto), pp. 269–91.

McDougall, P. and Oviatt, B. (2000), 'International Entrepreneurship: The Intersection of two Research Paths', *Academy of Management Journal* 43(5), pp. 902–6.

Mitchell, R., Buzenitz, L., Lant, T., McDougall, P., Morse, E. and Smith, B. (2004), 'The Distinctive and Inclusive Domain of Entrepreneurial Cognition Research', *Entrepreneurship Theory and Practice* Winter, pp. 505–18.

Mitchell, R., Smith, B., Seawright, K. and Morse, E. (2000), 'Cross-cultural Cognitions and the Venture Creation Decision', *Academy of Management Journal* 43(5), pp. 974–93.

Mitchell, R., Smith, J., Morse, E., Seawright, K., Peredo, A.M. and McKenzie, B. (2002), 'Are Entrepreneurial Cognitions Universal? Assessing Entrepreneurial Cognitions Across Cultures', *Entrepreneurship Theory and Practice* Summer, pp. 9–32.

Muzychenko, O. and Saee, J. (2003), 'A Phenomenological Study of Sub-contracting Small- and Medium-sized Enterprises and their Internationalization Strategies and Responses', *Journal of Transnational Management Development* 9(1), Series 1, pp. 3–19.

Mole, V., Dawson, S., Winstanley, D. and Sherval, J. (1993), 'Researching Managerial Competencies', paper presented at the British Academy of Management annual conference. Milton Keynes, September.

Muzychenko, O. (2006), *Competence Based Approach to Teaching International Opportunity Identification: Cross-cultural Aspects*, Proceedings of the annual Internationalising Entrepreneurship education and Training IntEnt2006 conference, San Paulo, 9–12 July.

Neisser, U. (1967), *Cognitive Psychology* (New York: Appleton-Century-Crofts).

Nisbett, R. and Ross, L. (1980), *Human Inference: Strategies and Shortcoming of Social Judgements* (Englewood Cliffs, NJ: Prentice Hall).

Oviatt, B. and McDougall, P. (1995), 'Global Start-ups: Entrepreneurs on a Worldwide Stage', *Academy of Management Executive* 9(2), pp. 30–44.

Parry, S. (1998), 'Just What is a Competency?', *Training*, June, pp. 58–64.

Ram, M. (2003), 'Editorial', *Entrepreneurship and Regional Development* 15, pp. 99–102.

Ruben, B.D. (1976), 'Assessing Communication Competency for Intercultural Adaptation', *Group and Organisation Studies* 1(3), pp. 334–54.

Ruben, B.D. and Kealey, D.J. (1979), 'Behavioral Assessment of Communication Competency and the Prediction of Intercultural Adaptation', *International Journal of Intercultural Relations* 3, pp. 15–47.

Saee, J. (1999), 'Managing across Cultural Frontiers: An Australian Perspective', *Journal of European Business Education* 7(8), pp. 3–69.

Saee, J. (2004), *Managing Organization in a Global Economy: An Intercultural Perspective* (Cincinnatti, OH: Thomson South-Western).

Samovar, L.A. and Porter, R.E. (1995), *Communication between Cultures* (Belmont, CA: Wadsworth).

Simon, M., Houghton, S.M. and Aquino, K. (1999), 'Cognitive Biases, Risk Perception, and Venture Formation: How Individuals Decide to Start Companies', *Journal of Business Venturing* 15, pp. 113–34.

Steensma, H.K., Marino, L., Weaver, K.M. and Dickson, P.H. (2000), 'The Influence of National Culture on the Formation of Technology Alliances by Entrepreneurial Firms', *Academy of Management Journal* 43(5), pp. 951–73.

Stephan, W. and Stephan, C. (1996), *Intergroup Relations* (Boulder, CO: Westview Press).

Timmons, J. (1994), *New Venture Creation*, 4th edn (Boston, MA: Irwin).

Timmons, J., Zacharakis, A. and Spinelli, S. (2004), *Business Plans that Work* (New York: McGrawHill).

Trompenaars, A. and Hampden-Turner, C. (2000), *Riding the Waves of Culture* (London: Nicholas Breasley Publishing).

Yamada, Y. (2004), 'A Multidimensional View of Entrepreneurship', *Journal of Management Development* 23(4), pp. 289–320.

Zahra, S., Ireland, R. and Hitt, M. (2000), 'International Expansion by New Venture Firms; International Diversity, Mode of Market Entry, Yechnological Learning, and Performance', *Academy of Management Review* 43, pp. 925–50.

Chapter 30
Change Management – Realizing the Transformation

David J. Newlands

Introduction

This chapter introduces the key issues associated with planning, forming a task force, implementing, monitoring and sustaining change. Change is a primary dynamic in organizations that wish to survive, compete and emerge as the leader. Change is not the same as routine managerial activity. Change must be based on perceptions, insight, managing and arbitrating conflict, engaging the creative talents of people, managing fear and resistance to change, creating a common vision, taking responsibility, planning, communicating, determining targets and objectives, balancing key performance measures against a philosophy of combining both rapid and continuous improvement.

> The only person who likes change is a baby with a wet nappy (diaper).

For international managers to operate effectively they have to understand the prerequisites of change including: understanding of ethics, negotiation; approaches including supply chain and purchasing management; methods including financial appraisal and value at risk analysis; tools including total quality management; planning and preparing including entrepreneurship and growth strategies. These have been reviewed earlier in chapters earlier in this handbook.

In the external environment, the seasons of the year come and go relatively predictably and new generations are born while older generations die off. According to an ice plug taken from the Antarctic, the planet we live on has experienced eight Ice Ages over the last 300,000. Without the influence of man's induced greenhouse effects the next Ice Age should start in about 16,000 years.

Some of us are getting fit and staying in shape. Others are getting flabby, stiff and lazy with contentment. Some people may point out that we need to take some weight off for the benefit of our health. Excess weight can lead to heart disease, diabetes, high blood pressure and cholesterol levels that can either shorten life expectancy or inhibit the quality of life enjoyed. Still others are just pottering along, not being particularly proactive or lethargic. These individuals seem to be always the same – in a perfect state of health and fitness. We may not notice that change is happening. The irrefutable truth is that time is passing and we, as individuals, are getting older and will die at some time.

Languages historically have changed by about 5 per cent per century. In the latter half of the twentieth century, with the introduction of personal computers and the internet, the rate of change in languages has dramatically increased. With the advent of the internet, languages simultaneously have converged with the increased use of common terms used in information technology. Short text messages have promoted more elaborate codes, for instance, :-) is used for happy and contractions originally used in shorthand dictation are frequently used. Acronyms such as POS for supply chain people means *point of sale*, while for children busy on home computers it means '*parent over shoulder*, and looking at what I'm doing'.

Alan Chapman (1995–2005) suggests that: 'Change management entails thoughtful planning and sensitive implementation, and above all, consultation with, and involvement of, the people affected by those changes. If you force change on people normally problems arise. Change must be realistic, achievable and measurable.' This assertion moves to a humanistic perspective of change that is quite removed from F.W. Taylor's scientific approach. Industrial organizations however maintain their stance toward scientific techniques and issuing instructions – telling rather than selling. This is driven by the lack of choice in industry – if the customer specifies, for example, a level of quality, what choice does the company have but to achieve this? The only alternative is to find themselves other customers or reduce their workforce because they have lost key accounts – their bread and butter orders. McDonald's restaurant chains are typical of a high conformance environment. Skills are acquired over time and practiced. Conformance to hygiene, food preparation, cleanliness, customer interaction protocols and overall behaviour are critical to assure customer expectations are met in every outlet. Companies with high conformance requirements are Tayloristic almost by default because management and branch supervisors have assumed that there is only one right way and employees must conform to relatively rigid requirements. While it remains true that the customer is always right, the style of how management go about transferring skills, encouraging and motivating is crucial to the change effort. This is critical to encouraging enterprise, innovation and radical improvements to both manufacturing and service operations. Steeple (this volume) suggests smaller, more family oriented organizations may have the corporate flexibility to change and adapt as they grow.

Organizations including small and medium sized enterprises, large multi-national and international businesses and even governments and their agencies have similar characteristics to individuals. Sometimes, the intention to change and activities to rectify problems and introduce improvements comes too late. Survival is not compulsory.

Manual Uribe, Mexico's heaviest man weighs more than 85 stone (1190lbs, 541kg) and is one of the world's heaviest people. He asked doctors to operate on him – because he fears he will die otherwise. (SkyNews.com (2006), Heavy Weight, see http://www.sky.com/skynews/picture_gallery/picture_gallery/0,70141-1209659-1,00.html)

Industrial Change and Transformation

Industrial organizations aim to create a profit as a result of efficiently producing high value competitive and desirable goods at a low cost.

Adam Smith's (1776) book, first published over 200 years ago, looked at dividing labour into specialisms in order to dramatically increase productivity. As production techniques became widely available through similar industrial equipment, low cost labour in other countries was considered the key driver of competitive advantage. Producing more goods with less labour increases the productivity of a workforce. The amount of labour cost per item is therefore reduced. For almost two centuries, the underlying paradigm for most industrial organizations in countries with more expensive labour costs to compete was that they must increase productivity.

Whole industries and supply chains collapsed due to the cost advantages of lower cost countries.

- Lancashire in Northern England received cotton via a long inbound supply chain from India. Those cotton mills converted loose cotton into linen on massive weaving machines. Labour costs rose faster than inflation, reflecting the increased wealth of the region and the nation. The mill management eventually decided to upgrade their weaving machines. The old, rather inefficient machines were sold off – to start up companies in India. With the reduced logistics costs, lower labour costs and overheads, linen woven in India quickly became more competitive than the Lancashire equivalent. The Lancashire mills all closed. Most of the weaving machines were sold to companies located in Northern Italy. Roubaix in France also had lower labour costs than Britain. The last weaver in Roubaix closed in 2005.
- When Japan was opened up to trade after 1853, their government quickly funded Zaibatsu to build and operate fleets of cargo ships. Japan built ships in order to create a steel industry. Shipbuilding in the UK, Ireland, Germany and France, for example, declined and many civilian yards collapsed. Military power and secrets dictate that most battle ships and submarines still are built by shipyards in the nation that they will protect. Japan's capability to produce steel was later used to supply their dramatic expansion in automobile exports. Today, generally it is too expensive to build ships in Japan. Korea has taken over as a low cost producer of rapidly built ships.

Manufacturing organizations in the 1960s started to realize the need to control the amount of stock both within their immediate control and throughout the supply chain. During the 1980s just-in-time (JIT) based on the Toyota production system (Monden 1983) began to be promoted in the West and understood. Today JIT is not considered to be an order winner but an order qualifier. To have effective JIT requires many other attributes that come under the umbrella of lean manufacturing (see Chapter 8, 'Supply Chain Management'). The probability of ensuring supply to customers is a key performance indicator that promotes holding stock and managing inventory systems. A more contemporary measure is days of supply. This is a figure that is calculated by taking the current daily production demand and dividing by total stock. If the figure rises above 30, stock turns are down to 12 per year. Stock turns at Toyota during the early 1980s were at least 72 per year. Dell Computer manages with minutes of stock. Their return on investment consequently is one of the best in the industry.

External influences such as legislation dramatically can change technical and performance requirements. Lead-free petrol in automobiles was introduced. Recent directives[1] have been implemented in micro-electronics to eliminate lead solder and promote recycling.

Since organizations and the individuals that work for them have to compete, they are competing against the creativity and innovations their competitors implement. Each organization can cut their cost base, increase the attractiveness of their product or make their business different from offerings by rivals in their market.

---

1 In Japan, the White Goods Recycling Act limits lead content; in China the Ministry of Information Industry published 'Management Methods', implemented in 2006; in Europe Directive 2002/95/EC (RoHS) concerns the restriction of the use of certain hazardous substances in electrical and electronic equipment. Chapter 4 of the EU directive limits or bans the use of mercury, cadmium, hexavalent chromium, polybrominated biphenlys (PBB) or polybrominated diphenyl ethers (PBDE).

Companies that have become aware of the need to re-align their activities are also aware that they can no longer maintain bureaucracies based on pyramidal hierarchies. During the 1980s and 1990s, most companies cut costs to remain competitive by reducing the number of people they employed. Simultaneously, the amount of outsourcing undertaken by companies also has increased. Suppliers are considered to be experts in what they do and hence, as they implement new ideas, they change and improve performance. Both strategies aim to increase productivity – a major factor in win-win relationships.

> Everyone said that it couldn't be done,
> But he gritted his teeth and set to it –
> And he tackled the job that couldn't be done,
> And he couldn't do it.
>
> Icarus
> (quoted in Grahame (1975))

Success can be dangerous. 'We've been successful, so why should we change?' Decisions made today are based on yesterday's data and affect tomorrow. How accurate is the data? What stated or tacit assumptions have been made, about the future? About the way things will be done? About what is needed?

Strategic management concepts suggest that company values should remain constant. Everything else, including organizational objectives, strategies and practices, is a candidate for infrequent negotiation and frequent change (Ebert and Griffin 2003).

Change can happen when:

- things appear for the first time, become plentiful, scarce, or disappear;
- things start, get faster, get slower or stop;
- things become unstable or uncomfortable;
- things are not measured, understood or planned;
- the unexpected unexpectedly occurs;
- common sense isn't commonly used;
- what is expected is superseded;
- additional features become the primary reason for the product use – unintentional market segment and product class creation;
- consequences of an action cause a far greater reaction which negates the effects of the first action;
- intuition and facts lead to conclusions;
- firm associations have been made in the mind, rather than when facts have been learned;
- awareness is achieved and individuals realize that the current situation is unacceptable;
- people take liberties, atrocities take place, positions are threatened and the current state is crisis.

Change can be imposed by external influences such as interest rates, mergers and acquisitions, conflicts, prejudices and misunderstandings.

Any *planned* change happens at least twice: once in the imagination and then in reality. The trick is to ensure that plans are drawn up, that the future state is described and that fear is eliminated or at least counselled. Each individual will need to come to terms with the change. Everybody in the organization should keep these key questions in mind:

- *Why do it?* Nike advocate 'just do it'. However, is there a valid reason for doing the activity? What would happen if it wasn't done? Once it is clear why it is done, the second key question is …
- *Why do it that way?* What alternative methods, techniques, materials, designs, configurations and sequences are possible? It is important to identify these by brainstorming – there are no wrong answers at first as the emphasis is on idea creation. Then the ideas are grouped and analysed for potential application and modification, appraised for cost and profit, and then detail reviews are undertaken.
- *How can we learn from mistakes?* Pointing fingers and blaming doesn't help in the long term. Who is really to blame? The person pointing a finger has one finger pointing out and three fingers pointing back at them. The first objective is not to attach blame. Instead, the aim should be to understand what went wrong and design a system or process that ideally stops the error from happening, detects errors and immediately puts out an alert signal and stops further errors from happening. Benchmarking can be used to identify mistakes, together with comparative good and poor performance. Projects and mistakes should be analysed and a 'lessons to learn' document created, shared and stored. In the United Kingdom, to show value for money, benchmarked key indicators are used to show how good schools, hospitals, police forces, fire brigades, ambulance services and other government-funded services perform. The measures emphasize, for example, grades achieved, waiting times, number of people served, surgery survival rates, percentage of reported crimes solved and reaction times as well as financial measure including cost per employee and cost per appliance or crew.
- *What are the customers' requirements?* Customers have needs and demands. These should be the primary driver to justify why things are done. If the customer doesn't appreciate the value of an activity or component, they should either be done or made and removed from further services and products. If services are needed but are not appreciated by customers, time should be made available to create new processes to automate, modify or eliminate these activities. For example, re-engineering makes it unnecessary for a customers calling from a phone with caller recognition technology to have to recite their customer reference number. By the third ring, customers' data can be booted and reviewed by telephonists. The call centre staff should be able to answer the call by saying 'Hello Mr Smith. My name is David. How can I help you'. If components are needed, and the design is mature – it does what is needed at a minimal cost – no further product design time should be invested to improve the part.
- *What are the in-house core competencies?* SWOT analysis helps management to analyse their situation in terms of Strengths and Weaknesses, and competitive Opportunities and Threats. To be competitive, companies have focused on their core competencies – the skills and processes that they are best at. These should provide a competitive advantage because the company understands and adds more value from these activities than its competitors do. Companies' strategic decisions may be to try to improve their weaknesses to try to raise their performance up to that of their competitors. An alternative strategy is to invest heavily in their strengths, to make them even better, faster and cheaper than their competitors in a narrow field of activities. Attracted by the prospect of reducing their

costs, companies that are competitors in the market may become value chain customers in order to get services and products. Renault and Nissan, for example, compete in the market place and collaborate on product design and process efficiency.

- *What product will we need to produce?* Management must make strategic decisions to invest in processes that add value. Equally importantly, they must decide what not to do themselves. Management must use its purchasing or procurement professionals to delegate at a business to business level by awarding contracts for creative, service, consultancy, financial and manufacturing activities to outside organizations that include suppliers, contractors, competitors, collaborators, design houses, professional, academic and research institutions.
- *How will it be put together?* This question covers a range of fields including modular design, contact points, fixtures and fittings, automated or manual assembly, single or multiple direction part mounting. Computers, cars, aeroplanes and ships are now built from modules. These major blocks are systems. On computers they include power systems, hard drives, batteries, floppy and CD/DVD drives. Car modules include power train (engine, gearbox and axles), suspension and brakes, seating, safety and control (steering wheel and mechanism, dashboard, airbags, sensors) and lighting (interior and exterior front, side and rear). Aeroplane frames are constructed in parts, typically nose, centre section, tail fin, large and small wings, fuselage extension sections, undercarriage, power plants, navigation and flight control systems. The key issue is that customers, particularly B2B customers who buy fleets of products, can specify the supplier of the modules. It is pointless, therefore, to build to stock finished goods as these will invariably require modifications prior to delivery. The stockholding cost would also financially cripple the business. To minimize stock and improve customer service, just-in-time pull systems are used to reduce costs by outsourcing module assembly to specialized suppliers, reduce the order fulfilment cycle time and improve quality. To make more and reduce the cost per unit, products must be assembled ever more quickly. Component part counts therefore must be reduced in order to minimize the 'hand time' required to assemble goods. Screws can be designed out of a product and replaced by catches, integrated hinges and fastenings. Hand time can be reduced further by designing goods to be assembled from only one side. Pizza- and Big Mac-type products are assembled from the base up. They do not require time to turn the product over to add parts to the other side.
- *Who will put it together?* IBM learned that anybody with a screwdriver could do the final assembly for a computer faster and cheaper than they could. They found they could make more money making and selling memory modules than making the entire computer. Dell, Nokia, Toyota and many other manufacturers have specialized in final assembly and testing products. This allows them to configure the product specifically to the exact customer requirements. They buy in almost all hardware, software and printed and packaging materials. Automobile constructors tend to retain the vehicle shell design and part manufacturing activities in order to keep the direction they have taken the styling as secret as possible.
- *How to align suppliers and contribute to the performance enhancement effort?* Suppliers have been selected for their ability to design, produce and deliver quality goods and services. Their costs must continuously be driven down in order to remain globally competitive. Assemblers and first tier suppliers are developing their own capabilities and their suppliers in order to enhance the performance of their supply chain. Chapter 28 reviews supplier development.

- *How will we get it to the customer?* The time it takes to make and deliver a standard product is usually different, and much longer, than the time the customer is willing to wait. If demand is almost instantaneous, in order to assure a reasonably high level of customer service, companies must ask themselves how much stock they should keep, at what level of completeness the stock is held and where to keep it. An alternative strategy is to develop rapidly reacting supply chains that can respond quickly to changes in customer demand. The business model may need to be redefined in order to be more flexible, rapidly satisfy customers' needs and minimize capital investment. Most businesses are based on an information, production then payment cycle. Information on customer orders is needed to control the supply chain. Products are made according to the order. Customers pay for products, or recognize they incur the cost, when they receive goods. Dell Computers challenged this model. They take the credit details along with the product order. They then assemble only the processing box of the computer. External screens, keyboards, mice, printers, scanners and other parts of the order are collected by a third party logistics services provider that delivers a set of boxes to the deliver address. This model eliminates the need to hold finished goods. Dell receives the money before it manufactures the goods. Customers accept a few days lead time to have a computer built to their specification, configured with software they need and delivered where they need it. In this market, customers understand that waiting a few days is better than buying a computer off the shelf with out-of-date technology.

Organizational Change

Change in organizations can be painful. At some time in their existence they will need to grow, reduce numbers, become more diversified or focused on core competencies, be a technology leader or follow as a 'me too', be a supplier to imposing customers, be a strong customer to less powerful suppliers, be in need of scarce resources, have an over abundance of stock or resources that have a short window of high sales value, and react to otherwise unforeseen circumstances.

A critical effect to be overcome is 'bystander apathy'. Individuals may feel a sense of social drive to do as others do. They may not be familiar with what to do in a given situation and 'put their heads in the sand' and try ignore what is going on or going wrong. Individuals may not like to take charge of others, give orders and instructions, ask for assistance, believe it's someone else's job and responsibility to deal with the issue. Analysis paralysis can also set in, which could be perceived as apathy. Observations are made and analysis is undertaken. The lead time to reach a decision can be extended indefinitely as a result of procrastination. In Mexico, the phrase 'a dog with two sandwiches' is used to describe a person who cannot make up their mind concerning two or more tempting offers.

The job for life policy so venerated and envied in Japan during the 1980s evolved into 'a job for as long as you want it'. Constructive dismissal is illegal. However, if underperforming individuals cannot easily and cheaply be dismissed, alternative extremely menial work is found for them. Their salary may be maintained at the previous position level for a given time period, say two years. After this, the pay scale for the job is implemented. This gives the employee ample time to retrain or find alternative employment while still earning a living. Employees can seldom accept the pay scale re-adjustment and tend to leave soon after the end of the two year period, if they haven't left before.

The total quality management and lean production era became apparent in the early 1980s. The concept of choice is important here. Do management and workers really have a choice but to comply with customers expectations on quality levels, cost and cost reduction targets, delivery lead time and reliability? The choice in the short term is 'do or do not'. If they don't accept and adopt these improvement schemes, they have chosen to accept they will not be awarded contracts and must either go out of business or find alternative customers.

Conflicts between individuals or groups in organizations can result in fear, lack of communication, working to rule, overt confrontation, resistance, walk-outs, sabotage, low productivity, lost customers, lower revenue and poor financial performance. Conflicts can also serve to create understanding and learning, new plans, better methods of measurement, revised criteria and routes for employee recruitment and promotion, recognition and procedural agreements, improved approaches to decision-making, more teamwork in place of group think, reduced levels of management hierarchy and bureaucracy, improved management and workforce leadership and empowerment.

Armenakis (1999) provides a comprehensive literature review on how organizations change.

Nissan

In 1953 Nissan workers were locked out when they went on strike. A second new union was formed with a new leader. Nissan stated that it recognized the new union, that there was only room for one union in the company, and that all management, engineers and shopfloor workers would be part of it. The original union collapsed because, when workers went back to work, they automatically joined the new union. By eliminating a 'them and us' division, the company accepted a fresh start and new ways of working together. Nissan has not had strike action which has halted production since then.

More recently, Carlos Ghosn was seconded from Renault to Nissan. His job was to turn the company around. Nissan was effectively giving away €1,000 in losses with every car produced. Ghosn took over when Nissan owed over one trillion yen. He asked his key employees to draft proposals that would radically change the business. There were no sacred cows that were to be left untouched. He rejected initial proposals as not aggressive enough. Ghosn gave these employees three months to make their proposals. He then reviewed them, went on national television and announced what Nissan would be doing to turn its fortunes around. Nissan employees watched this broadcast and were then informed by his team of the details that were to be implemented. Nissan reduced its debt, rationalized its product mix, improved product designs, reduced part costs at suppliers and increased sales. They went from making a loss on every vehicle to making a gross profit of 20 per cent (Magee 2003).

Ghosn didn't save Nissan. He allowed and supported Nissan employees and suppliers to save the company themselves.

A second strategy to build on this success, known as the Nissan 180, was revealed and periodically updated by Ghosn (2002) once the goals of the rescue had largely been achieved. The company has since released further improvement plans and is expected to continue releasing strategic improvement schemes and achieving success.

Scargill versus Thatcher

In trying to protect their members, trade unions represent their interests and may take industrial action to force management to accede to their demands. During the early 1980s, Arthur Scargill was president of the National Union of Mineworkers in the United Kingdom. They clashed with Margaret Thatcher's government over plans to liberalize trading agreements with other nations in order to have a free and competitive energy market. The union went on strike for nearly two years. Effects of this were felt across the economy: the families of the strikers built up huge debts by borrowing to cover their household expenses, financial support in the form of handouts to members nearly bankrupted the union, no coal was extracted and stocks ran down, customers in need of coal started importing or switched over to cleaner fuels such as natural gas, the government didn't receive pension, social security or tax contributions from workers or their employers. Deep extraction mines are more common in Britain. As the business was not making money, pumps used to drain water from the mines were switched off. By the time the miners gave up their protests and were ready to go back to work, it became apparent that most of the mines were full of water. It was deemed uneconomic to pump the mines dry, so most of the mines immediately were decommissioned. Thomas (2005) provides acidic comments in his chapter that reviews these events.

Strategic Change

Corporations can decide to radically change their business, their core field of revenue generation and the nature of their competitive advantage.

Radically Changing Business

Holding companies control various types of businesses. They can direct investment into different opportunities, to create competitive advantage as a result of superior products, technology and process capabilities. Holding companies can close down or sell off unprofitable assets, potentially failing companies and highly profitable going concerns. Essentially they operate as corporate business angles, funding ventures that may be high risk, low investment cost, high revenue and high margin activities. Deciding to relocate or divest a site is a radical change, at least for those who are employed at a site that will be closed down or sold off. Labour laws and costs of laying off employees vary. This can affect decisions relating to which site to close. It is frequently noted that workers in the United Kingdom are cheaper to dismiss than on the European mainland.

Changing Core Fields of Revenue Generation

Nokia is now known as a worldwide super power in the mobile phone transceiver and base station sectors. Nokia is a town in Finland. The people there owned shares in their town's business. Nokia started as a rubber, sugar and food producer. The business branched out to refine and sell petrochemicals. Nokia bought Salora – Salo Radio. Salo also is a town in Finland. Salora made walkie-talkies for the Finnish army. Salora bought Technophone, a British mobile phone manufacturer in Hampshire, England. Salora started to make mobile phones on a technology transfer basis. In the late 1990s Nokia decided to devolve itself and focus its core activities on mobile phones and base stations. This type of strategic business change is a means of extending a business existence.

Changing Competitive Advantages

Rather than competing on similar points and key performance indicators, they may create new indicators that enable them to differentiate themselves. Significant emphasis on these KPIs to enhance their performance may lead to increased sales both to end users and to their apparent competitors because businesses that can not compete collaborate in alliances to obtain capabilities they do not possess.

Technical vs Cultural Change

Technical change is typified by engineering and includes industrial projects: civil construction and ground work and mechanical and technological progress. Computing technology has progressed in terms of hardware performance, memory expansion and computational power. Software, in terms of operating systems and functionality, has become more robust and useful to clients. Networks, particularly local area networks and the internet, have become a principal source of data to search for solutions, suppliers, customers.

Cultural change affects people. Candidates and new employees are selected and trained based on the ability to adapt to the company values (see Chapter 8). People in organizations now constantly have to acquire new skills and assume different responsibilities and roles. Management processes and systems cannot be too rigid and inflexible or the decisions reached will be based on unrealistic conclusions that are the product of out-of-date data and evaluations that have unrealistic assumptions and inappropriate criteria. Organizational structures change. Hierarchies have become flatter or have been redefined into matrices.

Change initiatives can be a mixture of both technical and cultural aspects. For example, People, Systems and Organization (PSO) aims to balance the needs of the organization and the needs of customers, suppliers, employees and subcontractors in a process that is conducive to sustained peak performance. This is achieved by having the people as the basis of the processes and experiences. Human relations management appears to be moving toward this perspective.

As technical advances may be made by outside organizations, purchasing management may decide to outsource technology creation projects or change supplier in order to take advantage of higher technology products, better production processes and lower unit costs. Organizations and governmental purchasing functions have been active since the 1960s in various countries and business sectors to develop enhanced supplier performance. This has involved managing change and training programmes that involve suppliers in establishing, planning and implementing their own change programmes. These programmes are designed to create performance improvement across the supplier base, and improve the overhead structure by enabling them to serve their customer base more effectively. Chapter 29 on supplier development examines these inter-organizational performance enhancement projects.

The Coping Cycle

Kirt Lewin (1951) created an ice-water-ice analogy to explain changes in performance and confidence starting prior to change and ending with the enhancement being fully integrated in the organization's way of doing things. The proposal starts with ice, which is hard and brittle. The ice melts to create a fluid and chaotic environment. As the change finishes, ice reforms to consolidate and create relatively permanent forms and structure. Five stages are recognized on the coping cycle: Denial, Defence, Discard, Adaptation and Internalization. In the unfreezing stage, industrial organizations may eliminate rewards for current behaviour. During the transition phase, the organization instigates a search for or movement towards new choices and sells their benefits. The refreezing phase forces new organizational cultures to be adopted and become part of the way things are done there. New reward systems are set in place to sustain and embed the behaviours.

Individuals affected by change initially deny any need to change because the current system is sufficient. 'Is the change really necessary?' Resistance then becomes more explicit in order to defend and protect the hierarchy, employees' jobs and managers' power base. When they understand, fear disappears because the many negative perceptions that created the fear are corrected. People will then come to accept that change is inevitable. They can choose to be involved, continue the pretence that change will not happen to them, live in the hope that things will go back to the way they used to be, become saboteurs, leave the company, or become active members of the change initiative. Once it is realized that the old ways and things are no longer appropriate or available, confidence suffers. This, in turn, reduces performance. Individuals must come to terms with it, imagine the end result and understand the benefits. Eventually, after much persuasion of the benefits of changing over and drawbacks of resistance, the motivators who created the resistance are won over. New objectives are accepted and skills are acquired to achieve them. The learning curve effect starts to become apparent. Changes are made to adapt the original processes, objectives and skills training to the current situation. Confidence is restored in part when the people go out on visits to meet others in organizations that already use some or all of the new ideas and methods. As performance increases, pride returns. If the work now performed is in line with employees' self-fulfilment needs (Maslow 1954),[2] the new practices become apart of 'the way we do things around here'.

The five stages identified above are related to the learning cycle. Individuals may or may not be aware, and may or may not be capable.

Critique of the Coping Cycle

Performance may already be very low due to the uncertainty surrounding worker's jobs and the future of the business. Once they know what the plan is, they may pick up moral and become more motivated. If there is a management buy-out or a business activity is spun off to employees so that they become a supplier, motivation to find other customers and raise their income in a competitive business context can result in significantly improved performance, even though no significant investment has been made in equipment, technology or processes.

The coping cycle typically is associated with Tannenbaum and Schmid's (1958) continuum of leadership behaviour.[3] The leader autocratically states that change is to happen. A resistance develops and this must be overcome to coax productivity back up to levels previously achieved. Productivity may surpass that of the old system. Most diagrams of the coping cycle do not show significant gains, such as the order of magnitude changes expected by Hammer and Champy (1993). The effect of the learning curve is not expressed in the coping cycle. This later phenomenon shows a cost decay that should result from learning over time. Leaders' behaviour may be anything but autocratic. They may be sympathetic, listening and taking immediate action to improve a worker's job and work place ergonomics (Nelson et al. 1998). Such action

---

2   http://en.wikipedia.org/wiki/Maslow's_hierarchy_of_needs.

3   A summary of this is given at http://www.businessballs.com/tannenbaum.htm. Links are given to several other contributors on leadership and motivation.

can create ripple effects; other workers realize management is finally listening and they make more suggestions.

The performance can actually improve once everyone knows what the score is. When Rover Group was nearing closure, performance and quality actually improved. This perhaps is linked to Elton Mayo's Hawthorne Effect (Mayo 1937, 1949).

Awareness and Capability

'Ignorance is bliss', so a saying goes. This state allows the individual to exist without care or concern for issues, debates, events, methods, performance, competitive pressures, long-term survival, success or satisfying customers.

> Perceptions vary. Sometimes the very question is loaded. For example, is the glass half empty or half full? This is a loaded question. It presupposes that the response is framed within the context of pessimism and optimism. Negotiation theory requires that we search for alternative answers. Changing the context, for example where we in a pub, I would suggest that the glass is twice as big as it needs to be (for my beer, whisky, etc. and therefore needs perhaps some ice or a chaser) or that it's your round!
>
> What other frames of reference are there that will lead to more alternatives?

Perception is the medium between experiencing life or acquiring knowledge and taking responsibility to do something constructive. Gestalt (Houston 1993)[4] is the German used to describe the focus of perception. A common example of changes to perception relates to something bought by an individual that might take pride of place in their home. After a while, the good becomes 'part of the furniture' and isn't noticed. When anyone remarks on the item, good feelings associated with the process of purchasing the good are relived by the owner. Perhaps a detailed story may be related about how it was found, the luck involved and how it came to be in their possession.

Once an issue, challenge or opportunity is identified, individuals can assess if they are capable of dealing with it. The individual at this stage understands there is a need to improve but is incapable of doing anything immediately about the issue. Formal training may be necessary, for instance, to gain a better understanding, skills, tools, methodologies, processes for planning, methods of control and to lead others. As the individual's capability increases, they will become good technicians. This perspective applies to perfectionist sports as well. For example, rather than being regarded as experts, First Dan black belt marshal artists are considered ready to start to learn. True expertise comes later, when the practitioner doesn't consciously think about what they are doing. Instead, they instinctively react based on their long experience and rehearsed technical practices. The film *The Last Samurai* starred Tom Cruise. To beat his instructor, he was told not to think so much.

Trainers must codify and explain the secrets of their success. This forces experts to explain, simplify, provide advice, analogies and stories in order to convert raw untrained people into good technicians.

Wickens (1995, 1997) described a four-stage model used to make explicit the capabilities of high performance individuals. The first stage individuals are taught how to perform a task

---

4   The first five years of the *Gestalt Journal* are online at http://www.gestalt.org/.

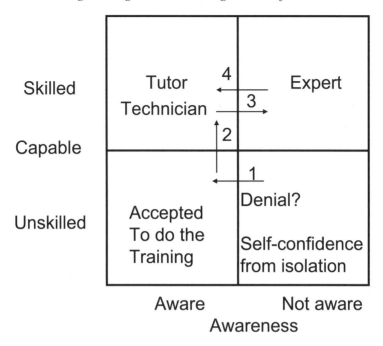

Figure 30.1   Awareness and capability matrix

to the required quality level. The second stage the learner becomes faster and can perform the task within the specified time as a proficient technician. The third stage involves being able to train others to the same level. The ultimate level of achievement involves being able to improve the process. A training progress sheet graphically shows the level of achievement for each individual against the range of activities. Some companies use the four sides of a square, others use a diamond.

Teams of High Performance Individuals

Special teams may be assembled from the people available. The range of skills and personal working preferences may not form the ideal team. Team dynamics are linked to the stage of their development: forming, norming, performing, adjourning and mourning (Tuckman 1965). Tannenbaum and Schmidt (1958) developed a continuum of leadership behaviour that ranges from pure authoritarianism through to perfect egalitarian collaboration based on contributions by group members. The leader may decide to take control. As collaborators become more proficient and increase performance, trust may be established that enables the leader to take a more back-seat role. Authority to dominate may not be present in various situations and hence the leader must ask for contributions, ideas, assistance and empower the group to take charge of aspects.

Thomson (n.d.) identifies several factors and levels of complexity associated with change programmes.

Jobs may be lost. In this case it is imperative that managers ensure that the people will be looked after, assisted to find alternate work or helped to start their own small enterprises. This assistance demonstrates to those who remain with the company that they will also be looked after.

Acquiring skills implies that new things will be learnt:

- old skills are no longer used and must be replaced with techniques that may have to be demonstrated by instruction and then tried;
- there is a need to read around the area;
- learned, new tools need to be mastered; and
- people will become responsible for new things including performance criteria, relationships with their new 'customers', understanding the impact of their actions – particularly concerning quality, cost and delivery.

In the automotive industry, employees are graded by their ability in four criteria, the ability to:

1. do the work to quality;
2. do the work to quality and in the prescribed time;
3. do the work to quality, within the time and be able to teach others to do the same;
4. do the above, plus the ability to improve the process.

These four levels create a 'closed box' that is visually displayed in the enterprise (Wickens 1995). If there is a staff shortage, qualified individuals can be selected to fill in. In the chase to constantly improve, companies have endorsed the belief that every individual involved in an activity knows the current state – they are the expert. Companies now that have the ability to improve the process have two jobs:

1. to do the work; and
2. to improve the work that they do.

For this reason, following on from 'one minute management' (Blanchard and Johnson 1982) individuals and teams should not just do something, they should sit there and think. They should consider redesigning the process, using a blank piece of paper and employing the concepts found in business process re-engineering. The key question they are asked is 'If we were to invent this company or process today, what would it look like?' This frees each individual up to use their imagination; they are not limited to 'what is', they can look to the future and dream up 'what could be'.[5]

Change can be implemented 'top-down', that is, employees are directed by authoritarian senior management whom have decreed what shall be. The business managers may request suggestions and recommendations from more junior employees in a 'bottom-up' initiative. The most typical flaws in these schemes are a lack of recognition of receipt of the idea, long periods when analysis is undertaken and little reward or recognition for the individual that recognized the opportunity. The middle managers may act as filters to information, recommendations and directives on the way up and on the way down. They may be trying to safe-guard their positions and power base that stem from the 'as is' situation at the expense of performance improvements.

According to Peter Drucker, individuals who wish to lead must have followers. For this reason, negotiation skills and acceptance of diversity are as vital as technical knowledge and vision. The leader must have a strong message, continuously communicate with passion, lead by example, understand the technical details, be honest about the changes and difficulties that are being faced, facilitate the change and be supported by sponsors in senior management in order to have the time and resources to work on the project. On the basis that converts are the

---

5   As George Bernard Shaw put it: 'You see things; and you say, "Why?" But I dream things that never were; and I say, "Why not?"': http://www.wisdomquotes.com/cat_dreams.html.

most evangelical, one of the first things a change leader must do is try to win over a powerful opponent.

Belbin (1981) used Benne and Sheats' (1948) early work on different roles and created a simplified group of nine roles, down from 27. These classifications have substantially remained intact. Belbin (2005) provides a web-based self-assessment test to determine individuals' preferred style and role. Similar tests are available using the Myers-Briggs Type Indicators.[6] Rotch (2005) provides a complementary set of roles to Belbin.

Kotter (1998) suggests eight errors that managers commonly make when they want to implement change. Managers of change typically:

- do not establish a great enough sense of urgency;
- do not forming a powerful guiding coalitions;
- lack a vision;
- undercommunicate the vision by a factor of 10;
- do not remove obstacles to achieving the vision;
- do not systematically plan for and creating short-term wins;
- declare victory too soon;
- do not anchor changes in the corporation's culture.

Kotter's recommendations are the antonym of these errors.

Roles that Individuals Play in Change

Individuals can say one thing, mean another and do something else. This incongruence can be observed most vividly in cross-cultural and mixed gender communications. Individuals usually listen but may require a year or more to make a mental simulation of what would happen and how. They may come up with suggestions that were recommended long ago, much to the annoyance and dismay of those who suggested the ideas. Managers and other employees can also play psychological games (Wild 1997)[7] including the blame game, the pending promotion game, and the annual surprise. A game that really kills off change initiatives is based on 'yes, but ...'. In business this is called 'the consultant game'.

The consultant game: a manager commissions a consultant to review the current situation in the organization. The consultant duly obliges by providing a huge written report detailing all the things wrong along with relevant recommendations to put things right. The manager then comes up with reasons why each of the recommendations cannot be implemented.

This premise of the consultant game is based on the ego state of the manager. The manager derives a pleasure from having more problems than the consultant has solutions. This serves as justification not to change the status quo.

Individuals act differently when alone than when they are in company. Large groups and crowds act as if the mass of people were a single organism. This can be:

---

6   Myers-Briggs Type Indicator: http://www.myersbriggs.org/ http://www.knowyourtype.com/.

7   This book is based on Berne (1964). An interesting chapter can be found at http://www.blonnet.com/businessline/2000/06/13/stories/041344pe.htm.

- a result of following the crowd – 'monkey see, – monkey do';
- spontaneous – Mexican waves at sporting events;
- catalytic, with one person doing something, then another and another until a cascade of similar activity is undertaken;
- planned by a small group of *agents provocateurs* in order to incite trouble – for example, systematic hooligans that attend sporting events,
- the result of social pressure to comply with norms that are considered to be a given – the icons of Western commerce include wearing a neck tie, collar shirt and suit. Due to the sheer presence of bicycles there, people visiting The Netherlands may experience the need to buy or ride one.

Teams differ from groups in the respect that teams accept and support diversity. In sports such as soccer individuals are specialists. This is unlike basketball where players can play in each role. Basketball stars' salaries are closer to a standard level than soccer players who, as individuals, command distinctly different transfer fees and salaries. Individuals retain their own views and contribute skills that benefit the whole team. Their weaknesses, or areas they feel uncomfortable with, are covered by other specialists. It is for this reason that cross-functional teams have become popular in organizations.

Dr Spencer Johnson (1998)[8] suggested there are four principle types of demonstrated behaviour defined by four characterizations:

1. Sniff is sensitive to change and has the instincts to recognize change is coming. Sniff has refined senses that he uses to search out new opportunities when the time has come to move on.
2. Scurry can move fast. This character will quickly move in the direction indicated by Sniff to find what they want.
3. Hem will continue to deny change is inevitable. He is frustrated because he thinks he deserves what he has always enjoyed, including status, comfort, wealth and profit. He persists with the belief that things will return to the way they were long past what, to an outsider, would be considered logical. He may never get back what was once plentiful and profitable.
4. Haw initially denies change is happening. He may suffer because he doesn't get what he wants or is used to. Eventually he faces up to the fact that change is inevitable or has already happened. He goes in search of something new to either replenish or replace what he had.

Johnson is not alone in suggesting that our own perception dramatically affects our behaviour. We must change the way we perceive ourselves (usually with a laugh), our environment and the situation. We must also overcome fear of the unknown because that paralyses initiative and motivation. W. Edwards Deming (1982) suggested that to be effective, managers have to eliminate fear, particularly fear of failure. He actively promoted Shewhart's (1931) change cycle – plan, do, check and act.[9] Hoshin Kanri[10] is a Japanese strategic management implementation version of Shewhart's cycle that starts with doing and finishes with planning.

---

8   To find out more about Sniff, Scurry Hem and Haw at http://www.WhoMovedMyCheese.com or, in the United States, call 1-800-851-9311.

9   http://en.wikipedia.org/wiki/Shewhart_cycle.

10   See http://www.mcts.com/Hoshin-Kanri.htm and http://membres.lycos.fr/hconline/hoshin_us.htm.

Achievement is important for the survival of the organization and the group. Using the blank sheet of paper technique, business process re-engineering (Hammer and Champy 1993) suggests that change projects can create staggering results – not just of a few percentage improvement, but rather in the region of a factor of ten:

- ten times more profit;
- one tenth of the time, money spent, materials required in stock;
- one tenth of the effort, people and administration;
- ten times better customer service.

When change is required, and if the change is significant enough that it requires a team to be put together to tackle it, a steering committee is usually convened to provide overall strategic guidance. It is required to appoint a project or change manager to 'champion' the project (internal and external). The steering committee must be composed of sufficiently senior staff, though not too many, from functions contributing resources and affected by the change. In many cases the committee should include representatives from key customer and suppliers. The change project manager who reports to the steering committee should also be a member of the committee.

Funds, people and other resources must be allocated. A 'litmus paper test' to find the best people for the project is to ask which person in the current activity is most needed every day. This person is probably networked to the other participants and thus is aware of the detail of the current situation and methods. People assigned to the change project must be liberated from their existing duties. It is imperative that they understand that their ideas are essential to the change project and that there is no 'glass ceiling'.

> Before Sir Roger Bannister broke the four minute mile everyone thought it was impossible. Within a couple of years more than 50 people had broken the four minute barrier. Since then athletes have continued to chip away at the world record. With improvements in training techniques and nutrition, the question begging to be asked is 'when will the three minute mile be a reality?'

An arbitrator may be appointed as a (sometimes quasi) third party either by management, customers, suppliers, consultants, recognized industry body or, for example, by governments, as a 'watchdog'. This role aims to resolve conflicts and disputes between function managers and people assigned to projects. The arbitrator can be assigned power to terminate, suspend and re-start the change using 'stop – pause – go' powers if it is deemed necessary, or to prescribe more resources in order to ensure performance targets are achieved. By monitoring progress and performance, the arbitrator can also define when bonuses and other motivating rewards can be given.

The steering group will define the vision or overall goal which is to be aimed for. Periodically they will want to know what is going on, how much progress has been made and how much it has cost. Therefore the change manager must report in a timely manner on agreed dates or at agreed milestones when activities are complete or performance targets have been reached. This discipline forces the members to have short-term goals that they *believe* they can accomplish. This contributes to the feeling of achievement and confidence. Both are necessary to sustain continuous improvement (kaizen) and reduce fear inherent to perceptions prior to radical change (kaikaku). If there is no sustained effort to improve, any initiatives can become fads that lead to 'one step forward and two steps back'.

Mr Arnold Schwarzenegger sustained his physique over an extended period. He thus was able to re-assume his role as a Cyberdine Systems Model 101 cyborg terminator.[11] His business colleague Mr Sylvester Stallone built his body up for the *Rocky* series and *Rambo II* and *III*. Mr Stallone subsequently bulked out for his role in *Cop Land*. Mr Stallone trimmed down and made a sixth *Rocky* movie. [11] At the time of writing (2007), rumour has it he plans to make *Rambo IV*.

Managing the Change

W. Edwards Deming (Chapman 1995–2005) provided a 14-step methodology to improve organizations' chance of surviving crises by focusing on working conditions, revolutionizing company culture, training workers, raising quality and collaborating with suppliers.

Getting workers to participate doesn't require just communicating or selling them ideas. Management must include those affected by decisions in the decision-making process. For management to get workers on a shopfloor to understand why the company wants changes may seem simple and straightforward. However, workers will probably start to resist in subtle or highly visible and crippling ways. Taking workers to another company that already has the changes or the machine in place allows workers to talk to other workers who are using the process. Workers talk to workers from different businesses more candidly than management would with their employees. Management must then allow time for employees to make their decisions and trust that the decision will be justified and in the employees' self-interest.

Managers may be faced with identifying how best to manage the change happen. It helps to break project into several stages:

- Create the steering committee (see chapters on negotiation, strategic management). Steering committees may be set up by management to oversee the smooth running of a change project. They may be composed of staff who are sufficiently senior to authorize activity and expenditure, and should include the project manager who will report to the committee. A representative of the main client may be on the committee as an advisor in order to ensure that the group remains focused and understand their customer's requirements better. Affected parts of the business should be represented and should select people who will contribute to and influence the outcome. 'Too many cooks spoil the broth.' To avoid unnecessary communication difficulties and 'make work' activities, the committee should not have too many members.
- Establish the need for change – show those affected why change is needed; financial performance, trends and known changes in the environment that will affect the business.

---

11 See, for example, http://www.schwarzenegger.it/gallery/musclegallery1/m573.jpg; http://www.schwarzenegger.it/gallery/musclegallery9/smg4.jpg.

12 See, for example, http://www.starpulse.com/Actors/Stallone,_Sylvester/gallery/1/; http://www.imagesjournal.com/issue04/reviews/copland.htm; http://www.sylvesterstallone.com/frontpage/photogallery/slygym.html.

It may be necessary to use creative accounting to create the justification (see Chapters 1 and 20 on international business and strategic cost management).

- Design a change that meets the immediate need and has potential for future development.
- Identify the impact the change will have on the organization – particularly from job cuts (see Chapters 3, 13 and 14 on managing the ethical company, employee relations and HRM impact on performance).
- Create the strategic, business and tactical level plans to implement the changes (see Chapter 2 on strategic management).
- Implement the change.
- Appraise the impact with regard to performance: quality, cost, delivery, efficiency (better, faster, cheaper and closer to the customer (Christopher 2005).
- Record the lessons to be learned – what went right, what went wrong, what could be done better, what didn't add value, where emphasis should be placed. Share best practice with others in the organization – hold seminars, include junior manager training modules.
- Recommend further actions, initiatives and projects.

Less conventionally, a change-team leader and potential team members together will define roles, expectations and responsibilities for each person on the team and others who provide limited contributions. Key questions asked can include:

- Who is *responsible* for the task?
- Who is going to provide resources – budget, time, money, facilities etc?
- Who is to *do* the new task?
- Who is will *decide*?
- Who is to *assess* progress?
- Who is going to motivate, guide, coach, facilitate, and train?
- Who is going to instil discipline or dish-out punishment?
- What will be *involve*d
  – Who must provide information and opinions?
  – Who could provide information and knowledge?
- Who must be *inform*ed of outcomes?

Taking the Monkey

A monkey has teeth, tails and hands. They are into everything, breaking, messing up and otherwise doing everything possible to take your attention away from things a manager should be working on. In conventional parlance, the manager is 'fire fighting' and when they find a problem they take the lead and solve it.

When an employee or other supply chain participant turns up with a problem, they are more than glad if you would take it from them and solve the issue. Managers must be prepared to resist this temptation. Instead, they should be calm and ask key questions of would be monkey dumpers:

- If you were me, what would you do right now?
- What options do I have to deal with this?
- Which of these options would you choose if you were me?

- What and who do we need to help us to do this, in terms of time, money, people and documentation/permissions?

The job of the change agent then is to approve the plan and give permission, supply resources and authorize the individuals to undertake the plan they themselves have significantly helped create.

It is less important to have accurate answers than to:

- identify what is missing and not yet known, specified or simulated;
- reflect;
- think about issues;
- cope with ambiguity; and
- communicate with others' ideas and opportunities.

Change managers must trust that others will do their best and make the right choices. They identify when it is best to avoid Tayloristic approaches that rely on issuing detailed instructions. Change agents should aim 'not to take the monkey'.

Conclusions

Survival is not compulsory. Start caring and keep all options open. The only people likely to keep their jobs in the future are those who help others to help themselves and those who work toward improving the situation. It is extremely important to start identifying potential savings. Typically, executives must identify savings of at least 15 times their annual salary in order to have the budget to pay their own salaries the following year.

> Identify the glass ceilings and smash them.
> Say, mean and do the same thing.
> Do not take the monkey!
> DO NOT TAKE THE MONKEY!
> Consult those affected by change and avoid Taylorism.
> Ask good questions and empower those involved or affected by the change.

Be prepared to work on the same issues year after year. Aim for sustained peak performance.

References

Armenakis, A.A. (1999), 'Organizational Change: A Review of Theory and Research in the 1990s', *Journal of Management (Yearly Review of Management)* May-June, http://www.findchapters.com/cf_dls/m4256/3_25/55307215/p1/chapter.jhtml.

Belbin, R.M. (1981), *Management Teams: Why They Succeed or Fail* (London: Heinemann).

Belbin, R.M. (2005), http://www.belbin.info/.

Benne, K.D. and Sheats, P. (1948), 'Functional Roles of Group Members', *Journal of Social Issues* 4(2), pp. 41–9.

Berne, E. (1964), *Games People Play: The Psychology of Human Relationships* (London/New York/Victoria/Ontario/Auckland: Penguin Books).

Blanchard, K. and Johnson, S. (1982), *The One Minute Manager* (Glasgow: Fontana).

Chapman, A. (1995–2005), 'Change Management', http://www.businessballs.com/change management.htm.

Christopher, M. (2005), *Logistics and Supply Chain Management: Creating Value Adding Networks*, 3nd edn (London: Pitman Publishing).

Deming, W.E. (1986), *Out of the Crisis* (Cambridge: Cambridge University Press).

Ebert, R.J. and Griffin, R.W. (2003), *Business Essentials*, 4th edn (Englewood Cliffs, NJ: Prentice Hall).

Ghosn, C. (2002), 'Nissan 180 Update and First Half FY 02 Preliminary Financial Results', speech text for 23 October, http://www.nissannews.com/site_library/corporate/ news/2002speeches/relautopasse2002102385935.doc.

Grahame, C. (1975), *How to Try Hard in Business without Really Succeeding* (London: George Allen & Unwin).

Hammer, M. and Champy, J. (1993), *Re-engineering the Corporation: A Manifesto for Business Revolution* (London: Nicholas Brealey Publishing Ltd).

Houston, G. (1993), *Being and Belonging, Group, Intergroup and Gestalt* (Chichester: John Wiley & Sons).

Johnson, S. (1998), *Who Moved my Cheese?* (New York: Vermillion, Penguin Putman Inc.).

Kotter, J.P. (1998), 'Leading Change: Why Transformation Efforts Fail', in *Harvard Business Review on Change* (Boston: Harvard Business School Press), pp. 1–21.

Lewin, K. (1951), *Field Theory and Social Science* (New York: Harper).

Magee, D. (2003), *Turnaround, How Carlos Goshn Rescued Nissan* (New York: HarperBusiness).

Maslow, A.H. (1954), *Motivation and Personality* (New York: HarperCollins).

Mayo, E. (1937), *The Human Problems of an Industrial Civilization* (New York: The Macmillan Company).

Mayo, E. (1949), *The Social Problems of an Industrial Civilisation* (London: Routledge and Kegan Paul).

Monden, Y. (1983), *Toyota Production System* (Atlanta, CA: Industrial Engineering and Management Press).

Nelson, D., Mayo, R. and Moody, P. (1998), *Powered By Honda: Developing Excellence in the Global Enterprise* (New York: John Wiley & Sons).

Rotch, S. (2005), 'Leadership: How to Get the Very Best from Your Teaching or Training Group', The Living Skills Library, http://www.livingskillslibrary.com/html/Leadership%20 3%20Roles.html.

Shewhart, W.A. (1931), *Economic Control of Quality of Manufactured Product* (New York: Van Nostrand).

Smith, A. (1776), *The Wealth of Nations*, reprinted 1986 (London: Penguin).

Tannenbaum, A.S. and Schmitt, W.H. (1958), 'How to Choose a Leadership Pattern', *Harvard Business Review* 36, March–April, pp. 95–101.

Thomas, T. (2005), 'Changing Role of Trade Unions', 22 April, http://in.rediff.com/money/2005/ apr/22guest2.htm.

Thompson, J.L. (n.d.), 'Strategic Change Management', Lecture notes, Chapter 24, http://www. thomsonlearning.co.uk/Businessandmanagement/thompson4/lecture24.htm.

Tuckman, B.W. (1965), 'Developmental Sequence in small Groups', *The Psychological Bulletin*: summary available at http://www.Businessballs.com/tuckmanformingstorming normingperforming.htm.

Wickens, P. (1995), *The Ascendant Organisation* (London: Macmillan Business).

Wickens, P. (1997), *The Ascendant Organisation*, IOM National Conference Proceedings.

Wild, R. (1997), *Games Bosses Play: 36 Career Busters your Supervisor may be Firing your Way and How you can Defend Yourself* (Chicago, IL: Contemporary Books).

Chapter 31

International Business Training using a Supply Chain Game

David J. Newlands

Introduction

This chapter discusses a realistic supply chain game. The structure is based on the mobile phone market and was originally conceived to teach managers and logistics planners the benefits of selecting various operating strategies. This constitutes design *of* logistics. The author then took this basic game and developed various options that represented more accurately the reality of the industry. The game was then used with product creation teams to explain design *for* logistics. The aim of these variants was twofold: to increase the awareness of product design on supply chain effectiveness and to promote the incorporation of certain strategically desirable design characteristics.

Children learn through play. Why should management and academics be any different? Peters (1994) pointed out that companies such as Microsoft actively promote playing and play time as an important means of sustaining peak performance and creativity.

Supply chain games (SCG) have been used to represent certain aspects of reality. Typically, initial conditions seem appropriate. Pre-production runs have generated some stock used at the launch. SCGs usually rely on there being stocking points with stock controllers ordering independently of each other and independently of the actual demand at the point of sale.

Production capacity may be constrained. Demands placed on manufacturing centres are the product of the various decisions and the timing of orders raised in the distribution chain.

The product may be made, assembled or released as finished goods based on a constant period.

The aim of the first round of SCGs invariably is to demonstrate the inadequacies and difficulties associated with traditional concepts, methods and paradigms. These include:

- the Forrester Effect and the Burbidge Effect;
- lack of communication between supply chain participants, particularly the planners and coordinators;
- the tacit assumptions inherent in the production process;
- multiple independent ordering echelons;
- economic order quantities and economic batch quantities;
- time delays between actual demand and re-ordering;
- second-guessing what has been sold;
- long distances between the various parts of the supply chain;
- early introduction of variants in the supply chain.

The Beer Game is a famous exercise that induces a single change in volumes from a constant level to another constant level of orders or demand. The instructor provides the rhythm necessary to coordinate the participants' activities. This approach controls for immediate responses and ensures a regular flow of information, even if there is no agreement between customer and supplier about the volume required. The free variable in the Beer Game is the number of goods ordered, despatched or made. The game is timed to stop prior to full recovery and stock records are kept to show how the participants have managed. A set of typical graphs is used to compare with the results obtained from the session.

There are limitations to this type of game. Anyone who has played the game or knows the point of sale demand profile can easily bias their decisions in line with this known quantity demand profile. The financial rules penalize failure to comply with or fulfil customer's requests for exaggerated demands. The Beer Game is available online, although the original version is still used for training groups.

Many electronic games exist. Participants may be groups or individuals tasked with certain responsibilities. Such games typically require many hours over an extended period to enter data and set up the base conditions. Some electronic games enable multiple businesses to operate in a given market. Sales patterns may be driven by historic market trends which are updated annually. Other games provide all participants with an equal playing field.

Many games focus almost exclusively on financial investment and performance to assess strategic investment decisions. Other games focus on sales and distribution strategies.

The live played version of the Beer Game enables participants to see what is happening, in real time. They may be able to identify areas of low performance. The reasons for this low performance may be misidentified, however. This is not possible with many electronic games. Only the results can be analysed, to identify trends and affects of decisions. Some analysis and information may be available to participants for a fee. However, the participants will not get an idea of the timescales, particularly reaction times between order and delivery. Electronic games have these set within specific probabilities of completion.

Supply Chain Representation

A real supply chain consists of a number of key elements:

- demand created at one or a number of points of sale;
- trade customers;
- regional and/or local distribution centres;
- value-adding distribution centres;
- border issues, border inspection and duty – customs and associated delays;
- manufacturing centres, with a jobbing, flow or batch strategy;
- suppliers – usually only first tier, though it is possible to have multiple layers;
- competitors who will take market share if demand is not satisfied;
- planning activities undertaken by various bodies within the supply chain in order to optimize their activities;
- financial results and other key performance indicators.

Each tier after the point of sale typically will have a stocking point and may well have planning and controlling activities. Figure 31.1 shows a representation of a typical supply chain game, from first-tier supplier through to the point of sale. The figure shows saw tooth diagrams associated with the activities undertaken by each organization.

Days of Supply

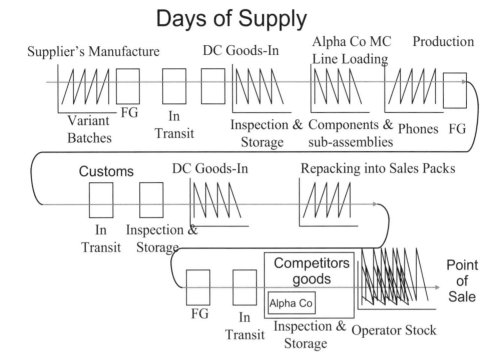

Figure 31.1 A representation of a supply chain

The angle of the saw tooth indicates rising or falling quantities for that particular stage or process. Suppliers build up stock. Once a batch is produced, it is transported. Materials in process and some safety stock may be present. The quantities and rate of build up or use of these may vary over time. During some phases of a product production life cycle, each part of the supply chain responds to its apparent demands by speeding up, slowing down or suspending activities until required again.

Safety and flowing stock may be increased or decreased during a game. If stock increases above the maximum liability, this extra liability cost may penalize that company's profit. If stock reduces, the 'current assets' of the company reduce. This reduces the value of the business because there is less capital in the business. As a consequence, the profit is reduced at the end of a period during which stock is reduced. Profit will return to an equivalent amount as that obtained under a stock rich environment; however, the obsolescence risk this profit has to cover is significantly reduced (Womack and Jones 1996; Newlands and Hooper 2001).

Suppliers produce their components, systems, raw materials or sub-assemblies. They perceive these as their finished goods – they get paid for them. The supplier may wish to carry stock at despatch in addition to stock in transit. A question arises of where or when these materials become the property of the manufacturing/assembly organization. The manufacturing centre may withdraw from stores materials owned and managed by the supplier. Equally, transfer can occur at the time of receipt or after goods have been inspected by a quality control team. These materials may be held in a goods in buffer until they are transferred to the manufacturing centre, where they are loaded into a buffer for the specific cell, workshop or line.

As materials are used, the raw materials buffer volume reduces, while the finished goods buffer increases. Eventually, a batch of finished goods is created. These are then available for transport to a distribution centre owned by, branded by, or franchised to the manufacturer. The finished goods may be cross-docked. The manufacturer's distribution centre may repackage the product into display item sets and can be instructed to undertake quality control inspections as a last chance filter before delivery to the trade customer.

Before the goods arrive at the manufacturer's distribution centre, they may need to be delayed, for example, by customs, product inspection, illegal substance searches (typically narcotics), illegal immigrant searches, paperwork verification, duty payments and value-added tax landing charges.

Once the products have been cross-docked, batches will be available to dispatch to the regional or local trade customer warehouses, or direct deliveries will be made to the points of sale. This will depend on the manufacturer' distribution strategy as well as access to the point of sale and the trade customer's logistics efficiency. When the manufacturer's goods arrive at the trade customers' warehouse, they are likely to be in competition with the manufacturer's competitors. The aim of some supply chain games is to maintain a given stock at the trade customer's warehouse in order to respond to demand from the point of sale. Most supply chain games use randomized (shuffled) cards to represent a given steady volume demand. The mix of products is known over a long period. For example, cat food has a given monthly demand because there are a given number of cat, and their owners buy the same quantity of cans per month. The manufacturer's marketing will know, to a reasonable level of in accuracy, how many of which flavour will be needed to be produced. The variable that is not determined is the sequence.

Most SCGs emphasize materials requirement planning (MRP), economic order quantities and economic batch quantities.[1] The games also put an emphasis on meeting a constant demand. Some games 'throw in' the extra complication associated with changes in demand created as a result of seasonality or marketing campaigns. Since the products are in direct competition with their competitor products, the actual rate of demand may vary significantly between the start of the game and the end. This can be based on the classic product life cycle model with:

- Early adopters paying high prices.
- Marketing driven sales campaigns that promote the product.
- New variants introduced to increase the product range after the product has been launched (using Pareto logic applied to volume and variant to prioritize the product design and introduction sequence).
- In the mature stage more competitors coming in to the niche to compete using modified versions of the original product.
- In the declining stage, profitability is reduced.

Many SCGs do not analyse data with a sufficiently mature cost model that can reflect the cost of lost sales due to loosing orders because the trade customer doesn't have the brand requested. More significantly, most SCGs do not take into account the cost of stock, obsolescence and logistics costs relating to the distribution channel design.

---

1 The effects of using these principles are reviewed by Newlands in Forrest Effect Solutions, in this volume.

Make, Assemble and Release

SCGs typically emphasize making, assembling or product release based on given time elapses and specific volumes. While making something is attractive, the game should be relatively cheap to operate, using materials and equipment relatively standard in training establishments and offices. This allows shopfloor workers to be taken away from their working environment and trained in concepts that raise awareness and promote their input. Training in another environment allows workers to understand and then correlate their understanding with their own practical examples and experience. This should facilitate their learning since they may feel less threatened and less dominated by the Tayloristic thinkers and can provide the trainers with feedback and suggestions to improve the realism of the game.

Making games typically use props such as paper, pencils, rulers, glue, scissors and guillotines. These readily available materials and equipment allow several simultaneous runnings of the game scenario in the same session. Participants may be broken down into 'departments', including participants representing designers, cutters, fabricators, assemblers, quality inspectors, suppliers and transporters, as well as customers. The emphasis in making games tends to be on lead time, process simplification, customer perceived defects, factory or material processor perceived quality, costs of production and costs of stock.

Assembly games use props that may have been bought off the shelf. Lego and Sticklebricks, for example, are used to represent modules. They need to be assembled in the correct sequence and in the correct configuration.

Some assembly games require participants to be responsible for particular colours of parts. Participants are not allowed to talk to each other. A master example may be present that has been glued together to ensure that it cannot be disassembled to inspect how it was put together. This would destroy their master but would give them insight into assembly procedures and sequences. In the real world that process is known as reverse engineering. Each participant must remember what sizes are required and how many of each. They must work out how to assemble their subassembly and then they must source these parts. Each participant goes to another room, picks up their chosen parts and returns. They assemble their part of the product and then offer it to the 'assembler' who must then ensure the subsystems are correctly put together.

Other types of assembly SCGs use fewer parts. They are presented to the assembler in buffer stocking locations. The assembler must put the parts together within a given period of time. This is the base line rhythm of the game. For example, if it takes 10 seconds to assemble a product, randomized demand at the point of sale also is set at 10 seconds. The theory behind this is that the production capacity is set at the average demand and hence the factory can make to and sell from stock. This strategy should, according to the theories of forecasting and rough cut capacity planning, fulfil the demand associated with variations in order quantities received at the factory. In reality, the waiting time and order to demand differences associated with batches create stock-outs of some parts and excess stock in other stockkeeping units (SKUs).

Ideally, there should be some 'time profit' built into the game. If demand is every 10 seconds, the product should be able to be built repeatedly in six to eight seconds, depending on the operator skill level and technique used. Knowing there is a time profit, the question to be raised is 'Why was the pipeline stock from the initial setting of the game used up?'

Material release type games do not reproduce value-adding activities (assembly). They are limited in that they can principally simulate accurate material delivery from a supplier. Quality problems can be included using a timer to release parts, materials, equipment or resources.

Supply Chain Game Simulated Effects

Orders received at manufacturing result from orders of either one or two per 10 second period, economic order quantity (EOQ) generated used at the trade customer of either three or five, depending on facilitators preferences at the time, and economic batch quantities (EBQ) of three or five of any one colour at the manufacturer's distribution centre.[2] As a result, orders back up because the factory has to complete each order before dispatch and because partial orders are not shipped. The extra waiting time is perceived as delay in delivery. This elapsed time uses up stock at the distribution centre and trade customer. As a consequence, the trade customer supplies competitors' products, even if this has a lower financial return on each transaction. In effect, the trade customer makes a sale and the branded good looses a sale. This directly affects their market share. In addition, the factory has been producing to orders received, yet other goods have been sold instead. This can cause significant difficulties in built-up finished goods stock obsolescence risk.

Game Modes

SCGs can be set up to represent various operations strategies. For example:

- making games represent engineer to order, make to order, make to stock, assemble to order;
- assembly games can represent make to stock and assemble to stock strategies;
- release games represent on-time delivery systems.

Some SCGs can represent operations paradigms such as traditional batch manufacture, jobbing, flow and continuous production. Some making and most assembly games can also represent mass production and lean production. Depending on the game's inherent flexibility, outsourcing and process optimization can be included, for example, suppliers pre-assemble modules. This leads on to when to introduce the point of variation. These SCGs, therefore, tend only to represent the design *of* logistics.

Supply chain simulations typically attempt to create Forrester Effects at various locations down the represented chain. They may change the ordering criteria, from economic order quantity and economic batch quantity to much smaller re-order quantities. These are economic if the company already has implemented quick change single minute exchange of dies (SMED) by Shingo (1985).

JIT promotes process flexibility. This avoids huge batch quantities being scheduled, together with their associated extended lead times. Just-in-time requires that each type of variant in the product mix should be produced every day.

Developed and Tested Game

The author was previously a consulting researcher as an internal supply chain specialist for a fast moving consumer electronics manufacturer (FMCEM). Part of this role put emphasis on training

---

2   Newlands provides a description of the Forrester Effect and some identified cures in Dynamic Instabilities: Causes, Effects and Solutions, in this volume.

product creation teams in design of and design for logistics. The supply chain game developed by this company focused on manufacturing modes such as make to stock, make to order and assemble to order. These modes were idealized product delivery process philosophies rather than operations strategies that reflected the move from mass, through lean to agile manufacturing. The study of design for and design of logistics continued after the original collaborative research.

As a result of more than five years of reflection and teaching supply chains, flexibilities inherent in the game infrastructure were identified. The game that originally served to show the basic Forrester Effect, stock control and heijunka (production levelling) has been developed. The game scenarios are now significantly more grounded and easier to understand than those ran with the FMCEM.

Emphasis in teaching the game can be on supply chain dynamics and also on change management. Playing the game facilitated participants to understand what to expect and also allows them to communicate the message to their co-workers.

Christopher (1997) teaches managers and logistics specialists the principal stages of how to get from a high stock, low return on investment supply chain. His approach shows four states of integration. The game as reflected in Figure 31.2 has three stages – mass, lean and agile. The rounds of the supply chain game used by the author go much of the way towards Christopher's evolutionary track. The manufacturer should develop closer relationships with their suppliers and with their customers. From a logistics practitioner perspective, it is interesting to note the development of the delivery practices from large batches, through lack of control, to smaller batches and eventually to JIT.

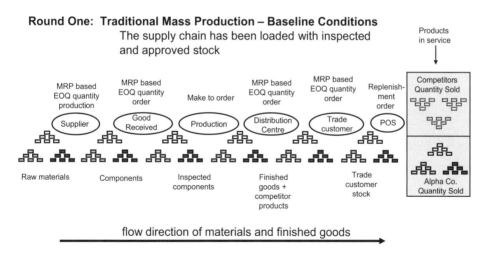

Figure 31.2   Stages of developing integrated supply chain

Source: Adapted from Christopher (1997).

The Brio Phone Game

An ideal environment involves small exam room type desks and chairs. This enables maximum flexibility and shows clearly how much space is saved by the end of round three (typically more than half the space is saved).

A mobile phone is constructed out of subassemblies and parts. Components are available direct from Brio. Three variants are produced: red, white and blue. Colour variants for wooden parts are painted after purchase. Blue caps for the radio antenna are standard. Yellow caps are used to track end-to-end cycles over the duration of the game. In round three, yellow caps are a variant.

Demand over the cycle of the games is constant; however, the sequence is randomized. Each phone represents about two hours manufacturing time, equivalent to 500 handsets. Losing sales therefore equates to significant loss in revenue.

Two minutes into each round, a second set of orders is released which represents a demand from an advertising campaign for one of the variants. This increase from one to two orders per time period is one form of Forrester Effect inducer. The number of campaign orders is constant, regardless of the variant chosen. At the end of the campaign, the drop in demand induces another Forrester Effect sequence, the waves being the inverse sequence of the first set. The net effect is to cause great difficulties in understanding replenishment needs at each stocking point. This then induces over-corrections via orders they release.

Game Rounds

First Round – Traditional Mass Production with Planning and Material Push

The first round of the game is typically based on mass production using material requirements planning, economic order quantities and economic batch quantities. It can be played with as few as seven players. If seven players are involved, a single courier will extract stock from each supplier and deliver. The manufacturing purchasing agent role will not be filled. There is flexibility to have up to about 19 participants depending on the size of the room and the 'make work' roles that are included such as sales, inspection, expeditious direct delivery courier, etc.

Location in widely different geographic regions can be suggested.

International truckers, long freight train journeys, aeroplane flights and large cargo/container ships are represented by people who walk from the order placer to the order completer with a tray and kanban-type card. They subsequently return with the completed order. A rule of the game is that they cannot transfer incomplete orders. This is an attribute of batch manufacture. If the batch is not complete, the economic quantity will not have been delivered and thus the cost of transport will be significantly higher than budgeted for.

At the end of each round, it is helpful to review what actually happened and identify potential areas of improvement. This does not just cover the physical aspects. It includes bonus and reward schemes, team work, value add versus cost add, process mapping to discover why the lead times are so long and comparisons between mass production and lean. Financial analysis is undertaken to calculate how much profit has been created by sales; how much profit has been eroded as a result of lost sales because competitor products have been supplied; and how much the profit is eroded due to now obsolete stocks.

Round 1, Management Planning Driven Production Material Push using MRP

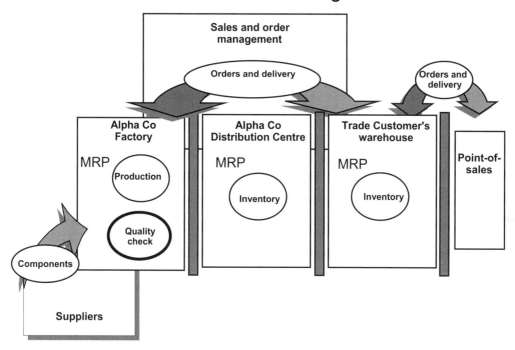

Figure 31.3 Management planning using MRP to push materials through a supply chain

Second Round – Lean Manufacturing

The second round aims to redesign the logistics infrastructure using principles from re-engineering and philosophies from lean manufacturing. It is necessary to engage the participants: to identify waste and non-value-adding activity. The easiest way to do this is to explain what value-adding activities are: making parts, changing the product, assembly, testing and packaging. All other activities are waste that can either be eliminated immediately or significantly reduced. A second suggestion is to use Honda's motto 'make where you sell, buy where you make'. It is important to explain that the point of sale is in a country trading or geographic region. As such, a transplant facility will be constructed to produce goods for the local market. The factory located in the original market of a lower cost country will continue to operate. Suppliers will be developed in each location where a plant is situated near a major market population. Location for these plants is related to 'population density of the region'. Central Europe, in a triangle between Liverpool, Hamburg and Paris, has the highest population density in Europe. Countries further away, for example Siberia, Finland and central Spain, have fewer large population centres and the overall population densities for those regions are much less.

Feedback and suggestions from participants are used to form an idea of what the value chain should look like. Concrete examples can be given; for example, the Nissan plant in Sunderland that groups suppliers around the assembly plant. If suppliers are not on the industrial estate, they are located within a radius that permits them to respond within the lead- time created when the vehicle is placed on the post-paint shop assembly line.

The aim is to reduce the work space and number of participants required and, as a consequence, increase the order response speed and thus reduce the raw materials, safety stocks, work in process and finished goods buffers. The principal casualties of the modifications are long-range transporters. Using small examination sized desks facilitates the negotiated reduction of fixed assets (in line with lean thinking's half the amount of space). Closing up the distances between suppliers, manufacturing plant and trade customer reduces the space further while virtually eradicating significant investment required in transportation, shipping and safety stock buffers.

Third Round – Agile/Mass Customization

The number of paid participants involved in making and distributing the products can be reduced from round one, using up to around 20 people, down to four in round three. A round three with three participants is possible; however, this is less efficient because the maker has to make and store, retrieve from store and supply in response to actual orders. This adds to the 'hand time' required to undertake all the activities, and hence increased end-to-end time. The net effect of too few people, therefore, is excessive lost sales to competitors.

Round three makes use of 'just add an egg' type marketing ploys and product designs that require customers to be involved (they aren't paid to add value to their product).

The third round of the game requires the product to be redesigned to fit into the new product delivery process. Variants are introduced after the sale has been made to the consumer at the point of sale. This reduces the necessary stocking of variants early in the supply chain and consequently reduces the amount of inventory carried at each stocking point.

The variations designed into Dell Computers, for example, are from the picking list. Hardware variants are kept to a minimum. Dell make their biggest contribution to profit by adding customer appreciated value because they plug a wire into the back of the computer and download individual customers' pre-selected software configuration. This allows them to provide their customers with products the customer can take out of the box and use with a very short commissioning lead time. Mobile phone accessory suppliers have started to use this type of post-sale configuration with downloaded images. Products at the fun end of the mobile phone market also permit the consumer to 'pop-on' covers to suit their attire. This allows quite significant mark-ups on the fashion accessories. With the electronic configuration paradigm, producers can revert to Ford's 'any colour as long as it is black' syndrome. In the case of Dell, this tends to be grey-covered laptops and black or beige computer boxes. Additionally, as with Dell, peripherals such as monitors, keyboards, mice, printers and scanners are collected by value-add logistics service providers and delivered together with the computer to the client. Dell also manufactures one computer at a time, regardless of the gross order volume requested by their client. In effect, Dell use heijunka (level scheduling) within their factory and down through the distribution to their client. As each machine is produced individually, and since module and component suppliers are aware of the exact number of machines sold, they can arrange deliveries using delivery kanban and replenish their dispatch buffers using manufacturing kanbans.

Reengineering Round

Participants can be asked to develop a version of their own based on:

- their knowledge of dynamics in particular industries;

- the mixing of props, such as hyperdynamic point of sale markets that require order sizes of one, three or five of any colour variant;
- transfer knowledge – when an order is known, someone relays this information to the team who are 'heads down' making products;
- production lead times versus customer expectations for the time elapsed between order and delivery dates (the p/d ratio) may be taken into account;
- outsourcing of standard parts and modules to local suppliers and transplants;
- designing a product that represents a complex assembly – an aeroplane, car, conveyor;
- designing product variants that simplify assembly by using a common process sequence, facilitate product mix and change over, improve quality and reduce time required.

Typical Facilitator Observations

Participants are expected to apply what they learn in theory. This typically does not happen. Supply chain game participants are seldom aware of both of these two effects. Even if they are, they may well not question the design of the supply chain before the first round of the game is played.

Participants do not disassociate themselves from their reality; nor do they actively ask questions such as 'what is going on here?' Typically they do not:

- correlate saw tooth diagrams to what they observe;
- tacitly apply MRP thinking (noted by Newlands in Forrester Effect Solutions, this volume);
- do not communicate. Even if they do communicate, this usually is only for a clarification of a single point or two rather than discussing, evaluating, comparing with experience, etc.;
- apply lean thinking concepts and principles straight away;
- apply mass customization/agile manufacturing.

Conclusions

Since reality is invented twice, once in the head and once in reality, playing simulation games that represent reality with a high degree of realism creates facilitates participants understanding, motivates them through involvement, and results in communication based on a common framework set of experiences.

The game can show financial benefits, and records can be kept of each game, the participants can appreciate the impact they can have on the profit and return on investment of the business.

The game is very useful when teaching change management, re-engineering, appreciation of the need to design both the product and the process, to identify non-value-adding costs, project management and leadership modes. Lessons to learn can be brought out from experiencing the various stages and relating these to elements of the game, both explicit and tacit knowledge in terms of what they observed and how they felt.

Participants may be asked to develop contribution proposals that help achieve the corporation's strategic goals. Learning offline enables experimentation and mental try-outs of changes that may then be rolled out for real in their company and across their business (including suppliers, customers and other stakeholders).

References

Christopher, M. (1997), *Logistics and Supply Chain Management: Strategies for Reducing Costs and Improving Services*, 2nd edn (London: Pitman Publishing).

Newlands, D. and Hooper, M. (2001), 'Cost Analysis for World Class Change, Part 1: Inventory Reductions for Profitability', *Control, Institute of Operations Management* March, pp. 17–20.

Peters, T. (1994), *The Pursuit of WOW!: Every Person's Guide to Topsy-turvy Times* (New York/London: Vintage Books/Macmillan).

Shingo, S. (1985), *A Revolution in Manufacturing: The SMED System* (Cambridge, MA: Productivity Press).

Womack, J. and Jones, D. (1996), *Lean Thinking: Banish Waste and Create Wealth in Your Corporation* (New York: Simon & Schuster).

Index